FAITH FOOD & FRIENDSHIP

Reflections and Recipes
from a Jesuit's Abundant Life

FAITH FOOD & FRIENDSHIP

WALTER J. SMITH, S.J.

This book is a memoir reflecting the author's present recollections of experiences over time. Its story and its words are the author's alone. Some details and characteristics may be changed, some events may be compressed, and some dialogue may be recreated. Some names and identifying characteristics of persons referenced in this book, as well as identifying places, may have been changed to protect the privacy of the individuals and their families.

Published by River Grove Books
Austin, TX
www.rivergrovebooks.com

Distributed by River Grove Books

Design and composition by Greenleaf Book Group
Cover design by Greenleaf Book Group

Publisher's Cataloging-in-Publication data is available.

Print ISBN: 978-1-63299-561-2

eBook ISBN: 978-1-63299-562-9

First Edition

For my family, whose love and support have provided nurture and support throughout my life and have always been the "wind beneath my wings." (Isaiah 40:30–31)

For my countless friends, at whose tables I have dined and in whose kitchens I have cooked, each of you has "satisfied my longing soul and filled me with such good things." (Psalm 107:9)

CONTENTS

PROLOGUE

Everything that lives and moves about will be food for you.

—GENESIS 9:3

It might be a bit unusual that a Jesuit priest who has spent nearly sixty years pursuing ministries of preaching, teaching, and managing academic and non-profit organizations would set aside time to collect memories that chronicle certain people, moments, and events—both public or private—that have shaped and formed his life. Even more remarkable is that he would choose to organize and present many of these recollections through the prism of foods and recipes for cooking and baking.

My goal is certainly not to write a comprehensive autobiography, in the common understanding of that term. The aim is more modest: to select certain stories and relationships from a full, rich, and abundant life, which account for some eight decades of life experiences, and present them as benchmarks or turning-point moments of that journey.

It is a bit ironic that food, cooking, and baking would be selected as major metaphors for this life review. Growing up in a second-generation Boston American Irish family that "ate" but never "dined," it is remarkable that I developed any interest at all in the culinary arts. My mother, by her own admission, was a terrible cook. She possessed few basic cooking skills and had even less interest in learning. My father—a World War II US Navy veteran and lifetime Boston firefighter—was a bit more open to learning how to cook, and after his retirement from fighting fire, he became more venturesome and successful in the kitchen. My immigrant grandparents brought with them rudimentary recipes from their native Ireland. Few were memorable or have survived in our family's culinary traditions.

Someone in the early 1940s must have given my parents a copy of the *Fanny Farmer Cookbook*. It was one of the few books that found a place in our home, an impressive hard-bound volume with ribbons that served as page markers. Fanny Farmer was herself a Bostonian who parlayed her cooking skills into a book first published in 1896, and it remains in print to this day. This compendium of recipes and the rudimentary techniques of cooking and baking became so popular that almost every new bride of that era received a copy as a wedding gift. I doubt my mother paid Fanny Farmer much attention. Many years later, she would recall she found me paging through its recipes and studying the color photographs, and even venturing to recreate some of its recipes on my own. I do recall using the book for another profane purpose: serving as an altar missal when I played "priest" celebrating Mass, and forcing my younger sisters to be both servers and congregation and to consume lemon-flavored Necco wafers that I purported to "consecrate" and distribute as holy communion.

My fascination with food and cookery was manifest early in my life in the most unlikely and inhospitable of human contexts. Little did I realize during those formative years just how much the kitchen and differing approaches to gastronomy and the culinary arts would contribute to a metaphor, weaving together the threads of a whole lifetime of experiences.

My years growing up in South Boston were nurturing, while at the same time, quite insular. Most of the families who lived in my neighborhood shared the same Irish socioreligious and ethnic traditions we did. There were a few Italian families and even fewer Lithuanian and Polish families in our parish community. Most of my friends ate similar stews and porridges; potatoes, bacon, and cabbage; soda bread, jam, and butter. All of our holiday meals were the same: a roast of beef or chicken or turkey; mashed potatoes and gravy, canned peas and carrots. Our Italian neighbors ate strange things like *brasciole* and *melanzane*, and our eastern European neighbors were eating novel things like *kielbasa* and *pierogis*. Not until I was in high school and college did my social networks broaden and my palate expand. I was introduced to exciting and undiscovered textures and flavors I never knew existed.

The journey of my life has been continuously punctuated and expanded by new culinary explorations and discoveries. I ventured outside the narrow confines and comfort zones of my family's origin as I blazed new trails in Europe, Asia, and Latin America. There I assimilated vastly new taste experiences.

This memoir, as did Fanny Farmer's original cookbook, collects recipes of a lifetime of discovery and integration, which are embedded in a select narrative about people and events that contributed to these culinary memories.

The Hebrew prophet Isaiah imagined God's kingdom as a grand banquet with "a feast of rich food and choice wines" (Is 25:6). In a time when food and drink were in short supply, Isaiah's image proved quite powerful. The one who prepares and invites to this extraordinary meal is "the Lord of hosts." The invitation to participate in the feast was extended to "all peoples." At this banquet, all the hopes of God's people would be fulfilled.

I am in good company as I set out on this adventure, when I realize that God has already suggested the metaphoric template I am now about to follow. Looking back on my own lifetime of discovery, I can affirm that God did not skimp on the good stuff. There has been plenty of butter and heavy cream, truffles and saffron, *aceto balsamico* and *jamón iberico de bellota*. Many are the aggregated and contrasting flavor profiles that have contributed to the balance and cadence of my life: the sweet and sour; the aromatic and spicy; the pungent and savory.

It takes a lifetime to appreciate its complexity. A good Parmigiano-Reggiano can take thirty-six to forty-eight months to mature; *prosciutto di Parma* requires two years of patient waiting. So, too, many things in life take time to mature. My formation as a Jesuit took a decade; my formation as a priest is still not complete. Life—like a good recipe—takes time, good ingredients, patience, and skill to perfect.

One of the amazing things about recalling and memorializing the stories and recipes in this memoir is the unimagined blessing it has been. This life review exercise has required a thoughtful and disciplined examination of decades of personal experiences, successful and failed experiments.

For many life projects, there were well-tested "recipes" to follow; for others, it was trial and error, to discover what works and what does not. New techniques and new recipes were attempted, tested, and modified along the way. Cooking, like life, is an exercise of permutations and combinations, successes and failures. Many of the recipes in this collection are the result of my personal creative efforts or bold attempts to mimic, adapt, or reproduce recipes for things I have been taught, tasted, or experienced. They have all been kitchen-tested and have received the praise of countless appreciative diners. I've provided many recipes with classic or novel titles in French, Italian, Spanish, or some other modern language, paying homage to their cultural roots. In these cases, I have also provided a descriptive English translation of the recipe's title.

A friend of mine, who is a very good cook, often quoted his own mother, who was her own worst critic. If a recipe did not turn out exactly as she thought it should, his mother would exclaim, "Failure!" In her judgment, the execution of a recipe was either a "success" or a "failure." I have had my share of frustration, discouragement, and disappointment—both in the kitchen and in life—but these ephemeral failures made me more appreciative of those moments of achievement, such as creating an exquisitely smooth hollandaise sauce or taking a perfectly risen chocolate soufflé from the oven.

In cooking—as in life—a timer will ultimately signal that the requisite time has elapsed. A memoir captures a bit of the story of how we got here. What we did or did not do to bring us to this moment. Did we follow every step of the recipe, use the proper ingredients, in the right proportions, and with a good balance of seasoning? What modifications might our experiences suggest in order to tweak the recipe for future cooks?

I invite you to accompany me on this journey in faith, food, and friendship, where prescient words from the author of the Book of Genesis will, it is hoped, prove true: "Everything that lives and moves about will be food for you."

Chapter 1

THE EARLY YEARS

Do not worry about your life, what you will eat; or about your body, what you will wear. For life is more than food, and the body more than clothes.

—LUKE 12:22–23

Jesuits have always hovered in the foreground and background of my life. As a youngster growing up during the first eight years of my life in Boston's South End, I attended Holy Trinity grammar school, which was staffed by a community of Franciscan sisters. Holy Trinity, a German national parish church, was administered by the Society of Jesus (the Jesuits). As early as second grade, in a class taught by Sister Regina Angelorum, I was learning the altar boy's Latin responses for the Mass under the patient tutelage of a diminutive, gaunt Jesuit priest, Fr. Ignatius Pennisi. Father Pennisi was well known for his patience as a tutor for boys like me who were memorizing the tongue-twisting responses of the Tridentine Latin Mass at the same time we were beginning to learn the rudiments of English grammar and syntax. This quiet Jesuit, who was a flutist, also dared to transform an inexperienced, nonmusical group of South End kids into a prize-winning drum and bugle corps.

The pastor of Holy Trinity was a garrulous and immense man with a deep baritone voice, Fr. Robert Carr, S.J. One of my earliest recollections from Holy Trinity is of a summer outing for altar boys, organized and led by Fr. Carr. We were shuttled by bus from the parish church on Shawmut Avenue to the Boston waterfront, where we boarded what was referred to as the "Nantasket Boat."

Nantasket in those years was a small seaside village located about ten miles south of Boston. The town hosted a small amusement park, with numerous concessions selling things like hot dogs, cold drinks, ice cream, and saltwater taffy.

I was eight years old, clearly one of the youngest in this group. For some unexplainable reason, I managed to get separated from the group soon after we disembarked from the boat and was left wandering on my own during the remainder of the day. I did know, however, that the return trip was scheduled to depart from the same pier at 4 p.m., so I figured I could at least rejoin the others at that time.

I spent the entire day in the penny arcade. My mother had given me a dollar for spending money. I bought a hot dog for ten cents and a soda for five cents and with hands full of pennies, I happily occupied myself with various games in the arcade. When Fr. Carr discovered me back at the pier, it was like a reenactment of the story of the prodigal son in the Gospels (Luke 15:11–32). The only difference was that at my tender age, I had not yet led a profligate life nor squandered my inheritance—but I had managed to go missing for six hours.

I later realized Fr. Carr had been a nervous wreck for the entire day. He had alerted the Nantasket police to be on the lookout for me. He had spent the entire day in a personal search to locate me. When he saw me standing by the pier he was relieved, not angry. He took me firmly in hand and quickly bought me all kinds of things to eat before we reboarded the vessel. He even purchased a big stuffed animal for me to take home. When we got back to the church, he insisted on walking me home to explain the day's saga directly to my parents. His concern and care were palpable.

When I got home, my mother asked me what I would like for supper. Spontaneously, even though it was midsummer, I said that I would like mac and cheese. Her version of this consummate comfort food was to combine melted American cheese with overcooked elbow macaroni. That day I was perfectly happy with what she made for me, and I've retained a love for the dish—but here is my version of that all-American standard. It is a bit more sophisticated in its approach and ingredients, and still able to comfort and console.

MACARONI AND CHEESE WITH A CONTINENTAL TWIST

Makes 4 servings

Ingredients

- 16 ounces penne or cavatappi dried pasta
- 1 tablespoon extra-virgin olive oil
- 6 tablespoons unsalted butter (for the sauce)
- ⅓ cup all-purpose flour
- 3 cups whole milk
- 1 cup heavy cream
- 4 cups shredded extra-sharp cheddar cheese
- 2 cups shredded aged Gruyère cheese
- salt, pepper, and grated nutmeg to taste
- 1½ cups panko breadcrumbs
- 4 tablespoons melted unsalted butter (for the topping)
- ½ cup grated Parmigiano Reggiano cheese
- ¼ teaspoon mild paprika

Method

1. Preheat oven to 350°F.
2. Lightly grease a large 3- or 4-quart baking dish and set aside.
3. Combine the shredded cheddar and Gruyère together in a large bowl and set aside (approximately 6 cups).
4. Cook the pasta a couple of minutes before it reaches al dente, following the packaging directions.
5. Drain, and then gently mix the warm pasta with olive oil and set aside to continue cooling while preparing béchamel sauce.
6. Melt butter in a deep saucepan and whisk in the flour over medium

continued

heat and continue whisking for about 1 minute, until bubbly and light golden in color.

7. Gradually whisk in the milk and heavy cream. Continue whisking until the sauce thickens (2 to 3 minutes). Add the salt and pepper and a bit of nutmeg.
8. Remove the saucepan from the heat. Add two cups of the shredded cheese into the sauce and continue whisking until smooth. Add two more cups of the shredded cheeses and continue to blend until creamy and smooth. Sauce will be smooth and thick.
9. Combine the cooled pasta with the enriched béchamel sauce until the pasta is thoroughly coated.
10. Pour half of the mac and cheese mixture into a well-buttered baking dish. Top with the remaining 2 cups of shredded cheeses and then cover with the remaining pasta mixture.
11. In a small bowl, combine panko crumbs, Parmigiano Reggiano cheese, melted butter, and paprika.
12. Distribute the mixture over the top of the casserole and bake until bubbly and golden brown, about 30 minutes. Serve immediately.

Without knowing it at the time, the seeds of my Jesuit vocation were first sown in the fertile soil of Holy Trinity parish. Many years later, on May 20, 1972, I would be ordained to the priesthood in the Society of Jesus. On that occasion I invited Fr. Carr, who was by then quite advanced in years, to robe me in the priestly liturgical vestments: stole and chasuble. Twenty-two years earlier it was he who had celebrated the Mass during which I first received Holy Communion from his hands. It just seemed the right thing to do. Robert Carr was the first Jesuit, among many, who would care for me personally, intellectually, and spiritually.

Our family moved to South Boston in 1951 when I was in the third grade. The early spiritual and intellectual associations with the Society of Jesus and its members at Holy Trinity Church left a formative and indelible imprint on my life.

In this new Irish enclave into which our family quickly assimilated, I was registered in the third grade at Nazareth School and became a member of Saint Brigid's parish. In those years in Irish-Catholic Boston, when one was introduced to a new acquaintance it was not unusual for them to ask: "What parish do you come from?" Parish membership was the defining, geographical locator.

Saint Brigid's had an interesting history. It was also the home parish of Cardinal Richard Cushing, a somewhat colorful character who served as the Archbishop of Boston from 1944 to 1970. Cushing was a prodigious fundraiser and builder of new churches, schools, and institutions. He was a major benefactor to both Boston College High School and Boston College. The cardinal archbishop quickly became a larger-than-life, fun-loving, and outgoing personality—a welcome relief to many in Boston from his predecessor, Cardinal William Henry O'Connell, who was an aloof and formal churchman who had wielded formidable influence as Boston's archbishop for thirty-seven years.

One biographer described Cardinal Cushing as looking like a tough, handsome Irish cop who behaved more like a ward politician than a high church cleric. Many recall that he was a trusted and revered friend and confidant to the Kennedy family. When John F. Kennedy was inaugurated in 1961 Cardinal Cushing gave the invocation, and two years later when the president was assassinated, it was the same Cardinal Cushing who presided at St. Matthew's Cathedral in Washington, DC, and at the gravesite ceremony in Arlington National Cemetery.

As a "Corporation Sole," the Archbishop of Boston could do virtually whatever he wanted with the funds and properties of the diocese. Our parish had been originally named Saint Eulalia. In 1933 a disastrous fire leveled the old wood-framed church building that adjoined the grammar school. Cushing, a successful fundraiser and famed builder, decided to erect a new church and rectory on a piece of property he had acquired on East Broadway, and to name it for his late mother, Mary Brigid Dahill Cushing—or so the story goes.

The cardinal's father was originally from Glanworth, County Cork, and his mother from Touraneena, County Waterford. The Dahills and Cushings had lived for many years on East Third Street in the City Point section of South Boston to which my family had relocated. My parents purchased a three-story brick building for $11,500. My maternal grandparents occupied the ground floor apartment and our family of five at the time occupied the three-bedroom, third-floor apartment.

My grandfather, John Joseph O'Brien, was a retired Boston firefighter. When my father returned from active service in the Navy during World War II, my grandfather helped him qualify for an appointment to the Boston Fire Department, where Dad served with great devotion until a service-related disability forced his retirement.

John O'Brien became quick friends with John Dahill, a maternal uncle of Cardinal Cushing. They had both emigrated from neighboring counties in Ireland and had instant rapport. I recall many summer evenings as a boy sitting on the grass at the base of the park bench on which these old Irishmen passed many an hour smoking their pipes and retelling and embellishing familiar stories—more characterized, I believe, by fancy rather than fact. Mr. Dahill was a very tall man, though by then bent by age. In fact, the cardinal strongly resembled his maternal uncle. They both had the same nasal sonority and stentorian bravado that unmistakably identified Mr. Dahill.

My grandfather's salvation in life was his fortuitous marriage to Rose Brown, whose family of ten hailed from the rural town of Enniskillen in County Fermanagh, in the basin of the River Erne in the north of Ireland. My grandfather was often wont to say that in marrying Rose he gave her two great gifts: He liberated her from the blasted north of Ireland and bestowed on her the name of the tenth-century king of Ireland, Brian Boru, founder of the O'Brien dynasty. O'Brien, the anglicized form of Gaelic *Ó Briain*, means "eminence" or "exalted one." John O'Brien had no trouble living up to his name.

My grandmother Rose spent her entire married life repaying the debt incurred from these "favors," both by her patience and forbearance. John O'Brien retired from the Boston Fire Department because of an ischemic stroke that left him with certain permanent physical and emotional disabilities. The stroke did not temper his acerbic tongue or soften his characteristic impatience.

I recall frequent reminders by my grandmother that my grandfather loved me. "But he never says those words, Nana," I protested. She was always quick to respond: "Irishmen never say those things, even though they feel them deeply."

"But my father says, 'I love you,' Nana, and he's an Irishman."

"Your father is American-Irish, not Irish. That's the difference."

Rose O'Brien was a very simple cook. Her daughter, my mother, was an even simpler one. Many years later, in 1975 when I was living in Rome, my mother informed me that she had received a Christmas gift of a gourmet Irish cookbook. I laughed at the very thought that Ireland was boasting of an haute culinary culture. Both my mother and grandmother thought that boiling was the best culinary route of attack for anything: potatoes, turnips, cabbage, eggs, meat, and poultry. And their approach to roasting was univocal: Keep a roast in the oven until every drop of fluid has evaporated. I did not see or taste a piece of rare beef until I had entered the Jesuits. At first, I thought the chef had forgotten to turn on the oven. In France, however, I quickly learned only to order meat either *bleu*, *saignant*, or *à point*.

One thing that my grandmother made very well was Irish soda bread. Irish soda bread is a quick bread, which requires no yeast. The necessary leavening comes from baking soda and buttermilk. I remember my grandmother's soda bread as dense, with a wonderful crust and soft interior texture, generously filled with plump raisins. I watched her make it many times, but I never saw a written recipe. Here is my reconstruction of Nana Rose O'Brien's intuitive approach to making this Irish staple.

NANA O'BRIEN'S IRISH SODA BREAD

Makes 8 servings

Ingredients

- 2 cups buttermilk
- 1 large egg
- 4½ cups all-purpose flour
- 3 tablespoons granulated sugar
- 1 teaspoon baking soda
- 1 teaspoon kosher salt
- 5 tablespoons very cold or frozen unsalted butter, cut into small cubes
- 2 cup raisins, plumped in hot water

Method

1. Preheat oven to 400°F.
2. My grandmother always made her bread in a 12-inch cast-iron skillet, but you can bake the loaf on a 11.5 x 16.5 nonstick silicone baking mat or on a parchment-paper-lined baking sheet. You could also bake

continued

the bread in a pie plate, but I really think the best crusting comes from a cast-iron skillet.

3. Combine the buttermilk and egg together, lightly beat, and set aside.
4. Sift and combine the flour, granulated sugar, baking soda, and salt in a large bowl.
5. Cut the very cold butter cubes into the dry ingredients with the tines of a fork or with your fingers until the flour mixture forms tiny peas.
6. Add in the plumped raisins and evenly distribute them throughout the mixture.
7. Add the buttermilk-egg mixture.
8. Gently work the dough together with a wooden spoon until it is too stiff to stir.
9. With floured hands on a lightly floured surface, form the dough into an 8- or 9-inch round loaf. Knead the dough for a minute or two to make sure all of the flour is moist. If the dough is too sticky, add some additional flour (a teaspoon or so).
10. Place the rounded dough in the prepared skillet or on the lined baking sheet.
11. Using a very sharp knife, make a cross (+) into the top. (My grandmother said that this was the time to say a quick Hail Mary.)
12. Bake the bread for about 45 minutes until golden brown. Keep an eye on it during baking: if the bread seems to be browning too quickly during the baking process (after the first 20–25 minutes), gently tent the loaf with some aluminum foil.
13. Remove the soda bread from the oven and allow the loaf to cool for 10 minutes in the pan before transferring to a wire rack.

Note: Buttermilk and cold butter are keys to the success of this recipe. If you do not have buttermilk, you can improvise by whisking together 2 cups of whole milk with 1 tablespoon of fresh lemon juice or white vinegar. Allow the milk and acid to sit together for about 5 minutes before using in the recipe.

My mother worked as a waitress for about thirty years, first as a union banquet waitress in some of Boston's large hotels and for some of the city's high-end caterers. Later, she would work for the University Club of Boston and for the final years of her service, at the Milton Hill House restaurant. With all of this exposure to fine food and dining, one might have expected her to have developed a more sophisticated palate and interest in cooking. Not so. In the Smith household, a traditional Friday evening supper was predictable. My mother would open a can of Campbell's tomato soup and pour it over a pound of Mueller's spaghetti—hardly haute cuisine.

Fortunate for our family, my father—in the tradition of other firehouse chefs—eventually became a far better and more venturesome cook. One Sunday, however, while my mother was attending the late morning Mass at St. Brigid's, my father was left to watch the children and tend to the roast of beef destined to become our family's midday dinner. My mother told him that when the roast was finished he should take it out of the oven and make the pan gravy. She instructed him to add a little flour to the drippings and a bit of water or more flour, depending on the desired thickness. My father, in utter frustration, kept adding more flour and more water until he eventually had produced a viscous glob of congealed starch, not at all looking like a smooth, velvety gravy. By the time my mother returned from the parish church Dad was exasperated, with a half-gallon of indescribable brown muck on the stovetop. It was a pretty quiet Sunday family dinner—an overcooked roast and no gravy.

The Smith household was certainly not an extension of Le Cordon Bleu.

Saint Brigid's, like Holy Trinity, quickly became the center of my life. Virtually all of the kids on my block were Roman Catholic and Irish. We had a few token Italian families in the neighborhood, but more than 90 percent of us were second-generation clannish Irish. Saint Patrick's Day in South Boston was like a national holiday and almost on a par with Christmas and Easter. The Smiths always hosted an open house in our home on March 17, which my mother said often did not end until the feast of Saint Joseph (March 19)! The apartment smelled of beer and smoke for days, with steady streams of relatives, neighbors, friends, and firefighters dropping in for a bit of hospitality.

There is a lovely tale about Saint Brigid, the Irish saint for whom our parish was named. As the story goes, Saint Brigid was once asked what her vision of heaven was. This was her reply: "I should like to have a great pool of ale for the King of Kings; I should like the Heavenly Host to be drinking it for all eternity." This vision of the Lord God presiding over a grand Irish drinking party may be profoundly offensive to all kinds of pious souls, but not to my mother or father. Many a Saint Patrick's Day in our home looked very much like Saint Brigid's vision of heaven.

At age six, I began taking introductory piano lessons from the Franciscan nuns at Holy Trinity. When we moved to South Boston my parents arranged that I continue keyboard lessons: piano, accordion, and organ. They purchased an old upright piano, which I was delighted to play during any free time that I had. They never had to encourage me to practice; I did it gladly and often.

I quickly learned dozens of Irish ballads and could play jigs and reels on the piano accordion and could keep up with even the most athletic of Irish step dancers. There is an old saying that the Irish are gifted in their feet for football (soccer) and for dancing. I always said it was a good thing that we owned the building in which we lived: the noise level, which included my accordion playing when a party was in progress, would exceed any reasonable decibel level.

I was fortunate to begin informal organ studies under the supervision of Mr. Fred Walsh, an elderly blind gentleman who was the principal organist at Saint Brigid's. With the naïveté and boldness of a twelve-year-old, I approached Mr. Walsh with a proposition. I had already gained some mastery of keyboard instruments—piano and accordion—and possessed a reasonable facility in sight-reading musical notation. So I asked Mr. Walsh if he would consider introducing me to the organ. In return, if I was successful, I might substitute for him for some services at the parish. He readily agreed to be my first organ tutor, and without any fee. I was amazed that Mr. Walsh had committed to memory such a vast amount of the organ repertory. He was blind from birth and had a highly developed sense of pitch and exceptional digital dexterity. With great patience, he detailed the mechanics of the small but excellent pipe organ at Saint Brigid's, explaining each of its ranks and stops.

He told me that the pipe organ is like a big box of whistles. Each pipe sits atop a wind chest, which is filled with compressed air provided by a bellows or blower. I watched as, with remarkable dexterity, he reached for each "stop" on the organ console. He explained that each one of these stops represents a set of pipes (a rank) of a particular tonal color, with a different pipe for every note on the keyboard. He demonstrated with an 8' flute, quickly running scales and letting me hear the pure sounds that emerged from the rank of flute pipes.

He methodically introduced me to the organ's pedal board and proper approaches to playing it effectively. I must say that at first, I really did not think I could do what Mr. Walsh was able to do so effortlessly. It was fun to play the pedals along with the rest of the organ, but I did not expect that it would be a workout too. Mr. Walsh required that I practice keyboard scales for hours, without touching the rest of the instrument.

After seemingly endless hours of keyboard exercises, he finally let me actually work on a piece of organ music. Nothing ever escaped his scrupulous attention and discerning ear. He heard every mistake, although he probably only commented on the most egregious ones. Before long I was picking up the service music for benediction and requiem masses. When he had sufficient confidence in my ability, he let me take over responsibilities for some of the services. I became his unofficial assistant organist, something I happily continued to do throughout high school and college, until I entered the Society of Jesus.

In fact, I had only two kinds of jobs during high school and college: music and food. In addition to assisting Mr. Walsh at Saint Brigid's, I also played the Hammond organ at an indoor roller-skating rink that featured ballroom-type dancing parties on Saturday afternoons.

My other jobs were all related to food and food service. As I noted earlier, my mother worked as a waitress. She was a waitress for so many years that my father jokingly used to quip that she and her friends had been servers at the Last Supper. During her tenure at the University Club of Boston, Mario Bonello was the executive chef. My mother got me occasional odd jobs with Chef Mario during my high school years, and for three summers I worked for him in Ogunquit, Maine, where he was executive chef at a seasonal hotel called Sparhawk Hall.

During my first summer I worked in the kitchen as a glass washer, graduating to the lofty role of *garde manger*. Although the title seemed awesome to a fifteen-year-old, it was nothing more than an entry-level cooking position that involved preparing salads or other smaller plates, which could be quickly assembled for service.

Later, I rotated to become an assistant to René, the pastry chef. He was a very kind French Canadian baker, trained in classic French patisserie. I worked alongside him in the day-to-day operations of the resort's pastry kitchen. In addition to making pastries and breads, he got me involved in assessing inventory and supplies and keeping the bakery sanitary and safe. Most exciting for me was when he involved me in helping him develop and test new recipes and alternative baking methods. I first learned the art of making pastry cream and buttercream from him. I learned firsthand about classic doughs: pâte à choux, pâte brisée, pâte feuilletée, and brioche.

Here is the simple way that René taught me to make the classic pâte à choux, the light pastry dough base used to make profiteroles, croquembouches, éclairs, cream puffs, French crullers, beignets, St. Honoré cake, and gougères.

PÂTE À CHOUX

Cabbage pastry

Makes about 1 dozen large eclairs or 2 dozen small puffs

Ingredients

- 1 stick (¼ pound) unsalted butter, cut into small pieces
- 1 teaspoon sugar
- ½ teaspoon kosher salt
- 1¼ cups all-purpose flour
- 4 large eggs, plus 1 large egg white
- 1 cup water

Method

1. Preheat the oven to 400°F.
2. Line sheet pans with parchment paper and spray lightly with vegetable spray.
3. Combine butter, sugar, salt, and 1 cup water in a medium-sized saucepan and bring to a boil.
4. Remove the pan from the heat and with a wooden spoon stir in all of the flour at once.
5. Return the pan to the stovetop and over a medium-high burner cook the mixture while continually stirring it for 3 to 4 minutes until it begins naturally to pull away from the sides of the pan. This cooking helps to dry out the dough before the eggs are added.
6. Transfer the mixture to the bowl of a stand mixer fitted with a paddle attachment. Pâte à choux must be beaten thoroughly, so using a

high-speed stand mixer is best. But you can do it with a handheld mixer, if necessary.

7. On low to medium speed, process the dough until it begins to cool down a bit before adding each of the 4 eggs (one at a time, until incorporated) and finally, the egg white. The paddle attachment helps the steam gently to escape from the dough and aids in its cooling. As you progressively add the eggs, allow each one to be beaten and fully incorporated into the dough before adding the next. Do not rush this step. The whole process may take up to 10 minutes.
8. You will notice that the dough begins to soften and lighten. Once the final egg white has been incorporated, the dough is ready.
9. The dough can be spooned or piped into desired shapes. Bake in the preheated oven for 25 to 35 minutes or until the outside is golden brown and crisp and the pastry sounds hollow when tapped.
10. Let the baked shells cool thoroughly before filling. If you want to use them with a savory filling, omit the sugar in the initial step above.

René impressed upon me the discipline of not opening the oven to peek for at least the first 15 minutes of the initial baking, lest the pastry might collapse. Believe me, he was absolutely right. I did this once early on in my apprenticeship, and we lost a very large batch of puffs. I learned this lesson well: be patient and trusting.

Saint Paul got it right, even though he was not talking about baking pâte à choux: "But if we hope for what we do not see, we wait for it with patience" (Romans 8:25).

Although temperamental and unpredictable, Mario Bonello was a first-rate chef, with advanced collateral skills in ice sculpture and elaborate vegetable carving. His buffets garnered national recognition for design and presentation. I watched him like a hawk with an eye on its prey. If imitation is the best form of flattery for a teacher, I have never forgotten the techniques that I learned from observing this culinary artist at work.

Our parish grammar and high schools were under the care of the religious congregation of the Sisters of Charity of Nazareth (SCN). Even though the congregation maintains its motherhouse in Kentucky, many of its sisters were recruited from the numerous excellent schools that the congregation staffed in the northeast. I candidly acknowledge that my academic career was firmly shaped and nurtured by these extraordinary women.

Sister Wanda Banks, SCN, had grown up in Saint Brigid's parish. She was the daughter of a military careerist. She had four brothers, two of whom went on to become quite distinguished Jesuit priests. Another brother, Paul, pursued a career in mathematics and as fate would decree, would teach me calculus during my freshman year at Boston College.

Sister John Robert (aka Sr. Wanda Banks), as she was then called, was my eighth-grade teacher. At the time she was about the same age as my mother, but she seemed to me to be much older. Her names in religion were strategically selected to honor her two learned Jesuit brothers, John and Robert. John had earned a doctorate in English literature and Bob, a PhD in classical languages and literature. Sr. John Robert obviously recognized some hidden potential in me and in several of my classmates and insisted on additionally drilling us in math and grammar. We were required to show up to her classroom early and stay later. She was a natural drill sergeant. She insisted that we take the qualifying examination for admission to Boston College High School. Founded by the Jesuits in 1863, it was acknowledged as the best private high school in Boston.

Sister John Robert also may have recognized certain spiritual sensitivities in me of which I was still unaware. On special occasions when one of her brothers was in town, she would insist that I come to the convent chapel to serve as acolyte at their masses. She never failed to keep me aware of their assignments and challenges. Fr. John Banks, S.J., who was fluent in written and spoken Arabic, was a missionary, teaching English literature at the Jesuit-run Al-Hikma University in Baghdad. Fr. Robert served as a tenured professor of classics at the College of the Holy Cross in Worcester, Massachusetts. With her unfailing encouragement and relentless drive for achievement, I did gain admission to Boston College High School.

In 1956, the pastor of Saint Brigid's was the Right Reverend Monsignor Patrick J. Waters, PhD. Monsignor Waters had been a senior professor of dogmatic theology and the history of philosophy at Saint John's Seminary in Boston before accepting this pastoral assignment. He was a very erudite man—well above the average intelligence level of most of his immigrant Irish parishioners. He came from a fairly affluent industrial Boston family and wanted to use some of his inherited financial resources to encourage the academic advancement of students from the parish school. Each year he offered a four-year scholarship covering tuition, books, and fees to a graduating eighth grader who had achieved the highest academic performance during the prior three scholastic years. When I graduated from Nazareth School in 1956, I was the fortunate recipient and beneficiary of Monsignor Waters's philanthropy.

Msgr. Waters believed in strict accountability. Recipients of his scholarship grants were required to bring their report cards to him for review after each quarter and discuss their current course work and future academic plans. He also maintained a significant personal library and would recommend certain books that he thought might complement the specific courses, particularly in the areas of classical languages and literature (Greek and Latin) and American and English Literature.

Matriculation into the world of Boston College High School was the single most important decision I made. More than any other life experience, BC High would open to me worlds that I might otherwise never have ventured to explore—intellectual, social, cultural, and spiritual. Earlier I noted that the Jesuits seemed to surround my life in important ways from the beginning—and that embrace was never more focused and sustained than during the four years of my secondary education at BC High where, as one Jesuit teacher reminded us during the first week of classes, "This is a place where boys become men."

In those halcyon years the faculty and administration of the school were comprised predominantly of Jesuit priests, scholastics, and brothers. In my first year, all of my five teachers were Jesuit scholastics and priests. I began to admire and appreciate the distinctive gifts of each of these men and also the things they shared in common. I spent a lot of time with these Jesuits in the classroom, in extracurricular activities, in spiritual experiences, and in social engagements.

And for the first time in my life I became associated with a group of fellow students—all young men—who came from familial situations and cultural experiences vastly different from the Irish cocoon in which I had so comfortably grown into adolescence. More importantly, these classmates were all my intellectual equals or superiors. During the last years of grammar school, I had been a big fish in a very small pond; now, I was a very small fish in a gigantic pond of more skilled fellow swimmers.

I took to the intellectual challenges that BC High offered, especially to the study of languages, history, and literature. I held my own in science and math, but I could not learn enough about ancient civilizations, their literatures and mythologies, and the histories and languages that were keys to their understanding and interpretation.

During a midyear written examination in geometry during my sophomore year, I was stricken with abdominal pains that had all of the earmarks of acute appendicitis. I was taken to a local community hospital in Dorchester run by the Daughters of Charity. Prepped and anesthetized for an appendectomy, I awoke to discover that the surgery never took place. Rather, a perceptive attending physician had diagnosed mononucleosis. I was hospitalized for a week as they addressed this illness.

Without fail, every single day during my hospital stay was highlighted by a brief visit from the rector of the BC High community, Fr. Francis J. Gilday, S.J. This man was legendary in the New England Province of the Jesuits. As the religious superior of the Church of the Immaculate Conception in downtown Boston—the site of the original high school—Fr. Gilday was instrumental in raising the necessary funds to purchase the land parcel in Dorchester and build the initial structures that became the new BC High. Despite his many other more pressing daily obligations, without fail, he appeared every day in my Carney Hospital room with words of inspiration and encouragement. Looking back, I now see how these visits by the #1 Jesuit at BC High gave me an unmistakable sense of what it means when Jesuits say that they are "men for others."

Fr. Robert E. Sheridan, S.J., entered my French classroom in the fall of my junior year and announced: *"J'entre dans la salle de classe; je regarde autour de moi, je vois mes élèves"* ("I enter the classroom; I look around me and see my students"). With those memorable words I began a love affair with all things French, and, as you will see later, a lifelong romance with *la cuisine française*.

Although Robert Sheridan was as Irish as my grandfather and probably just as old when he became *mon professeur*, he was affectionately known as *Mon Père* to everyone. He was only one of the characters I came to know and love in the Society of Jesus. From the perspective of his students he breathed, ate, and lived the French language and its literatures. I probably never worked harder to master a subject than I did in his introductory French class. I imitated everything *le Père* Sheridan said and did, and before long, I was beginning to speak and write the language of kings and nobles.

High school was a happy and growth-filled time in my life. My junior homeroom teacher was Fr. John W. Chapman, S.J., who like Sister John Robert, recognized potential about which I was unaware. Fr. Chapman selected four boys in our section for advanced work in both Latin and Greek. On Saturday mornings, one or twice a month, Fr. Chapman would call and invite us to come to the Jesuit residence at the school for two or three hours of intensive additional work on selected Latin or Greek texts—well beyond what the ordinary curriculum might require. At the end of these marathon sessions he would celebrate Mass in the Jesuit residence, and of course we would serve at the altar. Then he sent us merrily on our way.

Fr. Chapman had the distinction of introducing my palate to the taste of lobster. Once when he was visiting with his two unmarried schoolteacher sisters, Anna and Mary—who also lived near my home in South Boston—he invited me to join them for a dinner at the famous Anthony's Pier Four on Boston's historic harbor front. One of the restaurant's specialties was baked stuffed lobster, which all of the Chapmans urged me to try. I had grown up on a diet of haddock and fried clams from a concession stand at City Point, but we never tasted a lobster in our household. I have since developed my own signature recipe for this novel preparation, based on memories of my inaugural gustatory adventure into the world of this delectable crustacean. As you begin to enjoy what the cold waters along the Maine coast have produced, remember this verse from the psalmist: "Taste and see the goodness of the Lord" (Ps 34:8).

BAKED STUFFED LOBSTER

Makes 4 servings

Ingredients

- 4 (1¼ to 1½ pound) Maine lobsters

For the seafood filling

- 4 ounces fresh lump crabmeat
- 1 filet of haddock, cut into 1-inch cubes
- 8 ounces bay or sea scallops (quartered)
- 6 to 8 whole uncooked, peeled, and deveined shrimp
- 2 cups fresh breadcrumbs (best from a day-old French baguette)
- 2 tablespoons freshly squeezed lemon juice
- 2 teaspoons finely grated lemon zest

continued

- ½ cup fresh flat-leaf parsley, minced
- ½ teaspoon cayenne pepper
- ½ cup grated Parmigiano Reggiano cheese
- 1 stick (¼ pound) unsalted butter (melted and slightly cooled)
- sea salt and freshly ground black pepper

Method

1. Preheat the oven to 450°F.
2. Prepare the filling by combining in a bowl all of the seafood, along with the grated lemon zest, lemon juice, and minced parsley. In another bowl, mix the fresh breadcrumbs with the grated Parmigiano Reggiano cheese, cayenne, salt, pepper, and melted butter. Then gently add the breadcrumbs to the seafood and gently combine.
3. In a large pot, bring 10 cups of water to a rapid boil.
4. Now comes the part for those who are not faint of heart. Place the lobster on the cutting board belly-side down. With a strong chef's knife, insert the tip of the knife behind the lobster's eyes where the claws meet the body, and make one quick cut down. Continue to split the body and tail until the lobster is separated into two pieces. Under cold running water in the sink, remove the sand sack and the tomalley, roe, and the black intestine, but leave the tail meat intact. Repeat for all lobsters being used.
5. Remove the large claws from the lobsters and place into the boiling water and cook for 10 to 15 minutes, before removing them to a countertop to cool. Remove the meat from the claws and reserve.
6. Fill the cavities of the lobsters with the prepared filling, making sure to cover the tail meat with the seafood and crumb mixture. Place on a baking sheet and drizzle a bit of extra-virgin olive oil and melted butter over the prepared lobsters before placing the tray into the oven.
7. Bake in the preheated oven for about 15 to 20 minutes, until the topping is golden brown.

8. Sauté the reserved claw meat in a bit of melted butter to rewarm and garnish with some chopped fresh parsley. Distribute the claw meat on top of the baked lobsters and serve immediately.

As I was approaching the beginning of my senior year of high school, I began thinking strategically about college applications. In my class of some 360 boys, at the end of my junior year, I ranked second in terms of academic achievement. Bolstered by my academic standing, I reasoned that I would have good opportunities for college admission, and possibly even to be awarded a scholarship based on merit. Without informing my parents, one summer day in 1960 I took the subway to Cambridge and secured a catalogue and application form from the admissions department at Harvard College. I completed the required paperwork and brought the forms in early October to the principal, Fr. Ambrose J. Mahoney, S.J. Mahoney was a man of small physical stature; he was unceremoniously referred to by my classmates and me as "Mouse Mahoney." However, his stern posture and strict demeanor made him seem to us to be more than six feet tall.

When I appeared at his office door with the completed application forms in hand, he brusquely said: "What do you have there, Mr. Smith?"

"Father, I have completed the required application materials seeking admission to Harvard College. I need your recommendation."

To my utter astonishment and amazement, Fr. Mahoney swiftly seized the forms from my hand and just as quickly ripped them to shreds. "Mr. Smith: you are going to either Holy Cross or to Boston College. You choose."

I didn't tell anyone this story for many years thereafter. I chose to accept early admission and the very generous offer of a Presidential Scholarship from Boston College, which covered full tuition and fees. The tuition at Boston College at that time was $800 per year; more than a half-century later, tuition is $55,464.

In 1961, the president of Boston College was Fr. Michael P. Walsh, S.J., who himself had grown up in Saint Brigid's parish in South Boston. One of his sisters, Mary Walsh Hayhurst, was friendly with both my grandmother and mother; Mary's husband, Bob Hayhurst, worked with my dad as a Boston firefighter. The world of Jesuit influence kept reasserting itself.

If BC High was a big pond, the world of Boston College was a massive ocean. In my freshman Greek class I met students from other prestigious Jesuit high schools, like Regis in New York City and St. Ignatius College Prep in Chicago. For all of my knowledge of Latin and Greek, I was humbled to realize that others among my peers knew even more. We all came under the influence that year of an eccentric Jesuit professor of Greek, Fr. Carl Thayer, S.J., in a course that read the orations of Demosthenes, most notably his brilliant speech "On the Crown" (330 BCE). Fr. Thayer was erratic, sometimes plunging deeply into these classical texts, many of which he seemed to have committed to memory. At other times he would idle away class time excoriating the administration for some pending decision, like the prospective admission of women to the College of Arts and Sciences. Fr. Thayer—in an era well before the dawn of political correctness and women's liberation—believed that constitutionally, women were incapable of learning Greek. I would often encounter him slowly meandering around the campus between classes, silently rapt in his thoughts. Although I was still a naïve youth, I seemed to see beyond his obvious idiosyncratic behaviors and recognize a compassionate soul lurking beneath all his bluster. Although the classroom experiences were tense and unpredictable, I did come to appreciate the works of Sophocles, Euripides, Plato, and Demosthenes, thanks to this Jesuit's lifelong passion for their exquisite use of language and penetrating thought.

I came to understand that the ancient Greeks ate many smaller meals during the day, but the largest and most important meal of the day was dinner (δεῖπνον [deipnon]). I recall little mention of meals in all of the ancient Greek texts that I studied with Fr. Thayer and others, but I have many times made a version of this classic Greek bean soup, which I imagine that even Homer would have enjoyed.

FASOLADA

Classic Greek white bean soup

All the Mediterranean cultures seem to have some version of this simple soup, which still is considered to be the national dish of Greece, made with small white beans, a handful of vegetables, and copious amounts of extra-virgin olive oil.

Makes 6 servings

Ingredients

- 1 pound medium-sized white dried beans (cannellini)
- ⅔ cup extra-virgin olive oil
- 3 cups of finely chopped red onions
- 3 medium-sized diced carrots
- 3 diced celery stalks
- 3 finely chopped garlic cloves
- 2 bay leaves
- 28-ounce can diced San Marzano tomatoes
- 2 strips orange zest
- 1 teaspoon dried red pepper flakes
- 6 to 8 cups water
- salt and pepper to taste
- 3 tablespoons balsamic vinegar
- ½ cup chopped fresh flat-leaf parsley
- 1 cup of any small pasta (*stelline*, *acini di pepe*, *orzo*, *tubettini*, etc.)

Method

1. Soak the dried beans overnight. The next day, rinse and drain them.
2. Heat ⅓ cup olive oil in a Dutch oven or stockpot over low heat and sauté the onions, carrots, and celery together until wilted, about 10 minutes. Stir in the garlic.
3. Add the drained beans and toss to coat in the oil.
4. Add the tomatoes, orange zest, pepper flakes, bay leaves, and water.
5. Bring to a boil and then reduce heat to low and allow the beans to simmer for about two hours.
6. During the final 10 minutes, add the pasta to the thickened soup.
7. Before removing from the heat, correct the seasoning with salt and pepper.

continued

8. If you wish the soup to be even thicker and creamier, purée about 2 cups of the soup using an immersion blender and combine back into the soup. Blend in the remaining olive oil and finish with a few teaspoons of balsamic vinegar just before serving to add a bit of acidity.
9. Garnish with freshly chopped parsley and perhaps a bit of crumbled feta cheese.

Because the study of French had become such a passion during my final two years in high school, I decided to pursue French language and literature as a minor in college. Fortunately for me I met Fr. Joseph D. Gauthier, S.J., a French-Canadian Jesuit professor and scholar of the twentieth-century French novel. At the time he was the chairman of the romance languages department at Boston College. As a teacher and mentor, Fr. Gauthier ranks in my personal pantheon among the five most significant intellectual influences in my life. He was a master teacher: well-prepared, with an extraordinary command of his subject and an ability to engage with students, foster insights, and inspire future research. He opened for me the expansive worlds of André Gide and Jean-Paul Sartre, Albert Camus and Marcel Proust, François Mauriac and Georges Bernanos, Colette and Simone de Beauvoir, among others.

At Fr. Gauthier's recommendation, I also enrolled in a course offered by Professor Georges Zayed. Zayed had earned the prestigious Doctorat d'État Lettres/Sciences Humaines at L'Université Paris-Sorbonne and was an acknowledged specialist in nineteenth-century French poetry. Professor Zayed had been a visiting professor at Boston College from the University of Alexandria in Egypt. He was an accomplished and well-known poet and author in addition to being a brilliant teacher. I was mesmerized by his lectures. He never read a poem; he always recited them purely from memory. He once told us, "If you really want to understand a poem, you must make it a lasting part of yourself." To this day I still can recite from memory some of the poetry of Charles Baudelaire, Paul Verlaine, and Arthur Rimbaud, which Professor Zayed had invited me to make a place for in my heart. Some of these poets' words have been my companions now for more than a half-century.

I shared a philosophy, theology, and English class with a fellow student whom I had met during my first days at Boston College. Walter J. Woods had grown up in the affluent town of Wellesley and had graduated from Marian High School in Framingham. Owing to a practice of assigning seating in classrooms, Wally and I were located in the same general area of each of these classrooms, with surnames ending in "S" and "W." If his name had been "Adams," we may never have met.

We became most bonded in our shared English class with another colorful Jesuit professor, Fr. Arthur McGillivray, S.J. Tall and flighty, Fr. McGillivray had a penchant for the dramatic. Although his was a basic-level course in English language, literature, and writing, it could have been more properly titled a course in the prose of Elwyn Brooks ("E. B.") White, an American writer who had been a regular contributor to *The New Yorker* magazine and a coauthor of the English language style guide *The Elements of Style*, which Fr. McGillivray considered almost as important as the Bible. I think he must have murmured "Strunk and White" to himself in his sleep.

Fr. McGillivray also spent an inordinate amount of time in the course excruciatingly dissecting "The Hound of Heaven" by Francis Thompson. I still cannot fathom what it was about Thompson that so intrigued McGillivray. Thompson was a Roman Catholic who led an anguished existence, having given up seminary studies in preparation for the priesthood and later studying to become a physician. He was a guy who seemed never to have gotten his act together, living a meager life in London, ending up addicted to the drugs that were helping to manage his pain, and dying just before his forty-eighth birthday. From McGillivray's fascination with this man and his second-rate poem, you might have thought he was on a par with Milton or Shakespeare.

It seemed to Wally and me that Fr. McGillivray's thought was like a record needle stuck in a groove. In hindsight, I wondered if the prior night's cocktails in Saint Mary's Hall Jesuit residence might have clouded his memory for what he was teaching, since he seemed to be continuously circling back over the same materials.

At any rate, McGillivray's meandering thoughts gave Wally Woods and me more than ample material to process as our friendship began to mature.

When I first met Wally he had little interest in cooking or baking; his one culinary accomplishment was making onion rings in his parents' kitchen on vacation days. I recall a day when we were in a supermarket and he made the following comment: "When I'm walking up and down these aisles, all I see are jars and cans and boxes on shelves, and you see dinner!" When Wally later acquired a small New England salt box home in Wareham, Massachusetts, in the early 1980s he began to expand his skills in the kitchen, and today he is a very competent cook and bread baker.

One of his favorite dishes to make and serve is *Bucatini all' amatriciana*. There is a long tradition behind this classic recipe and many differing opinions about its origin. There is a pasta sauce, popular in central Italy, called *la gricia*, which is made with olive oil, guanciale, black pepper, and Pecorino cheese. Some folks claim that the people of Amatrice added tomatoes to the traditional *gricia* recipe and called it *amatriciana*. We both favor Marcella Hazan's directional approach to making this sauce, included in her book *Essentials of Italian Cooking*.[1] Here is my adaptation of a true gem of Italian cookery.

BUCATINI ALL'AMATRICIANA

Pasta with bacon, tomato, and Pecorino from Lazio

Makes 4 servings

Ingredients

- 2 tablespoons extra-virgin olive oil
- 1 tablespoon unsalted butter
- 1 medium, finely chopped onion
- ¼ cup dry white wine
- 2 ounces *guanciale* (preferable) or *pancetta* (substitute), cut into quarter-inch cubes
- 28-ounce can diced San Marzano tomatoes
- red pepper flakes
- kosher salt
- 1 pound bucatini pasta
- 3 tablespoons grated Parmigiano Reggiano cheese
- 2 tablespoons grated Pecorino Romano cheese

Method

1. Heat oil and butter in a Dutch oven over medium heat.
2. Add onion and sauté until softened and golden.

1 Marcella Hazan, *Essentials of Italian Cooking* (New York: Knopf, 1992).

3. Add red pepper flakes and bloom for one minute.
4. Add white wine and reduce slightly.
5. Add *guanciale* or *pancetta* and cook an additional minute.
6. Add tomatoes with about ¼ cup of reserved juice from tomatoes, along with a bit of salt.
7. Reduce heat and cook uncovered at a gentle simmer for 25 minutes. Adjust seasonings as desired.
8. While the sauce cooks, bring a large pot of salted water to boil. Cook the bucatini according to package directions to the al dente stage, less than 2 minutes.
9. Drain pasta and add to the Dutch oven with the sauce. Stir to coat pasta evenly and allow the pasta to complete its cooking in the sauce.
10. Turn off the heat, add the cheeses, stir to combine, and enjoy.

Despite all the intellectual and cultural stimulation that Boston College was providing, I was aware of other internal stirrings, which gradually became more insistent. When I had begun my organ studies with Mr. Walsh, he introduced me to the musical idiom of the *cantus firmus* in some of Bach's choral and organ works.

The *cantus firmus* functions as connective tissue within a work, expressing and reexpressing a dominant melodic line within a composition. It is the resonant, fixed melody to which other voices are added in a polyphonic work. The presence of Jesuits throughout my life have functioned like a cantus firmus, holding its entire storyline together as new stories and experiences progressively accumulated.

As my freshman year at Boston College was progressing, I more insistently began asking myself whether I might become a Jesuit priest. As quickly as these thoughts would surface in my consciousness, I tried to dismiss them. I dispelled this inner questioning with all earnestness, believing that I would most probably end up becoming a surgeon, lawyer, or a college professor. However, the growing attraction and fascination with becoming a Jesuit priest would not leave me.

Finally, I decided to visit with Fr. William Burke, S.J., a spiritual counselor whose office was located in a fairly remote area within Boston College's iconic tower building, Gasson Hall. I had never spoken with Fr. Burke, having passed by his office many times without summoning the courage to knock on the door. After several aborted efforts I eventually mustered sufficient inner fortitude to cross the threshold and expose my conflict to this wise guide of souls.

Burke was a very learned man whose vocabulary and literary allusions captivated me. He welcomed me and helped me quickly to get to the heart of my dilemma. After listening to my saga for some thirty minutes or so, he sat back in his chair and said: "You may have a vocation to the Society of Jesus." Hearing his words was paralyzing. I did not want a vocation to the Society of Jesus! I wanted to be told that these were fleeting fantasies and that I should get back to focusing on my courses in the arts and sciences.

"Well, what do I do now, Father?" Father Burke said he would make some follow-up appointments for me to chat with some other Jesuits, to test whether or not his intuition about my possible Jesuit vocation might be corroborated. He asked me to return the next day and he would have some appointments scheduled. The first appointment was with the dean of the college, Fr. John McCarthy, S.J. Few freshmen ever crossed the threshold of the office of the dean. What reason would one have? With trepidation, I entered the massive corner office in that historic Gothic building. McCarthy was a very reserved, ascetic-looking figure, tall and thin, but with a welcoming disposition.

"Fr. Burke tells me that you have an interest in entering the Jesuit novitiate," he said. How had that happened? On Monday I had been looking to dispel my notion that I was being called to be a Jesuit, and on Wednesday the dean was telling me that I was interested in entering the novitiate. Fr. McCarthy then proceeded to thoroughly interview me about my whole life. At the end of the session he suggested that I meet two other Jesuits for similar types of conversations. Little did I realize at the time that these conversations were actually formal screening interviews, which ultimately would lead to my admission to the New England Province of the Society of Jesus.

When the interviews at Boston College were completed, Father Burke, whom I later learned was also the province's director of vocations, arranged for me to take some written psychological examinations at the provincial headquarters on Commonwealth Avenue in Boston's historic Back Bay. I remember walking up to the front door of 297 Commonwealth Avenue on a late fall afternoon with the quiet belief that it would be here that I would finally discover that I really was not suited for the life of a Jesuit.

Throughout all of this, I had not told anyone about these exploratory discussions or proceedings. You can imagine my utter panic when I received a letter dated January 25, 1962 (the feast of the Conversion of Saint Paul), from the Very Rev. James E. Coleran, S.J., then provincial of the New England Province of the Society of Jesus, informing me that I had been accepted for entry to the novitiate at Shadowbrook in Lenox.

The new Shadowbrook novitiate was built on the estate formerly owned by Andrew Carnegie. The original mansion, which had served as the New England Jesuits' first house of formation, was destroyed in a catastrophic fire in March 1956. The new building served as a novitiate only for a dozen years because of changes set in motion by the reforms of the Second Vatican Council. The Jesuits soon determined that the spiritual, intellectual, and practical formation of its future priests for an active, apostolic ministry should not be pursued in remote geographical locations, but in places closer to where young Jesuits would soon work.

The provincial, Father Coleran, had been born in 1900 and, like me, completed his freshman year at Boston College before he entered the Society at Yonkers, New York, on July 30, 1919. Fr. Coleran's letter of acceptance further explained that I was to appear at Shadowbrook before 3 o'clock on the afternoon of July 30, 1962. What was I to do now? My innocent explorative conversation with Fr. Burke in early October had now culminated with a letter of admission to the first probation of the Jesuits. Was all of this a dream, or was this really happening?

I sat on this news for weeks before mustering the courage to tell my parents. I decided first to share this decision with my father. We had one family car—a black 1960 Pontiac Bonneville—which my father generously allowed me to use quite often. It happened that Dad had worked the night shift and I was scheduled to pick him up at 8 a.m. at the firehouse. When he got into the passenger's seat in the car, I told him that I had some important news to share with him. He suggested we drive to the nearby City Point beach. There we could talk freely.

Once there, I said, "I am going to leave Boston College at the conclusion of this academic year and join the Jesuits this coming summer." There was momentary silence as my words settled in.

"That is a wonderful decision," he said. "If God is calling you to this important vocation as a Jesuit priest, then you must follow your heart." I felt such relief in hearing my dad's initial words of confirmation and acceptance.

"I have always had deep admiration for the Jesuits," he went on. "It was a Jesuit priest, you know, who helped me with my decision to convert to Roman Catholicism." I guess I had remembered that fact, but it was so reassuring to hear my dad now linking these two events: his entry into the Church and my fledging vocation to the Society of Jesus.

And then he offered me counsel, which was both wise and liberating. "If this vocation is truly from God and you are willing to accept this gift, then I wish for you a happy and productive life as a Jesuit. However, no matter how strong your desires may be today, if you should ever discover that this is not the proper life for you, then I would hope that you will have the inner freedom to leave the seminary and pursue other life courses or professions."

My father, by every standard of the world, was not a learned man. He had not graduated from high school. He had entered the Navy and served in the Pacific campaign during the war. He was not a man of many words. But that morning, sitting by City Point in the early hours of a wintry Saturday, he had words and wisdom that ring as clearly in my mind and heart today as when God first put those words on his tongue to set me firmly on the pathway of my Jesuit life.

His final query was: "Have you told your mother?" I quickly said no. He asked if I wanted him to inform her. I said that I would like to tell her directly, which he immediately affirmed was the better course of action.

When I told my mother the same story, her response was equally affirmative, but decidedly balder.

"Well, finally!" she said. "I have been waiting for you to tell me this for a long time. I thought you would have entered the Jesuits after you finished at BC High. You have spent so much time with Jesuits, you are practically one of them already." Her final comments were even more hilarious. "When you graduated from high school last year, we bought you a set of luggage as a gift. Remember? Well, I had told Fr. Chapman of our plan, and he said, buy black luggage. When I asked you if we should get black leather, you said: 'No. I want tan leather.' We should have followed Fr. Chapman's advice, because now we will have to buy you a black leather suitcase for Shadowbrook. Your sisters can use the tan luggage."

When I left for Shadowbrook on that very hot day at the end of July, I told my parents not to give away my clothes or permit either of my sisters to move into my room. I expressed reservations that this would prove to be the right life for me and that I was entering the novitiate with an open but discerning heart. That was six decades ago. Fortunately, the intervening years have not only erased those lingering questions, but have confirmed the rightness of the vocational choice of an idealistic young man.

Chapter 2

THE LONG YEARS OF JESUIT FORMATION

Then Jesus declared, "I am the bread of life. Whoever comes to me will never go hungry, and whoever believes in me will never be thirsty."

—JOHN 6:35

When I entered the Jesuit Order in 1962, there were more than 1,300 members living and working within the New England Province. Most of these men received their early formation—the initial four years of a full course of studies of some fifteen years—at Shadowbrook, the former estate in Lenox, Massachusetts, where Andrew Carnegie lived and died. As noted earlier, in 1956 a disastrous early morning fire destroyed the old mansion and claimed the lives of four Jesuits. The remaining members of the Shadowbrook community were dispersed to the New York and Maryland provinces to continue their formation, while the officials of New England raised funds and developed plans to build a new residence on an adjacent parcel of land, with a commanding view of the Stockbridge Bowl.

The Jesuits welcomed me and my fellow novices on a sweltering July 30 afternoon, the eve of the patronal feast day of the founder of the Jesuits, Saint Ignatius Loyola. Waking up on my first morning at Shadowbrook, we were treated to the ceremony of the profession of vows of those men who had just completed the two-year novitiate formation, also called first probation. The day was full of other happy celebrations, culminating in a first-class banquet, the likes of which I had never seen before. I thought I had died and gone to heaven. So sumptuous was the feast that our master of novices, a 6-foot 5-inch giant of a man, Gerald O'Callaghan, S.J., strongly admonished us against writing home to our families describing in detail the bacchanalia that we had just experienced. I thought to myself, if this is the Society of Jesus, I have really chosen well!

I soon realized how truly exceptional that feast day celebration was. The ordinary fare was much more modest. I came to understand the Latin expression used to describe the day-to-day routine, including meals, *de more*—roughly interpreted to mean "boring, usual, and predictable."

There are hundreds of stories I could recollect from the initial three years I spent at Shadowbrook, but I want to focus on one person and one extraordinary relationship that was probably more central to my formation as a Jesuit than all the other intellectual and spiritual enrichment these years would afford.

The new Shadowbrook building had been the master project of the community's rector, Fr. Lawrence C. Langguth, S.J. While Fr. Langguth had great talent for building and construction, he was less skilled in interpersonal relations and social exchange. He knew how to fix a leak in a dripping pipe or get a heating system to function properly. He oversaw an impressive group of Jesuit brothers who collectively formed the operating staff of this massive building, augmented by the sweat labor provided by the two hundred or more novices and juniors who comprised the residential community. The faculty and administration numbered about fifteen other Jesuit priests. But everyone would agree: the brothers made the place run.

One of those brothers was already a golden jubilarian by the time I was fortunate to meet him: Brother Thomas Glennon, S.J. Brother Glennon was a native of Ireland, a proud man from Galway. He was of average height but strappingly built. Brother Glennon managed the farm and orchards, which produced from May through October the abundance of vegetables and fruits we enjoyed. Brother Glennon also oversaw the produce that was stored through the winter in impressive root cellars: potatoes, carrots, turnips, squash, and apples. In the winter months, he maintained a large green house that he had built in which he prepared seedlings for the next spring planting cycle. He was frequently the breakfast cook and occasionally substituted as *chef de cuisine* when Charlie, Shadowbrook's lay executive chef, was ill or on vacation.

As novices, we were regularly assigned to various jobs around the house or outdoors twice a day: after breakfast and in the early afternoon. One of the second-year novices was selected by the novice master as an executive coordinator of the novitiate and given the Latin title of *manuductor*, which roughly translates as "leading by the hand." The *manuductor* created the work schedules for the novices. I was very fortunate to find myself assigned with some frequency to assist Brother Glennon in one of his various outposts. I also found myself seeking him out during free time and lending him a hand, even when not assigned.

Tom Glennon was not an educated man, but he possessed an uncanny wisdom and practical spirituality. He took his role of edifying the novices (that is, not scandalizing them in any way by either his words or actions) quite seriously. Quite quickly, I found myself naturally bonding with this older Jesuit. I asked him hundreds of questions. At first he was circumspect and guarded about offering too much advice or counsel to a fledging Jesuit, but gradually, as our relationship matured, he told me more about his own life in the Society, about his prayer, his philosophy of work, his devotions, and so much more.

The only leisure he afforded himself was on Sunday mornings. I can remember summer and early autumn Sundays, when our windows might be open, listening to the sounds of Tom Glennon's violin as he played and sang old Celtic ballads. He would never have described himself as a violinist but rather as a fiddler, and he had a lilting, albeit quivering tenor voice. He was not a Pavarotti by any stretch of the imagination, but his voice was strong and soulful. On most Sunday mid-mornings, the novices were engaged in spiritual reading in their rooms for about ninety minutes. I must say that when Br. Tom was singing, I often closed my copy of *The Imitation of Christ* by Thomas à Kempis and quietly listened to his impromptu concert. I loved when he played and sang Schubert's *Ave Maria*. I could hear tender devotion and humble reverence in the vibrato of his voice. I know I benefitted more from this frequent Sunday morning distraction than I gleaned from whatever spiritual insights the readings of Thomas à Kempis or other ascetic writers might have provided.

I particularly relished time spent with Br. Glennon in late May and early June in the vast strawberry patch. I always tried to work as physically close to him as was possible. I often heard him praying aloud as he worked, reciting one Hail Mary after another. More than anyone else on the staff of the novitiate, Brother Tom Glennon was my formator-in-chief, and even more unlikely, my first cooking teacher. Whenever I work with strawberries—even today—I think about Tom Glennon. The recipe for this rustic French strawberry galette memorializes this giant of a Jesuit.

RUSTIC STRAWBERRY GALETTE

Makes 6 servings

Ingredients

For the pastry crust

- 2½ cups all-purpose flour
- ½ tablespoon granulated sugar
- ½ teaspoon kosher salt
- ½ pound cold unsalted butter, diced into quarter-inch pieces
- 6 to 7 tablespoons ice water

For the filling

- 2 cups fresh strawberries, sliced in half lengthwise
- 3 tablespoons granulated sugar
- 1 teaspoon orange zest
- 2 teaspoons freshly squeezed orange juice
- 1 beaten egg
- 1 teaspoon sliced almonds
- confectioners' sugar

Method

To make the pastry dough

1. Place flour, sugar, and salt into the bowl of a food processor and pulse a few times to combine.
2. Add cold diced butter and pulse the mixture until coarse crumbs form with some pea-sized pieces, then stop processing.
3. Initially, add 5 tablespoons of ice water and pulse just until moist clumps or small balls form.

4. Press a piece of dough between your fingertips and if the dough sticks together, you have added enough water. If not, add more water—a teaspoon at a time. Be careful not to add too much water or the dough will be sticky and difficult to roll out.

5. Transfer the dough to a clean work surface and gather together into a ball (it will not be smooth, but do not knead the dough). Roughly flatten and shape the dough into a 12-inch round disk. Cover with plastic wrap and refrigerate for about an hour before using in this galette recipe.

To make the galette

1. Preheat the oven to 400°F.

2. Line a baking sheet with parchment paper or a silicone mat.

3. Roll out the refrigerated pastry to a 14-inch circle and place on parchment paper or silicone mat. Refrigerate the dough while you prepare the filling.

4. Assemble the strawberry halves in a medium bowl. Sprinkle the sugar over the strawberries along with the orange zest and orange juice, and gently toss to thoroughly coat. Allow the strawberries to macerate for a few minutes.

5. Retrieve the chilled dough and arrange the strawberry halves, cut-side down on pie dough, leaving a 2- or 3-inch border of the pie dough. Scatter the sliced almond pieces over the arranged strawberries.

6. Begin folding the edges of the dough inward to partially cover the strawberries, forming a rustic border.

7. Brush the dough with the beaten egg wash, and drizzle with a bit of sugar. (I use some raw sugar crystals, but any sugar will do.)

8. Bake the galette for 30 to 40 minutes, until the filling begins to bubble and the pastry is completely golden.

9. Allow the galette to completely cool before serving.

continued

10. Dust with confectioners' sugar.
11. Serve tart with almond-flavored whipped cream and garnish with fresh mint leaves.

When the new Shadowbrook was constructed, it was providentially equipped with a kitchen that would be the envy of any first-class hotel. It had state-of-the art commercial stainless-steel appliances. It was meant to be able to provide three meals a day for a community of well over two hundred hungry young lads, as well as to wash and sterilize vast numbers of dishes, cutlery, and glassware. Apart from the professional chef and the brothers who filled in, the whole kitchen was efficiently staffed by the novices.

Cooking with Brother Glennon was an unforgettable experience. The man was a vigorous proponent of the school of thought "Waste not, want not," forcefully admonishing us not to waste *anything*. I suspect that some of his frugality came from his impoverished early life in Ireland where families had to make do with whatever meager things might be available. Besides, he toiled long and hard to produce so many of the fruits and vegetables that we might be too ready to discard.

I first learned the art of soup-making from this peasant farmer. When assigned to him, we would journey down to the walk-in refrigerator with a *plaustrum* (the Latin term for a service cart or trolley) and he would gather up virtually everything that had been left over from the prior couple of days. That is when the fun began. He would return to the kitchen with an eclectic array of foodstuffs and begin to plot his meal.

On one of those occasions, he suggested we bring the cart to the rear of the kitchen where there were enormous gas-fired cooking vats, probably with 100-gallon capacity.

"We're going to make a hearty soup," he announced. He instructed me to fill the cauldron with water, about half-full. Then he began emptying trays of leftovers into the water. He seemed not to worry whether lamb would combine with leftover meatloaf, or whether carrots and beats would properly marry. He then began adding cups full of seasonings, handfuls of macaroni shells, and handfuls of freshly chopped herbs. Then, with a long stainless-steel paddle in hand, he began to gently stir this massive mélange of ingredients, while occasionally singing a line from a favorite hymn as he gently blended together another version of "Brother Glennon's Mystery Soup."

BROTHER GLENNON'S MYSTERY SOUP

"Everything but the kitchen sink"

Makes 6 servings

Ingredients

- 1 teaspoon olive oil
- 1 cup chopped onion
- 4 ounces pancetta or chopped uncured bacon
- ¾ cup chopped celery
- 1 cup chopped carrots
- 2 cups diced butternut squash
- 1 teaspoon minced garlic
- ½ teaspoon of ground cumin
- ¼ teaspoon of paprika
- ½ teaspoon red pepper flakes
- 1½ cups chopped green beans
- 1 cup of uncooked rice or orzo
- kosher salt and freshly ground pepper
- 6 cups broth (vegetable, chicken, or beef)
- 28-ounce can diced tomatoes
- 2 cups loosely packed spinach or kale

Method

1. Prep all ingredients.
2. In a large stockpot, add olive oil, onion, pancetta, carrots, and celery. Sauté for 4 to 5 minutes until onions are transparent and fragrant.
3. Add diced squash, garlic, and all the spices and sauté again for another 2 to 3 minutes.
4. Add the diced tomatoes and cook for 3 minutes with the vegetables.

continued

5. Add broth, bring to a boil, then add rice or orzo.
6. Reduce heat to simmer and cook, covered, for about 20 to 25 minutes.
7. Add spinach or kale.
8. Cover and simmer for another 5 to 8 minutes or until greens are wilted.
9. Correct seasonings.

Shadowbrook's apple orchards were exceedingly productive, providing enough yield to generate gallons of fresh cider in the autumn and seemingly endless servings of apple sauce and apple pies. Among our community members was another Irish-born Jesuit brother, Tim Cummins, who was the house baker. All of our breads and desserts were prepared in Brother Tim's bakery. He had one apple dessert that became notorious among the younger Jesuits that we affectionately called "Brother Tim's Apple Bombs." The offering was pretty straightforward: He enveloped a peeled and cored whole apple in a simple egg-washed short pastry crust and baked it. He always served it with a hard sauce on the side (without the brandy). I think Br. Tim prayed over each apple dumpling he made. Maybe this phrase from the Book of Psalms is a fitting final word of gratitude for a great man of God: "Keep me as the apple of your eye; hide me in the shadow of your wings." (Psalm 17:8).

In fond tribute, I offer you my own reconstructed (and perhaps more palatable) version of Brother Tim's Apple Bombs.

BROTHER TIM'S APPLE DUMPLINGS

Makes 6 servings

Ingredients

For the pastry

- 2½ cups all-purpose flour
- 1 teaspoon salt
- 1 teaspoon granulated sugar
- 2 sticks chilled unsalted butter, cut into small pieces
- ¼ to ½ cup ice water
- Egg wash for pastry (1 egg, 1 teaspoon of water, and a pinch of salt blended with a fork)

For the apple dumplings

- 6 large baking apples (such as Granny Smith, Honeycrisp, or Crispin), peeled and cored
- 6 tablespoons unsalted butter
- ¾ cup dark brown sugar
- 1 teaspoon ground cinnamon
- ½ teaspoon ground nutmeg

For the brandied hard sauce

- 1 stick (¼ pound) very softened butter
- 1½ cup confectioners' sugar
- 2 tablespoons brandy

Method

For the pastry

1. In the bowl of a food processor, combine flour, salt, and sugar. Working quickly, add the small pieces of cold butter and pulse the mixture until it looks like small peas.
2. With the machine running, gradually add the ice water in a slow, steady stream through the feed tube.
3. Process for a few seconds until the dough holds together without becoming too wet or sticky. You can always add a bit more ice water

continued

if the mixture is too crumbly, but you cannot extract water if you add too much. You want to be able to form the dough into a ball, but not overwork it.

4. Flatten the dough into a rectangle, enclose in plastic wrap, and chill in refrigerator for at least an hour.

To make and bake the apple dumplings

1. Preheat oven to 400°F.
2. Lightly butter a 9x13-inch Pyrex baking dish.
3. On a lightly floured surface, roll out the pastry into a large rectangle (approximately 24x16 inches).
4. Cut the dough into six equal squares. Place an apple on each pastry square, with the cored top facing upward. Place a tablespoon of butter into each of the apples. With a teaspoon, add some brown sugar on top of the butter and, with your finger, force the mixture into the cored-out spaces.
5. Mix the cinnamon and nutmeg together and lightly dust the outer surface of the apples with the spices.
6. With a pastry brush, gently wet the outer perimeter of the dough with water.
7. With your fingertip and index finger, bring a corner of pastry square up to the top of the apple, then bring the opposite corner to the top and press together. Repeat the same technique with the two remaining corners and make sure they seal. With cupped hands, form the dough gently around the apple and be sure it is thoroughly sealed. Slightly pinch the dough at the sides to completely seal in the apple.
8. Place the six apples in the Pyrex baking dish, brush the dumplings with an egg wash and sprinkle with a little bit of granulated sugar.
9. Bake in preheated oven for 50 to 60 minutes.

To make the brandied hard sauce

1. Whisk the butter with a handheld mixer until fluffy.
2. Incorporate the confectioners' sugar gradually until thoroughly blended.
3. Add brandy and whisk again until fully combined.
4. You can serve the hard sauce immediately or store the covered bowl in the refrigerator. The hard sauce will thicken in the refrigerator, so bring it back to room temperature (about 30 minutes) before serving.
5. Serve the baked apple dumplings warm or at room temperature, with a bit of hard sauce on top.

Even though I came to Shadowbrook with some proficiency in piano and organ, I was not permitted to play keyboard instruments during my entire first year in the novitiate. The master of novices thought it was formative to subjugate certain natural interests and desires. Fortunately, by the time I completed the novitiate and entered the next phase of formation—humanistic studies or the "juniorate"—the new rector who succeeded Fr. Langguth was a proficient, classical pianist.

Fr. Thomas Lannon, S.J., quickly learned of my musical interests and talents and one day called me to his office with the proposition that he retain an organ teacher from Pittsfield who might help me to continue to develop as an organist. I was utterly amazed at this unexpected gift from heaven. Fr. Lannon also asked me if I might be willing to serve as one of the community's organists, to which I readily agreed.

I thoroughly enjoyed pursuing organ lessons in addition to my other studies in history, language, and literature. My role as one of the house organists got me into trouble on one memorable occasion. Between semesters, instead of giving me and my classmates a well-deserved break from classes and examinations, the dean thought he had a better idea: he engaged a film professor from Boston College to come to Shadowbrook in the dead of winter and involve us for a long weekend in an exhaustive study of Federico Fellini's masterpiece *La Strada*. Over the course of the weekend we viewed the entire film three times, interspersed with lectures and discussions of various themes and symbols. By Sunday afternoon we were worn out and tense.

The film has a memorable musical score by Nino Rota, with a haunting theme that is frequently reprised throughout. I was the scheduled organist on that Sunday night for the community service of Benediction of the Blessed Sacrament. In the quiet moments just before the priest takes the monstrance into his hand to impart the blessing, using a single solo flute stop I quietly played an improvised interlude, based on that unforgettable melodic line from *La Strada*. One by one my classmates began to giggle, and some began to laugh out loud. The faculty was perplexed, not understanding what had provoked this chain reaction of levity among the juniors. The novices, grouped on the left side of the chapel, were also puzzled. What was going on?

It did not take long for the faculty to uncover the mystery of the infectious and contagious laughter among the juniors. Fr. Lannon probably regretted the investment he had made in my continuing organ studies, although he may have been silently impressed by my rising improvisational skills.

Because of my intensive studies in the classics at Boston College during my freshman year, I was allowed to skip a year of the juniorate program. During the summer of 1965 I packed up my few belongings and prepared for the journey about forty miles away to Weston, where I would begin the third phase of Jesuit formation—the formal study of philosophy.

These were exciting years of change. The Second Vatican Council had been convened by Pope St. John XXIII in October 1962 and the synodal debates among the participating bishops were brought to a conclusion by his successor, Pope Paul VI, in December 1965. A new Order of Mass permitted vernacular languages to be used in public worship. Religious orders, including the Jesuits, were beginning to examine many things about lifestyle, formation, and ministries.

When I arrived at Weston in the summer of 1965, everything was in the final preparation stage to move the venue of our classroom experiences to the campus of Boston College. Even though we would still have special philosophy courses taught by our own Jesuit faculty, the whole teaching-learning engagement would take place in the more normal setting of a university campus, which I already knew so very well. Each morning, dressed in our long black cassocks and overcoats, we would pile into a yellow school bus driven by one of our Jesuit brothers for the half-hour commute to Chestnut Hill. The same bus would shuttle us back at day's end. In addition to our philosophy classes, we were permitted to enroll in other elective courses related to particular academic interests.

The prefect of studies in those years was Fr. James Leo Burke, S.J., a portly, wizening, and discerning older man who was a proverbial czar in deciding who studied what and where. One day, Father Burke sauntered into my room at Weston College to discuss my academic future. "I think it would be a good idea for you to enroll next summer in the intensive program in Russian language at Harvard," he informed me. This was the era of *Sputnik*, a series of earth-orbiting satellites that were launched by the Soviet Union beginning in 1957, and BC High was beginning to offer Russian language studies to its students.

Fr. Burke's suggestion caught me off guard. I replied, "If that is what you would like me to do, of course I will study Russian. But I was thinking that later on I might like to study for a doctorate in moral theology. I already possess a reasonable proficiency in French. Might it not be a better idea, then, that I earn a master's degree in French and teach high school French during regency? And French would be a more useful tool for the future study of theology."

Without blinking, he concurred that my proposition was brilliant. "Apply to the graduate French language program at L'Université Laval in Québec City," he said, "and I will make living arrangements for you at the Collège des Jésuites while you pursue this plan." It was decided: I would further my studies and teach high school-level French.

That is how quickly a decision was made that would so significantly influence the rest of my life. I thoroughly enjoyed my time in Québec and Paris, where I worked hard at mastering newly developing audiovisual methodologies for teaching French. I was able to take advantage of a newly established partnership between L'Université Laval and Paris's Sorbonne and to earn a master's degree.

During my student days in Paris, I lived in the historic Jesuit residence on the Left Bank at 42 Rue de Grenelle, located in the 7th Arrondissement in the shadows of La Tour Eiffel. It was a restive time in Paris in those days. My fellow students at the Sorbonne organized protests against capitalism, consumerism, and traditional institutions like l'Université de Paris and its methods of instruction and examination. The discontent of the students became contagious, quickly spreading among factory workers who initiated wildcat strikes throughout the country, involving some tens of millions of workers. These protests, demonstrations, building occupations, and revolts lasted the better part of two weeks and virtually shut down the whole French economy.

The Latin Quarter, where I lived and studied, became a virtual war zone, with students taking over university buildings, creating barricades, and burning the stately trees that nobly fortified Le Boulevard St-Michel. My final summer in France was spent in Rennes, in the heart of Brittany; there were no classes being offered in Paris as it gradually tried to get back to a sense of normalcy.

Perhaps even more significant for me was an unanticipated opportunity that living in Paris would present. On a lark one day, I walked into the reception area of a building on Rue du Faubourg Saint Honoré, which became the postwar home to the famous Le Cordon Bleu. Although the school has since moved to new and larger quarters in the 15th Arrondissement, Le Cordon Bleu, founded in 1895, remains one of the most élite cooking schools in the world.

In those years this venerable training school for chefs did not ordinarily offer admission or courses to nonprofessional chefs, who today constitute its principal source of revenue. Most of its students at that time were already proficient in the culinary arts, having completed apprenticeships in restaurant and hotel kitchens under the eye of accomplished chefs. With an attitude of "nothing ventured, nothing gained" I requested a brief, exploratory conversation with the school's *grande dame*. In my best French, I explained to an aging but still quite-in-charge Madame Élisabeth Brassart that I was a Jesuit student, living nearby and pursuing studies in French Language and Literature at the Sorbonne. I had an interest in cooking but no practical training or experience. Respectfully, I asked Mme. Brassart if it would be possible for me to audit a basic course in methods and techniques. Quite honestly, I could sense from her face and demeanor that while she understood what I was asking, she did not have a ready answer. She asked for time to consider my request and discuss the proposition with her colleagues; she vowed that she would have an answer for me the following week.

When I first met her, Madame Brassart was a petite and elegant seventy-year-old woman who not only spoke elegant French but also English, which was a help for me as I stumbled my way through our negotiations for this most unusual of requests. I found her warming up as we talked further. She was clearly intrigued by me—a boyish American, a Jesuit, and a culinary novice. Mme. Brassart, who managed the school until her retirement when she was eighty-seven years old, agreed to give me a fee-free opportunity to "audit" the introductory course under two conditions: I would need to purchase a set of Sabatier knives, similar to those being used by all of the other chefs-in-training; and, secondly, if I proved not able to keep pace with the other students, I might be asked to leave the course. What an unexpected gift this was! I actually grew fond of Mme. Brassart, and she of me.

Once accepted, I arranged with the cook at the Jesuit residence to become his unofficial volunteer helper so that I could hone my rudimentary skills outside of class. Thanks to Mme. Brassart's extraordinary belief in me, I was able to successfully complete a full training cycle at Le Cordon Bleu and gained an incalculable, firsthand introduction to the world of *la cuisine française*, which paved the way for a lifelong passionate fascination and engagement in the worlds of cooking and baking. At the completion of the course, Mme. Brassart presented me with *un Diplôme de Cuisine.* She died in 1992 at the age of ninety-five years. Until the end of her life, every year I sent her a Christmas card with *mes sincères remerciements e meilleurs souhaits.*

Fr. Burke's spontaneous agreement to a counterproposal that I study and teach French was a fortuitous one on so many levels. Had I studied Russian I might have become somewhat of an expert in making borscht, but thanks to Fr. Burke's support, I am able to share one of my first triumphs at Le Cordon Bleu, *soupe à l'oignon gratinée.*

SOUPE À L'OIGNON GRATINÉE

French Onion soup with melted cheese and crouton

Makes 6 to 8 servings

Ingredients

- 3 tablespoons unsalted butter
- 1¼ pounds thinly sliced onions
- 3 tablespoons all-purpose flour
- 1 cup of dry white wine
- ½ cup Cognac or brandy
- 6 cups water or chicken stock
- 1 bouquet garni (leek, parsley, thyme sprigs, and a bay leaf, tied together)
- salt and freshly ground pepper
- 12 slices of French baguette
- 3 ounces Gruyère cheese, grated (about ¾ cup)

continued

Method

1. Heat butter in large saucepan over medium heat.
2. Add the onions and cook very slowly until they become caramelized and deeply golden, about 20 to 25 minutes.
3. Add the flour to the caramelized onions and cook for 2 additional minutes, stirring frequently.
4. Add the wine, bring to boil, reduce the heat and simmer 2 minutes.
5. Gradually stir in water or stock, add the bouquet garni and season to taste with salt and pepper.
6. Bring to a boil, stirring constantly.
7. Reduce heat, add Cognac, cover, and simmer for 30 minutes.
8. Preheat oven to 400°F.
9. Arrange bread slices in a single layer on a baking sheet and toast in oven until golden.
10. Preheat broiler.
11. Remove the bouquet garni and ladle the soup into a deep, ovenproof casserole or individual bowls.
12. Float the toasted bread on top of ovenproof casserole or individual bowls and sprinkle with cheese.
13. Broil until cheese melts. Serve immediately.

In June 1967, the provincial invited me to spend the following two years as a teacher in the modern languages department at my alma mater, Boston College High School. Here I was, back as a Jesuit scholastic and a member of the faculty, living alongside many of my former Jesuit teachers as part of the Loyola residence community. It was both an odd and exhilarating experience. I was assigned to teach the junior and senior honors French classes. I had the best and the brightest students for my maiden voyage in the world of teaching.

I must say that the two years I spent in regency were among the happiest of my life. Teaching was pure excitement, at least for me. The students were not exactly thrilled by my ambition for them, but most of them were good spirited and went along with my youthful madness. To this day I remain close with a number of these students, having guided them through their college years, officiated at their weddings, baptized their children and grandchildren, and presided at the funerals of their parents and grandparents.

I was assigned by the principal to serve as moderator of the French Academy and we did some audacious things, including mounting the production of a comedic farce by Molière using the integral French text and employing period costuming and wigs, along with the music of François Lully to complement the choreography of the ballet scenes. We may not have risen to the standards of *La Comédie-Française*, but these efforts were testimony not only to youthful enthusiasm and inexperience, but also to my sheer immersion into the world of French language, literature, art, culture, and cuisine. Rightfully, my students thought I was mad.

Even more unlikely, I took on the coaching of BC High's fledging swim team. In those years swimming was not a varsity sport at BC High and the school did not have its own pool. I scraped together enough money to rent pool space in a local US Army and Navy facility in Charlestown where we practiced under conditions slightly better than in the open ocean, and I was also able to put together enough money to purchase Speedo suits for the swimmers, made in the school colors of maroon and gold. Miraculously, owing to their native talents and determination (and certainly not my coaching skills), the team won the Boston City Championship in its inaugural season. Today, swimming is one of the distinguished varsity sports at BC High. Its beginnings were most humble, and its neophyte coach could not have been prouder of his student athletes.

Being resourceful, I researched and quickly purchased a book by an accomplished varsity swim coach from Indiana University that contained many of his training and workout routines. With a whistle in my mouth, I replicated many of his training protocols with my young swimmers, pushing them through endless drills and repetitions. Miraculously, it all worked.

One time BC High was hosting a home meet, which meant that we were responsible for ensuring that we had qualified referees and diving judges. On the night before the meet, one of the diving judges called to say he was ill and could not make the event on the following day.

Quickly, I co-opted the services of another Jesuit scholastic, Don MacMillan. "I know nothing about diving," he said.

"No problem," I replied. "In the next thirty minutes I will teach you everything you need to know to qualify you to judge diving tomorrow." During the following minutes he learned what layout and pike positions are, the names of various dives, degrees of difficulty, the rudiments of a scoring system, and the key things to look for in rating a dive. The next day he performed brilliantly, surprising even himself at how consistently his scoring of individual dives was aligned with the other two judges. Once again, a Jesuit lived up to the ideal of being all things for all people. Nobody ever suspected that he was not a seasoned diving judge.

On a lark, during my first year of teaching I applied for a federally funded summer enrichment program for high school teachers of French and was selected to be a participant in the Saint Catherine's College (Minnesota) institute in France. I was the youngest and least experienced teacher in the program, but it was a magnificent opportunity, particularly to return so soon to my familiar haunts in Paris and have an opportunity further to immerse myself in the study of French history and culture under the tutelage of American college professors. I was barely twenty-five years old but was able to hold my own with people who had been teaching French for more years than I had been alive.

However, my final summer as a high school teacher proved to be the most significant. Working as I had been with juniors and seniors, I was often cast into the role of advisor and counselor—something for which I was scarcely prepared. Recognizing this deficit, I again asked the genial Fr. Burke if I might take some introductory graduate-level courses in counseling at nearby Boston University.

"Marvelous idea," he replied. "This will also be handy for you later when you more seriously take up the topics of moral theology. Guidance and counseling are important skills for future priests." With his blessing, I was off to register for my first two graduate courses in counseling psychology.

That summer Professor Duguld Sinclair Arbuckle, chair of the counseling psychology program at BU, was offering an introductory graduate-level course in the principles of counseling psychology. Dr. Arbuckle was the first chairperson of the department of counselor education and became affectionately known as the father of counselor education at Boston University.

Coupled with Dr. Arbuckle's course, I registered for a course taught by a Jewish clinical psychologist, Dr. Emmanuel Green, in theories of personality. These two intensive summer courses were offered in the late afternoons and early evenings. Because I was taking these courses exclusively, I had full days and weekends to do both the required and recommended readings. I devoured the reading lists and came to class a bit more prepared than some of my fellow classmates, most of whom were working full-time jobs and scarcely had any time to do the minimum amount of preparation.

Both professors soon took note of this eager beaver sitting in front of them. After a few weeks into the summer term, Professor Green asked me to stop by his office for a chat. "Who are you?" was his opening question as I sat down for our meeting. I explained to him my status as a Jesuit student, that I was teaching French at BC High and preparing to study theology, be ordained a priest, and eventually to earn a doctorate in moral theology.

Both Arbuckle and Green told me independently that I had natural gifts for psychology and counseling and suggested that if I was planning to take additional graduate-level courses, I might consider matriculating into BU's master of education program in counseling psychology. They reasoned that if I was investing my time and the Jesuits' money, I might as well earn the Ed.M. degree in counseling psychology. Dr. Arbuckle also hinted that the department might be able to defray some of the costs through scholarship and teaching assistantships.

When I brought this proposal back to Fr. Burke after that initial summer, he raised his eyebrows and said tentatively, "If you think you can balance all of that as you enter the next phase of the study of theology, then give it a try." In hindsight, I realize how much Fr. Burke believed in me and was willing to give me every opportunity to explore my interests and gifts to the maximum.

He did not have to say another word. I applied and was admitted by BU's Graduate School of Education to their Ed.M. program in counseling psychology and, by May 1971, I had another master's degree in hand.

Reflecting on all these serendipitous educational experiences and my mentors, I am reminded just how amazing combining and blending simple ingredients can produce marvelous results. Here is my take on a very simple French dessert, with a rather lofty name.

CLAFOUTIS AUX CERISES ET ABRICOTS

Baked cherry and apricot flan

Makes 6 to 8 servings

Ingredients

- 2 tablespoons unsalted butter, softened
- 1 cup all-purpose flour
- ¾ cup granulated sugar
- 5 eggs
- 1 teaspoon pure vanilla extract
- 1 cup whole milk
- 1 cup heavy cream
- kosher salt
- Cognac or brandy
- ½ pound dried cherries
- ½ pound dried apricots
- confectioners' sugar

Method

1. Plump both the dried cherries and apricot in a bowl with ¼ cup Cognac or brandy and hot water for about 30 minutes. Drain and pat dry with paper towels.
2. Preheat the oven to 350°F.
3. Generously grease a 9x13-inch ovenproof baking dish with the softened butter.
4. Lightly dust the interior of the baking dish with granulated sugar.
5. Combine flour and sugar in a bowl.
6. Add the eggs and vanilla and whisk until blended.

7. Gradually add the milk and cream, whisking continuously to avoid lumps.
8. Whisk in the salt and 3 tablespoons of Cognac or brandy.
9. Spread the cherries and apricot evenly over the bottom surface of the baking dish.
10. Pour the batter over the fruit.
11. Bake until the clafoutis is lightly browned and a knife inserted into the custard comes out clean, 35 to 45 minutes. Cool completely.
12. Sift confectioners' sugar over the top before serving.

In the autumn of 1969, I left my BC High classrooms on Morrissey Boulevard in Dorchester and crossed the Charles River to take up residence in Cambridge, where the Jesuits were embarking on a new experiment in formation: theological education would be provided for its students within the collaborative, multifaith venture known as the Boston Theological Institute. Previously, theological formation had been provided in the same Jesuit house of studies in Weston where I had gone in 1965 to study philosophy. Now, in a bold undertaking, the Society of Jesus had rented or purchased a number of properties in or around Harvard Square in which to house Jesuits students and faculty. Classes were cooperatively conducted on the urban campus on Brattle Street at the Episcopal Divinity School, previously known as the Episcopal Theological Seminary.

These were not peaceful times in Harvard Square. Opposition to the war in Vietnam and various forms of civil protest proliferated on college campuses throughout the country. MIT, Harvard, and Radcliffe were not immune. It was not unusual to smell tear gas in the air as police tried to disperse crowds that amassed in Harvard Square and nearby Cambridge commons.

Living in small Jesuit communities in Cambridge brought to the fore the latent cooking talents of many young Jesuit chefs. In this new experiment in communal living we directly shared responsibilities for all of the household tasks including food shopping, menu planning, food preparation, and cleanup. Some older Jesuits, critical of this new form of living, maintained that the scholastics should be investing their time studying theology and not "playing house." Some really good Jesuit cooks emerged from the Cambridge experiment. With my recent Parisian training at Le Cordon Bleu, I welcomed the opportunities to practice and improve my culinary skills.

On a weekly basis, our community of eight members would designate two shoppers to take the community car and go to the supermarket to buy the essentials for the upcoming week. Assigned cooks would determine their menus in advance to let the shoppers know what would be needed. Providing for eight hungry men for a week was no small feat of organization and shopping. Complicating the challenge was the fact that we lived in adjoining apartments on a fourth-floor walk-up. There was no elevator in the building. The designated shoppers could count on bringing twenty or so bags of groceries and produce up those stairs. The weekly foraging expeditions were scheduled during the evenings, when most of the community members would be at home to make lighter work of carrying those provisions.

One fall evening, my fellow shopper and I set out for the nearby 24-hour supermarket in Somerville. At 9 p.m. the store was virtually empty, except for one couple. "My God," I exclaimed to my fellow Jesuit when I recognized the couple, "there's Julia Child and her husband, Paul."

Julia Child was a towering woman—a full 6 feet, 2 inches in height. Her husband stood an inch shorter. The Childs lived right around the corner at 103 Irving Street, very near our apartment on Kirkland Street. Much later she would donate her entire Cambridge kitchen and its contents for permanent display to the Smithsonian National Museum of American History in Washington, DC.

At that time, Julia's inaugural cooking show, *The French Chef*, was debuting on WGBH, the public television network station in Boston. She was not yet the syndicated national celebrity she would later become, but she was already a recognizable figure. I had encountered her before while we were both shopping at Savenor's Market on Kirkland Street. Savenor's was a neighborhood butcher shop, and we often went there for special steaks or roasts. So did Julia.

That evening at the supermarket, as chance would have it, there was only one cashier on duty at the checkout counter. There we were with our two overburdened carts, loaded with every imaginable foodstuff. We were unloading the carts and processing them when the Childs pulled up behind us with a few items in their cart. Unable to contain her thoughts, Julia bellowed out in her inimitable voice: "My, you must have a very large family."

One of the lasting regrets of my life is that I did not speak right up, tell her our story, and invite the Childs to dinner. Somehow, I suspect Julia and Paul would have readily accepted. If so, this story would have had a much more interesting conclusion. *Malheureusement*, I became star-struck at that moment and politely acknowledged her comment, but failed to take the opportunity to offer to cook for her. I have repeatedly made many of her recipes during the more than forty ensuing years; here is my adaption of one of her favorites, *boeuf à la bourguignonne.*

BOEUF À LA BOURGUIGNONNE

Burgundy beef stew

Makes 6 servings

Ingredients

- 6-ounce slab unsliced bacon
- 3½ tablespoons olive oil
- 3 pounds lean stewing beef, cut into 2-inch cubes
- 1 carrot, sliced
- 1 onion, sliced
- salt and pepper
- 2 tablespoons flour
- 3 cups full-bodied red wine
- 2½ to 3½ cups beef stock
- 1 tablespoon tomato paste
- 2 cloves minced garlic
- ½ teaspoon dried thyme
- 1 crumbled bay leaf
- 18 to 24 white pearl onions
- 3½ tablespoons unsalted butter
- bouquet garni (4 parsley sprigs, one-half bay leaf, ¼ teaspoon thyme, tied in cheesecloth)
- 1 pound cremini mushrooms, quartered

continued

Method

1. Remove bacon rind and cut into *lardons* (pieces approximately ¼ inch thick and 1½ inches long). In a small saucepan, allow the *lardons* to simmer for 10 minutes in 1½ quarts of water. Drain and dry. Set aside.
2. Preheat oven to 450°F.
3. Sauté the blanched *lardons* in 1 tablespoon of olive oil in a Dutch oven set over moderate heat for 2 to 3 minutes to brown lightly. Drain and reserve.
4. Pat dry the beef with paper towels and season with salt.
5. Heat the residual bacon fat and some olive oil in the Dutch oven until almost smoking. Add beef, a few pieces at a time, and sauté until nicely browned on all sides. Reserve the browned beef along with the *lardons*.
6. In the same cooking fat, brown the sliced vegetables. Pour out the excess fat.
7. Return the beef and bacon to the Dutch oven and season with ½ teaspoon salt and ¼ teaspoon freshly ground black pepper.
8. Then sprinkle on the flour and toss again to coat the beef lightly.
9. Set the Dutch oven uncovered in middle position of preheated oven for 4 minutes.
10. Toss the meat again and return to oven for 4 minutes (this browns the flour and covers the meat with a light crust). Remove the Dutch oven and reduce the oven temperature to 325°F.
11. Stir in wine and a couple cups of beef stock, just enough so that the meat is barely covered.
12. Add the tomato paste, garlic, herbs, and bacon rind. Bring to a simmer on top of the stove.
13. Cover casserole and set in lower third of oven. Regulate heat so that liquid simmers very slowly for 3 to 4 hours. The meat is done when a fork pierces it easily.

14. While the beef is cooking, prepare the onions and mushrooms by heating butter and olive oil in a large skillet until it begins to bubble.
15. Add onions and sauté over moderate heat for about 10 minutes, rolling them so they will brown as evenly as possible. Be careful not to break their skins. You cannot expect them to brown uniformly.
16. Add ½ cup stock, salt, and pepper to taste and the *bouquet garni.*
17. Cover and simmer slowly for 40 to 50 minutes until the onions are perfectly tender but hold their shape, and the liquid has evaporated. Remove the bouquet garni and set onions aside.
18. Wipe out the skillet and heat remaining oil and butter over high heat. As soon as you see butter has begun to subside, indicating it is hot enough, add mushrooms. Toss and shake pan for 4 to 5 minutes. As soon as they have begun to brown lightly, remove from heat.
19. When the meat is tender, pour the contents of the casserole into a sieve set over a saucepan.
20. Wash out the casserole and return the beef and *lardons* to it. Distribute the cooked onions and mushrooms on top.
21. Skim fat off sauce in saucepan. Simmer sauce for a minute or two, skimming off additional fat as it rises. You should have about 2½ cups of sauce—thick enough to coat a spoon lightly. If the sauce seems too thin, boil it down rapidly. If it is too thick, mix in a few tablespoons of stock. Taste carefully for seasoning.
22. Pour sauce over meat and vegetables. Cover and simmer 2 to 3 minutes, basting the meat and vegetables with the sauce several times.

While residing in Cambridge and pursuing the study of theology, I thought it might be useful to gain some practical experience in counseling and psychotherapy. As with my earlier successful incursion into the world of Le Cordon Bleu, on a summer afternoon in 1970, without a prior appointment, I walked into a Victorian building on Sacramento Street, home to the Cambridge Guidance Center. I approached the receptionist to ask if it might be possible to have a chat with the chief psychologist.

"Do you have an appointment with Dr. Hirsch?" she inquired.

"No," I replied, "I am just interested in exploring with him possible nonpaid internship placements. I'm in the final year of my master's studies in counseling psychology at Boston University." Fortunately, on this quiet summer afternoon, Charles Hirsch, PhD, was free and perhaps curious enough about this bold fellow who had just walked in off the street unannounced, looking for a chat.

I was escorted to Dr. Hirsch's fairly sizeable second-floor corner office located in the rear of the building. His office might have been an original master bedroom in the home of a famous Harvard professor in the nineteenth century, but now, it looked like a clinician's space: walls of bookcases filled with scholarly books and journals, stacks of paper files, random chairs, a consulting couch, and a massive wooden desk. Dr. Hirsch welcomed me, and I immediately got to the point of self-introduction. He grew more interested as I peeled back the outer layers of the onion: a current Jesuit student of theology; earned degrees in philosophy and French language and literature, and finishing up studies in counseling psychology; a recent high school French teacher and swimming coach; interests in cooking and music; and now, exploring a possible counseling internship in a place I just happened to discover on a tree-lined side street in Cambridge.

This chance interview was the beginning of a mentoring relationship with Charlie Hirsch that spanned five decades until his death in 2018. We shared every important event in each other's lives from that day forward. Not only did Dr. Hirsch find a place that fall for me as a psychology intern on one of their three clinical teams, but he also became my most trusted career advisor from that moment forward. He introduced me to a staff psychologist on another team, Dr. Barbara Shea, who also became a dear friend. Not only would I later officiate at her wedding to Terry Fiori, but I would also baptize their three children.

Thanks to Dr. Hirsch, during the final two years of my studies for the Master of Divinity (M.Div.) degree, I was able to work as an intern at the Cambridge Guidance Center and later at Cambridge Hospital's Department of Adult Psychiatry. Those were exciting years in community mental health and group practice, and Dr. Hirsch was one of the pioneers in the community mental health movement. He opened up experiences and research opportunities that not only shaped my future career as a psychologist but also strengthened my application to the doctoral program in clinical psychology into which I matriculated immediately after my ordination in May 1972.

Ordination to the priesthood took place in the Pierce Chapel of the Cranwell

School in Lenox. I was ordained along with three other Jesuit friends, two of whom had taught with me during regency (one of whom was the diving coach wonder I had co-opted). The four of us had lived together in the Kirkland Street community from 1969 to 1972, and three of the four of us were alumni of Boston College High School. We were ordained by Jesuit Samuel Carter, who at the time was the Metropolitan Archbishop of Kingston, Jamaica.

When it was confirmed that Sam Carter, S.J., would be the ordaining prelate, I gradually broke the news to my parents. Though by no means bigots, my parents nonetheless were of a generation in which *black* people were not always held in the highest regard. "Why would that be a concern for us?" responded my mother. I thought silence would be my best response.

My godmother, who was seated directly behind my parents during the rites of ordination, recalled a verbal interchange between my parents after Archbishop Carter extended the greeting of peace to my mother. My mother's exuberant and uninhibited response was to hug the archbishop and kiss his cheek. After the archbishop returned to the sanctuary, my father exclaimed: "Mary, I never thought I would live to see the day that you kissed a black man."

"If I am going to begin," my mother retorted, "it's going to be with an archbishop!" I guess that I was not totally without justification in informing my parents in advance about the racial background of the ordaining prelate.

Since I would be engaged full time in doctoral studies for the next few years, the provincial thought it would be good for me to be fully immersed in priestly and pastoral pursuits during the summer of 1972. I was fortunate to find an opportunity to substitute as the residential Catholic priest chaplain at Mercy Hospital in Springfield. I spent ten weeks living within the hospital community, serving both as chaplain to the religious community of nuns who administered and served as nurses within the hospital as well as being available 24/7 to the staff, patients, and their loved ones. This was an immersion experience in the full range of priestly and sacramental ministries—a wonderful way to spend my first months as a priest.

I will briefly recount two stories from among the hundreds I can recall from that hospital chaplaincy assignment. The first involved a young married non-Catholic United States Air Force airman first class, David, whose wife had been admitted to the ICU with a severe brain trauma sustained in a catastrophic highway traffic accident. The couple and their ten-month-old son had just returned to Springfield from a brief vacation leave. When they got back to their apartment, the wife decided to go to the supermarket to restock their refrigerator after their two-week absence.

To do this she needed to enter the highway, travel two exits, and arrive at the supermarket. As she accelerated to enter the highway from the ramp, she collided with an eighteen-wheeler that was traveling at full speed. Her car was completely demolished. She was admitted to the hospital unconscious, with traumatic brain injuries. During her almost two-week ordeal, she never regained consciousness. Ultimately, her young husband, who had maintained a constant vigil at her bedside, determined to remove her from life support.

Although he did not claim to be religious, David had been raised in a fundamentalist Christian community in rural Texas. He felt terrible guilt for not going out for the groceries himself, and he was quick to interpret the events as God punishing him for not being as faithful as he could have been. He was traumatized by the prospect of having to raise a son without his mother. Separated from family and other supports, I became a lifeline for him during those difficult days.

Fr. Burke had been correct: counseling psychology would be a useful preparation for priestly ministry. During those days I relied on many of the things that Dr. Arbuckle had taught us in his principles of counseling and psychotherapy course.

I sat with David alone in the chapel after his wife had been removed from life support and died. In those quiet moments he was able to verbalize a prayer. Despite his profound sadness and the grief of his loss, he was able to express gratitude to God for sending me his way during the past several days. "Without Fr. Smith, I could not have gotten through this nightmare," he later stated to his parents who had come to the hospital to be with him. "With his help and guidance and encouragement, I know I will be able to be the best father I can be for Daryl." I did not sleep very well that night, but I was so grateful to have been able to be there for David in his moment of greatest need.

Another symbolic encounter was with a very old woman named Catherine who had been hospitalized with a bowel obstruction, only to learn subsequently that she had end-stage colon cancer. I brought her communion daily. She was a very devout woman, always sitting up with her hands folded as I approached with Holy Communion each afternoon. Because Mercy was a Catholic hospital, I was accompanied on my communion rounds by a nun carrying a lit candle in one hand and ringing a small bell with the other. You could hear us approaching along the corridors.

On this one particular day I approached Catherine's bedside and began reciting the preparatory prayers for the reception of communion. Then I held up the host before her eyes and said: "This is the Body of Christ, given for you, Catherine." She reverently took the host into her hand and looked at me straight in the eye, and before consuming the host she said: "And Father, the Body of Christ is also given for you—Amen." With that she devoutly placed the host in her mouth, closed her eyes in momentary silent prayer, and then reached out to take my hands and kiss them. She died that evening.

I found out from the nuns that her funeral Mass would be celebrated the following Monday at Saint Michael's Cathedral on State Street. It happened to be my day off from the hospital, so I decided that I would attend the funeral Mass. Catherine had never married; she was eighty-nine years old when she died. Populating that hollow nineteenth-century cathedral that morning was a scattering of people, most probably few of whom really knew Catherine. And there among them I sat, the last to have experienced and witnessed the power of Catherine's faith and to share in the fulfillment of God's promise that "whoever believes and hopes in him will never die" (John 11:26).

Armed with a treasury of pastoral experiences, I returned to Cambridge at the end of that summer to begin doctoral studies in clinical psychology at Boston University. It was a different school with a new faculty and I was ready and anxious to embark on this newest adventure. With four graduate degrees already earned, this represented in some sense a final academic hurdle. Clearly, I had put aside the earlier desire to study moral theology for this newly discovered behavioral science passion.

I enjoyed the course work and the faculty members who became my teachers. A significant number of the BU faculty were active clinicians and researchers. Some were associated with the Boston Psychoanalytic Institute. At that time, Boston University's clinical psychology department had a decidedly psychoanalytic orientation. I had spent a good part of my first summer with Dr. Green immersing myself in some of Freud's classic writings. I must say that while not becoming a Freudian purist, I did begin to understand much about human behavior through the lens and language that Freud supplied. Very quickly I began to fashion my own hybrid understanding of the human psyche, formed from an amalgam of insights from some of the leading clinicians and thought leaders of the nineteenth and twentieth centuries.

As I progressed in the program and passed the comprehensive examinations, I began to focus on what I might research for my doctoral dissertation. I knew that I wanted to select a topic where I would learn things I did not already know. By a process of elimination, I looked through my brief list of prior clinical exposures: work with children and adolescents at Cambridge Guidance Center; counseling with adolescents at BC High; community psychiatry rotation with adults at Cambridge Hospital. The one group with whom I had no prior clinical contact was the elderly. An emerging issue in the late 1960s and early 1970s was the topic of death and dying.

I ended up proposing a study of depression and death anxiety in a group of variably aged widows. In the end, I studied profiles of 120 women who had recently experienced the death of a husband. Through in-depth structured interviews, combined with some paper-and-pencil scales to measure things like depression and death anxiety, I gained fresh insight into the world of a cohort of older women and the grief they experienced in the aftermath of spousal loss.

In mounting this study I did not set out to focus my life's work in the fields of gerontology or thanatology, but once again the *cantus firmus* would play its part. In fact, these two issues would continuously reassert themselves as defining themes in my subsequent career choices and investments.

In May 1975 I became the Rev. Dr. Walter J. Smith, S.J. My graduation from Boston University occurred on Pentecost Sunday. Rather than be away from the parish community I was then serving in West Lynn on such an important day, I chose not to attend the commencement ceremonies. I quietly picked up my diploma from the office of the registrar the following week.

In the months prior to graduation, my provincial had begun conversations with me about my first postdoctoral priestly ministerial assignment. I had worked as an *ad hoc* consultant to the province during 1973 and 1974 as plans for a multitiered retirement community were being formulated. The province's goal was to convert the virtually abandoned building on Concord Road in Weston that had been our philosophy and theology student residence into a skilled nursing care and assisted living facility, as well as a spirituality and retreat center. With the Weston-in-Cambridge program successfully established, the New England Province needed to find a way to repurpose this flagship building.

Late in 1974, the provincial began to explore with me the possibility that I might assume responsibility as the religious superior of the residential community at Weston and serve as the founding director of the start-up nursing home. That proposal took me by surprise; I was only thirty-two years old. It did not seem prudent to ask such a young man to become the religious superior of men more than twice his age. While I was willing to undertake the development and management of the new assisted living and skilled nursing care facility, I suggested that a more experienced Jesuit be selected to serve as the religious superior.

We agreed in principle to this revised tentative plan and the provincial asked me to be ready to take this assignment by July 1975. He asked me to begin withdrawing from my other part-time commitments, which included teaching some psychology courses at Boston College and Boston University and my part-time employment as staff psychologist with the Cambridge Guidance Center. I began to terminate these responsibilities, with the goal of being free from all other responsibilities by Memorial Day.

In April, I learned that the Jesuit who had been named to become the religious superior at Campion Center had also expressed his desire to assume the directorship of the nascent nursing home project. That turn of events left me with a freshly minted doctoral degree in psychology and no prospective job. The provincial offered me a carte blanche to do whatever I thought might be most constructive. Since I had yet to complete the final year of Jesuit formation, called tertianship, I thought this might be an expeditious use of a free year while affording me the time to plan for full-time ministry beginning in the summer of 1976.

With great relief that I had quickly rebounded with a reasonable, tactical plan, the provincial approved my proposal that I spend the year in Rome, completing my tertianship under the direction and supervision of Fr. Edward Malatesta, S.J. From 1966 to 1977, Fr. Malatesta had served as professor of biblical spirituality at the Jesuit-run Pontifical Gregorian University in Rome. His specialty was in the letters of Saint John.

As fate would have it, my college friend Fr. Walter J. Woods, with whom I had served as a weekend supply priest at Sacred Heart parish in Lynn, was asked by Cardinal Humberto Medeiros to study moral theology in Rome in preparation for what would eventually become a more than twenty-five-year tenure on the faculty of Saint John's Seminary.

Here we both were—for different reasons, both missioned by our respective ecclesiastical superiors to Rome. We quickly booked passage on the final crossing from New York to Europe of the Swedish America Line *Gripsholm*. It was a twelve-day cruise, the first transatlantic ship crossing for both of us. We disembarked in Stockholm, activated our Eurail passes, put our trunks independently on the rails to Rome, and made a modest yet grand tour of Sweden, Denmark, and Norway before traveling south through Germany, Switzerland, and eventually making our way to the Eternal City.

It was on the *Gripsholm* that I first tasted the Swedish dish *Kroppkakor*.

Kroppkakor are large, hearty potato dumplings made by wrapping a potato-flour dough around some fried pork-product filling. Here is my version of this Swedish staple.

KROPPKAKOR

Swedish meat dumplings

Makes 6 to 8 servings

Ingredients

- 4 pounds unpeeled Yukon Gold potatoes
- 8 ounces finely chopped bacon
- 4 ounces coarsely chopped smoked ham
- 1 finely chopped onion
- 1 teaspoon coarsely ground allspice berries
- 1½ cups all-purpose flour
- 3 large egg yolks
- 3 tablespoons unsalted butter
- kosher salt

Method

1. Place the unpeeled potatoes in a large saucepan and cover with cold water by about 2 inches. Add 1 tablespoon of salt and bring to a boil. Reduce heat and simmer until tender, about 30 minutes.
2. Drain, and immediately return to pan. Allow the potatoes to cool and dry for about 15 minutes. Peel the potatoes and pass through a ricer, or finely mash. Reserve in a large bowl and allow to cool completely. Cover and refrigerate for a couple of hours or overnight.
3. Cook the bacon in a skillet over medium-high heat for 2 to 4 minutes. Add onion and allspice, reduce heat to medium, and cook until onion is soft, about 4 minutes. Add ham and cook until both bacon and ham are lightly browned, about 10 minutes. Let the meat and onion mixture cool.
4. Toss the cooled potatoes with flour and 1½ teaspoons of kosher salt. Gradually add the room-temperature egg yolks, stirring until incorporated. Using your hands, form the mixture into a ball.

5. Put ¼ of the potato mixture on a lightly floured work surface. Shape into a log that is 1¼ inches in diameter, then cut it crosswise into five 2-inch pieces. With floured hands, roll each portion into a ball and use two fingers to make a deep indentation in the center of the dough.
6. Place a heaping tablespoon of the cooled filling into the indentation, pinch to enclose filling, and press to seal. Flatten the ball slightly into a disc. Place on a parchment-lined baking sheet and cover with a clean kitchen towel.
7. Repeat the prior two steps until all the potato dough and filling are used.
8. Bring a large pot of salted water to a boil. Add about five dumplings at a time. Cook, stirring occasionally, until the dumplings rise to the surface, about 5 minutes. Using a slotted spoon, transfer cooked dumplings to a wire rack over a baking sheet. Continue to cook the remaining dumplings.
9. Heat butter in a large skillet until foamy. Gently sauté dumplings in batches, being careful not to overcrowd them, until golden brown, about 3 minutes per side. Add more butter as needed.
10. Cover the fried dumplings loosely with parchment and then foil to keep warm.
11. Serve with lingonberry jam.

Living in Italy was a transformative experience. I immediately threw myself headlong into the study of Italian by enrolling in an immersion course at Berlitz. I was assigned to live at the Collegio S. Roberto Bellarmino, a residential community for Jesuit priests and brothers who were studying for advanced academic degrees. The Bellarmino is located on the Via del Seminario, steps away from the Pantheon in the *centro storico* of ancient Rome and nestled in the shadow of the seventeenth-century Chiesa di Sant'Ignazio di Loyola in Campo Marzio. Italian was the common spoken language of the house. I concelebrated the 6:30 community Mass each morning in Italian. By simply showing up and jumping in, I began to learn the ordinary parts of the Mass by sheer immersion and repetition. Little by little, I began to catch words or phrases at table and recognized words and phrases in the evening newscast of RAI's *Telegiornale*.

By Christmastime I was able to celebrate public Mass in Italian with brief, carefully prescripted homilies. I made the full Spiritual Exercises in October under the magnificent blue skies of a Roman autumn. Thereafter, I cotaught a course at the Gregorian University on the Spiritual Exercises with Fr. Malatesta. He concentrated on the biblical and spiritual dimensions and I tackled the psychological dynamics. At his urging I also accepted the opportunity to develop and teach a six-week course at the Pontifical Regina Mundi Institute, founded by Pope Pius XII to serve as a continuing theological formation program for women religious.

In late November 1975, Fr. Malatesta one morning sheepishly confessed that he needed my help. It happened that he had accepted two commitments within the same time period: one assignment was to present a major talk in Milano, and the second was to give a series of three evening talks and offer Mass for a small group of Mother Teresa's novices at their modest home in the Tor Fiscale suburb of Rome.

Toward the end of their two-year novitiate, novices petition the Superior General for permission to take vows as Missionaries of Charity. Mother Teresa had granted their request and the four novices were preparing for their vow day on the upcoming feast of the Immaculate Conception at the Basilica di Santa Maria Maggiore.

Fr. Malatesta asked if I would take on this triduum of talks and masses, to which I readily accepted.

On the first evening when I arrived at the novitiate, I was greeted by the community's superior. She quickly advised me that Mother Teresa had come for a visit and specifically requested that she be permitted to participate with the novices in the triduum. Taken aback by this news, I asked the superior if Mother Teresa might like to give the talks.

"No," she replied. "Mother just wants to be with the novices and to benefit from your words, Father." So it was: I thought that I was preparing to speak with four novices and now I had a fifth guest: Mother Teresa of Calcutta.

Mother Mary Teresa Bojaxhiu, now known and venerated as Saint Teresa of Calcutta, was an Albanian-Indian Roman Catholic nun and missionary born in Skopje, then part of the Kosovo Vilayet of the Ottoman Empire. She died in Calcutta in 1997.

At the very simple community supper after Mass on each of the three evenings, I was seated next to Mother Teresa. I remember vividly on the first evening asking her this direct question: "Mother, how do you keep balance and perspective with the enormity of the needs of the people you care for?"

Her almost instantaneous reply has remained with me for the rest of my life: "Father, you can only care for the Christ who is in your arms at any given moment. There is no time to be distracted by anything else."

I suspect that in the toss-up, I got the better draw in Fr. Malatesta's double booking. I am sure his talk in Milano went brilliantly, but I got to sit next to a saint for three nights in a row.

Mother Teresa was not a foodie, but she did tell me that her mother said you should never enjoy a meal without sharing some of it with another. When I asked her what she enjoyed eating, she told me about a very simple dish called *Dal Chawal.* Here is my adapted recipe.

DAL CHAWAL

Indian lentils and rice

Makes 4 to 6 servings

Ingredients

- 1 cup split red lentils
- 1 finely chopped onion
- 2 ripe tomatoes
- 1 chopped green chili
- 1 teaspoon finely chopped garlic
- 1 teaspoon minced ginger
- ½ teaspoon ground turmeric
- ½ teaspoon cumin seeds
- ½ teaspoon coriander powder
- ½ teaspoon ground mustard seeds
- 2 tablespoons vegetable oil
- kosher salt

continued

- 3 cups water (in which to cook the lentils)
- 1 cup Basmati rice
- 2 cups water (in which to cook the rice)
- a pinch of salt

Method

To prepare the dal

1. Wash the split red lentils 3 to 4 times with water and soak for an additional 15 minutes.
2. Cook the lentils in 3 cups of water, along with the turmeric and a pinch of salt, over medium-high heat for about 20 to 30 minutes or until the lentils become soft and tender.
3. Heat oil in a frying pan over medium heat.
4. Quickly toast the remaining spices (cumin seeds, mustard, chopped green chili) for 15 to 30 seconds.
5. Then add onion, garlic, ginger, and cook for about 3 to 4 minutes, stirring frequently.
6. Add chopped tomatoes to the pan and cook further for 2 to 3 minutes.
7. Add the cooked lentil mixture and the coriander powder to the large frying pan and turn the heat to low, stir it well, cover the pan, and cook for 10 minutes until the dal becomes soft and is well incorporated.

To prepare the chawal

1. Wash rice 3 to 4 times with water.
2. Combine it with water and a pinch of salt and cook for about 8 to 10 minutes over medium-high flame.
3. Serve rice on a plate and pour hot dal over it.

The twenty-eighth superior general of the Jesuit Order was Pedro Arrupe. This charismatic Basque Jesuit had labored in Japan during the time of the bombings of Hiroshima and Nagasaki in 1945. Trained earlier in his life in medicine, Fr. Arrupe provided direct assistance to survivors of these horrific events.

In 1975, Fr. Arrupe was also serving in Rome as the president of the Unione Internazionale delle Superiore Generali (UISG), an organization that represents the superior generals of more than 200 male religious orders and congregations. Its purpose is to promote the life and mission of its priests and brothers in the service of the Church and to make the collaboration of its major superiors more efficient and their dealings with the Holy See and the hierarchy more fruitful. All superiors general of religious institutes or societies of apostolic life are members of the UISG. Fr. Arrupe asked Fr. Malatesta if, as part of my ministries during my tertian year, I might be available to help some of the major superiors.

I took on two assignments as a result of Fr. Arrupe's request. The first was to work with Cardinal Eduardo Francisco Pironio, who that year was *pro prefect* of the Vatican's Congregation for Religious and Secular Institutes (currently called the Congregation for Institutes of Consecrated Life and Societies of Apostolic Life). The kind and affable Argentinian Cardinal Pironio was promoted to prefect of the congregation and served in that capacity until 1984. I was fortunate to work closely with him during most of his tenure as the cardinal prefect. My second assignment was to help the superior general and general council of the Congregation of Christian Brothers (the Irish Christian Brothers) to develop a component of their six-month residential renewal program for their brothers from around the world.

Both of these assignments turned into much longer commitments, spanning the next decade or more. This also proved to be my first direct exposure to the special world that exists within the walls of the Vatican. Between 1975 and 1989, I had the privilege of working in some supportive roles with Pope Paul VI and Pope St. John Paul II.

The kindly Pope John Paul I only lived for a month after his election to the See of Peter. I had encountered Albino Luciani on a memorable occasion in the Basilica of San Marco on New Year's Eve in 1975 when he was the Patriarch of Venice, but he died before I had an opportunity to greet him as Pope John Paul I. He was a man much after the heart of our current Pope Francis. Luciani sold a gold pectoral cross that Pope St. John XXIII had given to him in order to raise money for special needs children. He encouraged his priests in Venice to sell their valuables to contribute to this cause and challenged them to live more simply and more humbly. During his tenure as Venice's Patriarch, Luciani founded a number of family counseling clinics to help the poor cope with marital, financial, and sexual problems.

My first encounter with Pope St. John Paul II was a few months after his election to the See of Peter on October 16, 1978. He was a very charismatic figure. When we first met he was a relatively youthful fifty-eight-year-old, strong and vigorous. During our initial encounter, on the eve of the publication of his first encyclical letter, *Redemptor Hominis* (March 4, 1979), Pope John Paul II put his right arm on my shoulder and with his clenched left fist he began punctuating points he wanted to emphasize by striking blows to my chest. "Priests must be distinguished by fidelity to our vocation." Another point and another punch: "We knowingly and freely commit ourselves to live in celibacy, and each one of us must do all he can, with God's grace, to be thankful for this gift and be faithful to the bond that he has accepted forever." He could not have been more animated or set on fire. I thought that if this Polish pope had another point to make, he most probably would succeed in cracking my sternum.

The Holy Father ended our inaugural chat by telling me how disappointed he had been when the then Archbishop of Krakow, Fr. Arrupe, had refused his requests to send Jesuits to work in his archdiocese. I thought to myself, "*We Jesuits had better fasten our seat belts, because this new pope is still ruminating on the way he felt spurned by the superior general of the Jesuits.*"

On another occasion, after a presentation in which I had played a very minor role, the participants in the meeting were gathered in a semicircle for the traditional *bacio di mano* (greeting and kissing of the pope's hand and ring). The Holy Father approached me and, with a twinkle in his eye, said in perfect English: "So young to be a professor!" To which I irreverently replied: "So young to be a pope." I got another of those affectionate punches as he threw his head back and laughed with great gusto.

Early on during my tertianship year in Rome, Fr. Malatesta introduced me to his friend Fr. Carlo Maria Martini, who at the time was the rector of the Pontifical Biblical Institute. Ed Malatesta and Carlo Martini were also colleagues. Carlo Martini was an imposing man, standing well over six feet tall, with a somewhat stern visage. I soon came to realize that behind the veneer of a serious New Testament scholar beat a zealous, compassionate, and pastoral heart. Ed suggested that during my long retreat I might wish to concelebrate midday Mass with Carlo, who regularly served as a chaplain to a community of religious sisters who lived near the Gregorian University. Although my Italian was still very limited, I gradually came to understand more of what Fr. Martini shared in his brief daily homilies to the sisters. Sharing these masses with Carlo Martini was the beginning of what matured into a friendship.

On subsequent visits to Rome I would reconnect with Carlo, often to share a meal in a local restaurant. He was a consummate linguist, speaking more than ten languages. I recall how direct and honest he was about his views on the Church. For example, he was very disturbed when Pope Paul VI issued his controversial encyclical on contraception, *Humanae Vitae,* which Carlo believed to be a mistake. One of the things I most remember from our many conversations was his approach to the sacred scriptures. He believed that the Word of God is simple, direct, and accessible. He said: "All we have to do is open our hearts and listen." I have never forgotten this counsel, and I must say that it has shaped my approach to preaching and pastoral care for the whole of my priestly life.

He moved across the Piazza della Pilotta from the Biblicum to become the new rector of the Gregorian University just days before the death of Pope Paul VI in 1978. A few months later, after the untimely death of Pope John Paul I, Karol Józef Wojtyła was elected pope on October 16. A little more than a year later, on December 8, 1979—the feast of the Immaculate Conception—the Holy Father traveled to Rome's Piazza di Spagna to honor the statue of Mary set atop the commemorative column in the Piazza Mignanelli, close to the Spanish steps in Rome. After the ceremonies were concluded, Pope John Paul II visited the Gregorian University and sat next to its rector, Carlo Martini, during dinner. I happened to be in Rome at that time for one of my regular consultative visits.

Within days of that encounter, Cardinal Sebastiano Baggio, the prefect of the Congregation for Bishops, called Carlo Martini to inform him that the pope wished to appoint Carlo to be the next archbishop of Milano. Carlo later told me of the events that rapidly followed. He asked Cardinal Baggio if it would be possible for him to discuss this appointment directly with the Holy Father. An early evening appointment was arranged, and Carlo met the Holy Father in his private study. Once seated, Carlo said that he proceeded to share with the Holy Father the numerous reasons why he should not become a bishop or assume pastoral responsibilities for the See of Milan. He said that the pope sat impassively in his armchair, with his elbow bent to support his chin attentively resting on his folded hand. He never once interrupted as Carlo methodically ticked through his list of reasons against the proposed appointment.

When he concluded, Pope John Paul II sat erect in his chair and with piercing eyes looked directly at Martini. "Father, the more you speak, the more certain I am that you are the right person for Milano. Furthermore, the Mass of your ordination as bishop is already set for the Feast of the Epiphany [January 6], in the basilica." The announcement of the appointment was released by the Vatican on December 29, 1979, the ordination followed a week later, and Carlo was installed as a successor of St. Ambrose in the historic fourteenth-century Duomo di Milano on February 10, 1980. John Paul II appointed Carlo to the College of Cardinals three years later in 1983.

I averaged about four trips to Rome each year between 1976 and 1988, spending about seventy days annually in combined work with the Holy See, the Christian Brothers, or some other religious orders or congregations. I also used the occasion of these trips—especially during the spring and summer months—to wander around Italy, giving particular attention to garnering new regional recipes and acquiring new cooking techniques.

Over the course of these many years, I have become quite knowledgeable about *la cucina regionale italiana*. It has been my *modus operandi* to search for a local *trattoria* and then inquire about *la specialità della casa*. Not only was the host often ready to share a recipe, but not infrequently I was invited back into the kitchen where either papa or mama would demonstrate *come si fa* (how it is done).

Close friends of Fr. Malatesta owned and operated a small ristorante just off the Corso Vittorio Emanuele, not too far distant from the Gregorian University. Fr. Malatesta was considered *famiglia* ("family") by this intergenerational clan whose origins were south of Rome in the hilly region of Abruzzi. Mama presided at the cash register, greeting guests and making sure everything in the dining room was *a posto*. Three married sons served as the principal *camerieri* (waiters). But papa was in full charge of the restaurant's tiny kitchen. One of his specialties was a dish called *Tortellini alla Papalina*. The antecedents of this dish goes back to the pontificate of Pope Pius XII, who requested a pasta dish that was both traditionally Roman but also somewhat inventive.

I loved this dish at first bite: the sauce is rich and velvety, the flavors meaty and earthy. My habitual inquiry at the ristorante—"*Come si fa?*"—brought me front and center to where papa proudly demonstrated the art of making *tortellini alla papalina*. This recipe is exactly as he made it, and as I have made it hundreds of times since then.

TORTELLINI ALLA PAPALINA

Roman pasta with cream sauce

Makes 6 to 8 servings

Ingredients

- 1½ pounds tortellini (traditionally meat-filled, but chicken- or cheese-filled are fine)
- 1 pound *prosciutto crudo* (cut thick and then diced)
- 2 ounces dried porcini mushrooms, reconstituted in 1 cup of warm water (strain and reserve the liquid)
- 2 tablespoons each butter and olive oil
- 1 cup grated Parmigiano Reggiano

For the sauce

- 3 cups chicken stock
- 1 cup heavy cream
- unsalted butter
- all-purpose flour
- ½ teaspoon kosher salt
- ¼ teaspoon ground white pepper

Method

1. Add 2 tablespoons each of melted butter and olive oil to a small skillet and quickly sauté the diced prosciutto, peas, and porcini mushrooms. Set aside.
2. Melt 3 tablespoons of butter in a heavy saucepan over medium-low heat. Add 3 tablespoons of flour and whisk for 1½ minutes (do not allow to brown). Gradually add the chicken stock, whisking constantly until it comes to a boil.
3. Add the heavy cream, salt, and pepper.

continued

4. Switch to a wooden spoon and stir constantly until sauce reaches the consistency of thick cream, about 15 minutes.
5. Cook the tortellini in a large pot of rapidly boiling and generously salted water, according to directions (3 to 4 minutes or until they all float to the top of the boiling water).
6. Drain pasta and combine with a generous portion of the sauce to coat the tortellini. Add to a serving bowl or plate individually, distributing the sautéed meat and vegetable mixture and garnish with freshly grated Parmigiano Reggiano.

One of my fellow Jesuits colleagues at the Bellarmino was Italian. His family originated from Bologna, one of the gastronomic epicenters of Italy. One day I was casually chatting with him about ragù alla Bolognese. His face was transformed as we began to discuss this. "You must come and meet my aunt," he said. "She makes the very best ragù alla Bolognese."

He did not have to offer a second time. We planned a quick trip to Bologna to meet Zia Maria (Aunt Mary), who operated a very small *hostaria* on a narrow back street in this northern Italian city. We both were welcomed by Zia Maria as if we were major dignitaries from Rome. I have eaten many good meals in my lifetime, but that visit to Bologna has to rank near the top of the list. With no formal training, Zia Maria was a natural cook with a personality as large as her girth.

A big pot of ragù alla Bolognese was already gently bubbling away on the back of her stovetop. Disappointed, I thought I would only get an explanation, not see the real thing produced before my eyes. Not so. She explained she made a big pot every day. What was on the stovetop was a finished version, ready for service. We were going to make tomorrow's fare now. Before we got started, with her beautiful Tuscan accent, she slowly explained to me that what we were going to make was the authentic ragù. Many people, she said, make a quick version of this sauce, but what she was about to teach me was the *ricetta antica*—the old traditional recipe, the pride of generations of Bolognese.

On the preparation table was a basket full of ingredients that looked like they were ready to be photographed by *Bon Appétit*. There were carrots that looked like they had been just pulled from the garden, still with visible remnants of the soil from which they had come. There were big, hefty onions, and celery so fresh that when it snapped, sweet water sprayed from its stalks. She had a generous handful of luscious San Marzano tomatoes, a bottle of a rich red wine, a bottle of milk, and dishes of meats: pancetta, pork, veal, and beef. She had a fresh nutmeg and a grating tool on the table. Everything was ready for my introduction to *come si fare il ragù alla Bolognese.*

RAGÙ ALLA BOLOGNESE

From Zia Maria

Makes 12 to 16 servings

Ingredients

- 2 pounds ground beef
- 2 pounds ground pork
- 2 pounds ground veal
- 2 cups dry red wine
- 6 ounces pancetta
- 2 tablespoons olive oil
- 3 medium onions, minced (food processor preferable)
- 4 celery stalks, minced (food processor preferable)
- 3 carrots, minced (in food processor with celery)
- 1 teaspoon salt or to taste
- 6 tablespoons tomato paste
- 28-ounce can crushed San Marzano tomatoes
- 2 cups whole milk
- 1 teaspoon nutmeg
- 4 large bay leaves
- 4 cups beef broth
- freshly ground pepper

continued

Method

1. Zia Maria began by combining by hand in a large mixing bowl the ground beef, pork, and veal. She poured about 2 cups of red wine over the meat and continued to work it in with her fingers until she felt that all of the meat had been thoroughly moistened.
2. Next, she roughly cut the pancetta and put it in a food processor with the minced onion. She worked it into a fine paste, which she called the *pestata*.
3. In a large heavy pot or Dutch oven (6-quart capacity), add 2 tablespoons of olive oil and the *pestata*. Place over medium-high heat and break up with a spoon to render the juices.
4. Once the *pestata* is sizzling away and is very aromatic, add the minced carrots and celery, stirring until they are all wilted and golden, about 5 more minutes.
5. Remove the pancetta and vegetable mixture to a bowl and reserve.
6. Turn the heat up a bit and add the meat mixture to the pan, giving it sufficient time to cook (to give up its raw, red color but not to brown) before adding back the vegetables. Add the bay leaves.
7. Cook on high heat, stirring frequently until much of the liquid (wine, meat juices, vegetable water) has dissipated (about 30 minutes). Begin heating up separately the other liquids (milk and broth) for the next steps.
8. At this point Zia Maria pushed the meat and vegetables aside with a wooden spoon to make an opening in the pot and quickly added the tomato paste to the bottom of the very hot pan, so that it could quickly sear. She stirred it around for a couple of minutes.
9. Then she poured in 2 cups of hot milk and thoroughly incorporated it with the tomato paste into the meat mixture, making sure to scrape all of the brown bits off that might be clinging to the bottom of the pan. Then she liberally grated the nutmeg over the whole pot, probably about a teaspoon in total. The aroma was intoxicating.

10. She explained that the addition of the milk—an essential step in this ancient recipe—helps to balance and neutralize the acidity from the tomatoes, which are the next addition.
11. Add the crushed San Marzano tomatoes, along with 2 cups of the beef broth or stock.
12. Bring the *ragù* to a slow, steady simmer. The surface area will continue to gently bubble away. Cover and let cook for at least 3 to 5 hours, checking and stirring about every 30 minutes. Add some additional hot beef broth as needed to maintain the liquid level of the *ragù* throughout the cooking.
13. Just before the ragù is finished cooking, correct seasonings, allowing at least 5 minutes of additional cook time for the spices to distribute. Remove the bay leaves and spoon off any access fat if using right away. If storing, leave the fat on to protect the sauce, removing some of it when it is cold before use. This is a health-conscious suggestion. Zia Maria reheats the congealed fat right in the sauce. "*Buon gusto,*" she said. "It adds to the great taste; why discard it?"

Even though his admonition was intended for a wholly different purpose, the words of Saint Paul to the Thessalonians could easily have been Zia Maria's counsel to me after she passed on the art and family tradition of her Bolognese treasure. Saint Paul wrote: "So then, stand firm and hold to the traditions that you were taught by us, either by our spoken word or by our instruction" (2 Thessalonians 2:15).

During the course of my tertian year in Rome, I began conversations about future missioning and employment opportunities with the three Jesuit universities in the New England Province. Eventually, I received two job offers: one from Boston College to teach in their graduate program, and another from Fairfield University to teach in their undergraduate program, where Fr. Tom McGrath, S.J., was the psychology department head. The provincial expressed a preference for me to accept the Fairfield University offer, no doubt owing in good measure to the fact that Fr. McGrath could be very persuasive.

At the same time, the rector of the Pontifical Gregorian University was plotting to recruit me to teach permanently in their Institute of Spirituality. Fr. Hervé Carrier, S.J., a French-Canadian Jesuit, was a forceful figure in the political world of the Roman Curia, and he was used to getting his way. When I informed him that my provincial had decided that I should return to New England and accept an appointment to the faculty of Fairfield, he bluntly rejoined: "Ignore your provincial's directive. I will speak directly with Fr. Arrupe about this."

"But Father, I can't *ignore* my provincial's expressed wish."

Fr. Carrier was unmoved by my rejoinder. "Ignore him. The Gregorians' needs will take precedence."

When Fr. Arrupe intervened to settle this dispute between a provincial and the powerful rector of the Gregorian University, Fr. General supported my provincial's judgment that I was more needed back in my home province. Fr. Arrupe reminded Fr. Carrier that the New England Province had been exceptionally generous in staffing the Roman universities (at the time there were already eight New England Jesuits serving in various administrative and academic assignments in Rome). In 1976, I was one of three New England Jesuits who had earned doctorates in psychology and the province had the responsibility for staffing three higher education institutions. It was settled: in August, I would join the psychology department faculty of Fairfield.

Two weeks prior to Holy Week, I was directing the annual eight-day retreats of two illustrious Jesuits, Fr. Gerald O'Collins, S.J., an Australian theologian who had been one of my teachers at Weston Jesuit School of Theology in Cambridge, and Fr. Bob Taft, S.J., a distinguished professor of theology and liturgy at the Pontifical Oriental Institute. During these retreats we were living together at the Jesuit Villa Cavalletti in Frascati, an eighteenth-century pseudo-Renaissance mansion and adjoining buildings, which at the time served as a spiritual retreat center and vacation house for Jesuits working, teaching, and studying in Rome.

During these days Fr. Arrupe also happened to be staying at Villa Cavalletti for meetings, and we found ourselves sitting together at supper one evening.

"I am glad that your assignment to return to your home province has been so amicably settled," Fr. Arrupe quietly remarked. "Will you be making your final vows before you leave the City?"

Momentarily flummoxed by his question, I respectfully replied: "Father General, you, more than anyone, knows that this decision is not mine to make."

With a smile he nodded affirmatively and continued: "Let me say it this way: if your provincial is agreeable, I would like to receive your vows here in Rome before you return."

The following day I wrote to my provincial, who quickly put the process in motion to prepare for the necessary approval and the ceremony of final vows that Fr. General Arrupe had suggested. On the morning of Trinity Sunday, June 13, 1976, in the actual rooms at the Gesù where Saint Ignatius wrote the Constitutions of Society of Jesus and later died, Father Pedro Arrupe, his successor, celebrated Mass and received my final solemn vows in the presence of twelve other Jesuits, including Fr. Malatesta, who graciously attended and joined in the concelebration.

The following day I left Rome on a pilgrimage to the Holy Land with an international group of priests from the Gregorian's Spirituality Institute, and then progressively—in the year of America's bicentennial celebrations—made my journey back to New England to begin my new mission as a professor of psychology.

My requisite formation and education as a Jesuit priest was now complete.

Chapter 3

ENTERING THE GROVES OF ACADEME

A generous person will prosper; whoever refreshes others will be refreshed.

—PROVERBS 11:25

Some people have commented facetiously that priestly ordination for a Jesuit is the reward for a life well spent. With such a long period of academic and spiritual formation, a Jesuit may appear ready for retirement by the time he has completed the full course of studies. In my case, I had completed the basic course of formation before presbyteral ordination in ten years—omitting a year of humanistic studies, a year of philosophy, a year of regency, and a year of theology. Of course, I added a few more years to complete the PhD in clinical psychology and tertianship, but I was still relatively young by the time I arrived at Fairfield University in Connecticut in the late summer of 1976, the bicentennial year of the birth of the United States.

Apart from my time in Québec and Paris and the year I spent in Rome, I had completed all of my formal education in the greater Boston area, either at Boston College, Weston Jesuit School of Theology in Cambridge, or at Boston University. I was an inbred Bostonian. Fairfield University was located on the geographical periphery of the New England Province, lapping the border of the New York Province. The Jesuit staff and their lay colleagues managed both a four-year college preparatory high school for boys and a well-regarded comprehensive university. Beautifully situated on a magnificent property overlooking Long Island Sound, Fairfield University has continued to grow in reputation for its academic excellence and extraordinary student body.

Arriving from Europe to the Fairfield University campus in August, I was quickly assigned to be a Jesuit housemaster in one of the student residences, Gonzaga Hall. There were two other Jesuits already serving as housemasters in that particular dormitory: Fr. Frank Moy, S.J., the campus minister of the university, and Fr. Patrick Cafferty, S.J., a professor of art. I found myself assigned to a floor of young women coeds.

One Saturday evening, a young lady was getting ready to go off with her date to a semiformal dance. She dropped by my room to show me how beautifully she was attired. The next morning, around 7 a.m., I was leaving the dorm to drive to the parish where I was assisting, and I encountered the same young woman who was just returning to the dorm. She looked quite different from the night before. Her hair was disheveled, and her party dress clearly had seen better days. The prior evening's festivities had ended up on the Fairfield beach where many junior and senior students rented houses.

"Good morning, Father," she sheepishly greeted me.

"What happened?" I replied.

"Well, let's just say that this dress has seen its last dance." I loved the youthful abandon and *joie de vivre* that I encountered virtually every day among these university students.

I was initially assigned to teach two sections of a course in lifespan human development and a senior-level introductory course in clinical psychology. The following semester, I taught two sections of abnormal psychology (one to nursing majors) and one section of introduction to psychology.

When I entered doctoral studies, I never imagined that I would be teaching undergraduate psychology. Rather, I had envisioned that I would be providing direct, community-based psychological services for poorer folks who might not otherwise have had access to such mental health resources. My earlier clinical experiences at the Cambridge Guidance Center and Cambridge Hospital had opened my eyes to the critical need for such mental health advocacy care. My service catchment area as an intern had included North Cambridge, where there was a significant concentration of people living at or below the poverty line and where the incidence of mental illness among children and adolescents was steadily on the rise. Although doing family interventional therapy was not easy with this population, we had mounted some interesting projects, with notable and encouraging results.

Being assigned to teach undergraduate psychology forced me to make a major mental adjustment. With reasonable ease, I began to understand and assimilate into the distinctive culture of the academy. I have long believed that there are two groups of people who often appear out-of-touch with the real world: members of the clergy and academics. At Fairfield, I was completely immersed in both of these worlds at the same time. I had to work hard to maintain a sense of perspective and humor.

Entering the world of the academy forced me to assemble all the ingredients of my formation into a new pot, blend seasonings, and hope for the best. Not too different from making a classic *Coq au Vin.*

COQ AU VIN

Braised chicken in wine

Makes 6 to 8 servings

Ingredients

- 3 pounds skin-on, bone-in chicken thighs and legs
- 3 cups red wine
- 1 bay leaf
- 2 to 4 fresh thyme sprigs
- 4 ounces diced smoked bacon
- 1 diced onion
- 1 peeled and diced carrot
- 8 ounces trimmed and quartered cremini mushrooms
- 2 minced garlic cloves
- 1½ teaspoons tomato paste
- 2 tablespoons all-purpose flour
- 2 tablespoons unsalted room-temperature butter
- 8 ounces peeled pearl onions
- ¼ cup chopped flat-leaf parsley
- kosher salt
- freshly ground black pepper

Method

1. Season the chicken pieces with salt and pepper. In a large bowl, combine the chicken with the wine, bay leaf, and thyme. Cover and marinate at least 30 minutes and up to one day.

2. In a Dutch oven or large pot set over medium heat, sauté the diced bacon pieces until browned and crispy, about 10 minutes. Remove from heat and using a slotted spoon, transfer the bacon to a plate lined with paper towels, reserving the rendered fat in the Dutch oven.

3. Remove the chicken from the wine marinade and pat dry thoroughly with paper towels. Reserve the marinade. Return the Dutch oven to the stovetop and heat the bacon fat over medium heat until it shimmers. Add the chicken, skin side down, in a single layer and cook until golden brown, about 5 minutes. Flip and cook until brown on the other side, about 4 more minutes. (Do not overcrowd the chicken—work in batches if necessary, adding a little olive oil and butter if you run out of rendered bacon fat.) Transfer the browned chicken pieces to a plate.

4. Add the diced onion, carrot, and mushrooms to the Dutch oven and season with salt. Sauté until the vegetables are tender and lightly browned, about 8 to 10 minutes.

5. Add the garlic and tomato paste and cook for about 1 minute, until you can smell the fragrance of the caramelized tomato and blooming garlic. Strain and add the reserved marinade. Bring to a boil over medium-high heat and reduce liquid to about half. Skim off any foam that may appear on the surface of the boiling liquid.

6. Add the chicken pieces, pearl onions, and half of the bacon. There should be enough liquid to just cover the chicken—if not, add a little water or some stock (vegetable, chicken, or beef). Cover and simmer over low heat until the chicken is tender, approximately 1 hour. Uncover, transfer chicken to a plate, and continue to simmer, about 10 minutes.

continued

7. Meanwhile, work the flour and butter together (*beurre manié* is simply a combination of equal parts softened butter and flour, mixed together in a small bowl to form a smooth paste, and used as a thickening agent in a sauce). Whisk the *beurre manié* into the stew. Continue to simmer until the sauce is thick enough to lightly coat the back of a spoon, about 2 more minutes.
8. Taste and correct the seasonings. Return the chicken to the Dutch oven and simmer until warmed through, no more than 5 minutes. Remove from heat and garnish with remaining cooked bacon and chopped parsley.

Fortunately, my boss and unofficial mentor was the wise and wary Fr. Tom McGrath, S.J. Tom had earned his doctorate in psychology at Fordham University and was one of the first trained Jesuit clinicians in the New England Province. He was the psychology guru of his time and a master teacher: smart, witty, engaging, and eloquent. I learned quite a bit from just observing how and what he did.

The psychology department employed a schoolmarm secretary, Mae Ferracane, who knew all the ins and outs of both the department and the university. As soon as I arrived, Tom introduced me to Mae, and I built a quick and strong relationship with her. Not only was she Tom's personal executive assistant, but she looked after the rest of us as well. She adroitly kept eight somewhat petulant psychology faculty members in line and managed to mother a legion of psych majors, holding their hands when they failed a statistics examination or were having difficulty navigating a personal relationship. She was clearly the connective tissue within the psychology department. When she retired, Tom hired another wonderful assistant, Claire Melish, a Fairfield resident and mother of three adult children. Without losing a beat, Claire took up where Mae left off.

In addition to attending to my teaching and housemaster responsibilities, I quickly figured out that if I wanted to be tenured, I would have to be attentive and responsive to research and service obligations. Apart from my doctoral research, I had not been involved in any other clinical research work, so I was clearly just off the starting block. Tom McGrath could not be terribly helpful to me. Although a full professor, he was the product of a different era. Tom had not been a researcher but a distinguished teacher and very popular lecturer. Where should I concentrate my research interests?

Because I was teaching a number of nursing students and premeds, I thought it might be helpful to consolidate some of my lifespan human development interests with issues surrounding death and dying. Over the course of the next two years, in some of my free time, I began to outline what might become a university-wide elective course in death and dying and possibly even a research book that collected some of the relevant learnings from psychology, medicine, allied health professions, and the social sciences. When I presented the course prospectus for departmental review and approval, my colleagues expressed significant interest and enthusiastically encouraged me to pursue it. There was nothing else being taught in the university that remotely touched on these topics. I got to work on fleshing out a syllabus and reading lists. I was beginning to carve out a niche for myself among the clinicians in the department.

When the course was first listed, I decided to offer it as a three-hour, fifteen-week course, taught from 7 until 10 p.m. once a week. The sixty places in the course were fully subscribed on the first day of registration. I attracted precisely the audience that I had hoped for: students aspiring to careers in the helping professions—medicine, nursing, psychology, and teaching. Students told me that after classes they would retreat to their dorms or the cafeteria and spend a couple more hours processing things said and experienced during the evening session. Some claimed they did not sleep well on the nights on which our classes were held.

These students could have probably benefitted on class nights from a midnight snack of these incredibly delicious, glazed ricotta cookies of Zia Maria—who had also first taught me how to make *Ragù alla Bolognese.* This is my adapted version of her mouthwatering ricotta cookie recipe. Zia Maria made these cookies without measuring anything. I watched her make the dough and I weighed the ingredients (or tried to estimate their weight) before she incorporated them into a mixing bowl. What is most remarkable about these cookies is how flavorful they are, how light and cakey, and how long a shelf life they have before hardening (if they are not immediately consumed).

ZIA MARIA'S GLAZED RICOTTA COOKIES

Makes 3 dozen cookies

Ingredients

- 2 sticks (½ pound) unsalted room-temperature butter
- 2 cups granulated sugar
- 1¾ cups whole milk ricotta cheese
- finely grated zest of a lemon
- 4 teaspoons vanilla extract
- 2 large eggs
- 4 cups all-purpose flour
- 2 teaspoons baking soda
- ¾ teaspoon kosher salt
- 4 cups confectioners' sugar
- 2 tablespoons fresh lemon juice
- ¼ cup to ½ cup milk

Method

1. Using an electric stand mixer with the paddle attachment, cream the butter with sugar until fluffy, about 2 minutes. Add the ricotta, lemon zest, and 2½ teaspoons of vanilla and beat well. Beat in the eggs one at a time. Scrape the sides of the bowl with a rubber spatula, then beat in flour, baking soda, and salt. Cover dough and chill for at least 2 hours. The dough can be refrigerated, before baking, for up to a week.
2. Heat oven to 350°F.
3. Line a couple of baking sheets with parchment paper or nonstick silicone liners. Shape tablespoons of dough into balls. Place cookie dough 2 inches apart on baking sheets and bake until pale golden on the bottom, about 15 minutes. Let cool on wire racks.

4. Melt remaining tablespoon of butter. Whisk confectioners' sugar to break up any large lumps, then whisk in melted butter, lemon juice, remaining 1½ teaspoons vanilla, and enough milk to make a spreadable icing. Dip or spread icing on cooled cookies, finish with sprinkles if desired, and then let set for at least 20 minutes before serving.

Years later, I encountered some former students—now established professional physicians and nurses—who told me how grateful they were for having enrolled in my death and dying course. They commented that it was the only comprehensive treatment of the issues of death and dying they had ever received. Nothing in nursing or medical school, they concluded, remotely touched on these topics in the ways that this course had.

Lectures and discussions were augmented by guest presenters who shared first-hand experiences. For example, I invited a mother, photographer Kathy DiGiovanna, whose daughter, Kara, had been diagnosed and treated for Ewing's sarcoma and eventually died from this deadly cancer at age twelve. Ewing's sarcoma tumors typically start in the bones but can also appear in other tissues and muscles. This primary cancer occurs most frequently in children and teenagers and is rarely seen in adults over the age of thirty.

Kathy spoke about Kara's thoughts and feelings and those of her other children who watched their younger sister battle cancer and eventually succumb to the disease. She described the emotional world in which she and her husband lived and how this event ultimately unhinged their marriage. Needless to say, the interest and relevance factors in this course were very high. This was real life, and the course allowed students to view it without filters or censorship.

Once launched, I offered this seminar every year thereafter. It quickly became one of the most sought-after courses among the university's offerings and skyrocketed my teacher evaluation assessments to among the top in the faculty. I kept enriching my own research and lectures with an eye to an eventual publication. In October 1985, my book *Dying in the Human Life Cycle: Psychological, Biomedical, and Social Perspectives* was published and enjoyed brisk sales for the next several years.[2]

2 *Dying in the Human Life Cycle: Psychological, Biomedical, and Social Perspectives* (New York: Holt, Rinehart and Winston, 1985).

The fusion of a personal, scientific, and scholarly interest began to anchor the direction of my career as both clinician and professor, uncovering my true bones as a priest and a psychologist. I am reminded of a popular southern Italian and Sicilian chicken dish called pollo alla scarpariello. The Calabrese restaurateur who first introduced me to this dish claimed that it got its name because of the chicken bones that can sometimes protrude from one's mouth as you eat, much like a shoemaker might hold tacks in his mouth as he works—as good an explanation as any for the dish's name. Anyone can cobble together these ingredients, and the result is truly delicious.

POLLO ALLA SCARPARIELLO

Shoemaker's Neapolitan country-style chicken

Makes 6 to 8 servings

Ingredients

- 1½ pounds fingerling potatoes, cut in half lengthwise
- 3 links sweet Italian sausage
- 6 skin-on, bone-in chicken thighs
- 2 large chopped onions
- 1 large chopped red bell pepper
- 6 garlic cloves, finely grated
- 1 cup dry white wine
- 1 cup low-sodium chicken broth
- ½ cup chopped Calabrese chili peppers in brine
- ¼ cup white wine vinegar
- 3 sprigs fresh rosemary or some crushed dried rosemary flakes
- 6 tablespoons extra-virgin olive oil
- kosher salt and freshly ground pepper
- chopped flat-leaf Italian parsley

Method

1. Arrange racks in upper and lower thirds of oven; preheat to 450°F.
2. Toss potatoes with 3 tablespoons of olive oil on a rimmed baking sheet; season with salt and pepper. Arrange seasoned potatoes cut side down and roast on lower rack until they are tender and browned, 20 to 30 minutes; set aside.
3. Meanwhile, heat remaining 3 tablespoons of oil in a large skillet over medium-high heat. Sauté the sausages, turning occasionally, until they are lightly browned on all sides, 6 to 8 minutes (they will not be fully cooked). Transfer to a plate to drain on a paper towel.
4. Season chicken well with salt and pepper. Cook in the same skillet until golden brown on both sides (6 minutes on the skin side, 3 to 4 minutes on other side). Chicken will not be fully cooked. Transfer to plate with sausage to rest.
5. Cook chopped onions, bell pepper, and garlic in same skillet over medium-high heat, stirring occasionally and scraping bottom of pan, until tender and beginning to brown, 10 to 12 minutes.
6. Add wine, deglaze pan of bits and scraps, and cook vegetables stirring occasionally, until reduced and you can no longer smell the alcohol, about 8 to 10 minutes.
7. Add broth, peppers, vinegar, and rosemary and bring to a boil; cook until slightly reduced, about 5 minutes.
8. Transfer vegetables and cooking liquids to roasting pan. Nestle chicken into onion mixture, then transfer roasting pan to upper rack of oven and roast chicken 10 minutes. Add sausages to pan, pushing them into onion mixture, and continue to roast until chicken is cooked through and an instant-read thermometer inserted into thickest part of thigh registers 165°F, approximately 5 to 10 minutes.
9. Finish with freshly chopped parsley and serve with roasted potatoes alongside.

As I was settling into my new life at Fairfield University, my friend Fr. Wally Woods was completing his doctoral studies in Rome and preparing for his return to his native Archdiocese of Boston, where he was to begin a distinguished career as professor of moral theology. His ministry at Saint John's Seminary would span the better part of the next twenty-five years. He proved to be an exceptional teacher, clear and organized, thoughtful and insightful. Wally understood well the historical evolution of doctrine and pastoral practice and how they shaped the moral teachings of the Roman Catholic Church. In 1998, he published *Walking with Faith: New Perspectives on the Sources and Shaping of Catholic Moral Life*. Beyond his technical competence he was also pastorally astute, fortified by the fruitful earlier years we had shared together in parochial ministry in Lynn and later by his postseminary teaching years as a pastor in Acton.

Once settled in Boston Wally decided to invest in a small home in Wareham, bordering the canal that serves as a gateway to the two bridges that provide direct access to the Cape Cod peninsula.

His little house, which he referred to by the endearing moniker "Le Manoir," proved to be a wonderful retreat for both of us during our early years of teaching. I would often spend weeks away from Fairfield during the summer academic recess as a resident in Wareham. When I had earned my first sabbatical semester leave, I used Wally's little house as a place in which to write one of my books. More than simply providing a place of refuge and rest, Le Manoir also provided a perfect venue to develop and further expand my culinary skills and repertory.

This recipe for stuffed pork chops quickly became a Manoir favorite. The secret of its success is the use of a good quality *Gorgonzola dolce*, and the chops are napped (coated lightly) with a sherry cream sauce.

STUFFED PORK CHOPS WITH GORGONZOLA AND APPLE WITH SHERRY CREAM SAUCE

Makes 8 servings

Ingredients

For the stuffing and the chops

- 4 tablespoons butter
- 2 tablespoons dried thyme
- 3 cups chopped Granny Smith apples
- ground black pepper to taste
- ¼ cup Gorgonzola dolce cheese at room temperature, crumbled
- 8 thick-cut pork chops
- 6 cloves garlic, minced

For the sauce

- 2 teaspoons extra-virgin olive oil
- ¾ cup crumbled Gorgonzola dolce cheese
- 2 cloves garlic, minced
- 12 tablespoons dry sherry
- 1 cup heavy cream
- ½ cup chicken broth
- salt and pepper to taste

Method

1. Preheat oven to 375°F.

To make the apple stuffing

1. In a sauté pan or skillet on medium heat, melt the butter and sauté dried thyme, chopped peeled apples, and salt and pepper until the apples are completely softened, about 15 to 20 minutes. During the final five minutes, add the 6 cloves of minced garlic.
2. Place the apple mixture in a bowl and add in ¼ cup of the cheese. The cheese will begin to liquefy in the stuffing within a couple of minutes.

To prepare the pork chops

1. Butterfly the pork chops by slicing them parallel to the plane of the

continued

chop from the fat side to the bone. Stuff each one with about 2 to 3 tablespoons of the apple mixture.

2. Place the chops on an ovenproof rack on a baking sheet, arranging them side-by-side with the stuffing sides pressed together. This will help to prevent the stuffing from exuding from the pork pockets. Bake the chops for about 30 minutes.

To make the finishing sauce

1. Heat the olive oil in a saucepan on medium heat, then sauté the 2 cloves of garlic until transparent (30 seconds).
2. Add ¼ cup of cheese and stir until it melts.
3. Immediately add the sherry and cook for an additional minute until combined.
4. Add the cream and ¼ cup of chicken stock, salt, and pepper.
5. Stir until well blended.
6. Reduce the liquid on medium high heat until the sauce begins to slightly brown.
7. Add another ¼ cup chicken stock and the remaining ½ cup of cheese; stir and allow to reduce and thicken a bit more.
8. Nap the finished pork chops with the sauce and enjoy!

When I first reconnected with Wally in Sacred Heart parish after my ordination in 1972, he possessed very rudimentary skills in the kitchen. I recall once asking him what he most liked to cook.

"Onion rings," was his spontaneous reply. I never saw anyone so enthusiastic about describing how he prepared a simple batter, sliced the onions, dipped them into the coating mixture, and then plunged them into heated vegetable oil. One would be led to believe that Escoffier himself was disclosing the intricacies of a complex preparation to hear Wally rhapsodize about his onion rings.

Through our association in the little Wareham kitchen and his willingness to function as sous chef on countless occasions, Wally gradually gained the knowledge, skills, and confidence to branch out from onion rings. He is instinctively a scientist and engineer at heart: he reads with attention to detail and he can logically execute a well-conceived and stated plan. For him, recipes became road maps; he followed them precisely and was more than once surprised at the favorable outcomes. Of course, this precision led him naturally to baking. Over time he became a fairly accomplished baker, especially in creating artisanal breads. Gradually, the kitchen equipment in Wareham began to reflect a shared passion for cooking and baking.

Over the course of my repeated trips to Rome and other Italian cities, the number of Italian-made cooking implements increased arithmetically: terra-cotta casserole dishes, Imperia pasta maker, espresso machine, and so on. Because Wally and I had experienced so many things together during our days in Italy, we often referred to kitchen items by their Italian names, for example: a ladle is a *mestolo*, and a large spoon is a *grande cucchiaio*. When we talked in the kitchen we naturally reverted to using Italian terms for many of the things we were using or preparing. On every return trip from Italy I loaded my luggage with things like dried porcini and pepperoncini and as much aged Parmigiano-Reggiano as I might hope to be able to safely bring undetected through US Customs.

We discovered things we had never seen or tasted before, like the Amarena cherry, which is a small, dark-colored, bitter fruit grown in the regions around Bologna and Modena (thus the Italian word for bitter, *amara*). Whenever we traveled together in Italy we were always on the hunt for the distinctive blue ceramic jar of the Fabbri family who, in the latter part of the nineteenth century, first developed the recipes for candying these luscious dark cherries and the delicious thick syrup in which they are preserved.

My very good friend and celebrity chef Lidia Matticchio Bastianich developed a special relationship with Amarena Fabbri, who became one of the sponsors of her public television cooking series. Lidia shared one of her original recipes for making distinctive ravioli featuring these delectable cherries, which make a sweet and savory dessert.

AMARENA FABBRI RAVIOLI

Sweet and savory ravioli filled with sour Italian cherries, adapted from Lidia Bastianich

Makes 6 servings

Ingredients

For the egg pasta dough

- 3 cups all-purpose flour
- 4 large eggs

For the ravioli filling

- ½ cup Amarena Fabbri cherries chopped in small pieces
- 2 tablespoons dark rum
- 1 large egg
- 2¾ cups shredded Montasio cheese
- 2½ cups shredded Fontina cheese
- 1¼ cups grated Grana Padano cheese
- ¼ cup fresh breadcrumbs
- ¾ teaspoon grated lemon zest
- ½ teaspoon grated orange zest
- ½ teaspoon chopped fresh thyme leaves
- ¼ teaspoon ground cloves
- Butter, grated cheese, and pepper for drizzling and sprinkling over the ravioli

Method

To make the pasta for the ravioli

1. On a marble or wooden work surface, pile the flour into a mound.

2. Make a well in the center of the mound.
3. In a small bowl, beat the egg with a fork until blended, and then pour it into the well.
4. Continue beating the egg mixture with the fork, gradually drawing in flour from the sides of the well until the egg has been absorbed by the flour.
5. Lightly flour the work surface again.
6. Knead the dough by pressing the heel of one hand deep into the ball, keeping your fingers high, then press down on the dough while pushing it firmly away from you. Turn the dough over, then press into the dough, first the knuckles of one hand, then with the other; do this about ten times with the knuckles of each hand.
7. Then repeat the stretching and knuckling process, using more flour if needed to prevent sticking, until the dough is smooth and silky, for about 10 to 20 minutes.
8. Place the dough in a small bowl and cover with plastic wrap. Let the dough rest for at least 30 minutes at room temperature.
9. Roll out dough either by machine or by hand into thin sheets.

To make the ravioli filling

1. Toss the Amarena Fabbri cherries with the rum. Let them stand, tossing once or twice, until the cherries absorb most of the rum, 20 to 30 minutes.
2. In a large bowl, beat together the egg and sugar. Add the remaining filling ingredients and mix well with your hands until thoroughly blended. Cover and set aside.

To prepare the ravioli

1. Lay one sheet of pasta dough onto a floured surface. Evenly space out tablespoons of the filling on the sheet, and then lay another pasta sheet

continued

on top. Press the dough around each mound of filling to remove any air and then cut out rounds with a 2 ½-inch round cutter.

2. Press the filling gently to fill any air spaces in the ravioli and press the edges firmly again to seal them tightly.
3. Arrange the ravioli in a single layer on baking sheets lined with lightly floured kitchen towels. Cover them with additional towels. The ravioli should be cooked immediately, or refrigerated or frozen.
4. When ready to cook, bring the salted water to a boil in a large pot. Add the ravioli to the water one at a time, stirring gently as you do.
5. Cook about 4 to 6 minutes in boiling salted water. Use a big skimmer or large flat slotted spoon to gently scoop out the ravioli, draining them well.
6. Place the ravioli on a serving platter or in individual bowls.
7. Drizzle the butter over the ravioli and sprinkle them with grated cheese and freshly ground black pepper.

With a continually developing culinary repertory, the Wareham house became a center for entertaining families and friends. Every Christmas season Wally would invite many of his seminary faculty colleagues to a festive dinner party, for which I would customarily be the menu planner and principal chef. These annual events became quite popular, and his colleagues would begin asking in October when the event was being scheduled so that they could be sure they would be free. Nobody wanted to miss this exceptional evening of fraternal conversation and culinary magic.

Two of the regular guests went on to become bishops. Alfred Clifton Hughes served as a rector of Saint John's Seminary before being ordained an auxiliary bishop of Boston in 1981. He later served as the bishop of Baton Rouge, Louisiana, before becoming the Archbishop of New Orleans in 2002. Al really loved these great banquets and marveled at the quality of food that could be produced in such a small kitchen.

A second regular guest was Walter James Edyvean, who served as an auxiliary bishop of Boston from 2001 to 2014. Walter also had earned a doctoral degree in theology in Rome in 1971 and served as a faculty member at Saint John's Seminary from 1971 to 1990, when he was named *capo ufficio* of the Congregation for Catholic Education in the Roman Curia. He loved to eat, and with all of the years he spent in Rome had become a great aficionado of *la cucina italiana*. He never missed a holiday dinner *au Manoir*.

Bishop Edyvean particularly enjoyed a wonderful Tuscan dish that I had first sampled in a small trattoria in Siena. I remember asking the gracious woman who was the restaurant's sole cook if she would be willing to share the techniques she used to make such a succulent roasted pork dish. She was thrilled to describe what she did.

Even though this dish is called an *arrosto*, it is cooked entirely on the top of the stove and not in the oven. Below I present a stove-to-table scenario. My *insegnante* (teacher) confided that she always makes this roast a day in advance of serving and refrigerates the finished roast in its sauce overnight. She claims that it is always better the next day: that the roast further absorbs the flavors of the sauce, the meat is easier to slice perfectly when it is chilled, and it reheats easily in the sauce.

Here is my reconstructed version of a Tuscan braised pork loin with milk.

ARROSTO DI MAIALE AL LATTE

Roasted pork with milk

Makes 6 to 8 servings

Ingredients

- 3½ pounds boneless pork loin, tied with butcher twine
- 8 sage leaves
- 1 large sprig fresh rosemary
- 3 garlic cloves
- ½ cup extra-virgin olive oil
- 3 tablespoons unsalted butter
- 2 cups whole milk
- sea salt and freshly ground black pepper
- fresh nutmeg

continued

Method

1. Rub the tied pork loin well with salt and pepper.
2. Add some olive oil and butter to a large enameled Dutch oven over medium heat. When the olive oil and butter begin to sizzle, add the loin to the pot and brown on all sides until golden. (This browning process will take about 15 minutes; do not short-change this time. So much of the flavor will come from this initial browning of the roast.)
3. Briefly remove the browned loin and pour off the remaining oil, but do not discard the fond (the brown bits clinging to the bottom of the pot). Stir in rosemary, sage, garlic, and a few grates of nutmeg and then add the whole milk. Return the browned roast to the pot and add a bit more milk until the liquid level is about midway up the sides of the roast.
4. Bring the Dutch oven to a boil and then immediately reduce the stove-top flame to its lowest setting and partially cover the pot with a lid, leaving it a bit askew.
5. Gently allow the pork loin to braise for at least 2 hours. During the cooking process, occasionally rotate the roast. When fully cooked to medium rare, the internal temperature of the roast will be about 150°F. I like the meat to be pink and tender; you might like it cooked more well done (another 30 minutes), but do not let the internal temperature rise to more than 175°F or it will become rubbery and virtually inedible.
6. Remove the meat to a platter, cover with foil, and allow to rest for 15 to 20 minutes. Discard the garlic, rosemary, and sage leaves from the milk sauce.
7. What remains in the pan is liquid gold. The cooking liquid will be somewhat thickened, with nutty-brown curds of the milky residue. If you like an even thicker sauce, at this point you can add ½ teaspoon of cornstarch to a couple of tablespoons of cold milk to make a little slurry, which you can then blend into the cooking liquid with a wire whisk and boil for a few minutes until the sauce naturally thickens even further. Sometimes, at this point, I add a splash of Cognac to further enhance the complexity of the sauce.

8. Strain the sauce through a wire sieve placed over a stainless steel bowl, and transfer the liquid into a heavy bottomed saucepan and keep warm over a low flame. Reserve the milk curds from the strainer. I sometimes include them as part of the garnish. They are delicious.
9. Slice the loin, nap with the sauce, and serve, garnished with some chopped flat-leaf parsley.

Many Jesuits also found their way to Wareham and enjoyed equally wonderful experiences. One of my religious superiors at Fairfield was Fr. Joseph D. Devlin, S.J., who—prior to his appointment at the university as its rector—had served as Catholic chaplain at Dartmouth College. Joe loved getting away from Fairfield and spending a fall or summer weekend in Wareham, where it was riotous laughter from the moment he arrived until he left to return to Fairfield. He was a magnificent human being, full of insights and stories, and with a passion for food.

In hindsight, I would say that Italian cooking became the normative fare at Le Manoir. Owing to his love for authentic, precise, uncomplicated, and tried-and-true recipes, Wally soon discovered the earliest published books of Marcella Hazan, who quickly became our authority for Italian cooking. Although I have branched out to embrace and learn from other culinary authors like Giuliano Bugialli, Mario Batali, and Lidia Matticchio Bastianich, Wally has remained a devoté of Marcella Hazan for his whole life.

Wally implicitly trusted an Italian woman who was first a scientist, having earned a doctorate in natural sciences and biology from the Università degli Studi di Ferrara. Marcella also was born and raised in an Italian culinary mecca, Emilia-Romagna. In the mid-1950s she married an Italian-born, New York–raised Jewish man, Victor Hazan, and together they relocated to New York City soon after their wedding. Wally always identified with Marcella because of the fact that prior to her marriage she focused exclusively on her studies and never cooked.

It was the year of my ordination that Marcella published *Essentials of Italian Cooking*. This book, along with its sequels, *The Classic Italian Cookbook* and *More Classic Italian Cooking*, became the bible of Italian cooking at Le Manoir.[3] Although

3 Marcella Hazan, *Essentials of Italian Cooking* (New York: Knopf, 1972); *The Classic Italian Cookbook* (New York: Harper & Row, 1973); *More Classic Italian Cooking* (New York: Harper & Row, 1978).

Marcella could be imperious and apodictic in her writing and teaching, her techniques proved to be reliable and her recipes were delicious and have stood the test of time. She remains a go-to authority for *la cucina italiana*.

Reading Marcella's recipes and stories and meeting her in real life, one could easily understand how her no-nonsense approach to cooking evolved. She oozed authoritativeness. "This is the way to do it," she would declare. "If someone tells you differently, they are simply wrong." Wally adored her confidence and authoritativeness.

I would venture to say that no other cooking guide had a more formative influence in the ways Americans cook Italian than Marcella Hazan: in terms of Italian fare, she was in many ways the equivalent of Julia Child for French cuisine. Over the course of many years I would say that I've made virtually every recipe in her early cookbooks, and I am still making things that I first tried years ago. Her recipes for tomato sauces have become staples of my basic culinary thesaurus.

I remember the first time on a Lenten Friday that Wally and I made her luscious tomato sauce that is enriched by what seems, at first reading, to be an inordinate amount of extra-virgin olive oil. When I read this recipe for the first time I was certain that there had to be an error, but blindly obedient to the *maestra* that Marcella was, I followed her method and was amazed by the result. I have made this recipe hundreds of time, each time equally delighted by the result.

SALSA DI POMODORO CON VERDURE E OLIO D'OLIVA

Tomato sauce with pureed vegetables and olive oil, adapted from Marcella Hazan

Makes 6 to 8 servings

Ingredients

- 2 28-ounce cans of imported Italian plum tomatoes, cut up, juice reserved
- ⅔ cup chopped carrot
- ⅔ cup chopped celery
- ⅔ cup chopped onion
- salt and freshly ground black pepper
- ⅓ cup extra-virgin olive oil

Method

1. Put the tomatoes in a saucepan along with the carrot, celery, onion, and salt, and cook with no cover on the pan at a slow, steady simmer for 30 minutes. Stir from time to time.

2. Add the olive oil, raise the heat slightly to bring to a somewhat stronger simmer, and stir occasionally, while reducing the tomato to as much of a pulp as you can with the back of the spoon. Cook for 15 minutes, then taste and correct for salt.

   Note: The steps above are Marcella's straightforward method. Over the years I have experimented with this recipe, and the following is my version of her classic method.

   I first sauté the aromatic vegetables in olive oil in a saucepan until they are wilted, but not browned (about 8 to 10 minutes). Then I add the tomatoes and juice and cook together for about 20 to 30 minutes. Finally, off the heat, I add a ½ cup of extra-virgin olive oil and, with an immersion blender, I bring the sauce together until the olive oil forms a smooth emulsion with the tomatoes and other vegetables. Then I correct the seasonings with salt and pepper. While I think Marcella's original recipe is excellent, I have come to like my variation even more. You be the judge.

A final note: I usually triple or quadruple the recipe when I make this sauce and freeze it in pint-sized containers. The sauce freezes beautifully and can defrost quickly in the microwave for an impromptu supper when guests arrive unexpectedly or when you crave something wonderful, but do not want to spend a lot of time cooking. ***Eccolo!***

Within the first weeks after I took up residence in Fairfield, I was on the hunt to find a parish where I might sink pastoral roots as a regular weekend associate priest. I took an assignment on my first weekend to preside and preach at Mass in Saint Luke's parish in Westport, Connecticut. This was a regular rotating supply call to the Fairfield Jesuit community. I chatted briefly with the pastor, Msgr. Thomas Driscoll, who was an alumnus of the North American College in Rome and, in addition to his pastoral responsibilities, also served as a canon lawyer within the diocesan tribunal in Bridgeport.

I asked Msgr. Driscoll to be on the lookout for a regular weekend pastoral assignment that I might consider. Fortunately for me, he had this request in mind when he shared lunch the following Tuesday with Fr. Vincent J. O'Connor, the pastor of Saint Catherine of Siena parish in Riverside, a part of the greater Greenwich community. Scrolling back through a lifetime of experiences, I now realize that this weekend call to Saint Catherine would become one of the most rewarding ministerial choices I would make in my entire lifetime. Ministry to the people of Saint Catherine's became an enduring pastoral engagement that has now expanded to almost five decades.

By his own confession, Father O'Connor was ordinary in virtually every way: intelligence, comeliness, preaching, and administration. But almost no one who knew him would concur with his self-assessment. Vinnie O'Connor embodied and personified the spirit of the Second Vatican Council. He evolved and professed a simple formula for pastoral care that I have reiterated countless times through the years. He maintained that in caring for others, there are ultimately only two relevant questions: "What do you need? How can I help you?" That dual formula summarized his whole way of proceeding as a pastor. As a young and impressionable neophyte in priestly ministry, I was like a sponge, absorbing everything that this extraordinary priest was willing and able to teach by both word and example.

Well before Pope Francis would emerge on the world stage with his exhortation to live more simply and love more generously, Vincent O'Connor was already there. He was pastor to a thriving parish in one of the most affluent communities in the United States, driving a small car where progressive rusting had eroded its floorboard to such a degree that you could see the roadway below as you drove along. He lived in the smallest room in the rectory on a twin-sized bed with a mattress in dire need of replacement. His closet contained a few long-sleeved black clerical shirts and a couple of pairs of black trousers. He had two black suits and a couple of sport shirts. That was about it.

His bookshelves contained theology titles. A decided emphasis in his modest collection focused on multifaith religious collaboration and liturgy. He collected the prayer books of many of the major religious traditions; he had multiple versions of the Passover *Haggadah* in Hebrew and English *and* a copy of the *Holy Koran* alongside multiple translations of the Holy Bible and the Jewish *Tanakh*. It was not surprising that at age sixty, Father O'Connor had enrolled in the MSW program at the Wurzweiler School of Social Work at Yeshiva University in New York City, America's only graduate social work school under Jewish auspices in a university setting. Two years later, in 1982, he successfully completed the program and was awarded the MSW degree.

He was known and admired in every religious community in Greenwich. He believed that showing up was almost more important than what you might say once you got there. He was virtually omnipresent, or at least it seemed so. Vinnie kept up a dizzying schedule, which might include brief pastoral calls to the Greenwich Hospital or to visit with residents and staff at the Nathaniel Witherell Center, a short-term rehabilitation and skilled nursing center operated by the Town of Greenwich. It was not an uncommon answer to the question: "Where is Fr. O'Connor?" to receive the reply: "He's at the hospital or nursing home."

Single-handedly, Father O'Connor convinced the administrator at Greenwich Hospital that they needed a full-time chaplain. He effectively promoted the candidacy of a young, recently ordained Congregational minister—the Reverend Catherine (Kitty) Garlid—to serve as the hospital's first board-certified chaplain, a role that she managed with great distinction and accomplishment for the following twenty-five years.

Because Vincent O'Connor passionately believed that interreligious cooperation enriched a community's life, he was in the vanguard to institute a monthly preaching visit by Christian and non-Christian clergy to the Saint Catherine's pulpit. I recall one occasion when he had invited the African American pastor of an inner-city Bridgeport African Methodist Episcopal Church to be the guest preacher. I was scheduled to celebrate the principal parish Sunday Mass and introduced myself and welcomed the visiting preacher in the sacristy before the procession commenced. In preparation, she instinctively applied fresh lip gloss to her lips. During the procession, she realized that she did not want bright red lips at the altar and whispered to me during the procession: "Do you have a handkerchief?" Reaching under the layers of my vestments and into the rear pocket of my trousers while trying to maintain decorum in the procession, I quickly handed her a clean handkerchief. She briskly wiped off the lipstick, leaving me with a handkerchief ready for the laundry and subject to a lot of explanation.

As one might expect, she preached with African American passion and gusto, something our congregation did not ordinarily experience. But they loved her and her message. When it came time for the Eucharistic prayer, she huddled up next to me and quietly asked: "Would it be all right if I concelebrate?" What was I to do? She was there. She obviously wanted to actively participate. So without any guile or malice, she read along with me for the remainder of the Eucharistic service.

Afterwards, I was scheduled to join Fr. O'Connor on a pastoral visit to a homebound parishioner, and we were driving together in his car along the Post Road in Greenwich. "Vinnie, there is something you need to know, because you may be getting a call later today from the bishop's office," I told him.

"What happened?" he inquired.

"Our guest preacher this morning concelebrated the Mass with me."

I thought he might swerve and drive off the road, but he maintained his calm and began to laugh. "If the bishop inquires, I will just pass it off as a young Jesuit's inexperience and poor judgment." But then he added, "You did the right thing. Charity always trumps every other option."

Fr. O'Connor loved New York City, and this was one of his few extravagant indulgences. He enjoyed the theatre and dining, especially when he was treating someone else to these pleasures. One time Walter Woods was visiting from Boston and Fr. O'Connor invited us to join him in Manhattan for a Saturday marathon, which included matinée and evening performances of two Broadway musicals with a dinner at the Four Seasons Restaurant in between. When we were seated for dinner, the maître d'hôtel presented him with an impressive wine list. He passed the imposing leather-bound book to me to make a selection.

Since we had all spent time in Italy (Father O'Connor had served as pastor in residence at the Pontifical North American College from 1974 to 1975), I thought I would choose a very modestly priced Italian white wine from the region just outside of Rome affectionately described as the Castelli Romani. I selected a young Fontana Candida from Frascati, which in Italy at that time would have cost a couple American dollars but was selling on the Four Seasons list for $45. When I announced my choice, Vinnie said: "Give me that list." He ordered a bottle of Corton-Charlemagne, which was one of the best wines I had ever tasted. Corton-Charlemagne is an exceptional white wine from the Côte de Beaune region of Burgundy. This delicious vintage is named after the Emperor Charlemagne, who once owned the hill of Corton on which the vineyards now rest.

"We're here to celebrate," Vinnie proclaimed. "Frascati is fine for a simple supper at home, but not for tonight." Corton-Charlemagne became for me a symbol—even to this day—of Vinnie O'Connor's singular largesse and magnanimity.

In the same vein, before Christmas every year, Father O'Connor would arrange a celebratory dinner in New York for all the priests who assisted at Saint Catherine's, in which I was always included. He often had his very close friend, Thomas W. Monetti, who for ten years was the food and beverage director at the Waldorf Astoria, arrange a festive dinner for all of us in Peacock Alley, a quintessential New York dining venue and one of Manhattan's most celebrated places to see and be seen.

The Waldorf Astoria is a New York City landmark, an enduring symbol of the city's glamour and opulence since it opened its art-deco doors in 1931. It began in the 1890s as two adjacent and competing hotels, operated by members of the Astor family: William Waldorf Astor and John Jacob Astor. Originally occupying the corner of Fifth Avenue on what is now the site of the Empire State Building, the quarreling cousins eventually put aside their differences and built a corridor connecting their hotels, which they called "Peacock Alley."

One of my stimulus-response associations with the Waldorf Astoria is its simple signature salad, which has been subject to an infinite number of interpretations through the years since it made its début in the late 1880s at this legendary hotel. Here is my adaptation of this classic dish.

WALDORF SALAD

Makes 4 to 6 servings

Ingredients

For the candied and spiced walnuts

- 2 cups unsalted walnut halves
- 1 egg white
- 1 tablespoon of a spice mixture (I use a combination of mild paprika, cayenne, cumin, ground fennel seed, and ground coriander, but you can use whatever spices suit your taste)
- 1 cup superfine sugar

continued

For the dressing

- ½ cup Greek-style plain yogurt
- ½ cup crème fraîche
- 3 teaspoons freshly squeezed lemon juice
- ¼ teaspoon white pepper
- ¼ cup walnut oil (you can also use olive or corn oil)

For the salad

- ½ cup peeled celery root (celeriac)
- 2 large Granny Smith apples, washed and unpeeled
- 2 large Gala apples, washed and unpeeled
- 1 dozen seedless red grapes, cut in half lengthwise
- ½ cup microgreens or celery leaves

Method

1. Preheat oven to 350°F.

To prepare the candied and spiced walnuts

1. Prepare the candied walnuts by combining the nut meats with the lightly beaten egg white in a large bowl. Combine the spices with a cup of sugar and mix with the walnuts until they are evenly coated. Spread walnuts onto a sheet pan that has been lined with parchment paper. Toast in the oven for about 20 minutes until the nuts have browned. Do not burn. Remove and cool.

To make the salad dressing

1. To make the classic dressing for this salad, combine the crème fraîche with the Greek yogurt in a glass bowl. With a whisk, add in the lemon juice and white pepper. Finally, drizzle in walnut oil and vigorously whisk until the dressing emulsifies.

To finish the salad

1. To prepare the salad, julienne the celery root and apples into matchstick-size strips. If you have a mandoline this job can be simplified, but you can achieve the same effect with a sharp knife.
2. Gently fold the dressing into the celery root and apple mixture until the ingredients are coated and well combined.
3. You can either individually plate the salad or compose it on an oval platter. The Waldorf Astoria classically serves it in a ring mold formation, with the cut grapes and candied walnuts arranged around the perimeter as garnish. Before service, tear a couple of celery leaves or scatter some microgreens on the top of the salad.

During one of our pre-Christmas dinners at the Waldorf, I passed by the hotel's venerable and well-used 1907 Steinway grand piano that was tucked away in the entry foyer to Peacock Alley. I noticed a small brass plaque on the piano that read "Some of the loveliest songs in American musical history were composed on this Steinway." The piano once belonged to Cole Porter, one of the hotel's former residents. When I inquired about the piano, Tom Monetti asked me if I might like to play the instrument. He did not have to ask a second time or coax me any further. Because it was holiday time, I sat down at the keyboard and played an improvised rendition of Irving Berlin's "White Christmas," for which I received applause not only from my dinner companions but also from many of the hotel's guests who had paused to listen to this impromptu concert.

After I finished, Tom graciously said that he was going to keep my contact information on his Rolodex just in case Daryl Sherman—who played the Cole piano in the Waldorf's lounge for some fourteen years until 2007—should ever need a replacement. That call to fill in for Daryl never came my way, or this story would be vastly improved.

It is funny how a certain meal becomes associated with a special memory. I remember tasting Veal Oscar for the first time during one of these unforgettable dinners. Veal Oscar is a relatively simple dish of *médaillons de veau* or pounded veal cutlets, asparagus, lobster, or crab meat and topped with a luxurious béarnaise sauce. The dish is named for King Oscar II, who was king of Sweden and Norway in the late nineteenth century.

Although this is not one of the signatures of the Waldorf Astoria, this is how I remember it from the first time I tasted it. I had a particular fascination for this preparation because it is crowned by béarnaise, one of the classic sauces I learned at Le Cordon Bleu. I recall that our *saucier* instructor told us that béarnaise sauce dates back to 1836, when a restaurant named Le Pavillon Henri IV opened in Saint-Germain-en-Laye, a western suburb of Paris. Chef Collinet created a sauce for the occasion and named it after the province of Béarn, where King Henri IV was born in 1553. Whatever its true provenance, it is certainly a sauce to have in one's culinary repertoire.

At one memorable New York City dinner party to which I had been invited, we were served a wonderful preparation of a classic Veal Oscar. This is my version of this classic French dish.

VEAL OSCAR

Sautéed veal cutlets with crabmeat and béarnaise sauce

Makes 4 servings

Ingredients

For the béarnaise sauce

- 3 large egg yolks
- 3 tablespoons champagne or white vinegar
- 1 tablespoon dry white wine
- 10 crushed black peppercorns
- 1 tablespoon finely minced shallots
- 1 tablespoon chopped fresh tarragon
- 1 stick (¼ pound) melted unsalted butter
- 1 teaspoon fresh lemon juice

- 2 tablespoons water
- salt and freshly ground black pepper

For the veal

- 1 pound thinly pounded veal cutlets
- ¼ cup all-purpose flour
- ½ pound lump crabmeat (or lobster)
- 2 tablespoons unsalted butter
- ½ tablespoon vegetable oil
- 12 fresh pencil-thin asparagus spears
- salt and pepper to taste

Method

To prepare the veal medallions

1. Cut the pounded veal cutlets into medallions, approximately 2 ounces each. A normal portion is about three medallions for each guest.
2. Gently feel through the lump crabmeat or lobster and remove any cartilage or shells.

To make the béarnaise sauce

1. Begin the reduction by combining the shallots, wine, vinegar, peppercorns, and tarragon in a saucepan and simmer over medium high heat until 2 tablespoons of liquid remains. Strain and discard the solids. Set aside.
2. In a heavy saucepan, melt and clarify the butter. Allow the butter to simmer for about 10 minutes until the water in the butter evaporates and the milk solids begin to coagulate on the bottom and sides of the pan.
3. Let the melted butter cool for a few minutes so that the solids naturally collect at the bottom of the pan. Skim off the foam on top

continued

and then either pour off the golden liquid, leaving the solids behind, or pour the entire melted butter through a cheesecloth-lined strainer. Retain the clarified butter and discard the milk solids.

4. Put the room-temperature eggs yolks and water into a heavy-duty saucepan. Off the heat, vigorously whisk the eggs and water for 30 seconds, whipping in lots of air.
5. Cook over very low heat, whisking constantly and scraping the bowl, until thick and voluminous. The whisk will leave tracks that hold for a few seconds.
6. At this point, take it off the heat and whisk rapidly for 30 seconds to cool slightly. In a slow stream, whisk in the clarified butter a little at a time to fully incorporate into the forming emulsion. Be sure the butter is not too hot, or it will break the emulsion.
7. To finish the sauce, whisk in 1 tablespoon of the shallot and wine reduction (or more to taste). Season with salt and pepper. Blend in some finely minced tarragon. Put the finished sauce aside in a bowl and cover with plastic wrap.

To assemble and serve the veal medallions

1. In a sauté pan with a little butter and olive oil, sear the veal medallions on both sides and place on a baking sheet arranged in six portions (three medallions to a portion).
2. Divide the asparagus into six equal portions and place the trimmed asparagus spears on top of each group of veal medallions.
3. Place equal amounts of crabmeat or lobster on top of the asparagus and season with salt and pepper. Place baking sheet into a hot oven (400°F) to heat up the asparagus and crabmeat. When hot, remove from oven; place each serving on dinner plates, top with béarnaise sauce, and serve immediately.

After one of Fr. O'Connor's memorable holiday dinner gatherings, the group of us priests walked over to Rockefeller Center to see the famous Christmas tree. Another Jesuit priest from India, Fr. Gilbert D'Souza, who was living at Saint Catherine's while working on a doctoral dissertation in scripture at Vanderbilt University, was tripped up by one of the sidewalk potholes that are part of the New York City terrain. He became both flustered and embarrassed. Fr. O'Connor quickly came to his defense. "Be kind to poor Gilbert; after all, there are no potholes in Pune!" Pune was Gilbert's hometown, the second largest city in the state of Maharashtra.

"No potholes in Pune!" We laughed about that phrase for years to come. It trickled off his tongue as if he had rehearsed that line for weeks. Whether it was the wine we had consumed at the Waldorf Astoria or his keen Irish wit, we laughed like a group of fools as we trekked together to see the holiday tree and lights in Rockefeller Center.

When Fr. O'Connor's brother, Msgr. William O'Connor, died in Boston in 1984, he called me. "Would you be able to come with me to Seymour to help me dress my brother's body for burial?" Naturally, I agreed. Vinnie's cousin was a local funeral director and was handling the arrangements. When a priest dies, he is clothed in the same vestments worn during Mass. Bill O'Connor had served as a chaplain in the military, retiring with the rank of colonel, and had been given the honorary title of "monsignor" because of his distinguished achievements during his career in the armed services. We put on Msgr. Bill's red cassock, a white alb and cincture, and the priestly stole and chasuble before his body was placed into the nearby coffin.

When this task was completed, Vinnie suggested that we stop for lunch before he drove me back to the university's campus. During lunch, Fr. O'Connor expressed his profound gratitude for the fraternal support I had been to him as he fulfilled a final charitable duty for his deceased brother. "Walter, I really want to do something tangible to repay you for your kindness. What would you like?"

I protested, saying that this was something any friend should be expected to do for another, especially one priest for another.

"No," he insisted, "I really want to do a favor for you. You can ask me for anything."

"Anything?" I countered.

"Yes, I mean anything."

"OK," I quickly rejoined. "Then allow the parish to celebrate your upcoming fortieth anniversary of priestly ordination, and let me be the coordinator of the arrangements." He was caught in his own trap.

"You Jesuits live up to your well-earned reputation for being sly and crafty," he said. "How can I deny you when you have caught me in my own game? Yes, you can celebrate the fortieth and you will be in charge of the arrangements." The genie was out of the bottle.

Vinnie O'Connor had been ordained to the priesthood on March 17, 1945, by Archbishop Henry O'Brien of the Archdiocese of Hartford. Even though an Irishman and a Jesuit was in charge of the festivities honoring another Irishman who had been ordained on the feast of the patron of all Ireland, Saint Patrick, we decided to plan the celebration to coincide with the feast day of the parish's patron saint, Catherine of Siena, and to host a major *festa italiana*.

The parish was teeming with many excellent cooks. Our little planning group created a relatively simple menu, developed the recipes, and got the local home cooks into production in their own kitchens. The centerpiece of the menu was *lasagna alla Bolognese*. I would guess that we had trays of homemade lasagna being stored in every freezer in Riverside, Connecticut, in preparation for the big *festa*. We rented dozens of electric ovens, which we had temporarily installed in the church's basement, and got an electrician to come in and power them up properly so that we did not burn the church down. We erected a huge green and white tent over the entire church parking lot and rented tables and chairs to seat the more than eight hundred guests we were expecting. The teenagers of the parish formed an amazing corps of servers. One of the women organized a group of ladies and together they made colorful matching aprons for all the servers. A local restaurant owned by one of the parishioners prepped enough salad greens to fill a backyard pool. We bought out an entire day's production of bread sticks from an Arthur Avenue Italian bakery in the Bronx. And we consumed more cases of Tuscan red wine than it would be prudent to count.

I even hauled out my accordion for the occasion, and instead of Irish jigs and reels I played every Neapolitan love song I had ever learned. It was a glorious parish-wide celebration, following upon a most extraordinary liturgy in honor of Santa Caterina da Siena, with woodwinds and brass winds accompanying our organ and parish choir.

And, to top it off, the parishioners presented their beloved pastor with a brand-new 1985 Toyota Camry, having without his knowledge removed his old car from the garage and delivered it to a scrap metal yard to be recycled. Fr. O'Connor was simply overwhelmed.

"Walter," he commented in a telephone call the next morning. "Now, I really must do something special to repay you." I cautioned him to be careful what he wished for.

"Touché," he quickly replied, still overcome by his feelings of immense gratitude. For once, he was the sole beneficiary of his people's love and appreciation, and of mine.

Within the year that same parish family would come back together for another celebration—this time for Fr. O'Connor's funeral. He was diagnosed with a life-altering illness, which in the course of four months claimed his life. As he was receiving treatment at Danbury Hospital, I visited him practically every day. One day, he asked me to bring paper and pen and he dictated detailed plans for how his funeral was to be celebrated, including instructions for the cremation of his body—a relatively new practice, long prohibited in the Roman Catholic Church. He asked me to preach at the main and concluding funeral liturgy.

After all of the details for Fr. O'Connor's funeral had been dictated and recorded, he asked two of the nurses on the floor to witness to the document lest there be any questions that these directives fully represented his intentions and desires. When we were alone, he said something quite important to me. Recall that at this point in my life I had been ordained for less than a dozen years, most of which I had spent in close association with this priest mentor.

"I have many close priest friends, Walter, but none of them, except for you, is able to be a priest to me," he told me.

By this statement he meant to convey that during these final weeks and months of his life I had been able to minister to him as well as to be his friend. On one particular occasion after we had celebrated Mass together in his hospital room and I imparted the final blessing, he took my hands into his and said: "For most of my life, I have been on the other side of the bed, where you now stand. I have said many of the comforting words you have just now spoken to me. I want to say to you that I am experiencing great consolation because I believe all the things you have just said. Thank you for being such an instrument of God's peace for me as I have been so many times in the past for others." My eyes spontaneously filled with tears.

When he died, the first text from the scriptures that flooded my heart on hearing the news of his passing were words from the prophet Micah: "To do what is right, to love justice and to walk tenderly with your God" (Micah 6:8). This was the text that formed the foundation of my homily that attempted to give voice to what had been an exceptional priestly ministry.

Among his final directives was also this one: "At a time that is convenient after the funeral, please arrange for a nice luncheon for all of the priests who came to the funeral and get Tom Monetti to supply a full case of Corton-Charlemagne and toast me." Mr. Monetti did supply the wine, and we spent a glorious afternoon eating lobster and drinking endless glasses of this elixir of the gods and sharing never-ending anecdotes about a man whom we affectionately called among ourselves "the bishop of Riverside."

Father Vincent J. O'Connor molded and remolded my understanding of priesthood and pastoral ministry more than any other single person. And in gratefully remembering him now, I am reminded of the very frightfully poignant and insightful words of the fourth-century archbishop of Constantinople and one of the Church's greatest teachers, Saint John Chrysostom: "And all men are ready to pass judgement on the priest as if he was not a being clothed with flesh, or one who inherited a human nature." But even more importantly, I still take great comfort in these words from the end of Matthew's Gospel: "His lord said to him, 'Well done, good and faithful servant. You have been faithful over a few things; I will set you over many things. Enter into the joy of your Lord.'" (Matthew 25:23).

Chapter 4

SALT THAT NEVER LOSES ITS TANG

You are the salt of the earth.

—MATTHEW 5:13

One of the first women I met when I began weekend ministry at Saint Catherine of Siena was Theresa ("Tess") Zadrosny. Do not be fooled by her Polish surname. She was born Therese Bologna in Riverside, Connecticut, more than a century ago. She died just before Palm Sunday on April 11, 2014, well into her ninety-seventh year.

For whatever work reasons brought Michael Zadrosny to southern Connecticut from his native Taunton, Massachusetts, he quickly caught the attention of Tess's keen eye.

"I am going to marry that guy," Tess told her friends.

"You don't even know him," they retorted.

"I may not know him, but I know that I am going to marry him." And marry him she did. Mike settled with Tess in Riverside and together they opened a small mom-and-pop variety store, Melfair Market, which also provided freshly butchered meat. Mike was an expert butcher and Tess, a superb home cook and baker.

The Zadrosnys raised their two children, Joe and Marianne. Marianne would later become one of Father O'Connor's parish secretaries before moving on later in her professional life to a distinguished career in business at US Tobacco and as managing director of human resources and corporate relations at Fieldpoint Private

Bank. Tess and Mike's son, Joe, married Eileen and raised a family of three sons in Vermont. Marianne, like her mother, has continuously resided and worked in the greater Greenwich community.

In every parish there are a couple of individuals who stand out not because they are natural leaders or seek the limelight, but because they become emblematic of the best of what the whole community represents. Tess was one of those kinds of people. Though relatively small in physical stature, she possessed a winning smile and a sparkling personality. Her parents had raised their family in this parish, which at the turn of the twentieth century was comprised predominantly of immigrant Italian families who had come from towns surrounding Naples in southern Italy.

If you were to stroll through Saint Mary's Cemetery in Greenwich, you could practice your Italian pronunciation by simply reading aloud the names that are chiseled into the headstones along its many pathways. Before I arrived at the parish in the fall of 1976, Tess's parents had died, but there were so many stories about Mariantonia D'Andrea Bologna and Nicholas Bologna. One of my favorites is a tale about their putative *jura possessionis* (the right of possession) of the pew they habitually occupied in Saint Catherine's church. Like many Catholics, the Bolognas sat in exactly the same pew every time they attended Mass. One time, Mr. Bologna was indignant when he arrived only to find someone else sitting in his place. "Excuse me," he said, "but you are sitting in my pew." Discreetly, the squatter removed himself and proudly the Bolognas claimed their proper place.

Tess must have inherited something of her father's sense of pride of place because Saint Catherine's became a real extension of her family. Every priest who ever served there experienced her motherly qualities. When you were assigned to Saint Catherine's, Tess adopted you, whether you knew it or not.

During the O'Connor years, Saint Catherine's became a very popular place to go for worship. The parish church offered a variety of liturgical styles: family-centered masses, folk music masses, and solemn choral celebrations with processions, incense, and an excellent vested choir. There were liturgical celebrations in Italian and French as well as in English. There was something for everyone.

The holidays of Christmas and Easter brought hundreds of additional worshippers to the doors of Saint Catherine's. The pastor scheduled masses not only in the main sanctuary but also in the church basement, in the adjoining school building's auditorium, and in the convent chapel. On these festival days life in the parish could only be described as organized bedlam, with celebrations taking place everywhere and at various times. We needed every priest, deacon, cantor, and musician we could engage to cover these demands.

On Christmas Eve, Tess began a lovely tradition of inviting all of the priests to her home for the customary Italian "Feast of the Seven Fishes." I had never encountered this tradition in Italy, but it was clearly an established tradition in many Italian American households as the quintessential Christmas Eve celebration.

The feast consists of a menu of seven different seafood dishes. Tess said that her mother referred to it as *La Vigilia di Natale*, the vigil of Christmas. She believed that the tradition harkened back to the antecedent Neapolitan Christmas Eve practice of abstaining from meat on December 24 and eating the many varieties of abundant seafood and shellfish that were available from the Bay of Naples. The most famous dish southern Italians are known for is *baccalà* (salted cod fish).

The following is my adaptation of a recipe that Tess often prepared. It is not for the faint of heart, since you need to start days in advance to rehydrate the salted cod. But the results are worth the patient efforts.

BACCALÀ DI NATALE

Traditional Christmas Eve salted codfish

Makes 8 to 10 servings

Ingredients

- 4 pounds dried salted cod, cut into 3-inch pieces
- 8 to 10 peeled and quartered Yukon Gold potatoes
- 1 cup extra-virgin olive oil
- 1 bunch celery
- 1 large diced yellow onion
- 2 cups good-quality pitted Italian olives
- 4 28-ounce cans diced San Marzano tomatoes
- 12 cups chicken broth

continued

Method

1. Place the salted cod pieces in a covered pot of cold water and refrigerate for at least 1 to 4 days, changing and refreshing the water frequently. At the end of the process, the water will appear clear and fish will almost be sweet when tasted.
2. In a large pot of cold water, place the potatoes. Bring the pot to a boil over high heat and cook for about 12 to 15 minutes or until potatoes are almost cooked through. Remove from heat and drain in a colander.
3. Heat the olive oil over medium heat in a large Dutch oven or stockpot. Add the diced celery and sauté for about 5 minutes, then add the onions and continue to sauté until the vegetables begin to wilt.
4. Add the olives and cook for an additional minute. Stir in the tomatoes and their juice. Bring the sauce to a boil before lowering the heat to a simmer. Finally, add the 12 cups of chicken broth to the pot and allow the sauce to simmer for another 20 minutes.
5. When ready for service, add the cooked potatoes and the soaked *baccalà* and simmer together for about 10 minutes or until the potatoes are reheated and the *baccalà* flakes easily.

Anyone who has ever prepared this elaborate holiday meal knows the countless hours of preparations required. But this never seemed to present a problem for Tess. She was the consummate hostess, with unmatched graciousness and charm. The dining room table was always beautifully set. Remember, on Christmas Eve the priests were doing double and triple duty, with only a couple of free hours between the early evening services and the midnight Mass. I recall how we would pile into the Zadrosny home and immediately be offered an array of appetizers and drinks. Soon thereafter we would be invited to table for what seemed like a never-ending menu of delicious dishes whose recipes had been handed down through generations of Italian grandmothers, mothers, and aunts.

Having experienced versions of this Christmas Eve bacchanal at several different Italian American homes through the years, I came to appreciate just how individualistic each family's tastes can be and how traditional preparations can vary. Tess resurrected a tradition that had grown dormant in her family and began preparing the full seven courses as a special treat for her priest guests. Ideally, a family should spend the whole of Christmas Eve together at table to do justice to a meal of these Herculean proportions, but we were men on a tight schedule, so everything seemed a bit rushed. Tess knew she had to have us back on the road to the church by 10 p.m., so the courses tended to pile quickly one on top of the other.

One of the younger priests, himself an Italian American of Sicilian ancestry, had a voracious appetite and we were dumbfounded by just how much food he could consume in a single sitting. Fr. O'Connor feared that young Fr. Joe Amato might later be vulnerable to vomiting during the midnight Mass because of the vast quantities of octopus salad, fried calamari, baked shrimp, spaghetti with clam sauce, and *baccalà* he forced into his expanding stomach.

After the magnificent repast Tess would parade out a medley of desserts, which looked like the display case of a fancy Italian bakery shop. On many a Christmas Eve we wished that we did not have any further services to conduct so that we could linger and savor the many delectable confections she had prepared. One of her signature confections was a flourless chocolate rolled cake—much like the French *bûche de Noël*—for which she was reluctant to pass on her recipe. However, when I quietly asked her to share this gem of a recipe, she weakened and passed it on to me. She curiously called this cake by its French name, *Roulade Léontine*, for which I later discovered many similar recipes. I must say that this cake, with endless permutations in fillings and garnishes, has remained a staple in my repertory for decades.

ROULADE LÉONTINE

Rolled flourless chocolate cake with cream filling from Tess Zadrosny

Makes 10 to 12 servings

Ingredients

For the cake

- 6 large eggs, separated and at room temperature
- ⅔ cup granulated or superfine sugar

continued

- ¼ teaspoon salt
- 1 tablespoon Dutch-process unsweetened cocoa powder, sifted
- 6 ounces dark chocolate

For the filling

- 1 cup heavy cream
- 3 tablespoons sifted confectioners' sugar
- 2 tablespoons Grand Marnier
- 1 teaspoon finely grated fresh orange zest

Garnish

- sifted unsweetened cocoa powder and confectioners' sugar

Method

To prepare the cake

1. Preheat oven to 350°F.
2. Oil a 15x10x1-inch baking sheet and line lengthwise with parchment paper, letting paper hang over both ends by at least 2 inches.
3. In a double boiler, melt chocolate with the water over very low heat, stirring. Cool melted chocolate to lukewarm.
4. Beat yolks, ⅓ cup sugar, and the salt in the bowl of a stand mixer fitted with whisk attachment, until thick and pale, about 5 minutes.
5. Fold in cocoa powder and melted chocolate until just blended.
6. Beat whites until they just hold soft peaks. Gradually add remaining 1/3 cup sugar and beat until whites achieve stiff peaks.
7. Gently mix one-third of the whites into melted-chocolate mixture to lighten the batter, then gently fold in remaining whites, incorporating them thoroughly.

8. Spread the batter evenly in the prepared pan and bake in the middle of the oven until puffed and the top is dry to the touch, about 15 to 17 minutes.
9. Transfer the baking sheet to a cooling rack. Cover the top loosely with a large piece of waxed paper and lay a dampened tea towel over the entire pan. Let stand 5 minutes, then remove wax paper and towel and cool completely. Loosen edges with a sharp knife.
10. Sift cocoa powder or confectioners' sugar over top of cooled cake layer and overlap two layers of wax paper lengthwise over cake. Place a baking sheet or serving tray over the paper and invert the cake onto it using the parchment paper to release the cake. When positioned, peel off the parchment paper on which the caked was baked. (Do not worry if cake tears or cracks a bit; trust in the Lord that it will hold together when it is filled and rolled.)

To prepare the filling

1. Beat the heavy cream with confectioners' sugar and Grand Marnier until it just holds stiff peaks. Fold in the orange zest.
2. Spread whipped cream filling evenly over the entire surface of the cake. Place a long platter or long cutting board next to a long side of the cake. Using the wax paper as an aid, slowly but decisively roll up cake toward you, forming it into a tight log, beginning with the top long side.
3. Carefully transfer the rolled cake log, seam side down, to the serving platter, using the wax paper to help slide the cake into position. (The cake may crack but will still hold together.)
4. Dust cake generously with additional cocoa powder or confectioners' sugar.
5. Cover loosely with plastic wrap and refrigerate until ready to serve. Use a serrated bread knife to cut the cake. I like to cut it on the bias, forming larger and more elegant pieces.

continued

Note: Although Tess always made this cake with the classic filling here, you can be creative and experiment. It is great to flavor the whipped cream with strawberry or raspberry purée; Cognac, Irish Cream, or Kahlua; rum or brandy. You get the picture. Experiment. The recipe is fail-safe and wonderful.

After the seemingly endless Christmas Eve feast there would be a beautifully wrapped gift for each priest, specially chosen to reflect individual tastes and styles. Tess and Mike provided this beautiful evening for several years until Fr. O'Connor died and the core staff of resident priests and assisting priests changed assignments. But appreciative memories of those magical Christmas Eve dinners with Tess and Mike and their family are vibrant and cherished.

Tess and Mike also traveled with me on a parish-sponsored pilgrimage that I organized and led to the Holy Land, followed by several days in Rome and Assisi. It was not an itinerary planned by professional tour operators. In hindsight, I realize that I packed far too much into the days and the trip became an arduous journey, even for younger folks. Most of the pilgrims, however, were well past sixty years of age. Not a single one of them complained and they were anxious to see and experience everything.

We covered all of the major points of interest in the Holy Land, stretching from Galilee to the Dead Sea and Masada. In Hebrew, "Masada" means a fortress. The bus left us off at the base of this ancient Jewish stronghold, and we climbed to the top. This is not a climb for the faint of heart. One of the older women in the group was wearing shoes with a three-inch heel that day—not exactly proper footwear for trekking up to the summit of Masada. Not only did she successfully make it up to the top, but she also made it down without an incident.

Next to Jerusalem, Masada is the most popular destination of pilgrims visiting Israel. It stands as a powerful and enduring symbol of Jewish resolve and determination—the final Jewish stronghold against a Roman invasion. More than two millennia separated us from those brave Jewish resisters and the fall of Masada, but standing there on that hot spring day we all felt united in spirit to these ancestors in faith, or as Pope St. John Paul II so beautifully said on the occasion of his first visit to Rome's Synagogue on April 13, 1986: "With Judaism therefore we have a relationship, which we do not have with any other religion. You are our dearly beloved brothers, and in a certain way, it could be said you are our elder brothers."

Subsequent days were also long and the sun was blazing, but my fellow pilgrims remained stalwarts. Our travels took us to the Golan Heights and ancient ruins of Caesarea Philippi. This place is mentioned in the Gospels of Matthew and Mark. Now virtually uninhabited, Caesarea Philippi remains an important archaeological site.

Most of us that morning were listening to our guide speak about the remarkably preserved Roman aqueduct. Running water was available to the old city of Caesarea, passing along its raised aqueduct. Herod built the aqueduct in the first century BC. Later, it was expanded by the Romans.

During the talk Tess huddled close to me and whispered: “Have you seen Mike? He seems to have disappeared from the group.” I looked around and behold, there was Mike, standing almost at the top of this aqueduct. How he climbed up that steep hill I still cannot explain, but there he was, seventy-five years young, standing like a proud mountain lion at the peak of this historic ruin.

This is the same guy who was constantly worrying about me not tripping on the cobblestones of the old City of Jerusalem. Polish guys from Taunton were made of very durable stock. Mike lived well into his nineties, and although he gradually gave up climbing to the top of Roman antiquities, he was still cleaning the gutters of his house from atop a forty-foot ladder well into his eighties.

One of my extracurricular involvements at Fairfield University was to serve as moderator, first of the Women’s Chorale and, later, of the University Glee Club composed of mixed male and female voices. Because of my association with Saint Catherine of Siena, every year Fr. O’Connor hosted the Glee Club for a pre-Christmas concert in the parish church during the first week of December. Very quickly this annual concert became a cherished holiday tradition, one that both the students and the parishioners eagerly awaited.

There would always be a scheduled rehearsal on the afternoon of the concert in the church, followed by a supper in the church hall prior to the evening’s presentation. Of course, each year for more than a decade, Tess happily took on the assignment to be the principal organizer and cook for this annual Glee Club dinner at St. Catherine’s. As undergraduates are wont to do, they devoured a delicious home-cooked meal, a welcome reprieve from the normal fare they consumed in the university’s cafeteria.

Many of the undergraduate singers got to know Tess during their four years in the Glee Club. In late October or early November, as they were learning the Christmas musical repertory, they would frequently ask me: “What is Tess going to prepare for us this year?” Not one to shirk away from a challenge, Tess knew of the kids’ expectations and she would outdo herself year after year. Escoffier could not have planned and presented more delicious meals than the ones she devised, and she loved the fact that all the Glee Club members called her "Tess." She was like a mother or kindly grandmother to them. I used to love to watch them hugging and kissing her before and after these annual dinners. I also relished watching her face radiating with delight during the concerts as her kids—all well fed—sang their hearts out, perfectly setting the tone for the approaching Christmas holidays for a most grateful congregation. And she loved the inevitable shout-out she would get from the music director, Carole Ann Coyne-Maxwell, when the musical director publicly expressed gratitude to the pastor and congregation for the hospitality and welcome the choir always received. When Tess's name was mentioned, the kids went wild with their own applause. Tess beamed with pride.

One of the many casserole dishes that Tess perfected was a classic recipe that many people think is Italian because of its name: *chicken Tetrazzini*. However, food historians trace the origin of this recipe back to the early years of the twentieth century. This American dish was created in honor of Luisa Tetrazzini (1871–1940), a Tuscan-born coloratura soprano who enjoyed a long career as an international opera diva, singing in both San Francisco and in New York. There is an unresolved debate whether this recipe was created by Ernest Arbogast—then chef at the Palace Hotel in San Francisco where Tetrazzini was a long-time resident—or by Louis Paquet, a renowned chef at the Knickerbocker Hotel in New York City. Whatever its origin, this dish became one of Tess Zadrosny's signature dishes.

CHICKEN TETRAZZINI

Baked chicken and pasta casserole

Makes 6 to 8 servings

Ingredients

- 9 tablespoons butter
- 2 tablespoons olive oil
- 4 boneless skinless chicken breasts
- 2 teaspoons salt

- 1 teaspoon freshly ground black pepper
- 1 pound sliced cremini mushrooms
- 1 finely chopped onion
- 3 chopped shallots
- 5 cloves minced garlic
- 1 tablespoon fresh thyme
- 1 cup dry white wine
- ½ cup all-purpose flour
- 4 cups whole milk
- 1 cup heavy cream
- 1 cup chicken broth
- ⅛ teaspoon ground nutmeg
- 1 pound dry fettuccini or linguine
- 1 cup frozen peas
- ½ cup chopped fresh Italian parsley leaves
- 1 cup grated Parmigiano Reggiano
- ½ cup fresh breadcrumbs, combined with ¼ cup ground almonds

Method

1. Preheat oven to 450°F.
2. Butter a 13x9x2-inch baking dish.
3. Cut the chicken breasts into small cubes. Season with salt and pepper.
4. Sauté the chicken pieces in small batches in some melted butter and olive oil until lightly browned. Drain on a paper towel and reserve.
5. In the same pan, sauté the mushrooms for about 8 minutes until golden in color. Add the wine to the browned mushrooms and simmer over medium-high heat until most of the liquid evaporates. Remove from heat and combine the cooked mushrooms in a bowl with the sautéed chicken.

continued

6. Sauté the onions, shallots, garlic, and thyme until the vegetables are translucent. Add the cooked onion mixture to the bowl with the mushrooms and chicken.
7. Add 4 tablespoons of butter to a saucepan over medium-low heat. Add the flour and whisk until the flour and butter combine to form a pale golden roux.
8. Whisk in the milk, cream, broth, nutmeg, salt, and pepper. Continue to whisk the mixture until the sauce thickens. Increase the heat to high. Cover and bring to a boil. Simmer, uncovered, until the sauce thickens slightly, whisking often, about 7 to 10 minutes.
9. Bring a large pot of salted water to a boil. Add the pasta and cook until it is about 2 minutes shy of the al dente stage; remove from heat and drain.
10. Blend the pasta with the cream sauce and add the peas and parsley along with the chicken, mushroom, and onion mixture.
11. Transfer the combined mixture to the buttered baking dish. Stir the cheese, ground almonds, and breadcrumbs in a bowl to combine. Sprinkle the mixture over the pasta. Dot with small pieces of butter and bake uncovered, until golden brown on top and the sauce bubbles, about 25 minutes.

When Father O'Connor, the patron of the annual event, died in 1986, the parish decided to memorialize this concert as the "Fr. Vincent J. O'Connor Holiday Concert." I am consoled to acknowledge that even now—decades later—the tradition continues at Saint Catherine's, even though Tess is no longer alive to fire up hearths and hearts with her loving care.

Besides her great accomplishments in the kitchen, Tess was a multitalented craftswoman. She seemed to be able to do almost anything that involved sewing or gluing. She used to collect discarded gaudy costume jewelry by the pound. With these junk fragments, she would make magnificent Christmas trees mounted on wooden panels that had been covered with stretched velvet and then beautifully frame these works of art in shadow boxes. It would take a book to catalogue all of the many items she crafted over the course of her lifetime.

Many of these items found their way to church bazaar sales or as gifts for newborn babies or homebound elderly persons. In her later years she volunteered her time as a craft teacher, working with people residing in assisted living or skilled nursing care facilities within the parish. Even though she was well into her eighties, she talked about her work with the "older folks."

"Tess," I once said, "you are one of those older folks."

"I still have all my marbles," she joked, "and I still drive." Age remained only a number for Tess Zadrosny.

On the last Christmas she was alive, she sent me in the mail a decorative pendant with four linked needlepointed squares, spelling out the word *Noël.* It was perfectly crafted. "I hope you like the *Noël* I made for you," were the words pinned to the gift. "As you can see, I am still at it." Fortunately, she remained at it right up to the end of her life. I love that her last artistic creation for me is a rendering of this Middle English word that means "a shout of joy."

On her ninetieth birthday, her family hosted a celebratory luncheon in her honor and asked several of her priest friends to come as guests. I was invited to say a few words in tribute. "Only say nice things about me," she counseled in advance.

There were only nice things that one could possibly say about Theresa Bologna Zadrosny. When she died there was a perceptible rent in the fabric of the parish community that nurtured her, and for which she cared so faithfully and tirelessly for her entire life.

. . . .

It was just after the conclusion of the Good Friday solemn service when Jim Sheridan, then a bright sophomore student at Brown University, approached me in the sacristy of Saint Catherine's. "Father, a good friend of our family is Terry Goodwin, a very successful Wall Street broker. I think he is interested in becoming a Catholic and you would be the ideal person to speak with him. May I give him your name and number to call?"

Without too much hesitation I agreed. During the ensuing year, every two weeks or so, Terry would drive up to Fairfield University after a long and demanding day on the trading floor at Wall Street and spend an hour or more discussing one or more aspects of Catholic beliefs and doctrines. During those months he virtually read through my entire personal theological library. I can imagine those Metro North commuter train rides from Greenwich to Grand Central with Terry buried in some work by Hans Urs von Balthasar, Dietrich Bonhoeffer, Hans Küng, Helmut Richard Niebuhr, Karl Rahner, Paul Johannes Tillich, or Josef Ratzinger. He must have gotten some very perplexed looks from others whose faces were buried in the *Wall Street Journal* or the *New York Times*.

It was my great privilege during the Easter Vigil almost a year after we had begun our preparations to receive Terry Goodwin into full communion within the Roman Catholic Church. As a symbol of his appreciation for the investment of time and effort in his pastoral preparation for this event, Terry presented me that evening with an engraved set of oval-shaped gold cuff links inlaid with lapis lazuli.

He was unaware as to its coincidental Jesuit connection; this particular stone is extensively used in the ornate and monumental altar in the left transept of the Chiesa del Gesù in Rome, in which the earthly remains of Saint Ignatius Loyola are inurned. Jesuit brother Andrea Pozzo, S.J., accepted the commission to design this altar in 1695. Materials include bronze, gold, silver, and many semiprecious stones, but most notably lapis lazuli. I have treasured Terry's gift and have worn those cuff links on virtually every special occasion since that time.

After several months of these intense study sessions, Terry mentioned that his wife, Candice, a Roman Catholic by birth, was getting a bit jealous of this exclusive relationship that we had formed and wanted to meet me in person. I was invited for dinner at their home, which was the beginning of a lifelong friendship with both Candice and Terry and their children and extended families.

Candice was a remarkable person. Born into an ethnic Italian American family in New Haven, Connecticut, she and Terry met as undergraduate students in a math class at Quinnipiac University, of which Terry later generously served as chairman of its board of trustees. Candice was bright, intuitive, passionate, and very direct. Among her many talents, three were especially notable: her extraordinary ability to do intricate needlepointing, her keen artistry as a photographer, and her zest and skill as a cook and baker. We found so many points of common interest.

I often compared her to Madame Thérèse Defarge, the character in *A Tale of Two Cities* by Charles Dickens who never stopped knitting. There were not too many other apt comparisons between these two women, although both Madame Defarge and Candice Goodwin were each a piece of work. As Dickens recounts, Defarge had a pretty tough childhood: her sister was raped by the Marquis St. Evrémonde; her father died of grief. Her brother was killed trying to avenge his sister's honor. Candice occasionally was dramatic, but nothing like Mme. Defarge. Their strongest common suite was with needle and thread and yarn.

Over the course of a quarter-century, Candice's output in museum-quality needlepoint art was prodigious. During those years she made enough Christmas ornaments to decorate an entire eight-foot tree. Each year she crafted special ornaments for each of her family members and close friends. She also needlepointed large Christmas stockings, pillows, and samplers, and a wide collection of standing Santa Claus masterpieces. Each of these needlepointed creations was beautifully finished in luscious velvets and silk brocaded fabrics and cording. Often when I would call her on the telephone during the evening, I would invariably find her nestled in the oversized chair she affectionately referred to as her "Queen Latifah chair," busy at work fashioning some future gift.

She also had a keen eye for photography. After a family trip to Italy, she made a judicious selection of some of her prize photos and made enlargements. She selected a variety of frames in which to display these works of art and I helped her to design a wall in her newly refurbished country kitchen to exhibit these extraordinary prints.

Each September she also loved to attend the US Open in Flushing Meadow Park, not just to see some of the best athletes in the world compete in this annual end-of-summer tennis tournament, but also to use her telephoto lens to capture some of the most exceptional action shots of the players. Reviewing a set of her work, I commented: "Candice, you seem to have a large number of shots of men's butts in this collection."

"Oh," she said, "you noticed. Professional tennis players have some of the best butts, only possibly outdone by Italian soccer players." This proves the old aphorism that "beauty exists in the eye of the beholder." She never lost her lifelong attraction to the male gluteus maximus.

One could always count on Candice for pure and direct communication. When I would be preparing for some foreign travel trip, I could routinely count on receiving two admonitions from her: "Don't sit on strange toilet seats," and "Remember who you are and don't let me read about you on Page Six."

Terry commented that I was one of the very few people Candice would actually allow to stand on her side of the preparation counter in the kitchen. She also would regularly take counsel or confer with me about a recipe or technique.

I once brought a rather simple homemade blueberry and apricot coffee cake to their home as a gift. Not only did she love the cake, but she insisted on adding the recipe to her growing collection.

BLUEBERRY AND APRICOT COFFEE CAKE

Makes 10 to 12 servings

Ingredients

For the streusel

- 1 cup packed brown sugar
- ⅔ cup all-purpose flour
- 1 teaspoon ground cinnamon
- ½ cup unsalted butter

For the coffee cake

- 2 cups all-purpose flour
- 2 teaspoons baking powder
- ½ teaspoon kosher salt
- ½ cup butter
- 1 cup white sugar
- 1 egg
- 1 teaspoon almond extract
- ½ cup milk
- 1 cup fresh blueberries
- 1 cup dried apricots, roughly chopped
- ¼ cup confectioners' sugar for dusting

Method

1. Heat oven to 350°F.
2. Prepare a Bundt pan with vegetable spray and dust with flour.

Making the streusel

1. Combine 1 cup of brown sugar with ⅔ cup of flour and some cinnamon in a medium bowl. Work ½ cup of cold butter into the sugar and flour with your fingers until the streusel mixture becomes crumbly. Set aside.

Making the coffee cake

1. Beat ½ cup of room-temperature butter in large bowl until creamy.
2. Add 1 cup of granulated sugar and beat until light and creamy.
3. Beat in 1 egg and the almond extract.
4. Gradually mix in 2 cups of flour, baking powder, and salt, alternating with the milk, beating well after each addition.
5. Spread half the batter into the prepared pan.
6. Cover with blueberries and apricots and add remaining batter.
7. Sprinkle the *streusel* topping over the surface of the batter.
8. Bake in the preheated oven for 55 to 60 minutes, until deep golden brown.
9. Remove pan to wire rack to cool.
10. Invert onto a plate after cake has cooled, and dust with confectioners' sugar.

Over the course of some thirty years I collaborated with Candice in the planning and execution of many holiday and special occasion dinners. I also watched Candice and Terry's two children, Heather and TW, grow into adulthood, marry, and assume themselves the roles of parents to their own children.

I spent many major holidays with the extended families. I recall on one Easter Sunday morning when I was celebrating the Eucharist with the Goodwin family in their living room, when unexpectedly Dr. Joseph Amato—a former priest and later a practicing psychologist—stopped by for an unannounced visit. Since we were just completing the liturgy of the Word, we paused and extended hospitality to this welcome guest and later resumed the Eucharistic celebration after he departed. Later that afternoon, young ten-year-old TW Goodwin said: "Father Smith, I loved the Mass we had at our house this morning."

Surprised by his spontaneous comment, I pursued the discussion a bit further. "TW," I asked, "what in particular did you like about the Mass?"

Not requiring even a moment to reflect, he replied: "I loved that we had an intermission in the Mass so that I could go out to the kitchen and snack on Mom's pizza rustica."

Candice enthusiastically embraced her Italian roots. Every spring, a week or so before Easter, she and Terry made a pilgrimage to Arthur Avenue in the Bronx, where there is a little ghetto of Italian specialty shops from which she could purchase all of the ingredients needed for the traditional Easter pie she called *pizza rustica,* although I have heard others refer to it as *pizzagaina* or in some dialects, *pizzagain.* Neapolitans sometimes use the dialect term *pizza chiena* (*pizza repiena*)—filled or stuffed pie—to refer to this holiday treat.

This pie takes some time to prepare and is not inexpensive, because it requires many high-quality ingredients: cubes of boiled ham, prosciutto, proscuittini (cured pepper ham), and capocollo, a salami made from the dry-cured muscle running from the head (*capo*) to the neck (*collo*) of the pig. The recipe also requires two additional cured sausage-like cold cuts: mortadella and sopressata. The pie also incorporates a variety of cheeses: a seasonal fresh basket cheese, ricotta, aged provolone, and a blend of Parmigiano Reggiano and Pecorino Romano.

Basket cheese (*forme di formaggio*) seems like a cousin to ricotta and mozzarella. This fresh milk Italian cheese is fashioned from the separation of the curds and whey; the curds get pressed together to form a compact ball and extract as much whey as possible. It is called "basket cheese" because it is often stored and quickly marketed in a small white plastic basket-like container. Many Italian specialty shops have this product readily available around Easter time because it is traditionally used in this recipe, but it is becoming a more popular year-round item.

Candice always made the pie on Good Friday morning, but no one in the family could touch it until Easter morning. Although the pie can be warmed, Candice always served it at room temperature.

PIZZA RUSTICA

Italian Easter meat and cheese pie

Makes 12 to 15 servings

Ingredients

For the yeast dough crust

- 5 cups flour
- ½ cup scalded whole milk
- ½ cup lukewarm water
- 3 tablespoons granulated sugar
- 2½ teaspoons dry active yeast
- 1½ teaspoons salt
- 5 tablespoons melted butter
- 3 tablespoons room-temperature butter
- 3 tablespoons room-temperature lard
- 3 tablespoons buttermilk or sour cream
- ½ teaspoon fresh lemon juice
- 1½ tablespoons extra-virgin olive oil
- 5 eggs

For the filling

- 1 pound fresh basket cheese
- 8 ounces fresh mozzarella, diced
- 1 pound fresh ricotta
- 1 cup cubed aged provolone cheese
- 1 cup freshly grated Parmigiano Reggiano
- ½ cup grated Pecorino Romano
- 4 ounces diced mortadella

continued

- 4 ounces diced prosciutto
- 4 ounces diced prosciutto
- 4 ounces diced capocollo
- 4 ounces diced sopressata
- 4 ounces of diced boiled ham
- freshly ground black pepper
- 5 large eggs, lightly beaten
- ¼ cup half-and-half or whole milk

Method

Preparing the dough (about 3 hours before you are ready to assemble and bake the pizza rustica)

1. In a small bowl, dissolve the yeast along with 1 tablespoon of granulated sugar in ½ cup of lukewarm water (about 105°F or warm to the touch). Stir in a bit of the flour (about ¼ cup) to feed the yeast. The yeast mixture will begin to come alive and bubble. Set aside for 10 to 15 minutes as it proofs.
2. In a small saucepan, scald ½ cup of whole milk until it begins to slightly foam and remove from heat and allow to cool (to about 85°F) before adding it to the yeast mixture. If it is too hot, it will kill the yeast.
3. In the bowl of a stand mixer, combine salt, 2 tablespoons sugar, and the remaining 4¾ cups of the flour.
4. Using the dough hook attachment on a stand mixer, add 3 tablespoons of butter and 3 tablespoons of lard and process until the fat is incorporated into the flour.
5. Add 5 eggs into the dough mixture. Knead on medium speed for 2 minutes. Add the melted butter and 3 tablespoons of buttermilk or sour cream.

6. Add the proofed yeast mixture into the flour mixture and continue to knead.
7. Add ½ teaspoon freshly squeezed lemon juice (this will aid elasticity and make the dough a bit easier to roll out and to stretch later on).
8. Continue kneading at medium speed for another 8 to 10 minutes. If dough appears too stiff and the dough hook is straining, add a few additional tablespoons of warm water.
9. Scrape the dough from the mixing bowl onto a work surface dusted with the remaining flour and using your hands—which you have lubricated with some olive oil—knead the dough for another 5 minutes. Dough will be light and airy, but somewhat sticky (hence, your oiled hands). As you knead, you may hear little "pops" as air bubbles break and new air pockets are formed.
10. Place the dough into a bowl smeared with olive oil, turn once to coat with oil, and cover with a damp cloth. Put the bowl in a warm, draft-free place to rise until the dough has doubled in bulk.
11. When the dough has doubled, punch it down and allow to rest for 10 minutes. Divide in half and roll and stretch out into two large oblong pieces.
12. Butter a large roasting pan (approximately 12x17) and line the pan bottom and sides with the rolled-out dough, with about a 2-inch overhang.

Making the filling

1. In a very large mixing bowl, begin by breaking up the basket cheese with your fingers. Add the mozzarella, ricotta, provolone, Parmigiano, and Pecorino cheeses. Combine all of the cheese with a wooden spoon or, as Julia Child would often say, with "an impeccably clean hand."
2. Prepare all of the meats by cutting the cold cuts into a small dice and gently combine with the cheese.

continued

3. Pour the milk and beaten eggs over the mixture and stir until thoroughly combined. When fully blended, spread the entire mixture on top of the dough and distribute evenly over the entire bottom surface of the roasting pan.
4. Roll out the remaining pizza dough to cover the entire surface of the roasting pan and seal all of the edges by folding over and crimping. Cut several decorative slits into the top of the pizza rustica and brush the entire surface with an egg wash (egg yolk and a bit of water).

Baking the pizza rustica

1. Preheat the oven to 400°F.
2. Bake initially for about 15 minutes at 400°F, and then lower the temperature to 325°F and continue baking for 45 to 50 minutes longer or until the top crust is deeply golden.
3. Transfer the pan to a wire rack to cool for 20 to 30 minutes.
4. Carefully invert the pizza rustica onto a platter or cutting board, and then reinvert it back onto the rack and allow it to continue cooling to room temperature. Cover with plastic wrap and refrigerate.
5. The pizza rustica can be served rewarmed in a microwave or at room temperature.

For a pre-Christmas supper at their home, Candice had purchased some peppermint stick ice cream to serve for dessert. I asked her if she would like me to make a quick and easy but delicious hot fudge sauce to accompany this seasonal ice cream treat. The hot fudge sauce required only a few ingredients that I knew she would have in her pantry and refrigerator. "Be my guest," she readily replied.

She loved the results and asked for the recipe. I scribbled the ingredients and method on a block of Post-its that I had in my brief case that were preprinted with the phrase: "From the Desk of God." I titled the recipe "Heavenly Hot Fudge Sauce."

She kept that original Post-it among her most treasured recipes and for the following decades she made jars of this hot fudge sauce as gifts for friends and relatives, always labeling these presents with the title I had suggested in jest when I first wrote out the recipe for her.

HEAVENLY HOT FUDGE SAUCE

Makes 6 servings

Ingredients

- ½ cup heavy cream
- 3 tablespoons cold unsalted butter, cut into small pieces
- ⅓ cup dark brown sugar
- ⅓ cup confectioners' sugar
- ½ cup strained Dutch-process cocoa powder
- a pinch of salt

Method

1. In a one-quart saucepan, over moderate heat, warm the cream and butter until melted and blended.
2. Add both sugars and stir until dissolved. Reduce the heat.
3. Add cocoa powder and a pinch of salt.
4. Stir briskly with wire whisk until smooth.
5. Store in covered jar or plastic container in refrigerator.
6. Reheat before use.

Candice volunteered regularly in the Neighbor to Neighbor program, a nonprofit organization established in 1975 that serves residents in need throughout the greater Greenwich area. Neighbor to Neighbor provides for the exchange of food, clothing, and basic living essentials in an atmosphere of kindness and respect. She carried on this quiet charitable work for many years, becoming a trusted confidante to the people who came in search of material support for their lives at Neighbor to Neighbor's discreet location in the Christ Church annex in Greenwich. In Candice Goodwin they always found a truly caring individual who was both ready and able to nurture their souls and spirits as well as to respond to their material requirements.

During one memorable Holy Week, I received a phone call from her in which she shared the news that she had just been diagnosed with breast cancer. A private person, Candice did not want others to know about her affliction. For the next couple of years, as she underwent surgery and chemotherapy, a very small handful of people discreetly formed her support team. I introduced Candice to one of my dear friends in New York City who was one of the city's premier breast oncologists, Dr. Anne Moore. Anne and Candice formed not only an excellent doctor-patient relationship, but Anne became (as she does with so many of her patients) a loving and trusted friend.

Initially, the cancer was successfully treated, and Candice faithfully saw Anne every six months thereafter, even though an annual check-up would have sufficed. Then, the unexpected happened: the cancer recurred, this time expressing itself in the bone. Ultimately it would spread to her brain and eventually it claimed her life in January 2011.

Looking now at her five beautiful grandchildren as they grow and develop, I cannot but think of how deprived they are not to have known their grandmother throughout their formative years. Although she has left behind a legacy of memories, needlepoint art, and photography, they will only know of her love, warmth, humor, and passion for life through stories like these, which inadequately celebrate the extraordinary woman she was.

Chapter 5

MINISTRY ON TWO CONTINENTS

So, whether you eat or drink or whatever you do, do it all for the glory of God.

—1 CORINTHIANS 10:31

Serendipity has been a recurring theme in my life. During the full year (1975–1976) that I spent completing my tertianship in Rome, I had numerous opportunities to meet and interact with the Jesuit superior general, the Very Reverend Pedro Arrupe, S.J. Earlier, I recounted how Fr. Arrupe had been the binding arbitrator between my provincial superior and the rector of the Gregorian University in the decision that led to my subsequent missioning at Fairfield University. I also talked about Fr. Arrupe's role in receiving my final vows as a Jesuit in Rome in 1976. Now I would like to talk a bit about the man who served as the twenty-eighth superior general of the Society of Jesus, and who was in great part indirectly responsible for my more than seventy trips to Rome over the course of twelve years of service as a consultant to the Holy See and to several religious orders and congregations.

I first met Father Arrupe personally during my second year of theological studies in Cambridge in 1971. He was visiting the New England Province and spent one evening during his visitation sharing dinner and conversation with our small Kirkland Street community, along with his American assistant, Fr. Harold Small, S.J. On that occasion, we presented Fr. Arrupe with the gift of a necktie. By that time, younger Jesuits had abandoned wearing cassocks and clerical attire and were dressing more casually. We often wore jackets and ties even to more dressy events. When Fr. General opened our modest gift, he smiled broadly and proceeded to drape the tie around his neck and fashion a perfect knot. We were quite amazed by his obvious familiarity and proficiency in tying a full Windsor. He chuckled aside to Fr. Small, musing: "What do you think the reaction of the fathers and brothers would be if I came to breakfast some morning at the Curia wearing this tie?"

Pedro Arrupe was born in 1907 in the Basque region of Spain. His early vocational aspiration was to become a physician. Before completing his medical education, he entered the Society of Jesus as a twenty-year-old. A mere five years after his entry into the Society in 1927, the Spanish government expelled the Jesuits, forcing the young Arrupe and his companions to complete their Jesuit course of studies abroad. But his most significant assignment came right after his ordination to the priesthood in 1938 when he was assigned to the Japanese mission.

The hardships and deprivations that he endured in Japan during the lead-up to the Second World War, including arrest and imprisonment, prepared him for his later responsibilities. From 1965 to 1983, he would be asked to lead the Society of Jesus as its superior general through the tumultuous years that followed the Second Vatican Council as the Church and the Society struggled to modernize their ways of proceeding.

God would call upon the rudimentary medical training the young Arrupe had received in Spain prior to his entry into the Jesuits on August 6, 1945, when a single American B-29 bomber flew over Hiroshima and dropped an atomic bomb.

Fr. Arrupe lived nearby and was serving as the master of novices. With some reticence, I asked him about that day during a dinner conversation I shared with him during our time together at Villa Cavalletti. He said that although the Jesuit novitiate was some distance from the epicenter of the bombing site, the building in which he and the novices were living shook when the bomb detonated, and its concussive force shattered the windows of the residence. He said that from his vantage point, the city of Hiroshima looked like one large blazing cauldron.

He told me that at that time no one knew anything about the dangers of being exposed to radioactive materials, so he blithely ventured closer to the edge of the inferno and offered assistance to people who had sustained serious burns, and he tried to comfort the hundreds of people who were dazed by the enormity of the devastation.

Modestly, as he recalled this story—then some thirty-one years after the virtual annihilation of Hiroshima—he still marveled that with such scant material resources, he and the Jesuits were able to care for so many innocent victims of the bombing.

Of the many superiors general under whom I have lived as a Jesuit, none has had a greater formative influence on me than Pedro Arrupe. He embodied for me the heart and mind of Ignatius. As general, he traveled constantly throughout the world, learning firsthand of the dreams and challenges of his brother Jesuits. I thought of him not as the superior general, but as the "Animator-in-Chief" of the Society of Jesus. In my judgment he was a cosmic optimist, always seeing more than one way to reach a desired goal. He simply had a can-do attitude that he enthusiastically conveyed to others, and his positive attitude was genuinely infectious.

Jorge Mario Bergoglio, S.J.—now Pope Francis—shares some of Arrupe's best traits. Pope Francis entered the Society of Jesus in Argentina as a novice on March 11, 1958, pronouncing his first vows as a Jesuit on March 12, 1960. He was teaching literature and psychology at the Jesuit High School in Santa Fe, the Colegio de la Inmaculada Concepción, when Father Arrupe was elected superior general. A year later, Bergoglio was assigned to teach at the Colegio del Salvador in Buenos Aires. Fr. Bergoglio was ordained to the priesthood on December 13, 1969. Soon thereafter, following in footsteps similar to those of Pedro Arrupe, Fr. Bergoglio served as the master of novices for the Argentinian province. In another appointment paralleling that of Pedro Arrupe, Jorge Bergoglio was named provincial superior of the Jesuits in Argentina from 1973 until 1979. I have a strong suspicion that, like me, Father Arrupe had a very strong positive influence on the young Jorge Bergoglio, shaping his understanding of social justice and supporting his lifelong dedication to the poor and marginalized.

Father Arrupe's primary concern was that the Jesuits commit themselves to advocacy and engagement to ensure that the needs of the poor be addressed. It was to Arrupe that the phrase "the service of faith and the promotion of justice" became a mantra of the mission of the Society of Jesus from 1975 forward to the present day. And this mandate was quickly embraced by the Society of Jesus in Latin America, and Jorge Bergoglio's work found a strong endorsement from Pedro Arrupe.

I visited with Fr. Arrupe in Rome on two brief occasions after his catastrophic stroke in 1981. Although he was unable to speak during the ten years that he lived in almost prayerful silence before his death on February 5, 1991, his eyes always communicated his infectious love of God and of his brother Jesuits. I certainly felt that love and encouragement. And every time that I return to Rome, for whatever reason, I always visit and pray at the final resting place of this modern-day saint in the Chiesa del Gesù.

The evening in 1971 when he visited our small community in Cambridge, we served Fr. Arrupe this French-inspired dessert, called a Paris-Brest. Culinary historians seem to agree that this confection—composed of a ring of pâte à choux, flavored with fleur de sel, topped with toasted sliced almonds, and filled with mounds of a rich crème praliné—was created in 1910 by pâtissier Louis Durand to celebrate the famous Paris-Brest-Paris bicycle race. The Durand family still operates its boulangerie-patisserie at 9 Avenue Longueil, 78600 Maisons-Laffitte, France, and they still offer Paris-Brest.

In his book *The Art of French Pastry*, Jacquy Pfeiffer, dean of Chicago's French Pastry School, notes that the crown shape may also "represent the head wreath that Greek athletes wore after a victory."[4] So, bike wheel or victor's crown, the dessert is still a crowd pleaser.

Whatever the origin of the confection, here is my adaptation of the dessert we prepared for Fr. Arrupe a half-century ago.

PARIS-BREST

A ring of choux pastry filled with praline-flavored cream

Makes 10 to 12 servings

Ingredients

For the choux pastry

- ¼ pound (1 stick) unsalted butter
- 2 tablespoons granulated sugar
- a pinch of kosher salt
- 1 cup all-purpose flour
- 1½ cups water

4 Jacquy Pfeiffer and Martha Rose Shulman, *The Art of French Pastry* (New York: Knopf, 2013).

- 5 to 6 eggs
- beaten egg, for glaze
- fleur de sel
- ½ cup slivered almonds, for decoration

For the pastry cream

- 4 tablespoons all-purpose flour
- ¾ cup granulated sugar
- 4 tablespoons unsalted butter
- 4 eggs
- a pinch of salt
- 2 cups boiled milk

For the praline-flavored cream

- 1 cup whole milk
- 6 eggs
- 1 cup granulated sugar
- 1 pound (4 sticks) unsalted butter
- 4 ounces of hazelnut-praline paste

For the Italian meringue

- ½ cup granulated sugar
- 5 teaspoons water
- 2 egg whites
- sifted confectioners' sugar

Method

1. Toast the slivered almonds in an oven preheated at 400°F until they turn golden.

continued

Making the pâte à choux

1. Boil water with butter, sugar, and salt.
2. Remove it from the heat and immediately add the flour and combine, then return to the heat and continue beating the mass.
3. Once the dough has formed and it has separated from the edges of the pan, transfer it to the bowl of a stand mixer with a paddle attachment.
4. Cool the dough on low speed before beginning to add the eggs, one by one, beating well to incorporate after each addition. The finished paste will be firm and glossy.

Shaping and baking the pastry wheels

1. Take a piece of parchment paper and trace two adjacent circles, 9 inches wide, then turn the parchment ink side down and place it on a baking sheet.
2. Fit a piping bag with a plain tip, approximately a half-inch wide in diameter, and then fill it with the prepared *choux* paste. Pipe the paste onto the drawn circles, then glaze them with a beaten egg and sprinkle each piped ring with toasted slivered almonds and a bit of the *fleur de sel.*
3. Bake on the middle rack of an oven preheated to 350°F for 35 to 40 minutes. When baked, turn the oven off, open the door, and wait for the rings to cool. Take out of the oven and place them on a wire rack to cool completely.

Making the pastry cream, hazelnut-praline crème au beurre, and French meringue fillings

1. While the choux rings are baking, prepare the pastry cream. In a separate bowl whisk eggs with flour, sugar, and salt. Bring milk to a boil then add it in thirds to the egg mixture, whisking after each addition to incorporate. Put the mixture in a saucepan and place it over medium heat, whisking it continuously until it boils. Boil for two minutes,

then remove from the heat and gently whisk in the butter. Pour the pastry cream into a bowl and cover with plastic wrap and refrigerate.

2. For the hazelnut-praline *crème au beurre*, boil the milk and whisk eggs with sugar. Temper the eggs with the addition of some of the boiled milk, then pour the tempered egg mixture into the milk, while constantly stirring. Proceed to stir until the mixture begins to boil then remove it from heat. Then whisk in the butter and the praline paste and allow to cool.
3. In a saucepan heat the sugar and water until they start to boil and the syrup reaches 250°F. With a hand mixer, beat the egg whites. When the egg whites begin to thicken and form soft peaks, pour the syrup into the egg whites, increase to full speed, and continue beating the meringue until it has cooled to room temperature.
4. Combine the three cooled creams into one by folding them together. Fill a pastry bag with the blended cream filling, which has been fitted with a large, fluted tip. Slice the *choux* rings horizontally in half with a serrated knife and pipe the lower halves with the cream, in a series of 2-inch-high mounds. Once piped, cover with top halves of choux rings and dust with confectioners' sugar.

I described earlier how Fr. Arrupe had personally enlisted my services to be of help to major superiors of male religious institutes, some of whom I was privileged to offer psychological consultation services. One such introduction was to a young and charismatic religious leader, Brother Gerard Gabriel McHugh of the Congregation of Christian Brothers, a worldwide religious community founded in 1802 in Waterford, Ireland, by Blessed Edmund Rice to educate youth, especially the poor. The Congregation received official approval from Rome in 1820.

Brother McHugh was a Canadian Christian Brother, born and raised in Saint John's, Newfoundland. He was elected superior general for two successive terms, having previously served as the provincial superior of the Canadian province of the Congregation.

In the 1970s, the Roman headquarters of the Irish Christian Brothers was housed in a modest but beautifully designed contemporary building on the outskirts of the City. The house was constructed on a lovely parcel of land whose entry drive was richly planted with stately cypress and pine trees and very fragrant nerium oleander shrubs.

Because the brothers are an international lay religious congregation, their leadership is drawn from diverse cultures including North and South America, Australia, New Zealand, India, Europe, South Africa, and Oceania. As part of the post–Second Vatican Council's mandate, which invited religious institutes to provide renewal opportunities for their members, the Christian Brothers in the 1970s created a half-year residential experience for their brothers that would not only update them theologically, but even more importantly, enrich them personally, emotionally, and spiritually.

It was to this residential renewal program that Brother McHugh invited me to invest my time and talents. What started initially as a single consultation in 1975 grew into a twelve-year relationship with the Brothers, which would bring me regularly back to their Roman villa and into many of their local provincial communities around the world.

There are three brothers in particular whom I would like to remember. These brothers formed a core team for the international renewal program. The first is Brother Gilbert Shea, fondly known as Fratello Gilberto, or simply, Gil.

Like Brother McHugh, Gil was also a Newfoundlander, but he spent the majority of his life as a brother living and working in Rome. He was completely fluent in Italian, gesturing liberally with his hands in every conversation and displaying all of the other acquired mannerisms that one might associate with a Latin temperament. He also loved to drive. He served for some years as an administrative associate in the papal household at the Vatican, and personally knew many of the curial cardinals and bishops and was beloved by many young recruits among the Swiss Guard. Because he was so adroit in moving around politically in the matchless world of Vatican City, the Swiss Guard were perplexed why he did not advance and become a bishop. They seemed not to note that he was a professed brother and not a priest. I am surprised that he did not snatch one of the Swiss Guard's halberds as a souvenir during his countless trips in and out of the Vatican.

This Newfoundlander loved to eat and quickly adjusted his palate to the Italian diet. Growing up on regular servings of cod and potatoes, I am certain that Brother Shea would have enjoyed my variation of these oven-baked cod fish cakes, albeit with an Italian twist.

TORTINI DI PESCE ITALIANE

Italian fish cakes with parsley caper sauce

Makes 8 servings

Ingredients

- 1 pound Yukon gold potatoes, peeled and diced
- 1 cup onion, minced
- 3 large garlic cloves, minced
- ½ cup celery, chopped fine
- 8 tablespoons unsalted butter
- 1½ pounds cod, boned and flaked
- 4 tablespoons all-purpose flour
- 8 tablespoons Parmigiano-Reggiano cheese, grated
- 1 teaspoon fresh thyme leaves
- 1 teaspoon fresh rosemary, finely chopped
- 1 teaspoon dried oregano
- ¼ teaspoon mustard powder
- ½ teaspoon Kosher salt
- Ground black pepper to taste
- ½ cup whole milk
- 1½ cups panko breadcrumbs

Method

For the fish cakes

1. Fill a saucepan with 4 cups of water and bring the water to a rolling boil. Add potatoes and cook for 12–15 minutes until the potatoes are soft but still firm. Drain and mash with 4 tablespoons of butter and 4 tablespoons of the grated cheese. Set aside to cool.

continued

2. Poach the skinless cod filet(s) in simmering salted water for about 8 minutes.
3. In a large saucepan, melt 4 tablespoons of butter and sauté the onion and celery over medium high heat until tender. Near the end of the sautéing, add the minced garlic and cook for an additional minute.
4. Turn heat to low and fold in flaked, poached fish. Slowly mix in flour, 4 tablespoons of grated cheese, dry mustard, thyme, salt, pepper, mashed potatoes. and milk. Gently combine all the ingredients carefully so as not to break up the fish.
5. Remove the pan from the heat and transfer the mixture to a glass bowl. Cover and refrigerate for one hour before forming the fish cakes for baking.
6. Preheat oven to 400°F.
7. Divide the mixture into roughly 8 equal portions.
8. Line a half sheet pan with aluminum foil and brush lightly with olive oil or cooking spray.
9. With floured hands, shape the portions into 8 fish cakes.
10. Combine the rosemary and oregano with the panko crumbs.
11. Coat each of the fish cakes completely with the seasoned breadcrumbs and place on the prepared baking sheets. Spray the top of the fish cakes with a vegetable or olive oil cooking spray.
12. Bake the fish cakes for 10 minutes and then gently flip and continue baking another 10–12 minutes until golden brown.
13. Serve with the caper-parsley sauce and some lemon wedges.

Caper-Parsley Sauce

Ingredients

- 1 cup extra virgin olive oil
- 1 egg yolk

- 6 tablespoons drained capers
- 6 tablespoons fresh Italian flat leaf parsley, chopped
- 6 anchovy fillets, chopped
- 1 teaspoon grated lemon zest
- ⅓ cup lemon juice, freshly squeezed
- 2 large garlic cloves, peeled and halved

Method

1. Blend all ingredients in a food processor until a coarse purée forms.
2. Season the finished sauce with freshly ground black pepper.

"Shea" is a difficult name for Swiss or native Italians to pronounce. Many of the Swiss Guard officers called him "Shay-ah." This caught on with his brothers, who affectionately referred to him as "Mr. Shay-ah." I once mused with Gil that should he ever be made a cardinal, his coat of arms would need to include a heraldic rendering of leather driving gloves and a car wheel, and that his motto might be: "*Girando Sempre,*" "Always Driving." Despite the menacing ways Italians drive through the ancient streets of Rome, Mr. Shay-ah never passed up an opportunity to ferry someone from one destination in the Eternal City to another. He loved being behind a wheel.

After he completed numerous positions at the generalate, including serving as house superior, Gil took on another responsibility later during his retirement years assisting Br. Sean Moffet, C.F.C., as a factotum at the Città dei Ragazzi (Boys' Town of Rome). He quickly became for Sean and the boys their Christian Brother "Zio" (uncle).

And nothing pleased Gil Shea more than an invitation to dine. One of the things that yoked him to Rome for almost his whole life was Italian food. He loved pasta in any form, and especially loved homemade *spaghetti alla carbonara*. Traditionally, this dish uses only five ingredients: guanciale (hog's jowl) or pancetta (pork belly), Pecorino Romano cheese, eggs, salt, and pepper.

I learned to prepare this dish from the Roman woman the Brothers employed as cook at their Roman headquarters.

SPAGHETTI ALLA CARBONARA

Pasta with egg, pancetta, Pecorino, and pepper

Makes 4 servings

Ingredients

- 3 eggs
- 1 cup grated Pecorino Romano
- 1 cup diced guanciale or pancetta
- salt and freshly ground black pepper
- 1 pound spaghetti (fresh or dried)

Method

1. Separate the egg yolks from the egg whites; beat the egg yolks lightly with a whisk, introducing a little bit of the egg whites into the mixture.
2. Freshly grate the Pecorino Romano cheese and add to the beaten egg mixture.
3. Grind a good amount of fresh black pepper into the egg and cheese mixture, along with a pinch of salt.
4. Place the egg and cheese mixture over a bain-marie (double boiler) with simmering water, not touching the bottom of the pot containing the eggs, and whisk briskly until the mixture thickens—almost to the consistency of a *zabaione* (light custard cream)—and remove from heat and cover.
5. Sauté the diced *guanciale* and remove to some paper towels to drain the grease. Reserve the residual cooking fat.
6. Cook the spaghetti to the al dente stage in a pot of salted boiling water. Reserve two cups of the pasta cooking liquid.
7. Drain the cooked pasta, add a cup of the egg-cheese cream, some of the reserved cooking fat from the *guanciale,* and mix. Continue to add the remainder of the egg cream sauce, the cooked *guanciale,* and

as much of the reserved pasta liquid as is needed to bring the finished dish to a creamy consistency.

8. Finish with a handful more of the grated Pecorino and serve immediately with some additional ground black pepper.

The Brothers who came to Rome to participate in the intensive international renewal program all shared one thing in common: they all worked very hard and derived much of their identity and satisfaction from success in their teaching and coaching work with young men in their schools. For many of them this was the first time in their religious lives that they had free time, and many of them developed psychophysiological symptoms during their Roman adventure. Most common among their complaints were sleeping and gastrointestinal disturbances, and visits into central Rome to consult with the English-speaking doctor were not infrequent.

One of the Brothers on the staff was Brother John E. Carroll, affectionately called by virtually everyone "John E." A native Irishman and skilled storyteller and actor, Br. Carroll could easily have been recruited from central casting for the numerous roles he played so well. He looked the part of an Irish raconteur, with a mane of wild, silver-white hair, rosy cheeks, sparkling blue eyes, and a bigger-than-life smile. Not only did he have the brogue of a Dubliner, but he was renowned for his ability to present a narrative tour of the thirty-two counties of Ireland (twenty-six in the Republic of Ireland and six in Northern Ireland), quickly changing accents as he spoke about the various sectors of the country. Truth to tell, he was a natural thespian at heart, a consummate minstrel, a bard of the first order. And to top it all off he was, during his lifetime, an irrepressible raconteur of the life and works of the Congregation's saintly founder, Blessed Edmund Ignatius Rice. Brother Carroll used to say that if the Christian Brothers were not able to canonize Edmund first in their own hearts, then the formal canonization of their founder would take a very long time. If the sanctity of Blessed Edmund Ignatius Rice was known and treasured by any single brother, John E. would certainly have been that Christian Brother.

But one of his lesser-known jobs was accompanying brothers participating in the renewal program to their medical consultations. At that time in Rome there was a British woman, an internist, who practiced at Rome's Salvator Mundi International

Hospital. Finding competent medical care in Rome from an English-speaking physician was no easy task. Salvator Mundi was the go-to place. Founded in 1947 by the Congregation of the Divine Redeemer, Salvator Mundi quickly became the preferred hospital of the popes and cardinals, and of many other VIPs, including Mother Teresa of Calcutta. It is conveniently located on the Gianicolo Hill, in very close proximity to the Vatican.

Because she was a native English speaker, Dr. Jeans was regularly consulted by many religious sisters, brothers, and priests from the predominantly English-speaking communities in Rome. Dr. Jeans looked like what one might imagine a nineteenth-century English schoolmarm to be: tall and gaunt, prim and proper, with hair neatly pulled back and carefully twisted into a tight bun and pinned in place at the top of her head; plain, not comely, with pince-nez eyeglasses precariously perched and squeezing the bridge of her nose.

One autumn afternoon, Brother Carroll accompanied four brothers on a regular weekly visit to Dr. Jean's consultation rooms. After she had seen the last of her patients, Brother Carroll engaged her in a genial, bantering conversation, as he was wont to do. In his exaggerated manner, he profusely expressed his appreciation for her great kindness and compassion to all of the Christian Brothers. "Oh Dr. Jeans," he concluded, "I don't know what the Christian Brothers would do without you." Without losing a beat, Dr. Jeans looked him directly in the eye over the rims of her glasses and replied: "On the contrary, Brother, I don't know what I would do without the Christian Brothers. You Brothers have become one of the most reliable sources of my income and livelihood."

John E. was an interesting blend of personalities. On the one hand, he was a deeply faithful man—pious, devout, and charitable to a fault. On the other hand, he was the life of any party, capable of captivating and commanding any audience in a matter of minutes. Like many Christian Brothers, he loved to eat. One of John E.'s favorite Italian dishes was *parmigiana di melanzane*, baked eggplant with melted Parmigiano Reggiano cheese. At their Roman home, the same wonderful cook who taught me how to make *spaghetti alla carbonara* often prepared this eggplant dish on Sundays for the Brothers, using the more traditional method of individually breading and frying each slice of eggplant.

I offer my own healthier, but equally delicious, grilled version of this classic dish.

PARMIGIANA DI MELANZANE GRIGLIATE

Grilled eggplant with basil tomato sauce and Parmigiano Reggiano

Makes 8 servings

Ingredients

- 4 or 5 medium-sized firm eggplants
- 4 eggs
- 3 cups fresh dried breadcrumbs
- 3 teaspoons mixed dried Italian herbs (oregano, thyme, rosemary, parsley)
- 2 cups shredded mozzarella cheese
- 2 cups grated Parmigiano Reggiano
- ½ cup grated Pecorino Romano
- 3 cups homemade tomato sauce

Method

1. Preheat the oven to 400°F. Cover a baking sheet with parchment paper, lightly sprayed with a vegetable or olive oil spray.
2. Wash and pat dry the eggplant. (I do not peel the eggplants, but you may certainly do so if you wish.) Then, slice them to about half-inch-thick circles.
3. Beat the eggs lightly and dip the eggplant slices into the egg mixture, and then dredge each slice in the seasoned breadcrumbs. Place the slices closely together, but not overlapping, on the baking sheet. You may need a second tray, depending on the volume of eggplant slices you are preparing.
4. Once you have the breaded eggplant slices arranged on the baking sheet(s), lightly mist the entire surface of the eggplant with an aerosolized vegetable or, preferably, an olive oil spray.

continued

5. Bake for 15 minutes before removing from the oven and turning each slice of eggplant. Return the trays to the oven and bake for another 15 minutes.
6. Prepare a rectangular Pyrex baking dish (approximately 2 quarts) by lightly coating with the vegetable or olive oil spray. Spoon some tomato sauce on the base of the dish and arrange a first layer of the baked eggplant slices. Generously sprinkle some of the Parmigiano Reggiano and Pecorino cheeses over the eggplant and add several dollops of tomato sauce over the cheese.
7. Repeat the process until you have created three or four layers of eggplant slices.
8. Top with a generous sprinkling of the grated cheeses and the remaining tomato sauce.
9. Bake for 20 to 30 minutes until the top layer of the casserole dish crisps and lightly browns. Allow the parmigiana di melanzane to rest uncovered for 15 to 20 minutes before slicing and serving.

One of the anchors of this triumvirate of the resident faculty of the Brothers' renewal program was a very cunning, wise, and discerning man named Brother Jeremiah Columba Keating, C.F.C., who later served as the superior general of the Congregation during the 1990s.

A self-made theologian, Columba became a trusted and inspirational leader of his fellow brothers. He was born in 1928 in Cahersiveen, a small town located on the banks of the River Fertha in the region of Skellig Kerry in County Kerry, Ireland. Cahersiveen is one of the more picturesque towns on the Iveragh Peninsula. One summer, when I set out to visit Br. Keating's family in Cahersiveen, I almost drove through the town without realizing that I had arrived. The whole town comprises less than a thousand people, with a boys' and girls' school and a single church.

True to the tradition of Kerry man, Columba was always asking questions. I recall once asking Br. Keating if the legend was true that a Kerry man never answers a question directly but counters by asking another question. "Whoever told you that?" was his reply.

Columba Keating was beloved by the men who came to participate in the Roman renewal program. They implicitly knew that he understood their struggles and doubts and always had their backs. He was also a consummate translator of and advocate for the hopes and ideals of the Second Vatican Council. He knew that the Christian Brothers needed to change their ways of proceeding. He had a judicious and skillful way of presenting difficult issues and was always genially armed with scriptural and doctrinal support for his challenging points of view on where the Church and religious life needed to move. And he had a wonderfully infectious sense of humor, and an enchanting, mischievous smile.

As I mentioned before, all the Brothers living at the *casa* of the Fratelli Cristiani at the Maglianella loved to eat. Even though they came from parts of the world where food tended to be quite bland and ordinary, most of them quickly grew quite fond of the Italian diet. The congenial Italian housewife and her lovely daughter employed as their cooks never disappointed. Outside the kitchen was a small garden where the women grew some vegetables and plentiful herbs. The rosemary bush was enormous, standing almost two feet tall and three feet in diameter, perfuming the whole garden with an incredibly memorable aroma. On many visits to Rome I would harvest long stems of rosemary from this bush, wrap them tightly in layers of plastic wrap, and smuggle them back to the States, where I carefully dried them.

In addition to the unrelenting work of managing the central governance of their Congregation, the Christian Brothers also staff and operate in Rome a quite successful English language private secondary school, Istituto Marcantonio Colonna. There was a beloved and legendary teacher and principal at the school who had spent most of his life in Rome, Brother Patrick Alphonsus Tarcisius Price. His religious name, Tarcisius, recalls a third-century Christian who was martyred during the brutal reign of the Roman emperor Valerian. Lore has it that Tarcisius, a young boy acolyte, had the responsibility of secretly bringing the holy communion to other Christians who awaited martyrdom in prison. He was discovered and attacked by a group hostile to Christians who beat him to death. His body is still venerated in the Church of San Silvestro in Capite in Rome.

By the time I came to meet Br. Tarcisius in person, he was already a golden jubilarian and morbidly obese. His girth was only matched by his garrulousness and bluster. The Brothers claimed that Brother Tarcisius never forgot a meal he had ever eaten and could regale you for hours on the theme of "things I have consumed." Without meeting him, I already had an affection for the man. Although not a cook, he clearly had developed an appreciation for gastronomy—more a gourmand than a gourmet.

Patrick Alphonsus Tarcisius Price was born in Ballyporeen, County Tipperary, on March 14, 1901—three days short of Saint Patrick's Day. His father, Henry Price, was head constable in charge of the police station at Ballyporeen. Br. Tarcisius's father, like Columba Keating, was a Kerry man, born at Aghalee near Aghadoe, just northwest of Killarney.

Br. Tarcisius completed his Christian Brother formation in Ireland and in September 1920 was missioned to go to Rome, where he spent the remainder of his life. Br. Tarcisius became an influential and well-known figure around the Vatican. He quickly established his importance with any new acquaintance by boasting that he "had witnessed the election of seven Popes, the rise and fall of Mussolini, the occupation and liberation of Rome, and the beatification and canonization of St. Maria Goretti!" This was exactly what he said to me when we were first introduced to each other.

He told me that in 1950, he'd met Cardinal Giovanni Battista Enrico Antonio Maria Montini. "That man," Br. Tarcisius later predicted, "will be the next pope." He had an uncanny knack of forecasting papal succession, and, true to form, in 1963 Cardinal Montini was elected Pope St. Paul VI.

Allow me a brief personal digression on the topic of Pope St. Paul VI. Paul VI was the first pope for whom I worked at the Vatican. I have for a long time considered him one of the great popes of the twentieth century. Montini returned from the See of Milan to that of Rome in a most critical moment for the Second Vatican Council. Paul VI presided over the final sessions of the Council, which had been convened by Pope St. John XXIII, moderated those concluding sessions with quiet and steady resolve, and governed the Church during the extraordinarily turbulent post-conciliar years. It is improbable that the Second Vatican Council would have completed its work, nor would the needed reforms within the Church set in motion by the constitutions and documents of the Council have had any chance of being implemented without his prudent, thoughtful, and courageous pastoral leadership.

I would like to share two fond memories of Paul VI. The first occurred on March 23, 1978, Holy Thursday—the final Liturgy of the Lord's Supper that the pope would celebrate. I happened to be in Rome for one of my frequent consultation visits and I was asked if I might like to assist at some of the papal ceremonies of the Sacred Triduum and Easter. Of course, I thought the invitation meant to assist in the distribution of holy communion to the faithful gathered for these liturgical celebrations. I receive a formal ticket of admission (*biglietto*) for the Holy Thursday event that was scheduled to be celebrated in the Arcibasilica di San Giovanni in Laterano, which historically has served as the cathedral of the pope, the bishop of Rome. All the ticket indicated was to arrive at a particular entrance to the basilica at a stated time, on the appointed day, *in veste talare* (attired in a clerical cassock).

I arrived early and was greeted by one of the members of the ceremonial corps of papal ushers, who led me through a labyrinth of corridors until we arrived at a room, which he indicated was my destination. When I entered the empty room I noted that it had been prepared for the vesting of the principal concelebrants of the Mass, including the distinctive mitre and pastoral staff ordinarily used by Pope Paul VI. I quickly concluded that I was in the wrong place and promptly exited the room, looking for another usher. After a while, I encountered another papal gentleman who looked at my ticket and escorted me back to the same room.

By the time I arrived back in the vesting room, the warm and congenial Cardinal Agnelo Rossi, prefect for the Congregation for the Evangelization of Peoples, was there, beginning to vest for the Mass. When I reentered the room, I explained to the cardinal that I was very confused. I thought I was expected to be a communion priest, but I had been escorted to this room, twice. The cardinal looked at my *biglietto* and he said that there was no mistake. The Mass would be concelebrated with the pope by six cardinals and six priests. I was one of the designated priest concelebrants. Still tentative, I waited until others arrived and, soon thereafter, I realized that I was indeed one of the designated vested concelebrants.

At the end of the Mass, the ailing and enfeebled Pope Paul briefly greeted each of the participants in the vesting room, offering each of us a small *regalo*—a pair of rosary beads in a leather case, embossed with the papal coat of arms. I was the last person in the line and unmistakably the youngest among the concelebrants. The Holy Father was being assisted to the exit when expectantly he turned back, and without saying a word, removed the white *zucchetto* from his head, folded it in half, and reached out to hand it to me. He smiled slightly, made a slight blessing with his hand, and hobbled off to the doorway. I still treasure that *zucchetto*.

A second story is about the day—some five months later—when I learned of the death of Pope Paul. In early August I was back in Italy for some weeks of consultations, prior to the beginning of the *Ferragosto*, the unofficial start of Italy's summer holiday season when the whole of Italy effectively shuts down until the start of

September. I had planned to enjoy a long weekend with some friends in Cattolica, a small seaside town near Rimini, along Italy's Adriatic coast. On Monday morning, August 7, as I was approaching the train station in Cattolica to begin my journey back to Rome, I noticed the bold headline on an Italian newspaper stand reading *"Morto Il Papa."* Pope Paul VI had died the previous night at 9:40 p.m., three hours after suffering a heart attack while attending a Mass celebrated on the Feast of the Transfiguration of the Lord in his private chambers at Castel Gandolfo, the papal summer residence, fifteen miles south of Rome. I attended the funeral of Pope Paul VI in St. Peter's Square on August 12.

As he had previously requested, the pope's coffin rested on a plain wooden platform in front of St. Peter's Basilica as Cardinal Carlo Confalonieri, then the dean of the College of Cardinals, led more than a hundred cardinals—all vested in red chasubles and white mitres—in a concelebrated Mass for the eighty-year-old Papa Montini who had led the church courageously during the preceding fifteen turbulent years.

Let me return now to the humorous story of Br. Tarcisius. I was also present in Rome when the Maglianella Christian Brothers community celebrated the golden jubilee of Br. Valerian Scanlon, who at that time was the director of the Brothers' Roman renewal program. Br. Valerian had been a former provincial of the eastern US province of the Brothers. Br. Tarcisius was invited as an honored guest at the jubilee festivities. The cook and kitchen staffed prepared a sumptuous meal composed of many courses, each complemented by very good local wines.

At the conclusion of the meal, Br. Tarcisius, with some obvious effort, pulled himself up to a standing position from his place of honor at the head table to offer a few words of appreciation and congratulations to the jubilarian, Br. Scanlon. In his toast he recalled with effusive gratitude a prior time when Brother Scanlon had hosted and entertained him at the provincial's headquarters located in New Rochelle, New York. The anecdote that follows provides indisputable corroboration that the legends about Br. Tarcisius were neither apocryphal nor exaggerated.

"I wish to salute Brother Valerian on this momentous occasion," he bellowed. "When he entertained me in New Rochelle, the cook prepared a most wondrous meal of succulent roasted turkey. The turkey had a crisp mahogany skin and was accompanied by several delectable side dishes including potatoes whipped with heavy cream and delicately finished with chopped scallion. There were carrots perfectly roasted and served in a sauce perfumed with Canadian maple syrup. The peas were floating in puddles of melted butter seasoned with fresh mint. There was a delicious bread dressing with chestnuts and sage and succulent sausage. And not to be forgotten was a curious American compote made with cranberries—a relish comprised of tart berries accompanied by apples, oranges, raisins, and walnuts all cooked together with brown sugar and orange rind until they married into a wondrous union of delicious memories. At the conclusion, the cook offered us a most perfect warm pumpkin pie accompanied by rum raisin ice cream." By this point there were murmurs and muted laughter rising from among the gathered brothers. Who but Br. Tarcisius could describe in such detail a meal he had eaten decades earlier?

Here is my own very easy-to-prepare recipe of that singularly American dish, which so delighted Brother Tarcisius's palate and about which he so enthusiastically rhapsodized.

FESTIVE CRANBERRY COMPOTE

Makes 10 to 12 servings

Ingredients

- 1 12-ounce bag fresh cranberries
- 1 cup superfine granulated sugar
- 1 cup light brown sugar
- 1 cup water
- 2 peeled, cored, and diced Granny Smith apples
- grated zest and juice of 1 lemon
- grated zest and sections from 2 navel oranges
- 1 ounce Grand Marnier
- 1 cup dark raisins
- 1 cup chopped walnuts or pecans

Method

1. In a saucepan cook the cranberries, sugars, and water over low heat

continued

for approximately 5 minutes or until the cranberries naturally begin to pop.

2. Add the diced apple, sectioned orange slices, citrus zest, and juice and cook for 10 to 12 more minutes.
3. Remove from the heat and add the raisins, nuts, and Grand Marnier.
4. Let cool, cover, and refrigerate until needed.

For more than a decade I enjoyed a wonderful international collaboration with the Christian Brothers and grew in my admiration for the exemplary ways in which they serve the Church and the world on six continents. We mostly know them for their laudable teaching and administering at elementary schools, secondary schools, and colleges. But the Brothers also have developed exceptional youth ministry programs that support parishes and dioceses. They are deeply committed to the works of social justice, serving the homeless and immigrants, and caring for the infirm and elderly.

Sadly, as stories of clergy sexual abuse gained global attention, the Brothers did not find themselves immune from this devastating discovery. Because their work so often centered on running schools and orphanages for boys, there were far too many cases of abuse uncovered as investigations and reports multiplied.

For example, in Canada alone, more than three hundred individuals alleged physical and sexual abuse by the Brothers while they were residents at the Mount Cashel orphanage in Newfoundland. These allegations of sexual abuse at this boys' home, founded and run by the Brothers in Newfoundland, led to a royal commission—the Hughes Inquiry—and other investigations that culminated in numerous arrests and court trials. In January 1993, the Christian Brothers in Canada reached a financial settlement with 700 former students who alleged abuse. The payout totaled some $23 million, which virtually bankrupted the province.

The year after Brother Keating completed his term as superior general, the Congregation of the Christian Brothers in Ireland published full-page spreads in Irish newspapers contritely apologizing to the thousands of alumni of their schools who had been abused or mistreated and offering remedial counseling and support. Because the Christian Brothers dominated Catholic education in Ireland for most of the twentieth century, there were more credible accusations made against the Brothers than against any other members of religious orders or congregations combined.

In 2009, the Brothers announced they would provide 161 million euros in reparations for child abuse in Ireland. This comprised a donation of 30 million euros to a government trust and 4 million euros donated to provide counseling services for victims. They also agreed that land owned by the Brothers and valued at 127 million euros would be transferred to joint ownership of the government and a trust that runs former Christian Brothers schools. In announcing this settlement, the Congregation stated that the settlement reflects the Christian Brothers' acceptance, shame, and sorrow for the roles that their members had played in the wide abuse of their sacred trust.

Other parts of the Congregation were forced to close institutions they had long cherished or to declare bankruptcy. Vocations to the brotherhood—as with many other similar groups within the Church—were negatively affected and some of their members were tried for crimes and incarcerated. Others elected to leave the Congregation.

This was an all too sad ending to what had been such an inspiring and engaging outgrowth of my Rome-based ministry with the Congregation of Christian Brothers. Without excusing the criminal behaviors of those Brothers who abused the boys who had been entrusted to their care, I must say without hesitation that the many other Brothers who have given themselves faithfully and selflessly to their ministries have lived up so well to the Congregation's motto *facere et docere* ("to do and to teach"). These words are drawn from the opening sentences of the Acts of the Apostles: "In the first book, O Theophilus, I have dealt with all that Jesus began to do and teach, until the day when he was taken up, after he had given commands through the Holy Spirit to the apostles whom he had chosen" (Acts 1:1–2).

I recall vividly being with a group of Christian Brothers when they were received in private audience at the Vatican with Pope St. Paul VI. In the course of his remarks to the Brothers, the Holy Father assured the gathered Brothers of the Church's deep appreciation for all they do and teach. But the pope went on to draw a wonderfully penetrating distinction. He told them that even more than what they do for the Church is who they *are* for the Church. With tenderness, he urged them always to be men of prayer and men of ever-deepening faith.

The Congregation of Christian Brothers is a community of deep and tested faith and these Brothers deserve the forgiveness, continued respect, admiration, appreciation, and affection of their many alumni and friends throughout the world who owe their moral formation, development, and vocational success to the astute education that the Brothers so generously and selflessly imparted to them.

The Brothers have a traditional way to bring activities to a close with a devotional exclamation: "Live, Jesus, in our hearts!" The others quickly reply in unison: "Forever." By these words, the Brothers continually pray that they will come alive from within the very core of their being and, as Saint Paul enjoined: "Have this mind in you, which was also in Christ Jesus" (Philippians 2:5).

In closing, I am reminded of these insightful words from an E. M. Forster novel: "Only connect the prose and the passion and both will be exalted, and human love will be seen at its height. Live in fragments no longer."[5]

"Live Jesus in our hearts, forever!"

---

5 E. M. Forster, *Howard's End* (New York: G. P. Putnam's Son, 1910).

Chapter 6

CHANGING COURSE

Gracious words are a honeycomb, sweet to the soul and healing to the bones.

—PROVERBS 16:24

Each year, a Jesuit meets with his provincial superior for a fraternal conversation called "an account of conscience." During this encounter a Jesuit candidly discusses issues in his life that he considers of importance so that the provincial may be able to direct and govern him better and guide him more effectively in his apostolic endeavors. When I met with provincial Fr. Robert E. Manning, S.J., on a cold February morning in 1988, I had no inkling just how radically life-altering that encounter would be. After we had spoken about all of the ordinary matters, the provincial made a bold declaration. He said that the Weston School of Theology in Cambridge, from which I had graduated in 1972, was actively searching for a dean, and he indicated that he wanted me to apply for the position. Taken aback by his suggestion, I argued that I was a clinical psychologist, not a theologian. He dismissed the protestation, indicating that my clinical background and academic experience were exactly the things that the school needed. In obedience, I did apply, was vetted, interviewed, and ultimately offered the position. When I reprised the discussion about this proposed career change later in the spring with Fr. Manning, he urged me to accept the offer, which I did.

After twelve happy and productive years teaching at Fairfield University and chairing its psychology department, the decision to leave a tenured-university professorship to move to Cambridge and become the academic dean of a professional school of theology was a big leap of faith. Both the Jesuit provincial and the school's president, Fr. Edward M. O'Flaherty, S.J., were convinced that my skills and talents would be well employed in this new administrative ministry. I blindly placed my trust in their judgments.

During the summer of 1988, I packed up my books and personal belongings and moved from Fairfield back to Cambridge and took up residence in an old Victorian house on Sumner Road that the school had recently purchased. In addition to settling into my new responsibilities as a dean, I also spent the better part of the first several months unexpectedly overseeing a major renovation project for a building that had been seriously neglected for more than a half-century. This project could have consumed an entire season of public television's celebrated series *This Old House*.

The deanship at Weston Jesuit School of Theology had been a revolving door. I was the fourth dean appointed in ten years, and my tenure, as you will learn, was not much longer than that of my predecessors. Fortunate for the school was the connective tissue in the Office of the Dean provided by Terry Lima, who for nearly three decades until her retirement in 2018 continued her work as executive assistant to the school's dean. Terry knew where all of the bodies were buried and made my transition easy, even though I was the first outsider to occupy that office. All my immediate predecessors had been selected from within the ranks of the faculty and later returned to their faculty positions once their terms of service as dean had ended.

So many aspects of the job engaged me immediately: the interfaith and ecumenical collaboration afforded by the school's active participation as a founding member of the Boston Theological Institute; the scholarship and sterling teaching abilities of the faculty; the breadth and depth of the library collections; the international mix of the lay and religious graduate students; the enthusiasm and talents of the Jesuit scholastics from the United States and around the world who were preparing for ordination to priesthood; and finally, the cultural and academic richness of Cambridge and Boston.

The richness, diversity, and attractiveness of this new ministry reminds me of a classic French soup that shares some of these same qualities.

SOUPE AU PISTOU

Provençale vegetable soup with basil and garlic condiment

Makes 6 to 8 servings

Ingredients

For the soup

- 1 cup dried cannellini beans
- 2 bay leaves
- 3 tablespoons olive oil
- 3 cleaned and sliced leeks
- 2 teaspoons minced fresh thyme
- 2 peeled and diced carrots
- 2 medium diced zucchini
- ½ pound green beans, cut on the bias into 2-inch pieces
- 6 cloves minced garlic
- 1 teaspoon sea salt
- 1 teaspoon freshly ground black pepper
- 1 cup fresh or frozen peas
- 1 cup orzo

For the pistou

- 1 clove finely minced garlic
- 2 cups fresh basil leaves
- ¼ cup extra-virgin olive oil
- 1 ripe heirloom tomato, peeled, seeded, and finely diced
- ¼ cup grated Parmigiano-Reggiano cheese
- a pinch of sea salt

continued

Method

1. Soak the cannellini beans overnight covered in cold water.
2. The next day, drain and rinse the beans. In a large saucepan filled with about two quarts of water, add the beans, along with two bay leaves.
3. Cook the beans on medium heat for about an hour, or until they become tender, adding more water if needed to keep them covered. Remove the beans from the heat and set aside in their cooking liquid.
4. In a Dutch oven or large stockpot, heat the olive oil over medium heat.
5. Add the leeks and cook, stirring occasionally, until they become soft and translucent.
6. Add the thyme, diced carrots, zucchini, green beans, garlic, and salt. Season with pepper and slowly simmer until the vegetables are completely cooked (about 20 to 30 minutes).
7. Add the cannellini beans and the liquid in which they were cooked, then the peas and orzo, plus two additional quarts of water. Bring the soup to a boil and simmer for a few more minutes until the orzo is cooked.
8. While the soup is cooking, make the *pistou* by pounding the garlic into a paste in a mortar and pestle (or use a food processor) with a generous pinch of salt. Coarsely chop the basil leaves and pound them into the garlic until the mixture is relatively smooth. Drizzle in the olive oil slowly, while pounding, then pound in the tomato and cheese.
9. To serve, add a generous spoonful of the *pistou* to each serving of the soup.

In the autumn of 1988 the Paulist Press published my book *AIDS: Living and Dying with Hope: Issues in Pastoral Care.*[6] The following year this book would garner recognition from the Catholic Press Association as the best pastoral book of

6 *AIDS: Living and Dying with Hope: Issues in Pastoral Care* (Mahwah, NJ: Paulist Press, 1988).

the year. The book grew out of the AIDS-related work that I had begun while at Fairfield University and my service on the first HIV education task force in the state of Connecticut.

When Catholic priests, religious, and laypersons who had become involved in many nascent HIV/AIDS ministries around the country formed a national support and continuing education alliance—the National Catholic AIDS Network (NCAN)—I became active in its leadership, eventually serving as one of NCAN's presidents. It was in that context that I first met Jon Fuller, S.J., a California Jesuit who had completed his medical education at the University of California Medical School in San Diego and pursued an infectious disease residency program at San Francisco General Hospital—one of the epicenters of the AIDS crisis—just at the time when the crisis was reaching epic proportions in that region.

In the year following the completion of his residency, Dr. Fuller was missioned to the Weston School of Theology in Cambridge to pursue his theological education—the final academic stage of Jesuit formation. As he was establishing himself in Cambridge as a student of theology, he was simultaneously recruited to join the staff and faculty of what was then the Boston City Hospital (now the Boston Medical Center)—America's first public hospital, located in Boston's South End, just across the street from the original Harrison Avenue site of Boston College (founded in 1863 with three Jesuit teachers and twenty-two students) and the Society's adjoining Church of the Immaculate Conception, consecrated in 1875.

I had been born in 1943 in an adjoining hospital, Massachusetts Memorial (originally called the Massachusetts Homeopathic Hospital), which moved to its site in the South End in 1874. Boston University would later acquire the hospital building and operate it, and in 1996 these two historic medical institutions merged to form the Boston Medical Center. The Boston City Hospital, according to its original charter in 1864, was "intended for the use and comfort of poor patients, to whom medical care will be provided at the expense of the city, and . . . to provide accommodations and medical treatment to others, who do not wish to be regarded as dependent on public charity."

It is remarkable to note that Boston Medical Center would become for Jon Fuller his life's mission. Now, after more than three and a half decades, Dr. Fuller has recently completed his service to patients and families in the institution's family practice and infectious disease programs. Jon became as much a part of New England as its famous clam chowder. Every New England cook has their version of this classic chowder. Here is mine, with a slight French twist.

NEW ENGLAND CLAM CHOWDER

Makes 4 to 6 servings

Ingredients

For the court bouillon

- 4 cups water
- 1 cup dry white wine
- 2 lemons, juiced
- 2 chopped yellow onion
- 1 rib chopped celery
- 2 minced garlic cloves
- 1 teaspoon black peppercorns
- 4 to 5 sprigs fresh thyme
- 1 bay leaf

For the chowder

- 3 strips thick-cut apple-smoked bacon (or pork belly)
- 4 tablespoons unsalted butter
- 1 large onion, cut into quarter-inch cubes
- 2 ribs celery, cut into quarter-inch cubes
- 1 teaspoon chopped fresh thyme leaves
- 2 bay leaves
- 2 Yukon Gold potatoes, peeled and cut into quarter-inch cubes
- ½ cup all-purpose flour
- 4 cups court bouillon (and whatever strained clam juice has been retained)
- 1 pound of gently chopped clam meat (fresh, frozen, or canned)
- Kosher salt and black pepper to taste

- 2 cups heavy cream
- 1 cup crème fraîche
- 2 tablespoons Pernod absinthe

Method

Making the court bouillon

1. Combine all the ingredients in a saucepan and bring to a boil over high heat. Reduce the heat and simmer for 8 minutes. Strain through a fine mesh, pressing against the solids.
2. If you are able to procure fresh cherrystone clams, poach 4 pounds of them in this broth and reserve 4 cups of the strained cooking liquid for use and incorporation into the chowder.

Making the chowder

1. Set a stockpot or Dutch oven over medium-low heat. Add the bacon or pork belly strips and cook, stirring occasionally with a wooden spoon, until the bacon crisps. Remove the bacon and drain on paper towels, leaving the rendered pork fat in the pot.
2. Add the butter, onion, celery, thyme, and bay leaves to the pot. Cook, stirring often, until onions are tender and translucent.
3. Return the crumbled cooked bacon to the pot and combine with the vegetables. Reduce the heat to low, add a cup of the court bouillon, and continue slowly cooking, stirring occasionally, while you prep the potatoes.
4. In a saucepan, boil the diced potatoes in salted water until they become tender, but not mushy. Drain and set aside.
5. Add the flour gradually to the vegetable and bacon mixture, stirring continuously, until the flour is thoroughly incorporated, and a paste begins to form. Stir and cook 5 minutes.
6. Increase the heat to medium and slowly begin to add the court bouillon

continued

into the mixture—one ladle at a time—incorporating it before adding more stock. Continue until 3 or 4 cups of the stock (and whatever clam juice may be available) have been added.

7. Increase the heat to medium-high and add the potatoes and clam meat. Keep stirring 5 minutes, until the clams are warmed through.
8. Add the cream and crème fraîche slowly; then stir in salt and black pepper, to taste. Finally, mix in the 2 tablespoons of Pernod absinthe.
9. Discard the bay leaves before serving.

One afternoon my executive assistant, Terry Lima, told me that Jon Fuller was on the phone and wished to speak with me. Jon was calling to ask for my assistance with one of his patients, whom we shall call Paul. As Dr. Fuller described the situation, Paul was a recently diagnosed AIDS patient in their outpatient program and he was proving to be a disruptive and noncompliant member of the treatment group to which he had been assigned. Dr. Fuller thought that I might possibly have the time and interest to accept Paul as a private, no-fee patient and use my skills and experience as a clinical psychologist to help Paul. I agreed, and the referral was made.

For the next fifteen months or so I saw Paul on a weekly basis in my office at the school. He was the youngest member of a fragmented family of seven siblings. His was a lower middle-class Boston family with a considerable history of family pathology, including alcohol and drug use, verbal and physical abuse, and criminal activity. At age fourteen, Paul ran away from home and eventually made his way to the West Coast. He proved to be a survivor, supporting himself in a myriad of ways: prostitution, procuring and selling drugs, deceit, manipulation, and larceny. Somehow, throughout his adolescent odyssey Paul had avoided arrest, conviction, and incarceration, but he was not able to protect himself from becoming infected by HIV.

At age twenty-two, he found himself back in Boston and a patient at the Boston Medical Center. Paul was an instinctively suspicious young man, of medium height, naturally muscular, and with all of the other classic features one might expect to find in a third-generation Boston Irishman. His family was of Roman Catholic background, although he had never been baptized nor raised in a religious environment.

When he arrived for his first appointment with me, he was obviously quite nervous and initially resistant. He was not very verbal or forthcoming, but gradually both his body's rigidity and speech softened, and he became more noticeably engaged in our conversations. Apart from the times when he was physically ill, he never missed an appointment.

One day, about seven weeks into our relationship, he arrived at my office, clearly animated and ready to talk.

"On the bus coming over here this afternoon, I thought to myself: 'I'm ready to work with this guy,'" he announced.

Somewhat astonished, I contained my surprise and gently pursued his declaration a bit more deeply. "Tell me, Paul, what do you think brought you to this insight?"

Without hesitation, he answered by painting a significant portrait of his life and experience. He noted quite matter-of-factly that he had never had an encounter with another man who ultimately was not looking for something from him: money, drugs, sex. As he was thinking about our relationship and how I seemed to be committed to helping him, he came to an insight, which he expressed in this way: "The thought crossed my mind that maybe this guy is for real; maybe there are some people in this world who genuinely care and are not looking for anything in return." For Paul, this was a watershed moment of discovery, and in hindsight, a turning point in our personal and therapeutic relationship. From that time on I needed to do very little to engage his conversation during our sessions, and he proved to be one of those patients who was both insightful and able to translate new knowledge into productive and transformative action. In the end, he turned out to be one of the best patients I ever cared for.

I could also see as the months moved on that Paul was expanding his network of acquaintances and friends, which included the school's receptionist, some of the graduate students he met in the waiting room and corridors, and especially my executive assistant, Terry. Her natural motherly traits facilitated a warm bond with Paul. They clearly liked each other a lot.

At the beginning of one session, Paul began with a question: "Both you and Dr. Fuller are both priests. Right?" I affirmed that we indeed were both Jesuits, and also that we were both doctors.

"Maybe I can use the 'priest' side of you guys," Paul said.

Intrigued, I pursued this statement more deeply. "Can you tell me a bit more what you mean?"

He went on to talk about something that had previously not been a topic of our conversations: the fact that he had never been baptized or received holy communion or been confirmed. He had never attended Sunday school or Mass, but he knew that his family was culturally Roman Catholic.

"I have been thinking a lot about God and my life," he said. "Do you think it might be possible for me to be baptized and to become a real Catholic?"

His desires and requests were unexpected; it was clear, nonetheless, that he had been thinking about these things for some time. I asked him if he had spoken with Dr. Fuller about this same thing and he said he had not. Without hesitation, I told him that I thought all of this was possible, and that we could clearly put this request very high on the "bucket list" of goals and objectives we had already been creating, alongside the more obvious tasks of ensuring medication compliance, securing independent housing, Medicaid support, and family reconciliation.

After some accelerated sacramental preparation, both Jon Fuller and I presided at an intimate celebration of a Mass in the seminary's chapel during which we baptized Paul, offered him first communion, and confirmed him in the Catholic faith.

In preparation of this milestone event in Paul's life, Terry asked me if I thought it would be appropriate for her to give Paul a special gift on that occasion. Recognizing that he was one of my patients, she sensitively inquired before making such an offering. When I explored what she had in mind, Terry revealed that when she was seven years old she had received her First Holy Communion at Saint Anthony Church, a Portuguese national parish to which her family belonged in East Cambridge. On that occasion she had been presented with a small white book containing devotional prayers. Through all of the intervening years, she had treasured this little memento of that special day in her life.

"I would like to give Paul my First Communion prayer book," she told me. Deeply touched by her desire, I encouraged her to share this meaningful gift with him and to tell him about the importance that this devotional object had for her. She did precisely that, and I think both Terry and Paul benefitted immensely from this loving act of giving and receiving.

For this special celebration, Terry brought a traditional Portuguese dessert called *pão de Deus*, or "Bread of God." These soft buns resemble a lemon-flavored brioche roll, topped with dried coconut flakes.

PÃO DE DEUS

Portuguese coconut buns

Makes 12 servings

Ingredients

For the buns

- 1 tablespoon active dry yeast
- 1 cup warm whole milk
- ¼ cup superfine granulated sugar
- 1 vanilla pod
- grated zest of one lemon
- 1 egg
- 4 cups plain all-purpose flour, plus more to dust
- ½ teaspoon *fleur de sel*
- 4 tablespoons melted and cooled unsalted butter

For the topping

- 2 eggs
- ½ cup superfine granulated sugar
- 4 ounces dried coconut flakes
- confectioners' sugar

Method

1. Activate the yeast by mixing it in a bowl with the slightly warmed milk and sugar. Leave the yeast to proof for about 10 minutes.
2. With a sharp utility knife, slit the vanilla bean lengthwise and scrape the seeds from the vanilla pod. Zest a lemon. Add the vanilla beans and lemon zest into the proofed yeast mixture, along with a lightly beaten egg.

continued

3. In a stand mixer fitted with a paddle hook, combine the flour, salt, and melted butter with the yeast mixture. Process until the ingredients come together into a rough, sticky dough. Change the attachment to a dough hook and knead for approximately 5 minutes. (If working by hand, combine the ingredients until a sticky dough ball has formed.) Transfer the dough onto a floured work surface and, with floured hands, begin to knead the dough, for about 10 minutes.
4. When the dough is soft, stretchy, and elastic, place it in a lightly oiled bowl, cover with plastic wrap, and leave it in a warm place to rise for an hour or so until it has doubled in size.
5. Deflate the risen dough with your knuckles and divide the mass into twelve equal-sized pieces. Roll each one into a smooth ball. Place the formed balls on a large ungreased and floured baking sheet, cover with a clean kitchen towel, and allow to rise in a warm place for an additional half hour.
6. When ready to bake, preheat the oven to 350°F.
7. Brush the top of each bun with an egg wash. Then combine one beaten egg with the sugar and coconut flakes to form a paste. Top each bun generously with the coconut paste mixture and smooth it using your hands, distributing it evenly and securely on the top of the buns.
8. Place in the oven and bake for 20 minutes until the buns are lightly golden and the coconut flakes are browned.
9. Remove from the oven and transfer buns to a cooling rack. When cool, lightly dust with powdered sugar.

It was equally gratifying and consoling that Paul's mother was both willing and interested to be present for this celebration, along with one of his sisters and Paul's nephew. This small family remnant became an encouraging sign of the reconciliation that was also gradually being reestablished between Paul and his family of origin.

For this occasion I prepared a very special first communion cake, which we shared, along with the *pão de Deus*, in an impromptu reception after the Mass concluded. Because it was early springtime, I decided to make a classic French *génoise* sponge cake, filled and frosted with fresh strawberries and a French buttercream. It was a great treat for Paul and his guests, and it was for some of the members of the school community the first evidence that the dean knew how to bake! Here is the recipe.

VANILLA GÉNOISE LAYER CAKE WITH STRAWBERRY FRENCH BUTTERCREAM

Makes 10 to 12 servings

Ingredients

For the génoise

- 2 cups sifted cake flour
- 4 tablespoons superfine sugar
- 1 pinch kosher salt
- 4 tablespoons melted unsalted butter
- 8 large eggs
- 1 cup granulated sugar
- 3 teaspoons pure vanilla extract

For the strawberry French buttercream

- 1 cup granulated sugar
- ½ cup water
- 8 large egg yolks
- 1 pound (4 sticks) unsalted butter, cubed and softened at room temperature
- 1 teaspoon vanilla extract
- a pinch of salt
- 1/4 cup pureed and strained strawberries
- halved strawberries for garnish

continued

Method

Making the genoise

1. Preheat oven to 350°F.
2. Grease a baking pan with a vegetable spray and line the pan with parchment paper and lightly spray the paper. Leave about a 2-inch lip of paper at each of the ends to facilitate removal of the cake from the baking pan.
3. Sift together 2 cups of cake flour, 4 tablespoons superfine sugar, and a pinch of salt into a mixing bowl.
4. Place 8 eggs into the mixing bowl of a stand mixer and place it briefly over a saucepan of simmering, not boiling, water. Do not let the bottom of the bowl touch the simmering water. Coddle the eggs, gently hand whisking them (do not let them scramble) for a couple of minutes before whisking in a cup of granulated sugar to the mixture.
5. When the sugar is incorporated, immediately place the bowl onto the standing mixer and with the whisk attachment, beat on medium speed until the mixture becomes pale yellow in color and falls off the end of the whisk attachment in long ribbons (about 4 to 5 minutes). Add the vanilla extract and blend to incorporate.
6. In three additions, fold in the flour mixture to the beaten eggs and sugar until just incorporated. Try not to overmix or deflate the batter.
7. Place about 2 cups of the batter into a bowl along with the melted butter and combine the butter with the batter.
8. Gently add this butter-batter mixture back to the main batter and fold it in by hand.
9. Pour the batter into the prepared pan and with a spatula, gently spread it evenly over the whole pan.
10. Immediately bake for about 25 to 30 minutes or until the top of the génoise is a light brown.

11. Allow to cool in the baking pan on a rack for about 10 minutes and then invert onto another rack and gently peel away the parchment paper. It is best to invert the cake again onto another rack so that it cools with its top up. Let the génoise cool completely before cutting and frosting.

Making the strawberry French buttercream

Note: I learned the technique for making this classic French butter cream at Le Cordon Bleu. It is a luxurious, smooth, rich multipurpose filling or frosting. There are an infinite number of adaptations and flavorings possible. Because it is made with an egg-yolk foam, which my teachers referred to as pâte à bombe, it has a yellow color which can, of course, be tinted by the addition of strained fruit purées such as strawberries or raspberries.

1. Combine the sugar and water in a medium saucepan. Warm over low heat, stirring until the sugar has dissolved and the syrup is clear. Increase heat to medium-high and allow syrup to come to a boil.
2. Meanwhile, place 8 room-temperature egg yolks in the bowl of a stand mixer fitted with the whisk attachment and beat until thick and foamy.
3. Cook the sugar syrup until it registers 235°F on a candy thermometer, which bakers often refer to as the "blow" or "soufflé" stage, where the boiling sugar creates small bubbles resembling snowflakes.
4. At this point, immediately remove the sugar syrup from the heat.
5. With the stand mixer running at the lowest speed, slowly drizzle the hot sugar syrup into the bowl with the yolks: do not pour the syrup onto the whisk, or the syrup may splatter against the sides of the bowl. Instead, pour it in a steady stream along the inner edge of the bowl.
6. Once all the syrup has been completely added and incorporated, increase the mixing speed to medium and continue whisking until the bottom of the bowl feels cool to the touch and the yolk mixture has cooled to room temperature. This will take about 2 to 3 minutes.

continued

7. While still beating on medium-high, add the butter, a few pieces at a time. Don't be alarmed if the mixture appears to be thinning. As the butter is incorporated, it will gradually thicken and peak. Add in vanilla and salt. Continue mixing until the buttercream looks smooth and creamy, about 5 minutes. (If the buttercream separates, keep mixing: it will come together eventually.)
8. Lastly, add in ¼ cup of puréed and strained strawberries. This will both flavor and color the buttercream.
9. If you are ready to frost your cake now, the buttercream is ready. If not, then refrigerate the buttercream, covered with plastic wrap. To use buttercream that has been refrigerated or frozen, allow the bowl with the buttercream to come to room temperature and then quickly whisk or beat again until the buttercream becomes smooth and spreadable.

In putting together Paul's cake, I spread a thin layer of buttercream on the bottom génoise and spread some seedless strawberry preserves over the entire surface of the buttercream. Then I placed the second génoise cake layer and frosted the top and edges with the remaining buttercream. I garnished the top with halved fresh strawberries.

Over time, Paul and I were able to address many of the other major items on his bucket list. Despite his personal efforts to restart his life, the virus progressively began to overwhelm him. One day—eighteen months after we had first met—I received a call from Jon Fuller that Paul had been rehospitalized and that his condition was rapidly deteriorating.

"I think Paul would like to say goodbye to you, if you have the time to visit him today," he told me. Even though I was preparing to leave the following day for a conference in South Bend, Indiana, on the campus of the University of Notre Dame, I quickly reorganized my schedule and opened up time to get to the hospital.

I found Paul in a severely weakened state with virtually no energy, scarcely able to speak. His respirations were labored and quite shallow. He was clearly in the final days or hours of his young life. I saw his eyes and smile brighten when he saw me. I chatted with him briefly, offering him a prayer and a blessing. As I was preparing to leave his bedside, I could see that with all of the energy that he could muster, he was reaching up to grasp my hand and to draw my face closer to his.

"When I first met you," he whispered, "you told me that you would stick by me until the end. You have done that. Thank you and I love you." Those were the last words that Paul spoke to me. He died peacefully that night.

During my years as the dean of Weston Jesuit School of Theology I had many wonderful experiences of ministry and collaboration. We strengthened and improved the school's policies and procedures, enhanced opportunities for faculty development, instituted and funded lecture series, and expanded student services and any number of other achievements.

But this one professional and pastoral engagement remains an iconic memory of those years in Cambridge. For me, Paul was a living example of the words of Jesus as recorded in Matthew 11:28: "Come to me, all of you who are tired and have heavy loads. I will give you rest."

After three years serving in this administrative position as dean, I was becoming restive. While the work was worthwhile and my colleagues were accomplished and committed, I could not imagine spending my most creative years in this somewhat insular academic environment. The school's president, Fr. O'Flaherty, and I discussed and debated these issues over many weeks before coming to a mutual agreement that I would complete my service as dean at the end of academic year 1990–1991.

What might I do next?

Chapter 7

TAKING A BITE OF THE BIG APPLE

Then God said, "I give you every seed-bearing plant on the face of the whole earth and every tree that has fruit with seed in it. They will be yours for food."

—GENESIS 1:29

It was a brisk sunny early spring morning in 1991 when Fr. Edward O'Flaherty, S.J., president of Weston Jesuit School of Theology, walked into my office with a document in his hands. "This prospectus for a nonprofit leadership position in New York City arrived in this morning's mail and it looks remarkably like you," he said.

"I am really not interested in considering a new job possibility right now, Ed," I replied. "I am looking forward to my planned sabbatical this coming academic year at Santa Clara University, where I have been offered and accepted a Bannan Jesuit Faculty Fellowship." In those years, Santa Clara University recruited Jesuit scholars as Bannan Fellows, providing them with an opportunity to write books, pursue research projects, and offer lectures and conferences covering a variety of topics to the campus community. This fellowship program helped Santa Clara further its reputation as a place that fostered intellectual rigor and inquiry around questions of Catholic identity and Jesuit mission. In a highly selective process, I had been invited and accepted to be a Bannan Fellow for the academic year of 1991–1992. I was anticipating pulling together my extensive research in gerontological psychology and writing a new college-level textbook, while at the same time planning for my next professional commitment.

"Well, put this document into your briefcase and at least read it over and let me know if you would like me to nominate you as a prospective candidate for this national search," Ed counseled. I agreed and hastily put the collected papers in a folder for later browsing. It was a nice gesture on Ed's part, but I really did not have much interest in pursuing a new job opportunity at the time.

That night I sat down and began reading through the well-written case statement for a newly created position of executive vice president and chief operating officer for a multifaith healthcare, research, and education nonprofit organization based in Manhattan called the Hospital Chaplaincy. The search document energetically described an organization with a clear and articulate mission, a strategic direction, and a leadership succession plan, and outlined the thirty-year history of the organization along with the broad goals the governing board was hopeful a next generation of leaders might help the Hospital Chaplaincy to achieve.

As I carefully read through this fifteen-page expository document, I surprisingly felt a warming attraction, connectedness, and growing enthusiasm for the organization's mission and management objectives. Included in the presentation was a brief biography of the Chaplaincy's copresidents, Carolyn and John Twiname. People often ask me in retrospect what initially attracted me to the Chaplaincy. My answer is immediate and has never changed: the mission of the organization, and the personal witness and commitment of this charismatic couple who had led it since 1983.

Carolyn Anderson Twiname grew up in a family of two children in Illinois, just north of Chicago. Her father, Harold Anderson, was in the newspaper business. He syndicated various newspaper columns, cofounded the Gallup Poll with George Gallup, and also syndicated comics like *Rex Morgan, M.D.,* and *Mary Worth*. Carolyn's only sibling, a brother who was five years older than she, Roger, had committed suicide when he was eighteen years old, during his freshman year at Yale University.

Carolyn was raised in a Protestant Christian community church. Her father's parents were from Sweden and professed to be very conservative Baptists, although her parents did not attend church frequently. On her own, during high school, Carolyn attended a Congregational church and sang in the choir, although she did not have much of an aptitude for singing. She once told me that it was this experience that early on taught her when to keep her mouth shut. As you will discover shortly, this was not a lesson that her spouse-to-be ever learned.

She believed that the roots of her multifaith sensitivity were shaped during her time at Cornell (where she transferred in her junior year of college). She joined an organization named Cornell United Religious Work, which encouraged all religions to work together. Carolyn recalls that the organization provided a common space for many religions to conduct worship services, and she concluded that despite our differences and beliefs, we could all get along together.

Carolyn met John Twiname soon after she transferred in her junior year to Cornell. She recalls sitting in the lobby of the Student Union Building when a confident, lanky guy came bouncing in, talking and laughing with everyone. Carolyn turned to her friend and without further reflection simply said: "That's the man I'm going to marry."

Her friend was astonished and replied, "But that's not the guy you're pinned to." One thing about Carolyn Twiname is this: she is decisive.

A natural sleuth, she quickly identified who he was. Twiname, a senior, was president of the student union. Maneuvering quickly, Carolyn got herself onto the student union board of directors and finagled their first date in May, prior to his approaching graduation in June.

Their coming together as a couple might have been like marrying a nectarine with a blackberry. The result, as you will see, can be quite delicious.

CROSTATA DI NETTARINA E MORA

A rustic nectarine and blackberry tart

Makes 6 to 8 servings

Ingredients

For the crust

- 1¾ cups all-purpose flour
- ¼ cup coarse cornmeal
- 3 tablespoons granulated sugar
- 1 teaspoon grated orange zest
- ¾ teaspoon kosher salt
- 2 sticks (½ pound) cold unsalted butter, cut into half-inch cubes
- ⅓ cup or more of ice water

For the filling

- ¼ cup granulated sugar
- 1½ teaspoons cornstarch
- 4 firm pitted nectarines
- 1-pint basket blackberries
- ½ teaspoon almond extract

For the baking and finishing

- egg wash (1 beaten whole egg)
- raw sugar for dusting
- warmed apricot preserves for finishing glaze

Method

Making the free-formed crust

1. Combine the first five ingredients in a food processor and pulse to blend for 5 seconds.
2. Add the cubed butter pieces to the processor bowl and pulse until the butter combines with the flour and cornmeal and forms small pea-sized clumps. Do not overblend the dough.
3. Add about half of the ice water until the dough comes together, gradually adding more water if the dough seems too dry.
4. With your hands, gather dough into a ball; flatten into an 8-inch disk. Cover with plastic wrap and chill in refrigerator for at least 1 hour.
5. Roll out dough on lightly floured sheet of parchment paper to 14-inch round, turning the dough disk occasionally to prevent sticking.
6. Slide rimless baking sheet under parchment. Transfer dough on parchment to refrigerator. Chill until the dough firms slightly, about 30 minutes.

continued

Making the filling and baking

1. Stir sugar and cornstarch in medium bowl to blend. Combine fruit and almond extract. Allow the fruit to macerate until juices begin to release, stirring fruit occasionally, about 30 minutes.
2. Preheat oven to 375°F.
3. Transfer baking sheet with dough to work surface. Let stand 8 minutes to allow dough to soften slightly, if too firm to fold.
4. Spoon fruit and juices into the center of the dough. Mound the fruit in the center, leaving a 4-inch border all around. Brush the border of the dough with egg wash.
5. Begin forming the border by lifting and pinching the dough to form vertical seams. Continue around tart, pinching a seam every 2 inches to form a standing border. Fold border down over fruit. Brush the folded border with egg glaze and sprinkle with raw sugar.
6. Place the baking sheet with free-form tart in the oven. Bake until crust is golden brown and fruit filling is bubbling at edges, about 55 minutes.
7. Remove from oven; slide large metal spatula under tart to loosen from parchment.
8. Brush fruit and outer crust with the warmed apricot preserves. Slide tart onto cooling rack. Cool 45 minutes before serving.

John Twiname—the love of Carolyn's life—was born on December 27, 1931, in Mount Kisko, New York. An only child, John grew up in Chappaqua, which was a virtual farming community at that time. In the years after the Great Depression, John's father was fortunate to find a steady job in New York City working on the dock of the B. Altman and Company store. He remained employed at B. Altman for the remainder of his life. John's mother worked for twenty years or more at the *Reader's Digest* and came to know DeWitt and Lila Wallace intimately.

Like Carolyn, John was the product of an eclectic religious formation. He remembered attending a Quaker Sunday school. After completing an hour of religious education each Sunday, he would often walk down the hill to the Baptist church where his mother played its pump organ.

During his final year of high school in 1949, John submitted a single application to college—Cornell University—for the simple reason that his cousin told him that he was going there. His uncle was an alumnus, but no other member of John's family had graduated from college. John received some scholarship assistance and off he went, viewing the campus for the first time when he entered it on the first day of his freshman year.

At Cornell, John joined ROTC and accepted an obligation of two years of active service in the army when he graduated in 1953. He never really returned to Chappaqua after 1949, but there was that fateful meeting with Carolyn Anderson a month before he was set to graduate. As he remembers the events, she literally swept him off of his feet. He admits that he almost did not graduate that June because he was spending every evening with Carolyn and not getting his papers finished, and not preparing properly for the upcoming final examinations.

Carolyn contracted hepatitis and did not return to Ithaca for her senior year at Cornell. Instead, she finished her education and graduated from Northwestern with a bachelor's degree in education. John entered the army later in the summer of 1953.

Their relationship matured through letter-writing over those intervening two years before they eventually married in 1955. After their wedding they headed to Boston, where John had been admitted to the MBA program at the Harvard Business School, from which he graduated in 1957.

Carolyn taught for a year before becoming pregnant with the first of their three daughters. Together they further explored their life of faith, first at Memorial Church on the Harvard campus, where John recalls hearing the Rev. Dr. Arthur George Buttrick—preacher to Harvard University from 1955 to 1960—exclaim in a sermon: "I doubt, therefore, faith lives," which was a clever turn of a famous phrase of Descartes's. Later the Twinames attended services the Old South Church in Boston, where John finally realized that "Morning Has Broken" was not a Cat Stevens original but a solid Congregational hymn! It was during the early years of their marriage that they finally began to discover and live their faith together.

After graduate school their lives progressed through a number of jobs and moves, the birth of two more daughters, and an eventual move to Washington, DC, where Carolyn's former high school friend Donald Rumsfeld was then a congressman and had floated John's name for a position in the Nixon administration in the now defunct Department of Health, Education, and Welfare, whose work today is carried forward by the Department of Health and Human Services. His job was the assistant secretary's deputy in welfare, which was social services. His task was to help her reform the conglomerate that John Gardner, as the previous secretary of the department, had put together involving rehabilitation and child welfare, welfare payments, an administration on aging, the Cuban Refugee Program, mental retardation, and many other programs. It was quite a lift for John and quite an opportunity. Meanwhile, Carolyn returned to graduate school and earned a master's degree in government and public administration.

The Twinames left government service to move to New York City when John accepted a position at the American Health Foundation, which he held for three years. As he was approaching his fiftieth birthday, he discerned a call to public ministry. Accepting sponsorship from the Madison Avenue Presbyterian Church, John pursued a full-time, three-year Master of Divinity program at Union Theological Seminary before being ordained at their church by the Rev. Dr. David H.C. Read, an internationally renowned preacher, scholar, author, and ecumenist who retired from the church after serving for thirty-four years as its senior minister.

About the same time that John was ordained to the ministry of the Gospel, the Hospital Chaplaincy's board was searching for an experienced executive who might help them to revitalize an organization that was on the brink of financial disaster. When Carolyn learned of the Chaplaincy's need and this singular opportunity she offered a suggestion, which clearly was inspired: Why not propose to the board that they might consider hiring both John and Carolyn as coexecutive directors?

Wisely, the board accepted their novel proposal and the Twinames brought their vast collective experiences, personal and business connections, and faith-inspired commitment to help rejuvenate and refocus the mission of the Hospital Chaplaincy.

One of their first strategic decisions was to transform what was essentially a Protestant Christian organization into a multifaith ministry. They identified key Jewish leaders and began concerted efforts to win over Jewish academic leaders and to convince them of the opportunities to make clinical pastoral education a constitutive element of rabbinic formation.

Secondly, they turned their attention to establishing a sound financial base for the Chaplaincy though assertive fundraising, including a capital fund development effort. To this end they led by example, committing a substantial portion of Carolyn's own family's inheritance to the Chaplaincy's first capital campaign. Unabashedly, they called on some of their former Cornell and Harvard Business School classmates and Washington friends to aid in both advisory and charitable roles. Already a number of these individuals had achieved great prominence and success in several Fortune 500 companies. In a similar way, they made significant outreach to numbers of foundations and private philanthropists to support the work of the Hospital Chaplaincy. And lastly, they worked vigorously to convince local hospitals to become partners in a vision that would enhance the scope and breadth of the spiritual care services that could be provided in a professional way within their institutional settings.

Much of the vision, energy, and passion that drove these notable achievements were inspirationally captured in the document that Fr. Ed O'Flaherty had serendipitously put into my hands on the spring morning in 1991, and which I read that same evening. At the end of the document the Hospital Chaplaincy had listed, on a single page, the experiences and traits of the person they aspired to recruit to a newly created position. Although they were searching to appoint an executive vice president and chief operating officer, the board was intentionally screening for the organization's next CEO, since they fully expected that this appointment would trigger an orderly transition of executive leadership as Carolyn and John Twiname prepared for retirement. As I read through the list, I realized that I could put a checkmark next to virtually every item on that page. Fr. O'Flaherty was right: this position description did look a lot like me.

Reluctantly, I had to admit I was hooked. When I returned to the office on the following morning, I went straight to Ed O'Flaherty's office and handed him revised copies of my résumé and curriculum vitae and said that with the provincial's agreement, I would be open to becoming a possible candidate for this leadership opportunity. Fr. O'Flaherty smiled broadly and seemed pleased that he had been prescient in his initial judgment about this job. He said he would be happy to write a letter to the search firm indicating his strong support for their active consideration of my candidacy for the position.

I had almost forgotten about this interlude when, out-of-the-blue, I received a phone call in early May from the head of the firm conducting the search on behalf of the Hospital Chaplaincy. He invited me to New York City for a one-on-one interview to be hosted at the University Club in Manhattan. The meeting was cordial and energetic, but appropriately noncommittal on either side. Another two weeks elapsed before I was extended another invitation, this time to meet with a representative delegation of the board of trustees, including the current copresidents, Carolyn and John. We had an interesting and engaging three-hour conversation, and

I recall doing much of the talking during this long session. At the end of the session the headhunter escorted me to the elevators; he told me that he would chat with me soon. I bid him adieu and headed back to LaGuardia airport where I boarded a shuttle flight back to Boston.

When I arrived back at my residence in Cambridge the phone was ringing. It was Bob Longley, the headhunter, asking if I could return to New York the following day. That was not possible for me because of scheduling conflicts, but I did agree to a return visit during the following week.

The third encounter proved to be a marathon day of meetings with key staff, more trustees, and a quiet dinner with the Twinames in the Cayuga Room at the Cornell Club on East 44th Street. I remember that evening enjoying a perfectly roasted duck à l'orange. When John heard me ordering the duck, he too decided to join me in the same selection. Although our dinner conversation was intense, I could not help but to recall with the Twinames the story of my first exposure to the preparation of this very classic French dish. They were fascinated in discovering this gastronomic aspect of my interests and experiences.

Here is my version of a recipe for a succulent roasted duck breast, along with a rich brown sauce perfumed with oranges. Fortunately, today it is not too difficult to procure *magrets*, or really large duck breasts. They are almost twice the size of an ordinary duck breast; a single *magret* can easily serve two persons. So if you cannot find a *magret*, then cook an ordinary duck breast for each of your guests.

MAGRET DE CANARD À L'ORANGE

Moulade magret duck breast with orange sauce

Makes 6 servings

Ingredients

- 3 duck breasts (*magrets*)
- 2 navel oranges
- ¼ cup Grand Marnier
- salt and pepper, to taste

For the orange sauce

- 2 tablespoons granulated sugar
- ¼ cup red wine vinegar
- 1 cup freshly squeezed orange juice
- 1½ cups chicken stock

To thicken the sauce, make a slurry of 3 tablespoons of port wine with 2 tablespoons of arrowroot or cornstarch.

Method

1. Preheat oven to 350°F.
2. Prepare the oranges by first peeling with a very sharp paring knife or a sharp vegetable peeler. Try not to get the pith, which can be somewhat bitter. Once you have removed large strips of orange peel, with a very sharp knife julienne them so that you have very thin slices.
3. Blanche the julienned orange strips for about two minutes in a small saucepan with boiling water. Transfer them to a small bowl and add the quarter cup of Grand Marnier and cover with plastic wrap and allow them to absorb the flavor of the liqueur.
4. Next, section the two oranges and reserve the pieces and pulp in a bowl with a little bit of the fresh orange juice.
5. Finally, prepare the sauce by combining the sugar and red wine vinegar together in a saucepan and whisk over medium high heat until the mixture turns a deep mahogany color. Add the orange juice and chicken stock and continue whisking over medium heat until the sauce reduces in volume (this will take 6 to 8 minutes, so be patient and keep whisking). Once reduced, remove from heat and set aside to be finished later.
6. Preheat your oven to 350°F. Take your *magrets* and, with a very sharp knife, score the tops of each breast. The incisions should be deep, but only into the thick fat layer and not into the flesh of the duck breast. I make multiple diagonal cuts, first in one direction and then in the

continued

other, forming diamond shapes. Liberally season both sides of each breast with kosher salt and freshly ground black pepper.

7. In a large preheated sauté pan on high heat, add about a tablespoon of vegetable oil and immediately place the duck breasts scored-side down and sear for 3 to 5 minutes until they become golden brown and crispy. Do not move them while they are searing. When the skin is seared, turn the breasts over and continue sautéing on the reverse side, on medium heat, for another four or five minutes, before removing from heat.
8. At Le Cordon Bleu, my instructor suggested at this point to puncture the underside of the duck breast with a paring knife. He counselled that this aids the even cooking of the breast in the oven.
9. Lightly cover the surface of the sauté pan with aluminum foil and place the pan in a preheated 350°F oven for another 4 to 5 minutes, until the inside meat is pink, not red.
10. Remove from the oven and remove the duck breasts to a tray and cover them with aluminum wrap to keep warm as they rest.
11. Drain most of the fat from the sauté pan and over medium heat on the stovetop, deglaze the pan with a bit or water or chicken stock, scraping up the *fond* (the burnt, brown bits that cling to the pan). Now add the orange sauce you had previously prepared and reduced in volume and reheat it while whisking (do not bring to a boil). To finish, add the additional liquid (i.e., the juice and Grand Marnier) from the julienned orange strips and from the orange sections. Continue whisking over medium heat until the sauce reduces a bit more. If you wish, add a slurry (port and arrowroot or cornstarch) and cook the sauce until it further thickens.
12. Carve the duck breasts horizontally into nice slices, pour some sauce over the top of the meat, and place some of the orange julienne slices and orange sections on top of the meat.

By the end of this most enjoyable evening, John and Carolyn enthusiastically invited me to become the Chaplaincy's executive vice president and chief operating officer. Their verbal offer was soon followed by a written contract. With the enthusiastic support and approval of the Jesuit provincial, I accepted the position and agreed to a start date in mid-September 1991.

That decision led to a twenty-six-year ministerial engagement with the Chaplaincy, which comprised collaboration with six board chairmen and almost 250 trustees.

The first board chairman, under whose watch I was hired, was Donald J. Keller, a former grammar school classmate of Carolyn Anderson Twiname. When I was initially interviewed by the delegation of trustees prior to my appointment, Don Keller asked me a very poignant question: "Do you think that your interests, career trajectory, and the permission of the Jesuit community will allow you to stay with the Hospital Chaplaincy for at least three to five years?"

I answered affirmatively, but honestly thought at the time that I would probably not spend more than five years with the organization. In my wildest imagination, I would never have dreamed that I would go on to serve the Chaplaincy as its CEO for more than a quarter-century.

A perfect marriage was being formed, almost like the pairing of prime veal chops with a good French Calvados, the *eau de vie.*

CÔTES DE VEAU AU CALVADOS

Veal chops with apple brandy sauce

Makes 4 servings

Ingredients

- 4 veal chops (bone-in)
- salt and pepper
- 2 tablespoons flour
- 1 stick (¼ pound) unsalted butter
- 2 tablespoons Calvados (apple brandy)
- ¼ cup tomato paste

continued

- ½ cup heavy cream
- 2 egg yolks
- 1 teaspoon fresh lemon juice
- ¾ cup dry white wine

Method

1. Preheat oven to 400°F.
2. Season veal chops on both sides with salt and pepper. Let stand for 15 minutes, to allow the salt to be absorbed into the meat.
3. Then lightly coat the seasoned chops with flour, brushing off any excess.
4. Add a few tablespoons of butter to a large hot skillet. When melted, add the chops to the skillet and brown for approximately 4 minutes on the first side, and for 2 minutes on the opposite side. Add some additional butter if needed. Remove from the skillet and place the chops in a baking pan fitted with a wire rack insert. Cover loosely with aluminum foil to keep warm.
5. Over low to medium heat, add an additional tablespoon of flour to the skillet and whisk into the residual cooking butter and pan drippings. Quickly add the tomato paste and allow it to caramelize. Add the white wine and whisk all of the ingredients together to blend well. Allow the sauce to come to a boil and continue whisking for 3 minutes to burn off the alcohol in the wine and slightly reduce the volume of the sauce base. Set aside.
6. Place the partially cooked veal chops, uncovered, into the oven for 5 minutes to complete cooking.
7. Melt 6 tablespoons of butter in a small saucepan and set aside.
8. In a bain-marie (double boiler) set over hot water, beat together the room-temperature egg yolks along with the lemon juice. Whisking constantly, slowly add the melted butter a few drops at a time to form a liaison with the egg yolks. When the butter has been incorporated,

remove the pan from the water bath, add the Calvados, and stir in the heavy cream. Introduce this mixture into the reduced tomato-wine base and return briefly to the heat, blending all of the elements. Strain the finished sauce through a fine mesh sieve and keep warm for service.

9. Remove the chops from the oven. The internal temperature of the veal chops ideally should be about 140°F. Pour the sauce around the exterior of the plated chops and serve.

When I joined the organization, it was modestly headquartered in a building owned by the New York Hospital near the corner of York Avenue and East 70th Street. The New York Hospital had acquired this somewhat dilapidated low-rise tenement building in an effort to control most of the real estate surrounding the hospital and medical school. Nurses working at the hospital occupied some of the studio and one-bedroom apartments in this building. The Chaplaincy eventually controlled the ground floor apartments and a studio on the second floor for a very small monthly rent. The entire administrative staff of the Chaplaincy in 1991 consisted of a handful of full-time and part-time employees in addition to the Twinames and me. The entire payroll did not exceed twenty persons, including all of the paid chaplains.

Carolyn and John Twiname not only handed on to me the leadership of a strong and vibrant nonprofit organization with excellent clinical partnerships and committed trustees and donors, but they also gave me a reasonable business plan to follow and further develop. Over the next decade, the Chaplaincy expanded and grew in organizational complexity. One of the strategic objectives, which the Twinames had earlier identified, was the need to find and purchase an adequate permanent home for the organization.

With bold determination, I plunged head first into the arcane world of New York City commercial real estate, which soon led to the purchase of a six-story, 14,000-square-foot building on East 60th Street near the corner of Second Avenue with unobstructed views of the Roosevelt Island tram and the Manhattan entrance to the Queensboro Bridge.

To make this dream a reality would require a small team of visionaries and donors.

Fortunately, Mary French Rockefeller and Laurance Spelman Rockefeller were only too willing to step up and lead this effort.

Before beginning to speak about this extraordinary couple, allow me to share my version of a dish named for Laurance S. Rockefeller's grandfather, John D. Rockefeller. There are many stories about how this preparation of oysters became associated with the elder Mr. Rockefeller. Most believe that the recipe originated in Antoine's restaurant in New Orleans, attributed to Jules Alciatore, son of the French-born restaurant's owner, Antoine Alciatore.

No one is certain how the name Rockefeller became associated with this dish, but one story claims that a diner, having tasted one of these baked oysters, said: "These are as rich as a Rockefeller!" Others have speculated the real reason for the name is because of the green color of the topping, which symbolized the sizable wealth of the Rockefeller family. Whatever explains the origin of the recipe and the attribution of its name, here is my version of what has become a classic.

OYSTERS ROCKEFELLER

Makes 4 to 6 servings

Ingredients

- 36 fresh live oysters
- 6 tablespoons unsalted butter
- 6 tablespoons fresh baby spinach leaves, finely minced
- 3 tablespoons minced shallots
- 3 tablespoons minced Italian parsley
- 5 tablespoons fresh breadcrumbs
- 1 teaspoon sriracha sauce
- ½ teaspoon Pernod absinthe
- ½ teaspoon fleur de sel
- lemon wedges for garnish

Method

1. Using an oyster knife, shuck the oysters and remove them from their shells, reserving the oyster liquor.
2. Discard the top shell and wash and dry bottom shells.
3. In a saucepan, melt the butter; add spinach, shallots, parsley, breadcrumbs, fleur de sel, sriracha, and Pernod. Cook on medium heat, stirring continuously for 10 minutes; remove from heat. Purée the mixture with an immersion blender. Allow to cool.
4. Preheat oven broiler.
5. Line a baking pan with crumpled aluminum foil and place the oyster shells to level within the indentations in the foil. Fill each of the shells with an oyster.
6. Put a bit of the reserved and strained oyster liquor on each of the oysters. Top each oyster with a spoonful of the puréed spinach mixture and spread the topping to the rim of the shell.
7. Broil approximately 3 to 4 minutes or until the edges of the oysters begin to curl and the topping starts to bubble.
8. Garnish with some chopped parsley and lemon wedges.

Laurance Spelman Rockefeller was born in New York City on May 26, 1910, the fourth of the six children of John D. Rockefeller Jr. and Abby Aldrich Rockefeller and the grandson of John D. Rockefeller, the founder of the Standard Oil Company and reputedly one of the world's richest men. Graduating from Princeton in 1928, Laurance subsequently completed two years of graduate study at the Harvard Law School. On more than one occasion Laurance told me that the most important and probably the best decision he ever made during his life was to woo and marry Mary Billings French in the Congregational Church in Woodstock, Vermont, on August 15, 1934. Together they raised a family of three daughters and a son: Laura Spelman Rockefeller Chasin, Marion French Rockefeller, Lucy Rockefeller Waletsky, and Laurance Spelman Rockefeller Jr. At the time of Mary's death at the age of eighty-six, she and Laurance had enjoyed sixty-three wonderful years of marriage. I can say without any risk of hyperbole that they were deeply in love until she breathed her last on April 17, 1997, at the New York Hospital-Cornell Medical Center. Laurance was a thoroughly engaging gentleman. His *curriculum vitae* includes many successful business and philanthropic ventures; one cannot think about conservation in America without tipping one's hat to Laurance. For more than a half-century he served on the board of Memorial Sloan Kettering Cancer Center and unquestionably became one of the organization's most generous lifetime benefactors. He was a successful venture capitalist and developer of environmentally sensitive resorts. But among all of these successes, perhaps what is least known about him was his interest in the life of the spirit and of the integration of spirit with mind and body.

Beginning in 1935, he began working in the family offices in Rockefeller Center, focusing on three genuine loves: philanthropy, conservation, and entrepreneurial business investing and development. And there was no place on earth that Mary and Laurance enjoyed more than their ranch in the shadows of the Grand Teton National Park in Wyoming. If you wanted to get Laurance chatting, one simply had to ask him about national parks. This topic could get him waxing lyrically for hours. Among his final earthly acts was the transfer of most of the land constituting his vast ranch in Wyoming to the National Parks and earlier, upon Mary's death, the creation of the Marsh-Billings-Rockefeller National Historical Park in Vermont.

With their passionate interests in health and spirituality, Laurance and Mary Rockefeller had been early and modest supporters of the Chaplaincy from its inception. When I first met them, I sensed a personal connection that clearly went beyond what one might anticipate of the relationship between donors and the CEO of a charity. That spark ignited what became a very significant friendship and close partnership—personally, professionally, and spiritually.

Early on, I discussed with Laurance the Chaplaincy's strategic need to establish a physical identity that was independent of the New York Hospital. The building in which we had been conducting our business had been declared unsafe for housing, and the hospital had informed us that we would need to find other arrangements. Fortuitously, a building on East 60th Street came to our attention. It involved a distress sale; the owners—who sold antique fireplace surrounds—were on the verge of declaring bankruptcy. Their asking price for the land and building was $1.5 million.

I called Laurance soon after I had initially toured the property and saw its potential usefulness to meet the Chaplaincy's present and future needs. He only asked two questions: "Where is it located?" and "How much are the owners asking?"

When I quickly answered both of his queries, he immediately said: "Walter, buy it today." I was startled, but quickly recovering, I further asked him if I could come over and discuss the matter a bit more in depth. Graciously he acceded to my request and invited me to join him and Mary later that same afternoon at his Rockefeller Center offices.

At our meeting I hastily reviewed the same information that I had conveyed earlier, and he could sense both my anxiety and my enthusiasm to move forward with this real estate transaction. "As I told you this morning, I think you should just make an offer and buy it," he said.

Listening again to his counsel, I replied: "I would feel a lot more confident in that decision, Laurance, if I knew that you and Mary are behind it."

Grinning broadly, but without losing a beat, Laurance looked at me directly and said: "How much do you want?"

Swallowing deeply, I answered: "Could you and Mary consider a gift of a million dollars?"

With a twinkle in his eye and a growing smile, he looked at Mary and turned back saying, "I think we could do that, and I will help you raise the additional five hundred thousand dollars that you will need to buy the property outright."

Within six weeks, Laurance and Mary made good on their verbal pledge and introduced me to a former secretary of treasury in the Nixon administration and Wall Street financier, William Edward Simon, who committed the remaining half-million dollars needed to ensure that the Chaplaincy would have its much needed new home.

These two donations provided the momentum to launch a really ambitious capital campaign. Prior efforts, apart from the Twinames' personal gifts, had raised several hundred thousand dollars. This campaign in 1995 raised $11 million, which helped us to completely gut and rebuild the entire interior of the building and to furnish and equip the new space.

The 60th Street building afforded the Chaplaincy the luxury of designing a nondenominational chapel space to welcome the coming together of people of every faith tradition. To fulfill that dream, we would have to evolve a design that was free of art and iconography partial to a particular religion.

Fortunately, I met a New York City–born artist, Eric Karpeles, who had a large installation at an AIDS conference that I was attending at Loyola University in Chicago. When I viewed Eric's work and soon thereafter met with him, I sensed that I had found an answer to my dilemma. I asked him two brief questions during our introductory meeting in Chicago: Did he have any current commissions, and did he have the energy to undertake a project of the scope required—namely, to create a multifaith chapel whose interior wall surfaces would all be oil-on-canvas paintings? He did not have a competing obligation and was clearly enthused to consider the challenge I was describing to him. The result was a magnificent work of art in what would soon become the Mary and Laurance S. Rockefeller Chapel of Hope and Remembrance.

Once I settled on the concept, I arranged a luncheon with Mary and Laurance at the Metropolitan Club. I recall that all three of us ordered the same dish that afternoon, a very simple but delicious entrée of filet of sole meunière. In tribute to the Rockefellers and the lovely memories of that momentous meal we shared together, I offer my simple version of this classic dish.

FILET DE SOLE MEUNIÈRE

Pan-fried sole filets with brown butter, lemon, and parsley sauce

Makes 4 to 6 servings

Ingredients

- 1 cup all-purpose flour
- 1 teaspoon kosher salt
- ½ teaspoon freshly ground pepper
- 1 teaspoon mild paprika
- ¼ teaspoon cayenne pepper
- 2 pounds fresh grey sole filets
- 2 tablespoons extra-virgin olive oil
- 6 tablespoons unsalted butter
- ½ cup dry white wine
- 1 freshly squeezed lemon
- 2 tablespoons finely minced flat-leaf parsley
- lemon wedges or slices to garnish

Method

Preparing and cooking the filets

1. Whisk the flour, salt, pepper, paprika, and cayenne together in an oblong baking dish.
2. Lightly dredge the filets in the seasoned flour mixture and pat to loosen any excess.
3. Preheat a large sauté pan over a medium-high flame and then add a little olive oil, along with some butter, to the pan.
4. In batches, gently place the fish in the pan and sauté for a couple of minutes on each side.
5. Remove the fish from the pan and place on an ovenproof platter. Cover the platter loosely with aluminum foil and place in a warm 200°F oven while you cook the remaining filets.

Making the meunière sauce

1. In a clean sauté pan over medium heat, add butter and allow it to melt in the skillet. As soon as the butter begins to bubble, quickly whisk in the white wine and lemon juice. Allow the sauce to warm for about 1 minute, swirling the pan to keep the sauce together.
2. Remove the fish from the oven. Pour the sauce evenly over the sole filets, sprinkle with chopped fresh parsley, and serve immediately accompanied by lemon wedges.

As our luncheon was drawing to a close, and with a certain measure of naïveté, I raised with the Rockefellers the prospect of naming the chapel in their honor. I had not sufficiently done my homework and did not know that rarely did they agree to have things named for them. In the few instances where something was named to recognize Laurance, these dedications had been done without his prior knowledge or assent—such as the Rockefeller Research Laboratories building on East 67th Street in New York City that houses some of Memorial Sloan Kettering's programs in cell biology, developmental biology, molecular biology, and structural biology, or the Rockefeller Outpatient Pavilion (sometimes called Memorial Sloan Kettering 53rd Street) that offers outpatient radiology and chemotherapy services in a comfortable, supportive setting. Both of these namings were unsolicited initiatives on the part of the board and executive leadership of Memorial. I was present for the dedication of both buildings as a guest of the Rockefellers.

"Would you allow the Chaplaincy, in recognition of your exceptional support and friendship, to name our multifaith chapel the Mary and Laurance S. Rockefeller Chapel of Hope and Remembrance?" I asked.

Without losing a beat, Mary replied, "I think that would be lovely."

Stunned by his wife's alacrity and enthusiastic response, he lovingly said to her: "Mary, I cannot ever remember a time when you announced a decision for us without first consulting me." Then, with a look of absolute pleasure and a broadening smile, he added: "I think Mary's response is inspired and we would be greatly honored by this gesture, Walter."

Laurance and Mary became friends, confidants, and advisors—they became virtual parents to me, without expressly setting out to do so. In Laurance I found an ever-ready motivator and strategist, always ready and willing to explore an idea or offer me a new way to frame a question. He was also so confident in my abilities and judgment that he frequently called upon me to accept a personal research assignment or investigative mission.

For example, he had a passionate interest in integrative medicine, at a moment in time when both the term and concept were somewhat alien in the circles of contemporary allopathic medical practice. He was becoming more familiar with and drawn to the work of a nontraditional physician, Andrew Thomas Weil. Dr. Weil was founder, professor, and director of the Arizona Center for Integrative Medicine at the University of Arizona. Andy and I are contemporaries; he was a student at Harvard while I was enrolled as an undergraduate at Boston College. After receiving his undergraduate degree in botany, Andy continued his medical education at Harvard Medical School and graduated in 1968.

Laurance was fascinated by Andy's passion for the innovative field of integrative medicine, which seeks to bring together a number of other modalities (herbs, massage, acupuncture, meditation, and other spiritual strategies) with conventional medicine. Weil was not without his critics and Laurance wanted an objective, firsthand assessment of his nascent program in Arizona.

Laurance asked me: "Would you have the time to go out to Arizona and spend a few days meeting with Andy and his colleagues and making your own informal assessment of the costs and benefits of what he is attempting to do, both clinically and educationally?"

Of course, I took up his request and did precisely that. When I reported back in detail, he was rigorously probative and expansive in his questioning. As a result of that visit and the increased confidence he had in what Dr. Weil was attempting to accomplish, Laurance increased his philanthropic contributions to Andy's seminal program.

Subsequently, in 1999 Laurance persuaded Memorial Sloan Kettering to develop an integrative medicine service that would offer a range of wellness therapies designed to work together with traditional medical treatments. It was his hope that these comprehensive, evidence-based complementary services would help relieve the negative physical and emotional effects of a cancer diagnosis and treatment and aid a patient's recovery and quality of life. To sweeten his request, he paid to get the program up and running.

Laurance asked me to serve on the Memorial Sloan Kettering steering committee that would ultimately recommend establishing this inaugural program in integrative medicine. I was appointed to serve as a member of the search committee, which recommended appointing Barrie R. Cassileth, PhD, as the Laurance S. Rockefeller Chair in Integrative Medicine.

Barrie has been a researcher and educator in the fields of alternative and complementary (integrative) medicine and the psychosocial aspects of cancer care for more than thirty years. Her multifaceted program continues to provide inpatient therapies at Memorial Hospital and its outpatient services at the Bendheim Integrative Medicine Center. The two-pronged research effort includes studies to evaluate the ability of specific complementary therapies to reduce symptoms associated with cancer and cancer treatments, and to investigate botanicals for potential antitumor effects. I know that Laurance would be very proud of how this legacy program has grown and become an integral part of patient care and research at Memorial.

Also an astute investor, Laurance taught me much about philanthropy and investments. One time I accompanied him—along with two of his grandchildren, Jacob Peter Waletzky and Naomi French Waletzky—to the dedicatory event of a holistic health center, which had just opened in lower Manhattan. It was a small, seminal, for-profit business venture led by the entrepreneurial son of a Memorial Sloan Kettering physician who had been Laurance's friend.

At Laurance's urging, I had previously provided some consultation to this young man and his other business partners as this complementary medical practice was in the early stages of its business planning and development. During a brief moment during the reception that evening, I was sitting alone with Laurance.

"It's wonderful that you have supported and invested in the development of this new healthcare venture," I said to him.

With losing a beat, he quickly turned his head to me and sternly said: "I thought you were more astute. This is not an *investment*; it is pure *philanthropy*. This place will be closed within a year. The business model is unsustainable. I only did this because of Bill [his physician friend]. His son will learn a lot from this venture. But I would never have invested in such folly."

I quickly learned the difference between sound, strategic investing and philanthropy. He was always teaching me.

With Mary, my relationship was a pure, spiritual companionship. She had been spiritually raised at the Brick Presbyterian Church in New York City, where her parents were married in 1907. Mary's faith and devotional practices were integral components of how she lived and related to others. Laurance often remarked to me that Mary was the spiritual glue that held together their whole family.

Mary was a tireless champion and supporter of the Young Women's Christian Association. Laurance once quipped to me that "Mary has spent her lifetime trying to keep the 'C' in YWCA." Beginning in 1951, her service to this organization spanned more than a quarter-century.

She was equally strong in keeping the Christian identity of the Rockefeller family in the forefront. Laurance humorously recalled that she would not countenance inviting the family to share Thanksgiving dinner before they first gathered around the piano where she played and engaged them in singing a hymn that was first introduced in Dutch Reformed churches around the turn of the twentieth century: "We Gather Together to Ask the Lord's Blessings."

We gather together to ask the Lord's blessing;
He chastens and hastens His will to make known.
The wicked oppressing now cease from distressing.
Sing praises to His Name; He forgets not His own.

Beside us to guide us, our God with us joining,
Ordaining, maintaining His kingdom divine;
So from the beginning the fight we were winning;
Thou, Lord, were at our side, all glory be Thine!

We all do extol Thee, Thou Leader triumphant,
And pray that Thou still our Defender will be.
Let Thy congregation escape tribulation;

Thy Name be ever praised! O Lord make us free!

On two occasions I was invited to share Thanksgiving dinner with the Rockefellers, and I was happy to add my voice to theirs as Mary led them in this hymn of gratefulness and praise. This is my version of a savory bread pudding that the Rockefellers' cook traditionally prepared for those celebrations.

CASSEROLE AU PAIN SALÉ

Savory bread pudding

Makes 6 to 8 servings

Ingredients

- 1 loaf day-old brioche, cut into ½-inch cubes
- 1 medium fennel bulb, coarsely chopped
- 2 sliced leeks (white and light green parts only)
- 1 pound washed and quartered cremini mushrooms
- 4 large eggs
- 1½ cups heavy cream
- 2 cups low-sodium chicken broth
- 4 ounces shredded Gruyère cheese
- 2 tablespoons unsalted butter
- 2 tablespoons olive oil
- 1½ tablespoons chopped fresh rosemary leaves
- 2 tablespoons chopped flat-leaf parsley
- 2 tablespoons finely cut fresh chives
- kosher salt and freshly ground pepper

continued

Method

1. Preheat oven to 250°F.
2. Place cubed brioche on a rimmed baking sheet and bake until the cubes become slightly dry, about 10 minutes. Remove from oven and cool.
3. Raise oven temperature to 350°F.
4. Butter a Pyrex or ceramic baking dish (about 3 quarts).
5. In a large sauté pan over high heat, melt 1 tablespoon butter with a couple tablespoons of olive oil. Season the mushrooms and sauté until they release their liquid and begin to brown. Remove from heat and put mushrooms into a bowl.
6. Return skillet to heat, add some additional butter, and sauté fennel and rosemary until the fennel softens and begins to brown. Then add the leeks and cook until all the vegetables are soft.
7. Return mushrooms to pan, add broth, and bring to a simmer. Season to taste with salt and pepper.
8. Transfer vegetables to a large mixing bowl and let cool slightly.
9. Beat eggs, cream, and chicken broth together. Mix in shredded Gruyère cheese.
10. Add the cubed brioche bread cubes and the creamy egg and cheese custard to cooked vegetables and gently stir to combine.
11. Transfer bread and vegetable mixture to the prepared baking dish. Bake in the center of the oven until golden brown and slightly puffed, 30 to 35 minutes.
12. Garnish with freshly chopped chives and parsley.

At noon one day, Laurance called to tell me that Mary had been hospitalized and that they would both appreciate a brief visit by me. Later that afternoon I stood at Mary's bedside at the New York Hospital, with Laurance devotedly attending to her on the other side.

After a brief conversation, Laurance sensed that Mary was tiring and discreetly signaled that I might begin to take my leave. "Wouldn't it be nice if we had a moment of prayer?" he announced. I quickly interpreted this to mean that a spontaneous prayer would be an appropriate way to conclude this pastoral visit. Hearing those words, Mary slowly, but quite resolutely, withdrew her hands from beneath the bedsheets and brought them to a folded position resting on her chest. With that she began to utter—to our shared amazement—the following prayer, which I paraphrase here:

> *Gracious and loving God. Thank you for the countless ways in which you have blessed me and our whole family through so many wonderful years. Thank you for bringing me into this extraordinary family and for the innumerable ways in which I have witnessed your grace and blessings. Not only do I pray in gratitude for all of these marvelous things, but I especially pray for our children and their children, whose faith is not as strong as ours. Help them to come to a deeper and personal understanding of how loving and wide your mercy and love is. Amen.*

As I looked across the bed to catch Laurance's eyes, I could see the tears that were forming and beginning to stream slowly down his cheeks. He had been expecting me to lead a brief prayer of blessing and then to quietly depart. What happened instead was that both of us witnessed the curtain of Mary's deep spirituality and faith being pulled back, only to reveal once again the breadth and depth of her soul.

Early on the morning of April 18, 1997, Laurance called me at home to share the news that Mary had died peacefully the night before. "The family has just gathered to make plans for her burial and memorial service," he said. "We will privately commit her body to the earth this weekend in the family's cemetery in Pocantico Hills, but we will gather for a memorial service in about a month at the Brick Presbyterian Church on Park Avenue. We are all agreed that we would like you to deliver a eulogy. I would like you, Walter, to reflect upon Mary's spiritual life. Nobody had a deeper connection to that dimension of her life than did you."

I did speak at Mary French Rockefeller's memorial service, and was the only non-Rockefeller who was invited to eulogize Mary's life. The entire service was videotaped and, in the years to follow, Laurance would often comment to me how he listened many times to the eulogy I had composed and shared with the congregation: "Each time I listen to what you said I find something new and comforting. You have been such a dear friend to both of us. Thank you."

On Mary's birthday each year (May 10), it had become my custom to send her a small nosegay of French lilac and lily of the valley—two of her favorite spring blooms. I continued this practice even after her death. Laurance called me on one of those subsequent birthday mornings to thank me for the little bouquet. "I am sitting in the bedroom that Mary and I happily shared for so many years; the three of us are here together," he said.

Four days before his own death on July 11, 2004, at the age of ninety-four, Laurance called me to tell me that he had just signed a check to secure his personal participation in the annual fundraising gala that the Chaplaincy hosts each November.

"Laurance, it is only the beginning of July and the benefit isn't scheduled to take place until November," I replied.

He said, "It is important to have lead donors who will encourage the participation of others. Even though I may not be able to be there is person—since I am not getting out many nights anymore—I want to be sure that I am seen as one of your faithful supporters." As providence would have it, Laurance Rockefeller's mailed check was delivered on the morning after he died.

His devoted household staff shared with me the events of his final Sunday morning. Suffering from congestive heart failure, he had been confined to bed. He summoned his small staff of assistants, whom he and Mary considered family, to gather around his beside. Devotedly, they always referred to him as "Mr. Laurance." One of his closest collaborators told me of his touching and inspiring final words to them. After thanking them most sincerely for their care and devotion—some of them had worked for the family for more than fifty years—he quietly told them with his characteristic enthusiasm: "I want you all to know that I very much look forward to the journey that lies ahead." He died peacefully later that afternoon.

Laurance once shared with me a personal story. When he was a young man, his mother, Abby Aldrich Rockefeller, presented him with a Bible, which he treasured. In the Bible his mother had written words from the prophet Micah. I would like to conclude this recollection about the Rockefellers with the words that Mrs. Rockefeller proposed as a bellwether for her son.

What does the Lord require of you
but to do justice, and to love kindness,
and to walk humbly with your God?

—Micah 6:8

I can offer no more eloquent tribute to my friend and mentor than to gratefully remember the innumerable ways in which he joyfully fulfilled God's requirement of him.

May Laurance's and Mary's souls be reunited and at rest. Amen. Alleluia.

Chapter 8

MANHATTAN MENTORS

Educate a young person in the way he should go,
and even when he is old, he will not depart from it.

—PROVERBS 22:6

Assuming the leadership of the HealthCare Chaplaincy brought me quickly into contact with some important medical professionals who not only became mentors and colleagues, but oftentimes my friends. Dr. Jimmie Holland was the chief of psychiatry at Memorial Sloan Kettering Cancer Center. A native Texan, Jimmie was a pioneer on many different fronts throughout her long and distinguished career. Some have rightly crowned her as the queen of the hybrid subspecialty of psycho-oncology, which focuses on the natural intersections between the medical treatment of cancer patients and a proper assessment, understanding, and treatment of the psychosocial and spiritual issues that attend a cancer diagnosis. Jimmie was an instinctive researcher, always raising concerns and seeking answers to difficult questions. She was also a superb teacher who attracted many bright psychiatric residents and fellows to her distinctive program at Memorial.

Working in tandem with Jimmie Holland was Kathleen M. Foley, M.D., a neurologist by training but more importantly, the inspiration and leader behind the first program in palliative care and pain management at Memorial Sloan Kettering. Later, Kathy would hand on some of her principal responsibilities at Memorial in order to accept George Soros's invitation to create and direct a seminal research fellowship program with the ambitious goal of preparing the next generation of leaders in palliative medicine and end-of-life care. The Project on Death in America wildly exceeded its ambitious goals, and many of the trailblazers in this field were mentored through Kathy's nascent program. If Jimmie Holland is the queen of psycho-oncology, then Kathy Foley wears a parallel crown as the queen of palliative and end-of-life care.

It was so exciting meeting and working with both of these women, beginning in 1991. Our friendship and collaboration have proven to be multidimensional, spanning more than a quarter-century. And through them, I was introduced to so many other interesting worlds and people.

One day Jimmie called to invite me to a very special luncheon at the Westchester home that she shared with her physician husband Jim Holland, a distinguished Columbia University oncologist and professor. Iona College, a comprehensive residential college run by the Congregation of Christian Brothers in New Rochelle, New York, had chosen Jimmie to receive an honorary degree at their forthcoming commencement. The college's president at the time was Brother Jack Driscoll, whom I had met on several different occasions because of my long-standing work as a psychological consultant to their religious congregation. Jimmie was hosting a very small luncheon at her home after the commencement and she very much wanted me to come.

Gladly, I accepted her gracious invitation. Jimmie served a delicious room-temperature sliced tenderloin of beef, sauced with a wonderful béarnaise sauce. Here is my rendition.

RÔTI DE BOEUF SAUCE BÉARNAISE

Roasted beef tenderloin with béarnaise sauce

Makes 6 to 8 servings

Ingredients

For the roasted tenderloin

- 1 beef tenderloin, approximately 2½–3 pounds
- 3 sprigs parsley
- 2 stems basil
- 4 chives

continued

- 1 cup extra-virgin olive oil
- freshly ground black pepper

For the béarnaise sauce

- 2 sticks (½ pound) unsalted butter, cut into ½-inch cubes
- 3 tablespoons minced shallots
- fleur de sel and freshly ground black pepper
- 2 tablespoons champagne vinegar or white wine vinegar
- 3 tablespoons dry white wine
- 3 large egg yolks
- 1 tablespoon (or more) fresh lemon juice
- 1 tablespoon finely chopped fresh tarragon

Method

Preparing the beef tenderloin

1. Finely mince the parsley, basil, and chives.
2. Add the minced herbs to the olive oil, along with a pinch of salt and freshly ground pepper; mix them well and allow the herbs to infuse the olive oil for about 15 minutes.
3. Place the tenderloin in a baking dish. Pour the herb-infused oil over the meat and massage the entire surface of the tenderloin with the oil. Cover the dish and allow the roast to marinate in the refrigerator for 12 hours or overnight, before bringing it back to room temperature for roasting.
4. Pat the roast dry with paper towels and preheat oven to 450°F.
5. In a large, very hot ovenproof skillet add 2 tablespoons of vegetable oil and carefully sear the roast on all sides until browned.
6. Transfer the skillet to a 450°F oven and continue to cook for about 20 minutes, or until internal temperature of the roast reaches 125° to

130°F. Do not overcook the roast. Use a meat thermometer to check for doneness.

7. Allow the roast to rest for 10 to 15 minutes, tented with a piece of aluminum foil, before carving.

Making the béarnaise sauce

1. Melt 1 tablespoon butter in a small saucepan over medium heat.
2. Add the shallots, along with a pinch of salt and pepper.
3. Stir in vinegar and white wine, reduce heat to medium-low, and cook until vinegar and wine is evaporated, 3 to 4 minutes.
4. Reduce heat to low and continue cooking shallots, stirring frequently until tender and translucent, about 5 minutes longer. Transfer the shallot reduction to a small bowl and allow to cool completely.
5. Prepare an immersion blender.
6. Warm the largest Pyrex measuring cup you have with hot water. Pour out the water and thoroughly dry the interior of the measuring cup.
7. Melt the remaining two sticks of butter in a small saucepan over medium heat until the butter is foamy. Transfer the melted butter to a bowl.
8. Combine egg yolks, lemon juice, and 1 tablespoon water into the warm dry measuring cup.
9. With an immersion blender, purée the egg yolks until smooth and slightly thickened.
10. With the immersion blender running, slowly pour in the hot butter in a thin stream, discarding the milk solids that may have settled at bottom of the measuring cup.
11. Continue blending until a smooth, creamy sauce forms, 2 to 3 minutes. Stir in shallot reduction and freshly chopped tarragon and correct the seasoning with salt, pepper, and more lemon juice, if desired.

As it turned out, the post-commencement luncheon party on the Hollands' front porch was a very small gathering indeed. Apart from Jimmie and her husband and Brother Driscoll, there were only two other guests: me and a New York City–born-and-bred Jewish real estate mogul, Jack Rudin.

Quickly I learned that Jack's father, Sam Rudin, had been the first Jewish trustee of Iona College, and that Jack had carried on the family's tradition by serving for many years as a trustee. In fact, it was Jack Rudin who had proposed Jimmie Holland for the degree of Doctor of Humane Letters, *honoris causa*. Jack was also a trustee of Memorial Sloan Kettering, where his first wife, Billie, had died in 1983 of a cancer-related illness. In his own telling, Jimmie Holland had been Jack's salvation while he coped with his own acute mourning and grieving in the aftermath of the tragic loss of his much beloved spouse. Over many years Jack had grown very close to Brother Driscoll, whom he publicly called his "Christian brother." So I was the newcomer in this elite group of friends. What a serendipitous day this proved to be.

There are no adequate words that capture fully the person of Jack Rudin. If ever there was a New York City icon, he fit the bill completely. After the death of his parents, Sam and May, Jack became the patriarch of a family that has been developing New York real estate for five generations. Along with his younger brother, Lew, the Rudins became indefatigable promotors of working partnerships and collaborations among city and state governments, business and professional groups, and organized labor. After the City of New York's near bankruptcy in the early 1970s, the Rudin family figured prominently in the city's rebirth and revival. During the fiscal crisis, Jack and Lew successfully argued that all the other real estate families should join with them in prepaying their real estate taxes to help rebuild the city's operating capital. As major owners, builders, and operators of both commercial and residential properties, the Rudins elevated the reputation of landlords (a word that Jack loathed).

Jack Rudin was born on June 28, 1924, in the Throgs Neck section of the Bronx. His mother, May Cohen Rudin, was a remarkable woman and a major influence on Jack and his understanding of philanthropy. His father, Sam Rudin (1896–1975), was the son of a Lithuanian Jewish immigrant grocer, Louis Rudinsky. In 1905, Jack's grandfather established the family in Manhattan with the purchase of a four-story brownstone on 153 East 54th Street. Jack used to muse that his grandfather chose this particular location and building because it was very near the Manhattan house in which John D. Rockefeller Jr. was raising his family.

Jack went to a public high school in Manhattan and for one year to City College before interrupting his studies to enlist in the army in 1942. He served in Europe in the army's 89th Infantry Division, was promoted to staff sergeant, and received the Bronze Star for heroic service before his discharge in 1946.

He came as close as anyone I have ever met to being the personification of goodness, kindness, and generosity. Before the end of our lunch with the Hollands that afternoon, I already felt the bonds of friendship locking Jack and me into a firm embrace. That actually proved to be a correct perception. Over many subsequent shared times and events over the course of nearly twenty years, the friendship between us enlarged and deepened.

"You're the first Jesuit whom I have gotten to know intimately," Jack once commented. How fortunate can a guy be? Jack really understood what the word "friendship" means, even though I suspect that hundreds of people in New York would claim Jack Rudin as their friend. Truth to tell, none of them would be lying.

The corporate offices of Rudin Management are located in the impressive 345 Park Avenue building, which Jack and his brother Lewis built on a city block that is bordered to the east and west by Park and Lexington Avenues and to the north and south by East 51st and 52nd Streets. If the story is true, Jack's father had attended public school on this very site. Jack's corner office offered magnificent sight lines of the city he loved passionately.

If there was one thing that May and Sam Rudin taught their sons, it was a deep and abiding love for the city that had offered their immigrant family such opportunities and notable successes. In the box in which I keep my cuff links and collar buttons, I have dozens of shiny gold apple lapel pins. Jack was always giving me one of these iconic pins—as well as to virtually anyone he met. He took the "I Love New York" campaign to heart, and he made his passion for his hometown visible with the Big Apple pins he commissioned and so liberally distributed to friends old and new.

The Rudin Management offices were also conveniently adjacent to the Four Seasons Restaurant, a former landmark originally located in the Seagram Building at 99 East 52nd Street. For many years, Jack and Lewis used the Four Seasons Grill Room as their private club for hosting friends, business associates, politicians, and wheelers and dealers of all sorts as their lunch guests. Jack regularly occupied one corner booth and his brother Lewis the other in this "power lunch" venue.

I was a very frequent guest, often joining with others whom Jack had added to his never-ending list of friends. Lunching in the Grill Room was like a walk through a list of the Who's Who of business and political movers and shakers, as well as entertainers and celebrities. And it seemed everyone knew Jack Rudin; he essentially held court from his strategic location in the restaurant. He enjoyed introducing me to many of these luminaries. He joked that it enhanced his standing to be seen with a Jesuit priest who, as he often described me, "is in charge of making sure that every person hospitalized in New York City—regardless of their beliefs—has compassionate care and counsel when they need it most." Could one pay for better press than this?

The Four Seasons Restaurant opened in 1969 as an American cuisine eatery, with seasonally changing menus. In the 1990s the restaurant's operation became the shared responsibility of co-owners Alex von Bidder (with whom I share a common birth date) and Julian Niccolini. Alex was born in Switzerland and grew up in the small mountain village of Grindelwald, in the Swiss Bernese Alps. Through the many receptions and meals and that I enjoyed at the Four Seasons, I came to know Alex well enough to invite him to serve on the board of HealthCare Chaplaincy. With his lifelong interests in yoga, spirituality, and holistic health, he became a natural trustee. He also became a very good friend.

Alex's business partner was a flamboyant Italian, Julian Niccolini. Julian was born in Italy's Tuscany region before he emigrated to New York in 1973. In notable ways, Julian became the public face of the restaurant, warmly greeting diners and each day arranging the strategically important seating chart.

One of the signature dishes Jack Rudin urged me to try was the legendary Four Seasons crab cake, the recipe for which Alex was more than happy to share with me.

FOUR SEASONS RESTAURANT CRAB CAKES

Makes 6 servings

Ingredients

- 2 pounds jumbo lump crabmeat
- ½ pound fresh cod filet
- 1 cup heavy cream
- 1 tablespoon Dijon mustard

- 2 teaspoons sesame oil
- 2 tablespoons minced Italian parsley
- 2 tablespoons minced chives
- 2 tablespoons julienned basil leaves
- juice of a half lemon
- salt and freshly ground black pepper
- olive oil and unsalted butter for sautéing

Method

1. Pick through the crabmeat, removing all shells. Try not to break up the large lumps of crabmeat.
2. In a food processor, purée the codfish to a paste and add ½ cup of heavy cream; continue to purée until cream is fully incorporated. Add more cream if needed. The mousse-like mixture should be smooth and shiny, yet firm enough to hold its shape.
3. Place this mousse in a metal bowl and gently fold in all the other ingredients except for the olive oil and butter.
4. Preheat oven to 450°F. With your hands, form 6 crab cakes.
5. Sauté the crab cakes in hot olive oil and butter until golden on both sides.
6. Finish by baking in a 450°F oven for 4 to 5 minutes.

I remember when Jack shared with me the news that he had fallen in love again. Soon thereafter I met Susan Salesky. Susan had worked in retail and had been a close friend to Jack's first wife. From the start, it was obvious what a difference Susan was making in his life. There was an extra sparkle in his eyes. Even after many years of marriage, I was always delighted by the way Jack would affectionately refer to Susan as "my bride."

One day, early in 2005, Jack called me to say that he and Susan had been invited personally by Pope St. John Paul II to attend a symposium in Rome to commemorate the fortieth anniversary of the Second Vatican Council's *Declaration on the Relation of the Church with Non-Christian Religions—Nostra Aetate*—that had been promulgated by Pope St. Paul VI on October 28, 1965. This document was the first of its kind in Catholic history to focus on the relationship that Catholics have with Jews. Its stated purpose was to invite a reflection on what humankind shared in common as people around the world were being drawn closer together.

Pope St. John XXIII had originally conceived the document as an expression of the relationship between the Catholic Church and the Jews. Over the course of several substantial revisions, the focus of the document was broadened to address relationships with several faiths. In many ways, for the first time in Catholic history, *Nostra Aetate* normalized relations between Catholics and Jews.

Although Jewish, the Rudins for two generations had been significant benefactors to the Archbishops of New York and to the archdiocese's many charitable endeavors. So it was not surprising that their names were included on the Holy See's guest list for this milestone anniversary event in Rome.

"I called the Vatican this morning to say that Susan and I would be delighted to accept the invitation on the condition that the Holy See would also extend an invitation to you," Jack told me. "Of course, they were happy to do this. Susan and I hope you will be our guests and join us for this special trip to Rome."

Gladly did I accept to share this historic moment. It was a glorious event. We stayed at the famous Hassler Hotel, located atop the Spanish Steps immediately adjacent to the church Trinità dei Monti. When we arrived at the hotel's reception desk, we were received as if we were old friends. Obviously, this was not the first time the Rudins had visited the Hassler.

At the Vatican's convocation we were seated in the second row, immediately behind some dozen cardinals. I introduced Susan and Jack to several of these cardinals I knew personally, including Bernard Law of Boston and William Keeler of Baltimore. Jack hit it off immediately with Cardinal Keeler, who had played a prominent role in advancing Jewish–Christian relations. After the meeting, which took place on a Thursday afternoon, Jack decided he wanted to host a *Shabbat* dinner the following evening. With some scurrying, we were able to secure a private dining room in a hotel on the Via della Conciliazione, steps away from Saint Peter's Square. Once arranged, there was the added challenge to invite people to join this impromptu dinner party. "Call Cardinal Keeler and invite him to join us," Jack requested.

I assumed that the cardinal would probably already have other plans, but I nonetheless found out where he was staying and called him. To my utter surprise and delight he was thrilled to receive the invitation, and without hesitation, he accepted to join us for the Sabbath dinner. When I told Susan and Jack that Cardinal Keeler would be joining us, along with some twenty other guests we were able quickly to assemble, Jack was beside himself with joy.

"You really do know your way around the City," Jack quipped. "You have cardinals at your beck and call." Even though this was far from the truth, I did not try to alter Jack's perception that I was a wonder worker.

The dinner proved to be great success. We had several priests and bishops in attendance, along with both Cardinal Bill Keeler and Cardinal Walter Kasper, who at the time was heading up the congregation that oversaw relations between the Church and non-Christian religions. As the toasts and impromptu speeches flowed throughout the evening, Jack beamed with pleasure. He was in his element as the consummate host.

Because it was Shabbat, we tried to include dishes on the hastily arranged menu that would be appropriate. Although the Rudins did not observe Jewish dietary laws, we nonetheless wanted to be sensitive.

Because we were in Rome, one item on the evening's menu was *Carciofi alla Giudia,* Jewish-style artichokes. This dish is very popular in restaurants in the neighboring Roman Jewish ghetto, just on the other side of the Tiber River from the Vatican. I've made this simple artichoke dish dozens of times through the years, and it is always delicious, and because of this association with Jack's Shabbat dinner, it is also memorable.

CARCIOFI ALLA GIUDIA

Jewish-style deep-fried artichokes

Makes 6 servings

Ingredients

- 12 small-to-medium-sized fresh artichokes
- 2 lemons
- peanut or canola oil for deep frying

continued

- 1 cup chopped Italian parsley
- ½ cup fresh basil leaves
- 2 teaspoons sea salt or to taste
- ½ teaspoon freshly ground pepper
- 10 cloves minced garlic
- all-purpose flour or matzo meal for dredging

Method

1. Trim the tops off the artichokes, working around the artichoke to retain their shape.
2. Place the trimmed artichokes in a bath of acidulated water (cold water with the juice of the two lemons). Soak the artichokes in the lemon water until ready to use, then pat dry with paper towels.
3. Hold the artichokes by the stems and gently tap against the countertop to loosen and open up the leaves.
4. Combine ½ cup of the olive oil with the parsley, basil, salt, pepper, and minced garlic and sprinkle the mixture between the leaves. Roll each artichoke in flour or matzo meal.
5. Heat a large pot, wok, or Dutch oven that has been filled with about 3 inches of peanut or canola oil. Deep fry two to three artichokes at a time for about 10 minutes, turning occasionally with long metal tongs. The artichokes will expand and puff up as they fry.
6. Serve hot, sprinkled with some sea salt.

Soon after I had met Jack Rudin he presented me with a little gift, which he said would be vitally important to the success of my work in New York City. It was a paperback copy of a collection of Yiddish expressions by David Rosten.

"Study this book, Walter," he insisted, "and you will find your way into the minds and hearts of the Jews of this city." I did just as he said, methodically learning one expression after another. Before long some of these phrases would naturally flow off my tongue, to the utter amazement of many Jewish associates and benefactors.

On one occasion, I was involved in a business negotiation with a Jewish real estate professional that became stalled and was seemingly going nowhere. I stopped, looked him directly in the eye and said: "OK, let's talk *tachlis*." This Yiddish word means getting to the main point, to the practical details, to the bottom line.

My business associate's eyes dilated for a moment. Then he grinned broadly and said, "Father, where did you learn that expression? I can see you are sharper than I had thought. OK, I will get to the point, as you suggest."

When I later told Jack of this encounter, he laughed heartily as he approvingly patted me on the back. "You're becoming a real New Yorker, Walter!"

Around Saint Patrick's Day each year Jack and Susan hosted a luncheon for their Irish friends at the Four Seasons. This annual event gathered about a hundred or more people together for a festive meal of smoked salmon, grilled Dover sole meunière, and Irish coffee. The Rudins were often the only non-Christians and non-Irish in the room. They always invited a pianist to play Irish melodies throughout the luncheon, and things got underway with the singing of the Irish national anthem in Gaelic along with a rendition of "The Star-Spangled Banner." Occasionally Jack engaged a piper, attired in an Irish kilt, to lead his guests from the preluncheon reception to the room in which the meal was to be served. The guest list often included the mayor and governor, the police and fire commissioners, and other notables who shared the commonality of Irish ancestry. Not infrequently, the Archbishop of New York was in attendance along with a good representation of priests, brothers, and nuns. For many years I was included on this select guest list and always looked forward to this annual celebration.

I recall on one occasion where traditional crème brûlée was made with Bailey's Irish cream. Here is my version of that recipe.

AN IRISH CRÈME BRÛLÉE

Makes 6 servings

Ingredients

- 2 cups heavy cream
- ¼ cup Bailey's Irish Cream liqueur
- 3 large eggs

continued

- 2 large egg yolks
- 1 cup superfine granulated sugar
- 1 teaspoon vanilla extract

Method

1. Preheat oven to 325°F.
2. In a saucepan, heat the cream and liqueur just until bubbles begin to form around sides of pan; remove from heat.
3. In a large bowl, whisk eggs, egg yolks, and ¾ cup of superfine granulated sugar until blended but not foamy. Slowly stir in hot cream mixture. Add the vanilla.
4. Place six 6-ounce broiler-safe ramekins in a baking pan large enough to hold them without touching. Pour the custard mixture into ramekins. Place pan on oven rack; add very hot water to pan, about halfway up the sides of the ramekins.
5. Bake 20 to 25 minutes or until a knife inserted in the center comes out clean; the centers will still be soft.
6. Immediately remove ramekins from water bath to a wire rack and cool 10 minutes. Refrigerate until cold.
7. To caramelize, sprinkle the baked custards evenly with remaining superfine sugar. Hold a kitchen torch flame a couple of inches above the custard surface and rotate it slowly until sugar is evenly melted and caramelized.
8. If you do not have a kitchen torch, you can caramelize the topping under the broiler in an oven by placing cooled ramekins on a baking sheet. Preheat broiler. Sprinkle custards evenly with remaining sugar. Broil 3 to 4 inches from heat 5 to 7 minutes or until sugar is caramelized.

When Jack's mother, May, died in June 1992, her funeral was held at Central Synagogue on Lexington Avenue. For the most part it was a traditional Jewish service, with customary prayers and eulogies. However, in tribute to the Irish legacy of the city the Rudins loved, the family had requested that the famous Irish ballad "Danny Boy" be sung at the conclusion of May Rudin's memorial service. I suspect this is the first and only time that a Celtic melody has ever been heard within that historic synagogue's walls.

Jack's father had begun a lovely tradition of occasionally sharing breakfast with the Archbishop of New York at the archbishop's residence. Beginning with Cardinal Terence Cooke, who served as New York's archbishop from 1968 to 1983, Jack continued that same tradition with Cardinal Cooke's successors, including Cardinal John O'Connor, Cardinal Edward Egan, and Cardinal Timothy Dolan. On the prearranged mornings Jack would show up at the cardinal's residence on Madison Avenue with a bag of warm bagels and sit down with the Archbishop of New York for a frank discussion of issues facing the city or nation.

I recall two interesting stories that Jack shared with me from these breakfast collations. The first involved Cardinal Egan, who was an accomplished classical pianist. Jack had been chatting with the cardinal about his musical interests and abilities. "They tell me that you're a pretty good piano player, your Eminence, but I don't see a piano here in your residence."

The cardinal politely replied that he had a concert grand piano on the second floor that he used for his practice.

"You need one down here on the first floor so that when you have guests you can play a tune or two for them. It will help to break the ice," Jack told him.

The cardinal did not know how to reply. "Look," said Jack, "why don't you get over to Steinway Hall on 57th Street and pick yourself out a new piano and send me the bill."

During lunch with me that same day, Jack asked me, "Do you think he will take me up on my offer, Walter?"

"I don't think so, Jack," I said. Jack was amazed, since he thought it was a great idea and might help the cardinal to become a bit more relaxed when people came to visit him at home. I tried to tell Jack that the cardinal was not a "piano player" per se but actually a classically trained pianist who was not given to public performance. Jack shook his head; the distinction was lost on him. "If I made you the same offer, you would be over to Steinway Hall this afternoon," he said. He had that right.

On another occasion, he was visibly upset by the early reports of clergy sexual abuse that were coming from the Archdiocese of Boston. He was quite disturbed by the ways in which the Archbishop of Boston, Cardinal Bernard Law, was publicly responding to these allegations.

"You're a friend of Cardinal Law," he said to me. "Call him this afternoon and tell him that Jack Rudin wants to pay for the continuing services of Howard Rubenstein [the renowned New York City publicist] to go up to Boston and advise the cardinal how best to handle this crisis."

I replied how thoughtful and generous an offer this was, but that I judged that the cardinal would not be open to such assistance, and even if he were willing to accept the gift of the counsel he would most likely not follow Howard Rubenstein's advice. Jack was not happy with this feedback, but he trusted my assessment. Later history would prove the case. Because of the negative fallout from his handling of these issues, soon thereafter Cardinal Law would be forced to resign his administration of the archdiocese in December 2002 and retreat to the safety of Vatican City, where he lived out the remainder of his life until his death in 2017.

Jack had previously met Cardinal Law on two separate occasions. On the eve of the beatification of Blessed Edmund Ignatius Rice, founder of the Irish Christian Brothers, Jack, along with a few other illustrious benefactors, was given a prestigious medal of recognition during a banquet at the Waldorf Astoria. I was an invited guest at Jack's table that evening in 1996, and Cardinal Law was seated at an adjoining table. During the course of dinner, Jack leaned over and whispered that he would very much like to meet Cardinal Law.

During a natural break in the dinner, I discreetly excused myself and went over to speak with the cardinal. "I am sitting with Jack Rudin, one of this evening's honorees, who has indicated that he would like to meet you. He has been a very good friend to the archbishops of New York and a very generous benefactor to many Catholic charities in the city. If I bring him over, you will need to give him your undivided attention. Are you willing to do this?" The cardinal seemed stunned by my bluntness and candor, but quickly recovered and said he would gladly meet Mr. Rudin. I brought Jack over and made the introduction, and the cardinal was good to his word, allowing Jack to regale him with stories and jokes. When Jack returned to the table he tersely commented: "A little self-important, but he seems like a pretty good guy."

Jack Rudin and Cardinal Law would subsequently find themselves as dinner companions in 2000 on the dais at another Waldorf Astoria event—the eightieth birthday dinner that Jack and others hosted for the then-ailing Cardinal John O'Connor. From my place in the ballroom, it appeared that Jack and Cardinal Law were getting along quite well during an animated dinner conversation. Later, Jack would give me a brief synopsis of their discussion.

"Your ears must have been burning, since I spent a good amount of time speaking with Cardinal Law about you and your great work in New York," he said.

I was somewhat amused, because although we were acquaintances, I did not consider Cardinal Law to be a close friend. But according to Jack's narrative, the cardinal had spoken about me as if he had known me intimately. "Walter," he had pompously said to Jack, "is the Archdiocese of Boston's gift to New York City." Jack told me that he whacked the cardinal on the back when he said this and replied: "Well, you certainly have gotten that right. Walter Smith is pure gold."

Jack Rudin was the purest of gold.

> *The souls of the just are in the hand of God and no torment shall touch them. They seemed, in the view of the foolish, to be dead; and their dying was thought an affliction and their going forth from us, utter destruction. But they are in peace. For if in the eyes of men, indeed they be punished, yet is their hope full of immortality; Chastised a little, they shall be greatly blessed, because God tried them, and found them worthy of himself. As gold in the furnace, he proved them, and as sacrificial offerings he took them to himself. Those who trust in him shall understand truth, and the faithful shall abide with him in love: Because grace and mercy are with his holy ones, and his care is with his elect.*
>
> —*Wisdom 3:1–6, 9*

Chapter 9

EXPECT THE UNEXPECTED

Even though I walk through the valley of the shadow of death, I will fear no evil, for you are with me; your rod and your staff, they comfort me.

—PSALM 23:4

It was just another midsummer evening at JFK International Airport in New York. TWA Flight 800 had just taken off for Paris, with 230 people from thirteen countries on board. Minutes later, around 8:30 p.m., the plane unexpectedly exploded, eight miles off the coast of East Moriches, Long Island. No one survived.

It was July 17, 1996. Like many others, I sat by the television that evening and early the next morning, trying to understand what happened, as theories of terrorism multiplied arithmetically. People were emotionally linking this tragedy to another event just before Christmas in 1988 when Pan Am Flight 103 disintegrated over Lockerbie, Scotland, killing all 270 people on board and for which a Libyan national, Abdel Baset Ali Mohamed al Megrah, was arrested and in 1992 convicted of mass murder.

The years prior to the TWA 800 tragedy had been punctuated by several horrendous terrorist acts, including the explosion in the World Trade Center's garage (1993), the bombing of the Alfred P. Murrah Federal Building in Oklahoma City (1995), and the bombing in Atlanta's Centennial Olympic Park (1996).

After exhausting investigations, we learned from the National Transportation Safety Board that the probable cause of the TWA 800 accident was a spark in its center fuel tank that eventually led to the explosion and brought down the aircraft.

What most captured my attention at that time, however, was how inadequately skilled were the local clergy of Long Island who responded to the surviving family members of the doomed passengers. There were many news interviews with these bereft relatives and with the members of clergy who were volunteering their time to try to be of comfort to them.

As the leader of a major chaplaincy care organization, I seriously questioned how prepared our own professional chaplains were to intervene in a large-scale crisis involving catastrophic loss of life. It is one thing to have trained clinical skills; it is wholly another thing in the face of a large municipal or national crisis to be able to apply them effectively.

Since ours was not only a clinical chaplaincy program, but also an education and research endeavor, I challenged our staff to discern how we might best train and equip our colleagues and students for this kind of large-scale crisis. With the ready support of the American Red Cross, all of our chaplains completed a specialized training program in disaster intervention. The HealthCare Chaplaincy also became an integral partner with the emergency and disaster management team of the City of New York. Our chaplains participated in staged drills alongside the police, firefighters, emergency medical professionals, and the city's crisis management leaders.

By the fall of 1998, every chaplain in our organization had been certified by the American Red Cross. Now we were prepared if a major disaster were to occur in New York City.

Three years later the unimaginable happened—not a high-rise fire in an apartment building or a derailed Amtrak train approaching Penn Station, but an air assault on the Twin Towers of the World Trade Center. Both towers collapsed within hours of the attacks.

I was settled into my offices on East 60th Street early on Tuesday morning on September 11, 2001. The night before we had hosted a dinner party to welcome new trustees who had joined our board. One of the participants, Don Christian, had celebrated his birthday on the balmy evening the night before. The following morning, as I was sitting at my computer writing email notes of appreciation to the trustee attendees, my executive assistant poked her head in and said: "Tune in to MSNBC on your computer; a plane just crashed into the World Trade Center."

I soon learned that it was not a small recreational plane that had made a navigational error, but an American Airlines Boeing 767 loaded with 20,000 gallons of jet fuel, that had careened into the North Tower of the World Trade Center. How could this have happened? It was a brilliant, clear, crisp morning. By the time I tuned in, every TV station was showing the gaping, burning hole near the 80th floor of the 110-story skyscraper that became an iconic image of that day.

Eighteen minutes later, while glued to the TV in the conference room next to my office, the cameras picked up a second Boeing 767—United Airlines Flight 175—heading down the Hudson River and sharply turning toward the World Trade Center. It barreled into the South Tower near its 60th floor. My heart almost stopped in horror.

I arose from the chair in which I had been sitting and asked my assistant to assemble our senior leadership team immediately, and I quickly reached out by telephone to the directors of pastoral care at our trauma hospitals in the city. We had been plunged into a crisis beyond what we could have ever imagined. America was under attack. New York City was in desperate need of care and support.

I knew our chaplains were well trained. Quickly, we marshalled forces to coordinate an effective response. The impact of the crashes caused massive explosions that poured down burning debris over the surrounding buildings and the streets below.

I received a call from the Reverend George Handzo, who at the time was directing our clinical service staff. He had been in lower Manhattan in the shadow of the Twin Towers for an early morning meeting on William Street at NYU Downtown Hospital.

He reassured me he was fine, and since all transportation systems in lower Manhattan were not functioning, he was making his way uptown on foot. He communicated that he was reaching out to all of our key clinical staff and would be back in touch once he had a better overall sense of what was happening.

Both NYU and the Weill-Cornell Medical Center had already set up their emergency triage centers in the expectation they would be receiving numerous people with burns and orthopedic injuries. With the collapse of the South Tower at 9:59 a.m. and the North Tower at 10:28 a.m., it became apparent that there would not be many survivors to treat. A third building in the World Trade Center complex—7 World Trade Center—collapsed at 5:21 p.m. as a result of fires generated by the collapse of the North Tower. Rather than treating survivors, we faced the grim prospect of 2,763 dead, including 71 police and security professionals and 343 NYC firefighters. Included in these numbers were the 147 passengers and 10 hijackers aboard the two airliners that had crashed into the Twin Towers.

At the time, the Office of the Chief Medical Examiner and the city's morgue were located together on First Avenue at East 32nd Street. They were situated between the main hospital building of the NYU Langone Medical Center and Bellevue Hospital. Bellevue, founded in 1736, is the oldest public hospital in the nation. It is the flagship institution of New York's public hospital system—the Health and Hospitals Corporation. It had developed an international reputation for its programs and training in emergency medicine.

The Office of the Chief Medical Examiner was responsible for handling the remains of the victims recovered from the World Trade Center disaster site. Throughout the day of the attack, bodies and body parts were being brought to the morgue. Before it would conclude its work some years later, the Office of the Chief Medical Examiner had collected nearly 20,000 body parts and about 290 intact bodies. The coroner's team identified more than 1,100 victims and issued death certificates without a body for another 1,600 victims.

There is a Latin inscription in the lobby of the city's morgue, which I first noticed when I entered that building on the afternoon of September 11, 2001: *"Taceant colloquia; effugiat risus; hic locus est ubi mors gaudet succurrere vitae."* Roughly translated, it says: "Let your conversations cease; let your laughter dissipate. This is a place where death delights in assisting the living." The original intent of this inscription was to underscore what can be learned from postmortem examinations, and how—in a broader sense—the dead can help the living by deepening medicine's understanding of diseases and pathogens.

But on that eventful night, I understood the inscription a bit differently. The massive loss of life we had just experienced that day was placing expectations and demands on this morgue and its staff beyond their physical and emotional capacity. The entire city had become a massive morgue where all conversations were muted. No laughter was heard. The survivors of the innocent victims of these terroristic acts were crying out to the dead for answers: "Where are you?" "Are you OK?"

Around 11 p.m. that night, exhausted from a day that was seemingly endless, I walked the few blocks back from the morgue to my apartment on First Avenue at East 22nd Street. From the south-facing window of my bedroom I used to be able to view the Twin Towers with their twinkling lights. That night, all I could see were smoldering towers of smoke dissipating into the night sky. I stood there silently, and for the first time that day, wept. *"Taceant colloquia; effugiat risus."*

It was at that moment I realized I had not eaten anything all day. Adrenalin must have kept me going. What could I prepare at this hour of the day that would be nourishing, light enough to eat immediately before going to bed? Most importantly, the preparations could not take much human effort. If I had a fuel gauge in my body, the needle would have been pointing to "empty." Quickly, the thought came to me: Why not make an omelette?

I had made literally dozens of *omelettes aux fines herbes* for the Jesuits at Rue de Grenelle when I was training at Le Cordon Bleu. It is about as simple as it gets, but my teacher insisted on a couple of things to ensure the success of this preparation:

make sure the pan is preheated (over medium heat, not too high); blend and bring to heat a small amount of butter with a little bit of vegetable or olive oil, but don't let the mixture burn; have the eggs at room temperature and beat vigorously; work quickly once the eggs hit the hot pan and fat; be attentive and patient and serve immediately when finished.

OMELETTE AUX FINES HERBES

Omelette with finely chopped herbs

Makes 1 to 2 servings

Ingredients

- 3 large room-temperature eggs
- a pinch kosher salt
- a few grinds of black pepper
- 1 teaspoon chopped herbs (parsley, tarragon, chives, chervil, or whatever you might have and like)
- 1 tablespoon olive or vegetable oil
- 1 tablespoon unsalted butter

Method

1. Using a fork or small whisk, beat the eggs, salt, and pepper in a non-reactive bowl until thoroughly mixed. Stir in the herbs.
2. Add the butter and the oil to a hot skillet over medium heat.
3. When the oil and butter melts and blends with the oil, swirl it around the pan, and add the egg mixture.
4. Stir continuously with a fork while shaking the pan for a couple of minutes to draw together very small curds of the eggs. Allow the runny egg liquid to stream back to the edges.
5. With your fork, gently loosen the forming omelette around the perimeter of the pan and allow it to cook undisturbed for 20 to 30 seconds

as the bottom surface forms a thin skin. Try not to let it brown too much. Loosen the bottom.

6. When most of the egg appears cooked, roll the omelette by folding over one side and then the opposite side, and with a quick twist of the wrist, confidently invert it onto a plate.
7. Garnish with some pieces of chives or a bit of freshly minced herbs or finely chopped tomato.

The next day, September 12, working in consort with the city's Disaster and Management team and the Red Cross, a reception and registration center was set up at 492 First Avenue in a building that houses the child reception center of the Administration for Children's Services (ACS), an agency that strives to protect, support, and promote the safety and well-being of the children, youth, and families of New York City. On that warm, early autumn day, the ACS lobby served as a place where hundreds of families had come in frantic search of news about their missing loved ones. It was the beginning of the proliferation of flyers with pictures of loved ones that were posted virtually everywhere in New York City.

Our HealthCare Chaplaincy administrative personnel staffed a desk in the registration area at ACS to receive these families; our chaplains and chaplaincy students were on hand to offer direct pastoral support and care. The waiting lines of distressed family members snaked out the door of the building and down and around the adjoining street. On several occasions that afternoon, police and fire vehicles sped along First Avenue carrying more bodies and remains to the morgue, which was located one block away from ACS. A painful, disturbing visual was the slow parade of three refrigeration trailers that moved in a convoy formation along First Avenue to augment the morgue's capacity to receive bodies and body fragments at an ancillary mortuary that was being established in the morgue's parking lot. Those refrigeration vans would remain in place for several months, from winter into spring.

To better care for these anxious family members and friends, our chaplains positioned themselves along the serpentine waiting line. They engaged people in casual conversation, responded to questions that had no answers, and made notes of specific needs and requests. One of our chaplains, Imam Yusuf Hasan—the first Muslim chaplain to be trained by HealthCare Chaplaincy who was certified as a professional chaplain and was a member of our clinical staff at Memorial Sloan Kettering Cancer Center—was prominently visible among the phalanx of our chaplains. I noticed that Yusuf was building a growing list of names in his small black notebook. When I inquired, he told me that this was his prayer list; he was telling families that he would bring their loved ones' names with him to his *masjid* (mosque) and pray by name for each person on his list. This single incident sealed for me not only the importance of a multifaith collaborative ministry, but also the fact that it could be practically achieved.

From those September days, death was continuously in the air. Over the next several weeks I would spend many evening hours after the workday was completed dropping into firehouses in central and lower Manhattan—places that had lost several of their comrades. Having grown up in a two-generation family of firefighters, I knew firsthand the fraternity that is emblematic of fire departments. Firefighters are a tight-knit group. They spend many waking and sleeping hours together and their work continually puts them in critical situations. I have lost count now of the number of funeral masses or memorial services for lost firefighters that I either presided, preached, or attended. I think it was somewhere around eighteen to twenty. Suffice it to say, there was a lot of mourning and grieving going on. The city that claims that it never sleeps appeared more somber and restrained than its normal fever-pitch tempo. People were becoming far more solicitous of each other.

In November, I attended an annual award celebration of the New York City Firefighter's Burn Center Foundation. For years, firefighters and their families had been raising money to support projects at the burn center at New York Presbyterian-Weill Cornell Medical Center. That year, in 2001, they had voted to make a grant to support the position of a full-time chaplain at the burn center. The chaplain whom we had recruited to fill this position was an African-American clergywoman. She happened to have been in the North Tower on September 11 for a training program, which was held on one of the lower floors. Miraculously, she was able to escape from the building. She walked back to the hospital—a few miles' distance—in her stocking feet. She had lost her shoes in the frenetic escape from the tower before the second plane made its approach. She was determined to be of help to others.

When I approached the foundation's president that evening to accept the check, he took the occasion to note what the Chaplaincy and I had been doing personally for firefighters and their families since the terrorist attack. He further told the audience about my grandfather's and father's service to the Boston Fire Department. The room exploded in sustained and deafening applause. Unexpectedly, tears began to stream from my eyes. Many eyes in the room were teary that evening. We all realized that for most of us, this was the first time we were laughing and socializing in months. This was a cathartic moment that we desperately needed.

Even in the midst of a tragedy of such enormous proportions, life finds a way to go on.

• • • • • • • • • • • • • • • • • •

"Honey, I need your help with this one." That was the way wedding cake impresario Sylvia Weinstock began one of the thousands of conversations that have dotted our friendship of some forty years. After raising three daughters in a Long Island suburb and successfully battling a diagnosis of breast cancer, Sylvia, along with her husband, Ben, sold their home and purchased a burnt-out shell of a building on Church Street in Manhattan's TriBeCa district. Ben skillfully oversaw the building's rehabilitation and transformation into a new business venture: Sylvia Weinstock Cakes, Ltd. Her iconic brand quickly became synonymous with the quintessential, artistic design of special occasion cakes. A roster of her clients and admirers reads like a Who's Who of the titans of Wall Street, Silicon Valley, and Hollywood—the movers and shakers of the business and entertainment industries, ambassadors and sheiks, as well as hordes of ordinary brides who dreamed of having a Sylvia Weinstock cake as the centerpiece of their nuptial celebrations.

"For what could you possibly need me, Sylvia?" I asked.

"I had a conversation in the office this morning with a lovely woman who is getting married at the beginning of December and she needs a priest to officiate at her wedding," she told me.

"Sylvia, you know I am not a 'gun-for-hire'-type priest."

"I know, Sweetie, but this is a wonderful person who needs to meet you. She is a Catholic and she is marrying a Protestant guy who had been previously married. Would you agree to at least meet her and guide her in the right direction?"

"I thought you only sold cakes. But I see that you are becoming a full-service provider," I joked with her. "Of course, I will meet her and see what I might be able to do for her."

That was my introduction to Kim Adrienne White. It was no exaggeration when Sylvia described Kim as a special person. One of the first of a generation of Wall Street women to break the proverbial glass ceiling, Kim had been a successful finance professional for twenty-five years. She worked as a partner at Moore Capital

Management, an investment management firm in Manhattan, and had become engaged to an equally wonderful guy, Kurt John Wolfgruber. Kurt had begun his distinguished career at JPMorgan Investment Management in various research, portfolio management, and management leadership roles. Later, he served as president and chief investment officer of OppenheimerFunds. Their wedding had been scheduled for December 8, 2001, at the Harmonie Club in New York, a mere four months from the moment in which Sylvia made the *Shidduch* (a Yiddish expression for "matchmaking") between Kim and me.

Coincidentally, I would later get to know Kurt much more intimately. After his marriage to Kim he was recruited by his alma mater, Ithaca College, to serve on their governing board, on which I also served as a trustee.

One cannot be in a New York City restaurant with Kim and not be interrupted several times by other friends and colleagues who are anxious to greet her or briefly pursue some business issue. Kim is as beautiful a person on the inside as she is physically lovely. Truth to tell, I fell in love with her at our first meeting. We met in the late summer of 2001 to discuss the interfaith ceremony that would take place in early December. I had been successful in inviting the Rev. Dr. Sarah Fogg, one of our hospital chaplain directors at HealthCare Chaplaincy, to co-officiate with me and to be the clergyperson-of-record for the signing of the marriage license.

Soon after our early meetings, the ominous events of September 11, 2001, happened, which, as described earlier, cast a pall over every aspect of New York City: its people, its institutions, and its spirit. No person in the city, it seemed, was spared some personal share in this human tragedy. Kim and Kurt were devastated by the loss of many close friends and colleagues.

Sometime in October, Kim and I spoke. "Do you think we should postpone the wedding?" she asked.

Without hesitation, I replied with a piece of wisdom I had learned from my Irish grandmother, Rose O'Brien: "Never change a happy event because of a sad one." Further, I told Kim that selfishly, I needed to celebrate the joyous occasion of their wedding: "For the past several weeks, everywhere I turn is filled with grief and mourning. I need to smile and be happy again, if only for a night." Whatever I said or the affect she heard in my voice was determinative: their wedding would go on as planned, and we would all try to smile again.

December 8 was a very cold early winter night in Manhattan, a city awash in the lights of the approaching holiday season. Kim meant what she had boldly declared: "I am forty-five years old and I have been waiting for this day for a long time. I am going to go all out on this wedding!" A good friend, the internationally acclaimed floral designer Preston Bailey, transformed the Harmonie Club room in which the ceremony was to take place into a winter wonderland. The center aisle looked like a magical forest of glimmering bare white tree boughs and branches that formed a continuous arch for as far as the eye could see. From these white-flocked limbs hung hundreds of tea light votive candles in gleaming crystal containers. The platform on which the ceremony would take place was framed by massive, exquisite white floral arrangements of orchids and roses, set off by soft mood lighting that bathed the entire room and subtly accentuated the gold leaf of the room's ornamental architectural details.

After a sensitive and personal interfaith ceremony, the wedding party and guests moved to the main ballroom of the club, which was decorated very differently. The room was awash in a riot of fall colors: gold, amber, yellow, orange, maroon, and purple. I told Kim that she must have killed off the entire flower population of a South American nation to procure all of the floral materials needed to adorn that festive room on their wedding night. And there in the midst of it all was a six-foot tiered wedding cake, laden with hundreds of similarly colored edible flowers, handcrafted from a gum sugar product and tinted to its proper shade. The flowers were artistically arranged in continuous cascades down the wedding cake—a true Sylvia Weinstock chef d'oeuvre.

I maintained a close personal friendship with Kim and Kurt. I recall one of the early occasions when I invited them to a dinner party at my apartment. Even though Kim rarely had time to focus on cooking, she nonetheless had an interest and passion about food. She and Kurt regularly dined in some of the countless emporiums of haute cuisine in New York City. That night I served a three-course dinner. Kim was ecstatic. She could not believe what came out of my home kitchen that evening.

"Honestly, I have not eaten a better dinner at Daniel's than what you served us tonight.[7] And the homemade Grand Marnier chocolate truffles are better than anything I have ever purchased from La Maison du Chocolat!"

Honestly, the truffles are really embarrassingly simple to make. Here is my recipe for the truffles, which Kim White professes are "to live for."

---

7 Daniel is a three-star Michelin-rated French restaurant in New York City, although sadly chef Daniel Boulud lost one of his stars in the 2015 ratings.

CHOCOLATE GRAND MARNIER TRUFFLES

Makes 18 truffles

Ingredients

- 12 ounces good bittersweet chocolate (with at least 60 percent cacao)
- ⅔ cup heavy cream
- 1 ounce Grand Marnier
- 1½ cups Callebaut or Valrhona cocoa powder for dusting

Method

1. Finely chop the bittersweet chocolate bars and put the chocolate pieces in a stainless steel bowl.
2. Bring the heavy cream to the boiling point in the smallest saucepan you have (to avoid as much evaporation of the liquid as possible), and do not let the cream scorch.
3. One of my pastry teachers at Le Cordon Bleu suggested boiling the cream twice or three times. He believed that the double or triple boiling deepens the *ganache* and extends its life. I would suggest you try it, but perhaps begin with more cream (¾ cup–1 cup) because the extra boiling will reduce its volume.
4. Pour the cream over the chocolate, allow the chocolate to begin to melt, and then gently stir with a whisk in concentric circles (don't beat or you'll add air to the ganache) beginning in the center of the bowl and working your way to the edge, until the *ganache* is smooth.
5. Let the ganache rest at room temperature for about an hour or more until it is thick enough to hold a shape.
6. You can either form the truffles with a very small ice cream scoop or pipe small rounds from a pastry bag (using 3/8-inch tip) onto baking

sheets that have been lined with either a nonstick silicone baking mat or parchment paper.

7. Put tray in refrigerator (1 hour) or freezer (15 minutes) until the chocolate mounds solidify.
8. Then, with a fork, gently roll the chocolate-coated truffles in the cocoa powder.
9. Put the finished truffles on a tray lined with waxed paper and refrigerate. Serve at room temperature.

On several occasions through the intervening years, I ventured out to Kim and Kurt's home in Southampton and enjoyed cooking in their magnificent chef's kitchen. At Kim's request, I once agreed to provide an informal "instructional" weekend of cooking classes, for some of the things that Kim was especially interested to learn to make. It is always amusing when she reminds me how I taught her the way to achieve good caramelization when cooking sea scallops. Kim and Kurt hosted several dinner parties to which they invited me to be their guest chef.

One Abruzzo peasant dish, not too well known in America, is the *Timballo alla Teramana*. Teramo is located almost a hundred miles from Rome, nestled between the Gran Sasso d'Italia, the highest elevation of the Apennines and the coastline of the Adriatic Sea. Blessed with a Mediterranean climate, Teramo is rich in vineyards and olive groves. A *timballo* is a drum-like pie constructed of layers of crêpes or in the local dialect, *scrippelle*. In between these layers are little meatballs (*polpettine*) or in dialect, *pallottine*, which are napped with a rich meat sauce and complemented by some spinach, artichokes, and a southern Italian cow's milk cheese called *scarmorza*. In Teramo, they make this *timballo* free-form, but I have made some adaptations to the traditional recipe and form and bake it in a springform cake pan. It is much like a lasagna, except one uses crêpes instead of pasta sheets and the fillings are a bit distinctive. It is worth the effort required to make this dish. If you are ever in Teramo at Christmastime, you will see this dish everywhere.

TIMBALLO ALLA TERAMANA

An Abruzzo meat pie

Makes 8 servings

Ingredients

For the ragù

- 1 chopped onion
- 1 grated carrot
- 1 stalk chopped celery
- 1 minced clove of garlic
- unsalted butter
- 1 tablespoon extra-virgin olive oil
- ½ pound ground pork
- ½ pound lean ground beef
- 1 cup dry white wine
- 2 tablespoons tomato purée
- 1 cup chopped mixed herbs (rosemary, thyme, parsley)
- kosher salt and freshly ground black pepper

For the tomato sauce

- 1 white onion
- 4 tablespoons extra-virgin olive oil
- salt and pepper to taste
- 1 cup fresh basil leaves
- 2 black olives
- 1 minced garlic clove
- ½ teaspoon red pepper flakes
- 28-ounce can San Marzano tomatoes, pureed

For the polpettini (mini meatballs)

- 1 pound finely ground veal
- 1 egg
- 2 slices white bread, soaked in milk
- salt and pepper to taste
- ½ teaspoon grated nutmeg
- 1 cup all-purpose flour

For the crêpe batter

- 2 large eggs
- ¾ cup whole milk
- ½ cup water
- 1 cup all-purpose flour
- 3 tablespoons melted butter
- butter, for coating the crêpe pan

For the fillings

- 2 cups fresh spinach, roughly torn
- 2 cups fresh or thawed frozen peas
- frozen artichoke hearts, thawed
- 2 balls diced fresh *fior di latte* mozzarella
- grated Parmigiano Reggiano
- sautéed mini meatballs

Method

Making the crêpes

1. Combine all of the ingredients together and whisk vigorously for a couple minutes to blend the batter.
2. Place the crêpe batter in the refrigerator for 1 hour to rest. This will

continued

allow the bubbles in the batter to subside so that the crêpes will be less likely to tear during cooking.

3. Heat a 9- or 10-inch crêpe pan or a nonstick skillet. Add a little butter to coat.
4. Pour a small amount of batter (¼ cup or less) into the center of the pan and swirl to spread evenly. Cook for 30 seconds and flip. Cook for another 10 seconds and remove to a cutting board or counter to cool.
5. Continue making crêpes until all of the batter is used. You should have about 25 to 30 finished crêpes.

Making the ragù

1. Sweat the chopped onion in a saucepan with a drizzle of extra-virgin olive oil and a pinch of salt.
2. Add the carrot, celery, and garlic and cook for about 5 minutes.
3. Then add 2 tablespoons of butter and the pork, combine with the vegetables, and cook for 5 minutes.
4. Add the ground beef, season with salt and pepper, and cook with the other ingredients for about 15 minutes, until the meat has browned.
5. Add the white wine and allow the alcohol to burn off.
6. Add ½ cup of water and the tomato puree. Mix well.
7. Then add some chopped rosemary and thyme and cook for another 15 minutes.
8. Remove from the heat and set the finished ragù aside.

Making the tomato sauce

1. Chop the onion roughly.
2. In a large saucepan, sweat the onion with some extra-virgin olive oil and a pinch of salt and continue to cook on medium heat until the onions begin to caramelize.

3. Add the basil, olives, and garlic to the onions and cook for two more minutes.
4. Add the red pepper flakes and cook for 1 more minute.
5. Add the puréed San Marzano tomatoes and some salt and pepper, and allow to simmer together for 15 to 20 minutes.

Making the mini meatballs

1. Combine the ground veal with the egg, nutmeg, salt, and pepper.
2. Squeeze the bread that has been soaking in the milk and, with your hands, combine the bread into the meat and egg mixture to fully combine.
3. Roll the mixture into small meatballs, no more than 1 inch in diameter.
4. Lightly dust the meatballs in flour and quickly fry them in olive oil and butter until they are golden and crispy.

To assemble and bake the timballo

1. Preheat your oven to 350°F and butter a 9- or 10-inch springform pan, and dust with breadcrumbs.
2. Reserve about four of the best-looking crêpes for the top of the *timballo.*
3. Place a layer of crêpes on the bottom and up a bit of the side of the pan (about three crêpes, slightly overlapping).
4. With a large spoon, spread a thin layer of the tomato sauce over the crêpes.
5. Add a layer of the mini meatballs, spinach, peas, artichoke hearts, mozzarella, and beef ragù and sprinkle with grated Parmigiano Reggiano.
6. Repeat to add multiple layers of crêpes, tomato sauce, ragù, and fillings until you have used up the ingredients.

continued

7. When the layering is complete, neatly arrange the final four reserved crêpes on the top.
8. Brush the top of the *timballo* with some melted butter and dust with some grated Parmigiano-Reggiano.
9. Put the springform pan on a baking sheet into a preheated 325°F oven and bake for 30 to 40 minutes.
10. Allow to rest for 10 minutes before removing outer ring and cutting to serve.
11. Serve with a bit of additional tomato sauce and grated cheese.

In January 2019, Kurt Wolfgruber was diagnosed with Stage 4 pancreatic cancer. This came as a shock, because he had been in excellent physical shape and health. The following six months before his death on June 17 were consumed with the many medical treatments that were meant to slow down the progression of this deadly cancer. I accompanied Kurt and Kim on much of this final journey. When death drew near, I was with them and their family in their Manhattan apartment and prepared the final meal that Kurt was joyfully able to share with his gathered family. And on June 25 at the Madison Avenue Presbyterian Church, I preached the homily at a memorial service that celebrated his life. Rest in peace, dear friend.

....

Earlier I introduced my friend Sylvia Weinstock. Sylvia was not the stereotypical Jewish mother in almost any way, but she was nonetheless an instinctive *yenta*—interested in everything and everyone. Nothing brought Sylvia more pleasure than being able to connect one person with another.

Sylvia married Ben Weinstock in 1949 and worked as a Long Island elementary school teacher while Ben pursued his law practice. As the mother of three daughters—Ellen, Amy, and Janet—she naturally became a cook and baker. As she plainly said, there was no one else to put dinner on the table, and Ben had a sweet tooth.

Ben and the girls loved skiing and the Weinstocks spend many weekends at Hunter Mountain, New York. As Sylvia tells the story, she became very proficient in après-ski. Those winter weekends at Hunter Mountain proved to be career-changing for Sylvia, who became friends with André Soltner, then the Alsatian thirty-four-year chef-owner of New York City's well-respected French restaurant Lutèce. The restaurant achieved a four-star rating from the *New York Times*.

Soltner nudged Sylvia to apprentice herself to the pastry chef, George Kellner, who operated a guesthouse on the mountain. It was a natural pairing. Sylvia quickly moved from being an apprentice to becoming Kellner's valued assistant. A natural business entrepreneur, Sylvia immediately started to market her new baking skills by providing local restaurants each weekend with dessert selections. These she had baked while her family was schussing on the trails of Hunter Mountain.

The Weinstock girls were in college when Sylvia was diagnosed with breast cancer. The cancer required a mastectomy and a course of chemotherapy three times a week. During the time of her recuperation and convalescence, the New York City kosher baker William Greenberg Jr. asked Sylvia if she could help him out by making special occasion floral cakes, which he had no time to do.

Greenberg began his bakery business on the Upper East Side of Manhattan by catering to the Jewish community and offering kosher cookies, cakes, and brownies. It was the place to go to find traditional Jewish sweets like hamantaschen, rugelach, cinnamon babka, schnecken, shortbread linzer tarts filled with raspberry preserves, apple strudel, and the wildly famous black-and-white cookies.

It was while working for Greenberg that Sylvia began to develop her signature handmade sugar paste flowers, from which Sylvia Weinstock Cakes was born. During all of the years I had known Sylvia, the ingredients of her essential business formula never changed: personal attention to customers, first-rate ingredients, tried-and-true recipes for her cakes and fillings, the best buttercream (no fondant or shortening-base frostings), and breathtaking, continuously inventive artistic design. I loved that others used to refer to Sylvia as the Leonardo da Vinci of cakes. Da Vinci is one of history's most diversely talented people; Sylvia rightly stands in the shadow that he has cast over the Western world.

Sylvia never lost sight of the fact that her career change—from being a mother and kindergarten teacher to her generation's impresaria of fabled cakes—was nurtured during a battle to heal and recover from breast cancer. People in need always quickly claimed her heart and attention; she was always seeking an effective way to be of help to those who struggled, whether it be a single parent, a person living with AIDS, or a newly arrived immigrant in need of a job.

Sylvia and Ben lived for years above her bakery. As noted earlier, they had purchased an abandoned midblock building in TriBeCa that became the production facility for Sylvia Weinstock Cakes. It also served as their primary residence. They set up a rather sophisticated mom-and-pop business on the lower floors, with the upper two floors and roof terrace of the building serving as their dwelling. When purchasing appliances for the commercial bakery, Sylvia bought an industrial range with a salamander broiler unit for her own apartment kitchen, as well as a heavy-duty industrial refrigerator. For one who enjoys cooking, Sylvia's kitchen was a chef's heaven-on-earth workspace—nothing glitzy or fancy, just perfectly designed and exceptionally well equipped. It was like having a small hotel kitchen in your own home.

When they acquired their property TriBeCa was a virtual wasteland—but since then, it has become gentrified and trendy. Condominiums in old commercial buildings now cost multiple millions of dollars. Sylvia and Ben always loved entertaining in their home. Their French country dining table comfortably accommodated eight or more people.

Over the years, Sylvia amassed a collection of old French copper pots and skillets, many with tin linings, some original. In addition to being a creative baker, Sylvia was also an intuitive and inventive cook. Everything in Sylvia's kitchen got used quite regularly. Even though she was ninety-two years old when he died on November 22, 2021, she loved to entertain right up to the moment of her death, and she did so with style, simplicity, and ease. There was never any pretense or effort to impress; she just selected recipes, skillfully prepared them, and presented good, hearty food, always served family-style.

Ben was always her reliable aide-de-camp. He was such a gentle soul. When he died at age ninety-three on May 13, 2018, he and Sylvia had been married for sixty-nine years. To me they always appeared like newlyweds, with a love story that had no beginning and no end. Ben adored Sylvia and encouraged her in everything she ever wanted to do. He delighted in her extroversion and extravagance, even though neither of those traits would ever be applied to him.

Ben was born in New York City, an army veteran of World War II. After graduating from NYU Law School in 1952, he established and ran a successful solo legal practice in Massapequa. He was fifty years old when Sylvia was diagnosed with cancer. Together they tried to figure out the answer to the "what's next" question, and

Ben decided to shutter his law practice in 1980, sell their Long Island home, move to Manhattan, and nurture his wife's venturesome dream.

Ben was the behind-scenes guy. He supported Sylvia's adventures. It was he who designed and engineered the infrastructure for her elaborate cakes, figured out the logistics of crating and shipping cakes all over the world, and delivered and set up finished cakes in hotels and homes all over Manhattan. Together, Sylvia and Ben traveled the United States and the world with her magnificent confections.

During dinner parties hosted in their Tribeca home Ben was the carver, sommelier, butler, and scullery maid. Sylvia presided from the head of the table, and Ben was frequently seated at her right hand. At these dinner parties through the years I met some of New York City's most interesting and fascinating people: writers and producers, editors and publicists, TV and sports personalities, movie and food critics, fashionistas and restaurateurs, and doctors, lawyers, actors, singers, dancers, and designers.

Among the hundreds of dinner guests with whom I dined at the Weinstocks over a quarter-century was the late Mimi Sheraton, the first woman food critic hired by the *New York Times*, a position she dominated for eight years. After Mimi left the *Times* in 1983 she wrote for a number of magazines, including *Time*, *Condé Nast Traveler*, *Harper's Bazaar*, and *Vogue*.

Before a trip that I was planning to Taipei in 2008, I recall chatting with Mimi at one of the Weinstock dinner parties about my travel plans.

"I will send you tomorrow a copy of a piece I published on the street foods of Taipei," she responded. True to her word, the next morning she emailed me a lengthy guide and review of some of her Taiwanese culinary discoveries from among the myriad food vendors that crowd along Taipei's back streets.

Months after my return from Asia, I met Mimi again at a surprise sixtieth wedding anniversary party that Ben's and Sylvia's eldest daughter, Ellen Weldon, was hosting along with her husband, Keith, in her Manhattan apartment. During a casual conversation, I described to Mimi a wonderful restaurant I had discovered in a night market in Taipei. Without a moment of hesitation, Mimi rattled off details about this restaurant, its precise location, and some of its specialty dishes. I was absolutely astounded that she had such complete recall of this establishment. "It's amazing that you know so much about what I thought was a serendipitous discovery," I said.

"Why should you be surprised? After all, it is my business to know these things," was her curt retort. No wonder so many restaurateurs lived in mortal fear when Mimi Sheraton controlled the food pages of the *New York Times*. Mimi once said that "if you want something from a far-off place, you go there and find it—there's an interaction between countries, between people of different nationalities; relationships are established, dependencies are established." She believed that food is an integral component of a culture: the seasonings, the flavorings, the ingredients. I could not have agreed more with her perspective and experience. Mimi Sheraton was a force of nature.

Returning the favor, I cannot enumerate the many dinners that I hosted at my apartment for Sylvia and Ben. And true to form, Ben was constantly in my kitchen, seeking to be of help with the carving and serving and clean-up. We dined together dozens of times each year, and I always prepared a dessert. Many people were amazed that I would dare to bake for Sylvia Weinstock. The truth is that Sylvia rarely ate desserts; but Ben had a sweet tooth, just like me.

Sylvia never refused the dessert course when she dined at my apartment, even if she only sampled the offering. I made a wide range of different things for her. One time, when tasting an orange buttercream, she put down her fork, looked me directly in the eye and said: "This buttercream is absolutely delicious; you could work in my bakery anytime. It's as good, if not better, than any buttercream I have ever made." Coming from Sylvia Weinstock, that was a great compliment.

In the fall of 2004 I was developing a new recipe for a pear frangipane tart, which I was hoping to make as Christmas gifts for friends during the upcoming holiday season. Ben and Sylvia were scheduled to come for dinner, so I decided to make this test recipe and to get her opinion. She gave it the thumbs-up.

PEAR FRANGIPANE TART

Makes 8 to 10 servings

Ingredients

For the tart pastry (pâte sucrée)

- 1¼ cups all-purpose flour
- ½ cup sifted confectioners' sugar
- ¼ teaspoon kosher salt

- 8 tablespoons chilled unsalted butter, cut into small pieces
- 2 lightly beaten egg yolks

For the frangipane

- ¾ cup lightly toasted and skinned hazelnuts
- ¼ cup sifted confectioners' sugar
- 1 tablespoon room-temperature unsalted butter
- 1 beaten egg
- 2 teaspoons liqueur (such as Frangelico, Grand Marnier, or Cognac)

For the fruit

- 4 firm Bosc, Anjou, or Bartlett (Williams) pears
- 2 lemons (juice and zest)
- 2 teaspoons raw sugar

Method

Preparing the pastry

1. Combine the flour, sugar, and salt in the bowl of a food processor fitted with the steel blade. Pulse several times to aerate and blend the dry ingredients.
2. Add bits of butter and pulse until the largest pieces of the mixture resemble peas.
3. Add the lightly beaten eggs yolks and pulse two or three times, just until the mixture looks moist and crumbly and comes together in a clump when you squeeze it. If the mixture seems too dry, lightly beat one whole egg in a separate bowl and add half of this to the dough, pulsing until it is incorporated. (My experience is that this is not necessary, especially if you use large eggs.) Nonetheless, the dough should be moist and crumbly.
4. Pour the dough directly from the bowl into a tart pan with a removable

continued

base, and quickly work the dough with your fingers to push it out, first against the walls of the pan and then the base. Cut a piece of plastic wrap and put over the entire pastry and continue to smooth out, using a small measuring cup to help flatten and shape the dough.

5. Tightly wrap the tart pan and refrigerate for a couple of hours before baking.

Making the frangipane

1. Process the hazelnuts in a food processor until finely ground.
2. Add the confectioners' sugar and pulse until blended.
3. Add the butter, and then pulse again until all ingredients are blended.
4. Add the egg and pulse to blend well.
5. Sift the flour over the mixture and pulse until just incorporated.
6. Mix in the liqueur and scrape the finished frangipane paste into a container.
7. Cover tightly and refrigerate until chilled and firm, about 2 hours.

Preparing the pears

1. Peel, halve, and core the pears. Toss the pear halves immediately with the lemon juice and lemon zest, to prevent browning. Cover with plastic wrap until the tart is ready to be assembled for baking.

Assembling and baking the tart

1. Preheat your oven to 375°F. Spread the frangipane on the base of the chilled unbaked tart shell. Arrange and embed the pear halves into the frangipane. Sprinkle with raw sugar.
2. Into preheated 375°F oven, place tart on baking sheet and bake for about 40 to 50 minutes until pastry is lightly browned and the frangipane is set.
3. Cool on rack before serving.

During the course of more than a decade, I never purchased butter for baking or cooking. I had my own supplier. Years before, Sylvia almost had a heart attack when she opened my refrigerator and saw the price label on a pound of unsalted butter. "Why are you paying more than five dollars a pound for this inferior butter when each week I purchase cases of Plugrá, a European-style butter that is slow-churned and creates less moisture content and has a much creamier texture when compared to average table butter?" I did not have a satisfactory answer.

Plugrá was Sylvia's butter of choice, and it soon became mine. The odd-sounding name is a play off the French words *plus gras*, meaning "more fat," with 82 percent butterfat compared to the normal 80 percent for most commercially prepared American butters. From that moment forward, whenever Sylvia came to share dinner at my apartment she didn't bring flowers or a bottle of wine, but instead she would schlep five or six pounds of Plugrá butter, a large container of hazelnut or almond flour, or an assortment of paprika that she recently picked up in a local spice shop. It was nice to have a purveyor of fine foods as a regular dinner guest.

To celebrate my sixtieth birthday in 2003, several of my friends hosted a Sunday afternoon luncheon in Connecticut. About forty family and New York and Connecticut friends gathered for the celebration. Sylvia insisted that she design and provide a cake for the occasion. Her design was magnificent. With ten or so layers of rich chocolate cake, filled with an exceptional raspberry buttercream (my favorite combination), she created a very realistic-looking three-foot-tall French copper stockpot, complete with cast-iron handles. The pot appeared to be filled with a soup that was bubbling up and spilling over its sides. A large wooden spoon, fashioned from sugar paste, was plunged into the simmering mixture. To the base of the cake, Sylvia added the legend, "His pot runneth over." How could I ever repay her kindness and creativity?

I became Sylvia's unofficial personal shopper on more than one occasion. Before departing on one of my many trips to Europe or Asia, I would nonchalantly ask Sylvia if there was something she might enjoy receiving. A fan of good quality costume jewelry, she quickly replied: "Buy me something big and chunky that makes a statement." From that time on, I regularly added to her collection of baubles with dramatic pieces from China, Thailand, Myanmar, Nepal, Indonesia, and Cambodia. We always chuckled knowingly when she was wearing one of these big pieces to some very fashionable New York City event, especially when a socialite would compliment her exquisite jewelry. Little did that woman know that I had picked up those stones for Sylvia from an Asian bazaar merchant for less than $25. Even though Sylvia stood a little more than five feet tall, she could wear almost anything with sophistication and elegance. In her own right, she was truly a grande dame. Ben and Sylvia were friends in every sense of the word. I cannot say strongly enough how much I loved them both—and miss them.

Chapter 10

STRENGTH AND BEAUTY

She is clothed with strength and dignity,
and she laughs without fear of the future.

—PROVERBS 31:25

"I want you to come to a benefit reception at a home on the Upper East Side for a new organization that I am establishing to promote better relations between African Americans and Jews." A casual invitation from a modern Orthodox rabbi, Marc Schneier, provided my introduction to the woman who graciously was hosting his friend-raising and fundraising event in her home on Fifth Avenue, just opposite the Metropolitan Museum of Art.

When I first met Dr. Mona Ackerman, I had a sense that we might possibly become friends. It did not take very long for this intuition to be confirmed. Even though there were some hundred or more people attending Rabbi Schneier's reception, Mona and I kept finding moments throughout the reception to visit and become more deeply knowledgeable about each other's life stories. We discovered that we were both clinical psychologists, teachers, researchers, writers, and extroverts. Before I left her apartment that evening, Mona said to me: "Walter, we are soul partners. We have to commit to meet very soon again and continue this conversation."

That was the beginning of a friendship that would deepen in so many ways, on so many levels, over the next several years until an unhappy diagnosis with ovarian cancer would cut short Mona's life at age sixty-six on December 5, 2012.

Mona Riklis Ackerman was born in Tel Aviv on May 22, 1946, to Judith and Meshulam Riklis. Along with her sister Marcia and her brother Ira, Mona emigrated with her parents to the United States, where her father became a wealthy man by pioneering leveraged buyouts and junk bond deals.

Mona married Irwin Ackerman in 1966 and together they became parents to a son, Ari, and a daughter, Gila. Mona graduated from New York University and, in her mid-thirties, in a career-changing decision, earned a PhD in clinical psychology from the Ferkauf Graduate School of Psychology at Yeshiva University.

Although she had divorced, Mona prized her family more than anyone or anything. Naturally, her children and grandchildren, her parents and siblings and their families, and her circle of intimate friends became the center of her life.

When I was invited into that inner circle of friends Mona was maintaining a small private psychotherapeutic counseling practice. Earlier, she had worked as a therapist at Bellevue Hospital. One of the things we soon discovered as a point of common interest was the care of persons with HIV/AIDS. Apart from her acquired clinical expertise, Mona possessed natural gifts of mind and heart. She was a very good listener. She was perceptive and smart. She was a natural soother and comforter.

I remember one day when she called me while I was in the office. I had become much like her older brother, her father-confessor. It was a very quick, animated, telegraphic midmorning conversation.

"Walter, I'm in love," she said. "Can we have lunch today?" I agreed.

We met a couple hours later at one of her neighborhood favorites, Café Boulud on East 76th Street. Mona was smiling radiantly. For years, my dear friend had contentedly lived a virtually celibate life. Without any warning, things had changed.

"There is a man in my life," she exclaimed. She went on to say that she had gotten to a point in life where she was beginning to accept the probability that she might never again find love. Richard Cohen called her assumption into question. "I don't know where things will go in this relationship, but Richard certainly has changed the equation," Mona told me. Richard, who wrote a weekly political column for *The Washington Post*, took center stage in Mona's life. "I never ever expected to fall in love again," she confided. "But I have." At the end of lunch, she said: "You have to meet Richard."

I soon discovered why Mona loved him. Their relationship, like a very good wine, had slowly matured over time. By the time Mona shared with me her newly embraced love they had been quietly testing the waters, making sure their love was not simply attraction or infatuation.

Soon thereafter I met Richard, and in time many of the members of his immediate family, who hailed from the greater Boston area. Mona met her intellectual match in Richard. Their conversations were never frivolous, and their debates were stimulating. Their politics were similar, but sometimes conflicted.

Prior to Christmas one year, I invited Mona and Richard to join Sylvia and Ben Weinstock for dinner at my apartment. On the menu that evening I had planned to serve grilled veal chops with a morel reduction sauce.

When I presented the entrée course, Mona exclaimed: "Walter, how did you know? Veal chops are Richard's favorite! This is amazing." In preparation for the upcoming holidays my apartment was already fully decorated, rivaling Macy's for lights and tinsel. And here I was entertaining four Jews.

Mona loved the holiday ambience but noted that I did not have a single live poinsettia plant in my entire apartment. "You need some poinsettias," she said. The next day, when I answered the door, two floral deliverymen laden down with poinsettias greeted me. The plants must have stood three feet tall, and there were four of them. When I unwrapped the packing paper they spread out to reveal virtual trees. Needless to say, they more than made up for the perceived deficit Mona had noted the evening before. On the accompanying note she had written: "Richard and I love you and wish you the merriest of Christmases. You are the best gift we will ever receive. Love from Mona."

CÔTES DE VEAU AUX MORILLES

Veal chops with morels

Makes 4 servings

Ingredients

- 4 veal rib chops (1¼-inch thick)
- 2 cups boiling water
- 1½ ounces dried morels
- 1 tablespoon vegetable oil
- 1½ tablespoons unsalted butter
- 1 smashed garlic clove
- 3 thyme sprigs

continued

- 2 minced shallots
- 2 tablespoons Cognac
- 1 cup crème fraîche
- 4 finely sliced chives
- 1 teaspoon chopped tarragon

Method

1. Preheat oven to 350°F.
2. Bring veal chops to room temperature for at least 30 minutes before searing and oven roasting.
3. Pour about 2 cups of boiling water over dried morels in a small bowl and soak until morels are softened, about 30 minutes.
4. Transfer morels to a mesh sieve set over a bowl to reserve the liquid. Gently compress the morels to remove excess liquid (do not squeeze out all the moisture).
5. Rinse the rehydrated morels to remove any remaining grit. Reserve morels and liquid separately, allowing any grit in the liquid to settle to the bottom of the bowl.
6. Pat the veal chops dry and season liberally on both sides with salt and pepper. Heat a large heavy ovenproof skillet over medium-high heat until hot. Add oil; when the oil begins to smoke, add veal chops and sear on one side for 2 to 3 minutes, and on the other for about a minute.
7. Add butter, garlic, and thyme to the skillet and baste the veal with the melted garlic-herbal butter.
8. Transfer skillet to oven and roast the chops, basting every few minutes, until an instant-read thermometer inserted horizontally into center of chop registers 130–135°F for medium-rare, 10 to 15 minutes.
9. Transfer chops to a plate to rest. Discard garlic and thyme, keeping juices and fat in skillet, and return to burner over medium-high heat.

10. Add morels and sauté for 1 minute; add the minced shallots and sauté an additional minute.
11. Take the skillet off the heat and add the Cognac. Ignite the Cognac and allow it to burn off the alcohol.
12. Return skillet to the range over medium heat and deglaze the pan by rapidly stirring and scraping up brown bits, until most of liquid has evaporated.
13. Slowly pour in reserved soaking liquid from the morels, being careful to leave behind the sediment in the bowl.
14. Add any meat juices that may have pooled on the plate holding the cooked chops, and on high flame, boil until the liquid has reduced.
15. Stir in crème fraîche, swirling to incorporate, and cooking until morels are lightly coated and liquid is slightly thickened.
16. Finally, stir in chives and tarragon and season with salt and pepper.
17. Serve the chops napped with the sauce and liberally garnished with the morels.

I cannot count the number of joyous family occasions that I spent with Mona and her extended family and close friends. None of these occasions was more significant than gatherings to celebrate Pesach (Passover). Her younger brother, Ira, would frequently assume the role of the leader of the Seder, having spent obvious hours carefully preparing its narratives and songs. And Mona, despite her demanding professional and social schedules, took special care in preparing many of the dishes that would be served to the twenty or more guests who would gather around the festive Seder table.

Over the course of many years, Mona had researched and collected any number of family recipes that went back a few generations. The Seder meal at her celebrations was always complemented by an enormous buffet, and each of the dishes featured little markers that gave the often-humorous name of the particular concoction. She featured dishes such as Rose's Stuffed Peppers, G*ddam Good Passover

Chicken Cannelloni, Middle East Spicey Meat and Potato in Beet Sauce, Grandma's Tchvechken, Knaidlach, Tzimmes Muffins, and Very, Very Chocolate Cheesecake.

Each year in anticipation of Passover, Mona would carefully select a meaningful personal gift that she would present to each guest at the Seder. One year, she had a sterling silver apple candy dish crafted by Tiffany and engraved with the date. Another year she had the state of Israel fashioned in crystal and then cut into several large pieces, as if a puzzle. All of the edges of these pieces of crystal were finely polished and then assembled in a blue velvet bag. Her gift carried its own meaning: Israel was divided and needed to be put back together. Each year's Passover gift not only demonstrated evidence of Mona's deep love for family and guests, but also had some lasting meaning.

One of her more creative Pesach gifting efforts centered on her growing collection of family recipes. On one Passover, on April 13, 2006, Mona presented each of us with a Plexiglas container in which were arranged a dozen or more prized family recipes. Each of the recipes was presented on a large card with a glossy picture of the finished dish, along with a detailed list of ingredients and step-by-step instructions on how to make the recipe. Here is one of those recipes, just as Mona presented it.

G*DDAM GOOD PASSOVER CHICKEN CANNELLONI

Makes 12 servings

Ingredients

- 1 whole, clean chicken boiled in its own broth, chicken (leftover from chicken soup), picked and shredded
- 4 onions
- 4 eggs
- 1 cup matzo meal
- ½ teaspoon kosher salt
- 2 tablespoons chopped parsley
- 3 tablespoons chopped fresh dill
- schmaltz*

- 1 package frozen peas and carrots
- shiitake mushrooms
- cremini mushrooms
- salt and pepper

**Schmaltz is rendered chicken or goose fat and is an indispensable component of traditional Ashkenazi Jewish cooking. It is available in jars in many specialty foods shops or online.*

Method

Making the crêpes

1. In a blender, combine eggs, matzo meal, salt, oil, and 1¾ cups of water and blend until smooth.
2. Then add parsley and dill to the batter and allow batter to stand for at least 2 hours.
3. Over medium heat lightly grease a 7-inch frying pan. It should sputter if water is thrown in.
4. Put about 1/8 of a cup of batter in the pan and quickly rotate the pan until it is thinly covering the bottom of the pan.
5. Practice will tell you when the edge of the pancake separates and browns. The crêpe can be easily turned by hand. Lightly cook the other side.
6. Repeat until the batter is all finished, about 15 crêpes.
7. Store crêpes with waxed paper until each crêpe is assembled.

Making and cooking the cannelloni

1. Fry the onions in schmaltz.
2. Add the cremini mushrooms and continue to sauté.
3. Add the shredded chicken pieces from the boiled chicken.
4. Add the frozen peas and carrots, and if desired, some prepared horseradish and some marinara sauce to taste.

continued

5. Season to taste.
6. Put a handful of the mixture on the crêpe and roll up, closing it like a blintz.
7. Put in a single layer in a Pyrex dish.
8. Cover tightly and refrigerate or freeze.
9. Before reheating, fry sliced shiitake mushrooms and put on top of cannelloni for taste and presentation.
10. Reheat, covered, on low heat, in the oven.

As Mona's sixtieth birthday was approaching her son Ari arranged for a surprise celebration in his SoHo apartment, which had a massive outdoor terrace. Having grown up with a consummate host for a mother, he instinctively knew how to arrange a fitting party. It was a perfect spring evening. What does one give to a woman who wants and needs nothing? I hatched a wonderful idea: I would create an original recipe in honor of her birthday and bring her the finished product as a tangible gift.

I set out to create a tart that would use some of the berries that were so abundant in springtime and early summer: luscious raspberries and blackberries; sweet wild strawberries and blueberries. Combining some classic approaches to fashioning a flaky pastry crust and a smooth pastry cream, I settled upon a fitting name for the confection: "A Berry, Berry Happy Birthday Tart." Enjoy every sumptuous bite!

MONA'S BERRY BERRY HAPPY BIRTHDAY TART

Created in celebration of the sixtieth birthday of Dr. Mona Ricklis Ackerman

Makes 8 to 10 servings

Ingredients

For the pâté sucrée (to line a 10- or 11-inch oblong tart shell)

- 1¼ cups all-purpose flour

- ½ cup sifted confectioners' sugar
- ¼ teaspoon salt
- 8 tablespoons chilled unsalted butter, cut into small pieces
- 2 large lightly beaten egg yolks

For the pastry cream

- 2 cups whole milk
- ⅔ cup granulated sugar
- 6 large eggs
- a pinch of kosher salt
- ⅓ cup all-purpose flour
- 2 teaspoons pure vanilla extract
- ½ cup whipping cream

Method

For the pâte sucrée

1. In a food processor fitted with a steel blade, combine the flour, sugar, and salt. Pulse a few times to blend the dry ingredients. Add the pieces of cold butter and pulse a few times to achieve the appearance of peas.
2. Add the lightly beaten egg yolks and pulse two or three more times, until the mixture appears moist and crumbly and comes together easily when you squeeze it. (If it is still too dry, then beat a whole egg and add a bit of the egg until the right consistency is achieved. It will almost never take the entire additional egg to become sufficiently moist.)
3. Now dust your fingers with some flour and press the dough evenly over the bottom and up the sides of the tart pan (with removable bottom). Wrap the whole pan and pastry in plastic wrap and refrigerate for a few hours or overnight.

continued

To bake the shell

1. Preheat oven to 375°F.
2. Prick the bottom of the tart shell all over with a fork.
3. Line the bottom with a piece of parchment or aluminum foil. Fill the liner with beans or pie weights and place the shell on a baking sheet.
4. Bake the shell in a preheated 375°F oven for 15 to 20 minutes, remove foil and weights, and return shell to oven for another 10 to 15 minutes, until golden brown all over. (Watch closely in the second baking cycle, since ovens vary, and the high butter-sugar content of the pâté sucrée makes it easy to overcook.)

To make the pastry cream

1. Combine milk and half of the sugar in nonreactive saucepan and bring to boil.
2. Meanwhile whisk egg yolks with the salt in a mixing bowl, then whisk in the remaining sugar.
3. Sift the flour into the wet ingredients and mix to combine.
4. When milk comes to boil, whisk about a third of it into the yolk and flour mixture, to temper.
5. Return the remaining milk to a boil and whisk the yolk mixture back into it. Continue to whisk until the cream is thickened and returns to a boil.
6. Take off the heat immediately and add the vanilla.
7. Transfer to clean bowl, cover with plastic wrap against the surface, and chill until cold.
8. To finish, whip the cream until it holds soft peaks and fold into the chilled pastry cream.

To assemble the finished tart

1. Fill the baked and cooled pastry shell with a generous portion of the finished and chilled pastry cream.

2. Arrange raspberries on the top in an artistic mounded display (I used 60 for Mona, of course).
3. Glaze with a bit of heated, strained, and slightly cooled raspberry or apricot preserves and dust with a fleck of sifted confectioners' sugar, and garnish with some fresh mint clusters.

Following Mona's earlier example, I photographed the finished tart and presented the ingredients and method on a similarly sized card as she had done in her Pesach recipe gift collection. I presented Mona with several copies of these recipe cards, along with one that had been matted and framed. I gave her a finished tart to take home and enjoy as she decompressed from her lovely birthday celebration. Among the many exceptional gifts she received from family and friends on that milestone birthday, none touched her more deeply than this humble but loving offering.

Over the years, as I intimated before, Mona had become as close as a sister to me. She shared moments of excitement as well as the more anxious ones. She took me into her confidence. Jokingly, she mused how a Jewish woman could become so comfortable "confessing" to a Catholic priest. She often fantasized about the books we might someday coauthor. Because she was heir to significant wealth, she had become a major philanthropist, and she even developed and taught a course at NYU on philanthropy.

Passionate about her Jewish roots, she immersed herself in any number of Jewish social programs. Had the times been different it would not have surprised me at all that Mona might have studied for the rabbinate. She was a deeply spiritual person, shaped profoundly by Jewish learning and tradition. No one ever had to teach her about the requirements of *Tzedakah*. In Hebrew, *Tzedakah* means "justice" or "righteousness," but it is understood by many of us simply as charitable giving. Being charitable is a mark of kindness or magnanimity or generosity. But for a faithful Jew, *Tzedakah* is a strict, ethical obligation. God requires *Tzedakah*; it is not optional. From her youth, Mona knew what was required and she never failed to exceed its expectations.

Mona was drawn to what I had been trying to accomplish in building a research program at HealthCare Chaplaincy that would seriously investigate the relationships between spirituality and health. When our seminal research efforts were getting started, Mona was right there with a pledge that would support several years of our efforts. When I was attempting to build a distinctive chaplaincy educational program—the Jewish Institute for Pastoral Care—within our multifaith organization, Mona wanted to be in the vanguard of early supporters. "Someday, I am going to become a student in this institute," she told me. "Perhaps, later in my life, I will become a Jewish chaplain myself."

While Mona was in the midst of worrying about her daughter Gila's recently diagnosed neurological disorder, her doctors discovered that Mona had ovarian cancer. Initially she minimized the threat posed by this diagnosis, and assured me and other friends who were privy to the news that everything would be fine. "I'm a fighter; cancer will not get the best of me," she insisted.

That would not prove to be a prophetic utterance. Although the early treatments seem hopeful, the cancer progressively spread and became more resistant to curative treatments. Inevitably Mona began to withdraw from social engagements, even with her closest friends. Email became a more normative way in which we communicated. She always remained hopeful, even as the cancer gradually chipped away at her life. Her last electronic birthday card to me was characteristically upbeat, although reading through the lines, I sensed it might be the last. The premonition proved to be true. Mona died on December 5, 2012, surrounded by Richard and her children. The world lost a truly magnificent person, and I lost a soul partner.

....

I was fortunate to have another strong woman in my life.

When I began to settle into my new life in New York City, my friend Joe Mullen said there was someone I simply had to meet. At the time Joe was a senior executive at MetLife, managing the western US operations from the Met offices in San Francisco. I had met Joe and Rollie Mullen when I first arrived at Saint Catherine of Siena parish in the fall of 1976. The company asked Joe to accept a West Coast executive assignment for a few years before he might return to their national headquarters in New York City. As it turned out Joe never returned to the East Coast, remaining in San Francisco for the remainder of his career and raising his children and grandchildren on that far distant shore.

Joe's corporate responsibilities frequently brought him back to New York City and he always planned for a lunch or dinner with me during these business trips. "You have to meet Sibyl Jacobson, who is the president and CEO of MetLife Foundation," he told me. Sibyl exercised various responsibilities during her MetLife career, but she was always involved with philanthropy and social responsibility.

Our introductory meeting was planned to take place in a small neighborhood Italian restaurant on the Lower East Side on one of the days in which Joe was flying east from San Francisco. Unhappily, his plane arrived later than scheduled that afternoon, delaying his arrival at the restaurant by ninety minutes. Both Sibyl and I arrived on time and quickly introduced ourselves to each other and settled into our reserved table.

It was the spring of 1992, and the local farmer's market in Union Square was teeming with fiddlehead ferns. Early on in our seminal conversation Sibyl remarked that she had been at the market the previous weekend and had brought home a basket of these furled fronds of young ferns, harvested early in the season before the fronds open and reach their full maturity.

In an animated way, this topic about fiddlehead ferns launched what would become a lifelong friendship. I talked about a handful of ways to prepare and pair these seasonal vegetables and even chatted with her about some of the dangers in eating ferns.

By the time Joe Mullen arrived at the restaurant, we were well into eating our meal and totally immersed in our conversation. "I can see you found each other, and by the look of things, my mission to introduce you to each other has already been achieved," he said. He could not have been more perceptive or correct.

At the time, Sibyl and her attorney husband, Frank Rosiny, lived in a large 14th-floor apartment in the private residential postwar Stuyvesant Town–Peter Cooper Village development on the east side of Manhattan, built and managed by MetLife. Together, the two housing developments comprise 11,250 apartments. Sibyl and Frank leased two connecting apartments on East 23rd Street, affording them two kitchens and three bathrooms. Even though Sibyl would never describe herself as an accomplished cook, she was interested in cooking and loved to entertain. I easily found a way into this scenario.

I was living in a single room within the Jesuit Community at America House on West 56th Street. Because America House was a full-service Jesuit community, all of the meals were served in a communal dining room, prepared by a professional chef and staff. Apart from weekends, there were scant opportunities to actually put on an apron and cook.

Sibyl and Frank gladly accepted my offer to come and cook for some of their dinner parties. Because of Sibyl's leadership position in corporate philanthropy, she met scores of prominent people in the world of the arts and entertainment as well as interesting people in the professions, higher education, and healthcare.

Sibyl was born into a Lutheran family in Iowa where she and her brother were raised. She later earned a PhD in English. Before moving to New York from the Midwest, she had been involved in education at the high school, community college, and university levels as a teacher and administrator before embarking on a quarter-century career heading MetLife Foundation. I often remarked that her tenure at Met surpassed that of all of the company's chairmen under whom she worked.

After collaborating in cooking several dinner parties at their home, we decided to challenge ourselves further by developing recipes for a series of Italian dinners. Each dinner would include four courses, each from a different region of Italy, and only use seasonal ingredients. Although challenging, we met and exceeded our expectations for these *cene italiane regionali.*

One of these dinners happened to intersect with the Fourth of July. Sibyl and Frank's apartment windows afforded a panoramic sightline for the annual Macy's fireworks display from three barges anchored in the East River. We decided that for this holiday midsummer dinner, we would prepare a buffet menu where each dish could be served at room temperature. Their guests were not only amazed by the fireworks but astounded by the sights and tastes of this gastronomic offering.

One of the simplest of the offerings got the most requests for a copy of the recipe. It was almost embarrassing to share such a simple preparation for an oven-roasted stuffed tomato served at room temperature.

POMODORI RIPIENI AL FORNO

Stuffed and roasted tomatoes

Makes 6 servings

Ingredients

- 6 large beef steak tomatoes
- 2 cups freshly grated breadcrumbs, from day-old Italian bread
- 1 cup arborio rice, cooked al dente

- 1 cup grated Parmigiano-Reggiano cheese
- 3 cloves minced garlic
- 6 tablespoons chopped fresh parsley
- 2 tablespoons chopped fresh oregano
- salt and pepper to taste
- extra-virgin olive oil

Method

1. With a serrated knife, carefully cut the caps off the tomatoes and reserve.
2. With a spoon, remove the tomato pulp to a large mixing bowl. Discard some of the seeds.
3. Add the rice, breadcrumbs, cheese, garlic, parsley, oregano, and salt and pepper to taste. Combine well with about a quarter cup of extra-virgin olive oil, until the mixture begins to hold together. Do not oversaturate.
4. Pat the interior of the tomatoes dry with paper towels and season with salt, pepper, and a little bit of grated Parmigiano Reggiano cheese.
5. Fill each tomato half with a mound of tomato, rice, and breadcrumb mixture and dot the top with a small dab of butter. Place the caps on the tomatoes.
6. Bake in a preheated 325°F. oven for 30 minutes until tops are golden brown. Can be served hot, cool, or at room temperature.

Frank Rosiny was raised in New York. He and his brother, Allen, followed their father, Edward, into the profession of law. Edward F. Rosiny had been born in 1908 in New York. After attending City College, Syracuse University, and New York University, he was admitted in 1932 to the bar. In 1934, he married Annabelle Steinman. In 1960, the Sony Corporation of America (SONAM) was established to oversee Sony's marketing activities in the United States. Edward Rosiny, a friend of Akio Morita, played the major legal role in the successful establishment in the United States of the Sony Corporation of America. When Mr. Rosiny died at age seventy on February 18, 1978, he was chief counsel, a director, and chairman of the corporate management committee of Sony.

I never had the pleasure to meet Frank's father, but I got to know his very colorful and engaging mother, Annabelle. Annabelle lived in Hollywood, Florida, but on occasion came to visit her sons and grandson in New York. As Annabelle was approaching her eighty-fifth birthday, Frank shared his desire to host a festive dinner at their home in her honor. It did not take a lot persuading for Frank and Sibyl to accept my offer that I plan the menu and cook the meal. So successful and appreciated was this venture that it turned into an annual tradition for the following few years until Annabelle's death at age eighty-eight on January 19, 1998.

I recall visiting with Annabelle in her condominium apartment the year before her death. We were sitting in a living room filled with paintings and sculptures and other objets d'art. She made a comment in passing about all of the accumulated stuff that was surrounding her. "We spent a lifetime in its acquisition, only to get to a point in our lives when it all becomes a burden," she told me. She reflected on her perception that neither of her two sons nor their families had much interest in any of these possessions, nor were they interested or knowledgeable about the provenance of many of these things. One example was compelling. Pointing to a small, enameled dish that was sitting on a stand on an adjacent side table, Annabelle asked me if I had any idea where it might have come from. To my untutored eye, it looked like something one might find in a souvenir shop in Tokyo. She invited me to examine the dish more closely. Taking it from the stand, I looked at it and turned it over. On the back was an inscription to her late husband from the former Emperor of Japan, Hirohito. The dish had been the emperor's personal gift to Edward Rosiny.

On one of these birthday bacchanalian dinners in honor of Annabelle I proposed that we might begin the dinner, which usually involved about a dozen or more guests, with an impressive presentation of a spectacular lobster soufflé. Many years before I had been introduced to Julia Child's recipe, and over the years I had evolved my own version of her classic presentation of a classic Hotel Plaza Athénée recipe from the nineteenth century, *Homard à l'Americaine*—lobster sautéed with tomatoes and Cognac.

LOBSTER SOUFFLÉ À L'AMÉRICAINE

A Julia Child classic reimagined

Makes 6 servings

Ingredients

For initial cooking of the lobsters

- 4 live lobsters, 1½ pounds each
- 2 large leeks
- 2 yellow onions
- 4 carrots
- 2 cups white wine
- 1 cup white wine vinegar
- 2 lemons
- 4 quarts water

For preparing the lobster stock (sauce Américaine)

- 3 tablespoons extra-virgin olive oil
- 1 large onion
- 1 large celery stalk
- 1 medium carrot
- 6 cloves garlic
- 2 tablespoons Cognac
- 1 cup dry white wine
- 1 large diced tomato
- 1 can (14-ounce) crushed tomatoes
- 2 teaspoons *herbes de Provence*
- 3 bay leaves
- 2 teaspoons paprika

continued

- 2 tablespoons freshly minced tarragon
- ½ teaspoon cayenne pepper
- ½ teaspoon fennel seeds

To finish lobster sauce

- ½ cup heavy cream
- 1½ teaspoons cornstarch, dissolved in 2 tablespoons of water
- 1 teaspoon Cognac

For the soufflé mixture

- 3 tablespoons chilled unsalted butter
- 3 tablespoons all-purpose flour
- 1 cup whole milk, warmed but not boiling
- 3 egg yolks (room temperature)
- 5 egg whites (room temperature)
- 1 cup Gruyère cheese, shredded
- 2 tablespoons Parmigiano Reggiano cheese, grated

Method

For the initial cooking of the lobsters (court bouillon)

1. Combine all the chopped vegetables in a large stockpot, along with the vinegar and 4 quarts of water. Bring to a boil and then reduce flame to a simmer. Squeeze the juice from the lemons and add them to the pot.
2. Add the lobsters, head first, and cover the pot. Bring cooking liquid back to a boil for another minute or so.
3. Take pot off the heat, keep covered, and allow the lobsters to steep in the hot liquid for another 10 minutes.
4. Remove lobsters from the pot, reserving at least two cups of the court

bouillon (cooking liquid). Put the lobsters on a platter or tray and allow them to cool to room temperature.

5. When sufficiently cooled to the touch, begin to remove and reserve the lobster meat and juices from the tail, claws, knuckles, and joints.
6. Remove the tomalley (green matter) from the lobster's body cavity and combine it with a couple of tablespoons of softened butter. Press this tomalley-butter mixture through a fine mesh sieve and reserve the residue for later incorporation into the sauce.
7. Cover all the lobster meat and whatever juices they may have yielded and refrigerate.
8. Chop up the lobster bodies and the shells and reserve for making the stock.

Making the lobster stock (sauce Américaine)

1. Heat the olive oil in a large Dutch oven; when oil is sizzling, sauté for a few minutes all of the chopped vegetables until they wilt and slightly brown.
2. Add the chopped lobster shells and sauté 3 to 4 minutes.
3. Pour in 2 tablespoons of the Cognac and tip the pan slightly toward the flame until the Cognac ignites. If this makes you nervous just use a wooden fireplace match, but be careful not to singe your eyebrows.
4. The flame will rapidly die down and extinguish. Add the white wine, all of the reserved lobster juices, the two cups of court bouillon, the diced tomato, the tomalley-butter mixture, and all of the seasonings. Bring the pot to a low simmer and let it gently bubble away, covered, for a half hour or more.
5. When the cooking is complete, strain all of the contents through a fine mesh colander or several layers of cheese cloth. Once strained, return the liquid to a saucepan and reduce over a moderately high flame until you have about a 1½ cups of highly concentrated stock.

continued

6. Just before you are ready to serve the finished soufflé, add heavy cream to the lobster stock reduction and whisk in the cornstarch slurry. You will note that the sauce will quickly begin to thicken. When that happens, remove from the heat and add the Cognac and perhaps a tablespoon of softened butter.

Making the soufflé mixture

1. Separate the eggs and add three of the yolks to a large mixing bowl.
2. Put the room-temperature egg whites into the bowl of a stand mixer and with the whisk attachment in place, beat until they form stiff, shiny peaks.

Making the béchamel

1. Melt the butter in a saucepan. Make a roux by adding the flour to the melted butter and whisking until blended and cooked (2 to 3 minutes). Remove the pan from the heat and add the warmed milk and continue to vigorously whisk. Return to heat and continue beating until the mixture thickens (if the milk is warm, this will happen quickly).
2. Take the saucepan off the heat.
3. While continuing to whisk the béchamel, add one egg yolk at a time until all have been incorporated. Now fold 1/3 of the egg whites into the sauce to lighten it. With a spatula, fold the remaining egg whites into the sauce (taking care to not deflate them), along with the grated Gruyère.

To form and bake the lobster soufflé

1. Preheat oven to 375°F.
2. On a large ovenproof platter, arrange six discs of buttered bread rounds (use a large glass or wine goblet and press the rounds from good-quality sliced white or whole wheat bread).

3. Place the rounds two by two, with the fifth at the top and the sixth at the bottom. Carefully arrange the lobster meat, equally apportioning the morsels on the six bread rounds.
4. Once completed, carefully spoon the soufflé mixture over the entire grouping, forming a complete, natural oval.
5. Sprinkle some grated Gruyère and Parmigiano-Reggiano over the formed soufflé mixture and quickly put the platter into the oven for 30 to 35 minutes.
6. Decorate the finished soufflé with two reserved claws and the tail shell and use one intact body shell for the head of the platter. Garnish with bunches of parsley and some lightly sautéed cherry tomatoes.
7. Serve the warmed lobster sauce as a luscious accompaniment to the individual portions that you will easily be able to serve from the whole soufflé. Why? Because you know precisely where the rounds are buried!

The morning of the dinner party, I asked Frank if he would go to Chinatown and find us one approximately four- to five-pound lobster. Frank had a penchant for buying far more than one either needed or requested, so we were quite explicit when we sent him off on his shopping mission. In the meantime, Sibyl and I were busy with other preparations, although we did fill the largest pot in the kitchen with water, which we set on the stove to bring it to a boil.

Within the hour Frank returned, quite delighted with his successful foray. He proudly announced that he had probably found the largest lobster in Chinatown: a monstrous crustacean weighing some eight to ten pounds. I was stunned by the size of this lobster, but even more confounded by the challenge of how we would deal with it.

Sibyl was not pleased with what Frank had purchased, but we nonetheless proceeded to deal with the creature by plunging it head first into the large pot of rapidly boiling water. The lobster was so large and powerful that as soon as its head was submerged in the water it repeatedly snapped its tail with such force that it projected itself out of the pot, landing on the stovetop. This unanticipated reaction startled us. With the help of kitchen tongs and towels, we were able to grab the lobster and force it back into the boiling cauldron, holding it down in the boiling water until it was finally subdued.

We had to use a novel cooking method because the lobster was much bigger than the largest stockpot could fully accommodate. First, we boiled the head and claws and then flipped it around and cooked the tail section with the head and claws protruding from the pot. How long does one cook an eight- to ten-pound lobster? We were on our own to figure this out. I was wondering whether a lobster of this age and size would be sweet and tender, or rubbery and tasteless. How would we artistically be able to crack open and remove the flesh without destroying the essential form and shape of the lobster? Fortunately, the dish proved to be tender, sweet, and delicious, once we conquered the obstacles encountered in its initial preparation. And in the end, Frank became the hero rather than the villain of the story. The presentation of this gargantuan crustacean that evening brought him many plaudits, and he still relishes telling the saga of this lobster soufflé.

For most of their married life, Sibyl and Frank maintained their single residence in Peter Cooper Village. At some point they decided they were going to look for a weekend home to purchase. They were very clear in setting the parameters of their search: it could be no more than an hour drive from Manhattan; it would need to be near the ocean; it would necessarily have to be low maintenance. What they ended up purchasing met virtually none of these requirements. The home they selected was in New Lebanon, in the Berkshires, about a two-and-a-half- to three-hour drive from Manhattan, located on the border between New York and Massachusetts. It was as far away from the ocean as one could imagine. The house was situated on a beautiful and large plot of land, with great open vistas of the neighboring hills and generously bounded by woodlands and wildlife.

Sibyl and Frank were like two children set loose in a candy shop. Before long, they were quickly adjusting to their new weekend community and adopted a more bucolic modus vivendi. The town was happily populated with other transplants from urban centers of commerce and culture who likewise had retreated to the sylvan landscape of Berkshire County.

Although now retired from his law practice, Frank was fully ready to embrace a wide and divergent range of new hobbies and activities: archery, fishing, bocce, skiing, still life and landscape oil painting, vintage movies, and much more. The amazing fact is that he proved to be good at all of them. These activities brought him into contact with groups of men he had never associated with before. For example, his bocce league was centered in an Italian American club. His name, Rosiny, was thought to be a corruption of Rossi or Rossini. He never let his friends think otherwise. He even decided to begin to study Italian, and within a reasonably short time he had attained a remarkable proficiency and an impressive command of vocabulary and idiomatic expressions, sounding as Italian as any of his bocce partners. None of them would have ever guessed he was descended from eastern European Jews.

Sibyl also started to develop some new passions: swimming, biking, and running. And beginning in the mid-1990s, Sibyl and I began inline rollerblading. She and Frank invested in rollerblading equipment and took a lesson or two at the Chelsea Piers complex in New York City. Frank soon lost interest in the sport and persuaded me to become Sibyl's rollerblading companion after work on weekday evenings. I purchased rollerblades and protective gear and I was ready to join Sibyl for this novel adventure. A couple of times a week, from early May until early October, the two of us rollerbladed along the scenic Hudson River walkway, following the same trajectory each time from Chelsea Piers on 23rd Street to Battery Park, where we often stopped for a sandwich and an iced tea drink, and then we shared a simple supper together before setting out for the return trip to 23rd Street.

The emergence of her midlife athleticism became a launching pad for Sibyl as a decorated triathlete. Soon after 9/11, Sibyl started running, biking, and swimming in earnest. I was amazed when she told me that she had registered for the Berkshire Y-Athon in 2004 and won in her age group. When I asked her what was driving her to do this, she simply said: "I want to do something on our weekends in the Berkshires that is a bit different and more challenging than what I am doing sitting at a desk in an office all week long." Her only regret, she once told me, was that she had not started racing earlier in her life, and not waited until we finally put on our rollerblades.

After her retirement from MetLife, Sibyl branched out, participating in international triathlons all over the world: New Zealand, London, Austria, Edmonton, Spain, and Switzerland—to cite just a few. She completed in the Ironman 70.3 championship in Zell am See, a picturesque Austrian town on Lake Zell, south of the city of Salzburg. As she edges close to age eighty, Sibyl is a two-time ITU Triathlon World Champion and a two-time Ironman 70.3 World Champion, and there is no evidence that she is slowing down.

My relationship with both Sibyl and Frank deepened even further after I leased an apartment in the Peter Cooper Village complex beginning in December 2000. Living only steps away from each other, we found even more opportunities to socialize. And I often spent holidays and long weekends with them in their Berkshire retreat.

I recall one particular Columbus Day. During the late summer, over a weekend brunch, Frank said: "Let's have a big open house on Columbus Day for our friends." Knowing Frank's penchant for the "more is better" philosophy, the guest list for the Columbus Day gathering quickly mounted to the point that they were anticipating hosting about eighty people in their home for cocktails and a buffet dinner.

They would gladly have engaged a caterer to handle this challenge, but we decided that I would design the menu and together we would produce the culinary event ourselves, making multiple trays of traditional lasagna alla Bolognese that we could make in advance and freeze. After all, we had a crowd to feed.

LASAGNA ALLA BOLOGNESE AL FORNO

Baked lasagna in the style of Bologna

Makes 10 to 12 servings

Ingredients

For the spinach pasta

You can purchase fresh sheets of spinach pasta from many Italian specialty stores, or you can make your own. If spinach pasta is not available, you can used dried boxed pasta sheets (lasagna bianca). In the style of Emilia-Romagna, we made our own green lasagna pasta sheets.

For the ragù

- 5 tablespoons extra-virgin olive oil
- 3 tablespoons unsalted butter
- 1 finely chopped carrot
- 1 medium finely chopped onion

- 1 finely chopped celery rib
- 1 thinly sliced garlic clove
- ¼ pound sliced pancetta, cut into quarters
- 1 pound ground veal
- 1 pound ground pork (not lean)
- ¼ cup tomato paste
- 1 cup whole milk
- 1 cup dry white wine
- 1 teaspoon salt
- ½ teaspoon freshly ground black pepper

For the besciamella

- 5 tablespoons unsalted butter
- ¼ cup all-purpose flour
- 3 cups whole milk
- 1½ teaspoons salt
- ½ teaspoon freshly grated nutmeg

Method

Making a simplified and quick ragù

1. Heat oil and butter over moderate heat and add carrot, onion, celery, and garlic, stirring until tender, 10 to 15 minutes.
2. Pulse pancetta in a food processor until finely chopped.
3. Increase heat to high and stir in veal, pork, and pancetta. Cook, stirring, until meat starts to brown, 10 to 15 minutes.
4. Add tomato paste, milk, wine, and gently simmer, uncovered, over low heat, stirring until almost all liquid has evaporated but the mixture is still moist, 1½ hours.
5. Add salt and pepper and remove from heat.

continued

Making the besciamella

1. Melt butter over moderate heat. Whisk in flour and cook, whisking frequently, until golden brown, 6 minutes.
2. Heat milk until about to boil. Add milk 1 cup at a time to butter mixture, whisking constantly until very smooth. Bring to a boil, whisking, then cook for 30 seconds.
3. Remove from heat and add salt and nutmeg. Cover with a buttered round of wax paper and cool, stirring occasionally.

Preparing and baking the lasagna

1. Preheat oven to 375°F.
2. Bring water to boil and add 2 tablespoons of salt. Have an ice bath ready to stop the pasta sheets from cooking and to cool them down.
3. Cook the fresh spinach pasta sheets for 1 minute. Transfer with a slotted spoon to the ice bath, then pat dry with clean a kitchen towel and hold for the assembly.
4. Spread a cup of the ragù thinly over bottom of a lasagna pan, and sprinkle with about 1½ tablespoons of the grated Parmigiano Reggiano. Cover with a layer of the cooked pasta sheets, slightly overlapping.
5. Spread ½ cup of the *besciamella* thinly over the pasta layer.
6. Repeat this process four or five more times until all the pasta sheets are used. On the final layer, sauce with about a cup or more of the besciamella and liberally sprinkle the top layer with grated Parmigiano Reggiano.
7. Bake, uncovered, until the top is browned and the sauces are bubbling, about 45 minutes.
8. Let stand at least 10 minutes or more before cutting and serving.

Frank was in charge of decorations for the Columbus Day gathering—and it was a big error of judgment on Sibyl's part to give over this mission to her husband. Frank seems to know every wholesaler in lower Manhattan, and he does not buy by the dozen; he purchases by the gross.

He had Italian flags of every size. Their long driveway was lined with flags; the living room had tricolor bunting. He had more clusters of plastic grapes hanging than might be found in a Tuscan villa. Sibyl could not believe what Frank produced by way of Italian décor, but prudently she remained silent in her disapproval, since she had delegated this aspect of the party planning to him.

The event proved to be a wild success. Frank had recorded music piped in everywhere. We heard strains of Puccini operas along with Neapolitan love songs. If you closed your eyes, you might for a moment believe you were in a gondola splashing along some back canal in Venice. Frank was attired like a peasant winemaker, a master of Barolo or Chianti Classico.

These theme parties gained traction to such a degree that I was called upon to help produce a Saint Patrick's Day bash as well as a Bastille Day outdoor extravaganza. Of course, Frank raised the bar so high with his inaugural event that he had to meet or exceed expectations in his follow-on productions. I must say that he did not fail to rise up to meet the challenge. In the course of time, he amassed a storehouse of décor.

Back when Sibyl and Frank became engaged, Frank's mother, Annabelle, told Sibyl something that would prove to be wildly prophetic: "Life with Frank will not always be easy, but it will always be interesting." Truer words could not have been uttered.

My life has been so deeply enriched by such a long and wonderful friendship with Sibyl Jacobson and Frank Rosiny. We all look back on that first conversation about fiddlehead ferns with such a deep sense of appreciation.

Chapter 11

BEHOLD, A GREAT PRIEST

Ecce sacerdos magnus, qui in diébus suis plácuit Deo: Ideo jure jurando fecit illum Dóminus crescere in plebem suam. Benedictiónem ómnium géntium dedit illi, et testaméntum suum confirmávit super caput eius. Ideo jure jurando fecit illum Dóminus crescere in plebem suam.

Behold a great priest who in his days pleased God: Therefore, by an oath the Lord made him to increase among his people. To him God gave the blessing of all nations and confirmed the covenant upon his head. Therefore, by an oath the Lord made him to increase among his people.

—THE BOOK OF SIRACH, 50

I recall the very first time, early in the fall of 1991, that I climbed the narrow winding staircase to arrive in the suite of rooms in the turret that served as the office and study of the rector of Saint Thomas (Episcopal) Church on Fifth Avenue. Soon after arriving at HealthCare Chaplaincy, I was briefed about its founding history. The original East Midtown Protestant Chaplaincy had been a conjoint effort by several prominent congregations in Manhattan to ensure that reliable Protestant Christian pastoral outreach and spiritual care would be available to hospitalized patients in the major eastside hospitals. Saint Thomas Church was one of the founding members of that coalition.

For many years Saint Thomas Church had continued its annual support to the Chaplaincy's works, but recently the rector, the Rev. John G. B. Andrew, had informed my predecessors that Saint Thomas would be gradually reducing and eventually reallocating its financial support to other social and educational ministries. My task that morning was to try to persuade Father Andrew to reconsider the church's philanthropic decision vis-à-vis the Chaplaincy.

I recall greeting the rector as I entered the capacious room at the head of that dark serpentine stairwell. In later years Fr. Andrew would also recall his first impressions as he met me. In his telling, he said to himself: "I have a sense that this priest and I will be friends for a very long time."

During our initial animated conversation, we talked about many things—the least of which was the continuing eleemosynary contribution to the Chaplaincy by Saint Thomas Church and its vestry, which Fr. Andrew quickly reinstated.

John Gerald Barton Andrew was born on January 10, 1931, in the village of Scarborough in North Yorkshire on England's North Sea coast. He spent much of his childhood living with his maternal grandmother in Anlaby, where he first became acquainted with the Anglican Church and Anglicanism's rich musical traditions, singing as a boy chorister at Saint Peter's Church and attending the all-boys Beverley Grammar School. He considered these early childhood experiences to be formative for his life of faith. By his own telling, the whole of his family, save for his grandmother, were "pagans."

In 1950, upon completion of officer training as part of his national service, John was commissioned into the Secretarial Branch of the Royal Air Force as a pilot officer. He was awarded a scholarship to Keble College at Oxford, where he read theology. After Oxford, he studied theology nearby at Cuddesdon College in preparation for ordination in the Church of England.

In 1956, John Andrew was ordained a deacon by Archbishop Michael Ramsey, who had been installed as the Archbishop of York in that same year. The following year, Michael Ramsey ordained John to the priesthood in the Metropolitan Cathedral of Saint Peter in York, commonly known as York Minster, one of the largest cathedrals of its kind in northern Europe. Fifty years later, on the anniversary of his ordination, I would host a festive celebration in honor of John's golden jubilee as a priest. We would gather with John around one large oval table—along with a cardinal, three bishops, and a number of Anglican and Roman priest friends—in the Rainbow Room, high atop Rockefeller Center.

After his priestly ordination, Father Andrew served as a curate in Saint Peter's Church in Redcar and assisted for a year and a half in the United States at St. George's-by-the-River in Rumson, New Jersey, before returning to the York diocese in 1960 as the archbishop's secretary-chaplain. When Michael Ramsey subsequently was appointed as the 100th Archbishop of Canterbury a year later on May 31, 1961, he brought John Andrew—who at that time was only thirty years old—along with him to Lambeth Palace to serve as his secretary. John served the Archbishop of Canterbury in that capacity for eight years.

Ramsey became very active in the Vatican II era ecumenical movement, and while Archbishop of Canterbury in 1966, he met Pope St. Paul VI in Rome. Famously, as they were preparing to part, the pope removed the ring he was wearing that day—the episcopal ring he had worn when he had served as the metropolitan Archbishop of Milano—and placed it as a memorial gift on the ring finger of the archbishop. This gesture symbolized the friendship between the two Christian leaders and the hope they cherished that this same friendship and affection would also come to transform the relationship between their churches. The pope had decided on this gesture the night before his final encounter with the archbishop but wanted the gift to be a surprise for Michael Ramsey. John Andrew worked behind the scenes with the Vatican officials to orchestrate the event. Among John's possessions was the box in which the Pope's ring had been contained. He decided to donate it to the Anglican Centre in Rome, which has continued to play an important role in furthering the relations between Rome and Canterbury in education, ecumenism, and shared mission.

Fr. Andrew spoke until his dying day with enormous affection about Archbishop Michael and his wife, Joan. Without any children of their own, the Ramseys had always treated John as their surrogate son. The archbishop depended on John Andrew for so many things. As a result, John exercised a very strong influence within the Lambeth household, and indirectly, among the members of the House of Bishops.

When the time eventually came, in 1969, for him to leave Lambeth at age thirty-eight, it was a bit disappointing that the only available appointment was to become both vicar of the Church of Saint John the Evangelist in Preston, Lancashire, and the rural dean of Preston, where he would minister during the following three years. Then came a life-altering invitation that would shape and define both his priesthood and ministry for the remainder of his life—the call to serve from 1972 to 1996 as the eleventh rector of St. Thomas Church, Fifth Avenue, where he was installed by the then-Bishop of New York, Paul Moore, on December 3, 1972.

I cannot count the number of times when I would hear Fr. Andrew say of himself that he was the luckiest priest in the Anglican Communion. With his early academic and ecclesiastical successes at Oxford and Canterbury, many wondered why he had not been selected to become the dean of a great English cathedral or a diocesan bishop. In some ways he found himself caught between the proverbial rock and a hard place. On the one hand, because he was an English, Anglo-Catholic priest leading one of the most prominent parishes in the Episcopal Church USA context, this may have effectively blocked any further advancement in America. On the other hand, at that time the Church of England appeared notoriously snobbish and reluctant to reclaim those like him who had seemingly deserted them by venturing across the pond and enviably had established themselves in prominent American parochial communities. Whatever the political or ecclesiastical explanation, John's highest American church honor was when the Bishop of New York, Richard F. Grein, promoted him on January 29, 1995, to be an honorary canon of the Cathedral of St. John the Divine—the equivalent rank to being named a monsignor in the Roman Catholic Church. A year later, when he would retire in 1996 from St. Thomas Church, George Carey, the Archbishop of Canterbury, awarded to Fr. Andrew the Cross of St. Augustine in recognition of his distinguished contributions to Anglicanism.

John Andrew was a very able and dedicated priest. His preaching was exceptional, and his messages were always delivered with passion and perfect timing. I would occasionally chide him that his charming British accent seemed to thicken on the short walk from the rector's chair in the sanctuary of St. Thomas to its high pulpit. The touch of Englishness that John Andrew brought to the pulpit of Fifth Avenue proved to be an element of his allure and remarkable success. I recall on one Advent Sunday Evensong his notice and admonition to the congregation about an upcoming service of lessons and carols. "I want you to come and join us and to sing your bloody heads off," he said. His charisma and turn-of-phrase were endearing gifts that he possessed and used to great effect.

Soon after an astronaut completed a daring and successful spacewalk, which had been televised around the world, John Andrew, in his sermon, compared the Incarnation to the image of that astronaut yoked by a lifeline to the spaceship: "God has tethered himself to earth." And in another memorable sermon he spoke about charism and grace of Christian baptism in terms of being indelibly tattooed: "When you've got it, you've got it."

John had a subtle talent for the theatrical and could create worship experiences that were, in his own words, "grand without being intimidating, precise without being precious." He had a very keen and aesthetic eye for ecclesiastical vesture, adding many beautiful chasubles and copes and altar antependia to the collections of

Saint Thomas Church. Many of these pieces he personally designed and had specially crafted by Watts & Co. Ltd. in London. Each of the vestments he designed had interesting historical antecedents. For example, one of the liturgical copes he commissioned was crafted from material salvaged from the ornate vesture worn by Michael Ramsey when he was enthroned as Archbishop of Canterbury. Later, I would suggest to John that he might present this cope as a gift to one of Archbishop Ramsey's former mentees who had just been appointed the thirteenth rector of Saint Thomas Church. Just prior to beginning his formal tenure in that post, the Reverend Canon Carl F. Turner, B.A., M.Th., had worked at the Exeter Cathedral heading its department of liturgy and music. After he had retired, Michael Ramsey served as Carl's mentor and friend during the time he was studying at Durham University and then at Oxford. The archbishop had arranged for Carl to spend two formative years in the United States while he was still a seminarian. This cope became a most meaningful legacy gift from the eleventh rector to the thirteenth.

In every sense of the word, John was a thoroughbred Englishman. He was a man who never countenanced the American expression of "shining one's shoes." John would announce that he was "off to get my boots blackened." Even though he spent much of his life attired in a black suit or cassock, he was always impeccably dressed. I recall one time inviting him, before he joined the Chaplaincy's board of trustees, to join me as my guest at a Chaplaincy gala, a formal black-tie event. "I will wear my Saville Row suit for that occasion," he stated. Untutored about such things at that time, I did not readily catch the importance of his reply, but I soon appreciated what he meant.

John always wore a fresh linen Anglican-style surplice for each choral evensong service at which he presided. To launder and press one of these garments requires considerable effort, so I thought it a bit extravagant for him to throw a single-use surplice into the laundry basket. Without losing a beat, he retorted when questioned about his practice: "I would never consider wearing a used shirt if I were to stand before Her Majesty, the Queen; why would I do less when I stand at the altar before the King of Kings and the Lord of Lords?" Case settled.

At the time John Andrew arrived as rector at Saint Thomas, the congregation might be fairly described as an affluent Protestant Episcopal New York City community, even though the church's magnificent architecture belies the fact that its liturgical practices were staid and simple. Progressively, John began the task of bringing the parish back into the liturgical mainstream of Anglo Catholicism. He changed the principal Sunday service from Morning Prayer to a Choral Eucharist. For the first time in many decades, one could smell incense wafting through the nave of the church. He established a chapel for the reserved sacrament and began to decorate the church with new statues, like Our Lady of Fifth Avenue, and with Byzantine icons. Daily Mass became a regular component of the parish's worship schedule. Unquestionably, there was a new rector at St. Thomas on Fifth Avenue. His life would be forever shaped on the corner of Fifth Avenue at 53rd Street in the iconic limestone building that is the home of the community of Saint Thomas. John Cardinal O'Connor, a former Archbishop of New York, got it precisely right when he told the visiting Pope St. John Paul II, in introducing him to John Andrew: "Your Holiness, this is my pastor on Fifth Avenue, Father John Andrew."

Not only did John excel as a liturgist and preacher, but he had a deep knowledge and appreciation of sacred music and provided new energy to its choir school. It surprised no one to see the priority that Fr. Andrew placed on music at St. Thomas and especially for the preservation and enhancement of its distinctive choir school to educate boy choristers. Founded more than a century before in 1919, Saint Thomas Choir School remains one of three of its kind in the world, and the only residential choir school for boys in the United States.

During his tenure as rector, the choir school arithmetically increased the numbers of its chorister alumni who went on to exercise important leadership roles among the professions, including as members of the clergy and musicians. Having such an important resource as the combined choir of men and boys and a celebrated organist, composer, and master of improvisation, Gerre Hancock, Fr. Andrew was able to make a measurable difference in the world of liturgical music. Gerre had been appointed organist and master of the choristers at St. Thomas the year before John became rector and served in that position until 2004.

Fr. Andrew introduced his New York congregation to the rich library of choral music that continually supported the liturgy. He reinvigorated the celebration of choral evensong. From the publication of its first vernacular Book of Common Prayer in 1549, the Anglican Communion has engaged through the centuries some of the best composers to provide inspiring settings for both the Liturgy of the Hours and for the celebration of the Eucharist.

There was no place John was more content than when he was at worship at Saint Thomas Church. He loved the liturgy of the Eucharist. He never found preaching or its preparation to be a burden, but a privileged joy. The psalms were an integral part of the fabric of his being. He virtually knew the psalter by heart, having begun to memorize the psalms when he was just a boy. At choral evensong, I often noted that he would put down his prayer book and sing the verses spontaneously and with gusto. He moved within the sanctuary with the grace of a dancer, with reverence and devotion. And he inspired generations of worshippers at Saint Thomas Church to love the Lord with full hearts and minds and voices.

It was a rare event not to see the vast nave of Saint Thomas filled with worshippers on a Sunday afternoon for the celebration of choral evensong. Not a few of the regular worshippers included a notable assembly of Jesuits and other Roman Catholic priests, drawn not only by the exquisite musical offerings but also by the singular preaching abilities of Saint Thomas's gifted rector. On many occasions, at John's invitation, I would vest and process with the St. Thomas clergy and participate in this Sunday evening prayer service.

John Andrew also proved to be a very capable administrator, overseeing a staff of more than thirty employees, with four or five curates and assisting priests, and building the register of enrolled parishioners to close to 2,000 members and with an annual operating budget of approximately a million dollars.

I recall one incident where he had experienced a misunderstanding with one of his younger curates. In a very matter-of-fact way he commented, "That young man fails to understand the root meaning of the word 'rector.' It comes, as you know, from the Latin verb '*regere,*' which means 'to rule.'"

Throughout the years of his rectorship, John recruited and appointed a number of priests who became associates with him in ministry at Saint Thomas Church. He was an exacting boss, holding them to a very high standard of excellence in their celebration of the liturgy, and in their preaching, pastoral care, and civic engagement. I remember one of his junior curates arriving at the church one weekday morning attired in a roman collar but wearing a lovely grey tweed jacket. Politely but firmly, John asked him to return home and properly dress in a black suit. "You look like a country parson," he admonished. "That is not how the gentlemen of the clergy dress here at Saint Thomas." The message was received.

John's generous hospitality was legendary in New York. He was the consummate social host. The rectors of Saint Thomas Church lived in a lovely home at 550 Park Avenue. During John Andrew's time, the rectory became a lively place of welcome and hospitality. John Andrew knew how to entertain. Not only was he an excellent cook and host, but he was also an unparalleled conversationalist and raconteur.

I remember an anecdote he once shared, attributed to his good friend and former parishioner Brooke Astor. Mrs. Astor was one of New York's best-known philanthropists and socialites. For many years she personally operated the Vincent Astor Foundation, which had been established by her third husband, Vincent Astor, who was the son of John Jacob Astor IV and great-great grandson of America's first multimillionaire, John Jacob Astor.

In speaking about John Andrew's spacious dining room, which could comfortably seat sixteen people for dinner and which was painted in a deep coral color and illuminated by dozen of candles arrayed in sconces along its walls and by candelabras graciously placed along the massive tabletop, Mrs. Astor exclaimed: "This is one of the most beautiful private dining rooms in all of New York." There was not a hint of hyperbole in her assessment.

I recall one time telling Fr. Andrew about my close friend Archbishop John Quinn, who at that time was the leader of the Roman Catholic Archdiocese of San Francisco. "Invite him to be my house guest," Fr. Andrew bellowed. On a subsequent planned visit to New York, Archbishop Quinn did indeed stay with John Andrew. About the same age and both bearing the name John, they got on famously. I recall a very special clergy-only dinner that John had arranged as part of the archbishop's visit, which happened to coincide with John Quinn's birthday. A dozen Roman Catholic and Anglican clergy made up the guest list for the dinner party. In a quirky decision, John Andrew insisted that all of the clergy be attired in cassocks, which meant that each of us had to bring proper vesture in attaché cases and change in his apartment before joining the reception. I remember advising John Quinn, who habitually traveled very lightly, that he would have to bring a ceremonial cassock and a mitre along with a house cassock for this trip. John Andrew had also invited the archbishop to be a guest speaker at choral evensong on the Sunday of his visit and proceeded to vest him in mitre and cope.

The dinner in the archbishop's honor was a howling success. Formal yet highly engaging, the conversation flowed liberally among the dinner guests. Many were the exchanged toasts and salutations. I recall that on that occasion John Andrew presented the archbishop with a Steuben crystal apple as a *bon souvenir* of his new friends in the Big Apple. A very accomplished classically trained pianist, Archbishop Quinn delighted us after dinner by sitting down at the grand piano in the rectory's large drawing room and playing from memory several of Chopin's nocturnes.

Throughout his life, John Andrew viewed entertaining as an integral part of his ministry. The table became an extension of the altar for him. I hosted him many times at my apartment at dinner parties with other friends. He was always a wonderful guest, adding depth and richness to any conversation in which he was a participant. At the conclusion of one of these dinner parties he was effusive in expressing his appreciation for the dinner, complimenting not only the culinary offerings, but also the table setting and décor. "You are a genius in the kitchen and a masterful host," he proclaimed. When I told him that I had learned everything I knew about planning and executing a dinner party from observing him, he quickly demurred. John Andrew, par excellence, set the bar high for gracious entertaining. For him, hospitality was an eighth sacrament.

Invitations to intimate and grand dinner parties in his full-floor Park Avenue apartment—and later, during his retirement, in his more modest residence on East 52nd Street—were greatly coveted. For many years, until his death, Fr. Andrew kept meticulous personally inscribed guest books chronicling the countless soirées he had hosted and the royalty, prelates, politicians, titans of Wall Street, and other notables who had dined with him. My name appears far too frequently among these pages. For many years I was on his A-list for important social gatherings, but I also received many impromptu invitations, always punctuated with the same question: "Would you be free to dine tonight?"

John loved to set an elegant dining table and through the years had amassed an enormous collection of dinner porcelain, crystal goblets, Georgian silver, and fine linens that would rival that of a royal residence. In particular, I recall that he possessed a set of charger plates bearing the arms of Lambeth Palace. I once jokingly asked him if he had stolen these plates from the palace during his time as secretary to the Archbishop of Canterbury. He quickly replied that they were a gift from Joan Ramsey on his departure from the archbishop's service in 1969. I took him at his word, but I still suspected he had grabbed them as souvenirs on his way out the door.

John fancied himself as a decent cook, and indeed he was. In his earlier years on Park Avenue he had the able assistance of a dedicated housekeeper and cook, whom he prided in training. Lonnie was reliable and faithful, and she produced many delicious meals. But frequently enough, John assumed principal responsibility as cook for his own dinner parties. He always served a first course in place—a hot or chilled soup, a plate of smoked salmon, a slice of paté, a small, composed salad—but the entrée and dessert courses were invariably offered buffet-style.

One of his favorite dishes—and one appreciated by generations of his dinner guests—was a chicken dish, served with a creamy horseradish sauce. In John's version, the chicken was often poached. Here is my adaptation of a John Andrew classic.

POITRINES DE POULET SAUCE AU RAIFORT

Sautéed chicken breasts with horseradish mustard sauce

Makes 4 to 6 servings

Ingredients

For the chicken

- 3 boneless and skinless chicken breasts, halved horizontally to make six filets
- 1 cup all-purpose flour
- 4 tablespoons unsalted butter
- 2 tablespoons extra-virgin olive oil
- 2 crushed garlic cloves
- salt and freshly ground pepper

For the horseradish-mustard sauce

- 6 tablespoons unsalted butter
- 2 finely minced shallots
- 4 finely minced garlic cloves
- 2 tablespoons Dijon mustard
- 3 tablespoons prepared horseradish
- 1 cup whole milk
- ¾ cup chicken broth
- ½ cup dry white wine
- 1 teaspoon freshly chopped tarragon leaves
- 1 teaspoon freshly chopped thyme leaves
- ½ teaspoon freshly chopped rosemary leaves
- ½ cup of crème fraîche or sour cream
- 1 tablespoon white wine vinegar

continued

- salt and cracked black pepper, to taste

Method

Preparing the chicken breasts

1. Season the chicken cutlets on both sides with salt and pepper. Dredge in flour, shaking off the excess. Set aside.
2. Heat the butter and olive oil, along with the crushed garlic cloves, in a large skillet over medium-high heat. Discard the garlic pieces once they begin to brown.
3. When the oil and butter is hot, quickly sauté the chicken breasts until they are lightly golden, about 2 to 3 minutes on each side, depending on the thickness of the chicken.
4. Transfer to a rectangular ovenproof casserole dish, with breasts only slightly overlapping. Keep warm.

Making the horseradish-mustard sauce and finishing

1. Preheat oven to 350°F.
2. In a saucepan, heat 1 tablespoon of butter with 1 tablespoon of extra-virgin olive oil and sauté the shallots for 2 minutes until tender. Add in the minced garlic and continue cooking for 30 seconds, until the garlic blooms. Remove the contents from the pan to a bowl and add the Dijon mustard and the horseradish and blend. Set the mixture aside.
3. In the same saucepan, melt 3 additional tablespoons of butter. When the butter begins to sizzle, add 2 tablespoons of all-purpose flour and blend with a whisk and cook for 2 minutes, to form a light roux.
4. Add 1 cup of milk and whisk together. The sauce will immediately begin to thicken. Then add ¾ cup of chicken broth and ½ cup of dry white wine or vermouth, and continue whisking until the sauce becomes smooth.

5. Add the prepared shallot-garlic-mustard-horseradish mixture and thoroughly incorporate into the sauce.
6. Off the heat, fold in the finely chopped tarragon, rosemary, and thyme leaves.
7. Add 1 tablespoon of white wine vinegar.
8. Fold in ½ cup of crème fraîche or sour cream; correct seasonings to taste.
9. Pour the sauce over the chicken breasts and bake, uncovered, for 15 to 20 minutes.

Early on in my growing friendship with Fr. Andrew, I asked him if he might consider serving as trustee on the governing board of HealthCare Chaplaincy. Without hesitation, he agreed. Throughout its history, the Chaplaincy had tried to ensure that one or two religious leaders drawn from among the many faith traditions in New York City would occupy seats on its board of trustees. Since St. Thomas Church Fifth Avenue was a founding partner of the HealthCare Chaplaincy in 1961, it was most fitting that Father Andrew, as its rector, should assume this governance responsibility as a Chaplaincy trustee.

John served with great energy and enthusiasm for six years, winning over many new friends among the other trustees for his prudence, wisdom, wit, civility, and gentility. However, he did not suffer fools gladly. If someone made a comment that he judged ill advised, he spoke right up with politeness and conviction. When I privately applauded him for something that he may have said by way of retort to someone's bombastic oratory, he replied: "I won't put up with such nonsense; I am simply too frightfully grand." Statements like that are seared into my memory and bring a smile to my lips when I recall these apodictic utterances. What can one say further to someone who is "frightfully grand"?

Father Andrew became a fixture at the Chaplaincy's annual fundraising gala, often serving as the clergyman offering the invocation or benediction. Because of his culinary expertise and discerning palate, I often asked him to serve on a small jury of tasters who would gather early each fall to select the menu for the November gala. He so enjoyed this chore. With great gusto he would dive into the various dishes and wines under consideration, offering his opinions about the merits or deficiencies of each offering until the small group reached consensus. Each year, one or other of the trustees whom I would ask to serve on the gala menu selection and tasting committee would invariably ask: "Will Father Andrew be joining us this year?" Unquestionably, he assumed the unofficial title of chair of this epicurean task force. In this role he was clearly in his element, sampling and pairing wines, weighing the pros and cons of entrée courses, and judging whether a chocolate dessert was preferable to a fruited one.

One of the dishes, prepared by the Cipriani family, always received his thumbs-up approval. This recipe for a *gratin di tagliolini panna e prosciutto*, which Arrigo Cipriani shared with me, now is a Cipriani classic. Arrigo is the son of Giuseppe Cipriani, who in 1931 founded Harry's Bar on the west side of the Piazza San Marco in Venice. The Cipriani family also opened up a large group catering operation in a former bank on East 42nd Street in New York City, which quickly became the site of many of the HealthCare Chaplaincy's gala events. Giuseppe was the creator of the Bellini (champagne and white peach nectar) and carpaccio (a dish of meat or fish, thinly sliced or pounded thin, and served raw, usually as an appetizer).

GRATIN DI TAGLIOLINI PANNA E PROSCIUTTO

Baked tagliolini with ham

Makes 4 servings

Ingredients

For the gratin

- ¾ pound dried tagliatelle or tagliolini (homemade green pasta is preferable)
- ½ cup prosciutto di Parma, cut into thin julienne strips
- ½ cup grated Parmigiano Reggiano cheese
- 3 tablespoons unsalted butter

For the besciamella sauce

- ¼ cup unsalted butter
- ¼ cup all-purpose flour
- 2 cups cold whole milk
- salt and white pepper

Method

Making the besciamella sauce

1. Melt the butter in a heavy-bottomed saucepan, over low heat.
2. Whisk in the flour and cook gently without browning, stirring constantly, about 3 to 4 minutes. Remove pan from heat and vigorously whisk in the cold milk.
3. When the sauce is well blended, return the saucepan to the stovetop and cook over medium heat, stirring constantly until it begins to thicken and becomes smooth. Use a wooden spoon and be sure to stir the sauce from the bottom and the sides of the pot.
4. Allow the sauce to come to a boil, then put the pot over simmering water and let it cook gently for another 10 to 15 minutes, stirring frequently.
5. Season with salt and pepper.

Making the pasta gratin

1. Preheat the broiler.
2. Bring a large pot of water to a rapid boil and add a tablespoon of salt.
3. Melt 1 tablespoon of butter in a large skillet over medium high heat and add the prosciutto, cooking the cured ham for just a minute.
4. Cook the fresh tagliolini in rapidly boiling water for 2 minutes, until it is al dente.

continued

5. Drain the pasta well and put the tagliolini into the skillet and toss it with the ham, add another tablespoon of butter, sprinkle with half the cheese, toss well.
6. Spread the pasta evenly in a 2-quart ovenproof casserole dish. Spoon the *besciamella* sauce over the top, sprinkle remaining cheese.
7. Place small pieces of butter over the top of the casserole.
8. Broil as close to the broiling element as possible, for 1 to 2 minutes, until golden and bubbly.
9. Garnish with additional grated Parmigiano-Reggiano and serve immediately.

John Andrew never lost connection with his roots in England, making regular trips back to Great Britain to visit with relatives and friends. While his mother was still living he made frequent trips to see her and his sister, Ann, in Whitby. For many years, Ann would spend Holy Week and Easter in New York, where I got to know her well.

During his tenure as secretary to the Archbishop of Canterbury, John became friendly with members of the royal family, including Queen Elizabeth II, Prince Charles, and especially Queen Elizabeth, the Queen Mother. On his trips abroad he would often be invited to share luncheon with the Queen Mother, who had served as the Queen of the United Kingdom from the time of her husband King George VI's accession to the throne in 1936 until his death in 1952. She obviously developed a great fondness for John Andrew, and John repaid her loyalty by fastidiously guarding any confidences he may have shared with the Queen Mother and not gossiping about things that he might have observed or witnessed. "We all know you are safe," the Queen Mother once said to him.

He did confide to me, however, what she told him when he left the archbishop's service and went to New York: "Whenever you are planning to be in London, do not hesitate to call and propose yourself for lunch." On one particular luncheon visit, one of the Queen Mother's ladies-in-waiting had been recently honored with the title of Dame of the British Empire. The new dame was present at the lunch table.

During the meal, the Queen Mother turned toward John and inquired: "Did you know that Frances Campbell-Preston, my lady-in-waiting, has recently been made a dame?" John said that he did not know what possessed him at the moment, but he began to sing, sotto voce, the first ling from the song "There Is Nothing Like a Dame," from the 1949 Rodgers and Hammerstein musical *South Pacific*. Without losing a beat, the Queen Mother picked up the melody and replied in song with the next line. Then together, with full voice, the two of them completed the refrain. With that, the Queen Mother raised her glass to salute the newly minted Dame Frances, who in John's telling became flushed and altogether disoriented by this musical outburst from her Royal Highness.

On another occasion, the Queen Mother queried why John had only taken one piece of veal from the serving platter that had been presented to him. He told her that he did not want to appear gluttonous. The Queen Mother hastened back the footman who was serving the meat course, and herself liberally piled additional slices of the thinly sliced veal onto his plate. What was being served that day at Clarence House was a cold veal dish with a creamy tuna sauce, *vitello tonnato*. This classic dish, originating in Italy's northeastern region of Piemonte, consists of aromatic boiled veal that is then thinly sliced and served in a tuna sauce with capers and anchovies.

VITELLO TONNATO

Sliced medallions of chilled veal in a tuna and caper sauce

Makes 8 servings

Ingredients

For the veal

- 2 to 2½ pounds top round veal roast
- 1½ cups dry white wine
- 1 stalk chopped celery
- 1 medium quartered onion
- 1 chopped carrot

continued

- 1 sliced leek
- 4 sprigs of marjoram
- 4 sprigs of thyme
- 2 bay leaves
- 5 black peppercorns
- 5 cloves garlic

For the tuna sauce

- 2 cans of Italian tuna, packed in oil
- 2 room-temperature egg yolks
- 2¼ cups extra-virgin olive oil
- 5 tablespoons freshly squeezed lemon juice
- 5 rinsed and patted dry anchovy filets
- 3 tablespoons drained and rinsed capers
- *fleur de sel*, to taste

For the garnish (optional)

- thin slices of fresh lemon
- thin slices of black olives
- Italian parsley leaves
- finely chopped hard-boiled egg
- capers

Method

To poach the veal

1. Poach the veal roast in a large saucepan with simmering water, wine, carrot, onion, celery, leek, garlic, cloves, peppercorns, bay leaves, and salt.
2. Cover the pot and allow the roast to simmer slowly for about 75 minutes.

3. Remove the meat from the liquid and allow to cool completely.

Making the tuna sauce

1. Place the tuna, capers, anchovy filets, and egg yolks in a food processor and pulse for about 30 seconds. Add the lemon juice and process for another 10 seconds. Correct the seasonings as desired.
2. With the food processor running, add the olive oil in slow stream, allowing an emulsion to occur and for the oil to be progressively absorbed. The finished sauce will look like mayonnaise.

To assemble the dish

1. Slice the veal as thinly as possible and arrange the slices on a large serving platter. Nap the top of the meat with the sauce, but do not oversauce.
2. Cover with plastic wrap and refrigerate for a few hours or overnight.
3. Garnish the platter as you wish with some chopped black olives, thin slices of lemon, some finely minced hard-boiled egg yolk, and some scattered Italian parsley leaves.
4. Serve additional tuna sauce on the side.

When the Queen Mother died at the age of 101 years and 238 days on March 30, 2002, John Andrew received a personal telephone call in New York from Queen Elizabeth II inviting him to join the family and the nation at her mother's funeral on April 9. John did attend the funeral in Westminster Abbey, and the Queen nodded to him in appreciation during the procession on that day as she walked behind the body of her deceased mother. John later would recount visiting the burial place of Queen Elizabeth in St. George's Chapel in Windsor.

In the 1996 New Year Honors, Fr. Andrew was appointed by Queen Elizabeth II as an Officer of the British Empire (OBE) for his charitable and community services in New York. This was a fitting recognition of both his strong ties to the monarchy and his major accomplishments in the New World. After John's retirement from St. Thomas Church in that same year, he chose to leave New York City for a time and move to a rather spacious apartment with a garden he had acquired in Bath. The multilevel residence was in a building that once had served as a summer home for Queen Charlotte (1744–1818). The stately house on Sydney Place was not far distant from Bath Abbey, a former Benedictine monastery first established in the seventh century, reorganized in the tenth, and rebuilt in the twelfth and sixteenth centuries.

I visited with John in Bath for a week during the summer of 1998. It proved to be a very rainy week. The roses in his well-tended garden were drowning and rotting because of the wet, dreary days and chilling nights. Notwithstanding the miserable weather it was a pleasant visit, with lovely meals and endless conversations. However, it was clear to me that this aging English cleric was not content, despite the beautiful and gracious surroundings in which he was then living. The Abbey clergy rarely called upon him as a preacher; few were his friends in Bath. I sensed that he longed to be back in New York and with the many people, like myself, who had become family to him. But pride was preventing him from moving back.

When I returned from that trip to England I spoke about John Andrew to Bishop Grein, asking if there might not be some useful work for him to do in the Diocese of New York. Providentially, the bishop spoke discreetly about an insistent need he had at that precise moment at Grace Church on Broadway to appoint an interim priest-in-charge to fill the vacancy of a rector who had unexpectedly resigned his ministry. I assured the bishop that if he asked John to consider accepting this interim position, I felt sure that he would seriously entertain the offer to return to ministry in New York.

The bishop called John in Bath and as expected, he quickly assented. Manna from heaven! Here was the opportunity for which unconsciously John had been looking. Without hesitation, he accepted the call to Grace Church. He would be back in his beloved New York City.

Fortunately, John was able not only to sell the Bath apartment at a slight profit, but the buyers were also interested to purchase whatever furnishings and décor that John might be willing to leave behind. He once quipped: "They were even interested to purchase an open jar of marmalade in the cupboard."

In 1999, John Andrew returned as the priest-in-charge of the historic parish of Grace Church in New York City, located on Broadway at the corner of East 10th Street. Some of his New York friends, learning of his return, offered to spruce up the very dreary parish house at Grace Church. In a matter of weeks they transformed and furnished the rectory and before long John was back preaching and entertaining, but now from a venue some fifty-five blocks south of his former residence on Park Avenue.

With dishes and glasses unpacked, he wasted no time getting back into the role of *hôte extraordinaire*. On one of those early summer evenings at Grace Church, John made a delicious cold fresh pea and mint soup—one of his signature dishes.

FATHER ANDREW'S CHILLED MINTED PEA SOUP

Makes 4 to 6 servings

Ingredients

- 6 cups good quality low-sodium chicken stock
- 1 small onion, studded with 2 cloves
- 1 clove garlic
- 1 teaspoon fresh tarragon
- 3 pounds freshly shelled peas or 3 packages frozen peas
- salt and freshly ground black pepper
- 3 cups heavy cream or Greek yogurt
- 6 fresh mint leaves
- A few mint leaves and crème fraîche for garnish

Method

1. Heat the chicken stock in a saucepan with the clove-studded onion, garlic, tarragon, and peas and about 6 mint leaves.
2. Cook until the peas are just tender. Remove and discard the onion.
3. Add salt and pepper to taste and purée in a food mill, blender, or food processor.
4. Enrich the soup by combining the cream or yogurt and chill in the refrigerator for 3 hours or overnight.
5. Serve well chilled and garnish with a dollop of crème fraîche and a generous sprinkling of julienned mint leaves.

As the search for a new rector was coming to a close and with it, John's ministry at Grace Church, Fr. Andrew's immediate successor at St. Thomas Church, the Reverend Andrew Mead—with the enthusiastic agreement of the vestry—offered John the well-deserved title of rector emeritus. This proved to be a most felicitous arrangement, providing John with an important ministerial reconnection to his spiritual home after his completed service at Grace Church, as well as affording him a way to continue enjoying social relationships with his vast network of friends and associates right up to the moment of his death.

When he left the rectory at Grace Church, Fr. Andrew moved into what would be his final residence on East 52nd Street. He occupied a small one-bedroom apartment with a large living and dining room, library-guest room, two bathrooms, and a small, windowed kitchen. He contracted to have some illuminated custom millwork built that housed his considerable collection of armorial porcelain and heraldic china. I must confess that I knew virtually nothing about the value or the provenance of most of these objects that were decorated with the coat of arms of either a family, institutions, or places. When he died, he bequeathed the entire valuable collection and so much more to Saint Thomas Church.

When he was preparing his advance directives, he approached me one day and asked if I would agree to serve as his healthcare agent and advocate—a request to which I readily agreed. I subsequent introduced him to Drs. Jean and David Case, internists who lovingly and with great solicitude cared for him for many years as his personal physicians. I exercised the role of health agent in earnest after an accident landed him in the hospital. While crossing First Avenue from his apartment on East 52nd Street early on an April morning to fetch a copy of the *New York Times*, John was struck by an automobile making a left-hand turn and was taken by the EMTs to New York Presbyterian Hospital for treatment of a shoulder fracture. Subsequently, he was transferred for rehabilitation to Saint Luke's-Roosevelt Hospital.

I visited him on Good Friday afternoon. His stomach was distended, and he was noticeably in physical distress. When I asked him a couple of routine questions, I quickly learned that he had not had a bowel movement during the ten days following his accident. Despite receiving stool softeners and enemas, he reported no relief. Speaking to the resident in charge, I politely asked if they had not considered doing an x-ray to rule out an obstruction in his bowel. The resident thought that mine was a reasonable suggestion and conferred with the attending, who ordered the x-ray. He was brought directly from the x-ray room to the operating room, where fortunately the chief of surgery was still around and successfully performed a resectioning. Had this not occurred, it is possible that he might have died that weekend.

After his discharge, Fr. Andrew was cared for most lovingly in his former home on Park Avenue by his successor, the Reverend Andrew Mead, and his most caring wife, Nancy. Nancy had looked after her own father during his terminal decline and was well able to deal therapeutically and compassionately with "the old rector." She nursed him back to health, encouraging him to a proper nutrition and exercise protocol that accelerated his recovery. More importantly, Nancy cared for his whole person: spirit, mind, and body. I believe that it was during this convalescence that John Andrew grew in deeper respect, admiration, and appreciation of this couple.

John Andrew habitually spoke of the congregation of Saint Thomas as his family. Over the years, I saw how truly related he became to so many individuals within that community of faith. James Booth and Frank Arcaro were among his most beloved "sons." Jamie, as he always called him, met John as a young man. Growing up in Kentucky, he was a Southern gentleman in every sense of the word. Bright, educated, talented, and well mannered, James epitomized everything one might long for in a son. Over the course of four decades James and his life partner, Frank Arcaro, showed increasing love and devotion to "the old rector," as John would often describe himself. They would often invite him to their home in Roxbury, Connecticut, for weeks on end, caring for him as if he was indeed their father. When they built a new home of their own design in Roxbury, they created a commodious wing in the house they called the John Andrew Suite. It became John's home away from home, beautifully appointed, right down to the smallest detail of including in the bathroom the aftershave cologne that John had consistently used since his adolescence in Great Britain.

On occasion I would be invited to join them, along with John, for a special holiday celebration. James and Frank are gracious hosts and superb cooks. Frank, especially, growing up as an only child in Medford, Massachusetts, developed an appreciation for both cooking and baking from his mother. He and James traveled extensively owing to their respective jobs as the president of Elsa Peretti for Tiffany and creative chief for Natori. Before Marcela Hazan gained recognition as a doyenne of Italian cooking, James and Frank were students hers, which opened up for them an increasing knowledge and appreciation of *la cucina italiana*.

During one two-hour car drive from Manhattan to their home in Roxbury, Frank and I became immersed in animated discussion about various approaches to ingredients and classic preparations of some French and Italian dishes. Having listened patiently for some time to this seemingly endless banter, John Andrew made the following declaration: "You two boys sound like debauched canaries." Of course, he was always appreciative of the fabulous dinners that frequently resulted from these spontaneous conversations. When James Russell Booth celebrated his sixtieth birthday on June 14, 2010, I created the following recipe, which I subsequently taught him during a private tutorial.

STRAWBERRY GRAND MARNIER CREAM CAKE

Makes 8 servings

Ingredients

For the cake

- 1¼ cups sifted cake flour
- 1½ teaspoons baking powder
- ¼ teaspoon kosher salt
- 1 cup superfine sugar
- 5 large eggs
- 6 tablespoons unsalted butter
- 2 tablespoons water
- 2 teaspoons vanilla extract

For the strawberry filling

- 2 pounds fresh strawberries
- 4 to 6 tablespoons superfine sugar
- 2 ounces Grand Marnier liqueur
- a pinch of fleur de sel

For the whipped cream filling and topping

- 8 ounces softened cream cheese
- ½ cup superfine sugar
- 1 teaspoon vanilla extract
- 1 tablespoon Grand Marnier
- a pinch of fleur de sel
- 2 cups heavy cream

Method

Preparing the batter and baking the cake

1. Adjust oven rack to lower-middle position. Preheat oven to 325°F.
2. Grease and flour a 9x2-inch round cake pan or a 9-inch springform pan and line with parchment paper.
3. In a large mixing bowl, by hand, whisk flour, baking powder, salt, and all but 3 tablespoons of the sugar.
4. Whisk in 2 whole eggs and 3 yolks (reserving the whites), butter, water, and vanilla. Whisk until smooth.
5. Using a stand mixer fitted with a whisk attachment, beat remaining 3 egg whites at medium-low speed until frothy, 1 to 2 minutes.
6. With machine running, gradually add remaining 3 tablespoons sugar, increase speed to medium-high, and beat until soft peaks form, 60 to 90 seconds.
7. Stir one-third of whites into batter to lighten.
8. Add the remaining whites and gently fold into batter until no white streaks remain. Pour batter into prepared pan and bake until a toothpick or wooden skewer inserted into center of cake comes out clean, 30 to 40 minutes.
9. Cool in pan 10 minutes, then invert cake onto a greased wire rack; peel off and discard parchment. Invert cake again and cool completely, about 2 hours.

continued

Making the strawberry filling

1. Cut in half 24 of the best-looking berries and reserve. Slice or quarter the remaining berries; toss with 4 to 6 tablespoons of sugar, along with the Grand Marnier, in a medium bowl and let sit 1 hour, stirring occasionally. The sugar and Grand Marnier will help macerate the strawberries, making them soft and generating liquid.
2. Strain the juices from berries and reserve (you should have about ½ cup). Put the strawberries in a bowl and use a potato masher to mash them; set aside.
3. In small saucepan over medium-high heat, simmer reserved juices until syrupy and reduced to about 3 tablespoons, 3 to 5 minutes. Pour reduced syrup over macerated berries, add a pinch of salt, and toss to combine. Set aside until cake is cooled.

Making the whipped cream filling and topping

1. When the cake has cooled, place cream cheese, sugar, vanilla, Grand Marnier, and salt in bowl of standing mixer fitted with whisk attachment.
2. Whisk at medium-high speed until light and fluffy, 1 to 2 minutes, scraping down bowl with rubber spatula as needed.
3. Reduce speed to low and add the heavy cream in a slow, steady stream; when almost fully combined, increase speed to medium-high and beat until mixture holds stiff peaks, 2 to 2½ additional minutes, scraping the bowl as needed (you should have about 4½ cups).

To assemble the cake

1. Using a large, serrated knife, slice cake into three even layers.
2. Place bottom layer on cardboard round or cake plate and arrange ring of 12 to 20 strawberry halves, cut sides down and stem ends facing out, around perimeter of cake layer.

3. Pour one-half of puréed berry mixture (about ¾ cup) into the center, then spread to cover any exposed cake.
4. Gently spread about one-third of whipped cream (about 1½ cups) over berry layer, leaving a half-inch border from edge.
5. Place middle cake layer on top and press down gently (whipped cream layer should become flush with cake edge).
6. Repeat with 12 to 20 additional strawberry halves, remaining berry mixture, and half of remaining whipped cream; gently press last cake layer on top.
7. Spread remaining whipped cream over top; decorate with remaining cut strawberries.

Fr. Andrew consistently introduced me to people as his closest priest friend. Many times he would declare that there was nothing essentially different in our beliefs as Christians and that nothing separated us—save certain circumstances of history, like Henry VIII and the Protestant Reformation.

When John Andrew's will was probated after his death, I learned from the executor of his estate that he had bequeathed to me his entire vast collection of dinnerware, along with a prized contemporary Russian icon of Christ that had been given to him as a gift on September 28, 1964, when the Russian Orthodox Patriarch of Moscow, His Beatitude Alexei, visited Archbishop Michael Ramsey at Lambeth Palace in London. I still treasure this image of Christ in Glory, which previously hung in Fr. Andrew's bedroom and now hangs in mine. As for the boxes of dishes and platters and tureens, I carefully sorted through the entire collection, repacked all the items, and regifted these heirlooms to many of John's other friends and former parishioners, who were thrilled and honored to receive these legacy possessions.

Over the course of the last few years of his life, Fr. Andrew's short-term memory progressively proved less reliable. Fortunately, his long-term memory was intact, allowing him to continue to regale his audiences—made up of new and older friends—with a rich tapestry of stories and experiences that it had taken him a lifetime to weave together. He cherished his boyhood memories growing up in York. He relished the recollections of successes and failures at Oxford and his early adventures as a young curate. He always said that his life had mirrored and fulfilled the Lord's promise of a hundredfold return. In his persona, John Andrew embodied the quintessential English gentleman: aristocratic in manner; reverential in piety; proper in dress and comportment; true and loyal in friendship. He was such a faithful priest. An aficionado of armorial heraldry and deeply schooled in its proper art forms, he was responsible for the design and registration with the College of Arms of many coats of arms that he had designed for friends and colleagues. Perhaps none provides a better conclusion to this recollection of a very dear friend and brother in the Lord than the following legend, which he chose to accompany the arms he created for Saint Thomas Church: "My heart is ready."

My heart is ready, O God;
my heart is ready,
And I will sing!
Yes, I will sing praise!
Wake up, my glory!
Wake up, harp and lyre;
I will stir the sleepy dawn with praise!
I will offer You my thanks, O Lord, before the nations of the world;
I will sing of Your greatness no matter where I am.

—PSALM 57:7–9

Chapter 12

A LONG JOURNEY

Two are better than one, because they have a good return for their labor:
If either of them falls down, one can help the other up.

—ECCLESIASTES 4:9–10

The portico and gently sloping piazza in front of Saint Catherine of Siena Church became for me the starting point of several lifelong relationships. My first encounter with Catey Long took place on that piazza. After the Sunday 10:30 a.m. Mass, I routinely greeted congregants as they were exiting from the Eucharistic celebration. On one brisk bright autumn morning in 1976 I noticed an attractive, blonde, impeccably dressed woman lingering on the periphery waiting for the crowd to dissipate before making her approach to speak.

"I'm Catey Long, and I just wanted to tell you how much I have enjoyed attending your masses," she said. "If you might be free and interested, my husband Mike and I are hosting a little gathering of friends at our home next Sunday evening to view and discuss Pier Paulo Pasolini's *Il Vangelo Secondo Matteo*, which Pasolini directed the same year we were married. I was wondering if you might be free and interested to join us to view the video and, over a casual buffet dinner, share some your own insights and reflections on the film?"

Pasolini's 1964 film *Il Vangelo Secondo Matteo* (The Gospel According to St. Matthew), which the Vatican City's newspaper, *L'Osservatore Romano*, much later in 2015 called the best film on Christ ever made, proved to be a most serendipitous entry point into a lifelong friendship with Catey and Mike Long and their families. We quickly discovered that all three of us had been born in the same year: Mike in

Oklahoma City; Catey in Little Rock, Arkansas; and I in Boston. Without knowing it at the time, we had all attended college together in the 1960s in the Greater Boston area: Mike at Harvard; Catey at Newton College of the Sacred Heart; and I at Boston College.

Catey and Mike met in 1964 during the summer between their junior and senior years while volunteering as support staff for a political campaign in Little Rock. They sensed a mutual attraction to each other, fell in love, got engaged, and were married in the monastic chapel of the cloistered Carmelites nuns of Carmel of St. Teresa in Little Rock on December 30, 1964, six months before their respective graduations.

Catey's mother, Betty Jane Howell, had vigorously opposed such a quick decision by Catey to marry and was dead set against the hastily arranged wedding that her daughter had proposed. Betty Jane strenuously wanted them to delay marriage until after their graduations. But Catey was as strong-willed as her mother. She appealed to her father, Gilbert, to help convince her mother to agree to the young couple's plans. Betty Jane relaxed her opposition. The wedding was quickly organized, thanks to the Carmelite nuns for whom Betty Jane had been a major benefactor.

After commencement Mike received the Harvard University Corning Glass Traveling Fellowship for 1965–1966, enabling Catey and him to visit over forty countries in Europe, the Middle East, Africa, and Central America. After working in various capacities for Ohio University and the Boston Consulting Group, Mike and Catey returned to Boston where he enrolled in the Harvard Graduate School of Business Administration, from which he received an MBA with distinction in 1971. From the Harvard Business School, Mike joined Brown Brothers Harriman & Co. (BBH) that June and became a partner in January 1984. Mike and one of his partners, Lawrence Tucker, cofounded the firm's merger and acquisition business at BBH.

Our lives finally connected a decade after graduation from college when, in 1975, the Longs moved from New York City and purchased their first home in Greenwich. By that time they had two children: an older daughter, Jane, and a toddler, Hampton.

When I connected with Catey and Mike in the mid-1970s, their parents were still living, and over the course of the following years, I got to know each of them. The Long family had migrated from Oklahoma to Little Rock, where Marsha Long continued her lifelong passion of providing piano instruction to younger children. Both of Marsha's children—Mike and Anne Long—were encouraged to learn to play the piano, but neither of them persevered and acquired the skill of their mother.

Marsha once confided to me: "Both of my children did acquire a deep appreciation for classical music, but they were just too lazy to learn to make music for themselves."

Marsha taught piano from the living room of her home, where she had two pianos—an upright, on which she played, and a baby grand piano, where her students would be invited to sit. She always believed the student should be invited to play the better instrument. When Marsha visited Catey and Mike in their Greenwich home, we frequently would play four-hand piano selections together on one of the two specially commissioned Steinway pianos that previously belonged to Cole Porter. One of these pianos—as mentioned earlier—graced Peacock Alley in the lobby of the Waldorf Astoria in New York City. The second of Cole Porter's pianos was in the Long's living room in Greenwich.

Gilbert Howell, an only child and a convert to Roman Catholicism, was a fascinating person. Born into a family of privilege, he was well educated and became a staunch Roman Catholic. The Howell girls were all raised as Catholics. Betty Jane, a lifelong Roman Catholic, was a liberated and thoughtful woman. She was bold and spoke forcefully about what she thought and believed. Early on in their family life Betty Jane became quite friendly with a Roman Catholic priest who became her guide and confidante until his death. The Howell girls grew up knowing and relying on Father James W. Nugent's ubiquitous presence and counsel. I often confided to Catey during the intervening half-century that consciously or unconsciously, I had somehow become her Father Nugent. Jane and Hampton grew up knowing me from their earliest years, and I have been with the Long family for virtually every milestone event during all of that time. I became almost as familiar to the Long children as chocolate chip cookies and cold milk. Here is my recipe for a familiar classic—made less than ordinary with some choice ingredients.

NOT YOUR ORDINARY CHOCOLATE CHIP COOKIES

Makes 2 dozen cookies

Ingredients

- 2 sticks (½ pound) unsalted room-temperature butter
- ½ cup superfine granulated sugar

continued

- 1½ cup packed brown sugar
- 2 eggs
- 2 teaspoons vanilla
- 2¾ cups all-purpose flour
- ¾ teaspoon *fleur de sel*
- 1 teaspoon baking soda
- 1½ teaspoon baking powder
- 2 Ghirardelli 92 percent intense dark chocolate bars (each bar 3.17 ounces)

Method

1. Preheat oven to 350°F.
2. In stand mixer fitted with the paddle attachment, cream on medium speed the butter, sugar, and brown sugar until fluffy.
3. Add both eggs and vanilla and beat for an additional 2 minutes. Add baking soda, baking powder, salt, and flour until fully incorporated.
4. With sharp knife, cut the chocolate bars into small, cubed bits and, with a rubber or silicone spatula, incorporate the chocolate bits into the batter, which will be somewhat dense.
5. Using a small to medium scoop, place rounds of the batter onto a parchment-lined baking sheet.
6. Bake for 12 to 14 minutes until the edges of the cookies are golden brown.
7. Remove from heat and allow the cookies to stay on the cookie sheet for an additional 2 minutes, before transferring the parchment paper with the baked cookies to a nonporous surface to complete cooling.

Catey was quick to establish family traditions. One of the most memorable was our tradition of spending the evening of December 23 together. This began during my first Christmas in 1976 with the Longs, when Catey and Mike invited me to join them for a family dinner. Before we ate, Catey put Hampton on my lap and gave me a child's book to read to him, saying, "Tell him the story of Christmas, Walter." Slowly, I read the illustrated book she had provided that recalled the Christmas narrative of Mary and Joseph's fateful journey to Bethlehem, the star and the angels, the shepherds, and the wise men. In its own way, this scenario has all the elements of a Norman Rockwell painting: Hampton resting on my chest, quietly attentive as I droned on retelling this familiar saga. By the end, he was fast asleep in my arms. Catey could not have been more happy. Jane, on the other hand, would have nothing to do with this. She was busy with other things, perhaps more focused on the approach of Santa Claus and what he might be bringing for her.

It was a real joy to be privileged to watch these two children—as the Gospel once said of Jesus—"grow in age, wisdom and grace" (Luke 2:52). As Jane and Hampton grew older, they both enjoyed helping me to prepare a home-cooked meal for our December 23 gatherings. I have the recollection of a snapshot that captured the three of us in their Greenwich kitchen. I was clothed in a red-checkered apron and the two children were huddled alongside me, watching as I sautéed and tossed mushrooms in a hot skillet for what would be eventually become a sea scallop soufflé.

SOUFFLÉ AUX PÉTONCLES GÉANTS

A sea scallop soufflé

Makes 6 servings

Ingredients

For the scallop mixture

- 1½ pounds fresh sea scallops
- 3 tablespoons unsalted butter
- ½ cup minced shallots
- 1 cup roughly chopped cremini mushrooms
- kosher salt and freshly grated black pepper
- 1 tablespoon chopped chives

continued

For the soufflé mixture

- 1½ tablespoons unsalted butter
- 3 tablespoons all-purpose flour
- 1½ cups whole milk
- kosher salt and freshly ground black pepper
- freshly grated nutmeg
- 3 separated eggs
- 1 cup grated Gruyère cheese
- 4 tablespoons fresh breadcrumbs (or dried Panko breadcrumbs)

Method

Preparing the mushroom, shallot, and scallop mixture

1. Preheat the oven to 350°F.
2. Prepare a 1½ quart ceramic ovenproof soufflé dish by buttering the bottom and sides and dusting the interior with the fresh breadcrumbs or Panko. Set aside.
3. Under cool running water, rinse the scallops, being sure to remove the side muscle if you find any still attached, and dry the scallops.
4. Melt the butter in a skillet over high heat and sauté the roughly chopped mushrooms. Add the shallots and continue to sauté until they soften and blend with the mushrooms. Remove and set aside.
5. Add some additional butter to the hot pan and sear the scallops for just a minute, to brown them a bit. They will continue to cook in the oven within the soufflé.
6. Add the scallops to the bowl with the sautéed mushrooms and shallots. Gently combine. Add chives and correct seasonings to taste. Transfer the mixture to the prepared soufflé dish.

Preparing the soufflé mixture

1. Melt the butter in a saucepan over high heat and whisk in the flour to

make a roux. Cook until the mixture is combined and the smell of raw flour disappears, about 2 minutes.

2. Add the milk and with a wooden spoon stir to combine. Bring the sauce to a boil and stir continuously, scraping the bottom and sides of the pan to prevent burning. As the sauce thickens, grate some nutmeg and reduce the heat, stirring occasionally.
3. Off the heat, beat in the egg yolks, one at a time, to fully incorporate.
4. Return briefly to the stove and cook for another minute or so.
5. Hold the sauce off the heat while you beat the room-temperature egg whites in a stand mixer (or with a handheld electric mixer) until the egg whites become shiny and stiff in soft peaks.
6. Fold about ⅓ of the beaten egg whites into the sauce mixture, combining well with the mushrooms, shallots, and scallops.
7. Then fold in the remaining egg whites, being careful not to deflate.
8. Finally, gently fold in the grated Gruyère cheese.
9. Pour the mixture over the scallops and shallots. Sprinkle on some additional breadcrumbs that have been combined with a couple of tablespoons of the grated Gruyère cheese.
10. Place the dish onto a cookie sheet and bake for about 30 minutes, until it puffs up and is nicely browned. Serve immediately.

As the children grew older, some of our pre-Christmas gatherings took place in the dining room of a local Greenwich country club. On one occasion Catey thought it might be interesting to include a woman she had recently met who was a divinity student. This proved not to be the wisest decision. Although the young woman was sincere, she was clearly not well-suited for her intended career in ministry. As her endless babble droned on, Mike's frowns grew deeper and more noticeable. The kids became antsy and Catey perceived the error of her ways. The only antidote to the evening was the spectacular French burgundy wine that Mike kept replenishing throughout the night.

When the dinner came to its natural conclusion, we all loaded into the Long's

SUV for the short ride back to their home. Once in the car, Mike began to release some of his pent-up frustrations from the evening by launching into a lengthy monologue. Momentarily distracted by his own thoughts, he missed a slight turn in the road and found himself barreling up a private driveway at 30 miles per hour. Fortunately, he caught his error and reflexively applied the brakes before we crashed into the garage door of some unsuspecting family's home. We still recall what could have been an even more memorable December 23 gathering.

The Longs' residence became a second home for me, and I never needed a special invitation to drop in and visit. One weekday, I happened to be in Greenwich for a parish meeting. Before returning to Fairfield, I decided to pay an impromptu visit to the Longs. On that particular day, Hampton was home from school. He had not been feeling well. When I arrived the housekeeper told me of Hampton's indisposition and that Mrs. Long was out in town attending to some business. I decided to check in on Hampton. I found him sitting at the kitchen island playing with his Union and Confederate toy soldiers. From his earliest youth, it was clear that Hampton Howell Long was a son of the South. He had, even by that young age, acquired an almost insatiable hunger to know everything one could possibly know about the Civil War. He staged and reenacted key battles of that war, displaying a remarkably accurate command of their details. I recall asking him some question about the Confederate flag. Without losing a beat he momentarily disappeared, only to return with an array of different Confederate flags and provide me with a tutorial about its evolution. This proved the rectitude of the old Latin aphorism *"Ex ore infantium, sapientia"* (Out of the mouths of children comes wisdom).

Later, I remember telling Catey to be patient with Hampton as she was dealing with some worrisome adolescent developmental issue. "In a very few short years, you will discover in Hampton a most interesting, charming, and engaging young man," I assured her. How prophetic those words have proven to be. He graduated from Harvard, completed a law degree at Vanderbilt, and settled with his veterinarian wife in Beaufort, South Carolina, where he established himself as a finance professional.

Jane Alexander Long was precocious and unpredictable. We must never forget that she descends from a matriarchal line of strong Howell women: beautiful, smart, insightful, and articulate self-starters. She almost effortlessly excelled in school. Whatever she attempted, she succeeded in mastering. For example, at one point she decided that she wanted to try competitive horseback riding. Before long, she was winning local and state competitions and proved to be an exceptional horsewoman. Her equestrian skills were varied: dressage, show jumping, and reining.

I recall an anecdote that Mike once shared with me. It seems that he had just completed arrangements to ship Jane's horse to Florida to get the animal away to a warmer climate during a frigid Connecticut winter. At 6 a.m. on one brutally cold winter morning, Mike stood shivering on the platform of the Greenwich train station as he awaited the Metro North commuter train to take him to his Wall Street office. In conversation with a fellow commuter he commented: "You know that you have made it when your daughter's horse is on a plane headed to a warm stable in Florida and you're freezing your butt off, waiting for a delayed commuter train in Greenwich." He did have a point.

Jane thrived at Yale where she majored in English, played lacrosse, and became an exceptional writer. She landed a summer internship with Robert De Niro's production company working for Jane Rosenthal who had been DeNiro's producing partner since 1988. She spent her entire professional life building Tribeca Enterprises and was a very demanding and exacting boss who became Jane Long's role model.

It is also where Jane met and eventually fell in love with Craig Stephen Gering, who worked at Tribeca as an executive assistant. At first sight, Craig did not immediately win her over. "He'd be standing there with fifty-seven notebooks and clipboards, and his headset connected to his belt, answering phones," she once said. All in all, Jane thought Craig was "a frightfully organized, frightfully smart, frightfully short man buried behind production schedules and unread scripts." He clearly grew on her. I recall Craig telling me that had a crush on Jane from the start, but he felt he had no chance with her. Jane had (and still does) the ethereal good looks and allure of a Gwyneth Paltrow.

After graduating from Yale University, the year following her summer internship, Jane was hired by Tribeca Productions. As fate would have it, in May 1995 she became Craig's assistant, who at that time was the director of production and development. To her great surprise, she found herself falling in love. I recall her mother keeping me apprised of this growing infatuation, as Jane began to see the sweet side of Craig Gering.

It wasn't terribly surprising when in the summer of 1996 Craig knelt down in the office, presented Jane with a gold foil cigar band, and proposed that they become a serious couple. They dated for another year before Craig—by then an agent at William Morris—proposed marriage with a real diamond ring.

This announcement pushed Catey into overdrive, and I had to hold her hand many times during the following several months as she planned the wedding of her only daughter. Although circumstances may have been different, the same Sturm und Drang that had earlier characterized her struggles with her mother, Betty Jane, would play out again as Catey negotiated the upcoming wedding plans with her own daughter.

I recall the day Catey had arranged to view a prospective venue on Wall Street for the wedding. Since the actual ceremony would also take place in this space, she had asked me if I might join her and to offer my own perspectives.

Catey had stayed the night before at the Mark Hotel on East 77th Street in Manhattan. When she departed from the hotel, she called me to advise that she would be picking me up shortly at my office on East 60th Street. During the short trip of seventeen city blocks from her hotel to my office, Catey bonded with her limo driver. When I joined them in the limousine, Catey introduced me to the gentleman and immediately launched into what I could only describe as a short synopsis of a pastoral problem that she felt I needed to solve for this poor guy. It seems that when the driver was a boy, the pastor of his parish had refused him and his friends permission to use the gymnasium for some pickup basketball game. As a result, he soured on the Catholic Church and had been alienated from his religious practice.

Catey has a remarkable ability to connect with people and skillfully interview them, and she has a lock-trap memory that catalogues and stores verbatim accounts of what has transpired in a conversation. She would have made a natural counselor, private investigator, or psychologist. "You have to help him straighten this out. He needs to find a way to reconcile this deep-seated hurt," she said to me.

I recall saying to her in astonishment: "Catey, you have only been in this limo for a few minutes. How did you get so deeply immersed in his personal life in such a short a time?"

"Never mind," she said as we were about to depart the car at the Wall Street facility. "Give him your card and work this out with him."

My friends the Cipriani family had acquired and were close to completing extensive renovations within an 1822 New York landmark building at 55 Wall Street. Over the years this edifice had served as home to the New York Merchants' Exchange, the New York Stock Exchange, the United States Customs House, and as headquarters of the National City Bank. The building is a breathtaking jewel of Greek revival architecture, with majestic columns and a grand 70-foot ceiling, crowned with a Wedgewood dome.

Catey loved the massive space at first sight. It was only steps away from the former headquarters of Brown Brothers Harriman—Mike's firm—at 63 Wall Street.

Mark, who was managing the Cipriani Wall Street facility, was also a good friend of mine. He had descended from a line of Swiss hospitality professionals, and he charmed Catey and quickly earned her confidence. If Catey selected this site for the planned February 27 wedding, it would be the first wedding held in the renovated space.

We ended that adventuresome morning by debriefing over a luncheon of *Pappardelle al ragù di anatra*, a Tuscan dish prepared with a combination of duck meat, garlic, tomato, red wine, stock, onions, carrots, celery, olive oil, rosemary, bay leaves, cloves, and juniper berries and served with a pappardelle pasta.

PAPPARDELLE AL RAGÙ DI ANATRA

Pappardelle sauced with duck ragù

Makes 4 servings

Ingredients

For the pappardelle

- Use either homemade, fresh, or dried pappardelle or fettucine, prepared to the al dente stage

For the ragù sauce

- 1 whole cut-up duck or breasts and thighs
- 1 onion
- 1 carrot
- 1 rib of celery
- extra-virgin olive oil
- 1 bouquet garni (rosemary sprig, bay leaf, juniper berries, whole cloves)
- white wine vinegar
- 1½ cups dry red wine (or Cognac)
- 4 cups of beef or chicken stock

continued

- 2 tablespoons tomato concentrate or paste
- 3 ounces dark chocolate (or a spoon of unsweetened cacao powder)
- freshly grated Parmigiano Reggiano
- kosher salt and freshly ground black pepper

Method

1. If using a whole duck, break it down into several pieces. Place the pieces in a bowl and cover them with a mixture of water and white wine vinegar. Cover the bowl with plastic wrap and allow the duck to marinate in the refrigerator for a couple of hours.
2. Discard the marinade and rinse the duck meat under running water and pat the pieces dry.
3. In a Dutch oven, heat a generous amount of extra-virgin olive oil and sauté the diced vegetables until they are soft and lightly caramelized. Remove from the pan and reserve.
4. In the same pot, add a bit more oil and over high heat, brown the pieces of duck on both sides for about 5 to 7 minutes.
5. When all the duck pieces have been browned, place back all the vegetables and combine. Add the red wine (or Cognac) and, over high heat, allow the liquid to slightly reduce.
6. Prepare a bouquet garni by enfolding in a double layer of cheesecloth the rosemary sprig, bay leaf, the juniper berries, and cloves. Add this to the pot plus about 4 cups of beef or chicken stock.
7. Over low-to-medium heat, allow the ragù to cook covered for 1½ to 2 hours, occasionally turning the duck pieces in the sauce during cooking and adding more stock if needed.
8. At the end of the cooking time, the duck meat will easily fall from the bones. At this point, carefully remove all duck pieces from the pot and allow them to cool at bit. Remove the bouquet garni from the sauce.
9. Remove and discard the skin from the duck pieces and, with two forks, shred the meat from the bones and discard the bones.

10. Add the tomato concentrate, chocolate, salt, and pepper to the sauce, and use an immersion blender to blend the sauce into a creamy consistency. If the sauce appears too thin, make a slurry with a teaspoon of cornstarch and cold water and incorporate into the sauce. Bring the sauce to a boil and reduce the heat.
11. Add the shredded pieces of duck meat back into the completely blended sauce and simmer gently, over low heat, for an additional 15 minutes. Taste and correct seasonings.
12. Finally, off the heat, add a couple of tablespoons of grated Parmigiano-Reggiano to the sauce and blend.
13. Toss the drained pappardelle with the ragù and serve, garnished with shavings of Parmigiano Reggiano cheese and chopped parsley (optional).

Because Craig is Jewish, Jane insisted that the marriage not be celebrated in a Roman Catholic church. Initially this was an irritant for Catey, but I convinced her that we would create a cathedral in whatever place they ultimately chose for the ceremony. Both mother and daughter had divergent ideas about what was desirable and required. In diplomatic ways, I had to play an ongoing mediating role between these two strong-willed women as the details of the wedding ceremony and reception evolved.

I was able to enlist the collaboration of a close personal friend, Rabbi Chuck Lippman, a Reform rabbi who had significant pastoral experience in officiating at marriages between Jews and Christians. Together we were able to design and conduct a seamless marriage ceremony that everyone felt was meaningful and respectful.

The wedding was a memorable evening. Guests entered this Wall Street temple on a red carpet, and every moment of the evening was chronicled by a team of photographers and videographers wearing hip black clothing and crowned with Madonna-like headsets. The wedding ceremony took place on a gardenia-scented mezzanine overlooking the banquet hall, with a brass sextet arrayed on a balcony close to the ceiling, blaring fanfare after fanfare. As drum rolls echoed like distant thunder, Jane ascended the staircase on the arm of a beaming father-of-the bride, Mike Long.

The reception and the dinner that followed the ceremony were flawless. Cipriani lived up to its stellar reputation. Instead of a large wedding cake, Sylvia Weinstock created a memorable dessert of individual cakes for each guest. Each of the cakes was finished in an opulent buttercream tinted a Wedgewood blue color. Sylvia also made a small cake for the bride and groom. After all the prewedding theatrics, the whole evening proved to be a success. Catey could not have been happier with it all, and both Jane and Craig were both relieved and thrilled.

Because of my increasing involvement at the Chaplaincy in fundraising, I did a considerable amount of entertaining. After living at the Jesuit residence America House for more than ten years, I received permission in 2000 to lease a rent-stabilized apartment in Peter Cooper Village. My First Avenue apartment became a venue for cultivating many prospective future trustees and donor prospects, as well as providing a venue for Jesuits looking for a place to stay while passing through New York.

When I signed the lease at Peter Cooper Village, Catey and Mike offered to help me set up and furnish the apartment and also offered me the assistance of one of their interior designers, Robin Upchurch. Robin had worked with the Longs on various projects, including the interior design and furnishing of their Quogue residence. She was a Southerner by birth. One of the items she donated to me for the apartment was a double pedestal oak desk she had been keeping in storage. The desk, which she believed was already more than a hundred years old, formerly belonged to her uncle, who had been a trial attorney in Georgia. Robin had had the desk slightly refurbished but pointed out some wear marks on the right lower drawer where this Southern gentlemen must have frequently rested his feet, probably while smoking a cigar.

Robin also knew of some items that the Longs had purchased but were sitting unused in basement storage. One of those was a six-paneled Chinese lacquered screen. Evidently, on one Saturday morning while doing some errands in Greenwich, Mike Long passed by an antique shop in which this screen was displayed in the window. He loved it and without consulting anyone, he bought it. When the screen was later delivered, Mike proudly displayed his proud purchase to his wife, who was less than thrilled with it. The screen eventually found its way to virtual exile in their basement. Catey was thrilled to see the Chinese screen move from Greenwich to New York. I loved it, and for sixteen years it was a prominent design feature of my combined living and dining room. Without the Longs, truth to tell, none of it would have happened at all.

Apples do not fall far from their trees of origin. To know Catey Long is to know her mother, Betty Jane Howell. Deftly twirling her glasses in one hand while keeping her gaze fixed on her conversation, Betty Jane was a force with which to be reckoned. She was never without an opinion or point of view. She relished delving into heady theological discussions, often with her son-in-law Mike Long, well into the wee hours of the morning.

Due to a serious illness that prevented her from traveling, Betty Jane had not been able to attend her granddaughter's wedding. We had been concerned that Betty Jane might die around the time of the wedding, and we had seriously discussed this possibility. Jane was able to visit with her grandmother in Little Rock after the honeymoon, climb into her bed, and regale her with all the details of the wedding—as only Jane Long could do.

When Betty Jane's husband Gilbert had died some years earlier after a valiant battle with leukemia, she reluctantly assumed the roles of both widow and matriarch. Soon thereafter she accepted a dinner invitation from a lifelong friend who himself had been widowed a year earlier. Bill Thompson was a charmer. Reaching across the table one evening in a restaurant, Bill affectionately took her hands into his and stared into her eyes. "Betty Jane, you are the sexiest thing I have looked at in a long time," he said. Betty Jane, in recounting this event to me some months later, told me that she went home that evening, stripped off all her clothes, stood naked in front of a full-length mirror, and asked herself aloud: "What the hell was he looking at?"

Their relationship matured rather quickly, and Bill soon thereafter proposed marriage. Betty was initially unsure whether it would be proper to get married again, less than a year after Gilbert's death. She did marry Bill and they enjoyed indescribable happiness for ten months, until Bill suddenly died, leaving Betty Jane on the brink of depression and despair. To have to bury two husbands within a relatively short period of time was too much grief for any person to have to bear. She became angry, grew despondent and a bit withdrawn—but she survived.

I was able to spend a few quality days with Betty Jane during the immediate weeks before she died. We had developed an unusual relationship. I suspect she saw the parallels between the bond she shared with Father Nugent and the one that Catey had forged with me over so many years. For lunch in her apartment I made a simple stuffed pear and Roquefort cheese dish, which I served alongside a small salad of baby arugula.

ROQUEFORT AND WALNUT-STUFFED ROASTED PEAR WITH SAUTERNES SYRUP

Makes 2 servings

Ingredients

- 2 Bosc pears, ripe but not overly soft, halved and hulled with a melon baller
- ½ teaspoon olive oil
- kosher salt and freshly ground black pepper
- 3 ounces Roquefort (or any blue cheese, such as Gorgonzola dolce, Saga, or Stilton)
- 2 tablespoons chopped toasted walnuts
- 3 tablespoons Sauternes
- thyme, for garnish (optional)

For the Sauternes syrup

- 1 cup Sauternes
- ½ cup granulated sugar
- *fleur de sel*

Method

1. Preheat the oven to 375°F.
2. Prepare the pear by slicing it in half and then removing the core with a teaspoon or a melon baller.
3. Rub each pear half with olive oil and season with salt and pepper. Nestle the pear halves in a gratin or Pyrex dish.
4. Make the filling by combining the Roquefort with the chopped walnuts. Mound into the cavities of the pear halves.
5. Add a couple tablespoons of Sauternes in the bottom of the gratin dish.

6. Bake the pears for about 30 minutes until the pear halves are soft, and the cheese is gently bubbly. Remove from oven and allow to cool slightly.
7. Meanwhile, make the Sauternes syrup by bringing the Sauternes and sugar to a boil. Whisk for a few minutes until the mixture is clear; all the sugar will have dissolved. Remove from the heat, add a few grains of fleur de sel, and put aside to cool.
8. Dress the baby arugula with a little olive oil and a few grains of fleur de sel, and plate.
9. When the pears are ready place them on the bed of arugula, drizzle with a bit of the Sauternes syrup and serve, garnished with a few leaves of fresh thyme or some micro greens.

I celebrated a Mass with Betty Jane and her daughters in Betty Jane's apartment after the first of our day-long discussions. Afterward, Betty Jane availed herself of the opportunity to speak. "We have just shared a beautiful and very meaningful celebration of the Eucharist. I just want to say one thing to y'all. Everything that we have just proclaimed and celebrated, I truly believe." Faith had given its final testimony.

That evening, the family had planned a simple dinner in Catey's youngest sister's home. Elizabeth lived in Little Rock with her husband, Ralph Patterson, and their two sons. Initially, Betty Jane had decided she would not attempt to attend; she had not been out of her apartment for many days. I told her that if she wanted to go to Elizabeth and Ralph's home for a short time that evening, she would be free to leave whenever she wished. After a little deliberation she decided to join the family. That would prove to be the final meal she would share with them. She rose to the occasion, drawing on all of her inner resources, and she sat at the head of the table and presided over the robust conversations.

The days after I left to return home were wonderful ones for Betty Jane and her four daughters. At my recommendation she gathered them, and systematically went through all of her possessions and designated to whom they would go. I think this exercise was a benefit not only to Betty, but to each of the girls.

Betty Jane died a scant several days later. I returned to Little Rock to preside at her funeral, which was celebrated in the Cathedral of Saint Andrew.

Mike Long served on many corporate boards. When one of these board commitments was scheduled in London, it generated an idea that Mike proposed to me: "Wouldn't it be nice for you to join Catey and me in London, and then we can travel together to Italy after the meetings are concluded, spending a week or so touring between Venice and Tuscany?" Once we all agreed, Mike set out about making the detailed plans. He personally researched and selected all the hotels and major dining venues. This trip turned out to be the fantasy vacation of all time. His selection of a five-star hotel in Venice put us directly on the Grand Canal. Catey and Mike's suite in this fifteenth-century palazzo hotel included a private outdoor terrazzo with a direct and unobstructed view of the Basilica di Santa Maria della Salute, a beautiful octagonal church that contains priceless paintings by Titian and Tintoretto.

One of our days in Venice was a Sunday. We attended the Italian high Mass that morning in the Basilica di San Marco. After Mass, Mike suggested that Catey and I take a leisurely stroll through the Piazza San Marco and through some of the adjoining streets while he returned to the hotel to order lunch. When we arrived back in the suite about forty-five minutes later, the terrazzo had been transformed into a private dining room, with bottles of wine chilling in silver ice buckets and two young *camerieri* attired in crisp white jackets standing ready to serve us the three-course meal Mike had arranged. We sat on the terrace for four hours, enjoying the ambiance and wonderful food, incredible wines, and sharing endless anecdotes and memories. There was a slight haze over the canal that afternoon, creating a mood and atmosphere that was almost ethereal. It was as if we had been captured in a Tintoretto painting ourselves.

This Venetian painter worked his canvases energetically, boldly, and swiftly, earning Tintoretto the nickname, *Il Furioso*. This recipe for spaghetti with zucchini, grape tomatoes, and dried pepperoncini is—like a Tintoretto painting—quick, colorful, zesty, and luxurious.

SPAGHETTI CON ZUCCHINI E POMODORINI

Spaghetti with zucchini, grape tomatoes, and red pepper flakes

Makes 4 servings

Ingredients

- 1 pound spaghetti, fresh or dried
- 2 pounds thin zucchini, sliced into ⅓ inch rounds
- 12 ounces tomatoes (grape or cherry), cut in half
- 3 tablespoons olive oil
- 2 cloves garlic, finely chopped
- 1 teaspoon pepperoncini (dried red pepper flakes), finely crushed
- 2 tablespoons butter, unsalted
- ¼ cup basil leaves, roughly torn
- ⅔ cup mild Provolone cheese, gently shredded
- ⅓ cup Parmigiano-Reggiano, grated
- ½ teaspoon black pepper, freshly grated
- ½ teaspoon Kosher salt

Method

1. In a large skillet, add the olive oil and then sauté the zucchini rounds until lightly browned on both sides (about 2–3 minutes). With a slotted spoon, remove the zucchini from the skillet and place on paper towels. Lightly salt and pepper and allow to drain.
2. Add the halved tomatoes to the same skillet, along with the garlic and red pepper flakes and quickly sauté (2 minutes). Remove the skillet from stovetop, season tomatoes with a pinch of salt, and allow to cool in the skillet while the spaghetti is cooking.
3. To cook the spaghetti, bring a pot with 3 quarts of salted water to a rolling boil. This is a bit less water than is normally used, but it will produce a cooking liquid with a higher starch content, which will be helpful in producing a creamy sauce later. Cook the pasta to a minute shy of the al dente stage, following cooking instructions.
4. Before draining the spaghetti into a colander, conserve 1½–2 cups of the pasta cooking water.

continued

5. Return the drained pasta to the pot. To the partially cooked spaghetti, add the sauteed zucchini, tomatoes, garlic, pepperoncini, shredded basil leaves, 1 cup of the reserved cooking liquid, and the butter.
6. Set the pot over a low flame and with a wooden spoon, continue cooking, stirring, and tossing the ingredients for about 60–90 seconds.
7. Remove from heat and add the provolone and parmesan cheeses. Stir energetically until the cheeses melt and the sauce becomes thick and creamy. Add additional cooking liquid as needed to achieve a smooth and velvety finished sauce.
8. Transfer the finished pasta to a large, warmed platter or individual plates and serve immediately, garnished with a bit of freshly grated black pepper and some grated Parmigiano-Reggiano.

From Venice we took a high-speed train to Florence, where we had the services of a car and a driver who had previously been a former member of the Carabinieri, Italy's national gendarmerie. In Florence, Mike had arranged for us to stay in a converted sixteenth-century palazzo formerly owned by one of the noble families of Firenze and now operating as a hotel. He allowed me to pick the dining venues in this ancient city, which I knew so intimately.

For lunch on that first day we went to a favorite trattoria in Fiesole, which provided us with a breathtaking panoramic view of the entire city of Firenze and the Arno River. Fiesole is a *comune* of Florence, located high above Florence about five or six miles northeast of the city. I suggested we try this pasta dish, a specialty of that town.

PENNE ALLA FIESOLANA

Penne with pea and prosciutto cream sauce

Makes 4 servings

Ingredients

- 1 pound penne

- 3 ounces finely minced *prosciutto*
- 1 tablespoon all-purpose flour
- 2 tablespoons unsalted butter
- 1 cup whole milk
- ½ cup heavy cream
- ¾ cup of frozen peas
- kosher salt and freshy ground black pepper
- grated Parmigiano Reggiano cheese

Method

1. Melt the butter, whisk in the flour, and cook until the roux becomes lightly golden.
2. Add the milk gradually until it thickens a bit. Then stir in the heavy cream and heat through, but do not boil.
3. In a large skillet, sauté the prosciutto in the remaining butter. Add the cream sauce and peas and keep warm over the lowest flame.
4. When pasta is almost al dente, reserve 1 cup of pasta water, drain the pasta, and add the pasta to the skillet with the sauce. If the sauce needs thinning, add a bit of the reserved pasta cooking liquid to ensure a creamy consistency to the sauce.
5. Increase the flame to high and toss the pasta and allow it to finish cooking in the sauce. Garnish with Parmigiano Reggiano and serve immediately.

The weather in Florence that first day was overcast and cool, with intermittent rain showers. Michael had planned for a very special dinner in a restaurant known especially for its *bistecca Fiorentina*, a T-bone or porterhouse beef steak.

This restaurant sourced its beef from an old breed of Chianina cattle, prized by Tuscans as Wagyu beef is revered by the Japanese. Catey was in favor of skipping lunch entirely, but Mike would not hear of it. I suggested we go to the Cinque

Amici trattoria that was owned and operated by some friends of mine to enjoy a bowl of their specialty soup, *Ribollita Toscana*, with some crusty peasant bread and a glass of their robust house wine, which was a blend of Sangiovese and Canaiolo grapes. Mike thought that was a splendid idea and Catey, like a good sport, went along. Both the *ribollita* and the vino took the chill off the day!

Every cuisine, it seems, has its own version of a vegetable and bean soup. This soup is very particular to the Tuscan region of Italy. The word *ribollita* actually means "reboiled." It seems that this was a leftover soup made from the reboiled *minestra* of the day before. The soup is thickened by adding leftover bread. Here is my version of this Tuscan classic. I try to reserve the rinds of Parmigiano-Reggiano cheese wedges (which keep well in the freezer). These add a nice complexity to this soup. If you do not have any rinds, add a bit more grated Parmigiano-Reggiano to the finished soup at service.

RIBOLLITA TOSCANA

A hearty Tuscan vegetable soup

Makes 6 to 8 servings

Ingredients

- 2 roughly chopped large yellow onions
- 3 chopped carrots
- 3 chopped celery stalks
- 4 finely minced garlic cloves
- a pinch or two of red pepper flakes
- salt and pepper
- 2 tablespoons tomato paste
- 1 bunch of chopped *cavolo nero* (Tuscan kale), ribs and stems removed
- 28-ounce can diced Italian (San Marzano) tomatoes
- 6 cups low sodium chicken stock
- 2 cans (15 ounces each) rinsed and drained cannellini beans
- 4 sprigs fresh thyme

- 1 bay leaf
- 1 or 2 Parmigiano Reggiano rinds
- extra-virgin olive oil
- 3 cups cubed, day-old rustic bread
- grated Parmigiano Reggiano cheese

Method

1. Heat a few tablespoons of olive oil in a Dutch oven or stockpot over medium heat. Add the onion, carrot, celery, garlic, and dried red pepper flakes and cook 7 to 8 minutes, stirring occasionally, until softened. Season the vegetables with salt and pepper.
2. Create a space in the middle of the pan and add the tomato paste and allow it to caramelize for a couple of minutes before incorporating it into the vegetable mix.
3. Stir in the kale. Tuscan kale is a bit smaller, darker, and more tender than the kale found in most American produce sections, but any kale will work; just remember to trim the leafy structure from the ribs and stems, which you should discard.
4. Cook the kale until it wilts.
5. Add the diced tomatoes, chicken stock, thyme, bay leaf, and Parmigiano Reggiano rind and bring to a simmer.
6. Place half of a can of the cannellini beans in a small bowl, along with a quarter cup of the soup cooking liquid, and mash the beans into a smooth paste.
7. Incorporate 1½ cans of cannellini beans, along with the bean paste, into the soup and stir.
8. Cover the pot and leave the lid slightly ajar to allow the steam to escape.
9. On low flame, cook the soup for about 30 minutes. Add the bread cubes and combine, cooking for another 5 minutes.

continued

10. Before serving, remove the thyme sprigs, bay leaf, and Parmigiano Reggiano rind. Adjust seasoning with salt and pepper.
11. Serve with a liberal sprinkling of grated Parmigiano Reggiano and a drizzle of your best extra-virgin olive oil and imagine you are in Tuscany on a chilly, rainy day.

Carefully pursuing his research in preparation for this trip, Michael had discovered the Relais La Suvera, a lovely sixteenth-century Renaissance villa set like a jewel among the undulating hills and picture-perfect Chianti vineyards, about twenty miles from the city of Siena and the town of San Gimignano and about a thirty-minute drive from Florence.

When our chauffeur brought us to the ancient courtyard of this villa estate, which once had been the sumptuous residence of Pope Julius II (Giuliano della Rovere, pope from 1503 to 1513), we were astounded. This five-star boutique hotel housed within its ancient walls more than nine centuries of history, art, and culture. We would be guests at this villa for the next three nights. Catey and I looked at each other in amazement; Michael was grinning like the Cheshire Cat in Lewis Carroll's *Alice's Adventures in Wonderland.*

Once standing in the courtyard, I could not help but notice the ancient church immediately to the right of the principal villa. This edifice also dated from the sixteenth century and was dedicated to San Carlo Borromeo, who had served as the Archbishop of Milano from 1564 to 1584 and as a cardinal of the Catholic Church. He was also an important figure in the Counter-Reformation.

We shortly learned from our chauffeur that the origins of La Suvera could be traced back to the High Middle Ages, when the building was a fortified castle situated in the territory of the Siena Signoria, in the fief of the legendary Countess Ava Matilda de' Franzosi, related to Clovis, the king of the Franks. And now we were guests here.

When we arrived at the reception desk Mike and Catey were immediately taken to the Pope's Suite, which was furnished with a majestic canopy bed with all the furnishings and trappings that harkened back to Renaissance times. I felt that Pope Julius II, himself a great patron of the arts and of artists, would have been pleased to have Mike and Catey occupying what were once his own private chambers. I was escorted to the

Duke of Genoa's Suite, dedicated to Ferdinand of Savoy, commander of King Carlo Alberto's Piedmontese army and great-grandfather to Princess Eleonora Massimo.

Michael had made reservations for dinner that evening in the villa's Oliviera restaurant. Catey was indisposed, so Michael and I dined alone. Without Catey to moderate his choices, Michael quickly persuaded me to join him in the proposed five-course tasting menu with paired wines. We sampled a warm salted cod dish, napped with a fennel cream. Next we were served a small roasted guinea fowl breast, topped with a piece of seared fois gras and arranged on a bed of arugula, all sauced with a rich balsamic reduction. This was followed by *gnocchetti*, small ricotta and flour dumplings combined with a lobster ragout and finished with a light pea cream. The entrée course was *maialino*—a roasted loin of suckling pig with an assortment of sautéed seasonal vegetables and some potatoes that had been roasted with hazelnuts. The dessert was a *tatin di mela*—a traditional apple *tarte tatin*, served with an accompaniment of vanilla gelato. We were embarrassed the next morning when Catey asked, "What did you boys eat last night?" With a slight smile, Mike said, "Oh, just a little pasta."

For the next couple of days we effortlessly meandered through the Tuscan countryside, visiting a number of lovely medieval walled towns and quaint villages. We stopped on these days for what we had mutually agreed would be more modest lunches. Our driver would often suggest a little *hostaria* or *trattoria*. Once seated and presented with the menu, Mike soon forgot our dining pact and would plunge ahead and order a three-course meal with *acqua minerale*, *vino bianco,* and *vino rosso*. So much for moderating our daily intake of food and drink! It was because of these experiences that Catey and I began to affectionately refer to Mike as the "Duca di Montepulciano."

Allow me to conclude these reflections on our Tuscan holiday by presenting my own version of a traditional Sienese Christmas cookie, Cavallucci di Siena. These crunchy, chewy, aromatic treats are often eaten on the Twelfth Night of Christmas, along with a glass of sweet, mulled wine.

CAVALLUCCI DI SIENA

Sienese "Horse Hoof" Cookies

Makes about 36 cookies

continued

Ingredients

- 1½ cups light brown sugar
- 2 tablespoons honey
- ½ cup water
- 1¾ cups all-purpose flour
- 1 teaspoon baking powder
- 1 cup shelled walnuts, finely chopped
- 2 ounces candied orange peel, finely diced
- 1 tablespoon anise seeds
- ¾ tablespoon ground cinnamon
- 1/3 tablespoon ground cloves
- Pinch of kosher salt

Method

1. Preheat oven to 325°F.
2. Combine dry ingredients (flour, baking powder, salt), fruit, spices, and seeds in a large mixing bowl. Set aside.
3. Put the sugar, honey, and the water into a saucepan and heat gently until the sugar and honey have dissolved and the syrup reaches the thread stage (measuring roughly between 225°F – 235°F on a candy thermometer).
4. Turn off the heat and remove pan from stove top.
5. Pour the hot sugar syrup into the mixing bowl with the other ingredients and mix with a wooden spoon until they are thoroughly combined.
6. Turn the mixture out onto a floured work surface and sprinkle a little flour on top. The mixture will be very sticky, so don't be afraid to add more flour as needed.
7. Form the dough into a log, about 1 inch in diameter, and allow the dough to cool on the work surface for about five minutes.
8. Cut the log into approximately 36 equal portions.

9. Roll each portion of the dough into a ball shape. Place the ball on a baking sheet lined with a floured piece of parchment paper.
10. Slightly flatten the balls a bit and then slightly pinch the ends to make an oval shape.
11. Bake the *cavallucci* for about 10-12 minutes. The finished cookies will be soft, but their crust will harden as they cool.

Beyond family and travels and a lifelong friendship, Mike and I also shared another important mission. Early on in my tenure at HealthCare Chaplaincy I asked Mike to serve on the board of trustees, to which he graciously assented. Initially he served a term of six years, spanning the executive leadership both of my predecessors and my earliest years as CEO. While she was working for Jon Kamen at RadicalMedia, Jane Long also served a term as our youngest trustee. Later, during the penultimate years of my service to the Chaplaincy as CEO, I prevailed on Mike to serve once again, this time as the board's chairman. Over the course of my final five years Mike deftly guided the board through some of its most important business decisions, including the recruitment of my successor. After noble service, we both retired from the Chaplaincy.

Serendipitously beginning on a church's piazza in Greenwich, my relationship with Catey and Mike Long—with their children and extended families, with their friends, neighbors, and business associates—is now counted not only in years, but in generations. I became their family priest. I officiated at their parents' funerals and inurnments, presided at the weddings of their children and nieces and nephews, baptized their grandchildren and grandnieces and nephews, and joined many family celebrations, reunions, and other special holiday events. I suspect it is rare these days for a priest to have the privilege of such a wide-ranging ministry within a family like this, but I must say I have gratefully savored each and every minute.

Give thanks to the Lord, for he is good; his love endures forever.

—PSALM 107:1

Chapter 13

STANDING STRONG, TOGETHER

Therefore, a man shall leave his father and his mother and hold fast to his wife, and they shall become one flesh.

—GENESIS 2:24

When the advancement of Dan Donahue's career at Merrill Lynch necessitated a physical move in the 1970s from Tacoma, Washington, to New York City, Dan and his wife, Judy, began the search for an ideal community in which they might raise their young family of three children. Judy Donahue became the family's chief search agent and her meticulous research led to their decision to settle in Riverside, Connecticut. Part of Judy's due diligence was also a to find a Roman Catholic parish community the Donahues could truly call home. Her strategy involved not only visiting a variety of churches and attending masses, but actually requesting an appointment to interview Fr. Vincent O'Connor, the pastor of St. Catherine's parish. I remember Fr. O'Connor telling me later that he had never been interviewed by a prospective parishioner before, but he found Judy to be smart, focused, amiable, and zealous. Dan had grown to trust Judy's natural intelligence, judgment, and assertiveness. Their joint efforts paid huge dividends, and St. Catherine's proved to be a spiritual oasis for the Donahue family.

Dan Donahue was born in Chicago on January 28, 1939. He was a firstborn son and attended the Dominican Fenwick High School in Oak Park. Upon graduation in 1956, Dan received a congressional appointment to the United States Military Academy at West Point. After his commencement from West Point as a commissioned officer in the US Army, he completed ranger and paratrooper training at Fort

Benning and Fort Campbell. He became a proud Airborne Ranger Infantry Officer in the 101st Airborne and 7th Infantry Divisions. During his military service, Dan was placed in charge of the Guerrilla Warfare Training School in Korea from 1962 to 1963.

Dan left the army in 1963, got married a year later, and accepted a position in finance at Merrill Lynch. During their first year of marriage Dan began working part-time on an MBA degree at the Booth School of Business at the University of Chicago. After beginning his career in Chicago, Dan was soon thereafter transferred by the firm to Tacoma, Washington, and eventually to Manhattan.

Judy Pardi Donahue completed her training as a registered nurse at Park Hospital School of Nursing and practiced nursing in Chicago before she and Dan wed. There is an old saying that "a good marriage is one where each partner secretly suspects they got the better deal." That would certainly be true of both Judy and Dan, but I suspect they were equal beneficiaries of their union.

Dan, with his rusty blonde hair and broad, infectious smile, looked like the map of Ireland; Judy, with her unbridled energy and passion, was unmistakably Italian. My Irish-born maternal grandmother, Rose O'Brien, would often refer to a marriage like the Donahues' as a "mixed marriage." As I came to know Judy and Dan more intimately during more than four decades, I grew to appreciate just how ideally matched they were. The stoicism and emotional reserve that are often both the blessings and curses of the Irish, were tempered in Dan's case by his complete immersion over the course of a lifetime in Judy's school of limitless affection, optimism, and unconditional love. This mixed marriage between an American Irish and an American Italian—a marriage that would span a half-century—reminds me of natural pairings, like tomatoes and basil.

GARLIC BASIL CHICKEN WITH TOMATO BUTTER SAUCE

Makes 6 servings

Ingredients

- 6 boneless skinless chicken breasts
- fleur de sel and freshly ground black pepper

continued

- ½ teaspoon dried thyme
- ½ teaspoon cayenne
- ½ cup extra-virgin olive oil
- 10 diced fresh Roma tomatoes
- 5 cloves of minced garlic
- ½ cup of freshly julienned basil leaves
- 1 stick (¼ pound) unsalted cold butter, cut into small cubes
- pasta of choice: spaghetti, linguine, or bucatini

Method

1. Lightly pound the chicken breasts to an even thickness.
2. Season the chicken breasts generously with a mixture of fleur de sel, freshly ground black pepper, dried thyme, and cayenne.
3. Cut the tomatoes in half, vertically, and reserve them in a bowl. Lightly salt them.
4. In a large skillet, heat the olive oil. Sauté and brown the chicken for 4 minutes on each side. Set aside on paper towels to drain and cool.
5. In the same skillet, with the cooking oil cooled a bit, add the tomatoes. Turn the heat to medium and allow the tomatoes to cook until they begin to break down and form a somewhat chunky sauce.
6. Add the garlic and butter and stir until the butter melts and is amalgamated into the sauce.
7. Add the chicken back in to soak in the sauce for a few minutes.
8. Just before serving, add the julienned pieces of basil.
9. Serve the breasts, finished with the basil-tomato sauce, or arrange the chicken breasts on a mound of buttered pasta enriched with the sauce.

West Point seeks to educate and inspire its cadets to cherish the values of duty, honor, and country. Dan Donahue learned these life principles well as a young man. They became the lodestar of his personal and professional life. I remember Judy telling me once that Dan may have taken off the uniform of an army officer in 1963, but he continued for the rest of his life to look like a soldier in civilian clothes. And she was not far from the mark.

Wherever Dan and Judy were, they were invested in the work of bettering life for their family, church, and community. The word "service" was an integral part of Dan and Judy Donahue's DNA and identity as a married couple. One never had to nudge either of them; when they saw a need, they were on it.

Like so many of my lifelong relationships, I met the Donahues for the first time at church in the late 1970s. This picture-perfect family of five surrounded me one brisk fall morning after Mass to introduce themselves. Recently settled in their new home on Normandy Lane in Riverside, they were also beginning the process of sinking their roots deeply into the rich and fertile soil of their new parish. What could be more natural than to meet one of the parish clergy? Even though I was only a weekend assistant in Saint Catherine of Siena parish, they wanted to get to know me, and more importantly, for me to get to know each of them.

At that time Dan was immersing himself in his new role in New York as Merrill Lynch's director of general services. Soon thereafter he would be promoted to become district director for all New England. In Greenwich, Connecticut, Dan would quickly engross himself in local and national politics, eventually serving as the chair of Greenwich's Republican Town Committee. With three middle-school- and high-school-aged children—Dan, Laura, and Joey—both Judy and Dan took an early interest in the Arch Street Teen Center. Not only did they find a parish community, but before long Dan was serving as the president of the parish council at St. Catherine of Siena.

Even though Judy was a full-time mother of three bright and energetic children, she found time to invest in an emerging health-focused relief and development nonprofit organization, Americares, that responds to people affected by poverty or disaster by providing medicine, medical supplies, and healthcare assistance. Judy not only served on the governing board of Americares as a trustee, but she volunteered on many overseas rescue missions as a professional nurse. I still have a framed photo of Judy holding a seriously malnourished and critically ill child in her arms—a portrait reminiscent of any number of Renaissance images of the Madonna and Child. At a risk to her own health and safety, she ventured internationally into remote areas, offering inoculations and medicine and urgent care to people who were victims of natural and human disasters. I know that these hands-on experiences in caring for the least of God's children were formative ones for Judy. The Gospel saying of Jesus

"Anything you did for one of the least important of these brothers and sisters of mine, you did for me" (Mt 25:40) sums up Judy's selfless work with Americares. Although Judy may have only practiced clinical nursing for a short time before assuming a full-time role as wife and mother to her young family, she never lost her professional identity as healer and nurturer.

Of the many charitable things that Dan Donahue did, one initiative stands out with particular vividness in my memory. He headed up Merrill Lynch's Scholarship Builder Program in Harlem. This program contracted with kids in Harlem's kindergarten and primary schools, promising the children that if they worked hard during their formative years and successfully graduated from high school, Merrill Lynch would guarantee a free ride to whatever college that accepted them. Under Dan's supervision and personal nurturing of this program, of the twenty-five boys and girls who were initially contracted, twenty graduated on time and benefitted from Merrill's pledge. Dan invested much of his time to ensure the success of this initiative in corporate philanthropy and community partnership.

Their oldest son, Dan, enrolled at the Brunswick School in Greenwich. Just as West Point espoused "duty, honor, and country," Brunswick's motto aspires to "courage, honor, and truth." I suspect that these aspirational values appealed to both Judy and Dan as they sought out a place for Danny to enroll. He thrived during his years at Brunswick and upon graduation was accepted for admission at Harvard College. I remember joining Judy and Dan for a dinner to celebrate Danny's commencement from Harvard at the landmark Boston restaurant the Locke-Ober Café, unquestionably one of the grand American restaurants at the time. (It surprisingly went out of business in 2017 after 137 years.) When Danny Donahue graduated from Harvard, Locke-Ober was a destination location to celebrate his accomplishments. In its 4 Winter Place location the restaurant had an impressive bar and a spectacular main-floor dining room with a raw oyster bar. That evening some of us ordered one of the old Locke-Ober's signature dishes, Lobster Savannah. Here is my adaptation of this famous entrée.

LOBSTER SAVANNAH

Lobster baked with mushroom and bell pepper sauce

Makes 4 servings

Ingredients

- 4 2-pound lobsters
- 2 tablespoons unsalted butter
- 12 large sliced white mushrooms
- 3 minced shallots
- ½ a red bell pepper
- ¼ cup Cognac
- ¼ cup cream sherry
- 2 cups heavy cream
- a pinch of paprika
- salt and freshly ground black pepper
- juice of half a lemon
- ¼ cup grated Parmigiano Reggiano

Method

1. Bring a large stockpot filled with water to a rolling boil over high heat. Place lobsters in the pot head first, cover tightly, and return to a boil as quickly as possible. Cook for about 10 to 12 minutes. Remove from water, drain, and allow to cool.
2. Remove lobster claws and knuckles, crack them open, and reserve the meat. Using heavy kitchen shears, cut a long 1½ inch-wide rectangle out of the top of each lobster body, extending from about 2 inches behind eyes to about 1 inch from tail. Keeping the body in one piece, carefully pry meat from tail and set aside. Remove any meat from body cavity, as well as the green tomalley (liver) and set aside. Rinse lobster bodies and reserve.
3. Preheat oven to 400°F.
4. Cut lobster meat into 1-inch chunks and set aside in a bowl with tomalley.
5. Place a large sauté pan over high heat and melt butter. Add the sliced mushrooms and stir until they begin to exude their juices, 1 to 2

continued

minutes. Add shallots and diced red pepper and stir until liquid has evaporated and vegetables begin to brown.

6. Remove the skillet from heat and add Cognac and sherry. Carefully ignite the alcohol and allow it to burn off.
7. When the flames subside, place the skillet back over medium-high heat and add the heavy cream, paprika, and salt and pepper to taste. Add lobster meat and tomalley (if using) to the sauté pan and gently whisk. Add lemon juice and adjust seasonings to taste. Allow the sauce to simmer until lobster is heated through and the sauce is slightly thickened, about 5 minutes.
8. Place reserved lobster bodies in a large baking pan. Place equal portions of lobster mixture in cavities of bodies and sprinkle with Parmigiano Reggiano.
9. Bake until cheese is lightly browned, 2 to 3 minutes.

Laura Donahue, not unlike her mother, is a complete love. Born on Bastille Day, she is as adventuresome as any of the revolutionaries who stormed that Parisian fortress in 1789. Laura was one of the first girls to break the proverbial glass ceiling and become an altar server at St. Catherine's parish. On one particular Sunday morning, she was assisting at the sung Mass and had the special role of being the thurifer, the acolyte who carries the incense and censer. The church was filled, the Mass was long, and the air perhaps was not circulating as well as it might have. Whatever the contributing factors might have been, Laura became light-headed and at a pivotal moment in the service, in front of a crowded church of family and friends, she fainted, and the ceramic censor she was holding crashed to the marble floor. Fortunately, she was not seriously injured, and she recovered pretty quickly. The reader that day happened to be one of the attending internists from the Greenwich Hospital, so Laura received immediate expert attention. But she was mortified. She believed that she had failed in this important ministry. She was back at her acolyte post the following Sunday.

I was thrilled when Laura applied and was accepted to my own alma mater, Boston

College, where she majored in English and minored in film studies. She maintained a 4.0 cumulative average and lived up to the university's motto, "Ever to Excel." Moving back to New York City after graduation in 1989, Laura found a position at Christie's as a new business proposal writer. Although she could have made a successful career there, Laura felt the draw to be an early childhood teacher. I recall meeting with her at my Fairfield University office to discuss graduate school options. She matriculated in 1996 into the Bank Street College of Education's Master of Science in Education program, where she specialized in early childhood and elementary education. She proved to be an exceptional classroom teacher at the Brearley School in Manhattan and later at San Francisco Day School and the Prospect Sierra School.

When Laura Anne Donahue and Michael Torrens McKeeman were married under a gazebo in the garden of the Ritz-Carlton Hotel in Half Moon Bay, California, on August 28, 2004, I was happy to preside at their nuptial Mass and to witness their vows. Later I would baptize their two sons, Connor and Ryan.

Recalling Laura and Mike's wedding at the Ritz brings back a memory of the Ritz's signature lemon pound cake that dates back to the 1920s in Paris, where hotelier César Ritz attracted August Escoffier—whom some have called "the king of chefs and the chef of kings"—to be his partner. While a student at Le Cordon Bleu I became familiar with Escoffier's 1903 *Le Guide Culinaire,* which remains one of my go-to resources.[8]

RITZ-CARLTON LEMON POUND CAKE

Makes 8 to 10 servings

Ingredients

- 3 cups all-purpose flour
- 1 tablespoon baking powder
- ¾ teaspoon kosher salt
- 3 cups granulated sugar
- 1 cup unsalted butter at room temperature

continued

8 Auguste Escoffier, *Le Guide Culinaire* (Paris: Émile Colin, Imprimerie de Lagny, 1903).

- ½ cup vegetable shortening at room temperature
- 5 large eggs at room temperature
- ½ cup milk
- ½ cup heavy cream
- 6 tablespoons freshly squeezed lemon juice
- zest of 1 lemon

Method

1. Preheat oven to 350°F.
2. Grease and flour a tube or Bundt pan or 2 loaf pans.
3. Sift flour, baking powder, and salt into a medium bowl. Set aside.
4. Using an electric or stand mixer, cream together butter, shortening, and sugar.
5. Add eggs one at a time, beating well after each one. Scrape down the sides and bottom of the bowl.
6. Add dry ingredients in three additions to butter mixture alternately with half of the milk and cream, beginning and ending with the flour mixture.
7. Beat at low speed until the batter is blended; do not overbeat.
8. Gently stir in lemon juice and zest.
9. Pour the batter into the prepared pan(s).
10. Bake until the cake is golden on top and a tester inserted into center comes out clean, 55 to 70 minutes (start checking after 55 minutes of baking).
11. Cool the cake in the pan. Using a sharp knife, gently separate cake from edges and inner tube.
12. Turn cake out onto rack.

Dan and Judy's youngest son is Joseph Patrick Donahue, whom I have known since he was six years old. Joey followed his older brother to Brunswick but then went west for college at Stanford University, where he received his bachelor's degree in biological sciences in 1993. He returned to New York to attend medical school at Columbia University College of Physicians and Surgeons. Because of his kind disposition and innate sensitivities, I fully expected Joey would have specialized in either in family medicine or pediatrics. He fooled me entirely when, after his internship at St. Luke's-Roosevelt Hospital Center, he completed orthopedic residencies at Memorial Sloan Kettering Cancer Center, the Alfred I. duPont Institute in Delaware, St. Luke's-Roosevelt Hospital, and University Hospital of Columbia College of Physicians and Surgeons. He accepted a fellowship in orthopedic sports medicine at the Stanford/SOAR Sports Medicine Fellowship Program before joining the Stanford faculty.

While Joey Donahue was still a medical student at Columbia, he proposed marriage to Katharine ("Kat") Alfond during an African safari in the spring of 1997. Soon after they returned from Africa, I got a call from Joey inviting me to meet Kat and join them for dinner at a lovely northern Italian restaurant on Central Park South. Kat is the middle child of a Jewish family from Weston, Massachusetts. As Joey and Kat talked together that evening I could see the synergies that they shared in terms of family values, dreams, and aspirations. But the end of dinner I found had another thing in common with Joey Donahue: I too loved Kat. Later when I met Kat's parents, Barbara and Ted Alfond, and her extended family, I understood why it was so easy to love Kat. The Alfonds are a wonderfully loving family.

I remember enjoying a wonderful risotto dish that night when I first met her, with fresh spring asparagus. Here is my version of this classic northern Italian dish.

RISOTTO CON GLI ASPARAGI

Risotto with asparagus

Makes 4 to 6 servings

Ingredients

- 1 pound thin asparagus

continued

- 5 cups chicken or vegetable broth
- 2 tablespoons extra-virgin olive oil
- 4 tablespoons unsalted butter
- 1 finely diced onion
- 1½ cups arborio rice
- kosher salt and freshly ground black pepper
- ½ cup dry white wine
- freshly grated Parmigiano Reggiano cheese

Method

1. Pour the broth into a saucepan and warm to a gentle simmer. Keep warm.
2. Prepare the asparagus by severing the ends of the spears and cutting the spears into about 1-inch segments. Add the discarded ends to the simmering broth to enhance its flavor profile.
3. Add 2 tablespoons of extra-virgin olive oil and 2 tablespoons of butter in a large saucepan and turn the heat to medium. When the butter starts to foam, add the onion and sauté until the onion is softened.
4. Add the arborio rice and stir in the butter, oil, and onion mixture for 2 or 3 minutes, and add salt and pepper.
5. Add the white wine and continue stirring for an additional few minutes until the wine is absorbed.
6. Add a quarter cup of the broth, stirring with a wooden spoon to prevent the rice from sticking to the pan. When the rice begins to absorb the liquid, add more broth.
7. Repeat this step of adding the broth and stirring, keeping the rice at the consistency of a dense paste, until all of the liquid has been added and absorbed. This will take between 18 to 20 minutes. Be patient and continue stirring and adding the broth.
8. After about 12 minutes into the cooking process, add the asparagus spears.

9. When the cooking of the risotto is completed, add a couple tablespoons of butter along with the grated Parmigiano Reggiano cheese. Cook another minute or two.
10. The risotto should be al dente (firm, and not too soft).
11. Serve with some additional grated cheese, and perhaps a bit of freshly chopped flat-leaf parsley.

Joey and Kat's interfaith wedding ceremony on the following September 27 at the Pierre Hotel in New York City, which I co-officiated with a rabbi colleague, Rabbi Bert Siegel, was a wonderful celebration of the beliefs and traditions they shared in common. The ballroom for their wedding reception and dinner had been transformed into a massive tent and the table decorations were memorable floral re-creations of jungle animals, all reminiscent of the safari adventure during which Joey and Kat had become engaged.

I so enjoyed getting to know Mrs. Pardi, Judy Pardi Donahue's mother, who spent increasing periods of time with the Donahues during the later years of her life. Having emigrated from Italy, Mrs. Pardi applied her remarkable sewing and embroidery skills as an expert dressmaker. As she grew older macular degeneration progressively robbed her of her sight, but visual impairment was unable to dampen her ebullient spirit. She spoke a mellifluous Italian.

On one of the numerous occasions that she visited with Judy and Dan, they brought her to the Italian Mass that I celebrated one Sunday a month in the parish for the Italian-speaking community. During a subsequent conversation that Judy had with her mother, Mrs. Pardi said, "He is such a lovely young Italian priest, Judy."

"Mama, he isn't Italian; he is as Irish as Dan Donahue."

"Impossible, Judy. He speaks beautiful Italian; he can't be Irish," Mrs. Pardi stated.

"He learned to speak Italian during his residency in Rome, but he definitely has strong Boston Irish roots, Mama."

"*Non lo credo* (I don't believe it)," her mother insisted. "Irish people can't speak Italian like that."

If Mrs. Pardi had tasted my version of *gnocchi alla Romana*, to which I was first introduced by my longtime friend, the restaurateur and celebrity chef Lidia

Matticchio Bastianich, Judy never would have been able to convince her Italian mother of my Irish ancestry.

GNOCCHI ALLA ROMANA AL FORNO

Baked Roman-style gnocchi

Makes 6 to 8 servings

Ingredients

For the gnocchi

- 5 cups whole milk
- 4 tablespoons unsalted butter
- 2 teaspoons kosher salt
- 1½ cups finely ground semolina flour
- ½ cup freshly grated Parmigiano Reggiano
- ½ cup freshly grated Pecorino Romano
- 2 large egg yolks

For the besciamella

- ¼ pound (1 stick) unsalted butter
- ½ cup all-purpose flour
- ½ gallon room-temperature whole milk
- ½ teaspoon freshly grated nutmeg
- 1 teaspoon freshly ground black pepper
- ½ pound shredded Taleggio cheese
- ½ cup grated Parmigiano Reggiano

Method

Preparing the gnocchi

1. Lightly grease and line a rimmed baking pan with parchment paper, slightly overlapping the ends of the pan. Lightly brush the top of the parchment with some melted butter or olive oil. (This will help to remove the gnocchi from the pan later.)
2. In a large (3- to 4-quart) saucepan, heat the milk, salt, and butter slowly to avoid over-boiling the milk or burning the liquid on the bottom of the saucepan. Using a whisk, blend in the Parmigiano Reggiano and Pecorino Romano cheeses.
3. Once the cheeses have melted, add in the semolina flour in a slow stream while vigorously whisking to avoid clumping. Switch to a wooden spoon and cook, while slowly stirring, for about 15 to 18 minutes, until the mixture becomes very thick and difficult to stir. It will no longer cling to the sides of the saucepan.
4. Off the heat, with wooden spoon, thoroughly incorporate the two egg yolks into the thickened mixture.
5. Spread the semolina mixture evenly onto the prepared pan and using a spatula, smooth the surface area. Allow the cooked semolina to cool, loosely tented with lightly oiled aluminum foil, and refrigerate for a minimum of 2 hours or overnight.
6. Once refrigerated and firm, invert the entire tray of semolina dough onto a countertop and peel away the parchment paper.

Preparing the besciamella

1. Melt the butter in a medium saucepan. Once the butter has melted, add in all the flour and whisk vigorously to avoid clumping for about 2 minutes until the mixture begins to bubble slightly and turns a pale golden color.
2. Slowly pour in the milk while continuing to whisk vigorously.
3. When the sauce has thickened, remove from the heat add the salt, pepper, nutmeg, and Taleggio and whisk to combine.

continued

To assemble and bake

1. Preheat oven to 425°F.
2. Grease a 9x13-inch ovenproof baking dish with a tablespoon of softened butter. Add about 1 cup of the *besciamella* sauce to the bottom surface of the baking dish.
3. Cut the semolina gnocchi into 2-inch squares and layer slightly overlapping with their points up (so that the squares look like diamonds); you will have three or four rows of overlapping diamonds at the end.
4. Nap each of the diamond-cut pieces of semolina gnocchi with a generous tablespoon of the *besciamella* sauce.
5. Sprinkle the surface of the gnocchi with grated Parmigiano Reggiano.
6. Bake the gnocchi for 25 to 30 minutes or until the *besciamella* sauce is bubbling and the tops of the *gnocchi alla Romana* are a beautiful golden brown.
7. Allow to rest for 10 minutes before serving.

In 2007, I received an invitation from Dan and Judy and three other couples from St. Catherine of Siena parish. What they proposed was that I might join them—as their guest—for trip to Tuscany to participate in a week-long cooking school run by cookbook author and chef Lorenza de' Medici. A week in a Tuscan cooking school turned into a dream adventure, which began in the Lungarno Hotel in Firenze that afforded magical vistas of the Ponte Vecchio and unbelievable Florentine sunsets.

Judy had arranged for our little group to revisit the Uffizi museum with a wonderful and knowledgeable docent. The Donahues had also made reservations for us to have a rare opportunity to tour the Corridoio Vasariano. The Vasari Corridor is an elevated passageway between the Palazzo Pitti and the Palazzo Vecchio. The corridoio was designed by Giorgio Vasari and constructed in 1565 at the order of Grand Duke Cosimo de' Medici. The Medicis wanted both safety and privacy as they moved by foot between their home at the Pitti Palace to their workplace, the seat of government in the Palazzo Vecchio.

We left Florence to travel to our residential cooking school, which was held in Lorenza de' Medici's historic home at Badia a Coltibuono, a former Benedictine monastery. Despite the frenetic class schedule each day, everything we did was fun. Like the cooking itself, each dish surpassed the next. Our instructor for the week was Guido, Lorenza's son.

Besides the cooking classes and sumptuous dining, we had a couple of other highlights during this not-to-be forgotten journey. We were invited one evening to dine with Baron Bettino Ricasoli and his wife, an aging noble couple who were living in the Ricasoli Firodolfi baronial apartments in the ancient Sienese neo-gothic Castello di Brolio. The Ricasoli family have been producing wine continuously from this vineyard estate since the year 1141, and Baron Ricasoli served briefly as Italy's twenty-eighth prime minister. Knowing that I was a Jesuit priest, he insisted that he personally provide us with a brief visit to the castle's lovely twelfth-century chapel of San Jacopo before we concluded our evening at the castello.

Serendipitously, our dream week coincided with Il Palio di Siena. We were invited to participate in three events connected with this annual horse race. First, we attended the *prova generale*, the trial race that occurs the evening before the actual race. That evening, after the *prova*, we joined the folks from one of the fifteen *contrade* (neighborhoods) and dined sumptuously with the *contradaioli* in the cobblestone streets of their neighborhood.

The next afternoon, the visual splendor of the events transported me back to the Middle Ages as we sat in reserved seats in the Piazza del Campo. The pageantry of the grand procession stimulated every sense, with the drummers, flag hurlers, and entourages of the various *contrade* parading within an arm's reach in front of us.

To be able to watch so closely *il mossiere* (the starter of the race) trying to get *Il Palio di Siena* off to a good start, with all the jockeys and horses in proper position, was unbelievable. And the drama of a photo finish to the race added to the spectacle.

During the summer months, one can find the Sienese dining on this very simple dish. Hand-rolled Tuscan *pici* are made with just flour, water, salt, and olive oil. Peasants in the countryside around Siena traditionally ate these long and irregular-shaped noodles dressed with a simple garlic and anchovy sauce and using breadcrumbs fried in olive oil.

PICI CON LE BRICIOLE

Sienese pici with garlic, anchovies, and breadcrumbs

Makes 6 to 8 servings

Ingredients

For the pici

- 1½ cups all-purpose flour
- 1½ cups semolina flour
- 1 cup warm water
- 1 tablespoon extra-virgin olive oil

For the dressing

- ¼ cup extra-virgin olive oil
- 2 cloves minced garlic
- 4 anchovy filets
- ¼ cup homemade breadcrumbs
- salt, pepper, and dried chili to taste
- grated Pecorino cheese (optional)
- fresh parsley, chopped (optional)

Method

Making the pici

1. Mix the all-purpose flour and semolina together on a clean work surface, forming a mound.
2. Create a well in the center of the mound and pour in the warm water and oil, and little by little, incorporate the flour with your hands.
3. Continue bringing the flour, water, and oil together until you end up with a smooth dough.

4. Set the dough aside to rest, covered with a bowl for at least a half hour.
5. Separate the dough into two pieces, keeping one piece covered. Roll one piece out into a 4-by-12-inch rectangle. On a well-floured surface roll out the first piece flat until it is about ⅛ inch thick.
6. Cut long strips about ¼ inch wide, and then with the palms of your hands or between your thumb and fingers roll each flat strip from the center outwards until you have a thick noodle, thicker than a spaghetti noodle.
7. Dust with semolina and set aside. Continue until you have finished cutting and rolling all the dough.
8. Heat a pot of water to boil the pasta.

Making the dressing

1. In a wide skillet, gently sauté the chopped garlic in half of the olive oil until it has softened and is about to turn golden. Add the anchovies and red pepper flakes and stir until the anchovies begin to melt. Do not to burn the garlic. Set aside.
2. Cook the pasta in the boiling salted water until al dente, about 3 minutes, depending on the thickness of your *pici*. Drain, saving some of the cooking water.
3. Add the drained *pici* with about a half cup of the cooking water to the anchovy and garlic mixture in the skillet and over a medium heat toss the pasta for one minute or so, adding more olive oil and the breadcrumbs, until combined. Serve immediately with some grated Pecorino and freshly chopped parsley.

Soon after meeting Judy and Dan I was introduced to Giselle Berube, Judy's former Park Hospital School of Nursing dean, who, while Judy was a nursing student, was a Roman Catholic nun and a member of the nineteenth-century French Canadian congregation Les Soeurs de Miséricorde. After leaving religious life during the tumultuous late 1960s, Giselle married and moved to Western Canada with her husband. Later, after she became widowed, she returned to live in Montréal to be closer to her family. The Donahues helped Giselle to find a senior living facility not too distant from the center of Montréal. Les Jardins de Renoir in Chomedey, Laval, proved to be an ideal, comfortable retirement home for Giselle. She had a light-filled one-bedroom apartment with a kitchen and bath, with views overlooking the Catholic parish church, located just across the street. Le Renoir provided a truly pleasant living environment, which Giselle cherished and deeply appreciated.

Giselle was an elegant woman, refined in every way. As a nun, she combined her deep faith and spirituality with her consummate skills as a clinical nurse and expert administrator. As an aging laywoman, she retained that wonderful blend of a contemplative immersed in every dimension of the world. Although living on a very modest budget (supplemented by the generous financial support of the Donahue family, who looked after her until her death), she remained elegantly coiffed and impeccably dressed.

On one occasion I accompanied Judy and Dan for a three-day visit with Giselle in Montréal, soon after Laura and Mike's wedding. My entry into Canada at the International Montréal-Trudeau airport was anything but smooth. Judy and Dan had passed quickly through their immigration review screening and moved on to the baggage claim area in the terminal, while I was detained by the immigration officer for further questioning.

"Who are you, and what is the intended purpose of your visit to Canada?" they asked. When I told the officer that I was a Jesuit priest, traveling with friends to visit a former nun who lived in a senior residence in Laval, I drew even further suspicion and was escorted to a private office for further interrogation. It seems that someone whose description I fit was purportedly traveling from New York to Montréal for some alleged criminal purpose—drug or weapons dealing or some other equally nefarious business. After almost an hour of delay and questioning, I was finally cleared to enter Canada. Judy and Dan were beside themselves, worrying that I had had a heart attack or had fallen and been taken to some hospital by ambulance. The border patrol officials would not let them reenter the zone in which I was being detained, nor provide them with any information about my whereabouts or why I was being delayed. When I finally emerged from the immigration area they were both relieved and full of questions. My simple reply was, "You will never believe the story."

It also happened that the Donahues had unredeemed courtesy coupons from Laura and Mike's wedding that afforded them several complimentary nights in a

Ritz-Carlton hotel. Judy and Dan decided to use this perquisite to treat Giselle and me to a long weekend in Montréal's Ritz-Carlton. Enthusiastically, Giselle accepted the invitation. On one of the evenings she recommended a very fine French restaurant in downtown Montréal where the concierge had successfully been able to book a reservation for the four of us. It was a quiet and very intimate dining establishment situated within an old nineteenth-century refurbished townhouse.

Before dinner, we were seated in a quaint lounge that had previously served as a first-floor drawing room in this beautiful mansion, complete with a crackling fire that warmed and gracefully illuminated the seating area to which we were invited. Once settled, Dan asked what we might like to drink. Without losing a beat, Giselle graciously but firmly declared: "A little bit of champagne would be lovely, Dan." Dan quickly ordered a bottle of fine champagne, which immediately drew a smile of contentment and approval from this grande dame.

The next day we visited L'Oratoire Saint-Joseph du Mont Royal, built because of the inspiration, vision, and persistent faith of Brother André Bessette, who was canonized by the Roman Catholic Church in 2010. First assigned to be a doorkeeper at the Collège Notre-Dame across the street from the future oratory, Brother André was subsequently asked to be the caretaker at a house of prayer, which he shepherded into existence on Mount Royal. He welcomed thousands of distressed people who were looking for a reason to hope. He listened to them and counseled that they pray to Saint Joseph in whom he had full confidence. Any number of miraculous healings took place on Mont Royal and many hearts were turned toward God. Giselle loved this place of pilgrimage and prayer.

During this visit Giselle accepted my suggestion that she tour the shrine in a wheelchair, which I volunteered to push. We stopped at every altar for a moment of prayer and reflection. Here was the contemplative Giselle, the same woman who hours before on the previous evening luxuriated on fois gras and truffles, champagne, and good Cognac.

On two other occasions, Judy, Dan, and I returned to Montréal to take on the role of chef de cuisine at Giselle's apartment, to prepare nutritious and delicious meals to fill her freezer for the long Canadian winter. We started these days with a carefully orchestrated trip to a local supermarket to purchase all the provisions we would need for our cooking marathon. On the menu were a variety of entrées, including classic dishes such as *Boeuf à la Bourguignonne*, rolled chicken breasts with a mushroom duxelles filling, *ragù alla Bolognese*, and a variety of other soups and stews. I am happy to share my personal recipe for Poitrines de Poulet Roulées.

POITRINES DE POULET ROULÉES AVEC DUXELLES SÊCHES DE CHAMPIGNONS

Rolled chicken breasts with mushroom duxelles and leeks

Makes 4 servings

Ingredients

For the chicken

- 4 boneless, skinless chicken breasts (8 ounces each)
- Dijon mustard
- lemon juice
- salt and pepper

For the duxelles filling

- ½ pound (about 2 cups) mushrooms
- 2 tablespoons minced shallots
- 1 small leek, white part halved lengthwise, washed and chopped
- ½ teaspoon minced fresh thyme leaves
- 2 tablespoons butter
- ½ cup dry white wine
- 1 cup beef broth
- 1 tablespoon each oil and butter
- kosher salt and freshly ground pepper

For the breading

- all-purpose flour
- eggs
- Panko breadcrumbs
- dried thyme
- unsalted butter

Method

Making the duxelles filling

1. Clean the mushrooms and finely chop.
2. In a skillet, sauté the mushrooms, shallots, and leeks in butter and oil over moderately high heat, stirring frequently. After 6 to 8 minutes, the mushroom mixture should start to brown. Season to taste with salt and pepper.
3. Add the herbs, wine, and stock to the mushrooms, and boil down rapidly until liquid has virtually evaporated.
4. Set aside to cool.

To prepare and bake the chicken breasts

1. Preheat oven to 350°F.
2. If the chicken breasts have the tenderloins attached, remove them and set aside.
3. Using a sharp knife, slice the chicken breasts in half horizontally.
4. Rinse a large zipper-lock plastic bag with cold water. Place each piece of chicken, laid out flat, in the bag, a one at a time. (The water will help to keep the chicken from sticking during pounding.)
5. Pound the chicken pieces to about ¼-inch thickness. Set aside.
6. When all the breasts have been pounded, season the inner portion of the poultry with salt and pepper and brush with a mixture of Dijon mustard and fresh lemon juice.
7. Spread evenly a portion of the prepared mushroom duxelles filling over each breast and roll up, like a cigar, seam-side down.
8. Lightly flour each rolled breast, then dip in beaten egg wash and finally coat lightly with the Panko breadcrumbs, which have been seasoned with the dried thyme.

continued

9. Place the rolled chicken breasts into a buttered oblong ovenproof baking dish. Once all of the chicken breast rolls have been arranged in the baking dish, drizzle the melted butter over the breadcrumb topping.
10. Baked for 30 to 35 minutes.

During the several hours we worked to prepare, package, and store these various dishes in Giselle's freezer—each with their reheating instructions—she sat contentedly in her chair by the window, smiling approvingly and appreciatively as we chopped and sautéed in her kitchen. Even though her eyesight was failing, she nonetheless took great comfort in her collection of spiritual books, most of which were amply underlined and annotated from years of prior contemplation and reflection.

Giselle played significant roles in the Donahue family's entire history. She inspired by the example of her life, praying for each of them continuously and serving as a loving, adoptive grandmother, an honor she immensely treasured.

When Dan retired, Judy anticipated that they would enjoy more leisure time together for travel and other activities. That was not to be. Soon after retiring from Merrill Lynch in 2006, Dan began sowing the seeds of a new private banking venture which two years later would become Fieldpoint Private Bank and Trust. His extensive network of relationships and the immeasurable trust he had earned over the course of his long career provided the human capital that made this new business enterprise possible. Dan nurtured the development of this novel private banking venture, recruited a corps of private investors and clients, built an impressive governing board, and did everything that was required to comply with state and federal regulatory guidelines. The new venture was successful. At the same time, he continued to find time for his many charitable and civic interests.

I recall sharing a dinner with Dan and Judy when he first told me about this embryonic banking adventure. He was animated as he talked about the challenges. In the years that followed Dan charted the bank's growth as its founding president, CEO, and chairman, and he shepherded this fledgling banking firm through the global financial crisis of 2007–2008. It proved to be one of the most challenging economic calamities in generations. Dan's integrity and human decency shaped a culture of service that set Fieldpoint apart in the financial services industry. Even today, Dan's imprint on

Fieldpoint is indelible. In January 2013 he became its lead director, and finally, in May 2014, he passed the leadership to another and became chairman emeritus.

When the children had begun to settle into their adult lives, Judy and Dan sold their home on Normandy Lane and bought a house on Country Club Lane on a promontory reaching into Long Island Sound, immediately adjacent to the property occupied by the Riverside Yacht Club. They lived there until after Dan's retirement from Fieldpoint in the spring of 2014, when they decided to relocate to California to be nearer their three adult children, their spouses, and their seven grandchildren.

For several years Judy and Dan had been making numerous extended trips to both Los Angeles and the San Francisco Bay area, and they had purchased a small pied à terre condominium in Pacific Palisades. The Donahues were beginning to formulate longer terms plans to sell their Riverside home and possibly establish permanent residency on the West Coast.

We shared a dinner together that September at which they mused about these future plans. In mid-October, they left Connecticut for California on one of their occasional trips, with plans to remain in Los Angeles through the Thanksgiving holidays. They had hoped to gather the whole family in December in Cabo San Lucas to celebrate Christmas together.

On October 21, 2014, without any prior warning, Dan Donahue suffered fatal coronary arrest. His death was instantaneous, with no time to offer any final farewells.

I presided and preached at a memorial funeral liturgy on November 22 in Connecticut. Saint Catherine of Siena parish church was filled to overflowing with family, friends, and colleagues on that bright Saturday morning. The eulogies that were offered painted essentially the same portrait of a man of exemplary virtue, sterling integrity, impeccable moral values, practical wisdom, unfailing devotion, serious gravitas, and eminently good Irish humor.

His remains were inurned in a beautifully designed columbarium at the old Cadets' Chapel on the campus of West Point. The academy provided full military honors and a fitting farewell on a bright autumn day for one of its very loyal alumni. I also bid adieu to a dear friend with whom I was so fortunate to accompany, along with Judy and his remarkable family, on a significant portion of our shared earthly pilgrimage.

I share this recipe for a bittersweet French lemon tart as a loving symbol of Dan and Judy's lasting imprint on my life and ministry. The finished tart has a firm, delicious crust infused with herbal Italian olive oil. The luscious lemon curd beams brightly like a Celtic smile—the sun that never sets.

TARTE AU CITRON CROÛTE À L'HUILE D'OLIVE

Lemon tart with olive oil pastry

Makes 6 to 8 servings

Ingredients

For the crust

- 1½ cups all-purpose flour
- 5 tablespoons granulated sugar
- ½ teaspoon kosher salt
- ½ cup extra-virgin olive oil
- 3 springs fresh thyme
- 2 tablespoons ice water

For the filling

- 1 cup granulated or superfine sugar
- ¼ teaspoon kosher salt
- 3 eggs, plus 3 additional yolks
- 1 tablespoon grated lemon zest
- ½ cup lemon juice (3 lemons)
- ¼ cup extra-virgin olive oil

Method

Making the crust

1. In a small saucepan, warm the ½ cup of extra-virgin olive oil. Off the heat, add 3 sprigs of fresh thyme and allow the herbs to infuse the oil as it cools, about 30 minutes.
2. Adjust oven rack to the middle position and preheat the oven to 350°F.
3. Whisk dry ingredients (flour, sugar, and salt) together to combine.

4. Remove the thyme sprigs from the oil and add the cooled infused olive oil and ice water and stir in the flour mixture. Blend until the dough begins to come together.
5. Using your hands, crumble three-quarters of dough over bottom of 9-inch tart pan with a removable bottom.
6. Press dough to even thickness in bottom of pan.
7. Crumble the remaining dough and scatter evenly around edge of pan, then press crumbled dough into fluted sides of pan. Press dough to even thickness. With a fork, prick the bottom crust of the tart.
8. Place the pan on a rimmed baking sheet and bake until crust is golden brown and firm to touch, 30 to 35 minutes, rotating pan halfway through baking.

Making the filling

1. About 5 minutes before crust is finished baking, whisk sugar, flour, and salt in medium saucepan until combined.
2. Whisk in eggs and yolks until no streaks of egg remain. Whisk in the lemon zest and juice. Cook over medium-low heat, whisking constantly and scraping the corners of saucepan, until mixture thickens slightly and registers 160°F or between 5 to 8 minutes of cooking time.
3. Off the heat, whisk in oil until it is incorporated. Strain the lemon curd through fine-mesh strainer that has been set over a bowl. Pour the curd into the warm tart shell.
4. Bake until the filling is set and barely jiggles when the pan is shaken, 8 to 12 minutes.
5. Let the tart cool completely on a wire rack, at least 2 hours.
6. Remove outer metal ring of tart pan. Slide a thin metal spatula between tart and the metal baking disk, then carefully slide the tart onto a serving dish.

In remembering the faithful life of Dan Donahue, these words of the prophet Isaiah come to mind:

No longer will you have the sun for light by day,
Nor for brightness will the moon give you light;
But you will have the Lord for an everlasting light,
And your God for your glory.

—ISAIAH 60:19

Chapter 14

A WONDROUS TAPESTRY

I want you woven into a tapestry of love,
in touch with everything there is to know of God.
Then you will have minds confident and at rest,
focused on Christ, God's great mystery.
All the richest treasures of wisdom and knowledge
are embedded in that mystery and nowhere else.
And we've been shown the mystery!

—COLOSSIANS 2:2–3

The twenty-six years of my life (1991–2017) that I invested in shepherding the diverse, multifaith works of the HealthCare Chaplaincy in New York City created a complex, unique tapestry of relationships and experiences. No memoir could possibly capture, chronicle, or describe all the individual threads that contributed to the woven masterpiece of a life's major work.

Over the years, I have heard various people compare life to a tapestry. When you examine the back of a tapestry, it often looks like a messy jumble of tangled knots and random threads of colored yarn. When you turn the tapestry over, you see an incredible image, fashioned in beautifully intricate patterns that have been created by a skilled weaver.

Life does not always reveal its integral beauty at an initial viewing. It is often difficult to grasp the full picture or understand why certain situations occur or how they ultimately fit in the scheme of the whole. At times life can seem to be a messy, tangled web, as is the reverse side of a tapestry. Yet when one looks back over the years, one gets a glimpse of the finished side and appreciates how God's skilled and artistic hands have been weaving a complex, magnificent, and lovingly designed tapestry.

I always viewed my work at HealthCare Chaplaincy as a ministry, not as a job. Because the Chaplaincy was a complex business enterprise, over the years I had my share of challenges and difficulties, joys and sorrows, successes and failures, high points and low points, incredible opportunities and seemingly impossible roadblocks to navigate. Looking back, I affirm God's hand in it all, slowly but inexorably designing and superbly weaving a remarkable tapestry from the discrete threads of these many experiences.

In 2012, as I was beginning conversations with the executive committee of the Chaplaincy's board of trustees about the need for them to think about and plan for executive succession, I serendipitously discovered an exhibition at the Seventh Regiment Armory that is located on Park Avenue on the Upper East Side of Manhattan.

New York is a remarkable place to live and work. Friends were continuously alerting me to exhibitions and lectures, Broadway and Off-Broadway plays and musicals, lectures and concerts. I read the *New York Times* religiously, and on weekends paid particular attention to the numerous arts and entertainment articles and reviews. But somehow notice of this current exhibition at the Armory had eluded me.

As I was hurrying to an appointment with my audiologist, Dr. Therese Deierlein, I noticed the billboard announcement of the event at the Armory. It piqued my interest. The exhibition was titled *The Event of a Thread*, presented by artist Ann Hamilton, whom I did not know. Ann is a visual artist who had built her reputation for large-scale, multimedia installations that simultaneously engage viewers on many sensory, intellectual, and spiritual levels.

The Park Avenue Armory is a massive red brick and stone structure designed in the gothic revival style by Charles Clinton and constructed as a national guard armory in 1880. It was beginning to show its age and needed both restoration and a new raison d'être. A private-public partnership was formed for this purpose. These folks raised the funds needed to undertake a major renovation of the Armory. The partnership now operates the building as a venue for exhibitions, artistic presentations, and cultural performances.

In 2012, the Armory's artistic director commissioned Ann Hamilton to create her large-scale installation. I decided to visit the exhibition. When I entered the Armory's cavernous space I was struck by numerous panels of white fabric and large wooden swings, which had been suspended from the Armory's original metal ceiling rafters. It looked as if each swing had been connected to another through a system of pulleys. As people sat on the swings and moved back and forth, the white fabric panels rose and fell to match the rhythm of their movements. As a result, these billowing sheets of fabric became a visual image of the connectedness of the people gliding on the swings rather than simply being barriers between them. Rather than "visiting" this exhibition, I quickly became directly immersed in this multisensory experience. Within this field of swings and fabric, all of us began to feel connected to the actions of one another and to the work itself.

Here was the metaphor for which I had been searching—a way to describe more than a quarter-century of relationships, events, and experiences in New York City. In this concluding chapter of reflections on my happy and productive New York years, I want to look at some of the "fabric panels" and "swings" from Ann Hamilton's installation that have contributed to the interconnectedness of my own quarter-century investments in the multifaith and multiethnic worlds of HealthCare Chaplaincy and New York City.

In this context, I recall one of the technical challenges I experienced at Le Cordon Bleu. We were asked to re-create the nineteenth-century confection *Gâteau St. Honoré*. This complex dessert celebrates St. Honoré, the Roman Catholic patron saint of bakers and pastry makers. The original recipe is probably more than two centuries old. We had been taught the 1846 approach of the French pastry chef Chiboust, who re-created this confection in his pastry shop located on Rue St. Honoré in Paris.

I associate this dessert with the rich diversity of my New York experiences because the Gâteau St. Honoré is composed of five different elements that combine into a glorious, show-stopper confection: *pâte feuilletée* (puff pastry); *pâte à choux* (cream puff pastry); *sucre caramélisé* (caramelized sugar); *crème chiboust* (a filling made by folding Italian meringue into a crème *pâtissière*); and *crème Chantilly* (flavored whipped heavy cream).

GÂTEAU ST. HONORÉ

Classic nineteenth-century pastry and cream confection

Makes 8 to 10 servings

continued

Ingredients

For the pâte feuilletée

There is excellent quality commercial puff pastry readily available in most supermarkets. I would suggest purchasing a box of two sheets of store-bought frozen puff pastry for this recipe.

For the pâte à choux

- ½ cup water
- ½ cup whole milk
- 8 tablespoons unsalted butter
- 1 teaspoon kosher salt
- 2 teaspoons granulated sugar
- 1 cup all-purpose flour
- 4 large eggs
- sifted powdered sugar

For the crème chiboust

- 2 cups whole milk
- 1 tablespoon granulated sugar
- 1 teaspoon vanilla extract
- 4 egg yolks
- 2 tablespoons granulated sugar
- 2 tablespoons all-purpose flour
- 2 tablespoons corn starch
- powdered gelatin (optional, for stabilizing the cream)

For the Italian meringue

- 4 room-temperature egg whites
- ½ teaspoon crème of tartar

- 1 cup granulated sugar
- 3 tablespoons water
- a few drops of lemon juice or 2 tablespoons corn syrup (which helps to prevent the sugar from crystalizing)

For the sucre caramélisé

- ¼ cup light corn syrup
- ¼ cup water
- 1 pound granulated sugar

For the crème Chantilly

- 2 cups heavy cream
- 1 teaspoon vanilla extract (or the scrapped seeds from 1 vanilla bean)
- 1 tablespoon confectioners' sugar

Method

Making the pâte feuilletée

1. Thaw one sheet of the puff pastry dough in the refrigerator overnight.
2. Roll the puff pastry sheet out on a lightly floured surface to ensure sufficient dough to cut an 8- or 9-inch diameter circle.
3. With the tines of a fork, dock (prick) the pastry generously to prevent dough from puffing up too much.
4. Cut pastry into an 8- or 9-inch disk.
5. Place the disk of puff pastry dough on a silicone mat or parchment paper to prevent dough from shrinking and keep refrigerated.

Making the pate à choux

1. Mix the eggs in a small bowl and set aside.

continued

2. Bring water, milk, butter, sugar, and salt to a boil in a medium saucepan.
3. Remove from heat. Using a wooden spoon, quickly stir in flour.
4. Return the pan to the stovetop and cook the flour over medium-high heat, stirring constantly, until mixture begins to pull away from sides of the pan (about a minute).
5. Transfer the dough ball to the bowl of an electric mixer fitted with the paddle attachment.
6. Mix on low speed for about 1 minute to allow the steam to escape and for the dough to cool down a bit. Then, on low speed, begin to add a portion of the lightly beaten eggs, allowing them to incorporate into the dough before adding more eggs. After all the egg mixture has been incorporated, the batter will form soft peaks when pinched with your fingers.
7. Preheat oven to 350°F.
8. Transfer the pate à choux into a pastry bag fitted with a 5/8-inch plain tip.
9. On a baking sheet fitted with a silicone pad or parchment paper, place the refrigerated puff pastry disk on one side of the pan. The other side of the pan will hold about 18 to 20 small cream puffs, which you are about to pipe.
10. First, pipe a thin half-inch-thick ring of pâte à choux dough onto the edge of the 8- or 9-inch puff pastry ring.
11. Pipe out 18 to 20 small puffs. With wet finger, smooth the tops and dust lightly with powdered sugar.
12. Bake the puff pastry ring and the pâte à choux small puffs on a rack arranged in the middle of the oven for about 40 minutes. Do not open the oven door during baking or the pastry may deflate.
13. Then turn the oven off, leaving the door ajar for another 15 minutes.

14. The small puffs can be removed, for they will not need more time to dry out.
15. Remove the pastry disk from the oven and let it cool completely on a wire rack.

Making the crème chiboust

1. Soak a gelatin sheet or dissolve powdered gelatin in cold water. Squeeze the water from the gelatin sheet.
2. Bring milk, sugar, and vanilla to a simmer in a saucepan.
3. Meanwhile, separately beat the yolks and sugar to blend. Add the flour and corn starch. Set aside.
4. Remove the saucepan from the stovetop. Pour the hot milk gradually into the yolk mixture, whisking constantly. Return the custard mixture to the saucepan and return the pan to the stovetop.
5. Over medium heat, bring the custard to a boil and cook for 2 additional minutes, whisking continuously. Turn off the heat and mix in the softened or dissolved gelatin. Cover the custard with plastic wrap and set aside.

Making the Italian meringue

1. In a clean stand mixer bowl fitted with the whisk attachment, add the room-temperature egg whites along with the cream of tartar.
2. Set the mixer speed to medium-low and beat. Using this method, the meringue will not fully form before you add the hot sugar mixture. The egg whites will remain in a somewhat liquid stage and slightly foamy.
3. To make the hot sugar syrup, cook the sugar, water, and lemon juice on medium high heat for about 5 minutes, covered.
4. Remove the lid and continue to cook until syrup reaches 240–250°F.
5. With the motor slowly running on the stand mixer with the egg

continued

whites, pour the hot syrup in a thin stream down the side of the mixer bowl. When all of the sugar syrup has been added, increase the mixer speed to high and whip until the meringue forms soft peaks.

6. Smooth out the reserved custard with a whisk and mix in one-third of the Italian meringue. With a rubber spatula, gently fold in half of the remaining meringue, then the other half.
7. Transfer the finished *crème chiboust* to a clean bowl, cover and refrigerate until ready to fill the cream puffs.

Making the caramelized sugar

1. In a small saucepan combine the corn syrup, water, and sugar.
2. Cover and cook the mixture on high heat for 5 minutes; this will self-clean the sides of the saucepan.
3. Avoid stirring the mixture until the light caramel stage is reached (about 340°F).
4. Remove the lid, reduce heat to medium high, and cook to the medium amber caramel stage (about 350°F). Do not allow the caramel to get too brown; at this stage, caramelization progresses quickly.
5. Immerse the bottom of the saucepan in ice cold water to quickly stop the cooking process.

Making the crème Chantilly

1. Whip all ingredients in a chilled mixer bowl to soft peaks.

To assemble the gâteau St. Honoré

1. In a pastry bag fitted with a plain tip, load some of the refrigerated *crème chiboust*. Fill each of the cream puffs from the bottom of the puff. Arrange the filled puffs on a tray. Put the remainder of the *crème chiboust* in the bowl and recombine.
2. Reheat the caramel so that it is fluid. Dip the heads of the filled cream puffs in the warm caramel and place them on a silicone mat, greased parchment paper, or a nonstick pan.

3. When the caramelized puffs have set, begin to assemble the cake. Dip each bottom puff in caramel and place them side by side on the ring of baked puff dough—about 18 puffs depending on the size of the pastry ring.
4. Fill a pastry bag fitted with a large star-tip with the remaining *crème chiboust.*
5. Fill the center of the gâteau St. Honoré by piping thick decorative concentric circles of the *crème chiboust.*
6. Finish the decoration of the confection by piping decorative rosettes of the *crème Chantilly.*
7. Refrigerate until time to serve. Best eaten the same day, but it will keep an additional day, refrigerated.

Into this New York City tapestry are woven the stories of some of the individuals who helped me with their friendship, counsel, and philanthropy. Allow me to reminisce specifically about a few noteworthy individuals who contributed mightily to my success not only as a nonprofit executive, but as a person.

Geoffrey ("Geoff") Bible was an anonymous parishioner at St. Catherine of Siena in Riverside, Connecticut. His wife, Sara, sang in the choir. I had become acquainted with their three adult children. Many years later, when I was beginning my ministry at HealthCare Chaplaincy, someone advised that I should reconnect with Geoff. Born in 1938 in Australia, Geoff joined Philip Morris as a finance manager in Europe in 1968. He left Philip Morris and spent a few years in the Geneva office of Ralph W. King Yuill, an Australian stock brokerage firm. He returned to Philip Morris in 1976. During the 1980s, Geoff became managing director of Philip Morris Australia, and then was brought to the company's corporate headquarters in New York City to head up the worldwide tobacco division. It was at that time that the family settled in Riverside and joined the parish. I had no knowledge of what Geoff did professionally; he was a quiet, discreet man. Two years after I arrived in Manhattan—the same year that I became the Chaplaincy's CEO—Geoff was promoted to become president and CEO of Philip Morris and soon thereafter added the title of chairman of the board of Philip Morris.

As soon as I reached out to Geoff for advice and support, he responded quickly and generously. He hosted me for several luncheon meetings in his private dining room at Philip Morris headquarters. He introduced me to many of the movers and shakers in the corporate world of New York City. My Chaplaincy colleagues were astounded to learn that the CEO of Philip Morris Companies had agreed to serve on the board of HealthCare Chaplaincy. During his tenure on the Chaplaincy's board, we were successful in recruiting other Fortune 500 CEOs to serve as trustees and to support the mission of HealthCare Chaplaincy. With Geoff's help, companies such as United Health Group, Ford, Berkshire Hathaway, General Electric, Home Depot, Bank of America, American Express, PVH, and PriceWaterhouseCoopers began to appear on our donor lists. One time Geoff told me that he was really impressed with the effective management and accomplishments of our little nonprofit organization. "The only thing that differentiates what you do and what I do at Philip Morris is the scale of our respective businesses," he said. Perhaps a bit of hyperbole, but I did appreciate his encouragement.

One moment in a long list of indelible memories was a time when Geoff stopped by my office to talk about a capital campaign that was in its planning stage. I was beginning to silently solicit major donors before the campaign was scheduled to go public and announce its targeted fundraising goal.

Because of his business demands Geoff would not be able to play a direct role as the chair or member of the campaign cabinet, but he wanted to express his support. Sitting at my conference table, he was effusive in expressing his support for the Chaplaincy's strategic plans, and without a further word he pulled a checkbook from the inner pocket of his jacket and began to write a check. He tore the check from the register, folded it, and handed it to me, saying, "Sara and I want to be lead contributors to this campaign." I thanked him and he left. When I unfolded the check to pass it on to our vice president for advancement, I noted that Geoff had written a personal check for $1 million. This is the kind of generosity that is synonymous with Geoff Bible.

Winston Churchill famously described the Australian accent as "the most brutal maltreatment ever inflicted upon the mother tongue." Geoff has not lived in Australia for many years, but he never lost his Australian accent. For me, he remains my closest Australian friend and confidant. And every time I prepare Australian rack of lamb, I think about Geoff.

CARRÉ D'AGNEAU AUSTRALIEN RÔTI

Australian roast rack of lamb

Makes 6 servings

Ingredients

- 1 day-old French baguette to make 1½ cups fine fresh breadcrumbs
- 3 tablespoons finely chopped flat-leaf parsley
- 2 teaspoons minced thyme
- 1 teaspoon minced rosemary
- 1 finely chopped shallot
- ½ teaspoon kosher salt
- ½ teaspoon freshly ground black pepper
- 4 tablespoons olive oil
- 3 frenched racks of Australian lamb
- 3 tablespoons Dijon mustard
- ¼ cup dry white wine

Method

1. Place the oven rack in middle position and preheat the oven to 400°F.
2. In a food processor fitted with the metal blade, pulse baguette to make fine breadcrumbs.
3. In a mixing bowl, combine the breadcrumbs, parsley, thyme, rosemary, shallot, salt, and pepper. Add four tablespoons of olive oil to the herbal breadcrumb mixture and mix well.
4. Prepare the frenched racks of lamb, removing some of the fat. Season liberally with salt and pepper. Allow to sit for 10 minutes, for the seasonings to be absorbed into the meat.
5. In a large heavy skillet, add some butter and olive oil and brown each

continued

of the racks of lamb (approximately 4 minutes). Be sure not to move the meat until it has formed a good crust.

6. Transfer the seared racks of lamb to a platter to cool slightly, as the remaining racks are browning.
7. Whisk together the white wine and Dijon mustard.
8. Liberally brush each of the cooled, seared racks of lamb with the Dijon-wine mixture. Using your hands, apply the herbal breadcrumb mixture onto the entire fat surface of the lamb, using your hand to press gently on the breadcrumbs to help them to adhere and compact.
9. Roast the lamb racks for approximately 15 to 20 minutes. Lamb is best cooked to medium rare (internal temperature about 130°F).
10. Allow the roasted racks to rest, gently tented with aluminum foil, for about 10 minutes before carving and serving.

During my years working in New York City, there were some 35,000 registered, not-for-profit organizations. Most nonprofits rely heavily on philanthropy to support their ongoing mission and works. HealthCare Chaplaincy was no exception. One of our major annual revenue sources was the annual Wholeness of Life Gala, usually held in November. The financial success of this yearly event was crucial to the fiscal health of the organization. This outcome hinged on whom we might be able to attract to be our principal honoree and the individuals who would agree to chair the dinner. On any single night in New York City, from September through June, there are dozens of these galas being held.

One of the early requests I made of Geoff Bible was to introduce me to some of the “king makers” in the New York City business community whom I might further cultivate as prospective friends for the Chaplaincy. In 1995, Geoff hosted a luncheon at his office during which he introduced me to Martin Lipton.

Before the meeting, Geoff provided me with a bit of useful background on Marty Lipton, whom he held in the highest personal regard. Marty was born in 1931 into a New Jersey Jewish family. When he graduated from Jersey Preparatory School in 1948, Marty was accepted into the Wharton School of the University of

Pennsylvania where he earned an undergraduate degree in economics in 1952. Even though he initially envisioned a career in investment banking, Marty applied and was accepted into the New York University School of Law. That experience began an almost seventy-year love affair with NYU and the law.

When he graduated from Law School in 1956, Marty clerked in the United States District Court for the Southern District of New York. He then entered the practice of law with the small NYC firm of Seligson, Morris & Neuburger, where worked alongside Leonard Rosen and George Katz, fellow NYU Law graduates. The law school invited Marty to become an adjunct member of its faculty. He taught corporate law and securities regulation. In 1965, in a career-changing decision and without developing a written partnership agreement, Marty joined his classmate-friends Rosen and Katz along with Herbert Wachtell, to form Wachtell, Lipton, Rosen & Katz. Their firm specializes in advising major corporations on mergers and acquisitions and matters affecting corporate policy and strategy. Every year since 1985, Marty has appeared in the National Law Journal's listing of the 100 Most Influential Lawyers in America.

Our introductory luncheon in Geoff's office was pure delight. From our initial handshake, Marty became genuinely interested in the work of the HealthCare Chaplaincy. He was intrigued to learn more about my relationship with Geoff Bible. Geoff was hyperbolic in his exuberant comments about my preaching at St. Catherine's, my personal importance to his family, and the early successes of the HealthCare Chaplaincy. The outcome of that luncheon exceeded expectations. Marty pledged he would "go to work" for the Chaplaincy and that I could count on Wachtell Lipton as an annual corporate contributor. I only wish every fundraising effort could have been this easy and productive.

During one of my follow-up meetings in Marty's office, I was exploring with him the possibility that he might interest one of his law partners to consider joining the Chaplaincy's board of trustees. I knew that with his involvement as the chair of the NYU governing board (1998–2015) and his investment as the chair (1990–2002) of Prep for Prep, it would not be prudent to ask Marty to serve directly on the Chaplaincy's board. Without losing a beat, Marty picked up his phone and called Ed Herlihy, asking him if he had some time to come to his office to meet me. Once seated, Marty made his own introduction of me and the Chaplaincy's mission and said, "Ed, I think it would be wonderful if you had the time and interest to join their board." Ed smiled and replied, "I would be honored to do that."

Early in the 1980s, Marty had persuaded Ed Herlihy to leave his position at the Securities and Exchange Commission in Washington, DC, to join Wachtell Lipton. Ed has been a partner at Wachtell, Lipton, Rosen & Katz since 1984, where he focuses on some of the largest and most complex bank and financial institution mergers and acquisitions and recapitalizations throughout the United States. Ed served with great distinction as a Chaplaincy trustee and became a close personal friend.

There was never any overstatement in what Marty Lipton promised, and he delivered on each of his commitments. During the remainder of my tenure as the Chaplaincy's CEO, Marty was always available for counsel and encouragement. We would regularly huddle together in the somewhat dark environment of the bar room of the former speakeasy the 21 Club on West 52nd Street, just a few steps down the street from his law firm's offices in the CBS building. The first time I dined there with him, I recall being struck by the unusual and eclectic décor of the room whose walls and ceilings were cluttered with antique toys and sports memorabilia. I later learned these were gifts from its patrons. The more than thirty cast-iron jockey statues that line the stairway and balcony above the entrance were also gifts from the restaurant's guests. Marty invariably ordered the 21 Club burger, a hidden pleasure that his wife, Susan, would surely have frowned upon. I asked the Club's maître d'hôtel what made this burger so special. Here is what he told me.

THE 21 CLUB HOUSE BURGER

A house classic burger with compound butter

Makes 12 servings

Ingredients

For the compound butter

- ¼ pound (1 stick) unsalted butter
- 2 tablespoons finely chopped basil
- 1 tablespoon minced thyme leaves

- 1 tablespoon chopped flat-leaf parsley
- freshly ground black pepper

For the garniture

- 1 vine-ripened tomato, cut into 6 slices
- 1 red onion, cut into 6 thin slices
- 1 tablespoon chopped basil
- 3 tablespoons extra-virgin olive oil
- 3 tablespoons freshly squeezed lemon juice
- salt and ground black pepper

For the burgers

- 2½ pounds ground chuck beef
- 1 tablespoon lemon juice
- a spice rub of finely ground black pepper, sea salt, paprika, cayenne, coriander, dill, garlic, and onion flakes
- good quality rolls (potato rolls)
- extra-virgin olive oil

Method

Making the herb compound butter

1. Place all the ingredients in a food processor and process until smooth. Gather the blended butter into a log; wrap in a piece of plastic wrap, twist ends of wrap, and freeze.

Preparing the garniture

1. Place all the ingredients in a bowl and gently toss to coat the tomatoes and onions with the basil, lemon juice, and olive oil. Season with salt and pepper and set aside.

continued

Making the burgers

1. Preheat the broiler in the oven.
2. Remove the compound butter from the plastic wrap and cut into six pieces.
3. Divide the meat into six equal patties and place a piece of the compound butter into each patty. Fold the meat over to cover the butter entirely and reshape the ground beef into an inch-thick patty. Be sure that the butter in not visible in the final patty.
4. Liberally season the patties with the spice mixture and set aside.
5. Brush the interior of the rolls lightly with olive oil and grill until lightly toasted.
6. Place the burgers in a skillet and broil approximately 4 minutes per side for medium-rare or to desired doneness.
7. Place each burger on a grilled roll.
8. Distribute garnishes (tomatoes and onions) on the burgers.

During the 1980s, Marty devised what has been described by some business and legal analysts as the "poison pill" strategy—a takeover defense used by publicly traded companies to discourage unsolicited acquisitions. Some legal historians are already referring to the poison pill strategy as the most significant piece of corporate legal artistry of the twentieth century.

I mentioned earlier that Marty's decision to go the law school at NYU was the beginning of a mutual love affair. Besides his teaching contributions to the School of Law, Marty served as a trustee and chairman of the law school's governing board for ten years. He joined the university's board in 1972 and served as its chairman from 1988 to 2015. During the years of his board chairmanship, NYU grew to become the largest independent research university in the United States with twenty-five schools including ten undergraduate schools and numerous graduate schools.

When Marty joined the NYU board as trustee in the 1970s, the university, like New York City's municipal government, was facing dire financial challenges. With

Marty's assistance, NYU President James McNaughton Hester successfully negotiated the sale of its University Heights campus to the City University of New York (CUNY). Later in the 1980s, Marty helped President John Brademas raise almost a billion dollars to invest in upgrading and building the Washington Square campus. In the decade of the 1990s, he helped President L. Jay Oliva begin focusing on the growth and expansion of NYU's national and international profile.

I recall sharing a lunch with Marty early in 2001 and an important conversation we had about presidential succession planning. For almost ten years, I served as a trustee of the Brennan Center for Justice at NYU School of Law. One of my fellow trustees was John Sexton, who had clerked for Chief Justice Warren Burger of the United States Supreme Court from 1980 to 1981 before joining the NYU law faculty. From 1988 to 2002, John served as the law school's dean. During my luncheon conversation with Marty, I introduced the topic of the upcoming presidential search, since Jay Oliva had recently announced his retirement. Quite casually, I spoke with Marty about how impressed I was with John Sexton and his tactical prowess in strategically positioning NYU's law school into the top tier rankings in the United States. "He would make a great next president of NYU," I said.

Without losing a beat, Marty looked me directly in the eyes and said, "Walter, I intend to do everything within my power to make that happen." Without undertaking a formal search, the NYU board elected John Sexton as its fifteenth president that same spring, and Sexton took over the university's leadership the following spring in 2002. He served as president until his retirement in 2015.

Over the course of his long legal career Marty represented and advised many CEOs and corporate boards, helping them to navigate through some of the largest merger transactions, change-of-control contests, and boardroom crises that they had to face, and he earned the admiration, respect, and friendship of many folks.

In that little primer of Yiddish expressions that Jack Rudin had given me, Leo Rosten describes a *mensch* as "someone to admire and emulate, someone of noble character." Rosten explained further: "The key to being 'a real mensch' is nothing less than character, rectitude, dignity, a sense of what is right, responsible, decorous." In my life Marty Lipton has been a real mensch—a mentor, counselor, encourager, supporter, protector, advocate, and most importantly of all, a loyal and faithful friend. He is the real deal, true *Menschlichkeit*.

One day, Marty suggested that I meet with one of his dear friends, Ken Langone, whom he thought could also be a help to me. Marty arranged for me to meet Ken at his 22nd-floor offices in the Seagram Building.

Kenneth Gerard Langone was born into a working-class family on September 16, 1935, in Roslyn Heights, New York. Within the first few minutes of meeting Ken, it was apparent that his great business success had not been able to erase the humble roots from which he had sprung. His father had earned his living as a plumber, his mother worked in a cafeteria, and his grandparents were immigrants from Italy. When I told him that my father had been a Boston firefighter and my mother a waitress, and that my grandparents were immigrants from Ireland, we achieved instantaneous rapport. Ken is one of the very few people in my life who decided from our first meeting to call me "Wally." I cannot explain why he settled on this nickname, but it became fixed in his mind. He never corrected the mistake.

Marty had briefly prepped me for the meeting, suggesting that I meet Ken in the morning before he became engrossed in other things. He also advised me to get quickly to the point with Ken, as he can easily become distracted. I was surprised that Ken was waiting for me as the elevator door opened into the lobby of the 22nd floor. Ken is a solid 6'2" imposing presence but with a genuine warmth and approachability that can be disarming. He greeted me as if we were old friends. Ken is also a very devout Roman Catholic. He attends daily Mass and speaks easily about his faith, but has a tongue that could embarrass a longshoreman or a laborer in the construction trades. Although he had never been educated by the Jesuits, Ken has an abiding respect for the Society of Jesus, even though he was quick to tell me that he liked the Franciscans better because they give short homilies, asked no questions in the confessional, and can complete a morning Mass at their church on 31st Street in twenty-two minutes. I knew we were off and running.

No sooner had Ken settled into his office chair when the phone began ringing on his desk. Without warning, Ken began bellowing through the large opening between his office and that of his assistant, "Pam, who is it? If Dick Grasso calls, put him right through." At that time Dick Grasso was the president of the New York Stock Exchange, and Ken was a trustee of the Exchange and chaired its compensation committee.

Pam Goldman has worked as Ken's executive assistant, crisis manager, advocate, counselor, hand-holder, gatekeeper, problem-solver, and troubleshooter for more than a quarter-century. She had joined him soon after her graduation from SUNY Albany. She has grown up alongside Ken. Pam knows what his every tone and gesture means.

Through the ensuing years, I got to know Pam socially and we have spent many weekends with her and other friends in the Hamptons. While we have enjoyed many meals together, by her own admission, Pam is not a cook. Although Jewish by birth, Pam will clearly qualify for canonization in the Roman Catholic Church for her patience and fortitude in keeping Ken Langone from not falling off a cliff. Not only is she completely devoted to him and he to her, but Pam also loves Ken's wife, Elaine.

The passing mention of Dick Grasso's name provided a good opportunity for me to jump back into the conversation. I began informing Ken about HealthCare Chaplaincy by telling him that Dick Grasso was one of our trustees. With that, Ken straightened up in his chair and became even more interested. This must be a serious enterprise. He was intrigued to know more about this Jesuit who was running it. I was able to get out my full elevator pitch, concluding that I would like to be able to tap into his experience and counsel from time to time. Mission accomplished.

Our initial introductory meeting was not protracted. Ken did have other things more urgent to address. "Father, I hate to end this meeting now, but I have to get back to making money," he said. I would hear that expression repeated many times again in the years that followed, and it would always bring a smile to my face. The irony is that he meant it. He once told me that even though he is a billionaire, there is still excitement in making money. This was true even though he and Elaine were among the first signatories in 2010 of the Giving Pledge, a campaign that encourages extremely wealthy people to contribute a majority of their wealth to philanthropic causes.

According to Aristotle's *Art of Rhetoric*, my meeting with Ken achieved three important goals. At the conclusion of the meeting Ken was still docile, open to learning more about yet another NYC charity that was looking for his support and endorsement. He was also benevolent, disposed to wanting to help me in ways that he could. And probably most of all, he was sufficiently attentive that he did not let the meeting conclude without inviting me to continue the conversation over lunch soon thereafter at San Pietro, one of his favorite midtown Italian restaurants. Over the years we would enjoy many lunches and dinners at other Italian eateries including Fresco by Scotto, Primola, Sistina, and Rao. Ken loved Italian cooking and he fancied himself a good cook, albeit one with a very limited repertory of dishes that he prepared.

One time, later in our relationship, Pam returned to the office on a Monday morning, raving about a meal that I had prepared for her and others the prior weekend at the Southampton home of mutual friends Kim White and Kurt Wolfgruber. As Ken listened to Pam blathering about the various recipes and dishes she had sampled, he suggested that perhaps he should challenge me to a cooking contest as to who could make the best meatballs. Pam said to him almost dismissively as she was returning to her desk: "Forget it, Ken, you would not even stand a chance." He never did challenge me, although it would have made this story even more interesting had he done so.

One of the dishes that the Russo family developed for their San Pietro restaurant menu is a version of the simple four-ingredient Roman dish *Cacio e Pepe*. The Russo family's version introduces a bit of egg yolk and *guanciale* into the classic dish, and they make a homemade black pepper *tagliolini* to accompany the enriched sauce. They call the dish *Tagliolini Cacio e Pepe dei Sette Re di Roma*. This is my reconstructed version of their offering, something Ken Langone occasionally ordered.

TAGLIOLINI CACIO E PEPE DEI SETTE RE DI ROMA

Black pepper tagliolini with guanciale and egg sauce

Makes 6 to 8 servings

Ingredients

For the black pepper homemade tagliolini

- 2½ cups all-purpose flour
- 4 large eggs, slightly beaten
- ¾ teaspoon kosher salt
- 1 tablespoon freshly ground black pepper

For the sauce

- ½ pound grated Pecorino cheese
- freshly ground black pepper
- ¼ pound small diced *guanciale*

- 3 egg yolks
- 1 small diced onion

Method

Making the homemade tagliolini pasta

1. Place flour, salt, and pepper in the bowl of a food processor. Pulse to combine thoroughly (about 5 pulses).
2. With machine on, and with the blade running, slowly pour in 4 slightly beaten eggs. Process until the ingredients come together, about 1 minute. Remove the dough ball from the food processor.
3. Transfer to a well-floured work surface and knead until dough is smooth and springs back when pressed with thumb, about 10 minutes. Wrap dough tightly in plastic wrap and refrigerate for at least 30 minutes.
4. Let dough return to room temperature. Cut into six pieces. Working with one piece at a time, keeping others covered, pass the pasta through a machine set at its thickest setting.
5. Reduce to the second setting and run through again. Fold dough in thirds (like a letter) and repeat the passing procedure from thick to more thin settings.
6. Set the finished dough sheet on a floured surface and dust with more flour. Repeat with remaining pieces.
7. Let pasta sheets dry until slightly leathery, about 10 minutes.
8. Run one sheet through the machine using the spaghetti-cutting attachment of pasta machine. (Alternatively, loosely roll sheets from short end to short end, and cut with a knife into eighth-inch strips.)
9. Shake out excess flour, place portion on a floured baking sheet, and sprinkle with flour. Repeat with remaining sheets.

Making the sauce

continued

1. Sauté the diced *guanciale* until softened and the fat has rendered. Set aside on paper towels to drain. Reserve the rendered fat in the sauté pan.
2. In the rendered *guanciale* fat, sauté the diced onion until golden in color but not blackened. Remove from the pan, drain, and combine with the cooked *guanciale.*
3. In a large mixing bowl, add the grated Pecorino and about 10 grinds of black pepper. Combine well.

To assemble the dish

1. In a pot of salted, boiling water, cook the homemade pasta. Cooking time in boiling salted water will be approximately 2 minutes, until al dente.
2. In a separate small bowl, combine the *guanciale* and onion mixture with ½ cup of the pasta cooking liquid. Add the three beaten egg yolks into the mixture and combine. Add a little bit more cooking liquid, if needed, and blend to combine well.
3. Transfer the cooked pasta to a serving bowl and combine with the prepared sauce, mixing well until the pasta further melts the cheese. Add a bit more pasta cooking liquid if needed to make the sauce smooth and creamy.
4. Mixing quickly and well is crucial. For a successful *cacio e pepe,* do not stop mixing too soon. At first the cheese may clump together, but do not be discouraged. Keep on mixing vigorously, adding a bit of cooking water if you need to so that the pasta moves around freely as the cheese melts entirely and clings uniformly to the pasta.
5. Add some additional grated Pecorino cheese and serve.

On one occasion that I was scheduled to share lunch with Ken, he had joined Cardinal Timothy Dolan, Archbishop of New York, for breakfast. Ken told me how distressed and preoccupied the Cardinal had been that morning about the structural problems and the overall deteriorating physical condition of St. Patrick's Cathedral on Fifth Avenue.

Perhaps a little-known fact is that the site on which the cathedral was constructed formerly belonged to the Jesuits until the beginning of the nineteenth century, when the Society of Jesus sold the lot to the recently established diocese of New York in 1813. Pope Pius IX had made the diocese of New York an archdiocese in 1850 and appointed John Joseph Hughes as its first archbishop. Three years later Hughes asked the architect James Renwick to begin work to design a cathedral in the gothic revival style, and in 1853 Archbishop Hughes blessed the cornerstone of the new cathedral, which was not completed until 1878 and consecrated in 1879.

Cardinal Dolan described to Ken how the roof was leaking, and certain other major issues with the deteriorating stonework and the antiquated heating and ventilation system. The cardinal was musing about how he would be able to raise the needed funds to do the kinds of rehabilitation and restoration work that would be needed.

I said to Ken, "The cardinal clearly wants you not only to be a major contributor of this project, but also he probably is going to lean on you to lead the capital campaign."

Ken looked me squarely in the eye and said, "There is no way in hell that I am going to do that. I'm already too involved in the medical center at NYU. I'm maxed out philanthropically." Not too much later, the Archdiocese of New York announced a major campaign to undertake an extensive restoration of the cathedral. The work spanned 2012 through 2015 and cost more than $177 million. Not only were Ken and Elaine Langone among the largest major benefactors of the cathedral restoration project, but Ken did end up chairing a very successful fundraising campaign.

When interviewed later about the project, Cardinal Dolan recalled that he had talked with a number of people about the challenge to restore St. Patrick's Cathedral. "You've got to go to Ken Langone. He is your man. And I did. He turned it around. He can call in a bunch of chits. He rallied people and got the job done. Thanks be to God that I went to him." Later, Ken would have to admit that I was right that the cardinal was setting him up for the big ask. Big-hearted as he is, Ken was thrilled to "get the job done," as the cardinal so aptly characterized the wonderful outcome. St. Patrick's now is a glistening gem for another century.

I did persuade Ken, after numerous conversations, to become an honoree at one of the Chaplaincy's annual galas. It was a couple of years after 9/11, and New York was beginning to regain its energy. (This was before the city later was plunged into the great financial crisis of 2008.) At the time of the Chaplaincy's dinner, Ken had been immersed in a lawsuit that was brought by the then–New York State Attorney

General, Eliot Spitzer, who was demanding that Dick Grasso repay the majority of a more than $140 million pay package he had received from the NYSE board. Spitzer alleged that Ken Langone, who chaired the compensation committee, had misled the board about the details of the recommended compensation package. It awarded Grasso incomparably more than other nonprofit CEOs. Ken was indignant with the actions of the attorney general and told me that he was prepared to spend $100 million, if he had to, in order to defend himself and Dick against this lawsuit. I said to him in reply, "Just think of all the better things you could do with that money than squander it on attorneys." He completely ignored my observation.

I had personally composed and read the citation to honor Ken Langone at the Chaplaincy's Wholeness of Life gala, detailing and lauding Ken for his many contributions in bettering the life of New York City and the nation. Ken delivered his brief extemporaneous acceptance remarks, dotted with his characteristic self-deprecating humor, as he graciously received the Chaplaincy's recognition to the applause of a capacity audience of friends and colleagues. I had just returned to the podium to continue the program when Ken unexpectedly took control again of the microphone. "By the way, Wally," he said, "would you mind sending a copy of your remarks about me to Eliot Spitzer?" With that remark the audience roared with laughter, rising spontaneously to their feet with ear-splitting applause. Ken was beaming, raising his arms and hands with the Nixonian "V" for victory. Later, in 2008, the New York State Court of Appeals would dismiss all claims again Grasso.

Dick Grasso also became a great friend to the Chaplaincy and to me personally. He served as a member of the president's advisory board and occasionally invited me to join him for lunch in the Oak Room of the beautiful Italianate townhouse of the Columbus Citizens Foundation on East 69th Street and Fifth Avenue. On one occasion I recall enjoying a delicious interpretation of a simple veal dish, *Saltimbocca alla Romana*, which literally means "jump in your mouth."

SALTIMBOCCA ALLA ROMANA

Sautéed veal scallopini with sage and prosciutto

Makes 4 to 6 servings

Ingredients

- 6 thinly pounded veal scallops
- 6 slices prosciutto di Parma
- 12 sage leaves
- 2 tablespoons extra-virgin olive oil
- 4 tablespoons unsalted butter
- ¾ cup dry white wine
- freshly ground black pepper
- all-purpose flour for dredging

Method

1. Lightly season the thin veal scaloppini with salt and pepper.
2. Place a single slice of prosciutto on top of each piece of veal.
3. Place a couple sage leaves on top of each of the scaloppini and secure the leaves and the prosciutto with toothpicks to the veal.
4. Dredge each piece lightly in the flour and set aside.
5. Heat the oil and 2 tablespoons of the butter in a large skillet over medium heat.
6. Add the veal to the pan, prosciutto side down.
7. Cook until browned and crispy, about 1 minute, then turn and cook the other side. Transfer the cooked scaloppini to a tray and cover with tented aluminum foil to keep warm.
8. Add the wine to the pan and deglaze, scraping any browned bits of meat from the bottom. Cook, stirring constantly, until the mixture thickens into a sauce, 1 to 2 minutes. Add 2 tablespoons of unsalted butter to the sauce and stir to incorporate and enhance the richness of the pan sauce.
9. Plate the scaloppini, remove the toothpicks, and top with sauce. Garnish with some basil leaves that have been quickly sautéed in melted butter until crisp.

In July 2003, I was asked to preside at the wedding in Cotuit, Massachusetts, of Brooke Herlihy and John Abbott Root Cooper. Brooke is the daughter of Ed and Patty Herlihy. The wedding was planned to take place at their summer home on the Cape, and many of the Herlihys' good friends were invited guests, including both Marty and Susan Lipton and Ken and Elaine Langone.

It happened that we were all staying at the same hotel, where the Herlihys had booked an incredibly large suite for me. When I encountered Ken Langone in the lobby on the afternoon before the wedding, his first question to me was this: "Have you said Mass today?" When I replied that I had not yet celebrated Mass, he replied: "Wonderful! What time shall we get together for Mass? Elaine and I have been on a cruise for the past week, and I haven't been to Mass in more than a week."

Recovering quickly, I suggested that we gather in my suite at 5 p.m. where I would celebrate the Eucharist. Ken was elated. He said, "I'll get Marty and Susan to join us."

"But Ken, Marty and Susan are Jewish. They won't have any interest in participating in a Catholic Mass on a Friday evening," I replied.

"Nonsense," retorted Ken. "They need the prayers and blessings as much as I." At five o'clock the four of them knocked at the door of my suite, and we celebrated Mass. Marty and Susan seemed to be both honored and happy to have been included in this intimate gathering; they knew how important Ken's Catholic faith was to him. This is a very cherished moment.

Brooke and Abbott's wedding was a memorable event. Everything about the wedding and reception worked out beautifully. I had flown to Boston from New York City and had visited with my family before renting a car and driving to Cape Cod for the celebrations. I had planned to return to Boston's Logan Airport on the day after the wedding and take the air shuttle back to Manhattan. For the only time in my life, I received not one but two offers to fly back to the city on private jets. I ended up returning on Ken Langone's plane, along with Elaine, Susan, and Marty. During that brief flight, Ken and Marty were chatting about the NYU Medical Center, whose board Ken had chaired since 1999. It was Marty who had persuaded Ken to join the NYU board after he retired from the board of his alma mater, Bucknell, and it was Marty who had urged Ken to turn his focus to the medical center. Ken agreed and told Marty that he would also make a $100 million anonymous gift to the medical center. Ken is not a guy who just writes checks; he wants to roll up his sleeves and get to work. And that is just what he did at NYU Medical Center.

I remember talking with Ken soon after he took over the chairmanship of the NYU Medical Center board. I candidly asked him, "Why did you take on such a major responsibility for a place that clearly needs a lot of reorganization, financial restructuring, and infrastructural rebuilding?"

Ken's answer was characteristically simple and memorable: "I have to help them raise a lot of money and I have to become their principal cheerleader." He brought to his work at the NYU Medical Center the same dynamism and passion that has contributed to Home Depot becoming the more than significant corporation it is today. He did the same thing he'd done in 1978 when he invested in Home Depot and became a cofounder with Arthur Blank and Bernard Marcus: he helped them to raise a lot of capital investment money, and he became their principal cheerleader.

HealthCare Chaplaincy provided the spiritual care services at NYU Medical Center, so I witnessed firsthand how personally involved Ken became in day-to-day operations of the hospital and medical school. Before long he knew everybody at NYU, from the doctors and nurses to the maintenance crews and the gift shop clerks. When the hospital hired Dr. Bob Grossman as its new dean and CEO, Ken wanted me to meet Bob.

I could see how Ken's enthusiasm for the medical center continued to grow, so it did not surprise me when I later learned that he and Elaine had determined to contribute another $100 million to the continued development of the hospital and medical school. What did surprise me a bit was that Ken had agreed to allow NYU to attach the Langone name to the institution, since Ken and Elaine much preferred anonymity in their philanthropy. But it is clear that both Marty Lipton and Bob Grossman persuaded Ken that the Langone brand would magnify the effect of Ken and Elaine's magnanimous gift. How right they were; the ensuing capital campaign attracted at least four additional gifts in the $100 million dollar range. Ken's genius and generosity has helped to transform NYU Langone into one of the nation's premier academic medical centers devoted to patient care, education, and research.

I have heard similar stories from many physicians who carry the indebtedness of their medical education well into middle age, gradually paying off hundreds of thousands of dollars of student loans. Ken mused what it would mean to have a tuition-free medical school, reasoning that it would put NYU Medical School on the map by creating a paradigm shift. After selling the board on the bold idea, he and Elaine made a third major gift of another $100 million when they announced that NYU would become a tuition-free medical school in 2018.

All of this from a guy who loves to tell the story of working as a day-laborer and digging ditches on the Long Island Expressway, which was constructed in stages starting in 1939, when the Queens Midtown Tunnel was built, until 1972, when the terminus in Riverhead was completed. You can now better understand the title of Ken's autobiography, *I Love Capitalism!*[9] He sent me a copy as soon as it was published. I was not surprised that a tribute from Marty Lipton was included on the dust cover: "I love Langone—I love him as a great philanthropist, a great businessman, a great citizen, a great friend; and now he has written a fascinating must-read book." Like the proverbial frosting on the cake, the book reminds me of this wonderful recipe for an amazing French buttercream, which can complement almost any cupcake or layer cake.

CRÈME FRANÇAISE AU BEURRE

French buttercream frosting

Frosts 24 cupcakes or one double-layer cake

Ingredients

For the pâte à bombe

- 10 large room-temperature egg yolks
- 1 cup granulated sugar
- 6 tablespoons water

For the crème française au beurre

- 1 pound (4 sticks) unsalted room-temperature butter
- 2 teaspoons vanilla extract

Method

Making the pâte à bombe

1. Put the room-temperature egg yolks in the bowl of a stand mixer fitted

9 Ken Langone, *I Love Capitalism!* (New York: Penguin Books, 2019).

with a whisk attachment and beat on high speed until thick and foamy (for about 8 minutes).

2. While the egg yolks are beating, combine sugar and water in medium saucepan. Heat over low heat while stirring until sugar dissolves. Increase heat to medium-high and bring to a boil. Cook until the syrup reaches 245°F and immediately remove from heat.

Making the crème française au beurre

1. With mixer running at lowest speed, slowly drizzle hot syrup down the side of the stand mixer bowl to incorporate into the creamed egg yolks.
2. Continue mixing until the bottom of the bowl is cool to the touch and the yolk mixture has cooled to room temperature. With a rubber spatula, remove from the mixing bowl and allow to continue to cool in another bowl on the countertop.
3. In a clean stand mixer bowl fitted with a clean whisk attachment, add the room-temperature butter and beat at high speed until it is thoroughly creamed.
4. Begin to incorporate the *pâte à bombe* into the whipped butter in about three different additions. Before the final addition, add the vanilla (or any other flavoring: orange extract, almond extract, strained raspberry purée, etc.) and continue mixing until buttercream is smooth and creamy and fully blended.

Over the course of my quarter-century at the helm of HealthCare Chaplaincy, I had the privilege of working alongside a few hundred incredible women and men who served as trustees or advisory board members. I shall remain eternally grateful for each of them—for who they are and for the many wonderful things they did. Here is a sampling of some of the amazing people whose stories and contributions are inextricably woven into the tapestry of my life.

I recall one day receiving a call from Fr. John Andrew in the late 1990s, asking a favor. One of his vestry members was writing a major article for *Newsweek* on the issue of clergy sexual abuse, which was just beginning to attract national attention. At the time, Jon Meacham was the managing editor of *Newsweek*; in 2006, he would be named editor-in-chief. Jon was interested in interviewing knowledgeable and informed clergy who could both help to fact-check his draft article and educate him further about this emerging story. Fr. Andrew recommended that he should speak with me. This was the beginning of my relationship with Jon.

Jon was born in Chattanooga, Tennessee, three years to the day before my ordination to the priesthood. He is a 1991 graduate of the University of the South in Sewanee, Tennessee, where he majored in English literature and was elected to Phi Beta Kappa. After working with Jon on that cover story for *Newsweek* we became friends, and he agreed to serve on the Chaplaincy's board of trustees. A devout, lifelong Episcopalian, he and his wife Margaret and their children were at that time living on the Upper East Side of Manhattan. They were active members of St. Thomas Church. His fascination with the world of politics led him in his monumental research into the lives of former US presidents that have included Thomas Jefferson, Andrew Jackson, Franklin Roosevelt, and George Herbert Walker Bush. Jon became a Pulitzer Prize–winning biographer and commentator: he is a talented and compelling storyteller who has deftly positioned history as a useful mirror in which to view and assess present social issues that challenge the soul of our nation and the diverse peoples who make up our union. More recently, he has helped President Joe Biden with formulating and drafting addresses to a nation in need of healing. How fortunate to have met and worked alongside Jon Meacham at the beginning of his illustrious career as writer, historian, biographer, and wise teacher.

In the year during which Jon began his service on the Chaplaincy board, I created these two recipes as Christmas gifts for our trustees.

CHOCOLATE HAZELNUT BISCOTTI

Makes about 3 dozen biscotti

Ingredients

- 1¾ cups all-purpose flour
- 1½ teaspoons baking powder

- ⅓ cup unsweetened cocoa, preferably Dutch process
- 1 teaspoon ground cinnamon
- a pinch of kosher salt
- ¼ pound (1 stick) unsalted room-temperature butter
- ½ cup firmly packed light brown sugar
- ½ cup granulated sugar
- 1 tablespoon instant espresso powder
- 2 eggs
- 1 cup toasted, coarsely chopped hazelnuts
- 1 cup dark or semisweet chocolate chips

Method

1. Prepare a baking sheet with a silicone pad or parchment paper.
2. Sift together the flour, cocoa, baking powder, cinnamon, and salt into a mixing bowl and set aside.
3. Combine the butter, brown sugar, granulated sugar, and espresso powder in the bowl of a stand mixer fitted with the paddle attachment.
4. On high speed, beat the ingredients until they are light, creamy, and fluffy.
5. Reduce the speed to low, add the hazelnuts and chocolate chips, and combine.
6. On low speed, add the flour mixture and mix until incorporated and a dough forms. Do not overmix.
7. Cover and refrigerate the dough for about an hour.
8. Preheat oven to 325°F.
9. Divide the dough in half and place the two halves on a prepared baking sheet, about 5 inches apart.
10. Using lightly floured hands, form each half into a log (about 3 inches wide, 12 inches long, ¾ inch high).

continued

11. Bake until firm to the touch, about 25 minutes (the logs will spread during baking).
12. Remove from oven and let cool slightly, for about 5 to 10 minutes, on the baking sheet.
13. Leave the oven set at 325°F.
14. Using a spatula, carefully transfer the logs to a work surface. Using a serrated knife, cut the partially baked logs on the bias, diagonal slices ½–¾ inch thick.
15. Arrange the slices—exposing both sides to the oven heat—on the baking sheets and bake for another 10 minutes.
16. Ovens will vary, so watch the biscotti. The desired result is crisp but still slightly tender to the bite.
17. Transfer the biscotti to wire racks to cool. They keep in airtight containers at room temperature for about 2 weeks.

PISTACHIO LEMON BISCOTTI

Makes about 3 dozen biscotti

Ingredients

- 1¾ cups all-purpose flour
- ½ teaspoon baking soda
- ½ teaspoon baking powder
- a pinch of kosher salt
- ¼ pound (1 stick) unsalted room-temperature butter
- 1 cup granulated sugar
- 3 tablespoons finely chopped candied lemon peel

- 1 teaspoon vanilla extract
- ½ teaspoon lemon extract
- 2 eggs
- 1½ cups unsalted shelled pistachio nuts

Method

1. Sift together the flour, baking soda, baking powder, and salt into a mixing bowl and set aside.
2. Combine the butter, sugar, candied lemon peel, vanilla, and lemon extract in the bowl of a stand mixer.
3. With the mixer on high speed, beat until light and fluffy. Mix in the eggs, one at a time, beating well after each addition. Reducing the speed to low, add the pistachios and combine.
4. On low speed, add the flour and mix until just incorporated. Cover and refrigerate the dough until well chilled (about an hour).
5. Preheat oven to 350°F.
6. Prepare a baking sheet with a silicone pad or parchment paper.
7. Divide the dough in half. Using lightly floured hands, roll each half on a lightly floured surface into a log (3 inches wide, 12 inches long, and ¾-inch high). Arrange the logs on the prepared baking sheet.
8. Bake until light brown and firm to the touch, about 30 minutes. Logs will spread during baking.
9. Remove from the oven and let cool slightly on the baking sheet (5 to 10 minutes). Leave the oven set at 350°F.
10. Using a spatula, carefully transfer the logs to a work surface.
11. Using a serrated knife, cut on the bias in diagonal slices that are ½–¾ inches thick.
12. Arrange the slices exposing both sides of the cookie on the baking sheets and bake until golden brown, about another 8 to 10 minutes.

continued

13. Transfer biscotti to wire racks to cool. Store in airtight container at room temperature for up to 2 weeks.

As a not-for-profit executive, one is continuously faced with the challenge of finding people who have the potential to become interested in the organization's mission, vision, and strategic objectives and who will have the energy, resources, and commitment to put those gifts to work for those worthy purposes. When one of my trustees told me about a fellow NYU Leonard N. Stern of Business graduate, who was then chairing the school's alumni council, I was anxious to meet Susan Jurevics. In a bit of informal research, it was soon discovered that Susan Lopusniak Jurevics was a 1989 graduate of the Jesuit-run College of the Holy Cross in Worcester, Massachusetts, where she doubled majored in studio art and art history. As did Ken Langone, Susan studied part-time at NYU to earn the MBA degree in marketing and international business, while she was working at her first job in brand marketing for Nickelodeon—at that time a decade-old company.

When I met Susan, she was well-established as Sony's senior vice president for global retail customer relationship management and brand marketing in what became a thirteen-year stint at Sony's New York City headquarters. She was immersed in many areas of branding and marketing at Sony that would later prove to be so enriching for HealthCare Chaplaincy.

I recall my initial conversation with Susan, who was intrigued to be reconnecting with a Jesuit almost twenty years after she left Holy Cross. Susan is smart and engaging. Our conversation was electrifying; she was full of questions and ideas. Within fifteen minutes, I had the sense she was disposed to accept the invitation to trusteeship. Most of the meeting time was devoted to figuring out just what I might ask her to do for the Chaplaincy. Before the meeting concluded not only had I asked her to consider becoming board member, but I also asked if she would be willing to chair the marketing and communications committee of the board.

With a characteristic broad and knowing smile she said: "Now I know for sure that I am talking with a Jesuit. Not only did you skillfully get a meeting with me; you knew exactly what you needed from this meeting, and you got it." Susan hit the ground running, and she never looked back.

In recruiting Susan, I hit the jackpot. She had it all: she was young and energetic, a senior executive of a major corporation, a digital leader at a time when the field was beginning to explode, an assertive and knowledgeable marketer with an engaging and entrepreneurial spirit, and a working mother of two children, Lucy and Maks. She had met her husband, Maris Jurevics, when she was a graduate business student at NYU. Maris is Latvian, and during their years as a family living in Brooklyn he had been deeply involved with the Latvian Evangelical Lutheran Church in Yonkers.

Although Susan's work at Sony was highly demanding, she gave considerable time and focus to her work at HealthCare Chaplaincy. She motivated her fellow trustees, mentored our management team, and innovated from within the organization, pushing the Chaplaincy forward into the new millennium. She once told me that one of the keys to her success was helping teams to become comfortable with uncertainty. In a nonprofit healthcare organization that relied on hospital budgets for much of its earned income, it did not get more uncertain. She was a natural motivator and team builder, and the Chaplaincy's branding activities became more disciplined and consistent, our communications crisper and more compelling. Our friends and donors looked forward to reading our newsletters and annual reports. Susan's imprint was on it all. Not only did she fit into the Chaplaincy's culture; she helped to shape and ground it. She brought together the diverse ingredients of HealthCare Chaplaincy's history and works, just as this recipe blends onion, garlic, wine, lemon, stock, cream, and braised shredded chicken into a memorable and rich sauce for pappardelle.

PAPPARDELLE CON POLLO BRASATO ALLA CREMA DI LIMONE

Pappardelle with braised shredded chicken and lemon cream sauce

Makes 4 to 6 servings

Ingredients

- 1½ to 2 pounds boneless, skinless chicken breasts and thighs
- 1 chopped yellow onion

continued

- 4 cloves minced garlic
- 1 cup dry white wine
- 2 cups chicken stock
- zest and juice of 2 lemons
- 1½ cups room-temperature heavy cream
- 1 pound pappardelle
- kosher salt and freshly ground pepper
- finely chopped herbs (basil, parsley, or tarragon)

Method

1. Preheat oven to 325°F.
2. Pat the chicken thighs and breasts dry with paper towels and season with salt and pepper.
3. Heat 4 tablespoons of olive oil in a large Dutch oven over medium-high to high heat. Add the chicken pieces to the pot (working in batches, so as to not overcrowd the pan) and sear until deep golden brown, about 5 minutes per side. Remove the chicken to another plate.
4. Add the onions and sauté until softened, about 6 to 8 minutes. Add the garlic and stir another 30 seconds. Pour in the wine and cook, bubbling vigorously, until reduced by half, about 5 minutes.
5. Add back the reserved and browned chicken pieces, along with any juices they may have exuded; add the chicken stock and bring to a boil.
6. Cover the Dutch oven and place on middle rack in preheated oven and cook for about one hour, until the chicken is falling apart.
7. Transfer the chicken to a bowl. Shred the meat, cover with aluminum foil, and set aside.
8. Add the lemon juice to the braising liquid and bring to a simmer over medium-high heat. Whisk in the room-temperature heavy cream in a slow, steady stream and completely incorporate into the sauce.

9. Continue simmering the sauce until it thickens enough to coat the back of a spoon, about 15 minutes.
10. Reduce heat to low. Add the lemon zest and season generously with salt and pepper. Add back the shredded chicken into the sauce.
11. Meanwhile, bring a large pot of salted water to a boil over high heat. Stir in the pappardelle and cook until al dente.
12. Drain the noodles and add them directly into the chicken mixture, tossing to coat. Allow the pappardelle to continue cooking in the sauce on low heat for a couple of additional minutes, to allow the flavors to blend.
13. Correct seasoning and garnish with freshly chopped herbs and serve immediately.

Susan taught me many things as we were planning for major involvement in the emerging field of palliative care. Many of our trustees, as experienced business executives, were less than venturesome. Susan, on the other hand, was of the opinion that one never has all the necessary data to make decisions. She was neither cavalier nor imprudent, but she was clearly comfortable moving in strategic directions where not everything was clearly defined. I admired her pioneering spirit. Much of the growth that she had been able to encourage in various business initiatives throughout her career had been tied to her risk-taking ability. She was assertive in asking questions at board meetings and in profiling choices that the board might consider in its decision-making.

It was totally in character when Susan decided, after highly successful and productive years at Sony, to accept J. K. Rowling's invitation in 2013 to become the founding CEO in London of Pottermore. This decision could have been disruptive for her young family, but Susan brought the same intentionality, values, and discipline to this decision that she has brought to every career choice she had made. I remember her comment that one's job or career has to be complementary to one's life, rather than the reverse.

For almost three and a half years, Susan helped Rowling develop her digital publishing, e-commerce, and entertainment company. Rowling may have amassed her fame and fortune imagining Harry Potter and a phenomenal world of wizarding, but Susan Jurevics helped her to expand that world in ways that Professor Albus Dumbledore—the legendary headmaster of Hogwarts School of Witchcraft and Wizardry and Supreme Mugwump of the International Confederation of Wizards—could never have imagined. Before Susan left London to return to the United States in 2017, she had helped Pottermore become one of the United Kingdom's fastest-growing global companies.

Because HealthCare Chaplaincy was so heavily invested in providing its services in a large network of New York hospitals, I was always looking to recruit physicians to serve as trustees. Referred to Dr. Anne Moore by one of her patients, I reached out to Anne and found that not only was she willing to talk, but she invited me for our initial meeting to share lunch with her in the faculty club at New York Hospital (now New York Presbyterian-Weill Cornell Medical Center).

Like me, Anne Moore is a member of the class of 1965. She received her undergraduate degree at Smith College before entering medical school at Columbia University's College of Physicians and Surgeons, from which she received her M.D. degree in 1969. During medical school she met Dr. Arnold Lisio, one of her teachers, who had received his medical degree from the University of Rochester Medical School in 1960. Anne and Arnie were married soon after her graduation from medical school in September 1969. They had two children.

When I met Anne in the faculty dining room at the hospital, she greeted me with a broad warm Irish smile. Once we were seated at a table she became fully engaged in conversation, erasing any doubt in my mind that this was going to be a difficult sell. Having done a bit of research in advance of our meeting, I was aware that Anne's father, John Denis Joseph Moore, had been appointed by President Richard Nixon in 1969 as the United States Ambassador to Ireland, where he continued in that post until 1975.

Anne was as Irish as her husband, Arnie, was Italian. Arnie's father, Anthony, was Italian-born; his mother, Dorothy, was Italian American. As noted earlier, my maternal grandmother, Rose, would have referred to such a union as a "mixed marriage." It was thought to be similar to blending beans with pasta.

The following recipe is a hearty peasant soup that is popular in the region of Naples. The unusual element of this recipe—which I developed from watching an older Neapolitan woman prepare her version of this classic *minestra*—is that the pasta and the beans are cooked together. Instead of using one type of pasta—commonly *tubetti*, small pieces of tubular pasta—this woman used a variety of dried pastas (basically whatever she had in her cupboard), which came together in a process she described in her inimitable dialect as "*minuzzaglia ammescata cu' 'e fasule.*" She said that she used either *borlotti* ("Roman") or cannellini beans for this dish, which had been soaked overnight, or for a minimum of eight hours. You can used canned beans but be sure to rinse them well a few times before incorporating them into the recipe, and cook the beans along with the pasta and reserve the cooking water. Here you have it: *Una pasta e fagioli cremosa, avvolgente, incredibilmente saporita che, in Napolitano, viene chiamata "azzeccata."*

PASTA E FAGIOLI

An original creamy Neapolitan version of past e fasul

Makes 8 to 10 servings

Ingredients

- 12 ounces dried borlotti or cannellini beans
- 12 ounces mixed pasta or tubetti
- 14 ounces diced canned San Marzano tomatoes
- 2 tablespoons tomato paste
- 2 cloves garlic
- 1 large diced onion
- 1 diced celery stalk
- Italian parsley
- 4 ounces diced pork belly (optional)
- kosher salt
- 1 bay leaf
- extra-virgin olive oil
- red pepper flakes

continued

Method

1. If using dried beans, soak the beans for at least 8 hours in cold water, and then rinse thoroughly.
2. Put the beans in a stock pot with 12 cups of cold water and a bay leaf. Do not add any salt, for it will toughen the beans. Cook gently for 2 hours. During the final 10 minutes of cooking, add the pasta. Drain the beans and pasta, discard the bay leaf, and reserve 4 cups of the bean-pasta cooking liquid.
3. In the same stock pot in which the beans and pasta were cooked, add some olive oil, and sauté the diced onion and celery until they begin to brown slightly. Add the minced garlic, along with the diced pieces of pork belly. Cook for an additional 4 minutes.
4. Add the diced San Marzano tomatoes and the tomato paste. Let them cook together on medium heat for another 10 minutes.
5. Add the beans and pasta to the tomato vegetable mixture, along with some of the bean cooking liquid (to make the soup as thin or as thick as you might wish) and cook together for about another 8 minutes.
6. Season the *minestra* with a bit of kosher salt, freshly grated black pepper, and some red pepper flakes and serve with a drizzle of extra-virgin olive oil. Add some freshly minced parsley on the top.

When the waiter presented the menu for our initial lunch together, Anne disregarded it entirely and told the server: "Bring me the club burger, medium rare." I ordered a Cobb salad and an iced tea. Anne must have noted a slightly surprised reaction on my face as she completed her order. She said: "My husband is an internist, specializing in cardiology. He rarely lets me eat red meat, so whenever he's not around I order it." I loved Anne immediately.

Anne is one of the most respected breast cancer oncologists in New York City. She is the medical director of the Weill Cornell Breast Center, professor of clinical medicine at the Weill Cornell Medical College, and an attending physician at New York Presbyterian Hospital. She readily accepted my invitation to serve for two successive terms as a trustee of HealthCare Chaplaincy. After her six years of service were completed, she suggested that she pass the trusteeship baton to her husband, Arnie, who himself served a full six-year term.

I got to observe Anne in other professional roles through the years. We were both fellows of the New York Academy of Medicine, where Anne was also a trustee. She was appointed by the New York Academy of Medicine to serve on the board of the New York Community Trust, a public charity and grantmaking foundation that seeks to better the lives of residents of New York City and its surrounding communities. The HealthCare Chaplaincy's work was enhanced by grants from this trust.

When Jacqueline Kennedy Onassis was in the final stage of her battle with non-Hodgkin's lymphoma, she was discharged in May 1994 from New York Presbyterian Hospital so that she could die peacefully at home in her Fifth Avenue apartment. She died the following night. In announcing her death on the morning of May 20, her son John said that she was surrounded by her family and friends and her books and the things she loved. Anne Moore was there with her.

Anne was one of four sisters. They had one brother, John. When John died, Anne asked me if I would preside at a private memorial service in the chapel of the Fifth Avenue Presbyterian Church at West 55th Street. Although baptized and raised a Roman Catholic, John D. Moore had become a member of the Presbyterian Church. With the pastoral sensitivity of the senior minister at the church, I conducted a memorial service for the family in what some folks called the "cathedral of Presbyterianism." As Anne would later say, "only a Jesuit could pull off a memorial service in such an elegant way that the Protestants thought the service was Protestant and the Catholics were convinced it was Catholic."

Arnie maintained a thriving private medical practice on Park Avenue throughout much of his professional life. He and Anne traveled extensively, making dozens of trips to Italy. He and I talked much about Italy and the Italian language, art, culture, and cooking. He was as enthusiastic and faithful a trustee of the Chaplaincy as one could ever dreamed of attracting. When Arnie and Anne returned to Rochester for his 50th class reunion in 2006, they established, in honor of his parents, the Dorothy and Anthony Lisio Prize. The annual award recognizes student excellence in some aspect of Italian studies. For his sixtieth reunion, Anne and Arnie provided a gift of $2 million to the University of Rochester to establish the Lisio Program in Italian Studies within the College of Arts, Sciences and Engineering. The award provided travel and immersion study opportunities in Italy for Rochester students.

Arnie was passionate about his Neapolitan roots. Many of the classic dishes of this region are simple, made with few ingredients, and have interesting stories. I am reminded of one very popular preparation called *Uova in Purgatorio* or as the Neapolitans say, *ova 'mpriatorio.*

Taking its inspiration from a Neapolitan fascination with the souls of the faithful departed—*il culto delle anime del purgatorio*—this classic peasant dish is a symbolic reminder of their fate. The eggs represent the souls of deceased persons in purgatory, who are seeking to be cleansed. The spicy tomato sauce is a reminder of the purifying flames of purgatory. The eggs bubble away in the red sauce until the whites are completely cooked or, one might say, "purified." The breaking of the yolks into the sauce symbolizes the extinguishing of the flames and the soul's final liberation on its final journey to heavenly bliss. It is Neapolitan folklore at its finest.

UOVA IN PURGATORIO OR OVA 'MPRIATORIO (NAPOLITANO)

Eggs poached in a spicy tomato sauce

Makes 4 to 6 servings

Ingredients

- 14-ounce can diced peeled tomatoes (or leftover marinara sauce or ragù)
- 2 cloves chopped garlic
- freshly ground black pepper
- 4 tablespoons extra-virgin olive oil
- 2 tablespoons minced Italian parsley
- 6 basil leaves, cut into a thin chiffonade
- 6 eggs
- grated Pecorino Romano cheese

Method

1. Heat the olive oil in a large frying pan over medium heat.

2. Sauté the finely chopped onion until it softens.
3. Add the garlic and sauté for 30 seconds.
4. Remove the pan from the heat and stir in the diced tomatoes or the leftover tomato sauce or ragù.
5. Return the pan to the heat and add about quarter-cup of water.
6. Add parsley and basil and season the sauce with salt and pepper.
7. Cook the sauce on medium-low heat until the sauce reduces by about half, about 15 minutes.
8. With a fork, make six wells in the sauce and add the eggs, one at a time.
9. Turn the heat to high and cook the eggs for about 8 to 10 minutes, until the whites are firm, and the yolks are set.
10. Remove the eggs from the pan, top with a bit of sauce. Garnish with some additional chopped parsley or basil, or some grated Pecorino Romano cheese.

New York City is such a fertile ground. When I was searching to interest a nursing leader to join the Chaplaincy's governing board, several people mentioned the name of Mary O'Neil Mundinger at Columbia University School of Nursing. At the time, Mary was already one of the longest serving deans at Columbia. At the time she retired, she had served as dean for almost a quarter-century. In her retirement, the dean emerita continues to impact the field of nursing as the Edward M. Kennedy Professor of Health Policy in Columbia's faculty of nursing.

I remember taking the subway up to West 168th Street to meet Mary for the first time. She had agreed to a meeting, although I was managing the expectation I would be successful in convincing her to lend some of her time to assisting me with the work of HealthCare Chaplaincy. Even before meeting her in person, I could see that we shared some things in common. She was doing for nurses and nursing practice what I was attempting to do for professional chaplains and chaplaincy practice. She was passionate about her work, in it for the long haul, and visionary. She unmistakably exuded leadership from every pore. Not only did Mary speak succinctly about the problems of providing quality healthcare, she also saw new pathways to address these issues. I suspect she identified similar qualities in HealthCare Chaplaincy as we spoke about the neuralgic issues that chaplains were facing in providing hospitalized patients with integrated care, which included spiritual care. Spirit, mind, body: she got it. She understood immediately we envisioned being a change agent in the face of momentous challenges from both clinicians and administrators, who might not appreciate the value-added proposition that we were espousing.

Mary was well on her way to getting the more-than-century-old Columbia School of Nursing onto a more stable financial foundation. Although still in its embryonic stage of development, I remember Mary speaking about her strategic ideas for a Doctor of Nursing Practice degree. That degree would eventually become the first clinical nursing doctorate in the United States. I shared my vision and plans for enhancing the clinical pastoral supervisory education program to include women and men from underrepresented groups in the profession of pastoral care, and I also envisioned the continuing academic formation of chaplain leaders by incentivizing the pursuit of part-time funded PhD and DMin education programs. We exhausted each other during our initial meeting. Even though I had traveled to Columbia with the sole goal of getting to know her, the meeting uncovered so many convergences of passion and interests that I wildly posed the question: "Would you consider being proposed to the Chaplaincy board for election as a trustee?"

Mary, with equal abandon, replied, "I would be honored to do so." The quick coming together of elements of experience and passion remind me of this French-inspired salad, which blends some unusual elements together for a remarkable and memorable outcome.

SALADE DE LA PASTÈQUE AU CITRON VERT

Watermelon salad with English cucumber, avocado, feta, and a lime mint dressing

Makes 4 to 6 servings

Ingredients

For the salad

- 4 cups cubed, seedless watermelon
- 1 large unpeeled English cucumber, cubed
- 2 ripe avocados
- 8 to 10 mint leaves, roughly shredded
- 1 cup French feta cheese

For the dressing

- grated zest and juice of 2 limes
- 2 finely minced shallots
- 2 teaspoons Dijon mustard
- 1 teaspoon granulated sugar (optional)
- ½ cup extra-virgin olive oil
- ¼ cup dry white wine
- salt and pepper

Method

1. Prepare the avocado by cutting in half and, with a large spoon, removing the flesh from the outer skin and cutting it in wide strips and then into cubes and tossing the pieces with lime juice, to prevent discoloration.
2. Place the chilled watermelon cubes, cucumber, avocado, and mint in a large bowl.
3. In a small bowl, whisk together the Dijon mustard, salt, pepper, and olive oil to form an emulsion; add white wine, shallots, sugar (optional) and lime zest and blend into the emulsion; add lime juice and whisk until fully incorporated.
4. Drizzle the dressing over the melon and cucumber mixture and toss to coat.
5. Sprinkle with crumbled feta cheese and serve.

Mary O'Neil Mundinger grew up in Fredonia, New York, and she received her undergraduate degree in nursing in 1959 from the University of Michigan. In 1958 Mary married Dr. Paul Mundinger, whom she had met at Michigan. Paul went on to earn a master's degree in biology at Michigan before going to Cornell, where he earned the PhD in ethology. When he was invited to pursue a postdoctoral fellowship at Rockefeller University in New York City in 1967, the family relocated to the town of Rye. Mary and Paul became parents to four children, Paul, Thomas, Ann, and Elizabeth.

Mary accepted a position in 1971 at United Hospital in nearby Port Chester as director of its nursing education department while simultaneously pursing a master's degree at Columbia University, which she received in 1974. She was accepted into the doctoral program and in 1981 received the PhD in public health from Columbia. She began her long and distinguished career at Columbia University. After completing her doctoral studies, Mary accepted an offer to direct the graduate nursing program. She then became associate dean of administrative affairs. In 1986 she was appointed assistant dean of the Faculty of Medicine and not much later was named dean of the School of Nursing, a position she held for nearly twenty-five years.

When I began my collaboration with Mary, she was already serving as a director of UnitedHealth Group. One of my former St. Catherine of Siena parishioners, Bill Spears, was also a director. Through him, I got to know UnitedHealth Group's Chairman and CEO, Dr. Bill McGuire, and his wife, Nadine. They became personal friends, advisors, and donors to the Chaplaincy. Mary continued her service on the UnitedHealth Group board for nearly two decades.

The most significant contribution Mary would make to the profession of nursing was her indomitable advocacy in promoting advanced nursing practice. She envisioned preparing nurses at the doctoral level to be practitioners, whom some folks facetiously termed "doctor nurses." Early on, Mary recognized the scarcity of family and primary care physicians. She imagined how advanced trained nurse practitioners could help to fill the void.

The Chaplaincy operated administrative offices on East 60th and 62nd Streets. In 1994, Mary established a seminal primary care practice staffed entirely by nurse practitioners. In 1997, she opened a midtown Manhattan practice near the Chaplaincy's offices on East 60th Street (Columbia Advanced Practice Nurses Associates) where the professional nurses received the same compensation for comprehensive diagnostic and treatment services that primary care physicians were getting.

You can imagine how Mary's bold initiative triggered both buy-in and strong push-back from within the medical community. Although diminutive in stature, Mary was a force of nature. To deal with medical skeptics who challenged the abilities of nurse practitioners to provide comparable care to that of a family or primary care physician, Mary proposed a two-year randomized outcome study. Using an ambulatory care setting near Columbia University, patients were randomly assigned to be evaluated and treated by either a physician or a nurse practitioner. When the results were published later in a peer-reviewed medical journal, it was just as Mary Mundinger had predicted: patient outcomes were comparable. Her great experiment was off and running. Now there are more than 350 doctor of nursing practice degree programs in the United States, including one at Boston College's Connell School of Nursing.

As the mother of the doctor of nursing practice, what Mary was able to accomplish reminds me of one of the staples of *la cuisine française:* blanquette de veau. This dish is hallowed in French cookery and might be rightly considered to be the mother of all French dishes. It is an incredibly simple, traditional dish—a quintessential example of how to use leftovers and standard pantry ingredients in a wonderfully creative way. All of the ingredients for this recipe, which dates back to the early years of eighteenth-century France, are cooked *en blanquette*, meaning that they are simmered in white stock or water with various seasonings resulting in a delicious creamy white sauce.

BLANQUETTE DE VEAU À L'ANCIENNE

Veal poached in a savory stock with a velouté sauce

Makes 6 to 8 servings

Ingredients

- 4 pounds boneless, trimmed veal shoulder, cut into 1-inch morsels
- ½ pound pearl onions (fresh or frozen)
- 9 cups chicken stock or bouillon
- 3 thyme sprigs
- 3 sprigs of parsley

continued

- 2 bay leaves
- 5 tablespoons unsalted butter
- 1 pound celeriac (celery root), peeled and cubed
- 4 carrots, peeled, cut into 1½-inch long sticks
- ½ pound cremini mushrooms, cut in half or quartered
- ½ pound trimmed haricots verts or green beans
- 3 tablespoons all-purpose flour
- ½ cup heavy cream
- 1 teaspoon freshly squeezed lemon juice
- fresh chives for garnish

Method

1. Bring a large pot of salted water to a rapid boil. If using fresh pearl onions, add the onions and allow them to blanch for 2 minutes. Using slotted spoon, remove the pearl onions from the pot and reserve in a colander. If using frozen, peeled pearl onions, thaw and set aside.
2. Add the veal morsels to the pot in which you blanched the onions and cook for 4 minutes. Drain the veal and rinse with cold water. Set aside.
3. Pour out the boiling water, rinse the pot of any grim or residual foam, and then return the veal to the pot. Pour in 8 cups chicken stock (or water with bouillon cubes) and bring to gentle boil. Reduce the heat to medium low and poach the veal, uncovered, for 30 minutes. Add the thyme and parsley sprigs and bay leaves and continuing simmering for 25 to 35 more minutes, or until the veal is very tender.
4. If using fresh pearl onions, cut the tops of the onions and peel the onions that had been previously blanched.
5. Meanwhile, in a Dutch oven, melt a couple of tablespoons of unsalted butter over medium heat. Add the pearl onions (fresh or thawed), celery root, carrots, and mushrooms and a cup of chicken stock. Cover

and cook until vegetables are tender and almost all the liquid has evaporated, about 15 minutes. Add the haricots verts or green beans and cook until just tender, about 2 additional minutes.

6. Drain veal, reserving 2 to 2½ cups of the cooking liquid (or additional chicken stock, if needed). Remove the bay leaves, parsley, and thyme sprigs and discard.
7. Add the drained, tender veal morsels to the vegetable mixture in the Dutch oven and stir to combine.
8. In a saucepan, over medium heat, prepare a roux by melting 3 tablespoons of unsalted butter and 3 tablespoons of all-purpose flour. Whisk the roux continuously until it becomes golden brown in color. Whisk in 2 cups of the reserved cooking liquid or stock and continue cooking until it thickens, and then add ½ cup of room-temperature heavy cream and blend thoroughly. If sauce is too thick, whisk in a bit more chicken stock. Adjust the seasonings and add some fresh lemon juice.
9. Pour the enriched velouté sauce over cooked veal and vegetables and gently blend. Garnish with chives if desired, and serve immediately.

Every nonprofit needs support within its board from accountants and lawyers. The HealthCare Chaplaincy was not only fortunate to enlist the early help of a PriceWaterhouseCoopers (PwC) partner, but I was able to ensure the support of the firm. It was analogous to a relay race. As one PwC partner was nearing the end of his term, he was encouraged to identify and pass the baton to another partner. And so it went. Among the wonderful PwC partners who became Chaplaincy trustees and treasurers of the nonprofit corporation was Donald B. Christian, who now is the leader for PwC's East Region, which includes the Northeast, Mid-Atlantic, and Southeast markets.

Don became a partner in the firm in 1997. A native of Jamaica, Don and his wife, Dawna, had relocated to New York City to assist PwC in building its consulting practice in the areas of business transformation, strategy, technology consulting, business performance improvement, and risk management. He was willing to supplement his PwC responsibilities with the added burden of trusteeship at HealthCare Chaplaincy. I remember hosting an orientation dinner at the Chaplaincy for new trustees and their spouses on September 10, 2001 (the night before the tragic events that would transform our city on the following morning). It happened to be Don's birthday that night, and we served a beautifully oven roasted leg of lamb.

GIGOT D'AGNEAU À L'AIL AU FOUR

Roasted leg of lamb with garlic

Makes 8 to 10 servings

Ingredients

- 6–8 pound leg of lamb, with bone in
- 1 tablespoon olive oil
- kosher salt
- freshly ground pepper
- 2 teaspoons dried *herbes de Provence*
- 6 cloves garlic
- 2 onions
- 2 bay leaves
- 1 roughly cut carrot
- 2 sprigs of rosemary
- 1 cup water

Method

To prepare the lamb

1. Remove the leg of lamb from the refrigerator at least 2 hours before preparation and roasting.
2. Remove the tough white skin on the surface, if needed.
3. Rinse the leg of lamb under cold water and pat dry with paper towels.

4. With a sharp knife, cross-hatch the remaining surface fat.
5. Rub the meat all over with olive oil, sprinkle liberally with salt and freshly ground black pepper, and rub some dried *herbes de Provence* over the top and bottom surfaces of the lamb.
6. Insert slivers of garlic in the cross-hatched cuts in the flesh, or as the French might say, *piquer la viande à l'ail.*

To roast the lamb

1. Preheat the oven to 425°F.
2. Place the leg, cross-hatched fat side down, in a roasting pan and scatter around it 4 onion halves (cut side down), rosemary sprigs, bay leaves and pieces of carrots.
3. Place the lamb in the oven and roast at the high temperature for about a half hour, to form a crust.
4. Remove the lamb from the oven and pour off any accumulated fat from the pan.
5. Reduce oven temperature to 375°F. Return the lamb to the pan, this time with the browned cross-hatched side up.
6. Add a cup of water into the pan and continue roasting, with the aromatic vegetables, for 45 to 50 minutes, or until the internal temperature of the lamb reaches 135°F (medium rare).
7. Remove the lamb from the oven and discard the vegetables. Cover the roasted lamb with foil and allow it to rest for 20 minutes so that the juices can flow back into the meat before carving.

Dawna Christian became as enthusiastic about the mission of HealthCare Chaplaincy as did Don. When she showed up for a Chaplaincy gala in the final days of the ninth month of her pregnancy with their first child, I was astounded. "How did you manage to get here, Dawna?" I inquired.

Without losing a beat she said, "I feel very secure. Some of the best doctors in New York City are in this room tonight, so I will be in such good hands should I go into labor." She delivered their son the next day, having enjoyed the banquet the night before.

When Don was transferred by the firm to assist in the management of their Washington, DC, operations, he enlisted Roy Weathers, another up-and-coming PwC partner, to take the baton from him.

Roy Weathers grew up in Blacksburg, South Carolina, and was in 1989 a first-generation graduate of Winthrop University. During an introductory accounting course, a guest speaker from PriceWaterhouseCoopers talked about the firm and the accounting field. After graduation, Roy earned a master's degree in accounting from Clemson University, was recruited to PwC, and began his career in the firm's Atlanta offices before moving to New York. In 2002 he was named partner. When Don Christian coaxed him into being a Chaplaincy trustee, Roy was the New York metro tax leader for the banking and capital markets and insurance sectors as well as the firm's chief diversity officer.

During his tenure on the Chaplaincy's board Roy met and married Rebecca Weathers, a senior manager and brand strategist at PwC. Rebecca has a Jesuit connection, having earned her MBA degree at Fordham University's Gabelli School of Business.

When Roy's term was ending, he saw an opportunity to pass the baton to a newcomer to the PwC family, Jude A. Curtis. Jude was a New Englander who grew up in Salem, Massachusetts, and in 1977 graduated from St. John's Preparatory School in Danvers. He graduated in 1981 from the College of the Holy Cross in Worcester, where he met classmate Elizabeth ("Liz") Galligan of Wallingford, Connecticut, whom he later married. After Holy Cross, Jude enrolled in the National Law Center at George Washington University where he graduated with honors. When Jude accepted the position with PwC, he and Liz—along with their three daughters, Mary, Kate, and Maggie—settled in New Rochelle.

When Roy Weathers proposed HealthCare trusteeship to Jude, he was anxious to meet with me to discuss the opportunity. We agreed to a breakfast meeting in one of the commuter restaurants surrounding Grand Central. Meeting Jude was like reconnecting with a friend of many years. Jude had worked in the Jesuit dining room while at Holy Cross, where he not only became familiar with many Jesuit priests and brothers, but also came to understand what makes Jesuits tick. Before long, we were beginning to identify many people we knew in common. An avid Red Sox fan, Jude could not understand how I had become a Yankees fan and had effectively lost my Boston accent. Before he had finished his breakfast, Jude was committed to carrying on the PwC tradition and said an unqualified and exuberant "yes" to the invitation to become trustee, treasurer, and the chair of the finance committee.

Successfully recruiting Jude was only part of the blessing. Very soon thereafter, I met Liz. Liz Galligan Curtis grew up in a large Catholic family in Connecticut. Liz was one of the early women pioneers at the College of the Holy Cross, graduating in its first coeducation class of 1976. It has always thrilled me to listen to her recollections of her undergraduate days, especially the memories of her Jesuit teachers and the life lessons she took away from her educational and religious experiences.

Liz also shared with me her passion for food and cooking, and she and Jude never turned down an invitation to dine at my apartment in the city. Someone once said of Jude there was nothing that he did not enjoy eating or drinking. Liz is far more discriminating. She was always fascinated by and appreciative of the menus prepared for them.

One evening, around the Christmas holidays, I had made some roasted almonds, which I then enveloped in chocolate ganache and rolled in a spiced confectioners' sugar. As a gift, I had prepared small bags of these almonds for my guests. Liz fell in love with them. She told me that she had to hide them at home so that Jude would not inhale all of them on one of his nightly clandestine ice cream forays. These confections are so simple to make and can easily become habit-forming. The chocolate-coated almonds can also be rolled in a Dutch-process cocoa as well as the spiced confectioners' sugar.

CHOCOLATE SPICED ALMONDS

Makes 8 servings

Ingredients

For the almonds

- 2 cups whole almonds

For the chocolate ganache

continued

- 1 cup heavy cream
- 8 ounces roughly chopped semisweet or dark chocolate
- 1 teaspoon pure vanilla
- 1 teaspoon Cognac or Grand Marnier

For the confectioners' sugar and spice finish coating

- 2 cups sifted confectioners' sugar
- ½ teaspoon Saigon cinnamon
- ½ teaspoon allspice
- ½ teaspoon freshly grated nutmeg

Method

1. Prepare the chocolate ganache by pouring the heavy cream (having been heated to the simmer-stage in a nonreactive saucepan over medium heat) over the chopped chocolate. Leave for about 5 minutes. Stir in the vanilla extract and Cognac or Grand Marnier. Whisk the ganache and allow it to come to room temperature. Cover and refrigerate.
2. Set a rack at the middle level of the oven and preheat to 350°F.
3. Spread the almonds on a cookie sheet and roast until the nuts are lightly toasted (about 10 to 15 minutes). Watch and do not allow to burn. Remove from oven and cool completely.
4. Remove the ganache from refrigerator and allow to come to room temperature.
5. Working with clean bare hands or plastic gloves, imbed each almond in a small portion of the chilled ganache, roll to shape, and place on waxed paper–lined trays.
6. For the final coating, roll the chocolate-covered almonds liberally in a mixture of confectioners' sugar (or cocoa, if you prefer) that has been sifted together with the spices.
7. Store in airtight containers or sealed plastic bags.

During my tenure at the helm of HealthCare Chaplaincy, I served for ten years on the governing board of Ithaca College. During this time I witnessed the concluding years of the tenure of its first woman president, Peggy R. Williams, the full-term of her successor, Thomas R. Rochon, and the inauguration of the successor president, Shirley M. Collado. I loved everything about my years of service as trustee of this comprehensive college, but most especially, the relationships that I was able to forge with many of my fellow trustees. Several of these women and men became supporters of HealthCare Chaplaincy, and two of them eventually joined the Chaplaincy's board.

One of these was George E. Pine, who joined the board of his alma mater in 2000. At the time he was president of ABC Radio Sales, a division of Interep Company formed in 1998 to serve as the exclusive sales company for ABC Radio. Headquartered in New York City, Interep was the largest sales and marketing company solely for radio advertising. At Ithaca College as a student George had managed the campus radio station, WICB radio, earned his degree in television-radio, and began his professional career as a media planner with Ogilvy and Mather Advertising. He acquired his first radio station in 1979, and successfully owned and operated radio stations in Florida, North Carolina, and Mississippi.

George's wife, Claude-France, was born in Monaco and was a fashion designer. Claude became more interested in the work of the Chaplaincy than she did in Ithaca College during the time that George had served as trustee. Claude-France and I quickly became friends, sharing many common interests including French language and literature, cuisine, and wine. George and Claude maintained a New York apartment that faced the sculpture gardens of the Museum of Modern Art, just a half-block down the street from the University Club, where George served for a term as its president.

I enjoyed many conversations and delightful meals with both Claude-France and George. Claude-France was a good cook; no doubt she learned many things from her mother. On numerous occasions I shared social occasions with Claude-France's sister, Maguy Maccario Doyle, who at that time was serving as the consul general of Monaco in New York. Maguy shared many of her sister's passions, especially for food and wine. Maguy invited me to many cultural and fundraising events at the consulate on Fifth Avenue. From both sisters, I learned much about Monégasque cuisine.

Claude-France spoke often about her mother's prowess in the kitchen and as a host. Growing up in Monte Carlo, both Claude-France and Maguy remember with fondness Sunday dinners that were always feasts. Their mother would prepare a multicourse meal including an appetizer, fish and meat, delicious wines, and of course dessert. They also remember accompanying their mother to buy the provisions for these meals. Their home was located not in the historic center of town, but about twenty minutes away in the hills. These Sunday dinners routinely welcomed a dozen or so guests who always enjoyed the incredible dishes that Claude-France and Maguy's mother would create. I could see how this early exposure to classic French and Italian-inspired cooking trained their palates, making them both discriminating connoisseurs of food and wine.

Much of Monégasque cuisine reflects a combination of regional Mediterranean cooking, with clear hints of French, Spanish, Portuguese, and Italian. One of the dishes to which Maguy introduced me is *la bourride.* If one were casually asked to name a fish stew or soup served along the Monaco and French Riviera coastline, the most likely answer would probably be *la bouillabaisse à la provençale. La bourride* is perhaps less widely known, but equally delightful.

La bourride is a very simple fisherman's dish, made from the leftovers of the catch of the day. The soup broth is thickened with an aïoli—a garlic-based mayonnaise—and served with some crusty grilled bread and the addition of a few potatoes, carrots, mushrooms, and leeks for a hearty and delicious lunch. This is my version of a *bourride*, finished with the classic aïoli in the Provençale style.

LA BOURRIDE À L'AÏOLI MARSEILLAIS

Provençale-style fish stew with garlic aïoli

Makes 6 to 8 servings

Ingredients

For the fish stock (bouillon de poisson)

- 2 tablespoons unsalted butter
- 4 pounds fish bones with heads (gills removed)
- 3 thyme stems
- 4 parsley stems

- 3 whole peppercorns
- 1 whole clove
- 1 bay leaf
- 1 stalk chopped celery
- 1 diced carrot
- 1 chopped onion
- 1 cup dry white wine
- 1 gallon cold water

For the aïoli

- 2 teaspoons fresh lemon juice
- 4 cloves minced garlic
- 2 egg yolks, at room temperature
- a pinch of kosher salt
- 1 teaspoon Dijon mustard
- 1¼ cups olive oil

For the bourride

- ¼ cup extra-virgin olive oil
- 1 teaspoon fennel seeds
- ¼ teaspoon piment d'espelette powder (or ground cayenne)
- 2 cloves minced garlic
- 2 roughly chopped leeks (white parts only)
- 2 roughly chopped onions
- 1 bay leaf
- 1½ cups dry white wine
- 4 cups fish stock (bouillon de poisson)
- 2 pounds firm white fish (halibut, monk fish, sea bass, cod)
- kosher salt and freshly ground black pepper, to taste

continued

- 2 teaspoons minced flat-leaf parsley

Method

Making the fish stock (bouillon de poisson)

1. In a large pot over medium heat, add the butter.
2. When the butter is melted, add the fish bones, carrots, celery, onions, leeks, parsley stems, thyme, bay leaf, peppercorns, and clove; sauté, stirring often, until the mixture is fragrant, about 3 to 5 minutes.
3. Add the white wine and cook until it has reduced to half its volume, about 5 minutes.
4. Add the water and bring the stock to a simmer for 40 minutes, making sure the broth does not come to a full or rapid boil.
5. Strain the broth, pressing on the solids. Remove and discard the solids. Set aside.

Making the aïoli

1. In a large heatproof bowl set over a saucepan of simmering water, whisk lemon juice, garlic, egg yolk, and salt until it begins to thicken, 2 to 3 minutes.
2. Off heat, whisk the Dijon mustard into the egg mixture.
3. In a steady drizzle, slowly whisk in the olive oil to form a smooth emulsion and eventually, a thickened mayonnaise. (This blending can also be done in either an electric blender or food processor, with the motor running.)
4. Transfer aïoli to a bowl and set aside.

Making the bourride

1. In a Dutch oven, heat the olive oil. Add the fennel seeds and *espelette* or cayenne powder and cook until the seeds and spice begin to bloom.
2. Add the leeks and onions and sauté until softened.

3. Add the garlic and cook for 30 seconds.
4. Add the fish stock, white wine, and the bay leaf and bring to a boil.
5. When the liquid and aromatics are boiling, reduce the heat to medium low and add the fish.
6. Cook the fish until firm (about 3 to 4 minutes).
7. Off heat, blend in some of the aïoli.
8. The soup can be enriched by the addition of some steamed fingerling potatoes and thinly sliced carrots, finished with some chopped parsley, and served with some grilled crusty bread rubbed with a clove of garlic. The remaining aïoli can be offered as a supplemental garnish.

On one occasion, I had invited George and Claude-France to join me for a special dinner party at my Manhattan apartment with eight other guests. They readily accepted my invitation and Claude-France insisted that she and George select and provide all the wines for the evening. She carefully reviewed with me the menu that I was proposing and selected magnificent wines that everyone enjoyed—far better than I could have selected or afforded to serve.

For the reception before dinner, I was making an hors d'oeuvre that Chef Daniel Boulud offers in his eponymous flagship East 65th Street restaurant—*les gougères*. A gougère is a savory baked choux pastry. On hearing of my plan, Claude-France said, "We must drink a Lucas Carton Demoiselle champagne with the gougères." She then proceeded to tell me the story of how this champagne was developed.

Since 1924, Lucas Carton—an esteemed Parisian restaurant—has sat just opposite L'Église de la Madeleine at 9 Place de la Madeleine. In 1993, Chef Alain Senderens, one of the fathers of *la nouvelle cuisine,* asked his good friend Paul-François Vranken to create a special cuvée of champagne that he could proudly serve his guests and would complement many of his dishes. Monsieur Vranken created a special reserve champagne—Demoiselle.

Senderens had worked at La Tour d'Argent and Lucas Carton, until he purchased the restaurant in 2005 and renamed for himself. He was the chef at Lucas Carton from 1985 until 2005, when he acquired major ownership of the restaurant partnership and renamed it Senderens. Chef Senderens favored a more modern version of

French cuisine that was less wed to classic buttery sauces and more open to incorporating flavors and products from other national cuisines. He relied on high-quality, locally sourced fresh ingredients.

Claude-France Pine had discovered Demoiselle when Sherry-Lehmann, New York City's leading Park Avenue wine retailer, began importing the champagne and was marketing it at exceptionally reasonable prices for such a delicious, quality French champagne. I loved the taste of the wine, as did all our guests that night. As Claude-France knew it would, Demoiselle was a perfect complement to the gougères. I have used many similar recipes to make these hors d'oeuvres; this is one that captures my own combination of ingredients and methods.

GOUGÈRES

Gruyère cheese puffs

Makes 12 servings

Ingredients

- 6 tablespoons unsalted butter, cut into pieces
- 1 cup water
- ¾ teaspoon kosher salt
- a pinch of nutmeg
- 1¼ cups all-purpose flour
- 4 large eggs
- 1½ cups grated aged Gruyère cheese
- ½ teaspoon freshly ground black pepper
- 1 large egg yolk
- fleur de sel

Method

1. Preheat oven to 400°F.
2. In a saucepan, combine the butter, salt, and nutmeg. Add 1 cup water and bring the liquid and fat to a boil.

3. Remove saucepan from heat and add flour, stirring to combine.
4. Return pan to stove and cook the mixture over medium heat, stirring vigorously with a wooden spoon, until mixture pulls away from sides of pan and forms a ball, about 2 minutes.
5. Continue to cook, stirring vigorously, until a dry film forms on bottom and sides of pan and dough is no longer sticky, about 2 minutes longer. Remove pan from heat and let the dough cool slightly, about 2 minutes.
6. Place the cooled dough ball in a food processor fitted with a steel blade. With the motor running, add one egg at a time, allowing each egg to fully incorporate into the dough. Repeat until all four eggs have been incorporated.
7. Blend in the grated cheese and pepper.
8. If you have a pastry bag, fit it with a round tip and spoon the dough into the bag. If you do not have a pastry bag, place the dough into a gallon plastic storage bag and cut a ½-inch opening diagonally at one of the lower corners of the bag.
9. Pipe small rounds of the dough, spaced 2 inches apart, onto a silicone pad or a parchment-lined baking sheet. With a wet index finger, smooth the tops of the pastry rounds.
10. Mix an egg yolk with a tablespoon of water and brush the rounds with the egg wash. Add a few flakes of fleur de sel on each round before baking.
11. Bake the gougères until puffed and golden and dry in the center (they should sound hollow when tapped), 20 to 25 minutes.

As I think about these numerous occasions of dinners shared with friends through the years, I am reminded of the wisdom of an old proverb that says, "It's not what's on the table that matters. It's who are in the chairs."

Chapter 15

LIFE IS BUT A WEAVING: COMPLETING THE NEW YORK TAPESTRY

My life is but a weaving
Between my God and me.
I cannot choose the colors
He weaveth steadily.
Oft' times He weaveth sorrow;
And I in foolish pride
Forget He sees the upper
And I the underside.
Not 'til the loom is silent
And the shuttles cease to fly
Will God unroll the canvas
And reveal the reason why.
The dark threads are as needful
In the weaver's skillful hand
As the threads of gold and silver
In the pattern He has planned
He knows, He loves, He cares;
Nothing this truth can dim.
He gives the very best to those
Who leave the choice to Him.[10]

---

10 The author of this poem is believed to be American minister, composer, and hymn writer Grant Colfax Tuller. It was made popular in the writings of Corrie ten Boom, a native of the Netherlands who was imprisoned by the Nazis in Ravensbrück concentration camp for her aid to Jewish citizens during World War II.

I begin this chapter with a poem made popular by a Dutch Reform Christian woman, Corrie ten Boom, who, along with her sister Betsie and their family, were members of a war time resistance movement—they offered the shelter of their Amsterdam home, along with the little food and money they had, to Jewish and Gentile refugees. For some years, the ten Boom family members were imprisoned by the Gestapo and its Dutch counterpart.

In recalling these people and events, I am taking another careful and appreciative look at the finished side of the tapestry. As I am recording these select memories of my New York years, the world is celebrating the 500th anniversary of the death of the great Renaissance painter Raphael, who died on Good Friday in 1520 at the age of thirty-seven years. A contemporary of Michelangelo, Raphael received a commission in 1515 from the de' Medici Pope Leo X (1513–1521) to create tapestries to hang on special occasions on the lower walls in the Sistine chapel. Raphael completed his drawings (cartoons) for these ten tapestries, depicting events in the lives of Peter and Paul, which are described in the Acts of the Apostles. The tapestries were woven of silk, gold, silver, and woolen threads in Belgium in the studios of Pieter van Aelst. It is likely that Raphael never got to see these finished works hanging in their proper location, as they were completed but not installed until a few months before his death.

On numerous occasions while serving as a consultant for the Holy See, I passed by one or other of these tapestries, which are part of the permanent collection of the Musei Vaticani (Vatican Museums) and are kept behind protective glass in a gloomy hall in the Pinacoteca Vaticana (Vatican Picture Gallery). Like so many things in life, we can engage with people and events, paying fleeting attention to their beauty, meaning, or importance.

One of the hidden joys of my lengthy tenure as the president and CEO of HealthCare Chaplaincy was the opportunity to get to know and work alongside some incredible men and women who voluntarily served as trustees of the organization. I worked with six board chairmen: Don Keller, Bill Donnell, Bill Spears, Gene Zuriff, Larry Toal, and Mike Long. I could write volumes about each of these important leaders and about the impact they had on me and the growth of the Chaplaincy. But I will limit myself to some select recollections—mere threads from the larger and more complex tapestry.

When I was recruited to the organization, my predecessors, Carolyn and John Twiname, had been hard at work assembling a strong board of trustees. The board chair in 1990 was Don Keller, who had served as CEO of Kraft Foods. He and

Carolyn had been high school classmates in Chicago and their friendship remained strong through the ensuing years. Don was living in Greenwich, Connecticut, along with his lovely wife, Ginny. In the Chaplaincy's important search to identify and recruit an executive vice president and COO who would soon succeed the Twinames as CEO, Don also chaired the small selection committee.

Although enthusiastic about my prospective candidacy, he was concerned that if appointed, I wouldn't remain with the organization for more than a couple of years. He reasoned that my academic interests, coupled with the Jesuits' leadership needs, might thwart the Chaplaincy strategic succession plan. I assured him that if I were offered the position and accepted it, the Jesuits and I would honor this commitment with a significant investment of time and energy. I think that my eventual twenty-six-year tenure at the Chaplaincy more than satisfied my promise to Don Keller.

Not long after I began my work at HCC Ginny was diagnosed with cancer, which eventually claimed her life. I found myself becoming a chaplain and pastor to my board chair, helping him and his family deal with the same kind of grief that many of our client families also had to face. This actually became a hallmark of my ministry at HCC: the trustees frequently became direct beneficiaries of the very astute pastoral care that they worked so tirelessly to ensure for others.

Don Keller was succeeded as chair by Bill Donnell. Bill was a young entrepreneurial investor who had inherited significant wealth from his family's Ohio oil conglomerate businesses. He was a very loyal and committed member of the presbytery at Fifth Avenue Presbyterian Church, which at that time was in the throes of an internal dispute that eventually divided the congregation.

Bill is a natural reconciler and optimist. He is naturally a pastor, even though he had no formal education in theology or pastoral care. As a gay man living in New York during the height of the AIDS pandemic, Bill had many friends who were ill or dying. For these reasons, he enrolled in a basic training unit of Clinical Pastoral Education at NYU Medical Center under one of the Chaplaincy's supervisors, a Lutheran pastor, Paul Steinke. This CPE basic unit became Bill's introduction to the world of professional chaplaincy, and his pathway to becoming a trustee and eventually board chairman.

In his own words, Bill is "a bleeding heart if there ever was one." He was philanthropically invested in so many worthy ventures: the arts, healthcare, spiritual care, gay and lesbian rights, kids, schools, immigrants struggling to learn enough English to get a decent job, the homeless, preserving great architecture. Bill's challenge has always been to manage his time and resources to make the most of what he can do.

Bill's life of service, blending talent and treasure, reminds me of a basic principle of all cookery: achieving a simple yet perfect blend of good ingredients. Just like making a perfect frittata.

FRITTATA AL TALEGGIO CON PATATE, PORRI, E FAGIOLI VERDI

A Lombardy cheese omelette with potato, leek, and green beans

Makes 6 servings

Ingredients

- 3 leeks
- 1 Yukon Gold potato
- 1 yellow onion
- ½ cup green string beans
- 6 large eggs
- ¼ cup basil leaves
- ¼ pound Taleggio cheese
- extra-virgin olive oil
- sea salt and freshly ground black pepper

Method

1. Prepare all the vegetable, cheese, herb, and egg components:
    - cut and wash the leeks, and slice thinly (white and light green parts only)
    - peel, quarter, and thinly slice the potato
    - peel, halve, and thinly slice the onion
    - cut the tips off the green beans and cut on the bias into half-inch lengths
    - roll the basil leaves like a cigar and with sharp knife, cut into thick julienne strips

continued

- remove the outer rind from the cheese and cut into small pieces
- break and beat the eggs with a pinch of salt and some freshly ground pepper and add the julienned basil into the egg mixture

2. Preheat oven to 375°F.
3. Heat a teaspoon of the olive oil in an ovenproof skillet over a medium flame.
4. Add the leeks, potato, onion, and string beans and season with some salt and pepper. Cover with a tight-fitting lid and cook 15 minutes, stirring often. Lower the heat to medium-low and cook for 10 more minutes, or until the potato is tender.
5. When the vegetables are cooked, transfer to a mixing bowl, and cool slightly.
6. Add the egg mixture to the cooled vegetables and blend.
7. With a paper towel, wipe the skillet and then add a bit of olive oil and a tablespoon of butter and warm over medium heat to melt the butter.
8. Pour in the egg-vegetable mixture and scatter the Taleggio cubes over it. Cook over medium heat uncovered, for 10 minutes, or until the frittata is set and golden on the bottom.
9. Place the skillet into the preheated oven and bake for 5 to 8 more minutes or until the top is set and the cheese is melted and beginning to brown slightly.
10. Rest for a couple of minutes before cutting and serving.

Gene Zuriff had been introduced to the Chaplaincy by his congregation's rabbi, Harlan Wechsler. Gene was an amazing rainmaker for the organization, and we worked together closely. It was through Gene that my networking within the Jewish community expanded geometrically. Throughout his life Gene has been a phenomenal golfer, beginning during his high school days when he worked as a caddy at a golf club in Westchester, New York. He made many friends through golf, and although not a golfer myself, I walked the course with Gene and his friends numerous times as a fifth member of many a foursome. After his graduation from NYU and its School of Law in 1964, Gene married Riki Tananbaum, and they soon became parents to two sons, Laurence and Bryan.

When I met Gene he had been divorced for some years from Riki and was remarried to Lois Zuriff, a bright and engaging lawyer who herself was an excellent cook. Gene had purchased a weekend house in Bridgehampton that had a wonderful kitchen. Lois and I collaborated in producing some memorable Shabbat dinners. Quite unexpectedly, on a day in early April 1994, I received a frantic call from Gene who was in the emergency room at Bellevue Hospital.

"Can you come over immediately?" he asked. "Lois has died."

I left the office, hailed a cab, and traveled the few miles to the hospital on First Avenue and East 28th. He was disconsolate. During a routine gynecological examination that morning, Lois went into anaphylactic shock and could not be resuscitated. She was about to celebrate her fiftieth birthday and just had been named a partner in her law firm.

On the night of Lois's death, Gene asked me if I would speak the following morning at her funeral service. I was both honored and frightened. Honored, because of the cherished gift of friendship which I had shared with both Gene and Lois, and because of the opportunity to share the *bemah* with Rabbi Harlan J. Wechsler, whom I had come to respect and love as teacher, counselor, colleague, and friend. I felt honored because of the privilege and opportunity to celebrate in words the life of a woman of keen intelligence, disciplined piety, poetic imagination, cultured taste, inner and outer beauty, and urbane wit. But at the same time I was also frightened because I knew that in speaking of Lois and of the incalculable loss to Gene that I would shed tears of grief.

In the cab that night, returning to my America House Jesuit community on West 56th Street from Gene's apartment on Second Avenue at 58th Street, I settled thematically on what I would attempt to say at the funeral. I recalled comforting words attributed to one of Judaism's ancient rabbis: "Even when the gates of heaven are closed to prayer, they are open to tears." Arriving back at the Jesuit residence, even though I was exhausted from an emotional day, I sat at my computer and wrote the unedited text I would deliver the next day in the chapel of Campbell's Funeral Home on Madison Avenue.

For the next several months, I had to be a personal chaplain to my board chairman. In some meaningful ways, through these experiences we both came to a much deeper appreciation of the Chaplaincy's essential, multifaith mission. Here was a Jesuit priest caring pastorally for a conservative Jew, perhaps in ways that even his rabbi could not. Through these experiences and others, Gene and I became brothers.

When he began dating again, he would often invite me to meet some of these women. Gene was attracted to strong, accomplished, and powerful women: lawyers, judges, designers, architects, business executives. He seemed always interested in my impressions, which for obvious reasons I was reluctant to offer. However, when I first met Sherry Jacobson, I had a strong sense that this could be a great *Shidduch*, a perfect match. Indeed it was.

Sherry had been raised in an Orthodox Jewish family. Her father, Rabbi Bernard Jacobson, became a marvelous friend. When the rabbi was celebrating his ninetieth birthday, Gene and Sherry planned a family celebration in the private dining room of Maloney and Porcelli, one of the restaurants of the Smith & Wollensky Restaurant Group, of which Gene was president at the time. There had been some murmuring among the Orthodox family members about having this celebration for the rabbi in a non-kosher venue. Of course, Gene and Sherry had made every provision to observe the requirements of *Kashrut*, ensuring that all the food served would be fit for consumption by observant Jews who practice the religious dietary protocols rooted in Jewish biblical tradition. When Rabbi Jacobson got wind of the family's gossiping he was annoyed but managed to mask his displeasure. In delivering his words of gratitude and appreciation at the conclusion of the birthday dinner, he said with a certain degree of ironic pleasure: "I know that some of you have expressed concern about the observance of our dietary laws in planning for this celebration. I want to reassure you that every detail of this celebration has been under the strict supervision of Fr. Walter Smith." The guests did not know how to react: with horror, or with laughter. Rabbi Jacobson, even at age ninety, had the final word.

A couple years later, Sherry told me about the foot pain that her father was experiencing. She had taken him for consultations with a neurologist and a podiatrist. Nothing seemed to be able to provide him any relief. I was invited to spend the weekend with the Zuriffs in their Bridgehampton home. Rabbi Jacobson was also to be there for the Shabbat dinner. I asked him if he would allow me to do a bit of massage and reflexology on his feet. He agreed, and I worked on his feet for about an hour. That evening, after the traditional candle lighting ceremony, which Sherry performed, Rabbi Jacobson walked to the head of the table in the dining room and prepared to offer the Shalom Aleichem:

> *Peace be with you, ministering angels, messengers of the Most High,*
> *messengers of the King of Kings, the Holy One, Blessed be He.*

Come in peace, messengers of peace, messengers of the Most High,
messengers of the King of Kings, the Holy One, Blessed be He.

Bless me with peace, messengers of peace, messengers of the Most High,
messengers of the King of Kings, the Holy One, Blessed be He.

Go in peace, messengers of peace, messengers of the Most High,
messengers of the King of Kings, the Holy One, Blessed be He.

As he was concluding this prayer, he paused and said: "I want to share with you news of a recent miracle. You saw me walking into the dining room tonight with ease, pain-free. Fr. Walter Smith did for me what no doctor has been able. Through the miracle of his hands, he has put new life into these old feet."

Life can be sweet, like these Linzer cookies.

LINZER COOKIES

Almond cookies filled with raspberry preserves

Makes 18 to 24 filled cookies

Ingredients

For the cookie dough

- ½ cup unblanched whole almonds
- 1 cup (2 sticks) unsalted room-temperature butter
- ½ cup granulated sugar
- 1 large egg yolk
- 2 cups all-purpose flour
- ½ teaspoon ground cinnamon
- ⅛ teaspoon salt

For the filling

- ⅔ cup raspberry preserves

continued

- 1 tablespoon liqueur (I used Chambord)
- confectioners' sugar for dusting

Method

Preparing the dough

1. Place the rack in the center of the oven and preheat to 350°F.
2. Arrange the almonds on a baking sheet and roast until lightly toasted and fragrant, about 8 to 10 minutes. Allow the nuts to cool, then grind them with ½ cup of the flour in the bowl of a food processor fitted with the metal chopping blade. Reserve the almond flour.
3. In a bowl of a standing mixer fitted with the paddle attachment, cream the butter and sugar together at medium speed until light and fluffy, about one minute.
4. Add the egg yolk and beat until combined. Add the remaining flour, cinnamon, salt, and the reserved almond flour mixture and mix at low speed until just combined.
5. Scrape the dough onto a piece of plastic wrap, flatten slightly and chill until firm enough to handle (about 2 hours).

To bake

1. Preheat oven to 350°F.
2. Roll out the dough between two sheets of waxed paper to between an eighth- and a quarter-inch thick.
3. Using a cookie cutter of your choice, cut out the forms from the dough. Using another smaller cutter, cut a small circle in half of the cookies, through which later the raspberry filling will be revealed.
4. Bake the cookies on ungreased baking sheets (I use parchment paper or a silicone pad) until lightly golden at the edges, about 8 minutes.

5. Place the baked cookies on a wire rack to cool.
6. In a small saucepan, melt the preserves with the liqueur. Cool slightly, then spread a little of the mixture over the solid bottom cookies. Dust the incised top cookies with confectioners' sugar. Place a dusted cookie over each preserved-topped cookie and gently press together.

I shared several Seder meals with Sherry and Gene and their families. For two of these Seders, Rabbi Jacobson was the leader. I recall an endearing comment he made on the occasion of the first shared Seder. He said: "You know that I am Orthodox, and that most of the Seder is celebrated in Hebrew. Because you are with me, tonight I will be Reformed."

Sherry quickly interpreted her father's statement in this way: "That means he will say a few of the prayers in English!"

At the conclusion of the final Seder shared with the aging rabbi, he walked with me to the elevator in Gene and Sherry's apartment, thanking me for sharing this joyous occasion with him and the family. "This has been one of the happiest Seders I have ever celebrated. I'm getting to be an old man. If I am not here next year, you will need to lead the Seder." Overhearing these remarks from her father, Sherry began to cry. Later she told me that she had memories of how strict her father had been throughout her early years, and how rigidly he adhered to the requirements of Jewish life. To hear him tell a Catholic priest that he would pass the mantle of leadership of the Pesach Seder to him was such a testimonial to a humanity where differences are erased and the commonality of a shared faith in God triumphs.

This recipe for a popular Sicilian fried rice ball encases a surprise savory filling, affirming the old adage that "there's more than first meets the eye."

ARANCINI SICILIANI

Sicilian rice balls

Makes 12 to 18 rice balls

continued

Ingredients

For the rice

- 3 tablespoons extra-virgin olive oil
- 2 cups cannaroli or arborio rice
- 4 ounces dry white wine
- 4 cups chicken stock or broth
- 1 egg
- kosher salt

For the filling

- 4 ounces mozzarella, cut into ½ inch cubes
- a good tomato ragù or Bolognese-style sauce
- frozen petits pois or green peas, thawed and blanched

For the coating

- all-purpose flour
- 2 beaten eggs
- 1 cup whole milk
- dried breadcrumbs (homemade or commercial)
- grated Pecorino Romano cheese
- fresh basil leaves, for garnish
- extra ragù for dipping

For frying the arancini

- peanut or canola oil

Method

To prepare the rice

1. In a saucepan, heat the olive oil and add the rice all at once. Stir the

rice to coat in the oil, and cook the rice for about 2 minutes, continually stirring it.

2. Add the white wine and blend it into the rice. Then, with the heat on medium high, begin adding the heated chicken stock a little at a time, continuously stirring until all the stock has been used and the rice is cooked, yet still al dente. It will take about 15 to 20 minutes to cook the risotto.
3. Remove from heat and set aside to cool.
4. When the rice is cooled, add a lightly beaten egg to the risotto and mix well, then refrigerate the rice mixture for a few hours, or overnight.

To form the arancini

1. Assemble all the ingredients for the filling and coating: the cubed mozzarella, the ragù or Bolognese sauce, and the peas.
2. Using about ¼ cup of the cold risotto, place it in your slightly cupped hand and flatten it a bit; not too much, not too little. The goal is not to let the filling ooze out of the ball when shaped.
3. Place a small cube of the mozzarella, a scant half-teaspoon of the ragù, and a few peas in the center of the cupped rice.
4. Next, close the rice around the filling and gently form into a ball.
5. Mix the eggs and milk together gently.
6. Gently roll the shaped arancini in the flour; dip in egg and milk bath and coat completely in the breadcrumb and Pecorino-Romano mixture. Place on tray and set aside. Refrigerate for one hour before cooking.

To fry the arancini

1. In deep fryer or deep saucepan, add peanut or canola oil and heat to 350°F.
2. Fry the refrigerated arancini in small batches until they turn uniformly

continued

golden. Drain on paper towels. Keep warm in the oven (225°F) until all the arancini have been fried.

3. Arancini can be refrigerated after cooking and cooling, and reheated in a 350°F oven for 20 minutes.

One of Gene and Sherry's New York City and Hamptons friends had recently remarried. His new wife quickly grew fond of the Hamptons summer social circuit of entertaining. She hired a personal chef from France for the summer season and entertained virtually every weekend during July and August. Learning of my interest in French cooking, she invited me to one of her summer soirées. I could sense pretty quickly that her personality and directness was beginning to grate on some of her husband's longtime friends. She did have a somewhat annoying personality and could be a bit crude in her use of language. Despite having the services of an excellent chef preparing the fare at her dinner parties, longtime friends of her husband began declining invitations.

She had been rhapsodizing before the upcoming event to which I had been invited about how incredibly delicious was her chef's classic *tarte tatin*. She told me that she had particularly requested that he make this dessert for the dinner that I would attend. On the evening of the scheduled dinner, due to a violent thunderstorm that tore through the region, there had been a temporary power outage in the Hamptons. When I arrived at their home for the dinner, she informed me straightaway that the chef was upset because his *tarte tatin* had been in the oven when the power went out and it had not properly baked. But, she exclaimed, "It will still be wonderful." When the dessert was finally served it was good, but not remarkable. The base puff pastry was very soggy and the apples were overcooked. I ate the tarte quietly, until she confronted me with the question: "Well, what do you think of the *tarte tatin*?"

Discreetly, I said it that it was good, but it was not the best I had ever eaten. She excused herself and went into the kitchen, only to return saying that her chef challenged me to a bakeoff.

I was stunned by her declaration. "What did you tell him?" I asked.

"I told him that the priest said, 'your tarte tatin sucks.'" An outrageous remark. That was the last dinner invitation I ever accepted from her.

Here is my recipe for a *tarte tatin* that never made it to a bakeoff competition with the anonymous visiting French chef.

TARTE TATIN

Apples baked in caramel sauce with puff pastry base

Makes 6 servings

Ingredients

- 6 Granny Smith, Jonagold, Honeycrisp, Golden Delicious, or Braeburn apples
- ¼ cup fresh lemon juice
- ½ cup granulated sugar
- 1 vanilla bean, split lengthwise
- 2 tablespoons unsalted butter
- 1 tablespoon apple cider vinegar
- a pinch of kosher salt
- 1 sheet previously frozen puff pastry, thawed
- all-purpose flour

Method

1. Preheat oven to 425°F.
2. Peel and cut apples in half, removing their cores and seeds. Rub cut apples with some fresh lemon juice to prevent discoloring. Set aside in a bowl.
3. In a 9-inch heavy ovenproof skillet, distribute ¼ cup of the granulated sugar over the bottom of the pan and scrape in the vanilla beans. (Keep the discarded pods in your sugar jar to lightly perfume your sugar supply.)
4. Place the skillet over medium heat and melt the sugar, allowing it to begin caramelizing to a pale amber color.

continued

5. Once this happens, add the remaining ¼ cup of sugar and continue to allow the sugar mixture to caramelize to medium amber color.
6. Carefully, stir in butter, vinegar, and salt and arrange the apples—rounded side down—tightly together on top of the caramelized sugar and cook the apples for about 6 minutes on medium heat.
7. Remove the skillet from the stovetop.
8. On a lightly floured work surface, carefully unfold a thawed puff pastry sheet and lay it flat. With a sharp paring knife, using a 9-inch round plate or template, cut out a pastry disk that will fit flush inside the skillet and cover the apples.
9. Carefully place the puff pastry round over apples and transfer the skillet to the preheated oven.
10. Bake until the pastry puffs begin to brown (approximately 20 to 25 minutes).
11. Reduce the oven temperature to 350°F and continue baking for an additional 20 to 25 minutes.
12. Allow the *tarte tatin* to rest and cool for 5 minutes before carefully inverting the tarte onto a serving dish.

Bill and Joan Bogardus Spears were raising their family during the years in which I served as a weekend associate at Saint Catherine of Siena parish. Bill worked in New York in the wealth management firm of Spears, Benzak, Salomon, & Farrell. In 1994 Bill and his partners sold their firm, which at the time was managing about $3 billion in assets, to KeyCorp, one of the nation's largest banking companies. He served as chairman and chief executive officer of KeyCorp Asset Management from 1996 to 1999. In 1999, he cofounded Spears Grisanti & Brown. Later, he cofounded Spears Abacus Advisors LLC in partnership with Abacus & Associates and serves as the firm's chairman and chief executive officer.

In 1993, I recruited Bill to the board. He served as chairman from 1996 to 2000. Joan was diagnosed with ovarian cancer and valiantly battled with the disease. From the day of her diagnosis until her death in 2002, I was a spiritual support to Joan and Bill. On the day on which Joan died at home in Greenwich, I was at her bedside. At one point, I asked her if she might like for me to read some scripture aloud to her. She said: "Yes, you know some of my favorite passages." Indeed I did. During my time at St. Catherine's, Joan was the leader of the folk Mass on Sunday evenings, playing the guitar and functioning as cantor. She and I prayed often together. I opened the Bible that was on her bedside table and read from this passage in Mark 4:39–41.

> *So they shook him awake, saying, "Teacher, don't you even care that we are all about to die!" Fully awake, he rebuked the storm and shouted to the sea, "Hush! Calm down!" All at once the wind stopped howling and the water became perfectly calm.*
>
> *Then he turned to his disciples and said to them, "Why are you so afraid? Haven't you learned to trust yet?" But they were overwhelmed with fear and awe and said to one another, "Who is this man who has such authority that even the wind and waves obey him?"*

When I finished reading this story, I paused in silence. Joan thanked me for selecting this particular passage, which she said brought her immense comfort. She said that she had been fearful of her approaching death, and that this passage was so helpful. "I feel there is no longer any need to be afraid since Jesus and Bill and you are in the boat with me, and the seas are now beginning to calm." Joan died peacefully later that same night.

I celebrated a funeral Mass for Joan at the Church of Saint Michael the Archangel on May 28, 2002. In my homily on that occasion, I cited a poem from *The Growing Season* by another friend of mine, Carol Lynn Pearson, who wrote these words in the wake of the death of her husband from AIDS.

GOOD GROUND

I have seen love,
Fallen on unbroken ground,
Blow with the first wind.

I have seen love,
Laid in a shallow row,
Unearthed with the lightest rain.

But pain
Is a plow
That opens earth for planting.

My heart is ready now.
Hurt-furrowed, it has depths
Designed for sowing.

Oh, love that lands here
Finds good ground for growing.[11]

This is a dish that I prepared for a Spears family supper on the night that Joan died. The children and their spouses had gathered. They had purchased sea scallops for supper. There was butternut squash, fennel, and pears available. This simple dish is easy to put together and is a wonderful blend of ingredients that may not be ordinarily paired.

CAPESANTE SCOTTATE CON ZUCCA E PERE

Seared scallops with butternut squash and pears

Makes 4 servings

Ingredients

- 2 cups cubed butternut squash
- ½ cup pancetta
- 1½ cups thinly sliced fennel bulb
- 2 Anjou or Bartlett firm pears
- ½ cup dry white wine
- ¾ cup heavy cream
- 16 sea scallops (4 per person)
- extra-virgin olive oil

11 Carol Lynn Pearson, *The Growing Season* (Salt Lake City, UT: Bookcraft, 1976).

- unsalted butter
- fresh chives
- toasted pignoli (pine nuts)

Method

Preparing the squash and pancetta

1. Preheat oven to 400°F.
2. Peel and cut the butternut squash into 1-inch strips and then into small cubes.
3. In a mixing bowl, toss the squash cubes with olive oil, salt, and pepper. Spread them onto a pan, lined with aluminum foil, and roast for about 20 minutes until tender and slightly browned.
4. Cut the pancetta into a small dice and sauté in a large skillet with a little butter and olive oil until the pancetta is softened. Remove from skillet and drain on a dish lined with paper towels. Reserve the cooking fat.

Preparing the pears and fennel

1. Peel the pears and cut into strips and then into small cubes. Place in bowl with acidulated water (lemon juice and warm water) to prevent browning.
2. Separate the upper stalks from the white fennel bulb, conserving some of the fennel fronds for garnish. Using a mandoline or a fine slicing blade in a food processor, cut the fennel bulb into thin slices.
3. In the same skillet in which the pancetta was sautéed, add a bit more butter and oil and sauté the pear cubes until they begin to soften. Add in the fennel and continue to cook together for about 5 to 7 more minutes.

continued

4. Remove the roasted squash from the oven and combine with the pears and fennel and add the white wine. Cook for another few minutes to evaporate some of the alcohol from the wine.

To cook the scallops and assemble the finished dish

1. Into a very hot skillet, add a bit of butter with a tablespoon or more of olive oil. When the oil begins to smoke add the sea scallops, which have been patted dry with paper towels and seasoned with a bit of salt and pepper. Do not move. Cook for about 2 minutes until the bottoms are golden brown. Turn and cook for one minute on other side. Remove from pan to paper towel–lined plate to drain and keep warm.
2. To the vegetable and pear mixture, add the heavy cream and cook until the cream is heated through and amalgamates with the sauce.
3. Spoon the vegetable and pear mixture onto the dinner plate. Arrange four scallops on top; garnish with toasted pine nuts and some minced fennel fronds. Finish with a couple of lengths of overlapping chives.

Once again, I was thrust into the role of becoming a pastoral support to a widowed board chairman, bereft and uncertain of the way forward. Bill had served for twelve years on the board of his high school alma mater, Choate Rosemary Hall in Wallingford, Connecticut. He had established the Spears Endowment for Spiritual and Moral Education at Choate and had asked me to serve on its governing board. During a car trip to one of the board meetings in the months after Joan's death, Bill told me of a relationship he was pursuing with a Greek-born woman who herself had been widowed in 2000.

Bill was a bit concerned about how his family and friends might react to him dating another woman so soon after Joan's death. I observed that he had been grieving in anticipation of Joan's death during the prior two years of her battle with cancer. If he was falling in love again, I encouraged him to allow it to take its natural course. On Valentine's Day in 2003, I officiated at his marriage to Maria. Maria has proven to be a wonderful partner to Bill. He sold his large home in Greenwich, purchased a lovely apartment overlooking Central Park on Fifth Avenue, and began his new life together with Maria. Maria is a marvelous cook and host, and I shared many wonderful evenings with them and their friends. Maria always did some of the cooking for these family meals, drawing upon her rich Greek culinary background. She made frequent forays to the Greek markets in Astoria and shared with me some of her family recipes. *Spanakopita* was often a part of her dinner offerings. Here is one classic presentation of this delicious spinach pie.

SPANAKOPITA

Greek spinach pie

Makes 8 to 10 servings

Ingredients

For the filling

- 2 pounds washed, dried, trimmed, and coarsely chopped spinach
- 1 bunch scallions
- 2 cups crumbled Greek feta cheese
- ½ cup grated Greek Kefalotyri cheese or Parmigiano Reggiano
- 2 large lightly beaten eggs
- ½ cup finely chopped dill
- ½ cup finely chopped flat-leaf parsley
- extra-virgin olive oil
- unsalted butter
- freshly grated nutmeg
- fleur de sel

For the assembly

- 18 9x14-inch sheets frozen phyllo dough
- extra-virgin olive oil for brushing; more as needed

continued

Method

Preparing the phyllo dough and oven

1. Thaw the frozen phyllo sheets and keep at room temperature, covered with a clean kitchen towel, to prevent the dough from drying out.
2. Position the rack in the center of the oven and preheat the oven to 375°F.

Preparing the filling for the spanakopita

1. Heat a Dutch oven with a couple of tablespoons of olive oil over medium-high heat. Add handfuls of the spinach and cook, continually mixing the spinach as it wilts. Continue adding the spinach until all has been incorporated.
2. When all the spinach has been softened, transfer the spinach to a colander to drain and cool. When cooled, add the spinach to the center of a clean kitchen towel and form into a ball and squeeze between your hands, releasing as much of the water from the spinach as possible.
3. In the same Dutch oven in which the spinach was wilted, quickly sauté the chopped scallions, add back the hand-squeezed spinach, and cook for another minute or two to blend.
4. In a large stainless steel mixing bowl, add in the feta and Kefalotyri (or Parmigiano Reggiano) cheeses, along with the dill, parsley, nutmeg, salt, and pepper. Mix to combine. Then add in the cooked scallion and spinach mixture and fold to combine. Finally, add in the beaten eggs and blend with the whole mixture. Set it aside to cool thoroughly.

To assemble and bake the spanakopita

1. Prepare a 9x13x2-inch Pyrex baking dish by rubbing the interior surface with a bit of olive oil.
2. Working quickly, lightly brush one side of a sheet of phyllo dough with cooled, melted butter and lay it in the pan, buttered side up, and

off center so that it partially covers the bottom and reaches halfway up one long side of the pan (the edge on the bottom of the pan will be about 1 inch from the side).

3. Brush the top of another phyllo sheet and lay it buttered side up and off center so it reaches halfway up the other long side of the pan.
4. Repeat this pattern with 4 more phyllo sheets.
5. Next, lightly butter the tops of 3 phyllo sheets and layer them buttered side up and centered in the pan. Spread the filling evenly over the last layer.
6. Repeat the buttering and layering of the remaining 9 phyllo sheets over the filling in the same way you layered the previous batch.
7. With your fingers, gently push the edges of the phyllo down around the sides of the pan to enclose the filling completely.
8. With a sharp knife, score the top phyllo layer into 24 rectangles, being careful not to cut all the way through to the filling.
9. With a pastry brush, brush milk along all the score marks (this will keep the phyllo from flaking up along the edges of the squares). Bake the *spanakopita* until the top crust is golden brown, 35 to 45 minutes.
10. Let cool until just warm. Cut out the rectangles carefully along the score marks and serve.

When I asked my friend Dick Parsons, who had recently been elected chairman of Time Warner Inc., if he had any recommendations about someone we could invite to be a corporate honoree at an upcoming Chaplaincy gala, he immediately suggested Larry Toal, whom he had recruited to Dime Bancorp, Inc., and who had just succeeded him in 1997 as chairman and CEO. Dick said that he would be happy to make the introduction and encourage Larry to accept the invitation. Larry did not need any coaxing.

When I was escorted into his office on Fifth Avenue, Larry made me feel welcome and was very interested to learn about the Chaplaincy and my role in the organization's life. Not long into the conversation, Larry told me that he had a brother who was a Franciscan friar. The Toal family had lived in Astoria, New York. Larry graduated from Dartmouth College and later earned an MBA in finance from New York University. In the 1960s, Larry served as a US Navy lieutenant. On April 20, 1963—when I was still a Jesuit novice at Shadowbrook—Larry married Sheila O'Connor in West Hempstead, Long Island. Larry recalls that on the morning of their wedding, Sheila's father, Bill O'Connor, said to him: "Larry, she's all yours—credit card bills and all." I always remarked to Sheila how fortunate she was to marry a guy like Larry, whom I never heard raise his voice or get bent out of shape. He quickly adjusted to and always admired Sheila's innate sense of style and good taste. One time, when speaking with me about perfectionism and attentiveness to detail, he said: "I can recognize these traits in others because I sleep with a perfectionist."

Not only did Larry become our corporate honoree, but he joined the Chaplaincy's board and in 2000 was elected board chairman. He was a wonderful partner in advancing the work of the Chaplaincy. And in the course of our collaboration, Larry and Sheila became very close personal friends.

When I first met them, they were living in an apartment on East 57th Street near Sutton Place. Soon thereafter they moved to Park Avenue and became active parishioners in St. Ignatius of Loyola Parish at 83rd Street and Park Avenue. They built an impressive home in Connecticut, where I was an occasional weekend guest.

Their weekend house was not too distant from Tanglewood and every summer season I would accompany them to one of the concerts. Sheila loved to host a picnic on the great lawn before the concert. Weeks before an upcoming concert, she would begin planning in earnest for the picnic supper. She loved when I would volunteer to prepare the meal, and she always made the resources of her butcher available to me.

The Lobel family have operated a butcher shop at 1096 Madison Avenue at the corner of East 82nd Street for more than sixty years. They offered the best-quality meat money can buy. For one of these Tanglewood soirées Sheila suggested we might prepare a roast tenderloin, which we could pre-slice and serve at room temperature with some accompanying sauce or chutney. The beautifully butchered and tied beef tenderloin from Lobel was hand-delivered to my apartment in a Styrofoam container. When I saw the price of the roast, I gulped. And then I remember the words Mr. O'Connor spoke to Larry on the day of his marriage to Sheila and I laughed aloud.

FILET DE BOEUF RÔTI SAUCE À L'ANETH ET RAIFORT

Roasted filet of beef with dill and horseradish sauce

Makes 8 to 10 servings

Ingredients

For the sauce

- 6 whole scallions
- ½ cup dill
- ¼ cup extra-virgin olive oil
- ¼ cup freshly grated or prepared horseradish
- 3 French cornichons
- 1 tablespoon Dijon mustard
- 2 teaspoons Worcestershire sauce
- 1 teaspoon fresh lemon juice
- kosher salt and freshly ground black pepper
- 1 cup crème fraîche
- 1 finely minced hard-boiled egg yolk

For the beef

- 1 beef tenderloin (3½ to 4 pounds)
- kosher salt
- 1 tablespoon Dijon mustard
- 1 tablespoon Worcestershire sauce
- 1 medium clove garlic
- 1 teaspoon honey
- 1 teaspoon soy sauce
- 1 teaspoon finely chopped thyme
- freshly ground black pepper

continued

- 2 tablespoons extra-virgin olive oil

Method

To prepare the horseradish and dill sauce

1. Pulse the scallions, cornichons, and dill in a food processor until roughly chopped. Add the olive oil, horseradish, Worcestershire sauce, Dijon mustard, lemon juice, half-teaspoon of salt, and a half-teaspoon of pepper and pulse until just blended.
2. Transfer to a bowl, blend in the crème fraiche, and then fold in the finely chopped egg. Refrigerate for several hours to allow the flavors to meld. Season to taste with more salt, pepper, lemon juice, or Worcestershire.

To prepare and roast the beef tenderloin

1. If your butcher has not fully prepared the tenderloin for roasting, fold the thinner "tail end" of the tenderloin under to create an evenly thick roast, and secure the entire roast at 2-inch intervals with twine.
2. Rub the beef tenderloin thoroughly with 1 tablespoon or more of kosher salt. Enfold the tenderloin tightly in plastic wrap and refrigerate for a minimum of 2 hours.
3. Remove the beef from the refrigerator and allow to rest at room temperature for about an hour before roasting. Meanwhile, position a rack in the center of the oven and preheat the oven to 475°F.
4. In a small bowl, prepare the flavoring mixture for the roast by combining the mustard, Worcestershire sauce, garlic, honey, soy sauce, thyme, and a few grinds of black pepper and set aside.
5. Heat a flame-proof roasting pan over medium-high heat, using two burners if necessary. Add the oil, swirling the pan to coat, and then brown the beef on all sides and ends. Transfer to a cutting board to rest.
6. Rub the prepared flavoring mixture over all of the beef before returning

it to the roasting pan, and roast to an internal temperature of 120°F for rare (approximately 16 to 20 minutes), or 125°F for medium rare (22 to 26 minutes).

7. Transfer to a cutting board, tent with foil, and allow the roasted tenderloin to rest.

8. Remove the twine. Slice and serve. If you are intending to serve it cold or at room temperature at a later time, once the tenderloin has cooled, wrap it tightly in plastic wrap and refrigerate it for up to 24 hours, slice and serve *à froid.*

As my friendship with the Toals matured, we began celebrating our birthdays together. For my birthday, Sheila always managed to secure reservations in one of the hottest new restaurants in the city. She followed restaurant opening reviews as carefully as investors follow the stock market, and she knew who the new acclaimed chefs were and which restaurants were attracting food critics' interest. One year, for her birthday in 2008, I asked her what she might like me to prepare for a birthday dinner, which I was planning to host at my apartment for her and Larry and some four or five close friends. Without losing a beat in her response, Sheila exclaimed, "I'd love for you to do something Thai."

For several years, during visits to Asia, I had been progressively expanding my repertory of Asian gastronomy and had been experimenting with reproducing several dishes that I had sampled in places like Thailand, Vietnam, and Hong Kong. For Sheila's birthday I created a virtual Thai banquet of a number of small plates. To make the event even more special and because most of these dishes are finished at the time of service, I invited the dinner guests to join me in the kitchen between courses to observe the dishes being finished and assembled. I had completed, in advance of the dinner, all the laborious preparatory work. The menu that evolved proved to be a Thai tour de force: *Khanom Bung Na Goong Roy Nga* (shrimp and pork appetizer), *Khai Niao Sod Sai Kai* (steamed minced chicken sticky rice balls), *Tom Kha Het Mai* (spicy mushroom soup), *Pad Thai Goong Faawy* (Pad Thai), *Pad Phak Ruam Mitr* (seasonal vegetable stir fry), *Leap Moo* (ground meat with lime juice and fish sauce), and *Yum Nuea* (barbequed beef with a sweet, smoky hot sauce and vegetables). Sheila said it was one of the best meals she had ever consumed. It took me the better part of a day to assemble all of the various ingredients and to do all of the chopping, grinding, mincing, and dicing.

Pad Thai is considered by many to be the signature dish of Thai cuisine. It has been said that Thailand has not only a different curry for every day of the year, but also a different *pad Thai* for every cook in Thailand. This is the variation that I prepared for Sheila's birthday dinner.

PAD THAI GOONG FAAWY

Thai stir-fried rice noodles with shrimp and tofu

Makes 8 to 10 servings

Ingredients

- 8 ounces rice noodles
- 6 cloves finely chopped garlic
- 2 tablespoons chopped shallots
- 6 cooked shrimp, roughly chopped
- ¼ cup prepared fish sauce
- ¼ cup granulated sugar
- 2 teaspoons tamarind concentrate, mixed with 5 teaspoons water
- 1 lightly beaten egg
- ¼ cup chopped chives
- ½ cup finely chopped peanuts
- 1 cup bean sprouts
- 1 cup diced firm tofu, marinated in dark sweet soy sauce

Method

To prepare the noodles and the garnishes

1. Prepare the rice noodles in advance by soaking them in warm water

for about an hour or more, depending on how soft you prefer the noodles.

2. Mix a tablespoon of fresh lime juice with a tablespoon of tamarind juice and a tablespoon of fish sauce. Add this liquid mix to ½ cup of uncooked bean sprouts, ½ cup of chopped chives, and ½ cup of very coarsely ground roasted peanuts. Reserve this mixture to garnish the finished *pad Thai.*
3. Prepare several limes by cutting them into segments. Slice a cucumber into thin rounds, then halve the rounds. Arrange the lime segments and cucumber segments around the serving platter. Set aside for final service of the *pad Thai.*

To cook and assemble the pad Thai

1. Heat a little vegetable oil in a wok or large skillet and add the garlic and shallots, and briefly stir fry until they just show signs of changing color.
2. Sauté the chopped shrimp. Quickly add the remaining ingredients, except the egg and the bean sprouts, and stir fry (about 3 to 4 minutes).
3. As you stir fry the mixture, periodically add 1 to 2 tablespoons of water.
4. As you continue to stir fry with one hand, slowly drizzle in the beaten egg to form a fine ribbon of cooked egg.
5. Finally, add the bean sprouts and cook for no more than another 30 seconds.
6. Remove from the pan to the prepared serving platter and garnish with prepared garnishes.

The final person to serve as chairman during my Chaplaincy tenure was T. Michael Long, whom I introduced at some length in an earlier chapter. Michael took on this responsibility at a critical time of transition. He presided over the process to recruit an individual to succeed me, and to pass the chairmanship to another of the trustees. As I often said to Mike, at the end we were both like characters from a 1950s-era Western: good guys who arrive in a town struggling with some issue or other and resolve the grave problems besetting the place by subduing the bad guys and restoring some semblance of order. Then we remount our horses and head west in the direction of the setting sun.

Because HealthCare Chaplaincy was a multifaith organization whose founding in 1961 was the work of several east midtown Manhattan Protestant congregations, I developed during my New York years many deep and significant friendships with the city's clergy. One of my earliest contacts was with Rabbi Harlan Wechsler, who was the founding rabbi of Conservative Congregation Or Zarua. Harlan was the first Jewish clergyman the Twinames had consulted when they attempted to attract Jewish staff and students to the Chaplaincy. At the time, in addition to his ministry as a congregational rabbi, Harlan also served as a respected professor at the Jewish Theological Seminary (JTS).

Founded in 1886, JTS is one of the academic and spiritual centers of Conservative Judaism and a major intellectual center for academic scholarship in Jewish studies in the United States. Harlan was a member of the search committee that had recruited me to the HealthCare Chaplaincy. Some years after my hire, Harlan told me a humorous story about the search committee's deliberations after my final interview. In the course of their discussion, Harlan told the committee that he had already known me. He went on immediately to clarify that although he had just met me personally—along with the other members of the search committee—he knew of me through my writings. In fact, he told the committee that he was currently using one of my books as a required reading text in one of the courses he was currently teaching at JTS. Such a recommendation clearly impressed the group and added to their determination to recruit me to the Chaplaincy.

Through our friendship, Harlan and I came to know many people in common. We shared several funerals and wedding celebrations, and he was consistently supportive and encouraging in every initiative that I would take throughout my tenure with the Chaplaincy.

As did Harlan, I also became friendly with Rabbi Dr. Norman Lamm, a distinguished rabbi, philosopher, teacher, and author who from 1976 until 2003 was the president of Yeshiva University. Yeshiva is the nation's oldest comprehensive institution of higher learning under Jewish auspices. After leaving the presidency, Norman served as chancellor and *rosh ha-Yeshiva* of Yeshiva University's affiliated Rabbi Isaac Elchanan Theological Seminary from 2003 until his retirement on June 30, 2013. Rabbi Lamm died in 2020 at the age of ninety-two years.

It was my practice to send holiday cards and messages to my many Jewish friends, associates, and donors at Rosh Hashanah, Hanukkah, and Pesach. Unfailingly, Dr. Lamm would always reply with a handwritten message, frequently commenting on the breadth and depth of my familiarity with Jewish scholarship. He always made some reference in his notes to my religious sensitivity and insight. These regular exchanges deepened our bonds. When I needed a strong endorsement from a respected Jewish leader, I could always count on Dr. Lamm to be in my corner with an eloquent testimonial.

I shared a similar wonderful fraternal relationship with Rabbi Dr. Marc Angel, who from 1969 until 2007 served as the senior rabbi of Congregation Shearith Israel. Congregation Shearith Israel, the Spanish and Portuguese synagogue, was founded in 1654, the first Jewish congregation to be established in North America.

Marc and I became not only colleagues, but trusted friends. I got to know his wife, Gilda, and their children, especially their son Hayyim, who like his father was ordained to the rabbinate and succeeded Marc as senior rabbi until 2013. Gilda and I shared a common interest in cooking. She published a wonderful book in 1986 titled *Sephardic Holiday Cooking: Recipes and Traditions.*[12]

When the Congregation was preparing for a yearlong celebration of its 350th anniversary in 2004, Marc asked me to be a member of a planning committee that was charged to plan a public symposium on the topic of religious freedom. The committee had reached out unsuccessfully to several prominent prospective keynote speakers. In desperation, Marc called me and asked, "Who else can we think to invite?" I suggested we might reach out to Antonin Scalia, who at the time was an associate justice of the Supreme Court. Marc was thrilled at the thought, but quickly inquired, "Do you know him?" I acknowledged that I did not have a personal connection with him, but I knew someone who had clerked for him and added that Scalia had been a 1953 graduate of Xavier High School in New York, a 1957 graduate of Georgetown University, and had a son who was a diocesan priest.

The short story is that Scalia accepted the invitation and was the major speaker

12 Gilda Angel, *Sephardic Holiday Cooking: Recipes and Traditions* (New York: Decalogue Books, 1986).

at the Shearith Israel Symposium. Marc Angel asked me to introduce Justice Scalia on that occasion, which I gladly did. In the Q&A session, one of the attendees asked Scalia about his reputation of being the intellectual anchor of an originalist and textualist philosophy he espoused within the Court's conservative wing. I recall Scalia pausing briefly, looking directly into the questioner's eyes and saying with a growing smile on his face: "Young man, I may indeed be a textualist, but I am not a kook. Next question."

In speaking about the oldest continuously operating synagogue community in North America I am reminded of *Zuccotto alla Fiorentina*, the oldest known dessert in Florence. If the lore is to be believed, this confection was first served in the sixteenth century during a banquet in honor of Caterina de' Medici. Food historians think it was the creation of Bernardo Buontalenti—a true Renaissance man—who in addition to being an architect, sculptor, painter, military engineer, and designer also dabbled in the art of pastry making. Legend has it that the first zuccotto was made inside a military helmet, which is also called a zuccotto. Priests, bishops, and the pope today wear a smaller skullcap called a *zucchetto*—black for priests, red for bishops, and white for the pope.

The shape of this dessert also reminds many Florentines of the famous sixteenth-century dome designed by Filippo Brunelleschi for the Cattedrale di Santa Maria del Fiore, Florence's celebrated duomo. Here is my simplified version of this very old dessert.

ZUCCOTTO ALLA FIORENTINA

Florentine cake filled with cream, chocolate, and chopped nuts

Makes 8 to 10 servings

Ingredients

- 2 ounces whole blanched and skinned almonds
- 2 ounces whole hazelnuts, shelled
- 1 good-quality prepared pound cake (16 ounces)
- 3 tablespoons Cognac

- 2 tablespoons Maraschino liqueur
- 2 tablespoons Cointreau or white curaçao liqueur
- 8 ounces semisweet chocolate
- 2 cups heavy whipping cream
- 1 cup confectioners' sugar
- fresh raspberries or strawberries for garnish

Method

1. Prepare a 1-quart rounded-bottom Pyrex bowl by lining the inside of the bowl with a layer of plastic wrap, which will help with the unmolding.
2. Preheat oven to 375°F.
3. Place almonds on baking sheet and place in uppermost rack of oven for 5 minutes. Do not let the nuts burn, and do not turn off the oven when you take out the almonds. Chop the toasted almonds rather coarsely.
4. Put the shelled hazelnuts on a baking sheet and roast them for 5 minutes. Take them out and, using a dry towel, rub off as much of their outer skin as possible. Chop coarsely, as with the almonds.
5. Cut most of the pound cake into slices 3/8-inch thick. Divide each slice diagonally in half, making two triangular pieces.
6. Combine the Cognac, Maraschino, and Cointreau in a small bowl. Use a spoon or pastry brush to distribute some of the liqueur mixture over each piece of cake, reserving some of the mixture for later use. Do not oversaturate the cake.
7. Line the inside of the bowl with the moistened pound cake triangles, the narrow end of each piece facing the bottom of the bowl.
8. Make sure the entire inner surface of the bowl is lined with cake. If there are gaps, fill them in with small pieces of moistened cake, without worrying about the pattern they form.

continued

9. Coarsely chop the chocolate.
10. Put heavy cream into a very cold mixing bowl and whip the cream until it is stiff. Add the confectioners' sugar during the mixing process and flavor the cream as you desire (almond extract, vanilla extract, rum extract, etc.)
11. Add to the whipped cream the chopped almonds, hazelnuts, and chocolate bits and fold until incorporated.
12. Spoon half of the mixture into the cake-lined bowl, spreading it uniformly with the back of a spoon or rubber spatula. You should be left with a hollow in the center.
13. Melt two ounces of chocolate. Fold the melted and slightly cooled chocolate into the remaining half of the whipped cream and spoon it into the hollow.
14. Add cake pieces to completely seal the top of the bowl (when inverted this will form the base of the cake). Moisten the base with the reserved liqueur mixture, cover with plastic wrap, and refrigerate overnight or up to two days.
15. Remove plastic wrap and invert onto serving dish. Lift bowl away. Remove outer lining of plastic wrap.
16. Garnish with sifted powdered sugar or sweetened cocoa. Garnish with raspberry sauce, fresh berries, or chocolate-dipped strawberries.

By the time that I joined the Chaplaincy, Rabbi Dr. Ronald B. Sobel was already a trustee emeritus of the organization. As part of my general orientation I arranged to meet Ronald, who from 1973 until his retirement in 2002 was the senior rabbi of the Reform congregation of Temple Emanu-El. He then took on the title senior rabbi emeritus.

Rabbi Sobel, like those who would follow him in Temple Emanu-El's rabbinic leadership, was deeply invested in interfaith relations. In 1975, he was the first rabbi to preach from the pulpit of St. Patrick's Cathedral in New York City. In the 1980s he helped found the Yorkville Emergency Alliance, an interfaith, nonpolitical group of men and women who created, on New York's Upper East Side, a unique community organization to deal with the plight of the poor, the elderly, the homeless, and the hungry. I became involved with Rabbi Sobel in a group of multifaith religious leaders who met monthly, called "A Partnership of Faith in New York," an ambitious effort to establish and maintain a grassroots coalition of congregational clergy throughout all five boroughs.

Whenever we would meet, he would hug me and greet me with the words "Beloved Brother." Often during the years, I would ask him to host the annual meeting and convocation of the HealthCare Chaplaincy in his historic synagogue on Fifth Avenue. He never failed to open wide the Temple Emanu-El's doors to us.

In recalling my involvement with the Partnership of Faith I am also reminded of my friendship with Rabbi Peter J. Rubinstein, who joined Central Synagogue as its senior rabbi during the same year that I was appointed to HealthCare Chaplaincy. Peter and I worked together on many important projects, including the Partnership of Faith, which he chaired for many years. He regularly hosted the monthly gatherings at Central Synagogue.

Under his leadership and vision, Peter revitalized the Central Synagogue's liturgy and education programs. He was responsible for rebuilding and restoring its historic sanctuary, which in 2001 was virtually destroyed by fire.

At the final Yom Kippur services at which he presided prior to his retirement as senior rabbi in 2014, I surprised Peter by attending the morning service, which was held in David Geffen Hall in New York City's Lincoln Center for the Performing Arts. The congregation annually rented Lincoln Center's 2,738-seat auditorium—home of the New York Philharmonic—for its High Holy Day services, to accommodate the swell in members wishing to participate in these liturgical events.

Before the Shacharit service began, I went up to the stage to greet Peter and to express my solidarity and best wishes to him. I could see that he was very moved by this fraternal gesture. Before he began the formal services of Yom Kippur, he made some announcements to the assembled members who packed the auditorium's seats. I was seated with Howard Sharfstein, a trust and estate attorney, who at the time was Central Synagogue's president. Howard was also a Chaplaincy trustee and had been taking training courses at the Chaplaincy to qualify during his retirement to be a Jewish chaplain. Peter told the congregation that they were honored, as was he, by the presence with them of Fr. Walter Smith, S.J., the president of HealthCare Chaplaincy.

"Not only has Fr. Smith been a good and faithful friend to me throughout my rabbinate at Central, but even more importantly, he has been a great friend to the entire New York Jewish community," he said. With that, quite spontaneously, the entire congregation of more than 2,000 participants rose to their feet and applauded me. I was humbled and embarrassed by this outpouring of affirmation and affection. Later, as I reflected on this gesture, I realized just how much my many years of investment in building a spirit of interreligious respect and cooperation had yielded. Praise be to God. *Baruch Hashem.*

One of the clergymen who had served as an early chairman of the board of HealthCare Chaplaincy was the Rev. Dr. John Silber Damm, professor, seminary president, and longtime senior pastor of Saint Peter's Lutheran parish, located in Manhattan's Citigroup Center Building on Lexington Avenue at 53rd Street. John Damm was one of the first persons to whom John and Carolyn Twiname introduced me during the early weeks of my engagement at the Chaplaincy, and there was an almost instant rapport established between us. He was enthralled with the knowledge that I had come to my work at the Chaplaincy directly from being a seminary dean. His Lutheran colleagues would quickly affirm my judgment that John Damm was one of the most influential twentieth-century American Lutheran leaders in the reform and advancement of seminary education. He was both a liturgical scholar and liturgical pioneer, and played a major role in the development of baptismally centered Eucharistic Lutheran worship. Pastor Damm was a consummate mentor—a wise man, full of love and good humor—with a capacious heart open to everyone.

I remember sitting with him during the years following his retirement as senior pastor in the congregation at St. Peter's for a special occasion Sunday Mass. Before the service began we got to talking about the parish's columbarium, which he was instrumental in establishing within the sanctuary at St. Peter's. I casually asked him if he was planning, upon his death, to have his ashes placed in one of the niches in the columbarium. He replied that he intended to be buried alongside his parents in New Jersey. When I challenged him about this decision, he became quite introspective and quiet. I reasoned that he had pastored this congregation for decades, had shepherded the organic growth of its liturgical life, and had envisioned the importance of St. Peter's columbarium as an integral part of the sanctuary's architecture. He personally had engaged a St. Peter's congregant, architect, and friend, Ralph Price (who also served as a HealthCare Chaplaincy life trustee), to design the columbarium. Why would he elect not to have his cremated remains placed here among St. Peter's faithful, where they gathered in prayer? The service began and abruptly ended this conversation. At the end of the service, John turned to me and said: "Walter, your challenge to me has been profound. I have been praying about it throughout this entire Mass. Of course, you are right. I will change my funeral plans. My remains will be placed in St. Peter's columbarium. God has worked so powerfully through you today." John Damm's ashes now rest among his beloved parishioners.

O Lord support us all the day long of this troubled life, until the shadows lengthen, and the evening comes, the busy world is hushed, the fever of life is over, and our work is done. Then, in your mercy, grant us a safe lodging, and a holy rest, and peace at the last; through Jesus Christ our Savior and Lord, Amen.

Eternal rest grant John, O Lord, and may light perpetual shine upon him. Amen.

Because of John Damm's need to regulate his diet due to chronic diabetes, he was fastidious about what he ate and the portions he took at any meal. Notwithstanding his dietary vigilance, he loved this tri-flavored salmon mousse.

AVOCADO, SALMON, AND SPINACH MOUSSE

Makes 8 to 10 servings

Ingredients

For the avocado mousse

- 3 ripe avocados
- 2 teaspoons fresh lemon juice
- 3 teaspoons dry sherry
- a pinch of fleur de sel and freshly grated black pepper

continued

For the salmon mousse

- 1 pound skinless, boneless, freshly poached salmon
- 2 tablespoons freshly minced dill or 1 teaspoon dried dill
- fleur de sel and black pepper

For the spinach mousse

- 1 pound fresh baby spinach, quickly blanched and well dried
- a pinch of fleur de sel, black pepper, and some grated nutmeg

Additional ingredients

- 3 teaspoons unflavored powdered gelatin
- ¾ cup fish or chicken stock for dissolving the gelatin
- 2½ cups lightly whipped heavy cream
- 14–16 thin slices Scottish or Nova Scotia smoked salmon

Method

1. Dissolve the gelatin in the fish stock.
2. Line a loaf pan (metal or glass) with plastic wrap (to help with the eventual unmolding).
3. Inside the pan, lay thin strips of smoked salmon leaving enough salmon overlapping the edges to fold over the top of the mousse and enclose.

Making the avocado mousse

1. Purée the avocado with the lemon juice and sherry until smooth. Season and set aside in a bowl.

Making the salmon mousse

1. Simply purée the poached salmon until smooth. Season and place in a second bowl.

Making the spinach mousse

1. Purée the blanched spinach with the seasonings until smooth. Place in a third bowl.

To finish the three mousse preparations and to assemble the dish

1. Fold one third of the lightly whipped cream and one third of the dissolved gelatin into each of the three bowls, and thoroughly combine.
2. With a spatula, transfer the mixture from each bowl carefully into the loaf pan on top of the foundation of smoked salmon and, with an offset spatula, evenly distribute the contents in even layers, beginning with the avocado mousse, followed by the salmon mousse, and finishing with the spinach mousse.
3. Fold over the slices of salmon to enclose the mousse. Cover with plastic wrap and refrigerate.
4. Chill for 8 hours or overnight until firm.
5. Turn out onto a serving plate and remove plastic wrap. Serve chilled with some crème fraîche that has been mixed with some freshly chopped dill. Garnish with a sprig of fresh dill.

In 1692, four years after the establishment of the Dutch colony of New Amsterdam on the southern tip of the present-day island of Manhattan, a Dutch Reformed congregation was established in what is now called the Collegiate Church of New York. When the British replaced the Dutch in the governance of New York in 1664, King William III permitted the Dutch Reformed Church to continue its ministries, even in 1696 granting it a royal charter. That made Collegiate Church the oldest corporation in America.

When I arrived in New York to begin my ministry with HealthCare Chaplaincy, I soon thereafter received a call from the Reverend Dr. Arthur Caliandro, who had been serving as the fifth senior minister of Marble Collegiate Church from 1984. Arthur succeeded his predecessor, the Rev. Dr. Norman Vincent Peale, and he continued until his own retirement in 2009 as senior minister at Marble. Arthur called me to not only express his welcome but to invite me to have lunch with him, which was the beginning of a remarkable friendship.

Arthur had been recruited in 1967 to the ministry staff at Marble Collegiate Church by Dr. Peale and his wife, Ruth Stafford Peale. At that time he was a youthful pastor. When he retired forty-two years later he was a much esteemed pastor and preacher, beloved by many. Arthur's father had been a Methodist minister in Portland, Maine, where the Caliandro boys were raised. Arthur was one of three sons of Tomaso and Francesca Caliandro, immigrants from Italy. All three sons followed their father into church ministry.

When I became involved in searching to recruit and appoint a chief financial officer at the Chaplaincy, Arthur called to endorse one of his congregants who was on the short list of candidates for the position. The search ultimately came down to Susan Fischer and another eminently qualified finalist—both women. We had an excellent firm assisting us in conducting the search. The lead recruiter was a consummate professional who always maintained his objectivity in the process. The final interviews with Chaplaincy trustees took place in the corporate offices of Sibyl Jacobson at MetLife. Three trustees participated in a full morning of conversations with the two candidates. Afterwards, they debriefed with me and offered their assessments. Then the decision was mine.

I went to lunch with the recruiter. For the first time, I sensed he thought the decision would lean in the direction of a woman who had been a vice president in one of the city's prominent banking institutions. Her résumé was impeccable. "I have decided to offer the position to Susan Fischer," I told him. I noted that his eyes dilated as he gasped to catch his breath.

"Fine," he said, "but may I ask you to share with me what led you to your decision?" Without losing a beat, I replied that both candidates—in terms of their skills and personality—could easily do the job well. "In the end, what helped me to decide is my judgment that for Susan Fischer, this will not only be a job, but it will also be her vocation." Susan Fischer was one of my closest collaborators for more than ten years.

When I called Arthur to tell him of my decision, he was thrilled. After I told him about the search process and my personal discernment of Susan's special calling to ministry at HealthCare Chaplaincy, he exclaimed, "You are a very wise man, Walter." He told me that he recognized the very same qualities of mind and spirit in her. Soon thereafter, Susan was ordained to diaconal ministry at Marble Collegiate Church.

Among Arthur's legacy contributions to Marble Collegiate Church were his efforts to identify and promote the leadership of women like Susan to positions of consequence. Susan was a very close friend with the Rev. Dr. Florence Pert, who, at Arthur's prompting, became the first woman in the history of the Collegiate Churches to be ordained a minister. Susan was also an admirer and devotée of Sister Carol Perry, S.U., a Roman Catholic Sister of Saint Ursula.

Susan spoke so appreciatively about Sr. Carol that I had to meet her.

At Florence Pert's prompting, Dr. Peale had persuaded Sr. Carol to give some Sunday morning Bible study classes to Marble's congregants before the Sunday worship services. Reluctantly, Sr. Carol agreed to give six weeks of presentations and discussions. She remained at Marble for thirty-seven years. Arthur had been a junior member of the clergy at that time and grew to appreciate Sr. Carol's value to the spiritual life of the congregation. When Arthur became senior minister, he asked Sr. Carol to become Marble's full-time resident biblical scholar.

It did not take long for me to connect with Sr. Carol. During my tertianship year in Rome in 1975 I had taught a course for women religious at the Pontifical Institute, Regina Mundi. Sr. Carol recounted her story. "In the 1950s there was not a university in the world where a Catholic woman could study the Bible," she said, explaining that although the leadership of religious institutes kept petitioning the Holy See to train women to be theologians and biblical scholars, the Vatican kept saying no. Finally there was a concession. Although women at that time were still not admitted to attend or pursue degrees at the major Roman ecclesiastical universities, the Holy See did establish Regina Mundi as a place where nuns like Sr. Carol could study the Bible, theology, and ethics. In 1957, Sr. Carol joined about sixty other women religious from thirty-two countries to study sacred scripture at Regina Mundi. She went on to earn a master's degree at Notre Dame.

Sr. Carol was clearly a woman ahead of her time. As a sister of St. Ursula, she had followed the right charism for her. At the beginning of the seventeenth century, Anne de Xainctonge, a French laywoman, intended to do for the education of girls what Ignatius of Loyola, founder of the Jesuits, had done for the education of boys and young men. She was a revolutionary, offering free education to girls and paying no attention to ethnicity, race, or socioeconomic status. The nuns wore no special habits, did not live a cloistered life, and wore the simple attire of widows in the area. Like Jesuits, whose rule they adopted, the sisters were urged to go out among the people and serve in whatever social and pastoral ministries they could, especially as teachers and spiritual animators.

• • • • • • • • • • • • • • • • • •

So here, under Arthur Caliandro's watch, Sr. Carol Perry's ministry at Marble thrived, in the oldest place of worship of the Collegiate Reformed Protestant Church in New York City.

Arthur had also played a major role in establishing, along with Rabbi Ronald Sobel, the Partnership of Faith to strengthen the personal and professional ties among Protestant, Catholic, Jewish, and Muslim communities in New York City. Even after his retirement, one could count on Arthur's presence and active engagement in the early morning gatherings of this group in the atrium meeting room at Central Synagogue.

For me, Arthur was always a quiet, calming presence. He had the ability to listen deeply, without judgment, and with great sensitivity and compassion. His counsel was always discerning and wise. He never viewed black and white as polar opposites, but opportunities to find commonalties and unity, much like the stripes of a zebra are a unified whole.

TORTA DI ZEBRA

Italian Zebra Cake

Makes 6 to 8 servings

Ingredients

- 5 room-temperature eggs, separated
- 2½ cups all-purpose flour
- 1 cup granulated sugar
- 1 cup canola oil
- 1 cup cola (such as Coke or Pepsi)
- 2 teaspoons baking powder

- 1 teaspoon salt
- rum extract
- vanilla extract
- cocoa powder
- confectioners' sugar (for dusting)

Method

Preparing the cake batter base

1. Preheat oven to 350°F.
2. Butter and line with parchment paper (bottom and sides) a 10-inch springform baking pan.
3. In a stand mixer fitted with the whisk attachment, beat the 5 egg whites on medium speed for about 3 minutes. With the mixer running, slowly add 1 cup of granulated sugar.
4. Add the egg yolks and continue to mix for another 2 or 3 minutes.
5. Reduce mixer speed to low and slowly stream 1 cup of canola oil into the bowl.
6. Finally, add 1 cup of room-temperature cola.
7. Remove the mixing bowl from its stand and equally divide the wet mixture into two smaller mixing bowls. (If you have large-volume measuring cups, you can divide the batter into them. It will facilitate successively pouring the vanilla and chocolate batters into the baking pan, as recommended below.)

To make the chocolate cake batter

1. Using a fine mesh strainer, sift 1¼ cups of flour, 3 teaspoons of cocoa powder, a half-teaspoon of salt, and 1 teaspoon of baking powder into one of the smaller mixing bowls and blend to combine. Add a few drops of rum extract and gently mix. Set the batter aside.

continued

To make the vanilla cake batter

1. In a similar manner, sift 1¼ cups of flour, a half-teaspoon of salt, and 1 teaspoon of baking power into the second mixing bowl and thoroughly mix. Finally, add 1 teaspoon of vanilla extract to the batter and stir to combine.

To assemble the baking pan

1. Beginning with the chocolate batter, add 2 tablespoons of the batter to the center of the prepared cake pan. Then add 2 tablespoons of the vanilla cake batter on top of the spreading chocolate batter.
2. Continue this procedure, alternating 2 tablespoons of each of the mixtures, until all the batter has been distributed in the pan.

To bake the cake

1. Place the filled, springform cake pan in the middle rack of the preheated oven and bake for about 60 minutes, until the cake springs back when touched.

To finish and serve

1. Allow the baked cake to cool on a rack for 10 minutes before releasing the cake from the springform pan and removing the parchment paper liners.
2. Dust with confectioners' sugar, if desired.
3. Serve with some flavored whipped cream, fresh berries, or ice cream.

Whenever I pass by the landmark Tuckahoe marble building on Fifth Avenue at 29th Street, I remember with deep affection and appreciation a man who never failed to remind me—even on some of my darkest days in New York—that there is no life without light. Rest in that light eternal, Arthur—dear friend and mentor.

My predecessors at the Chaplaincy, John and Carolyn Twiname, had already begun to establish networks within the New York Muslim community. It was they who introduced me to Imam Izak-El Mu'eed Pasha, the resident imam of Masjid Malcolm Shabazz in Harlem. When I called Imam Pasha for an introductory meeting, he invited me to join him for the Friday *Ṣalāt al-Jumuʿah* prayer service at the mosque. I made the journey uptown to 116th Street, where I was warmly welcomed. On that Friday midday, I was the only white face in a room packed with more than two hundred black men, standing and kneeling in prayer. I listened to Imam Pasha give a powerfully moving sermon and exhortation to his assembled congregation.

Masjid Malcolm Shabazz was established in the mid-1950s by Nation of Islam Minister El Hajj Malik Shabazz, better known as Malcolm X, who led the congregation until 1965. Malcom X was succeeded until 1975 by Minister Louis Farrakhan. When the Nation of Islam founder Elijah Muhammad died in 1975, he was succeeded by his son, Imam Warith Deen Mohammed, who disbanded the Nation of Islam and began its radical transformation into a mainstream American Islamic movement united with Sunni Islam. He also renamed the New York City congregation Masjid Malcolm Shabazz, to honor the assassinated Malcolm X. In 1993 the Malcolm Shabazz community elected its first native-born New Yorker to become its spiritual leader, Imam Izak-El Mu'eed Pasha.

After the prayer service was completed, Imam Pasha invited me to join him in his office. He was very interested in the work of HealthCare Chaplaincy and was profusely grateful for our interest to offer imams opportunities to gain the requisite education and training to qualify for certification as professional chaplains.

Soon thereafter, I was frequently invited to meet and address various groups of Muslim leaders, including Imam W. Deen Mohammed, who until his death in 2008 became a friend and supporter. With Imam Pasha and Imam W. Deen Mohammed's encouragement, HealthCare Chaplaincy became a principal advocate with the national chaplaincy certification agencies to develop pathways for imams to become board-certified chaplains. Because imams do not have accredited seminaries or standardized training programs in theology and ministry to support their formation, they did not meet certain basic requirements for certification. This problem was also compounded by the fact that some imams did not have completed undergraduate or graduate degrees from institutions of higher learning. Imam Mohammed was grateful to have an advocate working with him to provide specialized education for his clergy.

The Chaplaincy educated the first imam to earn certification by the Association of Professional Chaplains, Imam Yusuf F. Hasan. Yusuf became our certification test case as we shepherded him through the rigors of completing four units of clinical pastoral education, interpreting to the credentialing agency his prior theological and pastoral education and formation and enlisting prominent Muslim leaders, including Imam Mohammed, to validate his qualification as an imam.

For more than twenty-five years, Al-Hajji Imam Yusuf Hasan, B.C.C., has served as a staff chaplain at Memorial Sloan Kettering Cancer Center in New York City, where he has specialized in pediatric spiritual care and ministers to young patients and their families. I recall one day inviting Yusuf to come for a conversation where I wished to discuss with him the importance of making the hajj. The hajj is a pillar of Islam, required of all Muslims once in a lifetime. It is a physically demanding pilgrimage during which Muslims seek to deepen their faith, wipe clean past sins, and start anew before God.

As he was our first Muslim staff chaplain, I was intent that Yusuf be encouraged and helped to make this journey. When he arrived for the appointment, I told him that because of his achievements in gaining board certification, he would undoubtedly become a national spokesperson for professional chaplaincy among his Muslim confrères. I told him that I knew that he would probably not have the time or the resources to make the hajj, but that HealthCare Chaplaincy was prepared to offer him both the time and the financial help to do this.

He journeyed to Medina and then Mecca, and with thousands of others, circled the Kaaba counterclockwise seven times while reciting supplications to God, then walked between the two hills traveled by Hagar. He spent a night in the valley of Mina and climbed Mt. Arafat, the mountain of mercy. Having completed this important pilgrimage, Yusuf now proudly has added an honorific title before his name—Al-Hajji Imam Yusuf F. Hasan, B.C.C.

Through my membership and participation in the Partnership of Faith I came to know Imam Shamsi Ali, an Indonesian-born Muslim cleric. After completing his undergraduate studies at the International Islamic University in Islamabad, Pakistan, Shamsi taught in Saudi Arabia. The Indonesian ambassador to the United Nations heard Shamsi giving a lecture and was impressed by both his learning and passion. He invited him to come to New York City to build a mosque for the Indonesian community in Long Island City. Along with his young wife, Mutiah Malik, and their growing family, Imam Ali permanently relocated to the United States in 1997. In 2003, he received a PhD in political science from the University of Southern California.

When I first met Shamsi he was the imam at NYC's largest mosque, Islamic Cultural Center of New York (ICC), located on Third Avenue at 96th Street. This mosque was directly opposite one of the long-term-care residential facilities where HealthCare Chaplaincy was responsible for the management of pastoral care services. Imam Ali was actively engaged in interfaith activities and dialogue, which demonstrated his civic engagement on how to be a contemporary Muslim in a pluralistic society. His openness and acceptance of others alienated him from some members of his congregation and its governors. One of the delights of life is seeing how diverse elements can be blended together to produce an amazing result—something you will find in this recipe for a cookie that blends chunks of chocolate with whole oats, salted pecans, and dried cherries.

CHUNKY CHOCOLATE OATMEAL COOKIES WITH SALTED PECANS AND DRIED CHERRIES

Makes 12 to 18 cookies

Ingredients

- 1¼ cups all-purpose flour
- ¾ teaspoon baking powder
- ½ teaspoon baking soda
- ¼ cup cocoa (preferably Dutch-process)
- 1¼ cups rolled oats
- 1 cup lightly toasted and chopped salted pecans
- 1 cup dried chopped cherries
- 4 ounces bittersweet chocolate, roughly chopped
- 12 tablespoons (1½ half sticks) softened butter
- 1½ cups dark brown sugar
- 1 large egg
- 1 teaspoon vanilla extract

continued

Method

1. Preheat oven to 350°F.
2. Line two large cookie sheets with silicone pads or parchment paper.
3. Whisk flour, baking powder, baking soda, and cocoa in medium bowl.
4. In second medium bowl, combine the oats, chopped pecans, cherries, and chopped chocolate chunks.
5. In a stand mixer fitted with the flat paddle, cream together the butter and sugar at medium speed until smooth, about 1 minute. Scrape down the sides of bowl with a rubber spatula.
6. Add a lightly beaten egg and the vanilla and continue beating on low speed until fully incorporated, about 30 seconds. Scrape down the sides of the bowl.
7. With the mixer running at low speed, add flour mixture until just combined.
8. With mixer still running on low, gradually add oat, nut, and fruit mixture until just incorporated.
9. Remove the bowl from the stand mixer and scrape down the sides of the bowl with a spatula and do one final manual mix of the ingredients.
10. With a tablespoon, form heaping rounds of the dough and place on the cookie sheets, spaced apart. Press lightly to flatten each dough round.
11. Bake 13 to 16 minutes until medium brown.
12. Cool the cookies on the baking sheets for 5 minutes, then transfer to wire rack and let cool completely.

One morning my office phone rang. It was Bill Spears, calling to request a pastoral favor. One of his business associates, Chris Grisanti, and his wife, Suzanne Fawbush, had just given birth to their first child, a daughter. Chris had been raised in a Roman Catholic family in Mamaroneck, New York. His maternal uncle, the Rev.

Paul M. Couming, who before his death had been a diocesan priest, had officiated at their wedding. Suzanne had been raised in a Southern Baptist family in her home state of Kentucky.

In his telephone call, Bill Spears asked if I would be willing to meet with both Chris and Suzanne and to talk with them about the issues surrounding the pending baptism of their daughter, Alexandra Noël Grisanti. This was the beginning of what would become a close relationship not only with Chris and Suzanne but with their four daughters, each of whom I baptized—Noël, Antonia (Tonie), Eliza, and Victoria (Tory).

The first of these baptisms occurred in their first, smaller New York City apartment on East 68th Street. Chris prepared for what he wanted to be a full-immersion christening of Noël. In their living room he had set up a large plastic garbage can, which he had carefully draped with white tablecloths to camouflage its exterior surface and lined the can with a large black garbage bag. He filled the container with hot water, fully expecting it to cool down sufficiently before the actual ceremony began. Fortunately, before beginning the baptismal rites, I put my hand into the water, only to realize that the barrel, which was well insulated, had maintained a temperature much too hot for a neonate's delicate skin. We quickly added some cold water to prevent poor Noël from receiving a first-degree burn at her christening. At the moment of her actual christening, in his enthusiasm, Chris presented his first-born daughter, holding her up before all the assembled guests completely nude, before plunging her into his homemade baptismal font. He was as proud as he could be of his triumph, both as a father and as a liturgical empresario.

This is not a picture that Noël, now a graduate of Amherst College with a degree in classics and head of the classics department at the Ethel Walker School in Simsbury, Connecticut, would like widely disseminated. But it is emblematic of both Chris's passion and ingenuity. The girls would often cringe when their father would squirrel himself away to compose the Grisanti annual holiday letter to be sent to family and friends, in which he would profile highlights from the girls' feats and foibles of the past year. Chris is a brilliant writer, with both wit and words that can turn the most ordinary of events into a memorable story—perhaps for the readers, but not always so for his daughters. In reading these missives, I would occasionally comment to Chris that it was miraculous that one of his girls had not committed patricide. Sheepishly, he would ask: "Do you think I went too far?"

Early on, the two youngest girls developed a passion for baking, which both

Suzanne and Chris encouraged. Eliza and Tory became quite good at their hobby. They continuously expanded their repertory of confections and they also increased the degree of difficulty of the recipes and techniques with which they were experimenting. On one particular occasion I introduced them to the recipe for roulade Léontine (see recipe in chapter 4). On a Saturday afternoon I taught them how to make this rolled, filled, flourless chocolate cake. It was a completely hands-on engagement, with me guiding and encouraging them as they separated eggs, melted and tempered chocolate, whipped egg whites, and created various fillings for this melt-in-your mouth showstopper. This cake has become a Grisanti staple, often showing up for special event and holiday family dinners, including their father's annual birthday celebration.

Suzanne once recounted a heartwarming story. As the girls grew older, she and Chris tried each year to take a special vacation alone. One year, as they were remotely preparing for one of these adventures—a tandem bike tour in Europe—they convened a family meeting in which they explored with the girls who they might like to look after them during their parents' absence. Suzanne went through a short list of prospective chaperones, to which she received consistent pushback, for a variety of reasons. The only two candidates who received unequivocal thumbs-up was Chris's former executive assistant and me. Suzanne said: "Isn't it remarkable that four teenaged and preteen girls would choose a Jesuit priest to be their live-in nanny." I must say, this vote of confidence did warm my heart.

As the Grisanti girls were growing up I was a frequent guest in their kitchen and at their family table. And I got to know their extended families. Suzanne's mother would occasionally make the journey from her home in Kentucky, especially at holiday time. Evelyn was a wonderful, frugal country cook, taking pride in her version of fried chicken. I was amused when Suzanne told me that her mother arrived two weeks before Christmas one year with a large suitcase filled with well-packed frozen chicken. Perplexed by this discovery, Suzanne asked her mother: "Did you not think that we can purchase good chicken parts in New York City?" Quickly her mother retorted, "I know you have chicken, but the prices they charge in New York City are outrageous." Case settled.

Evelyn was charmed that Chris and Suzanne's priest friend was an accomplished cook and she was happy to see that Suzanne's interest in cooking had been engaged. The fact that Suzanne had to feed a family of six was the real motive behind her reengagement with the culinary arts. Besides, Chris was a pretty accomplished chef in his own right. Very soon the Grisanti kitchen became a social gathering place to test new recipes and to create some rather phenomenal dinner parties for family and friends.

For many years Chris and Suzanne hosted a large preholiday party, which could attract as many as fifty guests. They always asked guests to consider bringing gifts of diapers, baby formula, baby food, blankets, and clothes to support the charitable nonprofit work of another mutual friend, Chris Bell, the founder of Good Counsel Homes. Since 1985, Chris and his supporters have helped about 10,000 homeless women and children move from a crisis situation and receive concrete help to build a brighter future.

Chris and I often shared the Steinway piano in their living room for a community Christmas carol sing-along. Noël, properly named for her emerging leadership role, would often coordinate and direct the ever-increasing number of children attending these holiday gatherings, for the annual rendition of the "Twelve Days of Christmas." I was always amazed at how skilled she was in keeping the kids on track, and how the chorus would always swell when they bellowed, "Five golden rings!"

Suzanne was interested in expanding her culinary skills, and we frequently found ourselves working together on family celebrations in their East End Avenue kitchen. She has been an incredible mother to her four daughters and a remarkable role model. I occasionally confessed to Chris that he was not the only man in love with Suzanne. Over the course of a quarter-century, I grew in my own admiration and love for her as well.

The origin of the recipe for crêpes Suzette and how this recipe got its name remains disputed. Even though the bible of classic French technique and cuisine, *Larousse Gastronomique*, discounts this explanation, I find it not only plausible but charming.[13] Lore situates the context for this classic dessert in 1895 at Monte Carlo's Café de Paris. The guest is the Prince of Wales, the future King of England, Edward VII. A young fourteen-year-old assistant waiter, Henri Carpentier, accidentally ignited the cordials in a chafing dish containing the crêpes for the prince and his dinner guests. The young table steward thought he had ruined the presentation, but he quickly tasted the sauce as the flames subsided. He thought the end effect was wonderful and proceeded to serve the crêpes *flambées* to these important guests. The Prince of

13 Prosper Montagné, *Larousse Gastronomique* (Paris: Libraire Larousse, 1938).

Wales apparently devoured the crêpes with a fork, only to switch to a spoon so as not to sacrifice a drop of the sweet syrup. The prescient young waiter told the prince that the dessert was called Crêpes Princesse. Recognizing that the word "crêpe" controlled the gender of the complement, "princesse," and that this was an honor meant for him, the prince made a further suggestion. Among his dining companions was a woman named Suzette. "Will you," the Prince of Wales queried, "consider changing the name from 'Crêpes Princesse' to 'Crêpes Suzette'?" Whether this story is fact or fancy, I love it and think it a suitable tribute to Suzanne Fawbush Grisanti, who has brought warmth, brightness, and richness to my life.

CRÊPES SUZETTE

Crêpes with an orange butter filling

Makes 4 servings

Ingredients

For the crêpes

- 3 eggs
- 1 cup all-purpose flour
- 1 cup whole milk
- ¼ teaspoon salt
- 1 teaspoon sugar
- ¼ cup cold water
- 1 tablespoon vegetable oil
- unsalted butter

For the crêpe butter filling

- 8 tablespoons unsalted softened butter
- ½ cup superfine sugar
- zest of 1 large, firm navel orange

- ½ cup freshly squeezed orange juice
- 3 tablespoons Grand Marnier or Cointreau
- 2 tablespoons Cognac

Method

To make the crêpes

1. In a food processor (steel blade) or blender, combine the eggs, flour, milk, salt, and sugar and process until smooth. With the motor running, pour in the oil and melted butter in a steady stream and incorporate. Pour the batter into a large measuring cup or bowl and allow to rest.
2. Heat a crêpe pan or nonstick skillet and lubricate with a little butter.
3. Add a few tablespoons of batter to the hot skillet and quickly tilt the pan to evenly spread the batter over the entire bottom surface.
4. Cook the crêpe until you notice slight browning on the edges. This will often take less than a minute to occur. With a spatula, loosen the edges of the crêpe and flip it over and cook for another 30 seconds.
5. Slide the finished crêpe out of the pan onto a trap and continue the process, making additional crêpes until the batter is used completely.

To make the butter filling

1. In a nonreactive mixing bowl and using a wire whisk, blend the softened butter with the sugar and whisk vigorously until the sugar is fully incorporated. Then add in all the orange zest and orange juice and blend completely. Set aside.

To assemble and finish the crêpes Suzettes for service

1. Place an oven rack in the top middle and preheat the broiler unit.
2. Using the largest ovenproof skillet that you have (or two, if needed), sprinkle the bottom of the skillet(s) lightly with some granulated sugar.

continued

3. Place about a rounded tablespoon of the butter filling in the center of each crêpe and fold in half and then into quarters and place in the skillet, allowing the crêpes to overlap each other slightly.
4. When all the crêpes have been assembled in the skillet, sprinkle the entire mass with some sugar.
5. Place the skillet in the oven and allow the sugar to caramelize. This will take a minute or two. Watch the pan and do not let the crêpes burn.
6. Transfer the crêpes to a service platter or to individual serving plates.
7. In a small saucepan, heat the Grand Marnier or Cointreau and Cognac. Ignite the alcohol and carefully pour the flaming mixture over the crêpes.

At Noël's baptism I met for the first time Chris's father, Eugene (Gene) Grisanti. Gene quickly became a friend and a great help to me in my work at the Chaplaincy. Gene was the child of a father who had emigrated from Sicily. Born in Buffalo, New York, Gene became first acquainted with the Jesuits when he attended Canisius High School. Those bonds were strengthened when he later attended the College of the Holy Cross in Worcester. Later, he would attend Boston University and Harvard Law School. Gene began his career at the law firm Fulton, Rowe & Hart, which had been formed in 1946.

Gene was also a passionate patron of the arts in New York City. During the time he served as chairman and CEO of International Flavors and Fragrances, Gene was also chairman of the board of the New York City Ballet and vice chairman of the New York Botanical Garden. For many years, he served on the boards of the Lincoln Center for the Performing Arts and the Metropolitan Opera.

One morning, Gene called me at the office and said, "I think I can help you with a renewable annual gift from a foundation on whose board I serve. Can you put together overnight a quick proposal for support?" I had a proposal messengered to him before the close of business that very day. For the next dozen years or more, we received a sizable contribution from the Ambrose Monell Foundation.

When Gene died on March 29, 2017, from a long and valiant battle with multiple myeloma, Chris asked me if I would help celebrate Gene's life with the family by speaking at a memorial service at the University Club in Manhattan. I was honored to do this.

In Gene's memory, I offer my version of a classic Tuscan recipe. Bologna has its classic ragù; so too does Firenze. In my version I like to use orecchiette ("little ears"), a pasta typical of Apulia, a region of southern Italy—a favorite destination discovery of both Chris and Suzanne during one of their little vacations. The name of this pasta comes from its shape, which resembles a small ear, capable of capturing this flavorful and rich meat Tuscan sauce.

ORECCHIETTE STRASCICATE ALLA FIORENTINA

Ear-shaped pasta with a Tuscan meat sauce

Makes 8 servings

Ingredients

- 3 stalks celery
- 2 medium carrots
- 1 red onion
- 2 ounces pancetta
- ½ cup extra-virgin olive oil
- ½ pound ground beef
- ½ pound ground pork
- ½ pound ground veal
- 1 cup dry red Tuscan wine (any sangiovese grape wine, like Rosso di Montepulciano)
- 28-ounce can San Marzano peeled tomatoes
- salt and pepper
- ¼ pound (1 stick) unsalted butter
- 1 pound orecchiette pasta
- ¼ pound freshly grated Parmigiano Reggiano

continued

Method

To make the battuta

1. Finely chop the celery, carrots, onion, and pancetta.
2. Sauté the vegetables and pancetta in olive oil in a large skillet over medium heat until golden.

To make the Tuscan meat sauce

1. Add the ground beef, pork, and veal to the battuta and continue to sauté until the meat loses its pink color. Add the red wine and cook until it evaporates.
2. Purée the peeled canned tomatoes in a food processor and add them to the meat mixture. Season the meat mixture with salt and pepper and continue to simmer slowly over a medium heat until the sauce has thickened, for an hour or more.
3. Fill large pot with water and bring to a rolling boil. When boiling add salt and cook the orecchiette, stirring occasionally, until al dente, according to packaging directions.
4. Drain the pasta and add it to the sauce. Add the butter and cook until melted and the pasta is coated, for 1 or 2 additional minutes.
5. Finish the served dish liberally with grated Parmigiano-Reggiano.

As I turn my attention now to Ken and Jincie Duane, I am powerfully reminded that a casual relationship can morph into a lifelong bond, one that offers enhanced meaning to the spiritual web of a human life. I first encountered Ken Duane during the early years of his career when he was helping designer David Chu develop the brand Nautica. Very quickly we found our common threads: we were Bostonians, Roman Catholics of Irish descent, and Boston Red Sox fans. Ken had graduated from the Augustinians' Merrimac College in North Andover, Massachusetts, where he studied finance and marketing. He married Jincie, a woman from sunny California, who for their entire marriage has been Ken's anchor and North Star. They have raised a family of two sons and two daughters, all scholars and athletes.

Almost as soon as I was beginning to establish our friendship, Ken was facing an important career decision for which he invited my insight and counsel. Guess, Inc. was looking to recruit him away from Nautica International, which at that time was one of the fastest growing sportswear apparel firms in the country. Guess wanted Ken to lead their worldwide sales and marketing efforts. Ken had been an invaluable partner for six years with David Chu in building the Nautica brand, and before that Ken had been senior vice president of sales and marketing at Hugo Boss. This was a significant career decision for him. We talked about it over the phone and later at lunch. It seemed clear that Guess was considering moving from a privately held company to a public one, and strengthening its executive team would make it more attractive to prospective investors.

As I listened to Ken talk about the pros and cons of this career move, he was fascinated that I seemed to know more about the industry than he expected a priest to know. I told him that I did not possess any particular insider information, but that I did regularly read the business section of the *New York Times*. He laughed in his characteristically energetic way. The Marciano brothers did woo Ken to join the Guess team, and in 1996 the company began trading publicly on the New York Stock Exchange. The whole apparel industry was experiencing a market slump. Nonetheless, many clothing firms like Guess were trying to cash in on Wall Street at that time, including Donna Karan, Calvin Klein, and Mossimo, which all had successful IPOs around that time.

Ken and I continued to stay connected, and he agreed to lend his time and treasure to helping me as a trustee at HealthCare Chaplaincy. I ended up going to more runway shows and Fashion Week social events than I could have imagined. For several years I attended the YMA Fashion Scholarship gala, which raises funds to support scholarships for promising fashion, arts, and business students. Dressed in a clerical black suit, I felt I was always a curiosity in these fashionista gatherings. But my network of acquaintances in the world of fashion and lifestyle brand design, manufacture, and sales industries began to expand exponentially as I encountered folks like Geoffrey Beene, Tommy Hilfiger, Reem Acra, Vera Wang, Carolina Herrera, and Oscar de la Renta.

My friend Sylvia Weinstock helped expand this web of relationships by introducing me to Connie Uzzo, the American market director for Yves Saint Laurent and his longtime business partner, Pierre Bergé. The list of contacts continued to build through the years: Donna Karan, Ralph Lauren, Michael Kors, Marc Jacobs, and Joseph Abboud. Through these connections I became friendly with the grandson of the original owner of Barney's New York, Gene Pressman, who later joined the Chaplaincy's board of trustees.

From Guess, Inc., Ken Duane was recruited in 1998 to Phillips-Van Heusen (PVH), where he became the division president of Izod Wholesale before being appointed CEO of Wholesale Sportswear and North America Wholesale. Once established in his new position at PVH, Ken introduced me to another Jesuit alumnus, Manny Chirico. At the time, Manny was the company's CFO.

Manny was an Italian American kid from the Bronx. He grew up an active parishioner in Saint Anthony's parish, where he met his future wife, Joanne. He graduated in 1979 from Fordham University's Gabelli School of Business. Manny then began his career in accounting at Ernst & Young, got married, and with Joanne raised three sons—all educated in the Jesuit tradition, one at Fairfield University and two at Fordham University. In 1993, PVH recruited Manny and in a series of progressive promotions within the company, he was named CEO in 2006 and in the following year, he was elevated to chairman.

It was clear from the beginning of my friendship with both Manny and Joanne just how firmly grounded they both are in their Catholic faith. As Manny began the transformation of PVH, you could identify his values in virtually everything he did. Early on, he expressed the company's values in terms of accountability, partnership, passion, integrity, and individuality. Under his watch, brands like Calvin Klein, Izod, and Tommy Hilfiger joined their established labels Van Heusen, Arrow, and Warner's.

With all of these responsibilities, Manny accepted an invitation to become a Chaplaincy trustee and to chair the finance committee. Remarkably, he found a way to attend board meetings and even subcommittee meetings. He helped to build the brand of the Chaplaincy just as he was making PVH an industry leader. Philanthropically he was invested, personally and corporately.

Manny and Joanne were intrigued that I had not only an interest in *la cucina italiana* but was also able to create the finished product. They joined me on several occasions for dinner in my apartment to sample some familiar and novel dishes from the repertory of Italian cookery.

On one occasion I prepared a dish that was a bit unusual in Italian American home cooking. Stuffed meats are a common feature of the *cucina* of Emilia-Romagna. In this preparation an entire *cotechino* (a large sausage of ground pork and spices) is sliced and incorporated into a large butterflied breast of turkey along with chopped spinach, Parmigiano Reggiano cheese, and spices, and sauced with a reduction of pan juices. Both Manny and Joanne loved this dish, with Manny even pronouncing it to be "healthy."

ROLLATINO DI TACCHINO ALLA BOLOGNESE

Butterflied and rolled turkey breast with pancetta, sausage, and spinach filling

Makes 4 servings

Ingredients

- 1 turkey breast
- 2 eggs
- 1 cup grated Parmigiano Reggiano cheese
- 1 pound fresh baby spinach leaves
- 1 cotechino
- 4 ounces diced pancetta
- 2 cups dry white wine
- olive oil and unsalted butter
- fresh rosemary
- salt and freshly ground black pepper
- nutmeg

Method

1. Preheat oven to 350°F.

To butterfly a boneless, skinless turkey breast

1. Lay the turkey breast flat on a cutting board. Holding the blade of a slicing knife parallel to the board, make a horizontal cut about halfway through the thickness of the meat.

continued

2. Continue cutting with your blade parallel to the work surface, creating two equally thick layers of turkey. Make sure not to cut all the way through the meat, stopping when there is still about an inch or two of meat remaining uncut.
3. You should now be able to open the turkey to lay flat, like an open book, to make a uniformly thick, large piece of meat.
4. Using a meat mallet, pound out any of the thicker parts so that the entire turkey breast is roughly the same thickness.

To make the omelette

1. Beat the eggs in bowl with Parmigiano Reggiano cheese; season with salt and pepper and cook the omelette in a skillet that has been greased with a bit of butter and olive oil. When cooked on the bottom side, carefully turn the omelette over and quickly cook the top side. Remove and cool on a plate.

To prepare the filling

1. With a sharp knife, slice the cotechino on the bias into thin pieces. In same skillet in which you made the omelette, quickly brown the cotechino slices on both sides. Remove the sausage pieces and place them on a paper-toweled plate to degrease and cool.
2. In the rendered fat from the cooked sausage, quickly add the spinach and cook until just wilted; remove and season with salt, pepper, and nutmeg. Set aside.
3. Cut the pancetta into smaller cubed pieces and cook for a few minutes with some chopped rosemary.
4. Season the underside of the flat butterflied turkey breast with salt and pepper. Lay the thin omelette on the breast, trimming and patching as needed. On top of the omelette, spread the wilted spinach across the surface. Add the cotechino slices. Distribute the pancetta and rosemary mixture.

5. Starting at one end, begin rolling the turkey breast tightly and firmly (but not so tight that the filling gets squeezed out).
6. You have a choice in how to roll the turkey breast. If you wish to make a long, thin rollatino, start your roll with one of the wide sides. This will give you a number of smaller rolled pieces when you cut the rollatino for service. If you prefer a thicker, shorter rollatino, begin rolling on one of the narrow sides.
7. Continue rolling until the entire breast is rolled up, then place it on your board with the seam side down.
8. Prepare several pieces of unwaxed kitchen twine and line them in a row on your work surface, about 1 inch apart, parallel to the edge of the countertop.
9. Place the rolled turkey on top of the twine, seam-side down, and tie each of the strings in a double knot.

To brown and roast the rollatino

1. Preheat oven to 350°F
2. Brown the rolled turkey breast on all sides, then pour in about 1½ cups of wine and reduce a bit.
3. Transfer the turkey breast to the preheated 350°F. oven and roast for 45 minutes. Allow the rollatino to rest, covered with aluminum foil, for at least 10 minutes, before slicing for service.
4. Deglaze roasting pan with a bit more wine or chicken stock and serve the slices of the rolled turkey breast with the pan drippings.

The founder of the Jesuits, Ignatius of Loyola, often ended his letters to Jesuits who were leaving for missions around the world with the words "*ite, inflammate omnia*"—"go, set the world on fire." Some folks might think that this expression is like a high school football coach's parting words to his players as they take the field for Saturday afternoon's game. But for Ignatius, these words meant so much more.

Manny recalls having heard these words for the first time from a theology teacher at Fordham University during his senior year. These words seared into his soul; he was still talking about their significance years later when he was running a major corporation. He understood them to mean that you have to find your special calling—in marriage and family; in parish and community; in society and business. Then, you have to make a difference.

"Set the world on fire" is a curious expression. We have watched wildfires consume millions of acres of woodlands and homes in a place like California. We have seen the world on the brink of destruction from the fires of hatred, resentment, racial injustice, greed, lust, and other passions that are consuming individuals and whole societies. Fire also purifies. We recall in the New Testament how tongues of fire at Pentecost brought the regenerating power of the Holy Spirit to a group of followers of Jesus who were paralyzed and immobilized by their fears, cowering and sealed off in a locked room. This Gospel image may have been in Ignatius's mind when he told his Jesuit companions to break loose from the things that are holding them back and to go, set the world on fire. He wanted everyone to be set afire with passion and zeal for the roles that God might be asking them to play in the worlds to which he was sending them. Manny heard this insistent message. Whatever he may have learned in Fordham's classrooms about social justice and responsibility, he certainly carried those lessons forward into his business life and decision-making. It also influenced the way he has lived his personal life.

I was edified one day when Manny called and asked if I might be interested and available to lead an Advent day of prayer for the members of his local Westchester parish. In that conversation I learned that Manny was a member of the parish's liturgical committee and was the organizer of this Saturday event, which involved two talks, some time for personal prayer, and the celebration of the Eucharist with a concluding homily. I accepted his invitation and when I mingled among the parishioners at the luncheon, following the Advent morning of prayer, I really came to appreciate just how involved both Joanne and Manny were in their parish.

Manny has always been a thoughtful business leader who saw his calling far beyond driving profitability, and we have had many far-reaching conversations about business development. In every conversation it was clear Manny was not simply focused on PVH's shareholders. He was acutely sensitive that a decision that might improve shareholders' financial positions might also have disastrous impact on workers and their families in Vietnam who would lose their jobs when a production factory was forced to close. He was always looking for ways to balance the long-term health of PVH and its shareholders with not neglecting attention to the personal well-being of employees. I always left a conversation with Manny edified by his values and commitment.

I would get to see this firsthand in a few of PVH's garment and footwear manufacturing facilities in Vietnam. I casually told Manny that on an upcoming trip to Asia I would have a stopover in Ho Chi Minh City—formerly Saigon, and currently Vietnam's largest city. That communication got his wheels turning. Manny had recently implemented across the company a range of policies governing how their suppliers and producers must provide clean, safe, well-lit work environments as well as offer support services for their employees. Manny thought that I could help by paying some impromptu visits to these factories, observing casually and making informal assessments of conditions and employee morale and well-being.

He told me he would make the local arrangements. When I arrived in the bustling, densely populated Vietnamese capital, one of Manny's local executives was at the airport. With a car and driver, we were able to navigate our way through crowded streets where motorbikes seemed to outnumber pedestrians. Ho Chi Minh City has a population of close to 9 million within the city proper, and more than 21 million living in within the metropolitan region.

My Vietnamese hosts appeared to have no understanding that I was a priest, not a PVH executive. All they knew what that the company's CEO had personally requested that I be treated well and shown some of the production facilities in and around Ho Chi Minh City.

Those were remarkable days for my first visit to Vietnam. No tour company could have provided what the PVH local managers organized. They asked about my interests. They were limited to three: the wartime history of the city, the church in Vietnam, and Vietnamese cuisine.

My hosts provided me with a memorable tour of the War Remnants Museum, where vestiges of the atrocities and tragedies of the Vietnam War were on display. It was an emotional experience. Much of my early formation as a Jesuit had taken place during the height of the Vietnamese conflict. Having a young, perfectly fluent English-speaking Vietnamese guide walking me through the evocative and emotional displays was an eye-opening experience. I distinctly remember seeing a display of weaponry and machinery and a model of the cages used to hold Viet Cong prisoners. Everywhere I turned, I saw relics of the ravages of war and of the devastation caused by US troops. What surprised me the most was how warm, welcoming, and forgiving the Vietnamese people were to an American visitor. I fully expected to encounter pushback, resentment, or even hostility. But it was just the opposite: my Vietnamese hosts were engaging, understanding, and accepting. I came away with a much better sense of what Vietnam and its people had endured during the war and how they managed to survive and thrive.

My hotel was located in the heart of the French colonial-era city that dates back to mid-nineteenth century. Under French rule the city took on character of a European capital, and French architecture, art, and cuisine became fused with the local Vietnamese culture and traditions.

My hotel was just a block away from Paris Square and Notre Dame Cathedral. Soon after the French occupied Vietnam in the early 1860s, they began construction of the neo-Romanesque Cathedral Basilica of Our Lady of the Immaculate Conception. The cathedral was completed in 1880 and has two dramatic bell towers, reminiscent of its older sister in Paris. It is still an active place of Catholic worship in a country that remains predominantly Buddhist.

The most amazing dimension of my brief days in Ho Chi Minh City was my immersion experience in Vietnamese cooking. It seemed my PVH hosts were continuously exposing me to yet another aspect of Vietnamese cuisine. They introduced me to an older proprietor of a Vietnamese restaurant, an older woman who spoke mellifluous French and displayed the mien of a French grande dame.

I remember my first bites of crispy, savory Vietnamese crêpes called *bánh xèo* ("ban-say-oh"). I sampled these delicious morsels as I soaked in soothing views of the Saigon River while chatting with my ever-gracious and solicitous Vietnamese hosts. Here is my re-creation of this classic Vietnamese street food.

BÁNH XÈO

Vietnamese sizzling crispy crêpe

Makes 6 servings

Ingredients

For the batter

- 9 ounces rice flour
- 3 ounces all-purpose wheat flour
- 2 teaspoons turmeric powder
- 1 teaspoon kosher salt
- 3½ cups water
- 1 can coconut milk (14 ounces)
- 1 lightly beaten egg
- 3 to 5 thinly sliced scallions

For the filling

- 1 pound pork belly
- 1 pound whole peeled and deveined shrimp
- 2 teaspoons kosher salt
- 1 teaspoon pork, chicken, or mushroom stock powder
- 1 tablespoon vegetable oil
- 3 minced garlic cloves
- 1 minced shallot

Vegetables to serve alongside the crêpes (your choice)

- mustard greens
- mint
- cilantro
- Vietnamese perilla
- sorrel
- lettuce
- bean sprouts

Other ingredients

- Vietnamese fish sauce dipping sauce
- Vietnamese pickled daikon radish and carrot

continued

Method

To prepare the crêpe batter and filling

1. In a large mixing bowl, whisk together the rice and whole wheat flour, turmeric powder, kosher salt, coconut milk, water, and egg until well combined and set aside to rest for at least one hour, or better, overnight. The longer the batter rests, the crispier will be the crêpes. Just before using, add in the green onions.
2. Boil the piece of pork belly until it is tender, and then cut into thin slices.
3. Wash and pat dry the peeled and deveined shrimp.
4. In a large skillet (preferably nonstick), heat vegetable oil on medium high.
5. Add minced garlic and shallot and sauté until fragrant. Add pork belly and cook for about 2 to 3 more minutes. Add shrimp into same skillet with the pork and lightly sauté until just pink (1 to 2 minutes).
6. Remove pork and shrimp from skillet and set aside.

To make the crêpes

1. Coat a large nonstick skillet with a thin layer of vegetable oil.
2. Immediately add some onions, a few pieces of pork, and shrimp. Sauté, lightly mixing until very lightly browned.
3. Pour in about ¾ cup of batter and quickly tilt and rotate the pan so that the batter is evenly spread over bottom and sides of the skillet. Add more batter if it is not enough to cover the filling and the pan.
4. Add some bean sprouts and cover the skillet for 2 to 3 minutes, or until bean sprouts are slightly cooked. The batter should also be slightly cooked and transparent around the edges.
5. Loosen the edges of the crêpe with a metal or silicone spatula. Drizzle a little more oil around the edges of the crêpe to promote browning.

Cook for another couple of minutes. Begin to loosen the edges of the crêpe.

6. Remove the lid, lower heat to medium, and wait for the crêpe to become crisp. With a spatula, carefully fold the crêpe in half, transfer to a plate, and serve immediately.
7. Repeat with remaining batter and ingredients.
8. Serve crêpes with fresh vegetables and herbs, pickled daikon and carrots, and a small bowl of Vietnamese fish sauce dipping sauce.
9. The crêpe is meant to be eaten with one's hands, by breaking off a portion of the folded pancake, wrapping it in a lettuce leaf, adding in some herbs, and dipping the crunchy little bundle into a fish sauce before consuming.

In Manny and Joanne Chirico I found examples of two people not only in love with each other and their boys, daughters-in-law, and grandchildren, but two people who realized they were connected to everyone and everything else in the world. They knew that they were parts of the whole and obligated to love and care for what the Lord had entrusted to them. Everything is interrelated—in time, space, and our very being. "Go, set the world on fire." Manny and Joanne have done it, trusting that the spirit of the living God would sustain them as they patch and reweave the web again and again.

One definition of spirituality is "the art of making connections." If my life has taught me anything, it is this: everything is related to everything else. In a casual conversation one afternoon with TV personality and bon vivant Regis Francis Xavier Philbin, I asked him if he might have a recommendation of someone we could possibly engage as an honoree for our annual major fundraising gala. Regis suggested that Al DeCrane would be an excellent choice. At that time, Al was the chairman and CEO of Texaco. When I asked Regis if he might make the introduction, he said: "Absolutely. Al and I were classmates at Notre Dame, Class of 1953. He's a good Catholic."

Not long after speaking with Regis I received a call from Al's executive assistant, confirming an appointment for me to meet the chairman and CEO in Texaco's

New York corporate offices. I made the 22-mile trek northeast to Harrison from Manhattan, rehearsing in my mind as I was driving just how I might approach this initial interview with Al DeCrane.

As I entered Al's spacious executive offices, he greeted me with a very warm handshake and a broad grin. "I'm going to make this so much easier for you, Father," he said. "I know from experience how calculating Jesuits can be, so to save you the effort, I will be your honoree, and Texaco will help ensure that your dinner is a success." He then invited me to sit down, and we spent an enjoyable half hour or more beginning what has been an enduring friendship.

After graduating from Notre Dame and having served a year as a first lieutenant in the United States Marine Corp Reserve, Al became familiar with the Society of Jesus. He attended the Georgetown University Law Center and received his law degree in 1959, and was admitted to the bar in the Commonwealth of Virginia.

One of the great added benefits in meeting Al DeCrane was coming to know his wife, Joan Hoffman DeCrane. Joan—mother to their six children—met Al during their undergraduate years in South Bend. Joan graduated in the same class of 1953, but from Saint Mary's College, a private Catholic women's liberal arts college founded by the Sisters of the Holy Cross. The St. Mary's campus is located across the street from Notre Dame. A natural extrovert, Joan showed an affinity for the mission of HealthCare Chaplaincy and was thrilled to accept an invitation to become a trustee. She quickly found her way onto our advancement committee and for several years she helped us meet many future friends and donors.

A trustee can soon become a beneficiary of the Chaplaincy's pastoral care. In 2008, Al and Joan's daughter, Stacie Elizabeth DeCrane Shaddock, age forty-nine, died in her Nebraska home surrounded by her husband and three children. This was a terrible shock to the entire DeCrane family. They were gratified for the support that they received, including from their new HealthCare Chaplaincy family.

It did not take Joan and Al long to learn of my interests in classical music and opera. In 1940, Texaco began its sponsorship of radio broadcasts of productions from the Metropolitan Opera House in New York. The company's sponsorship continued for sixty-three years. It ended in 2004 when Texaco merged with Chevron. One of the perks of the CEO of Texaco was the use of a private eight-seat parterre box in Lincoln Center's Metropolitan Opera house. On many occasions, Joan and Al invited me to be among their guests at memorable Metropolitan Opera productions. Their invitation to Saturday matinées often included a precurtain lunch in the Grand Tier Restaurant, followed by a first intermission dessert service, as well as special seating at the live broadcast of the "Opera Quiz" that took place during the 20-minute intermission. The format for the quiz was always the same: the host asks a panel of three experts a series of questions about opera submitted by listeners. Al kindly introduced me to Edward Downes, the son of one of the earlier quiz hosts, Olin Downes. Al also introduced me to Peter Allen, who for almost three decades was the voice of the Metropolitan Opera. Anyone who was a regular listener of radio broadcasts from the Metropolitan Opera would recognize in an instant Peter's unmistakable voice. When I met him for the first time in person, it seemed like we had known each other forever. Unknown to Peter, I had been listening to him for decades.

I told Al that his frequent invitations to join him and Joan at Texaco-Metropolitan Opera events at the Met had ruined me for life: sumptuous dining; never-ending introductions to other movers and shakers of New York business, arts, and society; the backstage meet-and-greet encounters with some of the leading opera performers of the late twentieth century, including Luciano Pavarotti, Leontyne Price, Plácido Domingo, Susan Graham, Bryn Terfel, Deborah Voigt, Renée Fleming, and Cecilia Bartoli. How could I ever again be content with a standing room ticket at the Met?

I did not first taste the rich French dessert called gâteau opéra in Paris, but in the Grand Tier Restaurant with the DeCranes. Opera cake consists of layers of biscuit *joconde* (thin layers of almond sponge cake, soaked with a coffee flavored simple syrup), filled with *crème au beurre au café* (coffee buttercream), decadent chocolate ganache, and topped with a smooth chocolate glaze. For an elegant finish, the cake's name (opéra) is inscribed on top of each slice and decorated with a touch of gold leaf.

This cake is not something one can quickly put together; it is a bit time consuming, though each step is relatively easy to accomplish. But the result is heavenly.

GÂTEAU OPÉRA

Almond sponge cake with coffee buttercream and chocolate ganache

Makes 6 to 8 servings

continued

Ingredients

For the biscuit joconde (almond sponge cake)

- 5 whole eggs and 5 additional egg whites
- ¾ cup ground almonds or almond flour
- ¾ cup powdered sugar
- ½ cup all-purpose flour
- 2 tablespoons melted unsalted butter
- 2 tablespoons granulated sugar
- ¼ teaspoon kosher salt

For le sirop café (coffee simple syrup)

- ⅔ cup water
- ½ cup granulated sugar
- 3 teaspoons espresso or instant coffee powder

For the chocolate croustillant

- 3 ounces semisweet chocolate
- 3 ounces pailletté feuilletine (you can use crushed sugar ice cream cones or corn flakes as a substitute)

For the chocolate ganache

- 6 ounces semisweet chocolate
- ⅔ cup heavy cream

For the crème au beurre au café (coffee buttercream)

- 5 egg yolks, room temperature
- ¾ cup granulated sugar
- 3 tablespoons water
- 2 teaspoons instant coffee powder
- 1¼ cup softened unsalted butter

For the glaçage au chocolat (chocolate glaze)

- 7 ounces semisweet chocolate
- 2 tablespoons vegetable or canola oil

Method

To make the biscuit joconde (almond sponge cake)

1. Preheat oven to 400°F.
2. With a vegetable spray, grease a baking pan. Then line the pan with parchment paper, allowing the parchment to overhang by an inch or so at each end of the pan. Lightly spray the parchment paper. This will help in removing the baked sponge cake biscuit from the pan.
3. In a stand mixer fitted with the whisk attachment, whip the egg whites and salt until foamy. Gradually add sugar and continue mixing until stiff peaks form. Transfer the stiff egg whites to another bowl.
4. Clean the mixing bowl and dry. Fit the mixer with the paddle attachment. Add the sifted almond flour and powdered sugar into the bowl. Add 5 whole eggs and beat until the mixture is creamy and fluffy.
5. Remove mixing bowl from the stand and with a spatula, fold the whipped whites into the almond flour mixture and add the cooled, melted butter.
6. Distribute and smooth the batter evenly within the prepared pan.
7. Bake for about 8 minutes until slightly golden. Do not overbake. Cool the sponge completely.
8. When completely cooled, remove the cake from the pan onto a work surface. Peel back the parchment paper and trim the edges of the cake, as needed. Cut the sponge cake into three equal pieces that will measure approximately 6x12 inches. Wrap the cooled sponge sections in plastic wrap to prevent drying out.

continued

To make the coffee syrup

1. Place the water, sugar, and coffee into a small saucepan. Stir to combine and bring to boil over medium heat. Set aside to cool completely.

To prepare the chocolate croustillant

1. Melt the chocolate over a simmering bain-marie (double boiler).
2. Add the pailleté feuilletine (or crushed sugar cone or corn flakes) to the melted chocolate and stir to combine.
3. Spread the croustillant on top of one of the sponge cake pieces. Refrigerate to set.

To prepare the chocolate ganache

1. Place the chocolate into a bowl. Heat cream in a small saucepan until it just comes to simmer. Pour the hot cream over the chocolate. Let sit for a minute. Stir until completely melted. Set aside to cool, at room temperature.

To prepare the coffee buttercream

1. Mix egg yolks in a heatproof bowl until they are creamy and become a light yellow color.
2. In a small saucepan, combine sugar with water and instant coffee and place on medium heat. Using a candy thermometer, measure the syrup's temperature. When it reaches 240°F pour it gradually over the creamy egg yolks, while mixing continuously. Continue mixing until the mixture is cooled.
3. Gradually add softened butter. Mix on low until the butter is incorporated and then mix on high speed until smooth and fluffy.

To assemble the opera cake

1. Take the croustillant-coated sponge cake layer from the refrigerator, flip on a serving plate with chocolate croustillant facing down and brush the sponge layer facing you with coffee syrup.

2. Spread half of coffee buttercream. Add another layer of sponge cake and soak well with coffee syrup.
3. Spread the cooled chocolate ganache.
4. Add the last layer of sponge cake and brush well with coffee syrup.
5. Spread the other half of the buttercream on top and even the surface using an offset spatula or cake scraper.
6. Cover and refrigerate the cake for at least 2 hours or even overnight.

To prepare the final chocolate glaze

1. Before preparing the glaze, place the chilled cake over a rack placed on a baking sheet lined with parchment paper. Melt the chocolate over bain-marie. Add oil and stir to combine.
2. Pour the glaze immediately over the chilled cake to create a smooth surface. Refrigerate for about 1 hour to set.
3. Using a hot knife, cut the edges of the cake and cut the cake into rectangular pieces.
4. Using the leftover chocolate glaze, write "Opéra" on each finished piece and decorate with a flake of edible gold leaf (optional).

One of the first trustees who reached out to me after my appointment to HealthCare Chaplaincy was Thelma Van Dyke Dinkeloo, widow of John Gerard Dinkeloo, a partner in one the country's most distinguished architectural firms, Kevin Roche, John Dinkeloo and Associates. Thelma, a mother of seven children, fifteen grandchildren, and three great-grandchildren, was born and raised in a devout Presbyterian family in Zeeland, Michigan. She and John married in 1943 and remained residents of Michigan until the mid-1960s. John and Kevin had been coleading Eero Saarinen Associates in Michigan until the death of Mr. Saarinen, when they decided to form their own firm. They changed the company name and set up business offices in Hamden, Connecticut.

Their work in New York City quickly became iconic. The Ford Foundation headquarters, completed in 1968, is a NYC-designated landmark, one of the youngest buildings to achieve such status. Roche, Dinkeloo was also responsible for creating in the 1960s the master plan for the Metropolitan Museum of Art, and the firm designed some of the Met's newer wings.

My first one-on-one meeting with Thelma was at the Metropolitan Museum, where she had invited me to join her for lunch in a serene private dining room on the fourth floor of the Henry R. Kravits Wing. The room has extraordinary tree top views of Central Park. Thelma greeted me at the front door of the Met and led me through some of the galleries that her husband, John (who had unexpectedly died in his sleep in 1981 at age sixty-three), had helped design and engineer.

We walked through the museum's Sackler Wing, which John and his associates had created to house the Temple of Dendur. This ancient temple, a gift from Egypt to the United States, was given to the Met in 1967 by President Lyndon B. Johnson and is one of the most treasured works at the Met. Even though I did not know Thelma well at this moment, I could sense her grief and emotion, almost a decade after her husband's death. As we strolled through these monuments to his architectural and engineering genius, she spoke lovingly about him.

When we settled into our table in the dining room, we began what evolved into a two-hour lunch. Thelma was such a spiritual woman with a deeply grounded faith. She spoke with insight and enthusiasm about the work of HealthCare Chaplaincy, about the formation and education of professional chaplains, and about the need for competent research to better understand the relationships between spirituality and health. This conversation with Thelma proved to be one of my most strategic orientation sessions as the Chaplaincy's new CEO. We became so engrossed in our conversation that I almost forgot to eat the lunch that was set before us—an exquisite steak tartare.

I was surprised to find this item on the menu of a private dining room. Thelma was intrigued by our ensuing conversation about this dish, which many believe to be a French creation. Although some famous twentieth-century French chefs like Auguste Escoffier and Prosper Montagné offered versions of recipes for what they call "*le steak à l'américaine*," the dish is believed to have originated in the seventeenth century in the region of contemporary Mongolia, an area controlled by the Tartars, accounting perhaps for its modern name. It was subsequently introduced to Europe by Russian mariners.

STEAK TARTARE

Chopped raw tenderloin of beef garnished with shallots, capers, cornichons, and parsley

Makes 4 servings

Ingredients

- 1 pound top-quality beef tenderloin
- 2 tablespoons sherry vinegar
- 2 teaspoons freshly squeezed lemon juice
- 1 teaspoon Dijon mustard
- 2 egg yolks (use pasteurized eggs, if possible)
- ¼ cup extra-virgin olive oil
- 1 tablespoon Worcestershire sauce
- 8 tablespoons finely minced shallots
- 3 tablespoons capers, rinsed and patted dry
- 3 chopped cornichons
- ¼ cup minced celery leaves (optional)
- 2 tablespoons finely chopped parsley (optional)
- kosher salt and freshly ground black pepper

Method

To prepare the tenderloin of beef

1. To make this recipe and to help protect the health of your diners, use only the best quality beef, preferably a tenderloin freshly prepared by a reputable butcher. Inform the butcher what you are intending to use the tenderloin to prepare.
2. At home, the tenderloin should ideally be washed, patted dry, tightly wrapped, and frozen for a day or two to reduce the risk of any harmful bacteria.

continued

3. Defrost the tenderloin in the refrigerator the day before use.
4. It will be easier slicing the beef tenderloin if it is firm and very cold. Start by cutting the roast into cubes and then, with a very sharp knife, mince the cubes finely. Some folks use the food processor for this final step, but you will achieve a better final texture if you mince the beef by hand with a chef's knife.
5. Place the minced beef in a nonreactive bowl, cover with plastic wrap, and refrigerate.

To prepare the dressing for the tartare

1. In a mixing bowl, combine the olive oil, lemon juice, sherry vinegar, Dijon mustard, egg yolks, Worcestershire sauce, and salt and pepper. Whisk until blended and emulsified.

To mix and plate the steak tartare

1. Traditionally, the French do not add any minced herbs into their preparation of tartare. Use the chopped herbs (parsley, celery leaves) as your preference and taste may dictate.
2. Add the prepared dressing to the minced beef tenderloin, and with clean hands, massage the dressing well into the meat.
3. Place the seasoned beef into a fine strainer that has been placed over a bowl. Cover the strainer with plastic wrap and allow the seasoned mixture to drain in the refrigerator for an hour or more.
4. Close to service time, add the chopped cornichons, capers, and chopped shallots (and herbs, if desired) to the seasoned beef. Mix thoroughly.
5. If you have a 3-inch stainless steel pastry ring, you can begin to plate the steak tartare as it is traditionally served. If you do not have a proper ring form, you can use an empty tuna can, opened on both ends, carefully washed, dried, and sprayed with vegetable spray. It works perfectly.
6. Garnish the formed steak tartare with some mâche or microgreens and serve immediately, accompanied with some thin toasted slices of a French baguette.

During our luncheon conversation, Thelma mentioned that she was enrolled in an art history course at the museum. Through this course she had become acquainted with another woman she thought would be an excellent person to cultivate for prospective future membership on the governing board. "Lucy McGrath is a Roman Catholic, also a widow, with extensive nonprofit board experience, and a wonderful person. The two of you would get along beautifully," Thelma said. She noted that in late November, the Brick Presbyterian Church on Park Avenue would be hosting a jazz concert featuring David Brubeck and his quartet. Lucy McGrath had already accepted to be Thelma's guest for this performance, preceded by an informal supper at Sarabeth's restaurant on Madison Avenue at 93rd Street. Thelma thought that this would be an ideal context for her to make an introduction of me to Lucy, and I readily accepted.

It was a curious coincidence that I was reconnecting with so many widows. My doctoral dissertation research had immersed me in a study of the grief and life circumstances of many recently widowed women. Thelma and Lucy had discovered common ground in their own experiences of loss and moving forward. Both women, despite their losses, were turning to life again—or, as another widow so poetically expressed it, "in concert with others, she hides her sad truth."

Lucy Patricia Flemming McGrath was a native New Yorker who married John Patrick McGrath in 1940 at Our Lady Queen of Martyrs Church in Flushing, Queens, and they later celebrated with family and friends at a gala reception in the Waldorf Astoria hotel in Manhattan. John and Lucy later became parents to four daughters—Mary Lucy, Irene, Elizabeth, and Lucy Joan—and grandparents to nine grandchildren. After a long illness, John McGrath died on March 2, 1989. I met Lucy two years later.

From all the stories I have heard from both Lucy and his daughters, John McGrath was soft-spoken, but nevertheless a powerhouse in New York's political and business communities. He had earned a law degree at the Fordham University School of Law before serving as corporation counsel to New York City's Democratic mayor, William O'Dwyer. Later he managed the campaign that elected W. Averell Harriman as New York's forty-eighth governor. John became one the architects of Long Island University's financial recovery and subsequent development and served as trustee from 1951 until 1966, during which time he chaired its board. In 1966 he joined the East New York Savings Bank. During these many years of John's public and private service, in addition to raising their daughters, Lucy became immersed in many charitable endeavors. She planned and hosted many successful social and fundraising events.

Our introductory meeting that evening at Sarabeth's was delightful. Lucy was an astute, poised, and engaging dinner companion. Throughout her life she had traveled extensively. She remained actively involved in numerous projects of the Roman Catholic community, both locally and internationally. A Dame of the Sovereign Order of Malta, Lucy was a prominent benefactor and patron of the arts at the Vatican Museums. She had helped the Holy See to establish its first United States chapter of Vatican Museums patrons. During our first evening together, we found an immediate intersection of experiences. Lucy had been involved in leading an effort to help restore Raphael's *Healing of the Lame Man* tapestry, and she spoke with enthusiasm and pride about the patrons' work in restoring Fra Angelico's frescoes in the private chapel in the Vatican of Pope Nicholas V, who had served the Roman Catholic Church as pope from 1447 to 1455.

Lucy also shared a common passion for opera. When she and John were raising their family, they had been neighbors and close personal friends with Richard and Sarah Perelmuth Tucker. Sarah's brother was Jan Peerce, an operatic tenor at the Metropolitan Opera. For three decades Richard Tucker had also been a leading tenor with the Metropolitan Opera Company. At an early age, his voice was recognized by the cantor of the Allen Street Synagogue on the Manhattan's Lower East Side. He encouraged Richard to develop his vocal gift. Tucker was later ordained as a cantor, and even during his later career at the Met, he sang for the High Holy Day services of Rosh Hashanah and Yom Kippur.

Lucy remained active with the Tucker family in preserving the legacy of this great American tenor by her capacity as a trustee and benefactor of the Richard Tucker Music Foundation, which supports and advances the careers of talented American opera singers. Every year the foundation sponsors one of the most highly anticipated events of the opera season, the Richard Tucker Gala. This annual concert brings together a rich program of recognized arias, duets, and ensemble pieces performed by some of the luminaries of the opera world—all supported by the orchestra of the Metropolitan Opera company and under the baton of a world-class maestro. The concert is enriched by the performances of present and past winners of Richard Tucker Awards. Lucy always purchased a row of tickets for this gala, and for some twenty years I never missed attending these events. I recall on one of these evenings that Leontyne Price sat in front of me, Justice Ruth Bader Ginsberg was seated in the row behind, and Cardinal Edward Egan, then Archbishop of New York, was across the aisle.

These events were always followed by a seated dinner for the major patrons and their guests in the atrium of the Lincoln Center concert hall. For the trustees and principal benefactors of the foundation, one of the operatic performers was often assigned as a table guest. Foundation president Barry Tucker would frequently ask me to offer an invocation at this festive dinner. As table companions through the years, I had the chance to chat with baritone Robert Merrill, sopranos Renée Fleming, Angela Meade, Beverly Sills, and Anna Netrebko, and tenors Joseph Calleja and Roberto Alagna. Lucy almost always seated me next to her at table, and our opera guest was seated on her other side. Sometimes I had to pinch myself to be certain that I was actually bantering with some of the people whose voices, performances, and recordings had thrilled me for years.

Lucy became a very committed trustee of the Chaplaincy, and introduced many friends and donors to the work of the organization. She used the extensive network of her personal contacts to broaden the reach of the Chaplaincy, and, as a trustee of some foundations and donor-advised funds, she was able to find new ways to support philanthropically many of our educational initiatives.

Among those whom Lucy introduced to the HealthCare Chaplaincy was her close friend Miriam ("Mimi") Fitzsimmons Meehan. Mimi was one of four children raised in the staunchly Catholic Fitzsimmons family in Brooklyn in the 1920s and educated at Manhattan's Convent of the Sacred Heart. She married William ("Bill") M. Meehan, who was a senior partner of the stock brokerage firm of M. J. Meehan & Company, which had been established by his father. Bill became a member of the New York Stock Exchange in 1935 when his father gave him $130,000 as a twenty-first birthday gift, which was the price in that year for a seat on the Exchange. Later, Bill would become a governor of the Exchange. The Meehans raised their family of two sons, Terry and Billy, and their two daughters, Joanne and Maureen, on Park Avenue in New York City and in an impressive East Hampton property that previously had been the childhood summer home of former First Lady Jackie Bouvier Kennedy Onassis. For more than four decades, Mimi was an engaged board member of Catholic Big Sisters and of the Convent of the Sacred Heart. Lucy enlisted Mimi to become a patron of the work of the Vatican Museums. And of course, Mimi never failed to be an enthusiast for the work of the Religious of the Sacred Heart and of her alma mater on East 91st Street at Fifth Avenue.

I fondly remember one of many enjoyable evenings spent with Mimi and Lucy. We had been together for an early Sunday evening concert at Lincoln Center, and Lucy had suggested a postconcert supper at Café Pierre in the Pierre Hotel. We arrived at the restaurant around 9:30 p.m., and there were very few guests remaining in the intimate rear dining room where we were seated. Lucy suggested that we begin with some champagne, along with a platter of assorted hot and cold hors d'oeuvres. The conversation was animated and full of laughter. Imagine the scene: two exquisitely dressed matronly widowed women and a middle-aged man dressed in a black suit and clerical collar.

When the menu arrived, I noticed that they featured a lobster bisque. Since it was already late in the evening, I thought this would be an appropriate selection. When the maître d'hôtel came to take our orders, the two women ordered filet mignon. When they heard me order the bisque, they turned to each other and politely snickered. Quickly Mimi said to Lucy: "He has to get up and work in the morning; we don't, so let's not be restrained." The bisque was perfectly delightful, and I was able to sleep well that night. There are many approaches to bisque de homard, but this recipe follows that of Escoffier.

BISQUE DE HOMARD

Lobster bisque

Makes 4 to 6 servings

Ingredients

For the fish fumet

- 1 pound fish bones
- 1 thinly sliced shallot
- 4 cups water
- ½ cup white wine or vermouth
- kosher salt

For the sauce veloute

- ¼ pound (1 stick) unsalted butter
- ¼ cup all-purpose flour

- 3½ cups fish fumet
- a pinch of sea salt
- a couple of grinds of black pepper
- a pinch of nutmeg

For the mirepoix

- 1 tablespoon unsalted butter
- ½ diced onion
- ½ diced carrot
- 2 tablespoons minced parsley
- 1 tablespoon minced thyme leaves
- 1 bay leaf
- 2 tablespoons Cognac
- ¼ cup white wine or white vermouth
- sea salt
- freshly ground black pepper

For the lobster

- 1½ pound live Maine lobster

Method

To prepare the fish fumet

1. Soak fish bones in a bowl of lightly salted cold water for 1 hour, changing the water twice as the bones soak. Drain the bones and pat them dry.
2. Preheat oven to 400°F.
3. Transfer the fish bones to a rimmed baking sheet lined with aluminum foil, and roast for 5 minutes.

continued

4. Transfer bones to a stockpot and add 4 cups water; bring to a boil over high heat. Add shallots and wine; reduce heat to low and let simmer for 10 minutes.
5. Remove from heat and let stand for 10 minutes.
6. Strain the liquid through a fine mesh sieve; discard all the solids.
7. Let cool completely. Freeze whatever of the fish fumet is not used in the recipe.

To prepare and cook the lobster

1. Fill a large stockpot with water and bring to a rapid boil.
2. Insert a sharp knife in the head of the lobster.
3. Drop the lobster headfirst into the rapidly boiling water. Cook for 8 minutes. Remove the cooked lobster and allow it to cool.
4. Skim whatever scum may be on the surface of the water and retain about 4 cups of the cooking liquid to use later if you should need to thin out the bisque.
5. When the lobster is cooled enough to handle comfortably, open the lobster over a large bowl that can collect the liquid and discarded shells as you remove the lobster meat.
6. Place all the broken and discarded shells and liquids into a food processor fitted with the steel blade, and pulse several times. Press the processed contents through a sieve and retain the residue lobster paste.

For the sauce velouté

1. Melt the butter in a saucepan over medium heat. Whisk in the flour all at once. Whisk to combine and cook for a few minutes until the mixture becomes a golden-colored roux.
2. Add the fish fumet to the roux, whisking vigorously. Season the sauce velouté with salt, pepper, and nutmeg. Bring slowly to a boil. Turn off the heat. Set the sauce aside.

To prepare the mirepoix

1. Heat the butter in a saucepan over medium-high heat.
2. Add the onion, carrot, parsley, thyme leaves, and bay leaf. Cook for several minutes until the vegetables and herbs are beginning to caramelize, stirring continuously. Remove and discard the bay leaf.
3. Deglaze the pan with some Cognac.
4. Scrape the bottom of the saucepan with a wooden spoon to loosen the *fond.*
5. Add salt and pepper. Add the white wine and reduce the heat to medium-low.
6. Allow the liquid to reduce in the mirepoix (the mixture of sautéed chopped vegetables) for about 10 minutes.
7. Remove from heat and set aside.

To assemble the lobster bisque

1. In a Dutch oven, add the lobster meat, lobster paste, sauce velouté, and mirepoix mixture, and with a handheld immersion blender, purée the entire mixture until it is completely blended and smooth.
2. Add additional fish fumet or reserved lobster cooking liquid to thin out the bisque to the desired consistency.
3. Add some pads of unsalted room-temperature butter or a couple tablespoons of heavy cream at the end, for additional richness. Correct seasoning. You may wish to garnish with a scant pinch of cayenne.

We were the final guests to leave Café Pierre that Sunday night. I recall standing outside the restaurant and saying farewell to Mimi and Lucy before hailing a cab on Fifth Avenue to return home. We had shared together a wonderful evening of music and dining. Mimi's final words to Lucy: "We have to admit it, Lucy, we are two very lucky dames." I kept chuckling to myself about this comment in the cab all the way back to my apartment. But in remembering Thelma and Lucy and Mimi I am also aware that after the deaths of their respective spouses, they had found ways to turn again to life and smile and laugh.

Chapter 16

A JOURNEY OF A THOUSAND MILES BEGINS WITH A SINGLE STEP

There is a time for everything,
and a season for every activity under heaven:
a time to be born and a time to die,
a time to plant and a time to uproot,
a time to kill and a time to heal,
a time to tear down and a time to build,
a time to weep and a time to laugh,
a time to mourn and a time to dance,
a time to scatter stones and a time to gather them,
a time to embrace and a time to refrain,
a time to search and a time to give up,
a time to keep and a time to throw away,
a time to tear and a time to mend,
a time to be silent and a time to speak,
a time to love and a time to hate,
a time for war and a time for peace.

—ECCLESIASTES 3:1–8

As I was approaching my seventieth birthday, I reprised earlier conversations with the chairman and members of the Chaplaincy's executive committee about the urgency of succession planning to recruit and appoint the organization's next leader. I had already been serving as the Chaplaincy's CEO for more than twenty years, when the average tenure of other nonprofit leaders in New York City was around seven years. As it had been some years earlier, the initial reaction from this small group of trustee leaders was respectful but still resistant. They told me that age should not be a factor in determining whether I stay or move on. "You're such a youthful and energetic seventy," one of the trustees said. "Things are going so well, and with your new knees, you can easily continue on until you're at least seventy-five." I had just recently had undergone successful bilateral full-knee replacements, which had indeed gone very well, and the surgery had restored both mobility and energy.

The trustees, nonetheless, did reluctantly agree to take my request seriously and begin planning for succession. Another year came and went, and the board still had not put in place a formal succession plan. Again, at my next annual review with the chairman, I raised my concerns, this time even more insistently. I told him that the nature and challenges of the job had evolved and that I was at a point where I was resolved that the time was right to step away and allow new leadership and new ideas to take HealthCare Chaplaincy to its next level. I also told him that I had been discussing these same issues with my Jesuit provincial superior, who agreed that the time was right to move on.

This decision ultimately came down to the difference between *can* and *want*. The trustees were unanimous, it seemed, in their collective judgment that I *could* continue leading the organization indefinitely forward into its future; what they were failing to appreciate was that I was telling them that I no longer *wanted* to do this. Leading a nonprofit organization—especially a large and complex one such as HealthCare Chaplaincy—is inherently stressful, and the obligations are unrelenting. The annual work cycles are inexorable and wearying: budgeting and forecasting, planning and assessing, cultivating and fundraising, hiring, firing, auditing, and reporting. There comes a time when one arrives at an honest realization that even when you can do what the organization needs, you may no longer want to do it.

Life is a story of transitions. One is constantly completing one chapter, only to move on to the next, until the story is finally ended. Transitions are never easy, even when carefully planned. I was certainly aware of this at the Chaplaincy. Over the course of a quarter-century under my leadership, we had never experienced a year when we did not balance the budget. Our growth curves were steady and, at times, accelerated. Our business partnerships were strong, and our education and research initiatives were prospering and effective. We had developed and executed four strategic plans that continually challenged the organization to rethink its priorities and refine its mission.

The board of trustees had grown comfortable with the status quo and pressing these candid conversations with them about executive leadership transition and succession was unsettling. I had built solid and enduring relationships with all of the key stakeholders and supporters, and the management team was firmly committed to the Chaplaincy's mission and objectives. And I had developed excellent relationships with generations of present and former trustees, and annual fundraising results continued to be impressive. To entertain the possibility of a major leadership change was hard to comprehend for many of the trustees.

Since they were good stewards and successful business leaders themselves, they knew that they needed to focus on one of their most important responsibilities as trustees: to recruit and appoint the chief executive officer. For me, it was not an easy decision to give up something in which I had invested the largest number of years of my Jesuit ministry and in which I had found both enjoyment and success. But the time was right.

As the board was formulating its plan, the chairman asked me if I might be willing, after a sabbatical, to remain employed with the organization for some additional time, serving as the organization's president emeritus and its first chancellor and assisting my successor with future fundraising and business enhancement activities. I thought this was a risky offer, since the trustees had yet to recruit and appoint a new executive and they could not know whether the new CEO would welcome having a long-tenured predecessor hanging around. Those older trustees, with longer institutional memories, recalled how smoothly the transition between the Twinames and me had gone, and how happy both Carolyn and John had been when I gladly kept them actively involved as "life trustees" for several years after their retirement from their executive leadership roles. With my Jesuit provincial's encouragement I accepted the board's proposal, with the understanding that the agreement could be terminated at any future time, either by me or by the Chaplaincy.

By midyear 2016, having been in my new role of chancellor for several months, I asked the new board chairman if we might arrange to have lunch together. During that meeting I shared with him my sense that it would probably be best for both the Chaplaincy and for me to retire definitively by year's end. I had concluded that the new CEO had a very different vision for the organization and its future, and I had the clear sense that I would not be of much help to him in realizing his strategic goals. Like so many items in a kitchen's pantry, we all have expiration dates and a finite shelf life—and I candidly realized that I had reached my Chaplaincy shelf life. In early October 2016 I submitted my resignation, effective December 31.

That decision set in motion the transition rituals from an organization that I had loved and stewarded for twenty-six years. It was the first time in as many years that I began to think about what I might do next. My first thought was to remain living and ministering in New York City, which had become home to me. Counting the years spent with the Chaplaincy and the dozen years I taught in neighboring Fairfield, I had lived for thirty-eight years in the greater New York region. In practical ways I had become a New Yorker, with loyalty ties to the New York Yankees, Knicks, Rangers, and Jets, and I had lost the remaining vestiges of a Boston accent.

In initiating conversations about future work as a Jesuit priest, the provincial—who had been one of my former students when I served as dean of the Weston School of Theology—suggested that he would like me to begin considering availability to serve as the next president of the province's principal long-term care facility in Weston and to become superior of its Jesuit community. He did not require me to decide at that time, only to begin thinking and praying about this prospective future mission. I have always believed that if one's heart and mind remain open, blessings will follow.

The immediate tasks at hand were to attend to the many personal, emotional, social, and practical issues involved in making this major life transition. This decision to conclude my service to HealthCare Chaplaincy did not just require small lifestyle adjustments. It set in motion a sweeping metamorphosis.

The ensuing months were challenging. One of the principal drivers of change was the fact that the lease on the rent-stabilized apartment in which I had been living in Peter Cooper Village was due to expire in mid-December. I decided to allow the lease to expire at that time, which meant that I would need to be prepared to vacate the apartment.

So began the process of downsizing, sorting, discarding, packing, and storing. These instrumental tasks paled in comparison to the far more difficult tasks of saying goodbye to people and places that had shaped the human landscape of my life for more than twenty-five years.

Among these tasks was sharing the news of my transition with Maria Fan, who had been my next-door neighbor in Peter Cooper Village for sixteen years. Maria had been born in Shanghai but raised in Hong Kong. She immigrated to New York, where her husband was employed as chief of the Chinese Interpretation Section at the United Nations. Maria also worked for many years as an administrative assistant at the UN while raising the couple's two children, Perry and Vicky. By the time I occupied the apartment adjacent to hers at the end of 2000, Maria had been widowed and was living independently.

Occasionally Maria would seek my assistance with some minor repair in her apartment. I would respond to her requests and most often was able to address her immediate concern. Even though I would rate my technical abilities to be average or below average, Maria thought I was a mechanical genius. She would often quip that her son, Perry, even though he had earned a baccalaureate degree in chemical engineering from Princeton University, could scarcely be called upon to change a light bulb.

Over the course of our time together as neighbors, we continued to deepen our friendship, which was an enormous mutual blessing. Perry and Vicky, too, were comforted to know that someone unobtrusively was looking after their mother. On many occasions I invited Maria to join one of the many occasions in my apartment when I entertained trustees and friends at dinner. Maria is a very sophisticated and astute person, with broad intellectual and cultural interests. For much of her adult life she had collaborated and entertained diplomats from around the globe, and she and her husband had traveled extensively. She was always a great dinner companion.

I recall once when my sister and her husband were visiting for a long weekend when I invited Maria to join us for a casual dinner. In preparation, I told my sister to be prepared that Maria would most likely come dressed to the nines, even though she only lived in the adjacent apartment and knew that this was a casual family dinner. There were broad smiles all around when I opened the apartment door that evening to greet Maria—who at the time was well into her eighties—attired in a perfectly tailored Chanel suit, wearing Salvatore Ferragamo patent leather bow pumps and carrying a small patent leather Fendi handbag along with a beautifully wrapped bottle of Dom Perignon champagne.

On many Fridays I would bake a pie, tart, cake, or cookies. Whatever I decided to make, I always doubled the recipe and made identical items for Maria, who had a secret sweet tooth. She tended to be a night owl, retiring quite late in the evenings and sleeping later in the mornings. She maintained an extraordinarily active social schedule with her friends, playing mahjong at least twice a week, attending lectures and cultural events, working out in a local gym with a trainer, and regularly shopping at Bloomingdale's or Macy's. Rain or shine, she was usually out of her apartment by noon and not back on many evenings until suppertime. Around midnight, she would often crave something sweet. Early one evening I rang her doorbell, holding a plate piled with still warm macadamia chocolate chip cookies. Her smile broadened as she gratefully accepted the gift saying, "I am so happy to receive these cookies. I was just looking around the kitchen and realized that I had nothing sweet left and that I would have to stop at the bakery tomorrow. This is a gift from heaven."

MACADAMIA CHOCOLATE CHIP COOKIES

Makes 36 cookies

Ingredients

- 2 sticks of unsalted room-temperature butter
- ½ cup granulated sugar
- 1½ cups packed dark brown sugar
- 2 eggs
- 2 teaspoons pure vanilla extract
- 2¾ cups all-purpose flour
- ¾ teaspoon kosher or sea salt
- 1 teaspoon baking soda
- 1½ teaspoon baking powder
- 2¼ cups semisweet or dark chocolate chips
- 1½ cups macadamia nuts

Method

1. Preheat oven to 350°F.
2. Toast the macadamia nuts, spread on a sheet pan, in the oven for 10

minutes. Remove and cool. When cooled, roughly chop the toasted nuts. Set aside.

3. On medium speed in a stand mixer fitted with the paddle attachment, cream the room-temperature butter, granulated sugar, and brown sugar until fluffy.
4. Add both eggs and vanilla and beat for an additional 2 minutes.
5. Add dry ingredients (baking soda, baking powder, salt, and flour) and mix on low speed until fully incorporated. Do not overmix.
6. Remove the bowl from the mixer, and by hand, with a firm spatula or wooden spoon, add the chocolate chips and cooled, chopped macadamia nuts and blend until well distributed. The batter will be thick.
7. Using a medium-sized cookie scoop, drop small mounds of the batter onto two baking sheets, lined with parchment paper, to form about 36 cookies. Slight press down the tops of the mounded cookie dough.
8. Bake for 12 to 14 minutes until the edges of the cookies are golden brown.
9. Remove from oven and allow the cookies to remain on the cookie sheet for an additional 2 minutes.
10. With both hands, carefully move the parchment paper with the cookies to a nonporous surface to continue cooling for several minutes before serving or storing.

I was convalescing at the end of October 2012 in my twelfth-floor apartment after my second knee replacement surgery when New York City was seriously impacted by Hurricane Sandy. Fueled by wind gusts that measured more than 100 miles per hour, a 14-foot storm surge from the East River flooded the area in which we were living. The entirety of lower Manhattan and some surrounding areas were without electrical power for several days. The large hospitals in the neighborhood, including the VA, Bellevue Hospital Center, and NYU Langone Medical Center, were closed and evacuated because their lobbies and basements were flooded and the emergency generators destroyed. The New York City public transit system was forced to shut down due to the flooding of many subway tunnels.

Several things, however, were in our favor. My pantry, refrigerator, and freezer were well stocked. All of our Peter Cooper apartments were equipped with gas ranges and ovens, so we could continue to cook and bake. We continued to have running water and could flush toilets and take cold showers. I had plenty of candles in my apartment, along with a battery-operated radio, so that I could get occasional news updates. The downside was that I could not recharge my cell phone, and without power I could not use the internet to communicate with my office, friends, or family.

In addition to Maria Fan, there were other older persons living in some of the other six apartments on my floor. On the first day of the more than week-long blackout, I invited Maria and the other older widowed persons to come at 6 o'clock to my apartment for a simple supper. Not knowing how quickly power might be restored, I decided first to prepare the meat items in my freezer that would defrost most rapidly and later to prepare items like the roasts, which would thaw more slowly.

Each night that week five of us dined by candlelight, and each of these neighbors appreciated not only the delicious home-cooked meals, but the unaccustomed opportunity the blackout afforded for social connectedness and conversation. These communal meals continued for many of the days in which we were without power, and it spared having to throw away items that would have spoiled during the prolonged recovery period as they defrosted.

When power was finally restored in early November my neighbors missed the nightly dining soirées, but they regularly spoke of those experiences. Few of them previously knew of the extent of my culinary abilities and marveled not only at the range of the menus, but at the diversity of the things they had sampled. Of course, Maria bragged to the others that none of this was a surprise to her since she had been the continuing beneficiary of my kitchen's delights for more than a dozen years.

One of the first things I made for the ladies was a linguine and scampi dish. I had an unopened three-pound bag of large frozen shrimp, which would thaw pretty quickly. With plenty of pasta on hand, this was an easy and delightful main course.

SCAMPI AL COGNAC CON LINGUINE

Linguine with shrimp and a Cognac-infused cream sauce

Makes 4 servings

Ingredients

- 1 pound fresh or dry linguine
- 16 medium or large shrimp (fresh or frozen)
- extra-virgin olive oil
- Cognac
- 14-ounce can puréed San Marzano tomatoes
- flat-leaf parsley
- sea salt
- freshly ground black pepper

For the broth

- 1½ cups dry white wine
- 16 shrimp shells
- 1 carrot
- 1 stalk celery
- I small onion
- 3 cups water
- extra-virgin olive oil
- salt and pepper

Method

1. Clean the 16 shrimp by removing and conserving the body shells from the shrimp. Devein the shrimp removing the black digestive tract from the back, wash, and place on paper towels to absorb any extra moisture.

continued

2. In a large saucepan, add some olive oil and, over medium flame, sauté the reserved shrimp shells. Add the roughly chopped carrot, celery, and onion. Add 1½ cups of dry white wine and cook until the liquid reduces by a half. Add 3 cups of water and allow the broth to cook for about 20 minutes. Using a fine mesh strainer, pour out the broth into a stainless steel bowl and reserve. Discard the solids.
3. In a Dutch oven, add a couple of tablespoons of olive oil and heat. When oil is hot, add 3 cloves of minced garlic and cook for 30 seconds. Add in the diced tomatoes, stir, and cook on medium heat for 15 minutes.
4. In a skillet, add another tablespoon of olive oil. When hot, add a tablespoon of minced garlic and cook for 30 seconds. Add the cleaned and dried shrimps, and sauté for a minute. Add in ¼ cup Cognac and cook for another minute. Remove from heat.
5. Cook the linguine according to package directions until about 2 minutes before the pasta reaches the al dente stage.
6. When pasta is ready, transfer the linguine to the Dutch oven with the tomato-based sauce. Add about 1 cup of the shrimp stock to the Dutch oven, toss the pasta in the liquid, and cook over medium heat for another 2 minutes.
7. When the pasta is finished cooking in the sauce, add in the cooked shrimp, correct the seasonings, and finish with a ½ cup of finely chopped parsley.

Chinese New Year in 2012 heralded the year of the dragon. Maria's son, Perry, and his family were happily resettled back in New Jersey after their extended assignment in Shanghai. I had invited the Fan family for a Lunar New Year dinner. Living on our floor in Peter Cooper Village that year were two Canadian Chinese men who had recently graduated from business schools and who were each pursuing year-long internships in Wall Street firms. As a neighborly gesture, I invited them to join us for the celebration. I was the only non-Chinese person around the table that evening. I did not attempt to produce any authentic Mandarin or Cantonese dishes that evening but decided to serve what I sensed everyone would very much enjoy—a roasted prime rib of beef.

Some years earlier a chef friend had introduced me to a cooking method for prime rib that seemed quite unorthodox, but it works well. The basic formula is to preheat your oven to 500°F, and then determine the precise cooking time by multiplying the exact weight of the roast by five and rounding the resulting number to the nearest whole number. Then cook the roast for precisely those minutes. For my Chinese New Year roast, for example, I had purchased a 4.5-pound roast (4.5 x 5=22.5 minutes). I prepped the room-temperature roast by inserting some cloves of garlic into the fat cap and generously seasoned the roast with an herbed butter mixture. I then put the beef into a roasting pan in the hot oven, uncovered, for 23 minutes. Then I turned the oven off and waited two hours before opening the oven door. This is really important. Do not be tempted to peek and open the oven door. The result was a perfectly pink rare to medium rare roast.

CÔTE DE BOEUF RÔTI AU JUS

Roast prime rib of beef in its natural juices

Makes 8 to 10 servings

Ingredients

- 4–5-pound prime rib roast
- ¼ cup softened, unsalted butter
- 6 cloves of garlic
- 1 tablespoon freshly ground black pepper
- 1 teaspoon herbes de Provence
- kosher salt

Method

1. Place the rib roast on a plate and bring to room temperature, about 4 hours.

continued

2. With a sharp paring knife, make some 2-inch slits into the roast and insert cloves of garlic.
3. Preheat an oven to 500°F.
4. Combine softened butter, pepper, and herbes de Provence in a bowl and mix until well blended. Spread butter mixture evenly over entire roast. Season the roast generously with kosher salt.
5. Roast the 4–5-pound prime rib in the preheated oven for 23 minutes.
6. Turn the oven off. Leaving the roast in the oven with the door closed, let it sit in the oven for 2 hours. Remove the roast from the oven, slice, and serve. (You do not have to allow for any resting time before carving when using this cooking method.)
7. The actual cooking times will vary depending on the size of your prime rib roast.

To capture some of the culinary traditions associated with the Lunar New Year celebrations I made some extra-long homemade spaghetti, which I simply sauced with a wild mushroom cream sauce. The long strips of pasta symbolize the wish for longevity. In fact, many Chinese call these "longevity noodles" (*chángshòu miàn*). They were a perfect accompaniment to the succulent prime rib of beef.

Our young Canadian guests were not only thrilled to have been invited to this family celebration, but they were astounded by the meal that had been prepared for them. One of the young men commented that it was the best Chinese New Year dinner that he had ever experienced. When Maria questioned him about his statement, he further explained: "Usually at family holiday celebrations, everyone is talking loudly and at the same time, and frequently, a heated argument ensues, and the volume gets turned up even more. Tonight, we all talked calmly with each other, listened to each other's stories, and enjoyed a perfectly wonderful evening together, with no conflict." Listening to him, Maria affirmed that he was absolutely right. In fact, they all concurred that most Chinese family celebrations were extremely boisterous affairs, and that this one, hosted by an Irishman, offered a welcomed change.

Even though I did not use the long traditional steaming method to prepare this adapted, Westernized version of *nian gao*, a Chinese New Year cake, the results still received appreciative reviews from my guests.

NIAN GAO

Traditional steamed Chinese New Year almond and coconut cake

Makes 8 servings

Ingredients

- 3 tablespoons melted unsalted butter
- 4 large eggs
- 3 cups rice flour
- 3 cups whole milk
- 2½ cups granulated sugar
- 1 teaspoon almond extract
- ¼ teaspoon fine table salt
- 2 tablespoons sweetened coconut flakes
- 2 tablespoons toasted slivered almonds
- 2 tablespoons toasted sesame seeds

Method

1. Preheat the oven to 325°F.
2. Butter and flour a 9-inch round springform cake pan.
3. Combine the eggs in a large bowl and lightly whisk.
4. Add the flour, milk, sugar, melted butter, almond extract, and salt.
5. Whisk briefly until the batter is smooth.
6. Pour the mixture into the prepared cake pan and place on a baking sheet in the oven.
7. Bake for 30 minutes.

continued

8. Remove the baking sheet with the cake from the oven and sprinkle the top of the cake with the coconut, slivered almonds, and sesame seeds.
9. Return the tray to oven and continue to bake for about 25 additional minutes, until the cake is set and golden brown.
10. Remove the cake from the springform pan and let it cool for 15 minutes before serving.

Maria Fan had several very close friends with whom she maintained a robust social life. It was not until she was well into her late seventies that she decided to give up driving. Some of her even older friends still maintained a driver's license and would transport her from event to event. One evening, after a particularly busy day at work, I decided to stop for take-out at Frank's, a small neighborhood Italian restaurant on First Avenue that was owned and run by Mexicans, only to find Maria and three of her friends enjoying an early supper at a table just inside the restaurant's front door. When I noticed her, I was at first startled to observe that she had two black eyes.

"What happened to you, Maria?" I inquired. The other ladies began to politely snicker when they heard my query and were anxiously focused on just how honestly she would reply. Maria recounted that she had joined her friends for an afternoon film at the local AMC Kips Bay movie complex on Second Avenue. Becoming momentarily distracted by the animated conversation in which she was engaged with her friends, Maria walked directly into a closed plate-glass door in the theatre, bruising her nose and precipitating a noticeable pooling of blood under the skin around both of her eyes. Even though she resembled a panda, the accident had not affected either her spirit or her appetite. As I was leaving the restaurant with my take-out order, Maria did ask one favor from me. "Walter, please don't tell Perry about this little accident. Otherwise, he will be driving up from New Jersey to be checking on me."

A similar thing happened a few years later. One evening, when I rang her doorbell to present her with something freshly baked from the oven, she opened her apartment door only to reveal her face even more bruised than what happened after her mishap in the movie theatre. On a routine trip to Chinatown the day before for a scheduled appointment with her hairdresser, Maria crossed one of the side streets, passing quickly between some parked cars. As she was stepping up on the curbside, she did not notice a bicycle that had been chained to a parking meter and she caught her foot in the spoke of the bike's rear wheel. She fell flat, face-first, to the ground. Miraculously she did not break any bones, but she sustained multiple scrape wounds and her eyes were blacker and bluer than before. She did lay low for a few days before she could no longer tolerate the enforced social isolation. Masked by a lot of concealer makeup, Maria was soon up and out. She was not about to allow a misstep in Chinatown to disrupt her admirably active life in the Big Apple.

As we had been friends and neighbors for sixteen years, Maria found the prospect of my anticipated move to Boston to be difficult. She commented that in her nearly six decades living in her apartment she had never had a next-door neighbor with whom she felt such mutual closeness and caring. As an aristocratic and sophisticated Chinese woman, Maria was not given to outward displays of emotion or exaggerated expressions of affection. But even this stalwart Asian woman could not restrain the tears that spontaneously filled her eyes.

I surrendered the keys and rights to my apartment on December 14, 2016. Maria had planned to spend the Christmas holidays that year with her daughter, Vicky, in California, and she was scheduled to depart New York on December 12. The night before her departure she rang my doorbell to say farewell, and again, with tears in her eyes, she gave me a tight, warm hug, making me promise that on return trips to the city, I would visit with her.

As I was preparing to leave New York, I was also trying to determine what I might do and where I would live between January and June 2017. Having enjoyed some prior ministerial experiences as a cruise chaplain on Holland America Line (HAL) ships, I explored the possibility of spending these several early months of the new year assisting.

God's providence went into overdrive. I discovered that during the penultimate year of its service in the HAL fleet, the *MS Prinsendam* would need a chaplain for two back-to-back cruises leaving Ft. Lauderdale, Florida, right after New Year's Day and returning in mid-May. The first cruise of some seventy-four days was a circumnavigation of South America and Antarctica, and the second a thirty-eight-day round-trip transatlantic cruise to the Mediterranean. I volunteered for this extended ministry and was happy when HAL confirmed my pastoral engagement as a member of the *Prinsendam*'s crew.

After sharing the Christmas holidays with my Boston-based family, I flew to

Florida on New Year's Day, and on January 3 boarded the *Prinsendam* and set off on a once-in-a-lifetime discovery tour of South America. During the cruise, I was required to celebrate Mass each day for the passengers. On weekends, I additionally offered a Mass for the Roman Catholic members of the crew, many of whom were either Filipino or Indonesian. Because of its itinerary and the duration of the journey, this cruise was considered a "grand voyage." In addition to the Roman Catholic priest on board, Holland America Line had also engaged the services of a rabbi and a Protestant minister, along with a number of other support staff, including a Tai Chi instructor, arts and crafts teacher, a bridge grand master, and a number of celebrity chefs. We quickly formed a nice friendship circle. It happened that the Tai Chi instructor was a practicing Roman Catholic who often became a lector at the daily and weekend liturgies. Her husband, a retired US Army brigadier general, joined us half way through the cruise.

Transiting through the Panama Canal was a wonderful experience. It some ways it became a symbol for me as I was preparing to move from one culture in New York City, in which I had made my home for the past twenty-six years, to another culture back in a place that had been home during my youth and early education.

How often would one have the opportunity to circumnavigate a continent of such breadth and complexity of languages, civilizations, ethnicities, climates, and culinary traditions as South America? In all, as we moved from east to west, we were preparing to make thirty-four scheduled ports visits in nine countries, two continents, and three Caribbean islands. We anticipated destinations in Ecuador, Peru, and Chile before cruising for three days among the bays and glaciers of Antarctica. Making our way northward once again from the bottom of the world, we would visit the Falkland Islands before moving on to Argentina and Uruguay, just in time to arrive in Rio de Janeiro for the fabled celebrations of Mardi Gras. No trip to Brazil would be complete without an extensive cruise to numerous destinations in the Amazon before returning through the Caribbean to Florida.

I was thrilled to discover among the senior staff on the *Prinsendam* a British-born culinary arts director with whom I had collaborated on a previous cruising assignment. This woman was married to a French-speaking native educator in Papeete on the Polynesian island of Tahiti. As soon as we encountered each other on the ship, she was quick to ask me if I would be willing to offer a series of cooking demonstrations for the guests during the cruise, to which I readily agreed. I had conducted some similar demonstrations on a voyage that we had shared through the Suez

Canal and Red Sea, touring around Indonesia and India. It happened that Catholic Mass on the *Prinsendam* was routinely scheduled in the same location in which the demonstration kitchen had been installed and in which daily movies were screened. Many of the Catholic guests were amused that on a given day at 8 a.m. I would be presiding and preaching at a Eucharistic liturgy, only to find me back in the same location at 11 a.m. dressed in a chef's coat, demonstrating methods and techniques to make some easy French or Italian recipe.

For my first demonstration on this cruise, I decided to prepare a typically Sicilian pasta dish that is easy to put together, and with which few non-Italians are familiar. This is a layered, baked pasta dish that uses simple ingredients like sardines, anchovies, cauliflower, onion, and fennel bulb, paired with tomatoes, Pecorino cheese, olive oil, pine nuts, raisins, and breadcrumbs made from grated day-old bread. It was always an intriguing recipe to present and much appreciated, because it was something completely new for many people.

BUCATINI CON CAVOLFIORE, SARDE, E FINOCCHIO AL FORNO

Bucatini baked with cauliflower in a sardine and fennel-infused sauce

Makes 6 to 8 servings

Ingredients

For the breadcrumb and cheese mixture

- 6 generous slices dried, day-old Italian bread
- ¾ cup freshly grated Pecorino Romano cheese
- freshly ground black pepper
- ¼ cup extra-virgin olive oil

For the tomato sauce

- 1 cup chopped onion
- 5 anchovy filets

continued

- 1 small 6-ounce can tomato paste
- 1 can (28-ounce) San Marzano peeled and puréed tomatoes
- salt and pepper
- 1 fennel bulb, with fronds
- 1 can (4 ounces) sardines, packed in olive oil
- ½ cup raisins
- ½ cup lightly toasted pinoli (pine nuts)
- ½ cup extra-virgin olive oil
- 3 cups water

For the cauliflower filling

- 1 entire head cauliflower
- 1 cup chopped onion
- freshly ground black pepper
- ¼ cup extra-virgin olive oil

For the pasta

- 1 pound bucatini (or perciatelli) dried pasta

Method

To prepare the breadcrumb and cheese mixture

1. In a food processor fitted with the steel blade, process the dried Italian bread pieces until they yield a fine crumb.
2. In a large skillet, add the olive oil and the breadcrumbs and mix to coat.
3. Cook the breadcrumbs over medium heat, continually stirring until the crumbs begin to brown. Do not overcook and burn. Turn the toasted breadcrumbs onto a baking sheet and spread to cool.
4. When the toasted breadcrumbs have thoroughly cooled, mix in the

grated Pecorino Romano cheese and set aside in a bowl for later use in assembling the dish.

To make the tomato sauce

1. Prepare the fennel bulb by cutting away the root and the upper stalks. Reserve some of the feathery fronds. Roughly chop the fennel bulb. In a food processor fitted with the steel blade, add the fennel bulb, the sardines and their packing oil, and some of the fennel fronds, along with ¼ cup of extra-virgin olive oil, and process until everything is well puréed. Set aside in a bowl.
2. In a large saucepan, sauté the onion in the olive oil until it softens. Add the anchovy filets and stir until the anchovies melt and blend with the onions.
3. With a wooden spoon, open up a place in the center of the pan and add the tomato paste. Cook the tomato paste for about a minute or two before blending with the onions and anchovies. Add about 2 cups of water, to thin the paste mixture.
4. Add the puréed fennel and sardine mixture to the sauce and stir to incorporate.
5. Add the puréed San Marzano tomatoes, along with the raisins and toasted pine nuts. (You may need to add another cup of water to the sauce, to thin it a bit more.)
6. Cook on medium heat, partially uncovered, for about 15 minutes. Correct seasonings.

To prepare the cauliflower

1. Prepare the large pot in which you will subsequently cook the pasta. Bring the water to a rolling boil and salt.
2. Remove the outer leaves, root, and stem from the head of the cauliflower and, with a paring knife, separate into large floret clusters.

continued

Carefully add the florets to the boiling water and allow them to cook for about 8 minutes, or until they are tender, yet still firm.

3. With a slotted spoon, remove the cauliflower to a mixing bowl and roughly chop them. Do not discard the cooking water.
4. In the same skillet in which you browned the breadcrumbs, add some olive oil and sauté the chopped onion. When the onion is translucent, add the chopped cauliflower to the skillet and sauté with the onion. Add about 1½ cups of the tomato sauce to the onion-cauliflower mixture and combine. Turn off the heat and set aside the mixture for later assembly.

To prepare the pasta

1. In the same boiling water in which the cauliflower was parboiled, cook the pasta for about 8 to 9 minutes. The pasta will not be fully cooked at this point but will finish cooking in the oven.
2. Drain the bucatini and mix well with about another 1½ cups of the tomato sauce to coat the pasta.

To assemble and finish the dish

1. Preheat the oven to 425°F.
2. Coat the bottom of 9x13x3-inch ceramic or Pyrex baking dish with about a cup of the tomato sauce and distribute about a third of the bucatini on the base of the dish.
3. Spread about half of the cauliflower mixture over the first bucatini layer, and then liberally distribute some of the breadcrumb-cheese mixture over the cauliflower.
4. Nap the surface with a bit of the tomato sauce, being carefully not to oversauce and saturate the dish.
5. Add a second layer in the same manner as the first.
6. Finally, add the remaining bucatini with a dusting of the breadcrumb-cheese mixture and some spoons of the sauce. Before baking,

push down the outer perimeter of the pasta in the dish, to prevent burning.

7. Reserve the remaining sauce and breadcrumbs for service.
8. Bake for 20 to 25 minutes. Allow to rest for 10 to 15 minutes before cutting into wedges for serving. Garnish with some additional tomato sauce and some of the remaining breadcrumb-cheese mixture.
9. Once out of the oven, let it rest before cutting into pieces (like lasagna) and serving.

When the ship arrived in Ecuador, I was invited to serve as a staff escort with a group of the passengers on an overnight excursion to San Cristóbal, the easternmost island in the Galápagos archipelago, where we had the most incredible introduction to the flora and fauna of this remote paradise. We rejoined our fellow passengers on the sixth day of our journey at the ship berth in the port of Callao in the heart of the Peruvian capital, Lima. There were several things on my short to-do list in Lima, including a visit to the Basilica and Convent of Santo Domingo, where the body of sixteenth-century Isabel Flores de Olivia (Saint Rose of Lima) is venerated. As a young girl, Saint Rose expressed the desire to become a nun—a choice that her father strenuously resisted. Nonetheless, at age twenty she took the Dominican habit and lived the life of a Dominican tertiary while continuing to dwell in her parents' home. Santa Rosa is the patroness of the Americas, of the poor and indigenous people of the Americas, and the much beloved patroness of the city of Lima.

I made the short pilgrimage to Santo Domingo with an Irish-born couple—a retired physician and his wife—who had raised their family in Buffalo, New York. Both of them proved to be regular participants in the ship's daily Mass. The wife was a very good cook and had a keen interest in the culinary arts. This proved to be a very important point of connection since she had done a considerable amount of preparation for this voyage and commanded an impressive amount of information about local cuisine.

I was surprised to learn during our trip to Santo Domingo that Lima is considered by some experts to be one of the gastronomical capitals of South America and is revered by some foodies for its vibrant culinary scene. I also learned that ceviche was invented by Peruvians and elevated to a high art in Lima. Of course, later that afternoon, when we were strolling around the town on foot, we noted just how many cevicherías there were and how plentiful were the folks peddling amazing varieties of fresh fish.

Being adventurers, we decided to stop for a late afternoon snack in a little restaurant before we returned to the ship, and there we sampled causa limeña rellena—a traditional Peruvian cold dish made with multiple layers of different ingredients, flavors, and textures.

CAUSA LIMEÑA RELLENA

Peruvian cold layered dish with potato, tuna, tomato, and avocado

Makes 6 to 8 servings

Ingredients

- 2 pounds Yukon Gold potatoes
- ¼ cup vegetable oil
- ½ large red onion
- 2 medium lemons, juiced
- 1 can tuna, packed in oil
- 1 large vine-ripened tomato
- 2 ripe avocados
- 2 hard-boiled eggs
- 8 olives
- 2 cups mayonnaise
- ½ cup minced parsley
- freshly ground black pepper
- kosher salt

Method

1. Peel, quarter, and rinse the potatoes and place them in a pot with cold water and boil them until they are soft enough to mash into a purée.
2. Season the mashed potatoes with salt, pepper, lemon juice, and vegetable oil. Blend well.
3. Drain the canned tuna and mix with the mayonnaise and the finely chopped onion and olives.
4. Using an 8-inch springform cake pan (with the bottom removed), lightly brush the interior sides with olive oil. Place the ring on a serving dish to begin assembling the dish.
5. Spread a first layer of about half of the mashed potatoes inside the ring on the serving plate. Add a layer of the tuna mixture, using it all. Then add all the diced tomatoes, and then the slices of the avocado.
6. Using the remaining mashed potatoes, carefully cover the filling, and with an inverse spatula, smooth out the top layer of the dish.
7. Cover with plastic wrap and refrigerate.
8. Carefully remove the springform mold and garnish with some hard-boiled egg slices, mayonnaise, and a touch of parsley to decorate the dish.
9. Cut into wedges and serve.

On the final night, as we were departing Peru and sailing toward Chile, the *Prinsendam*'s executive chef offered on the dinner menu a simple Peruvian marinated and grilled chicken dish with a delicious aji verde sauce. He paired the grilled chicken with a refreshing side salad. He was more than flattered when I asked him how the dish was prepared, and he quickly noted the ingredients and described the method.

PERUVIAN CHICKEN WITH AJI VERDE

Marinated and grilled chicken pieces with green sauce

Makes 6 to 8 servings

Ingredients

For the chicken

- 1½–2 pounds chicken (thigh or breast, boneless, skinless)

For the marinade

- 4 minced garlic cloves
- 2 tablespoons extra-virgin olive oil
- 2 tablespoons fresh lime juice
- 2 teaspoons honey
- 1 tablespoon ground cumin
- 2 teaspoons regular or smoked paprika
- 1 teaspoon ground coriander
- 1 teaspoon dried oregano, thyme, or marjoram
- 1½ teaspoons kosher salt
- 1 teaspoon light soy sauce

For the Peruvian green sauce

- ½ cup sour cream
- ½ jalapeño pepper, seeded
- 1 garlic clove
- 1 cup chopped cilantro
- ¼ teaspoon kosher salt
- ½ teaspoon fresh lime juice

For the avocado, cucumber, and tomato side salad

- 2 cups diced English cucumber
- 1 large ripe, diced avocado
- 12 cherry or grape tomatoes
- cilantro leaves for garnishing
- extra-virgin olive oil for dressing
- kosher or sea salt
- squeeze of lime juice

Method

1. Preheat a grill to medium-high.

To make the marinade

1. Mince the garlic and place it in a large mixing bowl.
2. Add the oil, lime juice, honey, cumin, paprika, coriander, oregano, salt, and soy sauce, and stir to combine well.
3. Add the chicken pieces to the bowl and stir to coat thoroughly. Cover with plastic wrap and marinate, for about 20 minutes.

To make Peruvian green sauce (aji verde)

1. Place all the ingredients in a food processor fitted with the steel blade. Process until smooth, scraping down the sides with a rubber spatula.

To cook the chicken

1. When the chicken has sufficiently marinated, grill the chicken pieces, searing on both sides. When seared, turn the heat down on the grill or move to a cooler side to allow the chicken to cook through, but do not overcook.

continued

To prepare the side salad

1. Make the salad by placing the diced cucumber in a wide shallow bowl. Add the avocado and the cherry tomatoes that have been cut in half. Sprinkle with salt and freshly ground black pepper and drizzle lightly with olive oil. Finish with a squeeze of lime juice and garnish with some cilantro leaves.
2. Serve the chicken, lightly sauced with the aji verde, and accompanied by some of the refreshing salad.

Our itinerary provided for a total of nine days in Chile, beginning with the northern port cities of Iquique and Antofagasta before arriving in the capital and largest city of Santiago. Santiago is an impressive city that is nestled in a valley and surrounded by the snow-capped Andes. The city center has stately colonial and neoclassical buildings, including its eighteenth-century Catedral Metropolitana along with the Palacio Arzobispal, the main residence of the then-archbishop, Cardinal Ricardo Ezzati Andrellom, S.D.B.

I joined a few of the ship's passengers portside on one of the hop-on, hop-off double-decker buses that offer sightseeing tours of Santiago. This was a wonderfully easy way to see some of the city's principal landmarks, especially the cathedral.

One of the things on my personal to-do list was to visit the Jesuit Colegio San Ignacio, which St. Alberto Hurtado Cruchaga, S.J. (1901–1952), had attended as a young boy. Fr. Hurtado was a Chilean Jesuit, a modern-day champion for the poor and human rights, who established El Hogar de Cristo—houses for the poor. His own father died when he was just four years old. The Hurtado family quickly found itself living on the margins of poverty. Alberto got a firsthand experience of what it felt like to be homeless, marginalized, and dependent upon others for the basic necessities of life. He was very grateful that the Jesuits offered him tuition-free admission to the Colegio San Ignacio. In high school he not only thrived academically, but more importantly, he began to discern a call to the Society of Jesus. He entered the Jesuit novitiate in 1923 when he was twenty-three years old and had fulfilled his military service and completed his studies in law. Ten years after his entrance into the Jesuit order, he was ordained a priest and went on to earn a doctorate in educational psychology in Louvain in 1935. Fr. Hurtado returned to his high school alma mater in 1936 where he taught religion, and also served as a professor of educational psychology at the Pontificia Universidad Católica de Chile.

More than his academic contributions, Hurtado is well-remembered in Santiago for his wide outreach to poor children, women, and men through the houses he established all over Chile to provide people in need with shelter and food and other practical assistance. Someone once observed that Fr. Hurtado was incapable of seeing someone in pain without wanting to remedy it. In 1950, he was diagnosed with pancreatic cancer and died two years later. When Fr. Hurtado was canonized by Pope Benedict XVI in 2005, he was only the second native Chilean to be venerated with sainthood, sharing this honor with St. Teresa of Jesus, O.C.D., of Los Andes (1900–1920). Besides my sharing an affinity with Alberto Hurtado as a fellow Jesuit, it happens that his liturgical feast day is observed on my birthday, August 18—the day on which he died.

I was able to find the school and the Iglesia San Ignacio de Loyola, a Renaissance-style church built in 1872 after the original edifice was destroyed by fire in 1863. The church is painted in tones of pale yellow and white and has two tall domed towers, one a clock tower and the other a bell tower. Fortunately, I arrived in the church just as Mass was beginning, so I was able not only to appreciate the architectural beauty of the nave and sanctuary, but to also hear the magnificent pipe organ. At the end of Mass, I had to hustle back to the center of Santiago to catch the shuttle bus that was conveying passengers back to the ship.

When I returned to the ship I was ravenous, since I had not eaten anything since breakfast. I was fortunate that the Lido restaurant was still serving a delicious caramelized shallot and butternut squash soup with beet crisps. One of the Filipino cooks, one of my weekend parishioners, secured the Holland America Line recipe for me.

CARAMELIZED SHALLOT AND BUTTERNUT SQUASH SOUP WITH BEET CRISPS

Makes 6 to 8 servings

continued

Ingredients

For the butternut squash soup

- 2 tablespoons unsalted butter
- 2 cups peeled and halved shallots
- 4 cloves peeled garlic
- 2 large butternut squash, peeled and roughly diced
- 4 tablespoons maple syrup
- ½ teaspoon ground allspice
- a pinch of freshly grated nutmeg
- 3 cups vegetable stock
- ½ cup heavy cream
- 1 sprig thyme leaves
- salt
- freshly ground black pepper

For the beet crisps

- 1 or 2 large peeled beets
- 1 cup vegetable oil
- flaked sea salt

Method

For the butternut squash soup

1. In a thick-bottomed Dutch oven, heat the butter over medium-low heat.
2. Add shallots and garlic. Cook very slowly, stirring gently until vegetables are golden brown. Add all the squash, 4 tablespoons of maple syrup, allspice, and nutmeg.
3. Cook slowly, covered, until squash begins to soften and the vegetables are coated in the syrup.

4. Add the stock and cream and bring to a light simmer.
5. Add thyme and season with salt and pepper. Adjust with more maple syrup, if required.
6. Let cool slightly and purée with a handheld immersion blender or in batches in a blender. Return to the pot and check seasonings once more.
7. Serve in bowls and garnish with beet crisps just before serving.

For the beet crisps

1. Preheat oven to 200°F.
2. With a mandoline, slice the beet(s) very thin.
3. In a thick-bottomed pan or cast-iron skillet, heat oil to 350°F.
4. Deep-fry small batches of beet slices until slightly browned at the edges.
5. Remove with a slotted spoon and drain on paper towels. Season with sea salt.
6. Place on a baking sheet in the preheated oven to dry out for an hour or leave overnight in a warmed oven, which has been turned off.

One of the visual highlights of this voyage were the two days we spent navigating through the Cockburn Channel. The *Prinsendam* was small enough to make the passage safely through the twin rocks that guard the entrance to this channel. The channel is part of a most scenic route, connecting the Strait of Magellan with the Beagle Channel. The coastline is breathtakingly rich in fjords and glaciers, with many picturesque waterfalls that cascade down the slopes of the cliffs into the channel's waters.

I had first heard about Ferdinand Magellan in the fourth grade at Nazareth School, when Sister Helena held us in rapt attention as she described in wonderfully vivid detail the daring explorations of this Portuguese navigator who set out from Spain in 1519 with a fleet of five ships in search of a western sea route to the Spice Islands. On this hazardous journey he discovered what is now known as the Strait of Magellan, and became the first European to cross the Pacific Ocean. And here we were, making our gentle way along these same straits, which bear his name.

On scenic cruising days like these I celebrated Mass for the passengers at 8 a.m., so as to leave their days otherwise unencumbered. Because of the natural beauty on both sides of the ship, my fellow passengers scurried to claim seats in the prime viewing areas, both inside the ship and on its open decks. When I arrived in the dining room for breakfast on that first morning in the Cockburn Channel, the dining room was sparsely populated. I got engaged in conversation with a young Filipino cook who that day had been assigned to the omelette station.

Ordinarily I eat a very light continental-type breakfast of some fruit and a roll. But on this morning, Allen said: "Father, I want to make a really special omelette for you—a Holland America special." He described it as a fluffy omelette with both asparagus and smoked salmon. As we were chatting, the dining room manager came along, looking to order his own breakfast. When I told him what Allen had just proposed, he decided to join me in sharing an omelette. We sat at a table for two near a window in the Lido dining room and Allen set to work at his craft. It was indeed a wonderfully light and flavorful omelette. Here is Allen's method for making this Holland America offering, which is ample enough to serve two or even three persons.

FLUFFY OMELETTE WITH ASPARAGUS AND SMOKED SALMON

Makes 2 to 3 servings

Ingredients

For the omelette

- 4 separated eggs
- 1 tablespoon melted unsalted butter
- ¼ teaspoon kosher salt
- ¼ teaspoon cream of tartar

For the asparagus and smoked salmon filling

- 1 teaspoon olive oil
- 1 thinly sliced shallot
- ¾ cup fresh asparagus pieces
- salt and pepper
- 1 ounce chopped smoked salmon
- ½ teaspoon fresh lemon juice
- ½ cup grated Parmigiano Reggiano

Method

To prepare the filling

1. Heat the oil in a 12-inch ovenproof nonstick skillet over medium-high heat until the oil shimmers.
2. Add the chopped shallot and cook until it is softened and begins to brown, about 2 minutes.
3. Add the asparagus pieces, a pinch of salt, and some freshly cracked pepper and cook, stirring frequently, until the vegetables are crisp-tender, 5 to 7 minutes.
4. Transfer the asparagus mixture to a bowl and stir in salmon and lemon juice.

To prepare the omelette

1. Adjust the rack to the middle position and preheat the oven to 375°F.
2. Whisk the egg yolks, melted butter, and salt together in bowl.
3. Place the egg whites in bowl of a stand mixer and sprinkle cream of tartar over surface. Fit the stand mixer with a whisk attachment and whip the egg whites on medium-low speed until foamy, 2 to 2½ minutes. Increase speed to medium-high and whip until stiff peaks just start to form, 2 to 3 minutes.

continued

4. Fold the egg yolk mixture into egg whites until no white streaks remain.
5. Heat another tablespoon of butter in a 12-inch ovenproof nonstick skillet over medium-high heat, swirling to coat bottom of pan.
6. When the butter begins to foam, quickly add the egg mixture, spreading into an even layer with a spatula.
7. Remove the pan from the heat and gently sprinkle the filling and Parmigiano Reggiano evenly over top of omelette.
8. Transfer to oven and cook until center of omelette springs back when lightly pressed, about 4½ minutes for a slightly wet omelette and 5 minutes for a dry omelette.
9. Run a spatula around edges of the omelette to loosen, shaking gently to release. Slide omelette onto cutting board and let stand for 30 seconds. Using spatula, fold omelette in half.
10. Cut omelette in half crosswise and serve immediately.

In the matter of a few days, we went from wearing summer-weight clothing in the streets of Lima to donning sweaters and windbreakers to contend with the strong, cold winds as we were entering the waters around Cape Horn in southern Chile's Tierra del Fuego archipelago, where the Pacific Ocean meets the Atlantic. Our Dutch-born captain was sober as he described the navigational challenges around Kaap Hoorn, the Dutch name for what the Chileans call Cabo de Hornos. The captain spoke matter-of-factly about a perfect storm of hazards we might encounter from the rocky coastal shoals, frigid winds, massive waves, stray floating icebergs, and strong, ice-choked ocean currents. At Mass the next day, there were several fervent prayers for the ship's captain and crew as he brought us safely into port at the bottom of the world in Ushuaia. From there, we would cross the Drake Passage to Antarctica. There were also prayers for the many seafarers who had in years past perished in ships that were destroyed while navigating these same formidable waters.

There was a little laughter among my table companions that evening as we were docked in Ushuaia when on the dessert menu appeared one of Holland America's signature confections, Grand Marnier Chocolate Volcano Cake. Was this a subtle nod to Cabo de Hornos? I think all six of us at the table ordered this rich, chocolate confection, and it was not difficult securing the recipe from one of my shipboard parishioners, who was one of the pastry chefs. It's a really simple cake to make.

GRAND MARNIER CHOCOLATE VOLCANO CAKE

Makes 6 to 8 servings

Ingredients

- 1 pound unsalted butter
- 12 ounces bittersweet chocolate
- 1 cup sugar
- ½ teaspoon kosher salt
- ½ cup flour
- ¼ cup cocoa powder
- 2 teaspoons baking powder
- 2 teaspoons Grand Marnier
- 1 teaspoon grated orange zest
- 3 whole eggs
- 3 egg yolks
- 3 egg whites
- pure vanilla extract

Method

1. Preheat oven to 375°F.
2. In a baking pan with about a 2- or 3-inch rim, arrange 6 to 8 oven-proof porcelain ramekins or Pyrex glass dishes.
3. In a double boiler over simmering water, melt together 12 ounces (3 sticks) of butter along with bittersweet chocolate. Set aside to cool to lukewarm.

continued

4. In a stand mixer with the whisk attachment, combine the remaining 4 ounces (1 stick) of room-temperature butter with 1 cup of sugar and beat until creamed and fluffy.
5. On low speed, add in eggs and egg yolks—one by one—mixing about 30 seconds between each addition.
6. Add the cooled melted butter and chocolate, the Grand Marnier, and the orange zest and mix until just combined.
7. Sift together the flour, cocoa powder, salt, and baking powder.
8. Add the dry ingredients into the butter, egg, and chocolate mixture and blend for 3 minutes at high speed.
9. With a handheld mixer, beat the egg whites and remaining quarter-cup of sugar and gently fold into the chocolate mixture, trying not to deflate the egg whites.
10. Fill each of the ramekins with the cake mixture and bake for about 15 to 20 minutes.
11. Serve with some softened ice cream or freshly whipped cream, flavored with some grated orange rind, and perhaps a splash of Grand Marnier.

How does one describe the awe-inspiring majesty of the earth's southernmost continent, which is both pristine and unspoiled? I am afraid that I will run out of superlatives in talking about Antarctica. The day and a half crossing of the Drake Passage was easy and uneventful. Later, in reflecting on the entire Antarctic exploration, the captain would comment that in his more than twenty years of making these journeys, our 2017 passage was the smoothest in memory and the days spent scenically cruising in Antarctica were among the best. For the three days we experienced brilliant sunshine, light winds, calm seas, and spectacular, rich displays of marine wildlife. Having a lecturer on board who was an experienced naturalist, we were introduced to colonies of penguins and many different species of seals, whales, and seabirds. It was incredible to watch albatrosses with wingspans of more than eleven feet soaring effortlessly over our ship, without so much as a flap of their wings.

For me, it was a picture of the ideal calm we all long for. And we were introduced to more species of petrels and prions than I can remember.

Our captain was able to take us through the eerie stillness of the iceberg-dotted waters of the bays and islands of the Palmer Archipelago, off the northern tip of the long Antarctic Peninsula. For me it was a deeply moving and spiritual experience, and I noted that even the ship seemed to grow reverently more quiet as we glided through these hauntingly silent coves and inlets. We were also fortunate to have some of the scientists who were assigned to the research stations on the continent board our ship and provide enriching lectures about the continent's marine and terrestrial ecosystems. These presentations by various geologists, geophysicists, glaciologists, and marine biologists amplified and enriched our collective understanding and experience of Antarctica.

We saw only a bare fraction of the 5.5 million square miles of ice cover that make up this continent. The experience brought back to mind "God's Grandeur" by the Jesuit poet Gerard Manley Hopkins, S.J.:

The world is charged with the grandeur of God.
It will flame out, like shining from shook foil;
It gathers to a greatness, like the ooze of oil
Crushed. Why do men then now not reck his rod?
Generations have trod, have trod, have trod;
And all is seared with trade; bleared, smeared with toil;
And wears man's smudge and shares man's smell: the soil
Is bare now, nor can foot feel, being shod.

And for all this, nature is never spent;
There lives the dearest freshness deep down things;
And though the last lights off the black West went
Oh, morning, at the brown brink eastward, springs—
Because the Holy Ghost over the bent
World broods with warm breast and with ah! bright wings.

Leaving Antarctica, we headed to Stanley Island in the frigid, South Atlantic Falkland Islands, which the Argentinians still refer to as Islas Malvinas. We arrived in port on a bleak rainy Sunday morning in the archipelago's remote capital. Walking on foot, I joined with a couple of other passengers in a worship service in the Anglican Christ Church Cathedral, much to the surprise of the presiding priest and the handful of local worshippers. I suspect that the collection box that day reflected the fact that a cruise ship had landed.

It was remarkable that there are virtually no trees on the island because of the relentless, prevailing winds, but as we walked along the main streets of Stanley, the little cottage-style homes all reflected their English roots, with small containers brimming with flowering, summer annuals. It felt as though we had arrived in the English countryside, even down to the local police wearing the traditional bobby's helmet. Folks from the ship were scrambling to find some British pounds to pay for the scones with local diddle-dee berry jam and coffee. When I inquired about Falkland recipes with the woman who ran a small café in which we had stopped to have a cup of tea and escape temporarily from the wind and rain, she spoke about a typical English-style lamb stew, which I scribbled down on a napkin.

FALKLAND ISLAND BRAISED LAMB STEW

Makes 8 servings

Ingredients

- 2 pounds boneless lamb pieces
- ½ cup extra-virgin olive oil
- 6 to 8 cups chicken or beef stock
- 1 large diced onion
- 1 clove minced garlic
- 3 tablespoons all-purpose flour
- 10 baby carrots
- 1 washed and sliced leek
- 1 sliced zucchini
- 6 chopped scallions (whites and green)
- salt and pepper

- fresh thyme leaves

Method

1. Preheat oven to 350°F.
2. Season the lamb pieces with salt and pepper and sauté in olive oil in a Dutch oven until well browned.
3. Remove meat from the pot and set aside. In the same Dutch oven, sauté the onions until they become translucent.
4. Add the flour and mix with the onions to cook off the flour taste and form a roux.
5. Add in the stock and bring to a boil, stirring continually.
6. Add back the browned lamb pieces and the other prepared seasonal vegetables and herbs.
7. Cover the Dutch oven with a lid and braise in a preheated oven for about 40 minutes, or until the meat is tender.

It was a delight to feel the warmth again as our ship arrived in the harbor of Punta del Este, a beach resort town in Uruguay. Some people have referred to this Atlantic coastal getaway as the St. Tropez or Monte Carlo of South America. Arriving as we did in the middle of February, when summer begins to slip into autumn, we discovered that many of the tourists who regularly flock to Punta del Este in December and January had already departed, leaving the beach promenades virtually empty. Most of my fellow passengers were content to simply take leisurely strolls along the long stretches of seashore, imagining that just a few weeks earlier, these same beaches and strands would have been packed with tourists spilling out of yachts, luxury hotels, and casinos to sunbathe and deepen their tans.

One of my memories of our brief time in this southern Uruguayan coastal town was my introduction to a popular local sandwich the Uruguayos call *chivito*. These supersized and very filling sandwiches were being sold in *chiviterías* everywhere. Being a culinary adventurer, I definitely wanted to sample one. I guess one could say that a chivito is to Uruguay what a cheeseburger is to the United States, or a cubano to the people of Cuba. It did not take long for me to discover that there are many permutations and combinations of ingredients used in this iconic sandwich, but through several animated conversations with some of the locals in Punta del Este who spoke a little English, I settled on this set of ingredients and methods of assembly to create an authentic chivito.

EL CHIVITO DE URUGUAY

Uruguayan steak, bacon, ham, and cheese sandwich

Makes 4 servings

Ingredients

- 4 large potato or bulky rolls, sliced horizontally
- 4 thinly pounded minute beef steaks
- 8 slices apple-smoked bacon
- 4 thin slices of boiled ham
- 4 slices mozzarella cheese
- 4 thin slices beefsteak tomato
- 4 sunny-side-up fried eggs
- Boston, iceberg, or romaine lettuce leaves
- 4 tablespoons ketchup
- 4 tablespoons mayonnaise
- kosher salt and ground black pepper
- 2 tablespoons butter

Method

1. Preheat the broiler unit in the oven.
2. In a large skillet over medium heat on the stovetop, cook the bacon until crispy. Remove from pan and drain on paper towels.
3. Quickly sauté the minute steaks in the residual bacon fat. When seared on each side, remove to paper towels to drain and lightly salt.

4. Pour off the bacon fat and wipe the fry pan with paper towels. Add a pat of butter to the warm skillet and fry the eggs as you desire. Traditionally the chivito is made with sunny-side-up eggs, but you can make the eggs over easy, if you prefer.
5. Spread the inside of the buns with a mixture of the ketchup and mayonnaise. Place the lettuce pieces on the bottom halves of the buns.
6. Top each sandwich with 2 slices of bacon, a slice of the beef, a slice of ham, a slice of tomato, and a slice of mozzarella.
7. Place the uncovered sandwiches under the broiler briefly just to melt the cheese and remove from the broiler.
8. Add a fried egg over the melted cheese and top with the other half of the bun.

On the following bright and sunny morning, we arrived very early in the nearby capital city of Uruguay, the picturesque city of Montevideo, on the Río de la Plata. Fortunately, the ship had docked within easy walking distance from the central square of Plaza Independencia and Montevideo's charming Ciudad Vieja or Old Town. The ornate Metropolitan Cathedral (Catedral de Montevideo), dedicated to the Immaculate Conception of the Mother of God and to the apostles Philip and James, was one of the first places we visited upon disembarkation. Situated on the Plaza Ituzaingo in the impressive center of the Old Town, the church served for more than two hundred years as the center of the Archdiocese of Montevideo, and home to its archbishop.

As we were about to exit the cathedral, by chance we encountered the Salesian Archbishop of Montevideo, Cardinal Daniel Sturla, whom I immediately recognized. The Uruguayan cardinal is a very good friend of Pope Francis and is a warm and friendly man with an easy smile. My fellow companions were impressed that the cardinal had stopped to chat with us informally and to offer some brief comments about the history of the cathedral building. We were amused when the cardinal informed us that the cathedral once had been used as a citadel. The cardinal also suggested that we might like to visit the Colegio Seminario and the Church of the Sacred Heart, which the Jesuits had built and run at the end of the nineteenth century. I was happy to accompany our little group to this school and church, which is still operating, educating some 1,800 young Uruguayan *porteños*, women and men from this port city.

By midday we headed to the Mercado del Puerto, the old port market where lunch opportunities were endless, with more grilled meat offerings than one could possibly image. Uruguayans love their asado, a carnivore's delight of barbequed meats and organ foods. We learned a lovely phrase from the man who was tending the grill station where we decided to dine. He wished for us "*Salud, dinero, amor, y tiempo para disfrutarlo*" (health, wealth, love, and the time to enjoy it). What better prayer could anyone make?

After our midday feast we needed to work off some of the calories before we strolled back along the riverside to the ship. We were advised to purchase some local *alfajores*, delicious sandwich cookies filled with dulce de leche. When we arrived back at the port, the custom agent asked me, "*Como estás, Señor?*" To which I could only reply, "*Todo bien, todo bien.*"

The next day was somewhat overcast as we arrived in the estuary of the Río de la Plata in Buenos Aires. The ship provided a complimentary shuttle bus that brought passengers and crew members into the heart of this cosmopolitan capital city of Argentina. The bus left us at the foot of a long walking street where shopkeepers were just beginning to open for a day of commerce. Before long, we arrived on foot in the Plaza de Mayo, with its many grand nineteenth-century buildings, including two that immediately claimed my attention. The first was the Casa Rosada, Argentina's equivalent to the White House. Of course, I had flashbacks to those famous pictures of Eva Péron, speaking passionately from the Casa Rosada's central balcony to the throngs of Argentinians gathered beneath. We all recall the memorable song "Don't Cry for Me Argentina" by Andrew Lloyd Webber and Tim Rice for the Broadway musical *Evita*, and Madonna's portrayal of this iconic woman in the film version in 1996. Eva is revered almost as a saint by the Argentinian people, who even a century after her birth still remember her passionate speeches and actions on behalf of the underprivileged and disenfranchised, whom she called *descamisados* (folks without shirts). I had a particular desire to visit the Metropolitan Cathedral of the Archdiocese of Buenos Aires, where Jorge Mario Bergoglio, S.J., had served as archbishop from February 1998 until his election as pope in March 2013. Walking from the Casa Rosada, I stood in the middle of the square in front of its massive white obelisk, the Pirámide de Mayo, where I had a panoramic view of the cathedral's façade, composed of twelve immense neoclassical

Hellenic columns representing the twelve apostles of Jesus. Atop these columns in a sweeping triangular frontispiece is a relief that recalls the reunion of Joseph—who had been sold into slavery by his jealous brothers to Egyptians merchants—with his father Jacob and his older brothers.

Like many cathedrals of its era, the interior naves and columns and its high, vaulted ceiling are richly decorated in neo-Romanesque and neo-baroque architectural styles. I was particularly struck by the archbishop's chair in the sanctuary. In many cathedrals the *cathedra*, or presiding chair, resembles the throne of a king or emperor, elevated and lavishly adorned. I do not know what the Buenos Aires cathedra might have looked like originally, but Cardinal Bergoglio had it replaced and for his fifteen years as archbishop he used a simple wooden chair as his cathedra. The chair still remains exactly where he left it when he departed Buenos Aires for Rome.

There are so many wonderful stories of Pope Francis, and he remains a very cherished person among the faithful of Buenos Aires. Like the name of the city itself, Pope Francis was for his people "Good Air." He was a simple pastor, living almost unnoticed among his people, forsaking the splendor of the archiepiscopal palace that adjoins the cathedral for a modest apartment in a working-class neighborhood. He took the subway and the buses rather than using a chauffeured car. He cooked simple meals for himself most evenings, often commenting that his people were poor and that he chose to live among them and like them. He was a tireless voice for social justice and frequently a thorn in the side of the Argentinian government.

Born, raised, and educated in Buenos Aires, Pope Francis entered the Jesuit novitiate in 1958 and was ordained to the priesthood in 1969. At the age of thirty-seven he was appointed to serve as the provincial superior of the Jesuits in Argentina, during a time of great unrest in both the civil society, the church, and among Jesuits. It was in 1992 that at the strong urging of Buenos Aires Cardinal Antonio Quarracino, Pope St. John Paul II appointed Fr. Bergoglio as an auxiliary bishop to assist the cardinal in the administration of the archdiocese. Five years later, again at the ailing cardinal's insistent request, Bishop Bergoglio was appointed as coadjutor bishop with the right to succession upon the cardinal's death, which occurred eight months later.

As is true of many cathedrals, the cathedral in Buenos Aires contains many works of art that attract a visitor's attention. One of my personal discoveries in the left nave was a relatively contemporary artwork—an image of the Christ of Good Love, *Cristo de Buen Amor*. I learned that it had been a gift to the cathedral in 1979 by two of Argentina's famous soccer players, Héctor Scotta and Daniel Bertoni. The Argentinians refer to this sacred image as the "Christ of the Footballers." It is no secret that Pope Francis remains a big fan of soccer and of Argentina's San Lorenzo national team. Although this gift was made well before Bergoglio became archbishop, I thought how he must cherish that image of Christ in front of which he passed many times.

From the cathedral, I walked the few short blocks on the Bolivar St. Montserrat to the oldest church in Buenos Aires, the Jesuit Iglesia de San Ignacio. The building still retains aspects of the seventeenth century during which it was constructed. It was completed in 1675. There is a French phrase that says, "*les murs ont la parole*"—the very walls tell the story. That is true of this historic building, which, after the expulsion of the Jesuits in the later part of the eighteenth century, served for a while as the city's cathedral. During the resistance against an early nineteenth-century invasion by British troops, San Ignacio housed soldiers and military leaders. During a period of social unrest in the 1950s the historic church was torched, but fortunately the fire did not destroy it.

Rounding out my two days in Buenos Aires, I was able to join a group that was touring the Teatro Colón. Being an aficionado of opera, I have made it a point to visit as many of the world's great opera houses as travels permit. In Italy, that involved performances in Milano's Teatro alla Scala, Napoli's Teatro di San Carlo, and the Teatro dell'Opera di Roma. I have been blessed to witness performances in London's Royal Opera House at Covent Garden and in the Sydney Opera House, and while a student in Paris, I scraped together enough French francs to attend performances at l'Opéra de Paris. On my one visit to Vienna, in addition to visiting the residence of Sigmund Freud, the other must-see was the Weiner Staatsoper, although unfortunately not for a performance. And of course I was the beneficiary of being invited to New York's Metropolitan Opera.

Even though it was not opera season, I wanted to visit the early twentieth-century Teatro Cólon in Buenos Aires. It was not a disappointing experience. I was able to join a small group of visitors, with an excellent, English-speaking guide, for a tour of the opera house building that included a visit backstage. The Colón has exceptional acoustics. Although the opera house had recently undergone a major restoration in 2010, it seemed as if we were stepping back into the late nineteenth century. The room's crystal chandeliers and gilt work were glistening.

One of the young people in our group was an opera student. The tour guide allowed her to sing the Puccini aria from *La Bohème*, "*Quando m'en vo' soletta.*" It is to be hoped that the experience was as unforgettable for the young soprano as it was for the appreciative audience of about a dozen tourists for whom her voice made the Teatro Colón come alive. Our tour guide mentioned some of the great singers of the twentieth century who had performed on this stage, including tenors like Enrico Caruso, Plácido Domingo, and Luciano Pavarotti. When the guide recalled the name of Richard Tucker, I felt a special closeness because of my friendship with his children and grandchildren.

That evening, back on the *Prinsendam*, the chef had prepared a menu of Argentinian dishes, including *guiso*, a rich stew. The Prinsendam's executive chef was more than willing to share his approach to preparing this thick, flavorful soup. I found the addition of the diced apricots to be a surprising, but delightful garnish. *Buen provecho!*

ARGENTINIAN GUISO

Argentinian beef and vegetable soup

Makes 10 to 12 servings

Ingredients

For the soup

- ½ cup diced beef
- ½ cup diced carrots
- ¼ cup diced sweet potato
- ¼ cup diced Yukon Gold potato
- ¼ cup diced butternut squash
- ¼ cup diced onion
- 5 cloves minced garlic
- ½ cup diced tomato
- 2 tablespoons tomato paste
- 10 cups beef stock

continued

- 2 tablespoons flour
- 2 tablespoons unsalted butter
- kosher salt
- ground black pepper
- 1 teaspoon minced thyme leaves
- 1 bay leaf
- ¼ cup frozen corn kernels

For the garnish

- ¼ cup chopped parsley
- ¼ cup dried diced apricots, briefly soaked in hot water

Method

1. In a large saucepan or Dutch oven, sauté the onion, thyme, basil, and garlic.
2. In a separate skillet, brown the beef on high heat.
3. Transfer the browned beef to the saucepan and combine with the sautéed onions. Add the tomato paste and caramelize.
4. Stir in the flour and cook for 5 minutes before adding the stock.
5. Bring the mixture to a low simmer and cook soup until beef is almost tender.
6. Add the tomatoes, carrots, potatoes, squash, and more beef broth to cover all the ingredients.
7. Season with salt and pepper to taste.
8. Cook over low heat for 15 to 20 minutes until all the vegetables and meat are tender.
9. Add the corn and check seasonings.
10. Serve in soup bowls and garnish with parsley and apricots.

Our ship docked in Rio de Janeiro just as the city was preparing for the culmination of Mardi Gras festivities. There were three things that I wanted to accomplish during our brief visit in Rio: to stroll the concrete promenade along famous Copacabana and Ipanema beaches; to witness the massive floats and parading samba schools in the famous Sambadrome; and to make a pilgrimage to the peak of the 2,300-foot Corovada mountain in the Tijuca Forest National park to pray at the feet of the iconic statue of Christ the Redeemer.

On the first morning I joined a couple of folks who shared my interest to walk and explore. We took the shuttle bus from the pier into the city center, which was located a few blocks from the beaches. It was a slightly overcast but sultry day. Fortified with hats and sunblock, we began our leisurely stroll along these world-famous beaches. Since it was the weekend before Ash Wednesday, the beaches were packed. It was a festival for the eyes, with so many scantily clad people sporting deep tans, all in a holiday mood. It was everything one might imagine Rio to be.

Along the strand we came upon a little food cart where there were piles of little cheese breads, which we discovered were called *pão de queijo*. Along with a bottle of cold water, they provided a perfect snack food. These breads require few ingredients and are simply made. The Brazilians use a local cheese, similar to a Mexican queso fresco, but I have found that a mild Greek or French feta or some ricotta salata or even some finely grated Monterey Jack work beautifully in this thin batter. A food processer or blender does all the work. Tapioca flour is readily available in many markets or online. Brazilians, I discovered, use a lot of tapioca flour.

PÃO DE QUEIJO

Brazilian cheese bread

Makes 18 cheese rolls

Ingredients

- 1 egg
- ⅓ cup extra-virgin olive oil
- ⅔ cup whole milk

continued

- 1½ cups tapioca flour
- 1 teaspoon kosher salt
- ½ cup of grated queso fresco, mild feta, ricotta salata, or Monterey Jack cheese

Method

1. Preheat oven to 400°F.
2. Grease a mini muffin tin. This recipe will make about 18 small cheese rolls.
3. In a food processor, combine egg, olive oil, milk, tapioca flour, salt, and cheese. Blend until a smooth, thin batter forms.
4. Allow the batter to rest for 10 minutes.
5. Fill the greased muffin tins with the batter and bake in preheated oven until puffy and golden brown, about 15 to 20 minutes.
6. Allow the cheese rolls to cool in the pan for 5 minutes before removing to a cooling rack.

The *Prinsendam* had prepurchased a block of tickets for the Sambadrome spectacular on each of the nights that the ship was in port. There are more than a hundred samba schools in Rio de Janeiro. I learned from the ship's location manager that these are not truly schools for instruction, but rather collections of people with a passion for samba performance. These groups work out their routines and costumes throughout the year in preparation for the massive parades in the Sambadrome during the Carnaval do Brasil.

I also discovered that foreign tourist tickets are very expensive, well beyond my budget: the ship was charging passengers $500 for each of these prime tickets for the open boxes in the Sambódromo Marquês de Sapucaí, and providing round-trip transportation to the colorful spectacle. I had resigned myself that I would have to settle for watching TV broadcasts of the events until, expectedly, one of the couples approached me on the days before we were due to arrive in Rio asking if I wanted to be their guest for this once-in-a-lifetime experience. I was astounded by their generosity.

There was a drenching rain on the night of the performance. I thought that the event would surely be cancelled, but as the old aphorism suggests, the show must go on. The ship provided us with hooded plastic rain ponchos and disposable plastic shoe coverings, and novel umbrellas that fit like crowns over our heads. There we were, watching one of the most famous events of Rio's Carnival in unrelenting, driving rain. But the samba schools danced on as if it were a perfectly clear late summer evening.

I had the haunting fear that if any of us developed pneumonia from sitting for several hours in the pelting rain, we would never forgive each other. And of course, the thought did cross my mind several times that for the privilege of sitting in an open box in a torrential rain, this couple had spent a small fortune for the three of us. The following night, the weather was dry and clear. When some of the passengers who had joined us on the rainy night in the Sambadrome asked me why I did not have greater influence with God over weather, I jokingly replied that as a priest I was involved in *sales*, not *management*.

Within walking distance of the ship's terminal there were many street festivals with continuous music and endless dancing. The Brazilians were extremely welcoming. They beckoned us to join with them in their merriment.

Early on the morning after our drenching debacle in the Sambadrome, three of us rented a taxi from the ship to the mountaintop site of Christ the Redeemer. The site remains a revered cultural icon for the people of Rio de Janeiro. Standing almost 100 feet tall on a 26-foot pedestal, the statue's outstretched arms seem to be embracing the whole world. The morning was clear, and the sun made the white, cross-shaped landmark image of Christ glisten.

Once again, we were fortunate. A few years earlier the statue had undergone a massive restoration, so we were treated to an almost pristine experience of its massive beauty. Arriving early in the morning was fortuitous. The waiting times to board the various elevators conveying visitors to the summit were minimal, as the crowds had yet to swell.

I was surprised to find that there was a small chapel that had been built into the base of the statue. In October 2006, on the seventy-fifth anniversary of the statue's completion, then Archbishop of Rio, Cardinal Eusébio Scheid, S.C.I., consecrated the chapel in honor of Our Lady of the Apparition. We had some time to sit quietly in this sacred space, to pray for a peace the world so desperately needed.

As we were taking some panoramic photos of the city of Rio de Janeiro from this incredible perspective, we encountered four members of the kitchen crew from the ship, including one of the Filipino pastry chefs who was a member of my Sunday worship community. When I inquired how they had managed to get away from their respective jobs to make the trek up the mountain, they said they were on an hour break and had hired a taxi to bring them to see this statue. The pastry chef was still in her kitchen whites. She told me that she had just completed baking trays of chewy brownies. As an acknowledged chocoholic, I had a particular fondness for brownies. I asked her if it might be possible to have a copy of Holland America's recipe. Although her recipe was for volume production, on the following Sunday, just after Mass, she passed me an adapted recipe.

CHEWY CHOCOLATE BROWNIES

Holland America Line

Makes 12 to 18 servings

Ingredients

- ⅓ cup Dutch-process cocoa
- 1½ teaspoons instant espresso powder
- ½ cup plus 2 tablespoons boiling water
- 2 ounces unsweetened dark chocolate, finely chopped
- ½ cup plus 2 tablespoons vegetable oil
- 4 tablespoons melted unsalted butter
- 2 large eggs
- 2 large egg yolks
- 2 teaspoons vanilla extract
- 2½ cups granulated sugar
- 1¾ cups all-purpose flour
- ¾ teaspoon kosher salt
- 6 ounces bittersweet chocolate, cut into ½-inch pieces

Method

1. Adjust the oven rack to lowest position and preheat the oven to 350°F.
2. Make a foil sling for 13x9-inch baking pan by folding two long sheets of aluminum foil; the first sheet should be 13 inches wide and second sheet should be 9 inches wide. Lay sheets of foil in pan perpendicular to each other with extra foil hanging over edges of pan, smoothing the foil flush to pan, and lightly grease the foil with butter.
3. Whisk cocoa, espresso powder, and boiling water together in large bowl until smooth. Add unsweetened dark chocolate and whisk until the chocolate is melted.
4. Whisk in oil and melted butter.
5. Whisk in eggs, additional yolks, and vanilla and blend until smooth.
6. Whisk in the sugar until it is fully incorporated.
7. Add flour and salt and mix with rubber spatula until combined.
8. Fold in bittersweet chocolate pieces.
9. Scrape the batter into the prepared baking pan and smooth the top.
10. Bake the brownies 30 to 35 minutes or until a toothpick inserted halfway between edge and center comes out with a few moist crumbs attached.
11. Let brownies cool in the baking pan for 1½ hours.
12. Using foil overhang, lift brownies from pan. Transfer to wire rack and let cool completely, about an additional hour. Cut into 2-inch squares.

I am certain that all of us harbor images of what travel on the mighty Amazon River might look like. To a great extent, mine was shaped almost exclusively by Johnny Weissmuller in his career-defining roles of Tarzan and later of Jungle Jim. On many Saturday afternoons in the late 1940s and early 1950s my mother or grandmother would take me to a movie theatre to see the latest MGM or RKO film of Tarzan, the Ape Man, clothed only in a loincloth, forever rescuing or looking after the ever-beautiful Jane, and Cheeta, the chimpanzee. I recall being mesmerized by the many TV episodes of Jungle Jim.

As our ship departed from the port city of Icorarci (Belém) in northeastern Brazil, a gateway to Brazil's lower Amazon region, I was expecting that the river would resemble my Jungle Jim images of yesteryear.

I expected the Rio Amazonas, as the Brazilian refer to it, to be a relatively narrow river on which our ship would have to carefully navigate. I was surprised by its width, the amount of traffic and commerce it supported, and the continually changing coloration of its waters. The Amazon is one of the world's longest rivers, spanning almost 4,000 miles from its headwaters in Peru to the place where our ship entered it as it spilled into the Atlantic Ocean.

During our days of scenic cruising—and especially as we ventured on smaller side-trip excursions more deeply into its rainforests—we saw many species of birds, reptiles, and animals we'd previously encountered only in captivity. I remember being in a canoe on one of our excursions along a jungle tributary, with the dense canopy of the forest shading us, when our guide pointed out with his paddle an anaconda swimming in the water near our boat. The snake must have been twenty feet or more long, with its thick, powerful, and menacing body moving swiftly through the water. The guide took it all in stride. On another excursion we got to swim with a *boto*, a pink-hued river dolphin. We were continually admonished to keep our hands inside the boat, lest piranhas relieve us of a finger or two.

For some of my fellow travelers, especially those more naturally skittish about creepy and crawly things, the Amazon's wildlife, flora, and fauna presented challenges. There were insects galore, exotic yet toxic plants, and more spiders, frogs, and snakes than one could begin to catalogue. One of our ship's lecturers reminded us that the Amazon rainforest's ecosystem is home to more than 80,000 plant species and 30 million animal and reptile species. This proved to be a staggering realization.

Our major destination on this Amazon discovery voyage was Manaus, the largest city in the Amazon and about nine hundred miles inland from the place where our ship entered the river. The three days and two overnights in Manaus afforded us many opportunities to explore some of the nearby tributaries and backwaters.

One of my personal objectives in Manaus was to visit the opera house. Who would expect to find a grand Belle Époque opera house in the middle of a jungle? The construction and history of the Teatro Amazonas is a fascinating story. With the invention of the automobile, demand for rubber increased. The rubber export industry in the Amazon boomed, and this boom created wealthy "rubber barons." In the latter part of the nineteenth century, some of these successful entrepreneurs partnered with the government to design and build this impressive concert hall. They engaged Portuguese engineers and architects to design a neoclassical building and hired an Italian architect to oversee its construction. The jungle opera house hosted its first production—*La Gioconda*—on New Year's Eve in 1897. The opera featured Enrico Caruso as the lead tenor.

When synthetic rubber was invented at the turn of the century, the fortunes of these major benefactors of the Teatro Amazonas were quickly depleted, and the newly built opera house closed down for the next ninety years. In 2001 the government decided to reinvest in this landmark. The opera house is once again welcoming orchestras, dance troupes, and singers to enliven its stage. Surprisingly, during the day the opera house is open to visitors to wander its halls, stairways, and loggias.

Our visit to Manaus was in the off season, so we were not fortunate enough to experience the opera house's acoustics. The interior is reminiscent of any similar opera house one might see in Europe; the rubber barons had done their job well. They filled the building with French furniture and Italian marble, and they crowned the opera house with an impressive tiled dome.

Many cultures have their version of fish stew, and the Amazon has its own. I sampled this simple dish in Manaus. For the life of me, I cannot tell which fish they used in this preparation, but it was delicious. The addition of freshly squeezed lime juice just before service brightened the flavors immensely.

MOQUECA BAIANA

Traditional Brazilian Amazon fish stew

Makes 4 servings

Ingredients

For the fish

- 1 pound firm, boneless white fish filet (halibut, cod, monkfish, snapper, or catfish)

continued

- 2 tablespoons freshly squeezed lime juice
- ¼ teaspoon kosher salt
- freshly grated black pepper
- 3 tablespoons extra-virgin olive oil

For the broth

- 1½ tablespoons extra-virgin olive oil
- 3 cloves minced garlic
- 1 diced onion
- 1 sliced red bell pepper
- 1½ teaspoons granulated sugar
- 1 teaspoon ground cumin
- 1 tablespoon mild paprika
- 1 teaspoon cayenne pepper
- ½ teaspoon kosher salt
- 14 ounces coconut milk
- 14-ounce can peeled crushed tomatoes
- 1 cup fish, chicken, or vegetable stock

Method

To prepare the fish

1. Cut the fish filets into 1½-inch cubes.
2. Combine the fish, lime juice, oil, salt, and pepper in a bowl. Cover with plastic wrap and refrigerate for about a half hour.
3. Heat a small amount of olive oil in a large skillet over high heat. Sauté the marinated fish pieces until a light golden brown. Remove from the skillet and set aside on a plate.

For the broth

1. In the same sauté pan used to sauté the fish, add a bit more olive oil and cook the onion until it becomes translucent, then add the garlic and cook for an additional 30 seconds.
2. Add the sliced red bell pepper and cook for another 2 minutes.
3. In a Dutch oven, add the stock, coconut milk, and crushed tomatoes, along with the sugar, cumin, paprika, cayenne, and salt.
4. Over medium heat, cook the broth for about 15 minutes before adding back the sautéed onion, garlic, and bell pepper mixture.
5. Simmer the broth for an additional ten minutes and correct the seasoning.
6. Add back the fish to the broth and reheat for about 2 minutes, and stir through another tablespoon of freshly squeezed lime juice before serving.

In mid-March when the *Prinsendam* arrived back at its berth in Ft. Lauderdale, most of the passengers were ready to disembark from their seventy-four-day odyssey in South America. I was preparing to welcome a new congregation of adventurers for the next leg of the journey for the round-trip Mediterranean voyage. We would return to this same Ft. Lauderdale port in mid-May at the conclusion of this long ocean odyssey.

To my great pleasure, as I was meandering around the registration lounge late one morning I encountered several individuals and couples who had traveled on previous cruises on which I had served as chaplain. It was like a grand reunion of friends who had not seen each other for several years. One of the gentlemen, who served faithfully in his home parish as a reader, immediately approached me and announced that he would be honored to fill this liturgical function whenever I might need him.

On the first evening on board I was scheduled to preside and preach at a 5 o'clock Mass immediately after the conclusion of the obligatory muster safety drill. As I was vesting, an older gentleman who was walking with a cane approached me and introduced himself. He was a retired diocesan priest from Florida who had served as a career US Army military chaplain. Although he did not wish to vest and concelebrate, he did say that he would be willing, if desired, to do the readings. He commanded a big, stentorian voice that he used to its full dramatic effect. The entire congregation was happy to welcome his ministry, and he seemed pleased to participate in this way.

The voyage across the Atlantic was smooth. We arrived as scheduled in the Canary Islands, the first of more than thirty ports of call in twelve countries. I had always imagined that the Canary Islands were so named because they must be sanctuary to millions of little yellow pleasantly chirping birds. Our staff destination lecturer quickly corrected my lifelong error by stating, quite authoritatively, that the name derives from the Latin phrase Insula Canaria, which roughly translated means "Dogs' Island." In other words, no pleasantly singing yellow canaries, but an island full of barking and yelping feral dogs.

The archipelago that makes up the Canary Islands is located about 70 miles off the coast of northwestern Africa. I was immediately struck by the beauty of the black-and-white sandy beaches, which gave clear indication of the volcanic origins. We visited Tenerife and its lively capital, Santa Cruz de Tenerife. We also called in at Las Palmas and Gran Canaria.

Many of the passengers were anxious to set foot on firm ground after the transatlantic crossing. The Spanish character and influence within these autonomous communities was unmistakable: if one closed one's eyes, it would not be hard to believe you were in Valencia or Barcelona. Noting the local menus, I quickly concluded that traditional Canarian food used abundant fresh vegetables that must grow well in the subtropical climate and rich volcanic soil of the islands. The preparations of many of the dishes were uncomplicated and delicious.

After enjoying a delightful lunch of simply prepared grilled sea bass and a salad, I was intrigued to taste a local dessert called bienmesabe, which our waiter translated as "it tastes good to me." It was a wonderfully pleasant, mildly sweet purée of ground almonds, egg yolks, lemon zest, and cinnamon served with a generous dollop of sweetened whipped cream.

BIENMESABE

Spanish almond cream dessert

Makes 4 to 6 servings

Ingredients

- 2¼ cups peeled and blanched almonds
- 1½ cups granulated sugar
- 2 cups water
- ½ teaspoon Saigon cinnamon
- 1 lemon
- 3 egg yolks

Method

1. Preheat oven to 375°F.
2. If using raw almonds, blanch and peel the almonds. If using already peeled and blanched almonds, proceed to the next step.
3. Place the blanched almonds on a baking sheet lined with aluminum foil and toast in oven for about 5 to 7 minutes. Keep an eye on the nuts and do not allow them to burn. Allow them to cool slightly.
4. Add the toasted almonds to the bowl a food processor fitted with a steel blade and process until finely ground.
5. In a saucepan, add the 2 cups of water and bring to a boil.
6. Add the sugar and stir to dissolve. Continue boiling until a thin syrup is formed.
7. Add the ground almonds, cinnamon, and finely grated lemon peel and stir to combine.
8. Reduce the heat to low, stirring constantly as the mixture cooks and thickens, about 5 minutes. Remove from heat and allow to cool.

continued

9. When the mixture has cooled for about 30 minutes, beat the egg yolks and then fold them into the pan, stirring constantly. Return pan to medium heat until it boils, then remove from stove and allow to cool.
10. Refrigerate until ready to serve.

When I did not see my fellow priest traveler at morning Mass in Gran Carnaria, I became concerned. I soon encountered his cabin companion, who told me the priest had become ill overnight and had been transported to the hospital. The hospital personnel determined to keep him hospitalized and under observation as the ship departed for its next port of call in Gibraltar. When he was judged stable enough to safely travel again, he returned back by air to Ft. Lauderdale and continued his care in a local hospital.

On a brilliant, sunny Sunday morning, our ship passed through the eight-mile-wide Strait of Gibraltar and dropped anchor in its port. We were the sole cruise ship in Gibraltar that day. Most of the businesses were shuttered, and the streets were nearly vacant.

I noticed that many of our crew members were making their way to the Ocean Village Marina and to its Casino Admiral, where they knew there was a free, strong Wi-Fi connection. I followed them only to find many of them sitting along the hallways of the casino, chatting with their friends and loved ones on FaceTime or Skype. The empty spaces reverberated with sounds of Tagalog, Bahasa Indonesia, and their many different dialects.

I did find a small restaurant open and I joined with another couple for a light lunch. When we asked the proprietor if he might suggest something that would be characteristic of Gibraltar cuisine he pointed to a dish called rosto, which I quickly discovered was a form of ragù served with penne. The chunks of carrot and potato were interesting elements of the dish, and it shaped a memory of this brief visit to Gibraltar.

ROSTO WITH PENNE

Penne pasta with braised beef and vegetables

Makes 4 to 6 servings

Ingredients

- 1 pound pork loin or beef (chuck or round)
- 10 sliced cremini mushrooms
- 2 vine-ripened tomatoes, peeled and diced
- 28-ounce can chopped tomatoes
- 1 tablespoon tomato paste (tomate triturado)
- 1 chopped onion
- 3 large peeled and sliced carrots
- 1 Yukon Gold potato, peeled and cut into small cubes
- 2 finely minced cloves of garlic
- ½ cup dry white wine
- 1 cup chicken stock
- extra-virgin olive oil
- salt and pepper
- 1 teaspoon granulated sugar
- grated Parmigiano Reggiano
- 1 pound dried penne pasta

Method

1. In a Dutch oven, sauté the chopped onions until soft and translucent. Add garlic and cook for 30 seconds to incorporate into the onions.
2. Add the diced tomatoes, carrots, mushrooms, and potatoes and cook for another 4 to 5 minutes, stirring continually.
3. Remove the sautéed vegetables to a bowl and set aside.
4. In the same Dutch oven used to cook the vegetables, add a bit of olive oil and brown the beef. Add the tomato paste, first to caramelize and then to combine with the beef.
5. Add the white wine to the beef, along with the chicken stock and bring to a boil.

continued

6. Add back all the vegetables, along with the diced canned tomatoes.
7. Add a teaspoon of sugar and combine.
8. Cover the pot and cook on low heat for about 40 minutes, until the meat is tender.
9. About 15 minutes before the sauce is ready, cook the penne in salted boiling water for about 10 minutes. (It will be slightly less than al dente at this point; the pasta will finish cooking in the sauce.)
10. Drain the pasta and add it into the Dutch oven with the meat sauce and cook for about an additional 4 minutes, until the pasta is tender and has blended with the sauce.
11. Garnish with grated cheese.

After leaving Gibraltar, we arrived in the old Spanish port city of Cádiz. We docked near the charming old city with its imposing late eighteenth–early nineteenth century cathedral. I had been asked to escort one of the groups of passengers on an excursion to the capital of Andalusia, the beautiful city of Seville. Our tour included a drive around Cádiz with a brief visit to the cathedral, which contained the body of Manuel de Falla, one of Spain's most significant twentieth-century composers and pianists. The bus trip to Seville took close to two hours. Once we arrived, we were free to wander in the picturesque Jewish quarter, where many of the homes were whitewashed. The flower boxes on their balconies cascaded with colorful and beautifully scented flowers. The air of the city was unmistakably perfumed with orange from its many citrus trees.

There was no scheduled lunch for the group, so we were on our own to find a place to eat. Lunch in Spain is served between one and four o'clock. After our long bus ride and walk around the area of Santa Cruz, we were ready to sample some tapas, and we found a little bodega not too far from the cathedral. In we ventured. Although the tiny bodega was crowded, the three of us were able to find a place at the bar. We sampled many different small plates and sandwiches. One of the plates I especially remember was *berenjenas fritas con miel de caña*: rounds of baby eggplant soaked in milk, lightly dredged in flour, fried, drained, salted, and then drizzled with some local honey. The platters full of many varieties of *montadito* sandwiches attracted our attention. These beautifully composed bite-sized open-faced sandwiches allowed us to sample some of the local cheeses and ham. The proprietor encouraged us to try his *vermút rojo*, which he served over ice cubes, along with a sliver of fresh orange. It was sweet and refreshing, and an excellent accompaniment to our memorable tapas lunch.

Before we rejoined our bus later in the afternoon, we visited the fifteenth-century gothic Santa María de la Sede Cathedral and its famous bell tower La Giralda, which has become an iconic symbol of the city of Seville. The Seville cathedral is the third largest cathedral in the world, and contains the tomb of Christopher Columbus. Finally, we visited the Reales Alcázares de Sevilla, a royal palace developed by the Moors with its remarkable arches, columns, and tile work.

When we arrived back on the ship, the kitchen staff had augmented the regular dinner menu with a delicious Seville specialty. Solomillo iberico de bellota is the luscious, air-dried pork tenderloin of local pigs. The distinctive flavor of this local pork no doubt is influenced by the diet of the pigs who graze in the nearby forest and gorge on the many acorns scattered on its forest floor. This recipe can easily be made with readily available and inexpensive pork tenderloins. The chef offered this version, enhanced with a Spanish whiskey that had been aged in rioja casks. Any good Scotch or American whiskey will work beautifully.

SOLOMILLO WITH WHISKEY, SEVILLE-STYLE

Sautéed pork tenderloin medallions with whiskey pan sauce

Makes 4 to 6 servings

Ingredients

- 2 pork tenderloins
- 8 cloves of garlic
- 1 small cut and quartered onion
- ¾ cup whiskey
- 1 cup chicken or meat stock

continued

- 2 teaspoons cornstarch
- ¼ cup cold water
- 1 tablespoon lemon juice
- 4 tablespoons extra-virgin olive oil
- 2 tablespoons unsalted butter
- fresh thyme sprigs and leaves
- kosher salt and freshly ground black pepper
- 1 teaspoon grated lemon zest
- chopped flat-leaf parsley

Method

1. Season the pork tenderloins liberally with salt, pepper, thyme leaves, lemon zest, and a couple of tablespoons of olive oil. Cover with plastic wrap and allow to marinate and come to room temperature for about an hour before cooking.
2. Cut the tenderloins crosswise into 1-inch medallions.
3. Brush a heavy skillet with 1 tablespoon of oil and heat. Sear the pieces of meat until nicely browned on both sides. Do not overcook; just brown.
4. Remove the browned medallions from the skillet and set aside.
5. Add another 2 tablespoons of oil to the skillet and reduce the heat to medium. Lightly crush the cloves of garlic to split the skins, but do not peel them. Add to the skillet with the wedges of onion. Sauté, turning frequently, until onion is well browned.
6. Add the whiskey to the pan. Carefully flambé the mixture until alcohol is burned off. Snuff the flame with a pot cover if needed.
7. With a spatula, loosen any *fond* in the skillet. Add the stock and a sprig of thyme.
8. In a small bowl, create a slurry by mixing the cornstarch in ¼ cup of cold water.

9. Stir the slurry into the whiskey in the pan and stir over medium heat until sauce thickens and becomes smooth.
10. Season to taste with salt and pepper.
11. Add the freshly squeezed lemon juice and the butter. Simmer the sauce 10 minutes.
12. Return the pork medallions and all the accumulated juices to the skillet. Finish cooking over medium heat, turning the medallions in the sauce for about 3 to 4 minutes.
13. Discard the large pieces of onion and the sprig of thyme.
14. Serve the medallions and its sauce, garnished with freshly chopped parsley.

To have our ship docked in Barcelona for two days presented an unparalleled opportunity to visit places within walking distance of the port, like the Basilica de la Sagrada Familia and La Seu, Catedral de la Santa Creu i Santa Eulalia (the Cathedral of the Holy Cross and Saint Eulalia), located in the heart of the Barri Gòtic, and other Catalan architect Antoni Gaudí gems like the Casa Vicens, Casa Milà, Casa Batlló, and Colonia Güell. It also made possible a very special trip to Montserrat.

On our first day in port, I took the train from Barcelona for the approximately one-hour trip, where I took the cable car up the mountains that afforded spectacular views of the Catalan countryside. My destination was the Benedictine monastery Santa Maria de Montserrat, which holds a very special place in the memory and history of the Society of Jesus.

In his autobiography, the founder of the Jesuits describes his experiences at this holy shrine. It has been a pilgrim destination for more than a millennium.

After Ignatius had left his ancestral home in Loyola, he set out in search of knowing what God might want of him. He was plagued with remorse for his past sins and failings and sought to be reassured of God's forgiveness. During his convalescence from his battle-incurred injuries, Ignatius had read stories about how Christian knights devoted the whole night before receiving knighthood to prayer before the altar of the Blessed Virgin Mary. Ignatius, too, wanted to follow their example, by praying in vigil for an entire night before the altar of Our Lady at Montserrat.

When Ignatius finally arrived at Montserrat, he first devoted almost three days to reflecting and composing a catalogue of his sins. He had confided to his confessor the desire and intention to forsake his former life and dedicate the remainder of his life to whatever God might require of him. And symbolic of his choice, he wished to divest himself of his horse, sword, and dagger, which he asked his confessor to place in the church.

On the vigil of the Annunciation in the year 1522, unobserved by anyone, he approached a beggar, removed his noble clothes, and offered them to the poor man. He then put on a pilgrim's tunic, which he had previously purchased, and entered the monastic church of Montserrat.

He spent the entire night in prayer before the altar of what today the Catalans call *La Moroneta*—a small wooden statue of the Madonna, seated with her son on her lap and holding a ball with her right hand. The faces of both the Madonna and her son are black, perhaps resulting from the darkening of the paint caused by smoke and incense. Ignatius, so his autobiography reveals, threw himself on his knees before the altar of the Blessed Mother of God, and there—sometimes kneeling or standing with his pilgrim's staff in hand—spent the entire night in prayer before leaving the next morning on foot to the town of Manresa, where he spent the next eleven months.

My pilgrimage to this sanctuary happened on a beautiful spring day. Every view of the natural beauty of the countryside was breathtaking.

A highlight of my visit was hearing the boy choristers. They gave a brief performance of Gregorian chants at 1 p.m. that day. Some years later, when I served as the superior of a Jesuit health center, I had the opportunity to renovate and furnish a worship space for the Jesuit community. I suggested we dedicate the chapel to Our Lady of Montserrat.

The following day I invited three of the ship's musicians, who were all Filipinos, to join me for a trip to the Basilica de la Sagrada Familia, which had been completed in 1981. It happened to be a Sunday morning. We left the ship right after an early breakfast. Departing from the dockside by taxicab, we arrived at the church. As we were walking around and admiring the exterior, we noted that people were streaming into what appeared to be a lower-level shrine. We followed, only to discover that they were a pilgrim group who were about to share in the celebration of Mass in the central chapel of St. Joseph in the basilica's crypt church. We slipped into this company and participated in the liturgy, even though it was celebrated entirely in Spanish. What an added grace this proved to be. After Mass we quickly visited all the adjacent chapels, including one dedicated to Our Lady of Montserrat, the patroness of Catalonia. To my great surprise and delight I discovered that the body of Antoni Gaudí was buried in the Chapel of the Holy Virgin of Mount Carmel. Gaudí, the architectural and artistic genius behind the Sagrada Familia, died in Barcelona in 1926 days shy of his seventy-fourth birthday.

After viewing the highly individualized sui generis styles that Gaudí employed in building this basilica and taking note of the continuing work by contemporary Catalan artisans to complete this masterpiece, we took a cab back to the historic center of town and strolled along La Rambla. By midday on this gorgeous spring Sunday, the tree-covered pedestrian boulevard was teeming with locals and tourists. We shared lunch in a little restaurant located on one of the side streets. I sampled what was described as a traditional Catalan dish called mandonguilles amb sèpia, which combines little meatballs in an unusual but delicious rich sauce made from squid.

MANDONGUILLES AMB SÈPIA

Catalonian meatballs with squid sauce

Makes 4 to 6 servings

Ingredients

For the albóndigas (meatballs)

- ¾ pound pork belly slices
- 1 pound chuck beef
- 1 small finely chopped onion
- 6 cloves minced garlic
- 1 egg
- chopped flat-leaf parsley
- 1 piece stale white or sourdough bread, cubed
- sea salt and cracked black pepper

continued

For the squid sauce

- ¾ pounds cleaned squid (no tentacles)
- 2 large chopped onions
- 4 firm tomatoes
- ½ cup fresh or frozen peas
- 2 cups fish, vegetable, or chicken stock
- anchovy paste
- 1½ cups dry white wine
- extra-virgin olive oil
- sea salt and cracked black pepper

For the picada (flavor-enhancing paste)

- 10 peeled and blanched whole almonds
- 2 chopped cloves garlic
- 1 tablespoon chopped flat-leaf parsley
- 1 slice stale bread
- 2 teaspoons sherry vinegar
- ⅛ cup cooking liquid

Method

Making the albóndigas

1. In a stand mixer fitted with the meat grinding attachment, process the pork belly (including skin) along with the beef. It is advisable to put the meat through the grinder two or three times. If you do not have a meat grinder, you can pulse the meat in a food processor and then finish by hand-mincing on a cutting board with a chef's knife. The goal is to have a well-minced meat mixture of pork belly and beef.
2. Put the meat into a mixing bowl and add the bread cubes, chopped onion, minced garlic, chopped parsley leaves, salt, pepper, and a lightly beaten egg. With clean hands, combine the ingredients thoroughly.

3. Roll about 20 small meatballs in the palm of your hand, then dust with all-purpose flour. Refrigerate for 30 minutes before frying.
4. In a large sauté pan, brown the albóndigas well in hot olive oil and drain on paper towels, then set aside.

Making the squid sauce

1. In the same sauté pan used to brown the meatballs, over low heat and very slowly, allow the onions to caramelize until they become deep mahogany in color. The *fond* from the previously cooked meatballs will also help to enrich the deep color.
2. When the onions are caramelized, cut the firm tomatoes in half horizontally and grate them, wet side down, using a box grater, and discard the top skin. Add the grated tomato pulp to the onions and mix to combine.
3. Add the garlic, anchovy paste, parsley, wine, and about a ¼ cup of stock. Season with salt and pepper and allow the alcohol in the wine to burn off in cooking.
4. Cut the cleaned squid into 1½-inch pieces and add the squid to the mixture. Turn the heat to the lowest setting and allow the fish to slowly cook in the mixture. Do not overcook.
5. Return the meatballs to the sauté pan and add more stock, so that they are almost submerged. Cover the pan and simmer at a low temperature on top of the stove for about 30 to 40 minutes.

Making the picada

1. In a small sauté pan, toast the peeled, blanched almonds and the bread cubes in a tablespoon of olive oil and butter until they begin to turn a light golden color.
2. In a food processor, combine the toasted almonds and bread, garlic, and parsley. Process until the ingredients are well blended. With the motor running, add the sherry vinegar through the feed tube,

continued

along with a few tablespoons of the squid cooking liquid, to make a smooth paste.

3. Transfer to small bowl.

To finish the dish

1. In the last few minutes of cooking, add the peas and the picada.
2. Cook for another minute or two and serve.

The sun was shining brightly on the calm waters as the *Prinsendam* glided into Monaco's beautiful harbor, which was filled with an array of impressive luxury yachts and sailboats. Since I did not have to celebrate Mass on board until early evening, I was ready to disembark from the ship as soon as it was cleared by the local customs officers. I had decided to discover Monte Carlo alone and began my tour by strolling along the Port Hercule. I happened upon the eleventh-century Église Sainte-Dévote. The church memorialized the patron of Monaco and guardian of the Monégasque soul. This fourth-century young Christian woman died for her faith during the terroristic reign of the Roman Emperor Diocletian. Her body, which was destined to be cremated, was rescued by other Christians who wanted to provide a proper burial for her. On a trip to bury her body in North Africa, the boat in which her corpse was being transported was miraculously directed in a storm into Monaco's harbor. She was buried on the site of the present-day church.

From there I decided to jump on a bus to see the other major sites of the city. We passed by the world-famous thoroughfare on which the Grand Prix race is run. The Grand Casino, with its impressive Place du Casino and palatial façade, was glistening in the sunlight as we continued the tour. I alighted at the Prince's Palace just in time to watch the changing of the guards who ceremoniously protect its principal entrance. From there, I walked along a beautiful sylvan path built on a rocky cliff overlooking the sea. Along the path there were many varietals of trees and plants that thrive in the exceptional microclimate of Monte Carlo. I noticed a sign pointing to the cathedral and I followed it. Soon I arrived in the small plaza in front of the white stone façade of the nineteenth century Roman-Byzantine Cathedral of the Immaculate Conception, more popularly known as the Cathedral of St. Nicholas.

For more than seven hundred years the history of Monaco has been linked to that of the Grimaldi family, and this cathedral has been their spiritual home. I was delighted to be able to pause and pray at the tombs of Prince Rainer and his American wife, Princess Grace Kelly.

After my visit to this ecclesiastical center of the Roman Catholic Church in Monaco, I walked the short distance to the Musée Océanographique. There I became enthralled with its exhibits of rare species of fish, corals, and especially those of whales. The building in which the museum is housed is like a monumental palace itself. The views of the city and harbor from its windows are spectacular.

After an exhausting day of touring on foot, I was happy to end my meanderings in the nineteenth-century Condamine Market and its inviting covered pavilion. My Monégasque friends had suggested that I try one of the local specialties. It reminded me of an egg roll. A *barbagiuan* is a little appetizer of fried dough, with a delicious filling of wilted chard, onion, and ricotta. The recipe is accessible and easy, and the result offers a delicious memory of Monte Carlo.

BARBAGIUAN

Monte Carlo fried vegetable-filled pastry parcels

Makes 18 to 24 pastries

Ingredients

For the pastry

- 2 cups sifted all-purpose flour
- ¼ cup extra-virgin olive oil
- 1 well-beaten egg
- ¼ cup water
- ⅛ teaspoon kosher salt

For the filling

- 1 tablespoon extra-virgin olive oil
- 1 small diced onion

continued

- 1 finely chopped leek (white part only)
- 2 Swiss chard leaves
- 1 cup fresh baby spinach leaves
- fresh or dried oregano
- ½ cup whole milk ricotta
- ½ cup freshly grated Parmigiano Reggiano
- salt and pepper
- 1 egg, for the egg wash

Method

To prepare the pastry

1. In a food processor fitted with the steel blade, add the flour and a pinch of salt and pulse for a few seconds to aerate the flour.
2. Add the egg and olive oil and pulse a couple times before adding water as needed to bring the dough together into a firm ball.
3. Remove the dough ball and knead for a few minutes on a lightly floured work surface. Wrap the dough in plastic wrap and refrigerate for 30 minutes.

To make the filling

1. Remove the Swiss chard leaves from their stems. Blanch the chard and spinach in boiling water for 30 seconds to wilt the leaves. Remove, drain thoroughly, and squeeze dry with paper towels. Chop and reserve.
2. In a sauté pan, cook the chopped onions and leeks until soft, but not browned.
3. In a mixing bowl, combine the chopped spinach and Swiss chard leaves with the cooked onions and leeks. Season with oregano, salt, and pepper. Add the ricotta, grated Parmigiano Reggiano, and a tablespoon of olive oil and blend thoroughly and set aside to cool completely.

4. Remove the dough from the refrigerator and on a lightly floured work surface, roll out the dough to a thin rectangle.
5. Using a floured 2- to 3-inch round pastry or biscuit cutter, cut out as many disks as you can (between 18 and 24).
6. Make an egg wash by beating an egg with a teaspoon of water or milk and brush each round.
7. Put a small amount of the filling in the center of each pastry round and fold the dough over to form a semicircle.
8. Gently crimp the edges of the pastry with the tines of a fork to achieve a good seal.
9. In a deep fry pan or saucepan, heat vegetable or peanut oil to 350°F. In small batches, fry the barbagiuans for about 5 minutes or so until they are brown and crisp.
10. Drain on paper towels.

As the *Prinsendam* was approaching the Italian port of Livorno on a bright spring Saturday morning, I felt as though I was arriving home. While many of the ship's passengers were heading off to day-long excursions in nearby Pisa and Firenze, I was keen to remain in Livorno. Despite my many previous excursions in Italy, I had never had an occasion to visit this western port city of Tuscany. I was enthusiastic to discover a bit of its history and, of course, to sample some Livornese cooking.

The ship's shuttle bus brought a few passengers to the Piazza della Repubblica, with its many monuments, shops, and restaurants. Since it was a strategic port during the Renaissance, the ruling Medici family had fortified Livorno with walls, ramparts, and towers. Some of the original sixteenth-century structures remain, particularly the splendid Fortezza Nuova, which is surrounded by picturesque canals that are reminiscent of scenes from Venezia. I found myself wandering aimlessly on these streets and canals, absorbing the sounds and sights. In the Piazza Micheli I stopped to study the impressive Monumento dei Quattro Mori (Monument of the Four Moors), which reminded me of Bernini's monumental study Fontana dei

Quattro Fiumi (Fountain of the Four Rivers), which dominates the center of the Piazza Navona in Rome. I knew that I was back in Italy.

Walking westward, eventually I arrived at the Piazza Grande and the city's duomo, la Cattedrale di San Francesco. The original duomo had been bombed during the Second World War and virtually destroyed. The contemporary cathedral was rebuilt on the same site, and is a close reproduction of its seventeenth-century predecessor.

After visiting the cathedral I walked south to the Terrazza Mascagni promenade, which on that warm spring day was idyllic. It offered many perspectives of the Ligurian coastline. The terrace itself is a work of art. Its curving stonework pavement extends the promenade for some 1,500 feet into the sea.

I was becoming weary and started looking to find a small trattoria or ristorante to sample some typical dishes of Livorno. I found a restaurant whose name immediately grabbed my attention: Ristorante il Cassettone della Nonna, "Nana's Big Closet." Looking at its posted menu, I noted that they were offering many local pasta and seafood dishes. I spent the next hour and a half enjoying a wonderful meal alone, watching the endless dramas that were spontaneously developing among the locals seated around me and with the engaging wait staff. Here is a version of a local fish dish that I sampled. The ingredients and preparation are simple, and the results are fabulous.

DENTICE ROSSO ALLA LIVORNESE

Livorno red snapper

Makes 4 to 6 servings

Ingredients

- 4 to 6 red snapper filets (preferably with skin intact)
- 2 diced onions
- 12 pitted and chopped black olives
- 2 tablespoons rinsed capers
- 2 tablespoons extra-virgin olive oil
- 28-ounce can diced San Marzano tomatoes

- 1 cup dry white wine
- salt and freshly ground black pepper

Method

1. In a saucepan, add some olive oil and sauté one of the diced onions. When it becomes translucent, add a can of diced tomatoes along with the white wine, and cook the sauce for 15 minutes. Season with salt and pepper and set aside.
2. Preheat the oven to 350°F.
3. In an ovenproof sauté pan that is large enough to hold the snapper filets, heat some olive oil over medium heat. Add the second diced onion and cook until it becomes translucent.
4. Add the olives and capers and allow to cook for an additional 2 to 3 minutes. Remove the mixture to a bowl.
5. Season the snapper filets with salt and pepper.
6. In the same sauté pan in which the onions, olives, and capers were prepared, add a tablespoon of olive oil and heat.
7. Place the red snapper filets skin-side down in the pan and allow to cook for about a minute before adding about a cup or two of the tomato sauce.
8. Add back the onion, olive, and caper mixture and distribute evenly over the filets.
9. Place the pan in the oven and bake until the fish is cooked through, about 12 to 15 minutes.
10. While the fish is finishing in the oven, rewarm the remaining tomato sauce.
11. Using a spatula, carefully transfer fish to serving plates and spoon the pan sauce over the filets.
12. Pass the additional tomato sauce in a sauce boat.

The rain was falling steadily as our ship docked on Sunday at its berth in Civitavecchia ("Old City"), Rome's port city on the Tyrrhenian Sea. For some of our guests this would be the end of their voyage on the *Prinsendam*; for the others, it was simply the end of one segment of a long Mediterranean journey. For me, it was an exciting junction since my sister Maryellen and her husband, Ed Steele, and a family friend, Dr. Charles Dela Cruz, would be joining the ship's company for the next segment of the itinerary from Rome to Athens with scheduled ports of call in Naples, Venice, Croatia, and some of the Greek islands before finally arriving in Athens on Easter Sunday.

My plan was to take the commuter train for the fifty-mile journey from Civitavecchia to Rome to meet Maryellen, Ed, and Charles, who were staying at the Residenza Paolo VI, immediately adjacent to Saint Peter's Square in the Vatican. This small boutique hotel was formerly an Augustinian monastery, which had been transformed into a hotel in the year 2000 for the millennial Holy Year proclaimed by Pope St. John Paul II. I dreaded the commute in the rain, especially on a Sunday when trains might not be running at full efficiency. At breakfast, by good fortune, I encountered one of our solo passengers who told me that he had previously arranged for a driver and guide and a large SUV to do some private touring in and around Rome for the day. When he heard of my plan, he asked me if he might bring me to the hotel. He further astounded me by suggesting that perhaps my family, friend, and I would enjoy touring Rome along with him for the day before returning together to the ship. This proved to be a pure gift from heaven. Not only did it relieve me of my commuting concerns, but it would also provide an easy way to transport my sister and the others to the ship, along with their baggage.

As we drove away from the ship that morning in the lashing rain, the Porto di Traiano (Emperor Trajan's Port) was fully enveloped in fog. Much of this port city had been destroyed during the Second World War, so what one sees today is mostly postwar reconstruction. During nice weather, it is pleasant to stroll along the promenade bordering the harbor.

We arrived at the Vatican around 11 o'clock in the morning, loaded all the baggage, made proper introductions, and set off on what would be a whirlwind tour. Dr. Dela Cruz, a Yale professor of critical care medicine and pulmonology, had escorted my sister and brother-in-law on a walking tour of the Vatican on the previous day and evening, and they had discovered a local trattoria for dinner. The Residenza

Paolo VI has a marvelous rooftop terrace overlooking the Vatican Basilica, Apostolic Palace, and St. Peter's Square, where they had enjoyed sipping wine on the previous mild dry spring evening. As we were departing the Vatican the dome of St. Peter's was wrapped in an ethereal cloud, and the rain continued to pelt against the ancient cobblestones of its famous square.

Our Italian driver and guide was perfectly fluent in English, and an exuberant storyteller. We were clearly not his first guests. I marveled at how skillfully he maneuvered the large Mercedes SUV through the narrow streets of the historic center of Rome, bringing us up practically to the front door of the Pantheon and to the edge of the Trevi Fountain. We whizzed by the Aventine Hill, the Circus Maximus, the Campo de' Fiori, and the Campidoglio, and we scarcely had time to blink as we sped through the Piazza Venezia and by the Victor Emmanuel II monument. Some Italians jokingly refer to this monument as a wedding cake. Our driver provided a riveting introduction to the history of the Colosseum, bringing to life the gladiators who once battled lions and tigers within its walls, and described sea battles that were staged there for the amusement of the emperor and the *populi Romani*.

He drove us to the top of the Gianicolo or Janiculum Hill, which on a clear day offers unparalleled vistas of the city and the Tiber. That day, *Roma antica* was all a blurry mess.

We were all happy to accept the recommendation from our driver of a place to pause for lunch in a local restaurant where he knew the proprietor. By then I was chilled to the bone and happy to find a minestra listed on the menu. Minestra is a hearty seasonal vegetable soup, occasionally flavored with a piece of pork, a ham bone, a little pancetta, or the rind from a piece of Parmigiano Reggiano—all to flavor the vegetables. Minestrone is a variation of minestra, and it was a poor person's sustenance, sometimes serving as the only component of a meal. You can use any seasonal vegetables in preparing this simple dish. Here is a version of the minestra I enjoyed on that chilly rainy day that uses beans and spring vegetables.

MINESTRA PRIMAVERA ALLA ROMANA

A spring Roman vegetable bean soup

Makes 6 to 8 servings

continued

Ingredients

- 1 onion, diced into small pieces
- 2 carrots, diced into small pieces
- 2 celery stalks, diced into small pieces
- 1 leek, washed and roughly chopped (white and green parts)
- 1 cup chopped zucchini
- 1 peeled and chopped Yukon Gold potato
- 6 cups water (or chicken stock)
- 2½ cups canned romano or cannellini beans, rinsed and drained
- 3 coarsely chopped cloves of garlic
- 8 peeled and seeded roma tomatoes, coarsely chopped
- freshly torn basil leaves
- soup pasta such as ditalini, orzo, or rotelle (optional)

Method

1. In a large Dutch oven, bring the water or chicken stock to a boil and add all the ingredients except for the tomatoes and basil. If you wish to add a ham bone or some pancetta, or a cheese rind, do that now.
2. Adjust heat to medium-high and cook uncovered for about 10 to 12 minutes. Test the potato for tenderness.
3. Add your chopped tomatoes and torn basil leaves and simmer for another 10 minutes or so. If using soup pasta, add this now. Check cooking time for al dente.
4. Add salt and freshly ground black pepper. Remove ham bone and/or remaining cheese rind.
5. The total cooking time for the minestra should be 20 to 25 minutes.
6. At service, you might wish to drizzle a bit of extra-virgin olive oil and garnish with a few red pepper flakes and some freshly grated Parmigiano Reggiano. Some crusty rustic bread is almost an essential accompaniment.

We arrived safely back to the ship so that Maryellen, Ed, and Charles could register and settle into their cabins before they joined me for the celebration of Mass on the Fifth Sunday of Lent for our old and new passengers.

On the following Monday morning the rains had ended, and bright sun had returned as our ship slowly navigated its way through the tranquil waters of the Naples Bay of Vesuvius. The *Prinsendam* docked right in front of the twelfth-century Castel dell'Ovo, the oldest surviving castle in Napoli. From the decks of the ship we could already sense the verve of the city as Naples was awakening after its Sabbath rest. The sounds were exuberant as well as chaotic as we disembarked from the ship.

Because this was the first visit of my sister and brother-in-law to Italy, I thought we might best begin our day of sightseeing by boarding a bus that had its *capolinea* right in front of the Castel dell'Ovo. We were able to secure front row seats on the upper deck of the bus, as the drama of Naples gradually unfolded before our eyes. Napoli was prepared to display all its sounds, aromas, and color—exciting all the senses. Our bus driver maneuvered through the narrow neighborhood streets, with other drivers impatiently honking their horns. My sister was astounded by how many houses were hanging out their laundry to dry—waving in the breezes from windows and balconies and pulley lines stretched between buildings. People on the streets were chatting or arguing or busily opening up their shops and markets.

Our tour itinerary included most of the historic and architectural places in the city, including several important churches. Among these, I was most interested to bring my traveling companions to the Jesuit Chiesa di Gesù Nuovo, which, at least in my judgment, is one of the most important and beautiful churches in Napoli. Our bus steered right into the square in which the church is located. The building that houses the church was originally the fifteenth-century palace of a prince of Salerno. The Jesuits acquired the palace in the latter part of the sixteenth century and invested fifteen years remodeling it to serve as the mother church of the Jesuits in Napoli. During the intervening centuries the church at times was staffed by Jesuits and Franciscans, but for Neapolitans, it has always been "the Jesuit church."

From its façade, one might not be prepared for the baroque ornamentations of the magnificent Renaissance church within. I was happy to provide commentary on the Jesuit themes reflected in the eleven chapels and the many frescoes, including those of the Sacred Heart, Blessed Virgin, Ignatius Loyola, Francis Xavier, and Francis de Geronimo, S.J., a Jesuit saint who was born in the city.

We also paused to visit the monumental metropolitan cathedral of Naples, La Cattedrale Metropolitana di Santa Maria Assunta—its landmark duomo. Even though the cathedral church is dedicated to the assumption of the Virgin Mary into heaven, the locals popularly refer to the cathedral as the Cathedral of San Gennaro (Saint Januarius). Not to be outdone by other cities, Naples boasts some fifty patron saints, but unquestionably the fourth-century martyred bishop San Gennaro remains *numero uno*. According to folklore, after Bishop Gennaro's beheading during the reign of Diocletian, his blood was collected by a woman who preserved it inside two containers. These flasks containing Gennaro's blood were kept in a safe behind the altar of the Chapel of the Treasure of San Gennaro in the cathedral. Three times a year, people flock to the cathedral to witness the liquefaction of the blood. Being superstitious by nature, the Neapolitans believe that a quick liquefaction is a sign of good luck, while a delay or failure are taken as negative omens.

My interest in this story is tied to living in Manhattan for so many years and participating every September in a colorful, vibrant, ten-day street festival of San Gennaro in Little Italy, in and around the actual liturgical feast observed on September 19. The streets around Mulberry Street in New York are hosts to processions, parades, vendors, and games, and the smell of sizzling sausages and deep-fried dough is everywhere. This local celebration dates back to the 1920s when Neapolitan immigrants in New York began gathering to celebrate a tradition with which they had been raised in their native Napoli.

I was also intent that my family see the cloister of the Monastery of Saint Clare, which dates back to the fourteenth century. What is amazing to the eye is the tile work that decorates the octagonal columns and the long benches of the cloister. The Majolica tiles that were painted in Capodimonte studios during the seventeenth century are unique, capturing scenes from everyday secular life in riotous colors. It is a breathtaking scene, especially on a bright, sunny day.

I also wanted them to see at least one *presepio* (Neapolitan nativity scene) during their visit to Naples. Santa Chiara has an impressive one, with its figures dressed in local eighteenth- and nineteenth-century styles and set in what appears to be an ancient ruin. The artistry continues, and one can find many beautifully crafted figures and nativity tableaux everywhere in Italy.

We paused for lunch in a little trattoria in the neighborhood of Santa Lucia, where there are pizza shops, bakeries, cafes, and restaurants everywhere. My sister ordered the classic pizza of Naples, the margarita, but I wanted to sample a relatively contemporary regional dish, spaghetti alla puttanesca.

SPAGHETTI ALLA PUTTANESCA

Spaghetti with tomatoes, capers, and olives

Makes 4 to 6 servings

Ingredients

- 1 pound spaghetti
- 2 tablespoons unsalted butter
- 3 tablespoons extra-virgin olive oil
- 6 rinsed and mashed anchovy filets
- 3 minced garlic cloves
- ¼ cup pitted sliced black olives
- 1 tablespoon rinsed and chopped capers
- 14-ounce can diced San Marzano tomatoes
- 6 chopped Roma tomatoes
- ½ teaspoon red pepper flakes
- 1 tablespoon chopped flat-leaf parsley
- salt and freshly ground black pepper

Method

1. Bring a large pot, filled with 5 to 6 quarts of water, to a rolling boil. Add salt to the water and add the pasta and follow package directions to cook to the al dente stage.
2. In a mortar, pound the garlic and anchovies with a pestle into a smooth paste.
3. In a large saucepan, heat the oil and butter over medium heat. Add the anchovy-garlic paste to the oil and stir with a wooden spoon to bloom (about 1 minute).

continued

4. Add fresh and canned tomatoes, sliced olives, and capers. Simmer the sauce over medium-low heat until thickened, breaking up tomatoes with a spoon. Season to taste with salt and pepper.
5. Drain the pasta and return to the same cooking pot. Add the puttanesca sauce and parsley, tossing everything together over low heat until sauce coats the pasta, for about 2 to 3 minutes.

Our ship entered the calm, clear, and shimmering waters of the Adriatic Sea—the northernmost arm of the Mediterranean—and headed for Dubrovnik. For my sister, who is a big fan of the award-winning HBO series *Games of Thrones*, the first view of the sun-drenched ancient walls that envelop the city was awe-inspiring. Dubrovnik was a principal filming location in Croatia for King's Landing, a fictional city in the series. Even folks who have never seen a single episode of this drama would quickly concur that Dubrovnik is one of the most beautiful cities in the world. Some guidebooks refer to the city as the "pearl of the Adriatic," and there is no hyperbole in that description.

Remarkably, the city's limestone streets are impeccably maintained. Its baroque buildings reveal stunning details of their architecture as the sun plays off the walls and roofs. Recalling sad memories of the bombing assaults that Dubrovnik's Old City had sustained in the 1990s during the Croatian War of Independence at the hands of the Serb-controlled Yugoslav People's Army and local Serb forces, I was expecting to find a deeply scarred city. But like a phoenix, the city had risen from its ashes and much of the structural damage it had sustained has been repaired.

The *Prinsendam* anchored in the bay, and we went ashore by tender boats, disembarking right in the heart of the Old City. Refreshed from a day at sea, we were all ready to explore this southernmost city of Croatia. The city reminds one of the back lot of a medieval town in Universal Studios, with charming shops and side streets nestled securely within its ancient city walls and ramparts. We were immediately struck by how quiet and tranquil the city was, and how friendly and welcoming the Croatian people are.

We approached the Cathedral of the Assumption of the Virgin Mary. This seventeenth-century baroque-style building occupied a site where predecessor cathedrals have stood since the seventh century, and like other buildings damaged by earthquakes and wars, the cathedral also has been restored and serves as the religious center for Roman Catholics in Dubrovnik. Early in the voyage, after the celebration of Mass on the feast of St. Blaise on February 3, I had blessed the throats of the ship's passengers and crew members. According to tradition, St. Blaise had cured a boy who was choking on a fishbone. When the boy's mother brought him to Bishop Blaise he placed his hands on the boy's throat, prayed to God, and healed him.

But the folks in Dubrovnik revere St. Blaise for other reasons. It may be the product of legend, but Croatians hold on to stories that have been passed on for more than a thousand years. Here is the story of St. Blaise as I heard it recounted in Dubrovnik.

In 971, on the eve of the feast day of this fourth-century bishop and martyr, there were Venetian ships anchored in Dubrovnik's harbor. The Venetians, it seems, were strategizing to lay siege to the city and plunder its resources, even though ostensibly they had stopped only to replenish their food and water supplies before continuing their journey eastward. As the story goes, a priest entered the opened doors of St. Steven's church that night, only to find—to his amazement—a heavenly army led by a man dressed in the vestments of a bishop, with a mitre on his head. When the priest asked the bishop for his name, he responded, "Blaise." The old bishop then instructed the priest immediately to warn the city fathers of the Venetians' plan to attack and ravage Dubrovnik. When the Venetians noted the increased defensive activities taking place on the well-fortified and armed city walls and saw the gates to the city being closed and secured, they figured that their plot had been discovered and quickly set sail.

As a result, St. Blaise became the patron saint of Dubrovnik, and since 972 the city has been celebrating February 3 in honor of their liberator and patron saint. I smiled when I noted a statue of St. Blaise in one of the deep niches of the façade of the cathedral, sharing equal honor with St. Joseph and the child Jesus. I was a bit more dubious when, in the cathedral's treasury, I discovered that they claimed to have relics of the head, arm, and leg of the saint. The reliquary conserving St. Blaise's head is contained within an eleventh-century imperial gold crown, studded with precious stones.

After all these ecclesiastical explorations I was more than willing to indulge my sister's desire to wander among the many shops of artisans along the streets, where she was delighted to spend all the Croatian kuna in her wallet. Meanwhile, Charles, Ed, and I explored a Franciscan monastery, library, and pharmacy, whose origins date back to the thirteenth century. Charles was fascinated to discover that this old Friars Minor pharmacy is the oldest still functioning pharmacy in Europe and the third oldest in the world.

When our little band of city wanderers regrouped, we found a common interest in searching out the Jesuit Stairs. In season five of *Game of Thrones*, the infamous "Walk of Shame" scene was filmed on the monumental baroque Jesuit staircase that descends from Gundulić Square to St. Ignatius Church and the Collegium Ragusinum, Dubrovnik's highly regarded Jesuit college. We all agreed this would be the next destination on our itinerary. The Jesuits have been in Dubrovnik since 1555; remember, the Society of Jesus had been established in 1540. At the request of the bishop, Jesuits established a school in Dubrovnik on this site only fifteen years after the Jesuits had been confirmed by Pope Paul III as a religious order within the Church.

This complex of seventeenth-century stairways and buildings may well be one of the most representative examples of baroque architecture in Croatia. The Jesuit Stairs reminded me of Rome's Spanish Steps, which lead from Piazza di Spagna to the church Trinità dei Monti. I was fascinated to discover that architect, Ignazio Pozzo, S.J., had been sent to Dubrovnik where he finalized the plans for the construction of the church. Stylistically, Dubrovnik's Church of St. Ignatius bears a resemblance to the mother church of the Society of Jesus, Rome's Chiesa del Gesù.

After a full morning of walking, historical discovery, and shopping we were ready to pause and enjoy lunch in one of the historic center's quaint restaurants. Following the recommendation of our very pleasant waiter, I sampled a traditional local seafood dish—buzara—mussels and shrimps cooked in a tomato-scented, wine seafood sauce.

MUSSEL AND SHRIMP BUZARA

Croatian seafood stew

Makes 6 to 8 servings

Ingredients

- 1 onion

- ½ cup extra-virgin olive oil
- ½ cup unsalted butter
- 1 teaspoon kosher salt
- 1½ pounds cleaned mussels
- 1 pound shelled and deveined shrimp
- 1 peeled and thinly sliced garlic bulb
- fresh rosemary, thyme, and oregano, chopped (to taste)
- freshly chopped Italian parsley
- 2 cups dry white wine
- 2 ripe tomatoes
- ½ cup fresh breadcrumbs

Method

1. In a large sauté skillet, combine the olive oil and butter and sauté the roughly chopped onion until soft and translucent.
2. Add the mussels to the softened onions. Toss to mix. When the mussels just begin to open, add about half of the thinly sliced garlic cloves. Continue tossing and cooking for a few more minutes until all the mussels have opened.
3. While the mussels are cooking, roughly chop two large juicy tomatoes into bite-sized pieces, lightly salt them, and add the tomatoes to the skillet.
4. Add the white wine. Stir and cook for few more minutes before adding the rosemary, thyme, and oregano.
5. Finely, add the prepared shrimps and the remainder of the sliced garlic. Let the shrimp cook for about 3 to 5 additional minutes before adding a half cup of the breadcrumbs, which will thicken the sauce and make it creamy. Garnish with freshly chopped parsley.
6. This can be eaten as a seafood stew or it can be combined with some small boiled potatoes, or even with some buttered egg noodles.

Refreshed and restored after a delicious lunch, we decided to walk the mile and a half circumference of the old city's famous medieval walls, which the locals refer to as *Dubrovački miri*. I alluded to these tenth-century fortified walls earlier in recounting the legendary story of St. Blaise. We paid an entrance fee of about $10 US, which I am certain helps to maintain these walls in their excellent condition. We started our casual stroll at the Pile Gate and walked counterclockwise. The afternoon sun was bright, but because it was still early springtime, it was a pleasant walk. In August, I suspect that one could become dehydrated in a very short time. Along the route we passed by several fortresses. The panoramic views of red tiled rooftops of the old city, the neighboring islands, and the Adriatic were stunning—a photographer's heaven.

Before bidding farewell and returning to our ship after spending a memorable day discovering Dubrovnik, we were enjoying some cold drinks and ice cream at a little beach café when we were approached by a young English-speaking local Croatian who persuaded us each to invest $10 to take a forty-five-minute tour with him in his boat, which was moored at the nearby dock. So the four of us piled into his boat for a delightful late afternoon tour of the harbor. He circled a beautiful small island just offshore and pointed out its natural caves caused by erosion. The warm late afternoon breezes were invigorating as we sped through the clear, cool waters before we exchanged a speed boat for the ship's tender as we returned to the *Prinsendam* to continue our voyage.

It was about 6:30 on Palm Sunday morning when the *Prinsendam* cruised past the famed Piazza di San Marco in Venezia. In the morning light the nearly vacant square created an ethereal aura, with its 300-foot *campanile* standing nobly against the brightening sky of a new day. The campanile was originally constructed by the Venetians as a lookout tower to survey ships approaching Venice and to guard this important portal to the city. On this quiet Sunday morning, the golden figure of the Archangel Gabriel seemed to be welcoming us home again.

When the ship reached its berth at the Venice cruise terminal, we were ready to set out on foot for a full day of exploration and discovery. I had enjoyed many previous visits to Venice, beginning in 1975, but this was a first visit for Maryellen and Eddie. The night before our arrival I had asked my sister what was on her must-see list in Venice. Her answer was quick and focused: "I want to take a ride through the canals in a gondola, with the boatman singing to me."

Venice is a nightmare for persons with disabilities, but for others, the city is perfectly navigable with a good pair of walking shoes and a map. We disembarked from our ship and a tram brought us to the nearby Piazzale Roma. My plan was that we would amble through the complex maze of alleys and small bridges and eventually arrive at the Rialto Bridge, where we could engage a gondolier to fulfill my sister's dream. Afterwards, we could enjoy an outdoor lunch with a view to the Rialto and make our way to St. Mark's Square before taking a water bus back to the Santa Lucia station.

Getting lost in the back alleys of Venice is actually a serendipitous adventure. Eventually these alleys open on to amazing squares and equally beautiful architectural structures, and it seems that every arrow one sees points to San Marco. When we eventually arrived at the Rialto Bridge, there was a gondolier available at the egress of the alley from which we had just emerged. After some vigorous bargaining, we agreed on the price for an hour of touring. Unfortunately he was not a singer, but we heard enough echoes of singing in the back canals to satisfy my sister's fantasy. Truthfully, I had never stepped into a gondola despite multiple visits to Venice, though I had used the water taxis and buses. The trip was fanciful, although the odors rising from the somewhat stagnant waters in the back canals of Venice mitigated the romantic aspects of the excursion. Nonetheless, Maryellen sat back and took in the sights, sounds, and smells, imagining herself to be a seventeenth-century Venetian *duchessa*, if only for a day.

The gondolier brought us back to the same place where we had engaged him, adjacent to a row of restaurants bordering the canals, in full view of the Rialto Bridge shimmering in the midday sun. We settled at a table for four under an ample rectangular umbrella and quickly surveyed the menu, which was amplified with great flourish by our multilingual Venetian waiter, who recited a litany of other special dishes that the chef would be honored to prepare for us. One of the dishes he mentioned was *bigoli in salsa*, which is a Venetian specialty. Made from simple ingredients, this dish is easy to prepare and quite savory. Bigoli is a pasta that may not be familiar to many Americans, but it is very popular in northern Italy. It is a somewhat thick extruded noodle, traditionally made from buckwheat flour dough that is combined with duck eggs. Today, bigoli are often made from a combination of whole wheat and semolina flours and duck or chicken eggs. Available in some specialty Italian stores, it can also be ordered online, fresh or dried. One can substitute any thick strand pasta, like pici or bucatini.

BIGOLI IN SALSA

Venetian pasta with onion and anchovy sauce

Makes 4 to 6 servings

Ingredients

- 2 finely diced yellow onion
- 6 ounces anchovies (about 20), packed in oil
- ¾ cup dry white wine
- 1 pound bigoli pasta (or some thick spaghetti, like pici or bucatini)
- 1 cup minced parsley
- ground black pepper

Method

1. Bring a pan with 4 to 5 quarts of unsalted water to a rapid boil.
2. Chop the onions as finely as possible, and over low heat, add them to a large skillet with a tablespoon of olive oil and sauté them until they become translucent. Do not allow them to brown.
3. Chop the anchovy filets as finely as possible, which will facilitate their melting and blending into the sauce. Add the chopped anchovies into the softened onions and stir to combine.
4. Add ½ cup of water and ¾ cup of wine to the onion and anchovy mixture and increase the heat to medium and cook the sauce for about 10 to 15 minutes to reduce some of the liquid.
5. Do not add any salt to the pasta cooking water, since the anchovies will provide all the salt that is needed for this dish. Cook the bigoli (or pici or bucatini) according to package directions, until about 2 minutes before it reaches the al dente stage.
6. When the pasta is ready, reserve a cup of pasta water and drain. Add the cooked pasta to the sauté pan and combine with the onion and

anchovy sauce and continue cooking the pasta in the skillet for another minute or two. Add a bit of the pasta cooking liquid, if needed.

7. Garnish with minced parsley (no grated cheese, please), and a good amount of freshly grated black pepper.

After enjoying this popular and tasty Venetian pasta, I was ready to continue in my tour guide role. After taking the obligatory pictures of the Rialto Bridge, we made our way through more passageways and bridges until we began to notice more high-end shops as we approached San Marco.

The Piazza di San Marco was quite different from our first glance of it earlier that morning from the starboard upper deck of the *Prinsendam*: now it was teeming with tourists and Venetian families on a brilliant sunny Palm Sunday afternoon. The lines outside the ninth-century Byzantine-style Basilica di San Marco snaked all the way back to the neighboring Palazzo Ducale (Doges' Palace). Initially, my travel companions were reluctant to stand in such a long line to see yet another church, but I did persuade them that it would be worth the patient wait.

While in line, I told them a little bit about the history of Venice's cathedral church. Originally it was built to receive the human remains of the evangelist St. Mark, who eventually became the patron of the Venetian republic. You see the golden winged lion—the icon of St. Mark—everywhere in Venice. I pointed out to them the replicas of the four horses that dominate the loggia of the façade, which had been brought back to Venice from Constantinople by returning crusaders. The original horses are preserved in the basilica's treasury. Those horses, like many of us, have moved around quite a bit. Most probably they were originally cast in imperial Rome and later moved to Constantinople. They were transported back to Venice in the thirteenth century only to have them plundered by Napoleon at the beginning of the nineteenth, after which he placed them above the Arc de Triomphe du Carousel. But following the Battle of Waterloo, the horses finally were returned to Venice.

I regaled my family with anecdotes of Angelo Roncalli (Pope St. John XXIII) and Albino Luciani (Pope John Paul I), who both had served as patriarchs of Venice before their respective elections to the See of Peter. They were especially charmed by my story of a chance encounter with Cardinal Luciano in this very basilica in 1975, three years before his election as pope, for a pontificate that would last a mere thirty-three days—the shortest in the history of the papacy.

The people standing with us in line were equally enthralled by our animated conversations and stories and before we knew it, we arrived at the doors of the basilica. My companions and our new friends were astounded by their first view of the basilica's breathtaking interior with the gilded mosaics that decorate its walls and ceilings, and by the Byzantine reliefs, many dating from the tenth to twelfth centuries.

Emerging from the basilica, I suggested that we take in the spectacle of the square by enjoying some midafternoon refreshments at an outdoor table in the world famous Caffè Florian. I am usually one to avoid anything like a tourist trap, but on this occasion, I succumbed. Florian has a more than three-hundred-year history and may be one of the oldest continuously operating cafés in Europe. Caffè Florian is quite expensive, but the weather was perfect and we needed to savor this special experience. My sister is a big fan of traditional English afternoon high tea, so we decided to order a sampling of biscotti, macarons, *tipici sconi inglesi* (scones), and a selections of *tramezzini* (finger sandwiches) accompanied by a fragrant blooming tea (*fiori di tè*).

Content with our whirlwind tour of this ancient capital, we boarded the waterbus and soon thereafter we were back on board. The five o'clock Palm Sunday liturgy on board was a surprisingly overflow crowd, especially since the ship was moored in Venice overnight. I had presumed that many of the passengers would have remained in the city for dinner. Regardless of their plans, there was standing room only for the liturgy and the passengers all left happily waving the palm branches that the ship had so providently provided.

On the dinner menu on board that evening was a popular Venetian dish I had not tasted before—ragù di coniglio con tagliatelle. Many Americans, like myself, may not be familiar with eating rabbit, but it is very popular in Italy. Rabbit is a mild and quite delicious meat, especially when prepared in a ragù.

When the Indonesian-born dining room manager, who had become a friend, passed by our table enquiring if everything had been to our liking, I was highly complimentary about the rabbit ragù. Not much later the executive chef, attired in impeccably clean kitchen whites and tall toque, appeared at our table beaming about what the manager had conveyed to him about my pleasure with the ragù. He described his method of preparation, and I am happy to pass on my version of how he and his staff created this scrumptious Venetian specialty.

RAGÙ DI CONIGLIO CON TAGLIATELLE

Tagliatelle with Venetian rabbit sauce

Makes 4 to 6 servings

Ingredients

For the rabbit marinade

- 2 cups red wine
- 2 cloves of minced garlic
- 1 chopped small onion
- 1 teaspoon crushed black peppercorns
- 1 teaspoon crushed juniper berries
- 1 sprig rosemary (or 1 teaspoon dried rosemary)
- 2 bay leaves
- 3 torn fresh sage leaves (or 1 teaspoon dried sage)

For the ragù

- 2½–3 pounds whole rabbit
- unsalted butter
- extra-virgin olive oil
- ¼ pound diced pancetta
- 1 diced onion
- 1 peeled and diced carrot
- 1 diced celery stick
- 3 sage leaves
- 1 sprig rosemary
- 1 cup dry white wine
- 2 cups chicken or vegetable stock
- 14-ounce can diced tomatoes

continued

- 1 tablespoon tomato paste
- Kosher salt
- freshly ground black pepper

For the pasta

- 1½ pounds fresh or dried tagliatelle

Method

1. If the rabbit is purchased whole, prepare by removing its hind legs, as you would with a chicken, by cutting through the meat and the spine where the legs join the body. Cut the front legs away from the ribs. Cut between the rib cage and the saddle (the saddle, or loin, is the region in between the hind legs and the rib cage) using a flexible boning knife. Discard the ribcage and trim away any loose flesh from the saddle. Cut the saddle into two pieces through the backbone.
2. Put the rabbit pieces into a zipped freezer bag along with a marinade of juniper berries, sage, minced garlic, chopped onion, a fresh rosemary branch, black peppercorns, bay leaves, and 2 cups of red wine. Marinate in the refrigerator for at least 2 hours or overnight.
3. Preheat oven to 325°F.
4. Remove the rabbit pieces from the marinade and pat dry. Discard the marinade and herbs.
5. Distribute the rabbit parts in a baking pan, drizzle with some olive oil, and bake for 30 minutes. The meat will be partially cooked at this point.
6. Remove, cool a bit, and shred the meat, discarding the bones. Set the shredded meat aside.
7. Heat the butter and oil in a large skillet set over a medium heat. Once hot, add the pancetta and pan-fry until browned and crisp, about 2 minutes. Remove to paper towels to drain and cool. Reserve the cooking oil and pancetta fat.

8. Add the onion, carrot, celery, sage, and rosemary and continue pan-frying until the vegetables are tender.
9. At this point stir in rabbit meat, add the wine, stock, diced tomatoes, and tomato paste. Once the sauce is simmering, reduce the heat to low and cover.
10. Cook the ragù for about 1 hour, stirring occasionally and adding more stock if the liquid reduces too quickly.
11. Taste and adjust the seasoning; discard the sage and rosemary, remove from the heat, and set aside.
12. Cook the tagliatelle according to packaging directions to the al dente stage.
13. When the pasta is ready, drain it and add to the ragù. Toss until the pasta is well-coated with the sauce. Serve with a sprinkling of the sautéed pancetta pieces and generously finish with some freshly grated Parmigiano-Reggiano.

The sole disappointment in the voyage was the not-unexpected cancellation of our port-of-call in Istanbul. Turkey had recently survived the bloodiest coup attempt in its political history on July 15, 2016, when a segment of the country's military launched a coordinated assault in several major cities with the intention of toppling the government and ousting President Recep Tayyip Erdogan. Erdogan reacted swiftly and vehemently, arresting thousands of military officials, pilots, police officers, civil servants, writers, and professors. They were accused of complicity in the plot to overthrow his government and removed from their respective jobs. Because of these tensions the US government had restricted travel to Turkey, and Holland America Line cancelled its scheduled port-of-call. My sister's oldest son is married to a Turkish woman whose parents live in Bodrum, and they had been hoping to meet our ship upon its arrival in Istanbul. Those plans had to be aborted and the ship reset it course for the Greek islands and for Athens.

In 2017, Orthodox Christians and Western Christians were celebrating the Sacred Triduum and Easter during the same week. The Christian Orthodox

Church follows the Julian calendar when calculating the date of Easter, while the rest of Christianity uses the Gregorian calendar. Also, as historians note, Orthodox Christians continue to adhere to a determination made in 325 by the Council of Nicea requiring that the annual celebration of Easter take place after the Jewish Passover, in order to maintain the biblical sequence of Christ's Passion. For us, this meant that as we were visiting the Greek islands during the week leading up to Easter, these communities would be observing the same holy days, both liturgically and culturally.

It was a challenge to prepare and celebrate the distinctive liturgical services of the sacred Triduum—Holy Thursday, Good Friday, and Holy Saturday—while the ship was pursuing its own entertainment and activity programs. However, for the ship's Catholic travelers, being able to celebrate these holy days alongside the Greek Orthodox faithful was an added grace.

As we entered the Ionian Sea, my mind was transported back to my days in high school and college where I first became immersed in the ancient Greek language and through it, some of Greece's literature, history, and mythologies and sagas of its battles, wars, and conquests. I remember vividly reading descriptions by Thucydides about Sparta's fear of the alliances and territorial expansion of Athens, which he viewed as the catalyst for the fifth-century BCE Peloponnesian War. It was the same Thucydides who describes a naval battle that involved ancient *Κόρκυρα* or Corfu, our first destination off the northwestern border of Greece. According to historian and military officer Thucydides, this battle in the Ionian Sea triggered the lengthy war that would ensue between Greece and Sparta.

Santorini—located in the southern Aegean Sea—is a photographer's dream with its whitewashed buildings and contrasting bright blue domes. I do not recall precisely where I first heard a description of Santorini as a place where there are more donkeys than there are people, more wine than water, and more churches than homes. Whatever the source, it is not hyperbole. There are hundreds of hard-working donkeys serving as taxis for tourists to get from the waterfront to the city proper. As to the churches, there seems to be a little chapel almost at every turn, with abundant icons and the smell of burning beeswax candles and incense. As we were passing one of these small houses of worship, a priest was chanting as he was vigorously incensing the icons with a censer with its twelve bells rhythmically punctuating his prayers as clouds of billowing frankincense encircled him. Some people have asked about the symbolism of the bells on an oriental censer. Traditionally, the bells symbolize the twelve apostles of Jesus, and express God's continuous invitation to gather in worship in God's holy place, which is the gateway to heaven and life eternal.

I do not know what may have prompted this association with heaven, but on board that evening the *Prinsendam*'s pastry chef was offering one of Holland America's signature desserts, a Grand Marnier chocolate mousse cake, which was perfected by Master Chef Rudi Sodamin. It is a luxurious, Grand Marnier-flavored mousse layered on a foundation of chocolate génoise. I adapted this recipe from one of Holland America's cookbooks, and it's now a standard feature in my own *répertoire pâtissier*.[14]

GRAND MARNIER CHOCOLATE MOUSSE CAKE

Makes 8 to 10 servings

Ingredients

For the chocolate génoise cake

- 4 tablespoons unsalted butter
- 1 teaspoon vanilla extract
- 4 large eggs
- ⅔ cup superfine sugar
- ⅓ cup sifted all-purpose flour
- ⅓ cup sifted unsweetened Dutch-process cocoa powder

For the Grand Marnier chocolate mousse

- 1 pound finely chopped semisweet chocolate
- 1 cup granulated sugar
- 10 separated eggs
- 2 tablespoons Grand Marnier
- sweetened whipped cream

continued

14 Holland America, *A Taste of Celebration* (New York: Rizzoli, 1986).

For the garnish

- 6 to 8 strawberries, hulled and cut into wedges
- semisweet or bittersweet chocolate curls or shavings

Method

Making the chocolate génoise cake

1. Preheat the oven to 350°F.
2. Butter a 9-inch round cake or springform pan, line it with parchment or wax paper, and then butter the paper liner and flour it.
3. In a small heavy saucepan, melt the butter over medium heat to clarify. Reserve the clarified butter and discard the residual milk solids. Add the vanilla to the clarified butter and set aside.
4. In a wide saucepan, bring about 1 inch of water to a bare simmer, adjusting the heat as needed to maintain it. Combine the eggs and sugar in a large heatproof mixing bowl big enough to sit on the pan. Do not let the bottom of the bowl touch the simmering water.
5. Using a handheld electric mixer or immersion blender fitted with the whisk attachment, beat until the mixture is pale in color, stopping two or three times to scrape down the sides of the bowl, until the eggs are lukewarm (105°F).
6. Turn the heat off and remove the bowl from the pan but leave the pan on the stove.
7. Off the heat, continue to beat the egg mixture at high speed until it is cooled and tripled in volume. The egg mixture will be thick and will form a slowly dissolving ribbon.
8. Place a sheet of wax or parchment paper on your work surface and sift the flour and cocoa powder together over it three times. Sift about a third of the flour and cocoa mixture over the egg mixture. With a rubber spatula, fold the flour mixture quickly but gently into the eggs

until combined. Add the remaining flour in the same way, one-third at a time, until all the flour is incorporated.

9. If the reserved clarified butter mixture has cooled, briefly set it over the pan of water on the stove to remelt it. Place the bowl of butter on your work surface and add about a cup of the egg batter to it. With a rubber spatula, fold them together and then scrape this mixture back into the remaining egg batter and fold. Scrape the batter into the prepared cake pan and level the surface.
10. Bake the génoise for 30 to 35 minutes, or until the cake begins to shrink slightly around the edges and the top springs back when pressed with your finger. Allow the cake to cool completely in the pan on a rack.
11. To unmold it, run a small knife or offset spatula around the edges of the cake and invert it onto a rack. Remove the parchment and turn the cake right side up.
12. Lightly butter the sides of a 9-inch springform cake pan and line the sides with a strip of parchment cut exactly to fit. Cut a ½-inch-tall layer of the chocolate génoise and place it in the bottom of the prepared springform pan. Set aside. Save any remaining génoise for another use.

Making the Grand Marnier chocolate mousse

1. Place the chocolate in a large bowl; set aside. In a small saucepan, combine the sugar and 1 cup water and place the pan over medium heat. As soon as the sugar has dissolved and the syrup begins to boil, remove it from the heat and pour it over the chocolate.
2. Let the mixture rest briefly to melt the chocolate, and then whisk until completely combined. Beat in the egg yolks, one at a time, stopping occasionally to scrape down the sides of the bowl, until they are fully incorporated. Beat in the Grand Marnier.
3. Place the egg whites in the very clean bowl of a stand mixer fitted with

continued

a clean whisk attachment. Beat the egg whites on medium speed until soft peaks form.

4. Use a large rubber spatula to transfer about a third of the whites to the bowl with the chocolate and fold them together to lighten the mixture. Very gently fold the remaining egg whites into the chocolate, taking care not to deflate them.
5. Pour the mousse mixture into the prepared springform pan and smooth the top. Place the pan, uncovered, in the refrigerator until it is fully chilled. Cover the surface with plastic wrap and continue chilling for several hours or overnight.
6. To serve, remove the outer ring from the springform pan and gently remove the parchment paper. Put the whipped cream into a pastry bag and pipe rosettes on top of the cake. Garnish with the strawberries and shaved chocolate.

Our *Prinsendam* celebration of Holy Thursday was held at five o'clock. Instead of the traditional rite of the washing of the feet, I invited all of the participants to share in the washing of each other's hands, which proved to be a very moving and humbling experience of fraternal service. Earlier in the day, on the island of Mykonos, we arrived early enough in the morning to observe the latter part of the vesperal divine liturgy of Saint Basil that was being celebrated in the church of Zoodochos Pigis or Megali Panagia, the Greek Orthodox Cathedral of Saint Mary the Great, which was located only a short distance from the island's tiny Roman Catholic church. This liturgy of Holy Thursday commemorates the institution of the Holy Eucharist. In the Roman Catholic Church, prior to the reform of the liturgy after the Second Vatican Council, the rites of Holy Thursday were celebrated in the morning. I was struck by the number of people of all ages who were present and participating in this service and who received holy communion. Though obviously seen as tourists who had wandered into the church, we were nonetheless made to feel welcome. The church was enveloped in incense and everyone was standing closely together, seemingly oblivious to life outside.

Located in a square filled with shops and restaurants, for locals, this place was clearly the place to be on this holy day. After our visit to the cathedral, we paused for a light lunch. I noticed that the Greeks who were sitting next to our table were eating what at first I thought was spanakopita, a traditional savory spinach pie. When I inquired of our server, who spoke very good English, she told us that the pie was kremidopita (κρεμμυδόπιτα), a local Eastertime favorite made with caramelized onions. It occurred to me that many cultures have onion pies—for example, the classic dish made in Provence pissaladière. We ordered the kremidopita along with a Greek salad and had the most enjoyable and memorable lunch in Mykonos. Here is my attempt to recreate this simple but tasty onion pie.

KREMIDOPITA

Caramelized onion Greek Easter pie

Makes 6 to 8 servings

Ingredients

- 6 large onions
- 3 tablespoons olive oil
- 1 tablespoon tomato paste
- 1 teaspoon sweet paprika
- sea salt
- freshly ground black pepper
- phyllo dough sheets
- unsalted butter

Method

1. Preheat oven to 400°F.
2. Peel the onions and cut in half. Then, slice each of the halves into strips.
3. In a large skillet over a medium-high flame, heat the olive oil. Slowly

continued

cook the onions until they soften and begin to turn a light, golden color.

4. Open a space in the middle of the onions and cook and caramelize the tomato paste for a minute or two before combining with the onions.
5. Add the salt, pepper, and paprika and combine.
6. Continue to cook the onion mixture for another 5 to 8 minutes.
7. Prepare a 9-inch square metal or glass baking dish by lining the pan in both directions with sheets of overlapping aluminum foil. Spray lightly with cooking spray.
8. Working quickly so as not to dry out the phyllo dough, initially cut five 9-inch squares of the dough.
9. Place one layer on the bottom of the pan and brush with melted butter. Repeat the process until you have built up at least five layers of the phyllo dough.
10. Evenly spread the slightly cooled onion mixture over the bottom phyllo base.
11. Cut five more squares of phyllo and place over the onions, alternating each layer with the melted butter.
12. Cut a final layer of the phyllo about 10 inches square, butter the top layer, and place the larger piece of dough over the top, folding down inside the edges of the pan, to seal the pie. Butter the top layer of the phyllo.
13. With a sharp paring knife, cut a small cross into the center, to allow steam to escape.
14. Baked in preheated oven for 35 to 45 minutes or until golden brown.
15. Allow the pie to cool for 10 minutes before carefully removing from the pan, using the aluminum foil "wings," and slicing.

As Easter Sunday dawned our ship was already berthed in the port of Piraeus, the main port of Athens and the largest commercial port in Greece. Because this was a major port of disembarkation for the *Prinsendam*—including the end of the voyage for my family and friend—I celebrated the Easter Mass at 7 a.m. in the ship's principal theatre. In preparation, I had enlisted participation from some of the ship's musicians to provide music, and from one of the ship's vocalists to serve as the cantor. Some of the ships, officers and crew did the readings and led the universal prayers, and a couple of the passengers acted as Eucharistic ministers. The young Filipino who was the ship's florist had decorated the sanctuary area with two large, impressive arrangements and he had repurposed some of the ship's large fern plants to augment the floral displays. The theatre was packed with more than three hundred worshippers. We sang many alleluias, and at breakfast afterwards, many of those who had attended the Mass said it was one of the nicest Easter services they had ever experienced.

My family had decided to extend their stay in Athens before returning to Boston. After they disembarked from the *Prinsendam* and reclaimed their baggage in Piraeus, I accompanied them for the short five-mile taxi ride from the port to a downtown Athens hotel where they had booked rooms for the next two nights. Once settled in their hotel rooms, we began to discover Athens on a warm, sunny, festive Easter Sunday afternoon. It was an idyllic day to show my travel companions a bit of Athens and its famous Pláka neighborhood. Many Athenians leave the city for Holy Week and Easter, so there was much less traffic than usual and less pollution from car and bus emissions. A relatively calm atmosphere pervaded the avenues and side streets.

I was hopeful that we might arrive in time to catch a bit of the divine liturgy in the Greek Orthodox Metropolitan Cathedral of the Annunciation (Καθεδρικός Ναός Ευαγγελισμού της Θεοτόκου), which is the mother church not only of Athens but of all Greece. As we soon learned, the cathedral doors were locked tight. We met one of the locals who told us what had taken place earlier that day. The cathedral's Easter Anastasi services had begun the night before, around midnight, when the archbishop emerged from the cathedral and proclaimed to those gathered in the plaza, "*Christos anesti*" (Christ has risen). Candles were then lit from the holy flame from Jerusalem, and almost simultaneously with the archbishop's proclamation, fireworks were set off. The light from candles was quickly passed among all the people who had come to church. As the holy flame was passed through the crowd, the whole plaza in front of the cathedral reverberated with the words "*Christos anesti*" and the response "*Alithos anesti*" (Truly, he has risen). Then the Divine Liturgy was celebrated, and people returned to their homes around 3 or 4 o'clock in the morning. We understood exactly why the doors of the cathedral were closed on Easter Sunday afternoon.

We moved from the site of the cathedral to the old neighborhood of the Pláka with its winding streets and beautiful buildings, one of the oldest historical neighborhoods of Athens. It is located very near the Acropolis. The aroma of roasting lamb was in the air and as we walked through the streets, it seemed that a whole lamb was roasting on open fires everywhere we turned. For forty days leading up to Easter, many devout Greeks had fasted and abstained from eating meat. We sensed that the celebrating families were ready for a meat-centered feast.

At an open-air taverna in a large square shaded by many fragrant trees, we settled down for a traditional Easter dinner. Central to the restaurant's offerings that day was the traditional roasted lamb served with mounds of oven-roasted potatoes, along with a medley of roasted spring vegetables. Most of us ordered this outstanding Easter lamb special. My recipe uses ingredients from the Greek pantry, but the basic preparation and roasting techniques are ones that my Irish maternal grandmother, Rose O'Brien, used and that I have relied upon for years.

GREEK-STYLE ROASTED LEG OF LAMB

Makes 10 to 12 servings

Ingredients

- 4½–5 pounds leg or shoulder of lamb
- 4 garlic cloves
- 1½ cups chicken stock
- ½ cup dry white wine
- 2 quartered red onions
- 1½ pounds fingerling potatoes, halved lengthways
- 2 quartered and seeded lemons
- 1 cup pitted Kalamata olives

- kosher salt and freshly grated black pepper
- dried or fresh oregano
- olive oil
- all-purpose flour

Method

1. Preheat oven to 375°F.
2. Prepare the lamb by vigorously rubbing all over with extra-virgin olive oil and seasoning liberally with a mixture of kosher salt, freshly ground black pepper, and dried or fresh oregano. With a sharp paring knife, make several 1-inch-deep incisions into the flesh and insert pieces of garlic. Then sprinkle the lamb with some sifted all-purpose flour, shaking off any excess.
3. Place the seasoned lamb in a large roasting pan fitted with a wire rack.
4. Add the chicken stock and wine around the lamb in the roasting pan and cover with aluminum foil.
5. Roast for 1 hour. Take the roasting pan from the oven and place on the stovetop. Remove the aluminum foil covering. Baste the lamb with the pan liquids. Arrange the fingerling potatoes, onions, lemons, and olives around the lamb. Recover the roasting pan with the foil and continue roasting for an additional hour.
6. During the last half hour of roasting, remove the foil and allow the lamb to brown.
7. The optimal internal temperature for a perfectly roasted leg or shoulder of lamb is between 130° and 140° Fahrenheit, for medium-rare to medium.
8. When the lamb is roasted to the desired temperature, remove the pan from the oven and place the roast on a carving board, covered loosely with foil, and allow it to rest for about 15 minutes before carving and serving.

continued

9. Transfer the roasted vegetables to an oven-safe serving platter. Cover with foil and return to the warm oven until ready to serve.
10. Strain the pan juices and skim any fat that may have accumulated. The pan juices are all that are needed for saucing, but they can be used to make a richer pan gravy if desired.

After our Easter feast, which was enhanced by street musicians and spontaneous Greek dancing, we strolled among many of the shops open for business. My sister carried away bags of embroidered linens and various Greek comestibles as gifts for her children, grandchildren, and friends.

Late in the afternoon I bid them farewell and returned alone to the ship. I would not see them again until I returned to the States at the conclusion of the transatlantic voyage. I later learned that after such a sumptuous early afternoon dinner they were looking for something light to eat that evening, but still authentically Greek. Their waiter enthusiastically recommended that they try what he described as a very special "Greek Easter soup—*magiritsa*." Charles and Eddie quickly said they would love to try it. My sister, prudently, opted for a large Greek salad. When the soup arrived, they tasted it. Very quickly, they began to look at each other quizzically.

"What's in it?" Eddie queried.

Charles said, "I'm not sure, but it looks to me like an animal's internal organs." They called back the waiter and asked him what was in this special soup. Proudly he said, "Oh, it's made from lamb offal: heart, liver, lungs, and intestines, along with a red onion, and flavored with olive oil and lemon." As he spoke, my sister later recounted that the men's eyes dilated, which the waiter quickly saw. "If you don't like it, I would be happy to replace it with something else on the menu," he said. They probably ordered a hamburger. So much for daring to ask for the local Greek specialty on Easter Sunday night.

As the *Prinsendam* departed Athens it made its way back through the Mediterranean, calling on ports in Malta and Granada before arriving at A Coruña, a Galician port city in northwestern Spain. As soon as the ship was in port and cleared for disembarkation, three of the passengers and I booked a taxi for a destination that all of us were anxious to visit: the cathedral church of Santiago de Compostela and its world-famous burial place of the apostle Saint James the Great. This religious site is the culmination of the Camino de Santiago pilgrimage made by many people of faith since the ninth century.

It was raining heavily on the day we made our pilgrimage by taxi from the ship to the shrine. Our cab driver, who spoke enough English to allow us to converse with him, said it rained a lot in that region of the country because of its geographical location on the Atlantic Ocean. He brought us practically to the entrance to the cathedral. When we entered, we were not surprised to find many other passengers and crew members from the ship gathered inside. It seemed that many of us shared the same objective during this brief port visit.

We were in for a special treat. Every day a Mass is celebrated at midday to celebrate the completion of the camino. People of every age and from every part of the world make this pilgrimage. El Camino de Santiago begins in France at Saint Jean Pied de Port and travels five hundred miles through four of Spain's fifteen regions, ending at the Cathedral of Santiago de Compostela. Even though we had not walked a single mile of the pilgrim's route, we nonetheless joined with that day's arrivals in a special pilgrims' Mass. At the end of Mass as a hymn was being sung in honor of St. James, a huge silver censer (what the Spanish call a *botafumeiro)*, probably 5 feet tall and weighing 170 hundred pounds, suspended from the ceiling and billowing with smoke from burning incense, was released. It swung back and forth over the congregation, creating dramatic clouds of smoke and perfuming the entire church. I had never seen anything quite so dramatic in a church service. It was worthy of a Verdi opera.

Each of us got a chance to climb the stairs to the cathedral and enter through the carved stone Portico de la Gloria, which millions of pilgrims before us had passed at the end of their journeys. Like them, we touched the twelfth-century center column, which bears an image of St. James.

All of us from the *Prinsendam* continued to talk about our visit to Santiago de Compostela for days. Each was struck by how many people—with hopes and dreams, prayers and petitions—had entered that same cathedral through the centuries.

Before our ship embarked on the final transatlantic leg of its long voyage, the *Prinsendam*'s final European port of call was to the Azores, an archipelago of islands in the Atlantic Ocean, about 1,000 miles off the coast of Portugal. For a day, we were in port at Ponta Delgada in São Miguel. Although the day was bright and sunny, there were brisk Atlantic spring breezes, which required a windbreaker in order to be comfortable. Our time ashore was only a few hours. It was enough time to explore the island on foot. Due to their isolated geographical location, the Azoreans' way of life appeared both frugal and self-reliant. I noted as we walked along the streets, there were very few restaurants. The produce markets offered limited products for sale.

Our meanderings brought us to the Campo de São Francisco, one of the city's main gathering places. We found a bench on which to sit and enjoy the view of the wrought iron grille work that seemed to be a shared characteristic of the balconies of buildings in the neighborhood. Many of the houses were whitewashed. The white contrasted dramatically with the black enamel of the grilles. We watched as workers strung lights on the limbs of the barren trees throughout the square.

One of the locals told me that these were preparations for the upcoming feast of Santo Cristo, a celebration that begins every year on the fifth Sunday after Easter. The beautiful church located on one corner of this square is the Igreja do Santo Cristo. Our new friend told me about the Cult of the Lord Holy Christ of the Miracles, or what she described as the Culto do Senhor Santo Cristo dos Milagros. It is a popular religious veneration of an image of Jesus Christ. She explained that this is an event in which everyone participates, with processions, songs, food, and family entertainment. It sounded as if Ponta Delgada hosted a country fair, complete with day and night entertainment, including carnival rides for the children. After her description I visited the church and was impressed by the beauty of its interior that rivaled the churches of Spain.

When I asked about foods that would be characteristic of the island of São Miguel, she described a simple, hearty sopa de couves—a soup made of beans, *chouriçāo*, potatoes, and kale and seasoned with red pepper flakes. Here is my rendition.

AZOREAN SOPA DE COUVES

Bean and kale soup

Makes 8 to 10 servings

Ingredients

- 1 pound washed and sorted red kidney beans
- 12 cups water

- 1 pound Portuguese chourição (or linguiça)
- 2 cups torn kale leaves
- 2 large Yukon Gold potatoes
- kosher salt and freshly grated black pepper
- ½ teaspoon (or more) red pepper flakes

Method

1. Soak the red kidney beans in water overnight. In the morning, drain and rinse the beans and allow them to drain in a colander.
2. Prep all of the ingredients for the soup:
   - Cut the Portuguese chourição into quarter-inch slices.
   - With a sharp knife, cut the kale leaves from their stalks and then tear the leaves into small pieces. Discard the stems.
   - Peel the potatoes and slice them laterally and then into sticks, and then into a large dice.
   - In a mortar, add the salt, pepper, and pepper flakes and pound with pestle until well blended. (In São Miguel, they tend to add more red pepper flakes to their sopa.)
3. In a large soup pot, add the 12 cups of water. Add the beans and bring to a boil.
4. When the water is boiling, add the chourição, cover the pot with a lid, reduce the heat to medium low, and simmer for about 30 minutes until the beans are fully cooked and tender. Occasionally stir the beans to avoid clumping and sticking.
5. When the beans are tender, add the torn kale leaves, the diced potatoes, and the spice mixture. Stir well to blend. Recover the pot and continue to simmer for another 20 minutes or more, until the potatoes are tender.

The return trip across the Atlantic was smooth and uneventful. After months of living, praying, and exploring together, we all appreciated the days at sea to consolidate our memories and to prepare to reengage our ordinary work and relationships. The entire four months at sea had provided a graceful time of transition and an opportunity to prepare for my new mission in caring for aging and infirm Jesuits at Campion Center.

Chapter 17

THE FINAL MISSION

Even to your old age and gray hairs, I am he who will sustain you.
I have made you and I will carry you.
I will sustain you and I will rescue you.

—ISAIAH 46:4

Yogi Berra was admired for his baseball prowess. He was also beloved as an American original because of his unique "Yogi-isms"—one of his best being the well-known "It's déjà vu all over again." That memorable quip captures a bit how I was feeling as my sister Maryellen drove me to the front door of Campion Center on a mid-May morning in 2017.

In 1973, while I had been a doctoral student studying clinical psychology at Boston University and living at Boston College, the provincial of the New England Province, Fr. Richard Cleary, S.J., invited me to partner with Fr. John Conklin, S.J., who was overseeing the renovations of the north wing at Weston College that was destined to become a fifteen-bed skilled nursing care facility and retirement residence for Jesuits. Later, Fr. Cleary asked me to draft the "determination of need" application through which Campion Center would seek to obtain its nursing home operating license from the Commonwealth of Massachusetts. In a letter dated February 22, 1977, Campion was granted its initial licensure by the Massachusetts Department of Public Health to provide Level II skilled nursing care. The establishing license was for a quota of fifteen beds to serve the healthcare needs of New England Jesuits who were experiencing acute episodes of illness, occasional needs for rehabilitation, or for palliative or hospice care during the final months of their lives.

In 1926, New England Jesuits separated from New York and became an independent province of the Society of Jesus. The province comprised at the time 492 Jesuits. When I pronounced my vows at Shadowbrook in 1964, the New England Province had reached a peak membership of 1,129 Jesuits. The present-day Campion Center building had originally been designed to serve as the new province's principal house of studies. For the next forty years, three years of Jesuit education in philosophy and four years in theology took place in that building. When the goals of Jesuit formation began to shift after Vatican II, the province sought to find new apostolic uses for this massive building. It ultimately determined that it could serve two useful apostolic purposes: as a healthcare residence for aging and infirm Jesuits of the province, and as a retreat and spirituality center.

Late in 1974, as I was completing work on my doctoral dissertation, Fr. Cleary asked if I would be available the following summer to become the first clinical administrator of the Campion Health Center. To prepare for that prospective new mission I resigned from the part-time clinical positions I had been holding at the time at the Cambridge Guidance Center and the Cambridge Hospital, and declined a proposed teaching appointment at Boston College. When Fr. George Drury, S.J., was appointed to be Campion's new superior with an expectation that he would focus his time and energy in developing the nascent retreat and renewal ministry at Campion, he asked the provincial if he might extend his oversight responsibilities as superior to also include the administration of the health center.

During a hastily arranged dinner on Good Friday 1975, the provincial told me of these unanticipated developments. He also offered me carte blanche to use the following year to prepare for another longer term apostolic assignment. Providentially, as I recounted in an earlier chapter, I was able hastily to arrange to complete tertianship in Rome with Fr. Ed Malatesta, S.J., at the Gregorian University (1975–1976). From that serendipitous turn of events unfolded a rich and diverse apostolic life that included university teaching and administration, consultation and strategic planning, travel and pastoral service, nonprofit healthcare executive leadership, and fundraising. Together these experiences would shape and define the following forty-four years of my Jesuit priestly ministry.

As in earlier conversations with a provincial in 1975, a similar dialogue in 2016 with a successor provincial (provincials ordinarily serve six-year terms) conspired to bring my life full circle. As I was concluding my tenure at HealthCare Chaplaincy in New York City, I had harbored fantasies of remaining in the city and engaging in some pastoral ministries and nonprofit consultations. The provincial, Fr. John Cecero, S.J., had other ideas.

When he first raised with me the possibility that I return to the Boston area and Campion Center as its CEO and religious superior, I was initially reluctant. By then, already in my mid-seventies, I did not relish the prospect of pulling up personal and professional roots in New York to take on another onerous executive responsibility. Running through my head were the words "Been there, done that." However, after months of prayer, consultation, and discernment, I told the provincial that I would be open to this new challenging mission if this was what he wanted me to do.

Throughout my six decades as a Jesuit, as this memoir has so amply borne testimony, the good Lord had given me so many opportunities to grow in knowledge and experience, especially in cognate areas of strategic planning, healthcare administration, sustainable development, and fundraising. I realized that these acquired skills could benefit the mission and future of Campion Center. What finally led me to the decision to accept the mission at Campion Center was the recognition that God was asking me to use my aggregated talents and experiences to help the province make prudential and strategic choices to ensure its continuing ability to provide astute care for its aging, infirm, injured, and dying Jesuit brothers. The provincial also wanted me to focus on how best to renovate and care for this iconic 1926 building.

As I was again walking up those familiar granite steps to enter Campion Center as its new leader on a bright spring morning, I recalled words once spoken by President Lyndon Baines Johnson: "Yesterday is not ours to recover, but tomorrow is ours to win or lose."[15]

I had lived in this building as a Jesuit student from 1965 to 1967, and during the intervening years I rarely had occasion to visit Weston. Today, Campion Center functions as a comprehensive continuing care retirement community for the USA East Province. In addition to providing a Jesuit community context for men who remain functionally independent and require minimal medical and nursing supervision, Campion Center is the sole comprehensive fully licensed healthcare facility operated by the Society of Jesus in the United States and Canada. In addition, it also staffs and manages an integrated conference and renewal ministry. It provides Jesuits with state-of-the-art medical, nursing, and rehabilitative care in a vibrant,

---

15 Thanksgiving Address to the Nation on November 29, 1963, a week after assassination of John F. Kennedy.

warm, and welcoming apostolic community. Campion Conference & Renewal also offers lay and religious seekers an expansive medley of professional, educational, and spiritual care programs and services that are rooted in the Spiritual Exercises of Saint Ignatius as well as in the Ignatian tradition.

The provincial was clear in stating what he hoped I, along with Campion's very talented and dedicated staff, would be able to accomplish during my tenure: imagine the future of Campion Center and translate that vision into comprehensive, apostolic, strategic, and tactical business plans. I pledged that I would invest my full energies to accomplish these specific objectives, and with a deep breath, I embarked on this new venture.

From its initial 15 licensed skilled nursing care beds, Campion Health & Wellness had grown to a facility with 34 licensed skilled nursing care and 36 assisted living beds. In addition, the total Jesuit community numbered more than 75 priests and brothers and a Jesuit and lay staff of about 115 employees. My first task was getting to know this extensive network of brother Jesuits, nurses, nurses' aides, social workers, therapists, dieticians, cooks, housekeepers, maintenance workers, and a considerable number of business professionals. The learning curve during my first summer at Campion was steep. By Labor Day, I knew almost everyone by name and function.

It also took some time to untangle certain legal and governance anomalies that had arisen during Campion's prior forty years of operations. With the help of experienced nonprofit healthcare lawyers, we were able to revise Campion's bylaws and streamline corporate operations and to reflect best not-for-profit corporate practices. And with a highly qualified and committed senior management team, we began the slow process of communal discernment about Campion's apostolic future.

In addition to the main building, Campion's campus includes the Grant Walker manor house. That manor house was on the property when the Jesuits purchased the estate in 1921. The entire property was owed by Mrs. Mabel Shaw Walker, and in addition to the manor house, the estate included 120 acres of land on both sides of Concord Road. The Jesuits purchased the land and buildings on November 17, 1921, for $110,000. The price has been negotiated down from an original asking price of $175,000.

At the time of purchase, the main family residence was only about ten years old. It had been built in 1911 to replace the original structure, which had burned to the ground. From its earliest days, the summer home of the Walker family was referred to by the Jesuits as "the mansion." A century later, that same nominal designation endures.

The mansion is a three-storied brick Georgian building with a wing of two stories to the left. Its wood-paneled ground-floor entry foyer and its four great rooms have been preserved. In Weston this mansion sits at the town's highest elevation, about two hundred feet above sea level. From its large rear veranda, in the 1920s one must have been able to see distant vistas of the cities of Cambridge and Boston. This perhaps explains why the Walkers referred to their manse as "Fairview."

Access to the second floor of the mansion, where the bedrooms are located, is via two magnificent dark oak stairways and railings. The rooms that make up the superior's apartment were located on the first-floor rear corridor in the two-story wing. Originally, they were most probably providing housing for domestic staff. The mansion has a large and impressive dining room with curved windows facing east, overlooking the rear garden. All the rooms on the ground floor have large fireplaces and original cast bronze lighting fixtures, which, at some stage, had been converted from gas to electricity. When the provincial residence at 297 Commonwealth Avenue was sold, its large dining room table and chairs were given to Campion Center. They found a new home in the mansion's dining room. The table comfortably accommodates twelve guests.

The original pantry over the years had been converted to a small kitchen fitted with mongrel, mismatched cabinets and vintage appliances. When I arrived, eight or nine Jesuits were living in the mansion and there were a couple of additional rooms to accommodate guests. Since the mansion Jesuit residents dined communally in the main refectory, there was little use made of the mansion's kitchen other than to store snacks or prepare a light meal.

During my initial summer, with the input and assistance of an amazingly talented maintenance department, I embarked on two in-house renovation projects. The department comprised a licensed plumber and electrician, two finish carpenters, two painters, and other workmen who could multitask among the building trades. The team's manager was a licensed contractor.

The first project in the main building was to refresh the large first-floor room that was being used by the Jesuit community as a chapel for daily Mass. In the days when the building had functioned as a house of studies, this was one of Weston College's largest lecture rooms. It had oversized windows facing east and south that drew in abundant light. Because this chapel served as a daily worship space for many aging Jesuits who were dependent on walkers and wheelchairs, the space needed to be reconfigured to accommodate their special circumstances. With the help of our maintenance team we redesigned the space, ordered what would be needed, and completed all of the renovations within six weeks.

The chapel, oddly, did not have a proper name; the Jesuits simply referred to it as "the daily Mass chapel." The restoration and renovation of the worship space included not only the principal gathering space with its adjacent vesting room and sacristy, but also the external foyer, where we created a small devotional chapel for the stations of the cross.

When the renovations were completed, which included new seating, lighting, air-conditioning, and sound system, the community gathered to dedicate the chapel in honor of Our Lady of Montserrat.

A second project undertaken that summer was the redesign and renovation of the 1950-era mansion kitchen. The room has two large east-facing windows, which admitted wonderful light and provided great natural ventilation. There was a large closet located in the adjacent corridor. It invited repurposing as a dry-storage pantry. The kitchen floor had been covered with a worn vinyl linoleum. The vintage yellow enamel electric stove and oven was scarcely functional. There was no gas line available.

Together with a couple of our craftsmen, we quickly developed a cost-effective design and plan to give this space new life as a working kitchen. Crucial to the plan was the counsel of our plumber, who said that if we located the range and oven between the two windows, he would be able to purchase a large propane tank that could be hidden away from the building. He said that it would be easy to trench a gas line to the tank and connect it to a new gas cooktop and oven. We relocated the positioning of the sink and dishwasher, the refrigerator and freezer, and designated the various workstations. Our carpenter stated he could repurpose the existing cabinetry, fabricate some new doors as needed, and refit some of the mongrel cabinets with new glass doors and hardware. We decided to use granite countertops for most of the new work surfaces and specified a six-foot butcher block countertop for one of the prep workstations. Our electrician recommended we rewire the entire kitchen to bring it up to code, drop the ceiling and install energy-efficient LED lights, provide under-cabinet lighting, and install multiple outlets to accommodate countertop appliances. We decided to repaint all of the cabinet surfaces with a soft white enamel product and all of the interior surfaces of the cabinets and drawers with a matte bright yellow color. The floor was retiled with semigloss white 12-inch ceramic tiles, which would be easy to maintain.

Once we agreed on a comprehensive plan for the renovation, we emptied the kitchen of all of its contents. We also discarded many cans and spices whose expiration dates were generally some fifteen years earlier. In less than a month from the initial planning team meeting, the new kitchen was operational. What a remarkable transformation it was.

To celebrate this amazing feat and to properly thank the men for their accomplishments, I invited the entire maintenance department and its manager to come to the mansion's dining room for a luncheon, which I cooked and served. I prepared a three-course meal for them, beginning with a pasta course of tortellini in a cream sauce. For the entrée, I prepared a chicken breast in the French style, with a Dijon mustard sauce. For dessert I made a chocolate rolled cake filled with a raspberry cream. Several of the men were taking photos of each dish with their iPhones and sending them to their wives. Throughout my tenure, I grew in admiration and appreciation for the breadth of skills these men possessed and just how dedicated each of them was to the mission of Campion Center. We were fortunate to have such a talented and committed cadre of tradesmen who not only kept the building safe and functioning, but who brought positive energy to the workplace—especially to their relationships with the Jesuit residents.

POULET À LA DIJONAISE

Sautéed chicken breasts with mustard and tarragon cream sauce

Makes 6 to 8 servings

Ingredients

For the chicken

- 4 boneless and skinless chicken breasts, halved horizontally to make 8 filets
- kosher salt
- cracked black pepper

continued

- 4 tablespoons all-purpose flour
- 2 tablespoons unsalted butter
- 3 tablespoons olive oil
- 2 crushed whole garlic cloves

For the dijonnaise sauce

- 4 tablespoons unsalted butter
- 2 finely chopped shallot
- 6 cloves minced garlic
- 2 cups dry white wine
- 3 tablespoons Dijon mustard
- 1½ cups chicken broth
- 2 teaspoons chopped tarragon leaves
- 2 teaspoons dried thyme
- 1 teaspoon minced rosemary leaves
- 1 cup heavy cream
- salt and cracked black pepper, to taste

Method

1. Pat the chicken breasts dry with paper towels.
2. Season the chicken breast filets liberally with salt and freshly cracked pepper. Dredge in flour, shaking off the excess. Set aside.
3. Heat the butter and olive oil in a large skillet over medium-high heat. Add the crushed garlic cloves and allow them to perfume the butter and oil.
4. When the oil is hot and the garlic begins to turn golden in color, remove the garlic and discard.
5. Sauté the chicken breasts until they are golden (2 or 3 minutes on each side). Transfer to a plate and cover with foil to keep warm.
6. Add another 2 or 3 tablespoons of butter to the skillet. Sauté the

minced shallots for about 3 minutes, and then add the minced garlic and cook for another minute or less, just until the garlic flavor blossoms.

7. Pour off the residual cooking oil, if any. Add the wine to deglaze the pan, scraping up with a spatula or spoon any browned fragments on the bottom of skillet. On medium heat, cook until the volume of the wine has reduced in half.
8. Add the Dijon mustard into the reduced liquid and blend.
9. Add the chicken stock and herbs. Bring to a boil, then reduce heat to medium. Allow the liquid to reduce a bit, perhaps another 4 minutes.
10. Over low heat, whisk in the heavy cream and continue to cook and gently stir until sauce begins to thicken. This will take about 3 or 4 minutes.
11. When the sauce is slightly thickened, return the sautéed chicken filets to the skillet. Simmer gently until chicken is heated through and sauce further thickens (because of the flour coating), about 5 minutes.
12. Taste the sauce and adjust seasonings.

In recalling the redesign and refurbishment of the mansion's kitchen, I am going to digress now and reflect in some depth about my love and friendship for the Bastianich family, who not only helped equip this new mansion culinary workspace but virtually stocked and restocked the new pantry.

Any regular viewer of cooking shows on public television has more than once welcomed Lidia Bastianich into their home. I met Lidia for the first time in 1991, soon after I had arrived at my position at HealthCare Chaplaincy in New York City. The restaurant Felidia, which she and her late husband, Felice, established in 1981 on East 58th Street near Second Avenue, soon became one of my favorite places. The food was authentically Italian, reminiscent of so many earlier gustatory adventures in Italy. In those years, prior to staking her claim as a celebrity TV chef, Lidia did much of the day-to-day cooking in what would become her flagship restaurant. One would often encounter her tableside in the dining room, where she would finish a pasta dish or sauce an entrée from a skillet that was warming on a gas burner atop a nearby trolley.

When the HealthCare Chaplaincy moved to its location on East 60th Street at Second Avenue, my office was two blocks away from Lidia's restaurant. Many of my friends and trustees became regular patrons and fans, and I would occasionally be their guests for lunch or dinner. Whenever I had occasion to entertain business associates, Felidia was always on the short list of preferred venues.

Lidia Giuliana Matticchio Bastianich grew up in northeastern Italy in a region that in the year of her birth in 1947, became part of Yugoslavia. Today the area is called Istria, in Croatia. In 1956 she and her older brother, Franco, fled with their mother, Erminia, to Trieste. They were later joined by her father, Vittorio. The family lived in refugee camps for the next two years before emigrating from Italy to the United States. With the help of Catholic Relief Services, they initially settled in Bergen, New Jersey, before permanently moving to Queens, New York.

Lidia was introduced to her future husband at her sweet sixteen party. In 1966, she married Felice Bastianich, who, like herself, had been born in Istria and immigrated to the United States. Their two children, Joe and Tanya, were born in 1968 and 1972, respectively. A year before Tanya's birth, Felice and Lidia Bastianich purchased and opened their first restaurant, Buonavia, in the Forest Hills section of Queens. Lidia's mother, Grandma Erminia, helped with the children while Lidia and Felice worked to keep their little restaurant profitable.

It was during the years managing Buonavia that Lidia ventured into the world of serious Italian cooking. She gradually moved the restaurant's menu away from Italian American classics, like spaghetti and meatballs with Sunday gravy, baked ziti, sausage and peppers, ravioli, lasagna, manicotti, and pizza to a more expansive menu of authentic regional Italian dishes. Because many of the Italian immigrants coming to America who settled in New York and Boston at the end of the nineteenth century were from southern Italy, Italian cooking became synonymous with heavy red sauces and an assertive usage of garlic and peppers. Many of the dishes were baked with abundant quantities of mozzarella. Lidia introduced dishes that she had learned from her grandmother, using a more expansive repertory of fresh ingredients, flavors, and seasonings.

By the time the Bastianiches opened their second restaurant, humorously named Villa Secondo, Lidia was gaining in her confidence and her reputation as an innovative cook. Lidia is a natural teacher, with a knack for making even complex recipes accessible to everyone. When the family decided to sell their two restaurants in Queens in order to purchase the Manhattan real estate on which to build and open Felidia, Lidia was not only an accomplished cook and restaurateur but also poised to be a television host, cookbook author, and celebrity chef.

In 1993, Julia Child invited Lidia to present a segment on her PBS series *Cooking with Master Chefs*. Lidia prepared a simple dish of orecchiette with broccoli rabe and sausages. The recipe was novel, and the cooking segment was well-received. In 1998, PBS offered Lidia her first series, *Lidia's Italian Table*. Since that time she has become an icon of Italian home cooking, inspiring generations of Americans to venture beyond meatballs and spaghetti.

As a tribute to Lidia's first step into culinary stardom, allow me to suggest a recipe that uses an ingredient that was relatively unknown to the American palate—rapini, or broccoli rabe. This green cruciferous vegetable with a slightly bitter taste that when paired with sweet Italian sausage becomes an instantaneous culinary success story.

ORECCHIETTE CON BROCCOLI RABE E SALSICCE

Orecchiette with sausage and broccoli rabe

Makes 4 to 6 servings

Ingredients

- ¼ cup extra-virgin olive oil
- 3 thinly sliced cloves of garlic
- ¼ teaspoon kosher salt
- 1 pound orecchiette
- ½ pound sweet Italian sausage
- 2 pounds broccoli rabe
- ¼ teaspoon red pepper flakes
- ½ cup grated Parmigiano Reggiano or Pecorino Romano

continued

Method

1. Bring a large pot of water to a rolling boil and cook the orecchiette according to package directions to the al dente stage (usually about 10 to 11 minutes).
2. In a large deep heavy skillet, heat the olive oil and then quickly sauté the thinly sliced cloves of garlic for about a minute, being careful not to burn the garlic.
3. Add the sausage meat (which has been removed from its casings) to the oil and garlic and cook, stirring, until golden, about 3 to 5 minutes. Add the torn or roughly chopped broccoli rabe leaves (not the stems), along with about a cup of the boiling pasta water.
4. Season with salt and the red pepper flakes. Cover the skillet with a lid and allow the broccoli rabe to steam while the pasta finishes cooking.
5. Drain the pasta, add it to the sauce, and toss gently. Add about half of the grated cheese and toss again.
6. Remove from skillet to a serving platter and finish with more grated cheese, a drizzle of olive oil, and serve.

When one begins to receive invitations to share family celebrations, one realizes that a friendship has moved to a different level of intimacy. Lidia's television audience has grown accustomed to her TV signature catchphrase, "*Tutti a tavola a mangiare!*" which means "Everyone to the table to eat!" Through the years, I have joined la famiglia Bastianich for abundant Thanksgiving dinners and Easter Sunday banquets that kept us gathered together at table for four or five hours. There were also birthdays and graduations and sweet sixteen parties for grandchildren. Probably one of the fondest occasions I recall was a midsummer invitation to celebrate Mass in the home that Lidia shared with her mother in Queens. During that Mass, which I celebrated and preached in Italian, Grandma Erminia received the sacrament of the anointing of the sick. At a family celebration two years later at one of the family's Manhattan restaurants, Del Posto, I greeted Erminia and remarked: *"Signora, si sta così straordinariamente bene."* ("You are looking remarkably well.") Without losing so much as a beat, Erminia replied, "Whatever prayers you said over me must have been very powerful, because, as you can see, I'm still here." Grandma Erminia lived to celebrate her one hundredth birthday and shortly thereafter died peacefully on February 21, 2021. *Riposa in pace, amata nonna Erminia.*

At one of these family celebrations I remember a simple dish of potato gnocchi, sauced with butter, hazelnuts, and shaved black truffles. I have tried to recreate the recipe. While truffles may not be easily available or affordable, I've found that a little bit of black truffle butter (D'Artagnan makes a really good product), along with fresh hazelnuts, creates a delicious alternate dish.

GNOCCHI ALLA NOCCIOLA CON TARTUFO NERO E BURRO

Potato gnocchi with black truffle and hazelnut butter sauce

Makes 6 to 8 servings

Ingredients

For the gnocchi

- 1½ pounds russet potatoes
- 4 cups sifted all-purpose flour
- 2 eggs
- 3 tablespoons unsalted room-temperature butter
- kosher salt

For the black truffle and hazelnut saucing condiment

- ¼ pound truffle butter
- ¼ cup roasted and skinned hazelnuts, roughly chopped
- shavings of black truffle (optional)

Method

To make the potato gnocchi

continued

1. Wash the potatoes to remove any residual surface soil and cook the unpeeled potatoes in boiling water for 30 to 35 minutes.
2. Drain the potatoes and allow them to cool a bit. Peel the skins from the cooked potatoes and cut them into smaller pieces.
3. On a clean countertop surface, sift 4 cups of flour into a mound. With your hand, create a well in the center of the flour.
4. Using a ricer, process the potatoes and gather in a mound in the center well of the flour.
5. Make another smaller well in the center of the potatoes and add the two eggs that have been beaten, along with a pinch of kosher salt.
6. With clean hands, begin to incorporate the flour and the potatoes and eggs. Little by little, add in bits of the softened unsalted butter.
7. Continue working the dough until all the ingredients are well blended and the mixture comes together and begins to feel a bit dry.
8. Take a piece of the dough and on a well-floured surface, roll it into a long cigar-shaped strip, about a half-inch thick. With a sharp knife, cut the individual gnocchi, about ¾–1 inch wide. Put the gnocchi on a baking tray lined with a floured kitchen towel that has been sprinkled with flour.
9. Repeat this process until all of the dough has been rolled and cut.
10. Allow the gnocchi to air dry for at least a half hour.

To cook and sauce the gnocchi

1. In a Dutch oven with boiling salted water, cook the gnocchi for a few minutes until they rise to the water's surface.
2. In a sauté pan, gently melt the truffle butter and hazelnuts. With a stainless steel Asian spider strainer or large slotted spoon, remove the cooked gnocchi and transfer to the sauté pan with the melted truffle butter and hazelnuts.

3. If you are fortunate enough to have a black truffle, shave some of the fresh truffle over the finished dish and serve.

Through the years I have grown especially close to Lidia's daughter, Tanya Bastianich Manuali. Tanya, like her older brother, Joe, received a Jesuit education. During their childhood, both Tanya and Joe made frequent visits to Italy. They literally grew up in their parents' restaurant kitchens.

As the scope of Lidia's businesses has grown, so too have Tanya's hands-on responsibilities. Tanya researched and coauthored many of her mother's books and oversaw the growing line of Lidia's pastas, all-natural sauces, and olive oils. She even found time to coauthor a book in 2014 with her brother that profiles many simple recipes for making healthy pasta dishes. It seemed that every time I shared lunch with Tanya, she was planning another TV series with her mother or exploring another commercial cookware venture with QVC. When I once commented on the quality of the pasta that was being marketed under Lidia's brand, I learned that Tanya's husband, Corrado, had identified the pasta-making *fabbrica* in Italy that produces Lidia's proprietary line. It uses the highest quality durum wheat. If a box of Lidia's pasta says nine minutes cooking time for al dente, it's exactly nine minutes.

The top shelves in the kitchen pantry at Campion Center's mansion were arrayed with high stacks of boxes, representing the nine cuts of pasta and nine varieties of sauces that were included in Lidia's initial marketing venture. And there were plentiful cans of San Marzano tomatoes and bottles of extra-virgin olive oil. The oil is produced from trees growing near Lidia's maternal grandmother's homestead in Istria. There were bottles of Bastianich wines, cans of salted anchovies, and jars of cured olives. There were delicious *amarene*—sour, wine-colored Italian cherries grown in Bologna and Modena, bottled in a rich syrup—and any number of other delicacies from the family's Italian food emporium, Eataly, where the store's motto is "We sell what we cook, and we cook what we sell."

Whenever I dine with Tanya, I notice that she is always evaluating dishes for their taste, originality, and presentation. Often enough we ended up dining in Felidia, where she maintained her business office. Part of the restaurant's success was Sicilian-born executive chef Fortunato Nicotra, who worked at Felidia from 1996 until its closing in 2021.

Although born in Sicily, he was raised in Torino and learned *la cucina Piemontese* firsthand as a young man. He has never drifted too far from his mother's Sicilian roots in his cooking. Fortunato is a master chef, artfully pairing traditional ingredients in novel ways and presenting them beautifully. One of Fortunato's signature dishes, which both Tanya and I have enjoyed together many times, is a tasty pear- and Pecorino-filled ravioli. Although I do not have his exact recipe, I believe he also uses a bit of fresh sage in the preparation of the filling.

RAVIOLI DI PECORINO E PERE

Pear and cheese ravioli

Makes 4 to 6 servings

Ingredients

For the pasta to make the ravioli

- 4 large eggs at room temperature
- 2½ cups flour (a blend of semolina flour and all-purpose flour)
- 1 tablespoon extra-virgin olive oil
- 1 teaspoon sea salt

For the ravioli filling

- 2 firm ripe pears (Anjou or Bartlett)
- 1 cup aged Pecorino Romano cheese, shredded
- 1½ tablespoons refrigerated mascarpone cheese
- 2 fresh sage leaves, finely chopped

For the cacio e pepe sauce

- 6 ounces unsalted butter
- 1 cup grated Pecorino Romano cheese
- coarsely ground black pepper

Method

To make the pasta sheets for the ravioli

1. In the bowl of a food processor fitted with the steel blade, add all of the ingredients. Pulse for about 10 seconds until the mixture reaches a crumbly texture.
2. Remove the dough and form it into a ball with your hands, then place the dough on a lightly floured work surface. Knead the dough for 1 to 2 minutes until it is smooth and elastic. (If the dough seems wet or sticky, just add in some extra flour. You want the pasta dough to be pretty dry.)
3. Form the pasta dough into a ball with your hands and wrap it tightly in plastic wrap. Let the dough rest at room temperature for 30 minutes. Use immediately or refrigerate for up to 1 day.

To make the ravioli filling

1. Peel and core the pears and shred them against the large holes of a box grater.
2. In a bowl, combine the shredded pears with the grated Pecorino Romano cheese and some minced fresh sage leaves and fold in the mascarpone.

To form the ravioli

1. Remove the plastic wrap from the rested pasta ball and cut it into four smaller sections. Cover the sections that you are not using to prevent drying and crusting.
2. Using your hands, shape one of the dough wedges into a flat disc. Flour the disc and begin feeding it through the pasta maker, set initially on its widest setting.
3. Once the sheet comes out, fold it into thirds, similar to how you would

continued

fold a piece of paper to fit in an envelope. Flour again lightly and feed it through the rollers 2 or 3 more times, still on the widest setting.

4. Then continue to feed the dough through the rollers as you gradually reduce the settings, one pass at a time, until the pasta reaches the desired thickness. For ravioli, you want the pasta sheet to be thin. If your dough sheet starts to get too long to handle, just cut it in half with a knife. The end result should be workable sheets approximately 12 inches long and 3–3½ inches wide.
5. Lay a 12-inch strip on a floured work surface. For each ravioli, scoop a scant tablespoon of filling, shape it round, and drop in place. Space the rounded filling along the length of the pasta, about 2 inches apart from each other.
6. With egg wash or water, wet the edges of the pasta strips and in between each of the rounds of filling. Place a second 12-inch strip on top of the filled sheet and with your finger, carefully seal the separations between the ravioli.
7. With a pasta wheel or sharp knife, cut the individual ravioli and place them on a tray fitted with a clean kitchen towel that has been lightly sprinkled with either flour or cornmeal.
8. Repeat process until all the filling has been used. Reserve any remaining pasta for a future use.

To cook the ravioli

1. In a Dutch oven filled with salted boiling water, cook the ravioli until they float to the surface (about 3 minutes).

To make the sauce and finish the dish

1. Heat the butter until simmering in a large skillet and thin the melted butter with about a cup of the boiling pasta water.
2. Gently transfer with a slotted spoon the cooked ravioli to the skillet and coat with the hot butter liquid.

3. Remove the skillet from the heat and sprinkle over the grated aged Pecorino, mixing gently so that the cheese begins to melt into a sauce, and then liberally grind coarse black pepper over the ravioli.

I cherish fond memories of a pre-Christmas dinner at my Peter Cooper apartment to which I had invited Lidia and Tanya. My dining table comfortably accommodated eight guests, so in accepting my invitation, the women expected that they would be joined by others of my friends and colleagues. They were delightfully surprised when they arrived on a cold, mid-December evening to discover that they were the sole invited guests. I had prepared a four-course dinner. Almost instinctively, Lidia asked if she could be of help in the kitchen, but I demurred, telling her that she was my guest and that I was the cook, server, and clean-up guy. We enjoyed a bit of prosecco before dinner, then spent the remainder of the evening at table.

Over the course of my many years living in New York, I had entertained many professional cooks and bakers at home. Some friends marveled that I seemed comfortable cooking and baking for restaurateurs, chefs, pâtissiers, cookbook authors, hotel food and beverage managers, and food critics. In the end, each very much appreciated opportunities to relax away from work and enjoy good food and drink in the company of congenial friends in a home environment. Few ever turned down an invitation.

Lidia told me after our evening together how much she had enjoyed the warmth of the evening and the serendipitous opportunity it had afforded to chat with her daughter while I was busy attending to things in the kitchen. Because of their busy schedules, they rarely had relaxed time alone—as mother and daughter—to catch up with their lives and activities.

As the entrée for this winter holiday meal, I chose to prepare ossobuco in a traditional Milanese style. I first learned about the preparation of ossobuco from Nonn' Angelina, the housekeeper and cook for an Italian parish priest who ministered in a mountain village in the Emilia-Romagna region of northern Italy. Since that time, I have always used her stovetop searing and braising method in preparing this dish. Some cooks use red wine and beef broth, but this recipe reflects the way this humble peasant cook first taught me, and I have always been pleased with the results. Lidia certainly gave the dish two thumbs up and sent her plate back to the kitchen with only the bare bone of the shank remaining. She had happily consumed every morsel of its gelatinous marrow.

OSSOBUCO ALLA MILANESE

Braised veal with vegetables and gremolata

Makes 6 servings

Ingredients

For the ossobuco

- 6 cross-cut veal shanks
- ¼ pound unsalted butter
- 1 cup dry white wine
- all-purpose flour
- 3 cups chicken broth
- 3 seeded and diced ripe red tomatoes
- 2 tablespoons chopped fresh rosemary leaves
- freshly grated nutmeg
- kosher salt and freshly ground pepper

For the gremolata

- 2 cloves minced garlic
- ½ cup minced flat-leaf Italian parsley
- freshly grated zest of an orange

Method

1. Pat the ossobuci dry with paper towels and season liberally with salt and pepper. With some butcher twine, tie each of the veal shanks so that they will hold their shape during the braising process.

2. Dredge the seasoned and tied veal shanks in flour and shake off any excess.
3. In a Dutch oven, melt the butter and brown the flour-dredged veal shanks on all sides.
4. When the veal shanks are browned, drizzle the meat with the wine and continue cooking to burn off the alcohol in the wine. Add the chicken stock, a few scrapes of fresh nutmeg, and some additional salt and pepper. Cook until the chicken stock begins to boil.
5. Reduce the heat to medium low, add the chopped tomato and the chopped rosemary.
6. Cover the Dutch oven and continue to cook on the stovetop for 1½ hours, basting the veal shanks every 30 minutes during the braising time.

To prepare the gremolata

1. In a small mixing bowl, combined the finely chopped minced garlic, parsley, and orange zest.

To serve the ossobuco alla Milanese

1. When the ossobuci are cooked, carefully remove the meat to a platter and cut, remove, and discard the twine. Cover the shanks with aluminum foil to keep warm.
2. Turn the heat to high and bring the cooking liquid to a rapid boil and allow it to reduce further.
3. Place a shank on a dinner plate, sauce with some of the reduced cooking liquid, and garnish with some of the gremolata.

I knew that Lidia enjoys simple fruit desserts. During the same week of this dinner party, I had received in the mail an early Christmas gift of a dozen incredibly succulent Royal Riviera pears. I decided to make an Italian cake, using some of those pears and a hint of fresh basil.

TORTA DI PERE E BASILICO

Italian pear cake with basil

Makes 10 servings

Ingredients

- 1¼ cup all-purpose flour
- ⅔ cup granulated sugar
- ½ teaspoon kosher salt
- 1¼ teaspoon baking powder
- 3 oz unsalted butter, melted
- 6–8 fresh basil leaves, thinly sliced
- 8 oz mascarpone cheese, room temperature
- 2 large eggs
- 1 teaspoon pure vanilla extract
- 1 lemon, zested and juiced
- 2–3 firm pears
- Apricot preserves or basil-scented simple syrup for glazing

Method

1. Preheat the oven to 350°F.
2. Peel and core the pears. Dice 1–2 pears into bite-size cubes and cut the remaining pear into ⅛-inch slices. Place the pears cubes and slice in separate small bowls and toss with lemon juice to prevent discoloration. Set aside.
3. Melt butter in the microwave for 30–40 seconds. Add in the sliced basil leaves and allow the basil to perfume the melted butter for 5 minutes. Remove the basil leaves from the butter and discard.
4. Brush a 9-inch springform cake pan with some melted butter. Reserve about 1 teaspoon to brush on the pears later.

5. Add the remaining melted butter to a medium mixing bowl along with mascarpone, eggs, lemon zest, and vanilla extract. Beat with a whisk until smooth, about 3 minutes.
6. Into a small mixing bowl, sift the flour, baking powder, salt, and sugar. Reserve about 1 teaspoon of granulated sugar to sprinkle on top of the batter before baking. Mix the dry ingredients together with a clean, dry whisk until they are well combined.
7. Add the dry ingredient mixture to the mascarpone and egg mixture and gently fold with a rubber spatula until fully combined. Then, introduce the diced pears into the batter and continue folding until well-integrated.
8. Immediately pour the cake batter into the prepared cake pan and smooth the surface of the batter with an offset spatula. Arrange the sliced pears pieces artistically on the top of the batter surface. Brush pears with the reserved basil-scented butter and sprinkle the reserved sugar over the entire surface of the pears and batter.
9. Bake for 45 minutes until the top is lightly browned.
10. Allow cake to cool completely before unmolding from the cake pan.

You may brush the cooled cake with a glaze of heated apricot preserves, some basil-scented simple syrup, or a simple dusting of sifted confectioner's sugar.

In 2012, I recommended that the board of HealthCare Chaplaincy approve awarding both Lidia Bastianich and Sylvia Weinstock lifetime achievement Wholeness of Life Awards. These remarkable women joined a group of prior recipients who had previously received the same recognition: actor Angela Lansbury, philanthropists Mary and Laurance S. Rockefeller, cosmetic industry executives and philanthropists Evelyn and Leonard Lauder, and business entrepreneur Ken Langone.

Lidia and Sylvia electrified the assembled guests in Manhattan's Mandarin Oriental hotel ballroom on that brisk November evening. A young manager from one of the Bastianich restaurants proposed marriage to his girlfriend during the gala. Upon hearing this news, Sylvia Weinstock spontaneously returned to the stage and took command of the microphone, not only announcing the engagement to the six hundred assembled guests, but also committing that her company would make the cake for the couple's wedding. She also called upon Lidia to pledge that the Bastianich family would supply wine from their family's vineyards in Friuli-Venezia Giulia and the La Mozza vineyard in Maremma. Among the more than twenty-five HealthCare Chaplaincy galas that I had hosted, this one unquestionably had the strongest feeling of family. This was due in no small measure to the spontaneity and graciousness of these two extraordinary women.

The executive chef at that time at the Mandarin Oriental was an accomplished Asian woman. Sylvia Weinstock knew her well, and the chef made an appearance on the evening of the celebration in the main ballroom to greet our two honorees. One of the entrées she had prepared that evening was a pan-seared branzino with wild mushrooms in a port wine reduction sauce. Even though this dish might seem complicated, it is quite easy to prepare.

PAN-SEARED BRANZINO WITH WILD MUSHROOMS AND PORT WINE REDUCTION

Makes 4 servings

Ingredients

For the branzino

- 4 skin-on branzino (sea bass) filets
- ½ teaspoon kosher salt
- 2 tablespoons extra-virgin olive oil
- 2 tablespoons drained and rinsed capers
- 3 tablespoons dry white wine
- 1 tablespoon unsalted butter

For the wild mushrooms

- 1 pound wild mushrooms (any combination of shiitake, porcini, hen of the woods, black trumpet, oyster, lobster, chanterelle, or morels)
- 3 tablespoons extra-virgin olive oil
- 2 tablespoons unsalted butter
- 2 thinly sliced shallots
- 2 cloves of finely chopped garlic
- ¼ cup dry white wine
- 2 teaspoons chopped mixed herbs (any combination of fresh rosemary, sage, thyme, or marjoram)
- ½ cup coarsely chopped Italian parsley
- sea salt and freshly ground pepper

For the port wine reduction sauce

- 3 tablespoons unsalted butter
- ¼ cup finely chopped shallots
- 1 cup port wine
- ¼ cup Dijon mustard
- 2 cups beef broth
- 1 tablespoon cornstarch
- 2 tablespoons water
- 1 tablespoon cold butter

Method

To prepare the wild mushrooms

1. Melt 2 tablespoons of butter along with 3 tablespoons of olive oil in a large skillet over medium-high heat. Stir in the shallots and cook for 2 minutes to soften slightly. Add the garlic and cook for another minute.

continued

2. Add the ¼ cup of white wine, along with the chopped mixed herbs.
3. Add the mushrooms, combine with shallots and garlic, and continue cooking until the mushrooms have released most of their liquid and are browned and tender.
4. Remove the mushrooms from the skillet, add the ¼ cup of chopped parsley, and set aside.

To make the port wine reduction sauce

1. In a saucepan, add the butter and when it is sizzling, add the shallots and sauté until softened and translucent.
2. Pour the port wine into the saucepan with the shallots and bring to a boil over high heat. Boil rapidly for about 5 minutes until the port has reduced.
3. Whisk in the mustard and beef broth.
4. Dissolve the cornstarch into a small bowl with 2 teaspoons of cold water and add the slurry in a stream to the boiling liquid, continually whisking to incorporate and thicken.
5. Remove the saucepan from the heat and whisk in another tablespoon or two of cold butter. Continue stirring until the butter has melted and emulsified in the sauce.
6. Add the sautéed mushrooms back into the sauce and keep warm.

To pan sear the branzino filets

1. Heat a large skillet over medium-high heat. Pat the filets very dry with paper towels and check to make sure there are no small bones remaining in the flesh of the fish.
2. Score the skin side of the fish with a sharp knife by making a couple of shallow diagonal incisions on each filet. Season the filets on both sides with the salt and freshly ground black pepper.
3. Add some olive oil and butter to the hot skillet.

4. When the olive and butter begin to smoke, gently lay the filets skin-side down into the skillet.
5. With a spatula, press down on each filet to make sure it is making good contact with the skillet's surface.
6. Sprinkle the capers over the filets, but do not disturb the fish or try to move the filets for at least 3 minutes.
7. With a spatula, gently flip each filet and cook for no more than another minute on the flesh side.
8. Remove the branzino, along with the fried capers, to a platter or dinner plates—skin-side up—and nap each filet with an ample serving of the mushrooms and port wine sauce.

One of the innovations I introduced to the Campion Jesuits, once the mansion kitchen became operational, was a regular Monday evening series of dinners that I promoted under the moniker "Mondays at the Mansion." For the first round of dinners I invited Jesuits from each sector of the community: those living in the skilled nursing care and assisted living center and those who were living in the active apostolic community. I created a simple, three-course meal that consisted of a soup or pasta and an entrée of fish, poultry, or meat, along with complementary side dishes and a dessert. Our guests arrived about thirty minutes before dinner for an apéritif and light hors d'oeuvres. I had the able assistance of Fr. Jim Mattaliano, S.J., the community's administrator, who not only had an insatiable appetite for the kind of good Italian home cooking he had experienced growing up, but also was a talented cook in his own right. In many ways he inspired and encouraged me to explore as much of the repertory of *la cucina italiana* that I might wish to attempt. And he was ever at the ready to procure whatever fresh ingredients might be needed to accomplish any proposed menu. I once told him that I believed that he could write the definitive book on where to find or purchase anything in the city of Boston and its environs. In a word, he was completely and reliably resourceful.

During the course of my years at Campion Center I worked my way through most of the recipes in Lidia Bastianich's cookbook, *Lidia's Celebrate Like an Italian*, and from the galley proofs of *Felidia: Recipes from My Flagship Restaurant* I would often tell both Lidia and Tanya that I could easily have qualified as a professional recipe tester for any of her books. More frequently, I was passing on rave reviews from the consumer Jesuits who were delighted by the variety of the menu offerings.

To maintain the alliteration established by "Mondays at the Mansion," during the summer months I offered a variation al fresco event on the mansion's expansive rear veranda, which were advertised as "Tuesdays on the Terrace."

After the initial series of events, we opened up the special dining evenings to other Jesuits who might be living in the greater Boston vicinity. Several men from Boston College joined us, as well as Jesuits who might be visiting the community. Even the provincial joined one of these dinners. One of the dishes I prepared for a winter dinner for the Campion Jesuits was Lidia's polenta torta with Gorgonzola and savoy cabbage. For me, this was a novel recipe. Lidia has always demonstrated a fondness for using cabbage in a variety of her recipes and presentations. The Jesuits loved the dish.

The concept for this preparation is straightforward. It requires pouring cooked polenta (cornmeal) into a springform cake pan and then refrigerating it. When set, the polenta cake is cut into three thinner layers. Using the same springform pan, the layers are successively filled with a prepared mixture of cooked, slightly mashed cabbage and potato, topped with crumbled Gorgonzola cheese, and baked for about three-quarters of an hour. As the Italians might say of this torta, "*deliziosa!*" This is my adaptation of Lidia's recipe.

TORTA DI POLENTA CON CAVOLO E GORGONZOLA

Polenta cakes with potato, cabbage, and Gorgonzola

Makes 6 to 8 servings

Ingredients

For the polenta

- 1 bag coarsely ground Italian yellow polenta
- ½ cup freshly grated Parmigiano Reggiano

For the cabbage and potato filling

- 2 large Idaho potatoes
- 1 head Savoy cabbage
- 2 teaspoons fresh thyme leaves
- 4 cloves roughly chopped garlic
- kosher salt
- freshly ground black pepper
- red pepper flakes

Other ingredients

- 1½ cup Gorgonzola dolce cheese
- ½ cup grated Parmigiano Reggiano
- 1 cup fresh breadcrumbs
- extra-virgin olive oil
- unsalted butter
- kosher salt

Method

To make the polenta cake

1. Butter the bottom and inside rim of a 9-inch springform cake pan.
2. Add 2½ cups of water to a medium saucepan. Bring the water to boil over medium-high heat.
3. While the water is coming to a boil, in a medium-sized bowl, combine 1 cup of coarse yellow polenta with 1 teaspoon of kosher salt.
4. Using a wire whisk, blend 1 cup of cold water with the polenta. Combining the polenta with cold water helps to keep it from clumping when it is added to the hot water.
5. Slowly add the polenta mixture to the boiling water, stirring constantly. The continual stirring helps the cornmeal mixture distribute well throughout the boiling water without clumping.

continued

6. Cook and stir until the polenta returns to a boil. Be attentive, because occasionally the polenta will spurt, sputter, and pop as it thickens.
7. Reduce the heat to medium-low and continue to cook for 25 to 30 minutes, stirring regularly with a strong wooden spoon until the mixture becomes thick and soft. By continually stirring the polenta, it will not scorch.
8. When the polenta is finished cooking, stir in about a half cup of grated Parmigiano Reggiano cheese and pour the mixture into the prepared springform cake pan.
9. When cooled on the countertop, cover with plastic wrap and refrigerate for a few hours or overnight.

To make the potato and cabbage filling

1. Peel the potatoes, cut them in half, and then into smaller pieces.
2. In a large saucepan filled a bit more than halfway with cold salted water, add the potatoes and bring to a boil. Reduce the heat and simmer for an additional 5 minutes.
3. While the potatoes are initially cooking, prepare the cabbage by removing the core and roughly chopping into pieces.
4. Add the cabbage to the potatoes and cook for another 15 minutes. Test the potatoes for tenderness.
5. In a large colander, drain the potatoes and cabbage, pressing out as much liquid as possible.
6. In a large skillet, heat some olive oil and butter over medium heat. Add fresh thyme leaves and garlic to the oil and cook for a minute or two until the garlic blossoms.
7. Add the cabbage and potato mixture to the skillet and with a wooden spoon, gently begin to fold together the ingredients with the herbs and garlic. Adjust seasonings with salt, pepper, and red pepper flakes.
8. The objective is to evaporate most of the residual liquid in the cabbage

and potatoes. As the cooking progresses, press the potato and cabbage mixture against the sides and base of the skillet to coarsely mash.

To assemble and bake the torta

1. Preheat oven to 400°F.
2. Remove the polenta from the springform pan.
3. Wash the springform cake pan and dry thoroughly. Butter the base and interior rim of the pan and coat with some fresh breadcrumbs, discarding any excess crumbs.
4. With a thin slicing knife, separate the polenta cake into three equal horizontal layers.
5. Begin assembling the torta by placing a layer on the bottom of the springform pan. Top it with about half of the filling and about half of the crumbled Gorgonzola cheese.
6. Repeat the layering process with a second disk of polenta, filling, and cheese.
7. Place the final layer of the polenta and press on it gently to compress the whole torta.
8. Brush the top polenta layer with melted butter and liberally dust the entire top with grated Parmigiano Reggiano.
9. Place the assembled torta on a baking sheet and bake for about 40 minutes. If the top layer begins to get too brown, lightly tent the pan with aluminum foil.
10. Allow the torta to rest for about 15 minutes before releasing it from the springform pan and removing the outer ring for cutting and service.

As a community of aging and retired priests and brothers, Campion Jesuits experience much of their shared common life at table. Holidays and special occasions are often celebrated by festive, gastronomic feasts. In recent years, Columbus

Day has come under public scrutiny. In America, Columbus Day has become for Italians what St. Patrick's Day is for the Irish. Some folks have suggested that the day be renamed Indigenous Peoples Day. Nonetheless, the Italian Americans continue to march proudly on Fifth Avenue in New York, marking the anniversary of Christopher Columbus's arrival in the Americas on October 12, 1492.

At Campion, I began a new traditional of hosting on the observed Columbus Day holiday what we called a "Festa Italiana." Because Columbus Day is a public holiday observed over a long weekend, our kitchen staff was often reduced in numbers. For dinner, some of the other Jesuits and I combined forces to prepare and serve a meal centered around a menu of three different pasta selections. Each year we varied the selections, preparing dishes that were not ordinarily part of the regular dining menus.

On one occasion I prepared different pasta dishes all focused around pesto. Pesto generally refers to an Italian sauce originating in Genoa, the capital city of Liguria, consisting of crushed garlic, pine nuts, basil leaves, and grated cheese, all blended with olive oil. There have been so many inventive ways in which other pesto sauces have been created. Here is a trio of recipes for pesto sauces paired with three different types of pasta.

TRIO DI PASTA CON PESTO GENOVESE, PESTO POMODORI SECCHI, E PESTO ARUGULA

Three pasta dishes with different pesto sauces

Makes 8 to 12 servings

Ingredients

For trenette or tagliatelle with pesto Genovese

- 1 pound trenette or tagliatelle, cooked according to package directions to the al dente stage, 1 cup of cooking water reserved
- 2 cloves garlic
- 2 tablespoons pine nuts
- 1 large bunch fresh basil leaves

- ½ cup grated Parmigiano Reggiano cheese
- 1½ tablespoons grated Pecorino Romano cheese
- ½ cup extra-virgin olive oil

For cavatappi with pesto pomodori secchi

- 1 pound cavatappi, cooked according to package directions to the al dente stage, 1 cup of cooking water reserved
- 4 ounces sundried tomatoes, reconstituted in 2 cups boiling water
- ¼ cup grated Pecorino Romano cheese
- ¼ cup toasted pine nuts or walnuts
- 2 cloves garlic
- ¼ cup extra-virgin olive oil

For the spaghetti with pesto arugula

- 1 pound spaghetti, cooked according to package directions to the al dente stage, 1 cup of cooking water reserved
- 3 cups arugula
- 1 cup flat-leaf parsley (no stems)
- ¼ cup salted shelled pistachios
- 2 cloves garlic
- 2 tablespoons extra-virgin olive oil
- 2 ounces Gorgonzola dolce cheese

Method

Making trenette or tagliatelle with pesto Genovese

1. Crush the garlic using a mortar and pestle. Add pine nuts; crush with the garlic. Add basil leaves gradually, making circular movements with the pestle until a smooth paste forms.
2. Mix Parmigiano Reggiano cheese and Pecorino Romano cheese using a wooden spoon. Stir in olive oil until the pesto is blended thoroughly.

continued

3. Add pesto to the cooked pasta and toss. If too dry, add a bit of pasta cooking water. Finish with some grated Pecorino Romano cheese.

Making cavatappi with pesto pomodori secchi

1. Reconstitute the sundried tomatoes in hot water then drain and squeeze them thoroughly dry.
2. Add the sundried tomatoes to a food processor and process until the tomatoes become a paste.
3. In a dry, very hot sauté pan, add the pine nuts and turn off the heat. Keep the pine nuts in the skillet so that they toast and not burn. Transfer to a plate to cool.
4. Add garlic, toasted pine nuts, and grated Pecorino Romano cheese to the food processor with the sundried tomato paste and pulse to combine.
5. Through the feed tube, with the motor running, drizzle in the olive oil until it forms a nice smooth consistency.
6. Toss cooked and drained cavatappi with the sundried tomato pesto. Add a bit of cooking liquid, if needed. Finish with some chopped parsley or basil chiffonade.

Making the spaghetti with pesto arugula

1. Clean and wash the arugula and pat dry with paper towels.
2. In the bowl of a food processor, add the arugula, garlic cloves, and pistachios. Pulse until fully blended and finely chopped.
3. With your hands, break up the Gorgonzola dolce cheese into smaller pieces and add to the bowl of the food processor.
4. With the motor running, drizzle in the olive oil and process until the pesto is well blended.
5. Toss cooked and drained spaghetti with the arugula pesto. Add a

bit of cooking liquid if needed. Finish with some grated Parmigiano Reggiano cheese.

One of the big adjustments I had to make when I moved from New York City back to the Boston area was to reassign my loyalties to the New England sports teams. During my long tenure in New York I had become a fan of the Yankees, Jets, Rangers, and Knicks. In Boston, to survive, I had to become a supporter again of the Red Sox, Patriots, Bruins, and Celtics.

Many of the Jesuits living in the mansion were avid sports fans, and on a game day all of the chairs in the common television room were occupied. Most popular, of course, were those Sunday afternoons during the fall when Patriots games were played. I began preparing light supper meals, usually some type of pasta that could be easily enjoyed while watching a game. This initiative was universally applauded and much appreciated. One weekend I wanted to attempt a new dish, something that I had seen but never actually made. The dish is called timpano, perhaps named because the finished dish resembles a kettledrum. Baked in a large stainless steel bowl that has been lined with a bread-like dough, the cavity is then filled with different pastas and sauces, savory meatballs, and cheeses. A timpano serves a large hungry crowd and makes a show-stopper presentation. It takes a bit of time to prepare, but it's worth the effort. And for an occasion such as a Superbowl game, it was an instantaneous and spectacular hit with the Jesuits.

TIMPANO FESTIVO

Dome-shaped bread crust filled with meatballs, sausage, and cheese

Makes 12 to 15 servings

Ingredients

For the impasto (crust)

continued

- 4 cups all-purpose flour
- 2 teaspoons kosher salt
- 2 teaspoons baking powder
- ¾ cup whole milk
- 1 cup olive oil
- 2 whole eggs
- 2 tablespoons grated Parmigiano Reggiano

For the polpette (meatballs)

- 1 pound mixed ground veal, pork, and beef
- ½ pound sausage meat
- 6 large slices dry bread
- ½ cup whole milk
- 1 egg
- ½ cup grated Parmigiano Reggiano
- ¼ cup chopped parsley

For the salsa pomodoro (tomato sauce)

- 1 medium onion, finely chopped
- 1 grated carrot
- 6 cloves minced garlic
- 28-ounce can whole or diced San Marzano tomatoes
- extra-virgin olive oil
- salt and pepper to taste

For the salsa besciamella (white cream sauce)

- 3 tablespoons unsalted butter
- 4 tablespoons sifted all-purpose flour
- 2 cups hot whole milk
- salt and freshly ground black pepper

- freshly grated nutmeg
- 3 tablespoons grated Parmigiano Reggiano

For the pasta

- 2 pounds mixed tubular pasta, such as rigatoni, tortiglioni, paccheri, or mostaccioli

Additional ingredients for the assembly

- 1 pound drained whole milk ricotta
- ½ pound diced provolone cheese
- 6 slices crusty Italian bread (day-old is best)

Method

To make the impasto (bread dough)

1. In a food processor bowl, add the flour, salt, and baking powder and pulse four or five times to combine the dry ingredients.
2. In another mixing bowl or large measuring cup, combine the wet ingredients: milk, olive oil, and eggs. With a small whisk or fork, blend the ingredients together.
3. With the food processor running, pour the wet ingredients through the feed tube and blend until the mixture just comes together in a ball.
4. Stop the processor and turn the dough ball onto a lightly floured surface and hand knead for another minute or two.
5. Cover the dough ball with plastic wrap and refrigerate for about 45 minutes or more, to relax the gluten.

To make the polpette (meatballs)

1. Preheat oven to 350°F.
2. Tear 6 slices of the day-old Italian bread into smaller pieces and add

continued

them to a mixing bowl. Pour the milk over the bread and allow the pieces of bread to absorb the liquid.

3. In a large bowl combine the ground meats, sausage meat, egg, Parmigiano Reggiano, parsley, salt, and pepper.
4. Using your hands, squeeze the excess milk from the breadcrumbs and add to the meat mixture.
5. Working with clean hands, combine all ingredients and shape into as many medium-sized meatballs as the mixture yields.
6. Place the shaped meatballs on a baking sheet that has been lined with aluminum foil and bake for about 20 minutes.
7. After 20 minutes, remove the meatballs from the oven and place on paper towels to absorb any residual fat.
8. When the tomato sauce has cooked for about 20 minutes, you will gently add the meatballs to the sauce.

For the salsa pomodoro (tomato sauce)

1. In a large saucepan, heat about 3 tablespoons of extra-virgin olive oil and add the chopped onions. Sauté until the onions are translucent, and then add the chopped garlic and cook for 30 seconds before adding the diced San Marzano tomatoes. Mix to combine. Bring the mixture to a boil and then lower to a simmer and allow the sauce to cook for about 20 minutes.
2. As noted above, add the meatballs to the sauce at this point and continue to simmer on low heat for another half hour or more.

For the salsa besciamella

1. Melt the butter in a heavy saucepan over medium-low heat. Add flour and whisk for 1½ minutes (do not allow to brown).
2. Gradually add the hot milk, whisking constantly. Season to taste with salt and pepper and stir constantly with a wooden spoon until sauce becomes the consistency of thick cream, about 15 minutes.

3. Grate in some nutmeg and add some freshly grated pepper. Off the heat, blend in the grated Parmigiano-Reggiano cheese.

To prepare the pasta

1. In a large pot, bring water to rapid boil and cook the pasta about 3 minutes less than what would be required for al dente. Drain the pasta and divide evenly into two mixing bowls.
2. Sauce one of the bowls of pasta with the tomato sauce (without the meatballs); sauce the other bowl of pasta with the besciamella sauce.

To assemble the timpano festivo

1. Allow the chilled dough to rest at room temperature for 15 minutes.
2. Prepare a 4-quart ovenproof stainless steel domed bowl by rubbing the interior of the bowl with softened butter and dusting the interior with some fine breadcrumbs, removing any excess remaining breadcrumbs from the surface.
3. With a slotted spoon, remove the meatballs from the tomato sauce and slice each meatball in half, and set aside.
4. Retrieve the drained ricotta from the refrigerator.
5. Preheat oven to 350°F.
6. On a lightly floured surface, divide the dough ball, using about three-quarters of the ball for a large, circular pastry disk and the remaining quarter for the bottom of the timpano.
7. Roll out the larger piece of dough into a circle large enough to fully full line the bowl, with about a 2-inch overhang. Roll the remaining quarter-inch piece into a smaller circle, which is large enough to form the bottom of the timpano.
8. Carefully arrange the larger dough in the bowl, with approximately 2 inches of dough hanging over the edge.

continued

9. First add in the pasta with the besciamella sauce and with your hands, distribute it evenly on the lower surface. Add the remaining sauce.
10. Arrange a layer of the sliced meatballs on top of the besciamella, along with the chunks of provolone cheese.
11. Distribute the drained fresh ricotta over the meatballs and provolone. Add a few dabs of the tomato sauce on top of the ricotta.
12. For the final layer, add the pasta mixed with the tomato sauce. Add a few dabs of additional tomato sauce and dust with grated Parmigiano Reggiano. Press down the pasta to form a smooth, even surface.
13. Place the smaller circle of dough on top of the pasta layer and with a finger dipped in water, trace the outer edge of the dough circle with the water. Fold over the 2-inch overhanging dough and carefully seal.
14. Cover the bowl lightly with aluminum foil and place the filled bowl on a baking sheet.
15. Bake for 1 hour and 10 minutes until the dough is golden and crisp.
16. Remove from the oven and let sit for at least 15 minutes.
17. Carefully invert the timpano onto a large cutting board.
18. At this point it would be best to cover and let sit for a few more minutes to allow the contents of the timpano to settle before slicing.
19. Serve with some additional tomato sauce and cheese, if desired.

Returning to Campion Center was a homecoming of sorts. Not only had I lived in the house earlier in my Jesuit formation, I had also shared earlier experiences working and living together with many of the Jesuits who were now members of the Campion Health & Wellness community.

Fr. Joe Duffy, S.J., had been principal at Boston College High School during the years in which, as a Jesuit scholastic, I had been assigned to teacher French to juniors and seniors. As he was advancing toward his ninetieth birthday, I approached Joe to ask if he would enjoy celebrating his birthday with a special dinner with several of his fellow Jesuits in the mansion. He gratefully accepted the suggestion, and I prepared a festive menu for the occasion.

For the first course that evening, I chose to prepare a dish that I have been making and enjoying for many years. I was introduced for the first time to this dish in France. It is a standard offering on the menus of many French bistros, but it was Julia Child's approach to coquilles Saint. Jacques à la Provençale that I have followed through the years. This is one dish that I could make in my sleep.

COQUILLES SAINT-JACQUES À LA PROVENÇALE

Sea scallops in a savory wine sauce

Makes 4 to 6 servings

Ingredients

- 1½ pounds fresh or defrosted sea scallops
- ¾ cup minced onions
- 1½ tablespoons minced shallots
- 2 cloves minced garlic
- salt and pepper
- 1 cup sifted all-purpose flour
- ⅔ cup dry white wine and vermouth
- 3 tablespoons water
- 1 bay leaf
- fresh or dry thyme
- 1 cup shredded Gruyère cheese
- extra-virgin olive oil
- unsalted butter
- sweet paprika

Method

1. Remove the small side muscle from the scallops, rinse with cold water,

continued

and thoroughly pat dry. Depending on the size of the scallops, cut them into half or quarter segments. Set aside on a plate lined with paper towels.

2. Cook the minced onions slowly in butter in a small saucepan for 5 minutes or so, until tender and translucent but not browned. Stir in the shallots and garlic and cook slowly for 1 minute more. Set aside.
3. Just before cooking, sprinkle the scallops with salt and pepper, toss in flour, and shake off any excess.
4. In a large sauté pan with some melted butter and olive oil, quickly cook the scallops for about 2 minutes to brown them lightly.
5. Add the wine and water into the skillet with the scallops. With a spatula, loosen whatever may have adhered to the bottom of the skillet.
6. Then add the herbs and the cooked onion, shallot, and garlic mixture.
7. Cover the skillet and simmer on very low heat for 5 minutes.
8. Uncover, and if necessary, boil down the sauce rapidly for another minute until it is lightly thickened.
9. Correct seasoning and discard the bay leaf.
10. Spoon the scallops and sauce into 4 to 6 buttered scallop shells.
11. Sprinkle with the shredded Gruyère cheese, dot with butter, and lightly dust with a pinch of sweet paprika.
12. Just before serving, run under a moderately hot broiler for 3 to 4 minutes to heat through the scallops and sauce, and to brown the cheese lightly.

I have also shared a long history with Fr. Bill Russell, S.J., who was also part of the community of Jesuits living in Campion's mansion. Bill was born in Winthrop, Massachusetts, but grew up in the town of Hingham. He entered the Society of Jesus in 1952 while I was still in grammar school. He completed much of his Jesuit formation and studies in France, where he had mastered the French language. This is where our path first intersected. In 1960, during my senior year in high school,

Bill was briefly assigned to teach French at BC High. He became my teacher. After his ordination in 1965 he returned to the United States and served as rector of the Jesuit Community at the Jesuit School of Theology at Berkeley in California, president of Cheverus High School, director of admissions at Boston College High School, province assistant for development, province vocation director, and superior of the Patrick House Jesuit Community in Kingston, Jamaica. In his retirement at Campion Center Bill continued to be actively engaged in a variety of pastoral ministries, caring for his infirm Jesuit brothers as well as for countless convents of retired religious women. He is an excellent raconteur and an even better homilist.

And there could be no greater fan of my cooking and baking than Fr. Bill Russell. Whenever I was at work in the kitchen, Bill would always stop by to sample a sauce in preparation or taste a pastry filling. Until he developed problems with walking that required the use of a cane, Bill was a regular volunteer waiter for the "Mondays at the Mansion" events. Although always maintaining his love for French gastronomy, he had acquired a fondness for pasta of any shape and sauced in any way. And he enjoyed anything made with chocolate. When I combined dark chocolate with Grand Marnier as the silky filling for an orange-scented olive oil pastry shell, Bill exclaimed, "*un marriage crémeux*" (a creamy marriage).

TARTE AU CHOCOLAT FONDANT GRAND MARNIER

Dark chocolate tart with Grand Marnier

Makes 6 to 8 servings

Ingredients

For the crust

- 1¼ cups all-purpose flour
- 5 tablespoons granulated sugar
- ½ teaspoon kosher salt
- ½ cup extra virgin olive oil
- 2 tablespoons finely grated orange zest
- 2 tablespoons chilled Grand Marnier

continued

For the filling

- 1 cup heavy cream
- 4 large eggs, separated
- 1 tablespoon Dutch-process cocoa powder
- a pinch of kosher salt
- 12 ounces finely chopped dark chocolate
- 1 teaspoon pure vanilla extract
- 1 teaspoon Grand Marnier
- 12 teaspoons melted unsalted butter

Method

Making the crust

1. In a small saucepan, warm ½ cup of extra virgin olive oil. Off heat, add the finely grated orange zest to infuse the olive oil as it cools, about 30 minutes.
2. Adjust oven rack to middle position and preheat oven to 350°F.
3. Whisk dry ingredients (flour, sugar, and salt) together to combine.
4. In a small glass, pour 2 tablespoons of Grand Marnier over some ice cubes to chill.
5. Add the cooled, orange-infused olive oil and zest along with the iced Grand Marnier (not the ice cubes) and stir into the dry ingredient mixture, blending until the dough just begins to come together. Do not overwork.
6. Using your hands, crumble ¾ of the dough over bottom of 9-inch tart pan with a removable bottom.
7. Press the dough to an even thickness in the bottom of the pan.
8. Crumble remaining ¼ dough and scatter evenly around edge of pan, then press crumbled dough into fluted sides of pan. Press dough to an even thickness.

9. Place pan on rimmed baking sheet and blind bake until the crust is golden brown and firm to touch, 30 to 35 minutes, rotating pan halfway through baking.
10. Remove from oven and allow the cooked pastry shell to cool completely before adding the dark chocolate Grand Marnier filling.

Making the filling

1. Prepare a large stainless steel mixing bowl, along with a fine mesh strainer. These will be used later to strain the chocolate custard mixture.
2. In a small saucepan (or in the microwave), melt the butter and keep warm.
3. In a medium-sized saucepan, combine the heavy cream, egg yolks, cocoa, and salt.
4. Cook the mixture over medium heat, continually stirring and scraping the bottom and sides of the pan with a silicone or flat wooden spatula until the mixture begins to thicken and become smooth. This will take about 5 minutes.
5. Remove the pan from the cooktop to a safe workspace. Into the hot custard add all the chopped dark chocolate, along with the vanilla extract and Grand Marnier, and gently whisk until the chocolate is melted and thoroughly incorporated. Then add the warm melted butter and blend completely.
6. Pour the warm chocolate custard mixture through the fine mesh strainer into the prepared mixing bowl and discard any residual solids left in the strainer.
7. With a spatula, transfer the strained chocolate custard mixture into the cooked, pre-baked tart shell and allow to set, uncovered, at room temperature for about 30 minutes.
8. Once cooled and set, refrigerate the tarte au chocolat for several hours or overnight.

continued

9. When ready to serve, remove the tart from the ring and transfer to a presentation dish.
10. You may wish to garnish individual servings with a dollop of Grand Marnier flavored whipped cream or crème fraîche.

Fr. Larry Corcoran, S.J., was a young Jesuit priest teaching English at BC High during my years of regency. Not only was he a popular classroom teacher, but he was an equally successful coach of the track team. When I asked to take on coaching responsibilities for the swim team, I would consult with Larry about how to navigate through the politics of dealing with the director of athletics.

Larry had earned a master's degree in English at Bread Loaf, Middlebury College's summer program in the mountains of Vermont. It was during these summers spent with the literary community of Bread Loaf that Larry nurtured what would become a lifelong passion for poetry and the written word. At Campion Center, Larry's room in the Skilled Nursing Unit was located adjacent to the elevator and directly opposite an exit to an external ramp. Rain or shine, three or four times a day, Larry would walk the short distance with the aid of his rollator and sit at the top of the ramp to enjoy a cigarette. During frequent encounters Larry always had a joke or a few lines of poetry or a sports fact to share.

Larry was a deeply spiritual man with a keen appreciation for the scriptures. On occasions when I would preside at a funeral or a special event, he would seek me out to express appreciation for a homily preached or for the quality of the liturgical music program. He had a surprising aesthetic sense. Whenever there was a special floral arrangement to decorate the chapel, he would never fail to express his thankfulness and praise.

Particularly edifying was Larry's sensitivity and support for his fellow Jesuits in the health center. As the health status of one of the younger men was declining, Larry made the effort to stop by his room each day to recite from memory lines from Yeats or Emily Dickinson. On one occasion I stopped by his room and found him writing some lines of poetry. As I entered his room he discreetly closed the folder, which contained reams of poems that he had written through the years but rarely showed to anyone.

His infirmary room was close to the main residential elevator, the building's rotunda, and the main chapel. During the Christmas season in 2019, I often encountered him on an afternoon sitting in the chapel. Each time, he would stop me to say how much the decorations lifted his spirit and contributed to his sense of joy. By New Year, he had developed pneumonia. When the nurse asked him if he wished to be transferred to the hospital, he declined. He preferred to live out whatever days remained at Campion. I noticed that he was not in his accustomed place in the chapel for the celebration of Mass on the Solemnity of the Epiphany. After Mass had concluded, I learned that Larry had died peacefully while we had been celebrating the feast day. As he closed his eyes on this life, he had been listening to one of Bach's Epiphany cantatas: "*Herr, wie du willt, so schicks mit mir*" ("Lord, as you will, so let it be done with me").

During my years as the religious superior at Campion Center I celebrated the funeral of twenty-eight members of the Campion Center Jesuit community. Each of these men would be deserving of several pages of recognition in this memoir. Each had a fascinating life story and an equally compelling curriculum vitae, such as Fr. Francis Sullivan, S.J., who for much of his professional life was professor of dogmatic theology and later dean of theology at the Pontifical Gregorian University in Rome.

Frank had been one of the concelebrants at the Mass celebrated by Fr. Pedro Arrupe in the *camerette di San Ignacio*, during which I pronounced final vows as a Jesuit on June 13, 1976. After retiring from his faculty position in Rome, Francis taught theology at Boston College before returning to Campion Center. At the time of his death in 2019, Fr. Sullivan was the oldest member of the Jesuit Northeast Province.

Perhaps among the more colorful characters at Campion was Fr. Bob Taft, S.J. "Taftie," as so many of his Jesuit brother referred to him, had been a professor of Oriental liturgy at the Pontifical Oriental Institute in Rome from 1971 until 2003. I got to know Bob well in 1975, and we remained friends until his death on November 2, 2018.

During the years just prior to his ordination to the priesthood at Weston, Bob was permitted to transfer from the Roman to the Byzantine rite. He was ordained in 1963 in that rite. He pursued doctoral studies in the same Roman institute in which he would spend most of his scholarly life. He both loved and hated Rome. He often complained about various aspects of Jesuit life at the Orientale, the inefficiencies of the Italian government, and the Machiavellian workings of the Vatican curia. One thing Bob never complained about was Italian cooking; he loved Roman restaurants. I would often join him on the discovery of some new trattoria or hostaria. He walked everywhere, and inevitably struck up a conversation with the *padrone* of some quaint ristorante.

On one of our gastronomic forays he introduced me to spaghetti alle vongole veraci by stating apodictically: "This is not the clam sauce you may have eaten before. This is the real Neapolitan classic dish." He was, of course, right. I had never eaten a clam sauce where the clams were served along with their shells, combined with the pasta, and where the sauce was nothing more than the cooking liquid. It's really the simplest of preparations, but is satisfying and delicious.

SPAGHETTI ALLE VONGOLE VERACI

Spaghetti with clams

Makes 4 to 6 servings

Ingredients

- 2 pounds fresh clams (such as littlenecks, topnecks, cherrystones, or manila)
- 1 pound spaghetti (or linguine)
- 5 cloves of garlic (3 lightly smashed and 2 finely minced)
- ¼ teaspoon red pepper flakes
- ½ cup chopped flat-leaf parsley
- 1 cup extra-virgin olive oil
- 1 lemon (grated rind and juice)
- 2 tablespoons unsalted butter
- kosher salt

Method

1. Clean and wash the clams. Dry on a clean kitchen towel and set aside.
2. Bring a pot of water to a rolling boil and add 1 teaspoon of kosher

salt to the water. Cook spaghetti for about 11 minutes, according to packaging directions, to the al dente stage. Reserve about ¼ cup of pasta cooking liquid.

3. In a large skillet with a cover, heat 1 cup of olive oil. Add 3 cloves of lightly smashed garlic to the oil, along with ¼ teaspoon of crushed red pepper flakes.
4. Add the clams to the pan, and with a spoon, distribute them evenly over the bottom of the pan, coating them in the hot oil. Cover the pan and cook for about 5 minutes, shaking the pan.
5. Uncover and with a spoon, move the clams around in the cooking liquid. Add about half of the chopped parsley to the pan. Recover the pan and cook for another minute or two. Remove any clams that may not have opened.
6. Through a fine mesh strainer placed over a stainless steel mixing bowl, pour off and filter the cooking liquid and reserve.
7. To the sauté pan with the cooked clams, add 2 tablespoons of butter, 2 tablespoons of olive oil, 2 cloves of minced garlic, the grated lemon rind, and lemon juice. With a spoon, swirl to combine before pouring back the strained cooking liquid.
8. Cook uncovered for another minute before adding the drained pasta. Over medium heat, toss the pasta with the clams and sauce. Add some of the pasta cooking water if needed. Cook for another minute.
9. Serve immediately, garnished with the remaining chopped parsley.

By the time I arrived at Campion, Bob Taft was living in the skilled nursing wing, diagnosed with advanced Alzheimer's disease. He still recognized me, and I could always elicit a smile from him. Because of his prodigious scholarship and substantial contributions to the Eastern churches, he had been honored by the Ukrainian Catholic Church in 1998 and named a mitred archimandrite. This honor permitted him to wear a crown or mitre, along with a pectoral cross. Other Eastern churches subsequently presented him with additional pectoral crosses. On one occasion, one of his brother Jesuits asked Bob why he wore two pectoral crosses. His simple, curt response was: "Because I can!" He actually confided to me that he was permitted to wear three pectoral crosses.

I remember receiving a call during the summer of 2017 from one of Bob's former students, the Very Rev. Mark Morozowich, dean of theology at Catholic University. Mark informed me that the president of the Ukrainian Catholic University in Lviv, Bishop Borys Gudziak, wished to come to Campion Center to present Bob with an honorary doctorate. At the time, New York-born Bishop Borys was also the apostolic exarch for the Ukrainian Catholic faithful of the Byzantine rite living in France, Benelux, and Switzerland. Mark and Borys came to Campion on a hot summer afternoon and presented Bob with the citation. Although not able to communicate easily, Bob seemed to understand the significance of the honor and was pleased to see two of his former students.

Before he retreated into the silent world of a person living with advanced dementia, Bob had formulated detailed instructions for how his funeral should be conducted. One of the sections of this briefing paper described how his body should be prepared and vested. By prior agreement, a fellow archimandrite in Washington, D.C., would oversee the proper prayers and vesting of his body at the funeral home and direct the preparations. When Bob died I dutifully called this priest, only to learn that he would be unable, for reasons of health, to fulfill this obligation. I asked my colleague Fr. Jim Mattaliano to accompany me to the funeral home where together we would complete these ritual tasks. In anticipation, I had researched the ceremonial prayers that accompany the proper vesting of a deceased Eastern rite priest. I arranged each of the priestly vestments, in the precise order in which we would place them on Bob's body. Vested in one of Bob's Byzantine stoles, I began the ritual blessings and vesting, and Jim assisted by responding to the prayers. When we had completed the vesting, we blessed the coffin and Bob's body was placed by the funeral directors within it. Finally, I placed two pectoral crosses on his chest, a blessing cross in his hand and the mitre on his head.

On the drive back to Campion, Jim inquired whether I had ever done anything like this before. "You seemed to know exactly what to do and what to say," he commented. I told him that until the night before I knew nothing about these ritual acts, but, thanks to the internet, I was able to download the proper prayers and instructions, and, like any recipe, I simply did what was prescribed. Somehow, I believe that Bob Taft was pleased that everything was done with dignity and precision.

Although I did preside at many funerals, at Campion Center there were many more joyful occasions to celebrate. I was surprised and pleased when one of the Campion Jesuits approached me with a request. He and six of his classmates were planning a reunion to celebrate at Campion their sixty-fifth anniversary as Jesuits. He was wondering if they might organize a special dinner in the mansion as part of their festivities, and if so, might I be available and willing to plan and cook the dinner? Without losing a heartbeat, I readily agreed.

I put together a menu that featured both Italian and French dishes. For the entrée course, I proposed a chicken dish that I had first tasted during a summer that I had spent study in Rennes, in Brittany. During weekends, I explored local sites nearby in both Brittany and Normandy. One of the items I sampled was a chicken dish braised in broth, cider, and Calvados, a local brandy made from apples.

POULET À LA NORMANDE, FLAMBÉ AU CALVADOS

Chicken braised with mushrooms, apples, and Calvados cream sauce

Makes 12 servings

Ingredients

- 5 tablespoons unsalted butter
- 3 peeled, cored, and quartered Granny Smith apples
- 1 tablespoon olive oil
- 4 pounds chicken parts (breasts, thighs, drumsticks)
- kosher salt and freshly ground black pepper
- 1 washed, cleaned, and broadly sliced leek (white and light green parts)
- ¼ cup Calvados (apple brandy)
- ¾ cup apple cider
- 4 sprigs thyme
- 2 bay leaves
- 1 cup chicken broth
- ½ pound cremini mushrooms

continued

- ½ cup crème fraîche
- 1 large egg yolk

Method

1. Wash and pat dry the chicken pieces, season liberally with salt and pepper, and set aside.
2. Heat 2 tablespoons of butter in a large Dutch oven over medium heat. When the butter begins to foam, add the peeled apple pieces and cook, turning occasionally, for about 10 minutes. Remove the apples from the pan and transfer to a plate and reserve.
3. Increase the heat to medium-high and add oil and an additional tablespoon of butter to the skillet. Brown the chicken parts, being careful not to overcrowd the pan; the goal is to brown and not steam. When the parts are browned, set aside and continue the process for all the chicken pieces.
4. If needed, add a bit more butter and proceed to sauté the leeks and shallots until they soften.
5. Remove the pot from the stovetop and carefully add the Calvados, and then ignite the pan to burn off the alcohol.
6. Return the pot to the stovetop and add the apple cider. Bring to a boil, lower the heat, and simmer until the liquid is slightly reduced, about 3 minutes.
7. Return the browned chicken pieces to the Dutch oven and add thyme, bay leaves, and broth. Bring to a boil; reduce heat, cover pot, and simmer, adding reserved apples back to the pot halfway through. Continue cooking until the chicken pieces are cooked through, about 20 to 25 minutes.
8. Meanwhile, heat the remaining 2 tablespoons of butter in a large skillet over medium-high heat. Add the mushrooms and cook, tossing occasionally, until browned and softened, 6 to 8 minutes; season with salt and pepper. Transfer the mushrooms to a plate.

9. Whisk the crème fraîche and egg yolk in a small bowl. Using a slotted spoon, transfer chicken and apples to a baking sheet and remove pot from heat.
10. Whisk the crème fraîche mixture into cooking liquid in the pot. Carefully add back the chicken, apples, and mushrooms and gently stir to combine.

I complemented this rich chicken dish with a presentation of oven-braised rounds of butternut squash, paired with onions and bacon. When I first learned to make this dish, I asked why it carried the description *boulangère.* This seemed to imply it had something to do with a baker (*boulanger*). My French instructor explained that in many towns people brought prepared dishes like this one to the local baker's oven to be cooked—so alongside loaves of baking bread was placed this casserole dish of squash and onions. Whether this explanation is fact or fiction I cannot attest, but the association with the baker survives in the dish's name.

COURGE MUSQUÉE BOULANGÈRE

Oven-braised squash with bacon and onions

Makes 8 to 10 servings

Ingredients

- 3 medium-size butternut squash
- 1 pound slab bacon, cut into quarter-inch cubes
- 3 large yellow onions, finely sliced
- 4 sprigs fresh thyme
- 1½ cups white wine
- 3 cups chicken stock
- kosher salt and freshly ground black pepper
- extra-virgin olive oil

continued

- 18 fresh sage leaves

Method

1. Preheat the oven to 375°F.
2. Remove the top and bottom pieces from each squash and peel away the outer skin.
3. On a cutting board, using a chef knife, cut crosswise slices of the squash, about ¾-inch thick. Remove whatever seeds and membranes remain from the center of the slices.
4. Once you sliced and cleaned all of the squash, liberally season the squash with kosher salt and freshly ground pepper and toss the seasoned slices in some olive oil to coat. Set aside.
5. Cut the slab of bacon into about a half-inch dice and add to a hot sauté pan. Cook until the bacon renders most of its fat. Remove the partially cooked bacon to paper towels to drain. Reserve the rendered bacon fat.
6. Arrange the slices of squash on rimmed baking sheets. With a pastry brush, lightly flavor the tops of the squash with a bit of the rendered bacon fat.
7. Add about half of the chicken broth and half of the wine to each of the baking pans. Distribute the thinly sliced onions between and among the slices of squash. Add the chopped thyme leaves, along with the bacon pieces. Season with salt and pepper. Cover the baking sheets with aluminum foil and place in the preheated oven.
8. Bake for 30 minutes, covered. Remove the aluminum foil and bake for a final 10 minutes (or until the squash is tender), to allow some final caramelization to occur.
9. Heat the remaining bacon fat in the sauté pan and fry the sage leaves. Remove the leaves from fat and allow to drain on paper towels.
10. Garnish the finished squash dish with some of the fried sage leaves.

Dessert was a traditional Sicilian cassata. In the United States this dessert has evolved to be an ice cream cake, often utilizing different flavors of ice cream, molded with cake strips. However, the classic Sicilian dessert is made with fresh ricotta, candied citrus peel, cherries, and pistachios.

CASSATA ALLA SICILIANA

Sicilian dessert with ricotta, candied citrus peel, cherries, and pistachios

Makes 8 servings

Ingredients

- ½ cup superfine sugar
- 1 tablespoon water
- 1 pound whole milk ricotta
- 3 ounces roughly chopped semisweet chocolate
- 2 ounces chopped candied lemon peel
- 2 ounces chopped candied orange peel
- 2 ounces glacé cherries
- 2 ounces blanched unsalted pistachio nuts
- 2 homemade or purchased sponge (génoise) cake layers (if you'd like to make it yourself, you can use the recipe for vanilla génoise layer cake in chapter 6)
- 1 cup sweet dessert wine, like a moscato or a vin santo

Method

1. Combine sugar and water in a saucepan and place over moderate heat until the sugar is dissolved. Set aside the simple syrup.
2. Push the ricotta through a sieve and mix with the sugar syrup, chocolate, candied fruit, and pistachios.
3. Prepare a small domed Pyrex or stainless steel mixing bowl by lining with plastic wrap, leaving an overhang to facilitate unmolding.

continued

4. Cut the sponge or pound cake in thin slices (⅜-inch), then cut into strips. Brush the cake strips lightly with the wine.
5. Line the bowl with the cake (using about two-thirds of the strips). Fill the center of the bowl with the ricotta, fruit, and nut filling.
6. Top with a layer of the wine-brushed sponge cake. (I often cut a round of sponge to fit the size of the bowl. It makes a smoother finished product, but it also works fine with just scraps of wine-soaked cake pieces.) When inverted, this layer of cake will form the base of the cassata.
7. Refrigerate several hours. Unmold onto a serving dish and pipe whipped cream decoration on the cake. I flavor the whipped cream with a very little bit of almond extract. Finish the decoration with whole blanched almonds or candied fruits, or in any way that you wish.

As I mentioned earlier, the centerpiece of my mission at Campion Center was to design and lead a process that would develop a multidimensional, comprehensive plan for Campion Center. To do this effectively, I enlisted the wholehearted engagement of the executive and management team in a lengthy process of spiritual communal discernment to deepen our shared understanding of the mission of Campion Center. As we were engaging in this planning, the Society of Jesus promulgated four universal apostolic preferences that would be normative for all Jesuit works going forward. Our apostolic plan would need to integrate these preferences. We redesigned Campion's website and began a rebranding initiative to enlarge knowledge and understanding of Campion Center's distinctive Jesuit apostolic mission.

All of us were committed to articulate a vision and propose a plan that not only would preserve Campion Health & Wellness's independent status as a Five-Star Center for Medicare and Medicaid Services (CMS)-rated LTC provider. It would also ensure that Campion Center would continue to serve as the principal licensed advanced care facility for Jesuits in the USA East Province.

Campion's Conference & Renewal center was already evolving from its earlier identity as a retreat house to an enlarged mission as a place where persons of all ages might encounter God through individual spiritual direction, single or multiday retreats, faith-sharing groups, spiritual direction supervision, spiritual conversation, and discernment. There was also to be professional development, conferences, public lectures and discussions, continuing professional education, civic community meetings, and shared workspace. Throughout our months of communal discernment of apostolic opportunities and priorities, the Campion team drew deeply upon the experience, education, imagination, inventiveness, and creativity of each other. Through this prayerful and reflective process, we filtered an abundance of data, zeroed in on critical facts, and came up with solutions to seemingly unresolvable dilemmas.

Once the plan took shape, we began to seek funding to implement some of its easier objectives. One of the more pressing immediate needs was in the area of rehabilitative services. We swiftly recognized that the space allocated to physical and occupation therapy and speech pathology was unable to meet the increasing need for these services. With the assistance of our maintenance professionals, we were able to develop a plan that would triple the available space for our therapists. With the consultation of experienced rehabilitation service providers, we made a list of needed equipment. We also created a working budget.

In my Christmas appeal that year to friends, I described Campion's needs. Before year's end we had received enough donations to fund the entire project. Three months later, we opened and blessed the enlarged treatment areas. Our Jesuit residents began receiving therapies in areas that ensured privacy and were outfitted with state-of-the-art equipment and technologies. We even had enough money left in the budget to be able to renovate and improve the lighting on the basement corridor. That work had gone unattended for more than fifty years.

When the Center's only access ramp was first constructed, there were no guidelines or mandatory requirements in place. By contemporary standards and regulations, the existing Campion Health & Wellness ramp would be considered dangerous and noncompliant. With the provincial's approval, we set about designing a ramp that would provide direct access into the main wing of the health center, one that would complement the architecture and finishes of the 1926 building.

We were able to find a masonry contractor, Paolo Fragale, who not only had the technical competence and craftmanship to undertake a project of that scope, but who also resonated personally with Campion's mission. Paolo had established Fragale Building Corporation in 1971. From my first meeting with Paolo and his son, Edoardo, I sensed that masonry construction was in the family's DNA. It started with Paolo's grandfather, who had been a stone mason in the late nineteenth century in Calabria, Italy. Paolo's two sons, Edoardo and Carlo, are carrying on the family's tradition of excellence. Edoardo worked on the Campion ramp project every day, rain or shine. The Fragales were able to match the brickwork on the original building, and Paolo created a new archway for the entrance to the ramp that mirrors what the original masons had done almost a hundred years ago.

When the ramp was formally blessed on the day before Thanksgiving in 2019, both Paolo and Edoardo were present for the ceremonies. The ceremony was led by Fr. Stephen Sanford, S.J., a wheelchair-bound resident of the health center. The Fragales were moved by the many expressions of gratitude voiced by the Campion Jesuits, some of whom they had gotten to know by name during the five months of the ramp's construction.

In honor of the Fragale family, I offer this very simple recipe for a Calabrese pasta dish, traditionally made with dried and salted cod. This recipe has been adapted to use fresh cod filets.

BUCATINI ALLA CALABRESE

Calabrian bucatini with cod in spicy tomato sauce

Makes 6 servings

Ingredients

- 2 pounds cod filets
- 1 pound bucatini
- 28-ounce can San Marzano whole tomatoes
- 1 onion
- 3 cloves garlic
- extra-virgin olive oil
- salt
- freshly ground black pepper
- red pepper flakes

Method

1. Fill a stockpot with water and bring to a rapid boil to cook the bucatini.

2. Wash and pat dry the cod filets. With a sharp knife, cut the fish into approximately one-inch cubes.
3. Cut the onion into a large dice. Peel and finely chop the garlic cloves. Pour the tomatoes into a large bowl and, with a clean hand, gently break up the tomatoes into smaller pieces.
4. In a large skillet, heat the olive oil and sauté the onion until it becomes soft and translucent. Add the minced garlic and cook until the fragrance blooms. Remove the onion and garlic mixture to a small bowl.
5. Add some additional olive oil and over medium heat, gently sauté the fish, being careful not to break up the pieces. Turn off heat and remove the skillet with the fish from the stovetop to stop cooking.
6. In a large saucepan, add the hand-crushed tomatoes and the onion garlic mixture, and begin to cook the tomatoes. After about 10 minutes reduce the heat to medium, add the sautéed fish, partially cover the pan, and cook for another 15 minutes.
7. Salt the boiling water and cook the bucatini according to packaging directions, to the al dente stage.
8. When the sauce is finished, using a wooden spoon, gently press the tomatoes and fish against the sides of the saucepan, breaking and crushing them a bit.
9. Add a pinch of red pepper flakes, if desired. Season with salt and freshly grated black pepper.
10. Reserve about a cup of the pasta cooking water and drain the bucatini. Add to the saucepan and gently combine, allowing the pasta to cook in the sauce for a couple of minutes. Add some additional pasta cooking water if needed to thin the sauce.

The principal entrance foyer to Campion Center had not been refurbished for dozens of years. It was poorly lit and gloomy. Among the many renovation and reconstruction tasks identified in the apostolic plan, this area was among what might be described as low-hanging fruit: things that were easy to do and required almost no effort or added resources.

We located in another part of the house two stately, impressive carved wooden chairs that had been abandoned. With some new upholstery, they could be repurposed. We selected a deep turquoise paint to create an accent wall to complement the fresh neutral painting of the remaining wall surfaces and ceiling. On the accent wall, we matted, framed, and displayed photographs of the Pope Francis and the Archbishop of Boston, Cardinal Séan Patrick O'Malley, O.F.M. Carm., and of Fr. Arturo Sosa, S.J., superior general of the Society of Jesus, and of the provincial of the province. A slender wooden statue of St. Edmund Campion, S.J., the center's eponymous patron saint, was moved from a niche in the dining room to the entrance hall and displayed against a fabric banner of turquoise. Our maintenance crew restored and polished the original marble floor. We purchased a round oriental-design carpet and placed a contemporary design table under the suspended chandelier, which had been cleaned and polished. The most dramatic element in the refurbishment effort was the purchase and installation of a large, all-weather custom-designed rug for the entrance portico. The rug's turquoise field was bordered in orange and emblazoned with the seal of the Society of Jesus in white to form its central medallion.

After the rug was fabricated and installed, most of the Jesuits admitted it brightened and transformed the space. It also made a dramatic statement by the boldness of its color. Some critics complained that people would be walking over the Jesuit seal, with the iconic name of Jesus prominently displayed in its center. I was quick to remind them that for centuries, in many of the churches of the Society, people had been parading over the same emblem in the marble floors of those houses of worship. Many of the guests and retreatants who entered the building after these renovations were completed were amazed by the foyer's transformation and highly complimentary of the hospitable environment these changes had created.

Sometimes, simple things can make a big impact. This experience reminds me of an olive oil cake that I sampled many times in Italy. We were taught a preparation for this traditional cake at Lorenza de' Medici's cooking school in Tuscany, and since that time I have experimented with dozens of similar recipes. Almost all recipes for this cake agree that its essential ingredients are eggs and flour, citrus zest and juice, milk, and good olive oil. This recipe seems to incorporate a lot of liquid. Somehow it all works together to produce a moist cake. As do I, you will make this recipe more than once.

TORTA ALL'OLIO D'OLIVA

Moist olive oil cake

Makes 6 to 8 servings

Ingredients

- 2 cups all-purpose flour
- ½ teaspoon baking soda
- ½ teaspoon baking powder
- 1 teaspoon kosher salt
- 3 large eggs
- 2 cups granulated sugar
- ¼ cup freshly squeezed orange juice
- 1¼ cups whole milk
- 1½ cups extra-virgin olive oil
- ¼ cup Grand Marnier
- 3 teaspoons finely grated orange zest
- ½ cup sliced almonds
- confectioners' sugar for dusting

Method

1. Preheat oven to 350°F and adjust the rack to the center position in the oven.
2. Butter the interior rim and bottom of a 9- or 10-inch springform cake pan. Cut a piece of parchment or waxed paper into a circle and place in the bottom of the pan. Place the paper liner in the pan and rub your finger over the surface of the paper. Remove the circle and flip it over, and place the buttered side of the paper liner face up.
3. In a mixing bowl, combine the flour, baking soda, baking powder, and salt, and stir to combine the dry ingredients.

continued

4. In the bowl of a stand mixer fitted with the paddle attachment, cream together the eggs and sugar.
5. Add the orange juice, milk, olive oil, Grand Marnier, and orange zest to eggs and sugar.
6. Add the dry mixture into the wet mixture. On low speed, beat until the batter is well blended. Don't be alarmed: the batter will be thin.
7. Pour mixture into the prepared springform cake pan. Distribute the almonds on the surface of the batter.
8. Place the springform pan on a baking sheet and bake for about 50 minutes or until cake springs back to the touch.
9. Allow the cake to cook for about 10 minutes on a wire rack. Then, using a kitchen knife, gently separate the cake from the perimeter of the pan before releasing the spring.
10. Remove cake from pan and continue to allow the cake to finish cooling before removing the base of the pan and discarding the parchment or waxed paper liner from the bottom of the cake.
11. Dust the top of the cake with a bit of powdered confectioners' sugar placed in a small sieve.

Although the Jesuits have been residents in the quaint New England town of Weston for a century, as a group we remained somewhat of a curiosity to many of our neighbors. We tended not to become entangled in the town's politics or engaged with the town's churches or clergy. Jesuits did assist at the local Roman Catholic parish of St. Julia's. After Vatican II, my predecessors at Campion Center had become members of the Weston Clergy Association and invited their fellow clergy to hold meetings at Campion. During my years in New York City, I had become an active member of its vibrant multifaith clergy association, the Partnership of Faith. I was anxious to build on those multifaith experiences and welcomed the opportunity to meet and collaborate with Weston's clergy. When the Rev. Dr. Thomas Wintle, the senior minister of the Unitarian Universalist First Parish of Weston, called me and invite me to lunch I was quick to respond.

I met Tom at Campion Center and accompanied him to the nearby Pine Brook Country Club, where we shared lunch and conversation among the few other guests in the airy dining room that overlooked the golf course and swimming pool. I learned that Tom had graduated from the University of Nebraska, earned a doctorate from the Chicago Theological Seminary, and had pursued graduate studies at Oxford and the Harvard Divinity School. He had held numerous positions of leadership within his denomination and had served as president and executive director of the Unitarian Universalist Christian Fellowship, the Evangelical Missionary Society, and the Senior Ministers of Large UU Congregations.

Tom was interested to learn that I had earlier served a term as dean of the Weston School of Theology, a member school of the Boston Theological Institute. Earlier in his ministry Tom had been a field education supervisor for the Harvard Divinity School and had served as a trustee of the Andover-Newton Theological School, both Boston Theological Institute sister schools. Most germane was that Tom had been ministering in Weston for more than two decades and was then the leader of the Weston Clergy Association. Not surprisingly, we became immersed in more substantive discussions of faith and practice. Quickly I came to appreciate that Tom was not the stereotypical Unitarian pastor of a white-steepled church on a New England town green, where ancient Puritan covenants continue to be recited faithfully every Sunday. He had integrated Christianity into his Unitarian Universalist life of faith. In his own words, he said that it was "within Unitarian Universalism that I became a Christian."

For almost a quarter-century, Tom had been enabling the members of his First Parish congregation to become Christians at their own rates. Within the historic faiths of Unitarianism and Universalism, Tom became a well-respected preacher of a creative, vibrant, and believable liberal Christianity, rooted in the ministry of Jesus. I immediately bonded to this man of faith and was delighted to become part of the local clergy association. Campion Center progressively became more open and engaged in the collaborative ministries of the local Christian communities within the town.

We helped to plan and host the annual interfaith service of prayer during the week before Thanksgiving. After one of these prayer services, during a fellowship reception in the rotunda outside the Chapel of the Holy Spirit, I became engaged in a casual conversation with an elderly gentleman who was a lifelong resident of the town and member of the Congregational Church. With a certain hesitancy, he confessed that this was the first time he had ever been inside Campion Center and was awed by the grandeur and beauty of our chapel. "I've driven past this building for more than fifty years. I always wondered what was inside," he told me.

His comments made a lasting impression. I realized just how distant and unapproachable we had appeared to our neighbors, and how impenetrable a fortress Campion Center was perceived by so many people. From that night forward, I was resolved to work much harder at changing the perception. We needed to replace remoteness with hospitality. Soon thereafter we were scheduling multiple concerts by the Rivers School and its impressive music conservatory in our chapel. The conservatory provides a high-quality music education program for its students and music instruction to more than nine hundred students of all ages from the Greater Boston area. We hosted concerts by local community choral groups, and the Jesuits at Campion Center were treated to performances by numerous instrumental groups from the Weston High School.

The image of Weston sitting on its isolated perch at the top of Concord Road, crowned by the impressive dome of its chapel, reminds me of the classic French dessert aptly called île flottante, "floating island." During his time serving as America's first ambassador to France in 1778, Benjamin Franklin wrote home, noting that he had been served a floating island. Here is my version of a dessert that has virtually disappeared from the menu of many French restaurants today. It is worth resurrecting.

ÎLE FLOTTANTE À LA CRÈME ANGLAISE

Floating island meringues and crème anglaise

Makes 6 servings

Ingredients

- ¾ cups granulated sugar
- 2 cups whole almonds
- 1 tablespoon orange blossom water
- 2 vanilla beans
- 3 cups milk
- 6 egg yolks
- 10 egg whites

Method

To make the almond praline garnish

1. In a small saucepan, combine 2 cups of sugar with ½ cup of water over medium-high heat.
2. Using a candy thermometer, cook the syrup until the temperature reaches the firm ball stage (245°F) or approximately 18 minutes, and then with a wooden spoon, stir in the almonds, orange blossom water, and the seeds from one of the vanilla beans.
3. Continue stirring until the mixture crystallizes (about 4 minutes).
4. Working quickly, pour the mixture out onto a parchment-paper-lined baking sheet, spread it evenly into a layer, and allow to cool. When cooled, break the almond praline into smaller pieces for a garnish for the îles flottantes.

To make the crème anglaise

1. Split the second vanilla bean and add it to 2 cups of whole milk in a saucepan and bring to a simmer over medium heat. Do not boil.
2. In a mixing bowl, whisk the egg yolks with ¼ cup of granulated sugar.
3. Next, temper the egg yolks by gradually adding about ½ cup of the heated milk into the egg mixture and whisking continually to incorporate.
4. When the eggs have been tempered, whisk the egg mixture back into the pot of simmering milk and continue cooking for 10 to 12 minutes, until the mixture thickens.
5. Remove the saucepan from the heat, strain through a fine sieve, and transfer to a bowl that has been placed over a large bowl with iced water. This will stop the cooking process.
6. Withdraw the vanilla bean pod from the strainer and scrape the seed into the strained custard before discarding the pod. (You can rinse the pod, dry it, and then place into your sugar storage canister.)

continued

7. Cool the crème anglaise to room temperature, then refrigerate until cold.

To make and poach the meringue

1. In a medium saucepan, combine the remaining 1 cup milk with ½ cup of granulated sugar and 8 cups of cold water and bring to a boil.
2. Reduce the heat to medium low to keep the simmering poaching liquid warm.
3. In a large bowl and using a hand mixer, beat egg whites to soft peaks for about 3 minutes.
4. Add ½ cup of granulated or superfine sugar and continue beating until stiff peaks form.
5. Depending on the size of the individual meringue you desire, form the île into an irregular sphere. You can use a metal measuring cup that has been lightly sprayed with a vegetable spray. Add the desired amount of beaten egg whites to the measuring cup and drop into the simmering milk and water cooking liquid.
6. Poach, carefully turning as needed, until the meringues are firm on the outside, 3 to 4 minutes, depending on size. Using a slotted spoon, remove and drain on a paper-towel-lined baking sheet.

To serve the iles flottantes

1. Divide the crème anglaise among shallow rimmed dishes (a soup dish is ideal) and top each with a poached meringue.
2. Garnish with shards of the almond praline.
3. In a small skillet, heat the remaining ½ cup sugar and 1 tablespoon water over high, and cook, stirring occasionally, until the color of dark amber, about 6 minutes.
4. Using a spoon, quickly and carefully drizzle the caramel over the meringues until set. Serve immediately.

While the Chapel of the Holy Spirit was being constructed in the 1920s, the rector made arrangements with a local organ company located in the town of Weston to design, build, and install an organ. The 108-year-old firm of Elias and George G. Hook and Francis Henry Hastings was a nationally known manufacturer of church and concert hall organs. It had moved from its earlier location in Roxbury to the town of Weston, and for some years it was the largest employer in the town, providing work for seventy of the town's 1,700 residents. Mr. Hastings had grown up in Weston in the mid-nineteenth century and played a major role in the decision to build and operate the organ building factory in his hometown. Hastings worked for the Hook brothers and after their death in the 1880s, he purchased their share of the business. He retained the Hooks' prestigious name as he reorganized the business. Hastings died in 1916, a few years before the Jesuits had acquired the property on Concord Road. It was most likely that Weston's rector at that time, Fr. Tivnan, S.J., negotiated with Arthur Coburn, the brother-in-law of Mr. Hastings, who took over management of the Hook & Hastings Company.

Hook & Hastings produced an estimated 2,614 organs. The organ at Campion Center, commissioned in 1926, was among the final instruments they built, installed, and voiced. It joined other prestigious instruments in Boston including those at Tremont Temple, the First Church of Christ Scientist, Saint Paul's Episcopal Cathedral, and the Jesuit Church of the Immaculate Conception. When I was a scholastic living in Cambridge I occasionally played the great Hook & Hastings instrument at the Immaculate Conception.

After Hastings's death in 1916, management of the company passed to Arthur Coburn, president, Norman Jacobsen, vice-president and supervising designer, and Alfred R. Pratt, secretary and superintendent—all associates of Hastings for two decades. In the late 1920s the company built its most famous modern organ, the Rockefeller Organ for the Riverside Church in New York City. The Riverside Church instrument took a year to build in Weston and more than nine months in 1931 to install and voice in New York City.

While the Jesuits at Campion had made efforts to maintain the 1926 organ, it was not in the best condition when I arrived there again in 2017. Several of the original ivory veneers on the keyboards were cracked, chipped, or missing. Some of the organ chambers had been rebuilt or refurbished. With the help of James David Christie, a world-class recitalist and organ teacher, I was introduced to another organist, Ann Sursa Carney of Mint Hill, North Carolina.

Ann is the daughter of the late David and Mary Jane Sursa of Muncie, Indiana. Until his death in 2003, Ann's father had been a banker, community leader, and philanthropist. The Sursa family were active congregants of First Presbyterian Church, where Ann's father and mother both served as deacons and elders. The family also made a gift of the six-hundred-seat Sursa Performance Hall, named in honor of Ann's parents. The Sursa family's generosity not only provided for the hall but also gifted its world-class pipe organ, designed and built by the Goulding & Wood Co. Ann met her husband, John Bernard Carney Jr., (called Brian) when they were both organ students at Oberlin Conservatory. Brian died a month before his sixtieth birthday on March 8, 2012.

In an extraordinary gesture of her own philanthropy, and in memory of her parents and husband, Ann committed to underwrite the costs of completely rebuilding and restoring Campion's 1926 Hook & Hastings organ and console. During several of her visits to Campion Center, I was happy to invite several of the Jesuits and other friends to join with Ann for some enchanting dinners, shared both in the mansion's dining room and on the terrace on a warm summer's night. Ann also was able to join with us for an intimate New Year's Eve dinner to welcome the year 2020. Besides music, Ann is a connoisseur of fine dining, and she relished many of the dishes that were prepared for these celebratory dinners.

One might not consider a pot roast to be a celebratory menu item, but this slow-cooked French preparation of a chuck roast, paired with oven-roasted radishes, makes for a memorable feast.

BOEUF BRAISÉ AUX RADIS

Braised beef with radishes, onions, and shiitake mushrooms

Makes 8 to 10 servings

Ingredients

- 4 to 5 pounds chuck beef roast or boneless short ribs
- ½ cup vegetable oil
- 10 peeled and sliced garlic cloves
- 10 large peeled and sliced shallots
- 1 pound stemmed shiitake mushrooms

- 1 bottle dry white wine
- 3 cups beef stock
- ½ cup pitted black olives
- 2 large bunches round red radishes
- 3 tablespoons extra-virgin olive oil
- kosher salt and freshly ground black pepper

Method

1. Prepare the beef by removing any large amounts of residual fat that may have been left by the butcher. Salt the beef liberally and wrap in plastic wrap. Refrigerate for minimally an hour or two, preferably overnight.
2. In a large, covered Dutch oven, heat a half cup of vegetable oil over high heat. With large kitchen tongs, carefully brown the salted and patted dry beef in the hot oil. Take your time with this step in the preparation; you want a deep caramelization of the beef. This browning process can take 15 to 20 minutes.
3. When the deep browning of the beef has been achieved, remove the meat to a plate and pour off and discard the cooking oil. Do not disturb the *fond* on the bottom and sides of the pan—this is pure gold flavor.
4. Return the Dutch oven to the stovetop over medium heat and add a couple tablespoons of fresh oil to the pot. Sauté the sliced shallots until they become softened, but not browned.
5. Then add the sliced shiitake mushrooms (discard the woody stems) and cook for about 5 more minutes before adding the sliced garlic. Cook for another two minutes before transferring the browned shallots, mushrooms, and garlic to plate.
6. Add about one-third of the bottle of white wine and the browned beef to the Dutch oven. Bring to a boil over high heat. Reduce to a simmer, cover, and let cook until the liquid is almost fully evaporated, about 20 minutes. Repeat this process two more times, adding one-third of the bottle of wine to the pot each time.

continued

7. After the last of the wine has been added to the pot, preheat the oven to 325°F.
8. When the final reduction of the wine has been achieved, return the shallots, mushrooms, and garlic to the pot. Also add the olives and the beef stock. On the stovetop, simmer the mixture until the beef stock begins to boil.
9. Cover the Dutch oven and place on the middle rack of the preheated oven.
10. Cook, basting and flipping the meat, for about 3 hours. Remove the pot from the oven.
11. Increase the oven temperature to 350°F.
12. Transfer the beef to a rimmed serving dish and tent the meat with aluminum foil to keep warm. With a slotted spoon or wire spider, remove the vegetables from the pot and reserve.
13. Skim surface grease from the braising liquid. If the sauce in the pot is not well reduced, place the pot back on the stovetop over medium-high heat and simmer the sauce until it thickens further. At this point you may also add a cornstarch slurry (1 teaspoon of cornstarch and 2 tablespoons of cold water) to help the sauce thicken. Correct the seasonings. Carefully add the beef and the cooking vegetables back to the pot and cover to keep warm over a very low stovetop flame.
14. On a large baking sheet, spread out the radishes (and their greens, if still attached) in a single layer. Drizzle with the olive oil and season generously with salt and pepper, tossing and rubbing to coat. Transfer to the oven and roast for 10 minutes or so, until the radishes are crisp-tender.
15. Remove the meat from the sauce and slice. Serve with the sauce and the roasted radishes.

I had learned in advance from the friend who introduced me to Ann that she, like me, was an *amateur de chocolat*—a chocoholic. Since my days at Le Cordon Bleu, I have used this simple, classic recipe for mousse au chocolat. The traditional preparation does not add Grand Marnier but I always add it, since I believe this liqueur to be a natural counterpoint to the bitterness of extra dark chocolate. I recommend using unsweetened dark chocolate (between 60 and 70 percent cacao), but this decision is purely a matter of taste. I paired this dessert with a small slice of a simple Italian torta di mandorle to which Lidia Bastianich introduced me.

MOUSSE AU CHOCOLAT GRAND MARNIER

Chocolate mousse flavored with Grand Marnier

Makes 4 to 6 servings

Ingredients

- 6 ounces quality dark chocolate (preferably more than 60 percent cocoa)
- 1 ounce Grand Marnier
- 3 ounces unsalted butter
- 4 eggs
- 2 tablespoons superfine granulated sugar

Method

1. Chop both the dark chocolate and the butter into smaller pieces.
2. In the upper container of a double boiler over simmering water, place the butter and chocolate, and gently stir the ingredients until they melt together and become smooth.
3. When melted, blended, and smooth, remove the chocolate-butter mixture from the double boiler, and off the heat, stir in the Grand Marnier and allow the chocolate-butter mixture to cool.
4. Separate 4 room-temperature eggs into yolks and whites.
5. In the bowl of a stand mixer, beat the egg whites with 1 tablespoon of sugar until the whites form soft but firm peaks. Set aside.

6. Add a tablespoon of superfine granulated sugar to the egg yolks and with a small whisk, beat the egg yolks and sugar until the sugar is combined and the mixture becomes pale yellow.
7. Transfer the beaten egg yolks to the cooled chocolate mixture and combine thoroughly.
8. Add a couple of tablespoons of the beaten egg whites to the chocolate mixture and whisk to thin the texture.
9. Lastly, with a large rubber spatula, gently fold in the remaining beaten egg whites, being careful not to deflate the egg whites as they are incorporated.
10. Transfer to a larger serving bowl or individual dessert glasses, cover with plastic wrap, and refrigerate for 4 to 5 hours.
11. Serve with a dollop of whipped sweet cream and some fresh raspberries or strawberries.

TORTA DI MANDORLE

Italian almond cake, adapted from Lidia Bastianich

Makes 6 to 8 servings

Ingredients

- 2½ sticks softened unsalted butter
- 1¾ cups all-purpose flour
- ½ teaspoon baking powder
- ¼ teaspoon kosher salt
- 1 cup granulated sugar
- 5 large eggs
- 1 lemon (grated zest and juice)

- 1 teaspoon almond extract
- 8 ounces blanched slivered almonds
- 1 cup semisweet chocolate chips
- ½ cup sliced almonds

Method

1. Preheat oven to 350°F.
2. Butter and flour the bottom and sides of a 9- or 10-inch springform pan.
3. In a food processor fitted with the steel blade, process the 8 ounces of blanched, slivered, or whole almonds until they effectively become an almond meal. It should yield about 2 cups of almond meal. (Don't fret if you slightly overprocess the almonds. Almond powder is still OK; just don't make almond butter.)
4. Sift together the all-purpose flour, baking powder, and salt onto a piece of parchment paper.
5. In a stand mixer fitted with the paddle attachment, cream the butter and sugar at medium-high speed until light and fluffy, about 2 minutes.
6. At medium speed, add the eggs one at a time, incorporating each egg thoroughly before adding the next and scraping down the sides of the bowl as needed.
7. Beat in the lemon zest, 2 teaspoons of freshly squeezed lemon juice, and the almond extract, and then raise the speed of the mixer to high and beat the batter until it becomes very light, a minute or more.
8. At low speed, mix in half of the sifted flour mixture, beating just until it is incorporated; beat in half the almond meal. Scrape the bowl and mix in the remaining flour and almond flour. Beat briefly at medium speed to make a smooth batter.
9. At low speed, mix in the chocolate chips just until they are evenly distributed. Scrape the batter into the prepared pan and spread it in an even layer.

continued

10. Distribute the sliced almonds over the top.
11. Bake, rotating the pan halfway through the baking time, until the cake is golden brown on top and a knife inserted in the center comes out clean, about 45 minutes. (If the surface almonds begin to darken too much during the baking cycle, lightly tent the baking pan with aluminum foil.)
12. Cool the cake in the pan for about 10 minutes on a wire rack.
13. Run the blade of a paring knife around the edge of the cake, then open the spring and remove the side ring.
14. Cool the cake completely before serving. Cut into wedges and serve.

When the north wing of Campion Center was originally being built, an underground passageway was constructed that joined the mansion's basement to the new facility. That passageway remains functional to this day. One of my predecessors as superior of Campion Jesuits was Fr. Paul Holland, S.J. During his tenure he may have made some improvements to this old passageway in terms of lighting or even paint. When I arrived at Campion, one of the Jesuits humorously referred to this passageway as the "Holland Tunnel." Fresh from a quarter-century of moving in and out of the Holland Tunnel under the Hudson River, which connects lower Manhattan with New Jersey, I found the allusion had a certain charm.

The first large room in the main building that one encounters upon exiting the passageway from the mansion is a space that has been used principally as a recreation room. In the 1920s it had served as an auditorium. This large room—used daily by both the Jesuit community and by Campion Health & Wellness Center's activities department—quickly found its way onto the to-do list. Because the apostolic plan envisioned repurposing the former house library—which occupied a premier space on the fourth floor of the central corridor—to become a comprehensive health and wellness pavilion, we needed to relocate the community's extensive book collection. Prior to my arrival at Campion, the library's collection had already been reduced to about 12,000 volumes. After careful consideration, our goal was to further reduce the collection to about 5,000 volumes. We would then incorporate the library into the plans for the renovated recreation room.

With the assistance of some additional fundraising appeals, combined with a testamentary gift from the estate of a deceased benefactor, we were able to put together the funds that would cover the costs for this project. Relying again on our skilled team of Campion craftsmen, we developed a comprehensive plan for the room. We invested some of the funds to equip the audio and digital systems for this room. This was to ensure that no matter where one might be seated within the room, one would be able to see and hear. Our carpenters were able to reuse much of the hundred-year-old oak originally used in fashioning the millwork in the library to fabricate new millwork to house and display the collection. All the new cabinetry had built-in LED lighting. This not only made it easier for aging eyes to survey the book titles, but also lent a warm ambiance to the entire room. All of the principal furnishings were fabricated in durable leather, and all of the tables had polished concrete tops. We were also able to construct two handicap-accessible bathrooms within the room. The exits to the exterior of the building and to the inner courtyard were ramped. This made access to the building easier and safer.

When the former ceiling was demolished in preparation for the renovation, our workmen make a frightening discovery: the existing eight-hundred-pound condenser unit providing the room's air-conditioning had been improperly installed. An earlier installer had used toggle bolts attached to the ceiling. Had there been any unusual vibrations in the building, the massive unit could have fallen. This would have injured or killed anyone seated below. Needless to say, the replacement units are properly installed and securely attached.

When Mark Delorey, the vice president for maintenance and operations, asked for my counsel on a color palette for painting the room, I immediately thought of one of the classic soups that I learned to make in France—leek and potato soup, or as the French call it, potage parmentier. The color palette I suggested to Mark was a warm white paired with a light green, taking its lead from the gradations found in a leek. It's a delightful and simple-to-make soup, using few ingredients but producing a memorable texture and flavor. Some people change the color by introducing carrots into the preparation, which is also delicious. But I stick with the classic method—just leeks and potatoes.

POTAGE PARMENTIER

Potato and leek soup

Makes 6 to 8 servings

Ingredients

- 2 large leeks
- 1 pound peeled and diced Yukon Gold potatoes
- 2 tablespoons unsalted butter
- 2 teaspoons kosher salt
- 6 cups chicken or vegetable stock
- 3 cups cold water
- ½ cup crème fraîche
- freshly ground black pepper
- 2 tablespoons minced fresh chives (for garnish)
- freshly toasted croutons (for garnish)

Method

1. Peel and cut the potatoes into small cubes and reserve in a bowl of cold water.
2. Cut the base from the leeks and remove the upper dark green parts of the plant. Cut the leeks in half diagonally and thoroughly wash the interior, ridding them of any sand or soil. Cut the leek into thin slices.
3. Melt the butter in a large saucepot or Dutch oven over medium heat. Add the leeks and sauté until any remaining water in the leeks evaporates and the leeks tenderize. Do not allow the leeks to brown.
4. When the leeks have sweated, add the stock and water and bring to a near boil. Reduce the heat to medium low and add the drained potatoes, along with the salt.
5. Partially cover the pot and cook over medium-low heat for about 30 minutes, or until the potatoes are soft and tender.

6. Remove from the stovetop and with an immersion blender, purée the potage until it becomes smooth.
7. With a fine mesh sieve over the large saucepot or Dutch oven, strain the puréed soup.

By February 2019, our executive and management planning team had concluded many months of communal discernment and planning and had completed the writing and editing of a comprehensive apostolic plan for Campion Center. The development of this plan was central to the mission that the provincial had ordered.

When we began this discernment and planning process, we spent weeks discussing just how we would go about the tasks and in defining what areas we would propose for our deliberation. We wanted the process to be inclusive, and each of the department heads committed to what would be a lengthy personal and communal engagement. We undertook the task of gathering data from our various areas of responsibility. This included reviewing earlier planning documents or analyses. We agreed to ask an experienced spiritual guide to assist our group in this discernment and planning endeavor. We invited Fr. Bill Barry, S.J. (1930–2020), a renowned spiritual writer and director and a former provincial of the New England Province, to assist the group as facilitator and animator. Bill readily accepted this assignment and faithfully accompanied the group for the ensuing months. Before we jumped into the work, Bill took time to educate the group about the history of Ignatian discernment in common and gave some practical guidelines about how individuals might pray or reflect on the group deliberations.

Bill stressed the importance of the group's willingness to pray. He readily acknowledged that some of the members of the management team might not be accustomed to praying in this way. Fr. Barry described prayer in nonthreatening ways, encouraging each of us to take some quiet time to ponder over the things that colleagues shared and to see if there might be feelings, thoughts, or reflections that arose from this quiet, private time that an individual might later be willing to share with the rest of the planning team. He talked about active listening and intentional speaking. What the team learned from this lengthy planning experience altered the way we interacted with one another from that time forward. Believers and nonbelievers, Jesuits and lay women and men, we grew to recognize and accept that the Spirit of God was actively at work in our midst and was clearly leading us forward. The planning experience fostered and strengthened a sense of mutuality and respect within the group.

The discernment and subsequent apostolic plan focused on the key areas of Campion Center's mission. In concentrating on the changing needs of the Health & Wellness Center, we were concerned by the increasing numbers of Jesuits who were presenting at admission or later were diagnosed with cognitive deficits or advanced cognitive decline. Of the Jesuits who were currently receiving care in our assisted living residence, 25 percent had a dementia diagnosis or a documented cognitive deficit. When we considered the census of the skilled nursing program, four men had a mild cognitive impairment and thirteen had a dementia diagnosis or serious cognitive deficit.

When we looked at the entire census of the Health & Wellness Center, 61 percent of the Jesuit residents already had diagnosed memory problems. There is mounting evidence that with advancing age come the increasing burdens of impaired memory. These often present alongside other comorbid conditions. Not infrequently, coexisting pathologies appear to increase the risk for dementia. We projected that many of the Jesuit residents with mild to moderate cognitive deficits would progress to develop dementia before they died. We all agreed the most critical clinical need within the USA East Province's healthcare continuum would be to create, license, and staff a specialized twelve-bed Health & Wellness Memory Unit at Campion Health & Wellness.

This became one of the final major undertakings during my remaining time as Campion Center's superior. Once the province had approved moving ahead with this element of the plan, we interviewed three architectural teams with significant successful experience in designing facilities of this type. We also consulted regularly with the Massachusetts Department of Public Health to meet all requirements. We selected the Concord-based firm of LWDA and began work. Within a very tight schedule the architects developed conceptual designs, and with the help of construction estimators, were able to develop budgets for the project. These received the province's approval.

I had not been physically in the offices of the Department of Public Health since the mid-1970s, when I first worked on Campion Center's initial determination of need application. I felt as if I had come full circle as I began making the case in 2019 with the public health officials for reducing the number of assisted living beds and adding licensed memory-care beds.

Over the ensuing months, Mark Delorey and I, along with the director of nursing and the health center's executive director, spent many hours with the architects, engineers, and interior designers hammering out the details of the memory care unit. The east–west wing of the third floor of the health center was demolished. Our lawyers were hard at work, collaborating with the Department of Public Health to ensure the requisite approval for the project, and the construction drawings for the memory unit were finalized. Mark, in addition to his other responsibilities, took on the coordinating role of construction manager and began the process of soliciting and reviewing bids from construction firms that had experience in building facilities like this within occupied spaces.

One of the principals with whom I worked in developing this memory unit project was Ruth Neeman, a registered architect with more than thirty years of experience in planning, design, and research focusing exclusively on environments that enable elders and support independence and aging with dignity. Born and raised in Israel, in addition to speaking English and Hebrew Ruth shared a common interest and passion with me for the Italian language and its numerous regional cuisines. Along with conversations about the design of innovative memory supportive care environments for those living with cognitive impairment, we also pursued discussions about her advanced Italian conversation classes and cooking.

Ruth was fascinated by one of the recipes I shared with her for a not-so-well-known ragù associated with the region of Genoa. Like the famous meat sauce of its neighbor in Bologna, this Genovese sauce requires many hours of slow simmering to develop the complexity of its rich flavors, but this ragù Genovese uses only a few ingredients, principally onions and beef. The recipe reminded me of how a project like conceiving and building a memory unit required many hours of patient attention and care to bring it to realization.

RIGATONI ALLA GENOVESE

Rigatoni with a Genovese meat sauce

Makes 8 to 10 servings

continued

Ingredients

- 6 ounces diced pancetta
- 2 ½ pounds beef chuck, cut into cubes
- 1 cup diced celery
- 1 cup diced carrot
- ¼ cup tomato paste
- 1 bay leaf
- 1 cup white wine
- 4 pounds yellow onions, sliced
- 2 pounds red onions, sliced
- kosher salt and freshly ground black pepper
- extra-virgin olive oil

Method

1. Heat about ¼ cup of olive oil in a large Dutch oven over medium heat. Cook the pancetta until it renders most of its fat and the pieces begin to brown. Remove the browned pancetta with a slotted spoon and set aside. Reserve the cooking fat.
2. Over high heat, add all the cubed beef pieces and season generously with salt. With a wooden spoon, toss the meat in the oil and fat to coat. Cover the pot and allow the meat to begin cooking and browning. After about 10 minutes, remove the cover and stir again. Continue cooking uncovered, allowing the liquid released from the beef to evaporate, and the meat will further brown during the 10 to 15 minutes of cooking.
3. Reduce heat to medium-high. Add the sofrito (chopped celery, carrots, and browned pancetta) and season again with salt and freshly ground black pepper. Mix together with the beef and cook for about 5 minutes.
4. Add 3 tablespoons of tomato paste, a bay leaf, and a cup of white wine. Stir to combine the ingredients.

5. With a wooden spoon, scrape up the *fond* from the bottom of the Dutch oven and cook for a few minutes to allow the alcohol in the wine to dissipate.
6. Add the sliced onions. It will seem like there are more onions than one could possibly imagine in a recipe, but there is no mistake. If all the onions don't fit into your pot, cook the first batch until they reduce in volume and then add the remainder.
7. When the onions are all in, reduce the heat to medium, cover the Dutch oven, and cook for 30 minutes without stirring. After 30 minutes, stir onions and meat until well combined. Cover again and cook another 30 minutes.
8. After this initial hour of cooking and blending the onions with the beef, give another good stir of the pot, reduce the heat to low, and cook the sauce, uncovered, for 8 to 10 hours, stirring occasionally.
9. During the long simmering, skim off fat as mixture cooks. If sauce seems to reduce too much, add some water or beef broth as needed to maintain a sauce-like consistency. Cook until beef and onions appear to melt into each other.
10. Think of this sauce as a marriage of a classic ragù Bolognese with a French soupe à la oignon.
11. Best served with al dente rigatoni that is finished in the sauce and served with grated Parmigiano Reggiano.
12. This recipe makes enough sauce to generously accompany about 2 pounds of cooked pasta, like rigatoni, and any leftover ragù freezes perfectly.

Much of my time and attention at Campion was invested in promoting social engagement with my aging Jesuit brothers. We put considerable energy into ensuring spiritual engagement, especially their participation in the daily, Sunday, and special feast day celebrations of the Eucharist. With the support of our dieticians and food service colleagues, we were attentive to providing a welcoming dining experience for our men to help them maintain a healthy and satisfying life. Many of the activity programs were targeted to intellectually stimulate the Jesuit residents, knowing that active cognitive engagement slows cognitive deterioration and decline significantly. Without consistent spiritual, intellectual, and social interaction, Jesuits, as do other older persons, can experience a variety of debilitating conditions including loneliness, depression, and an increased risk of dementia. Many of my conversations with staff focused on ways in which we could assist the resident Campion Jesuits holistically to maintain health and wellness through active engagement and social interactions with their fellow Jesuits and with the staff. Most importantly, we worked to foster a sustained experience among the Jesuit residents that they remain a part of the larger mission of the Society of Jesus.

I cannot say enough about the competence and dedication of the more than 115 people who help to make Campion Center the amazing place that it is. During my years there I grew in knowledge, admiration, and appreciation of just how much each of these women and men are invested in the total well-being of the Jesuits for whom they care. Some of the staff have worked at Campion for a quarter-century or more. Every year, we celebrated the milestone service anniversaries of our employees. Large numbers of these individuals have received ten-, fifteen-, and twenty-year service pins. I found this quite remarkable, since the turnover rate in long-term care facilities can be a real problem, ranging from 55 percent to 75 percent for nurses and aides. It was very comforting to know just how dedicated our staff is to the care and well-being of the men. This same spirit and dedication extends to the housekeeping staff, the kitchen and dietary personnel, and the laundry and maintenance workers, as well as the professional caretakers and rehabilitation therapists. This was all summed up one day when I overheard one of our Jesuits say to the aide who was assisting him to get dressed: "You are the apple of my pie." I walked past that room with an enormous, grateful smile on my face.

In the spirit of Campion's working ethos, here is one of my favorite variations on the American classic apple pie. This one combines apples with golden raisins plumped in brandy and is enveloped and baked in a buttery, flaky crust.

APPLE RAISIN PIE

Makes 6 servings

Ingredients

For the double pie crusts

- 2½ cups all-purpose flour
- ½ teaspoon kosher salt
- 2 sticks chilled and diced unsalted butter
- ½ cup ice water
- 1 teaspoon apple cider vinegar

For the apple filling

- ⅓ cup golden raisins
- 3 tablespoons brandy
- 6 Granny Smith apples, peeled, cored, and cut into wedges
- 3 teaspoons vanilla extract
- ⅔ cup packed dark brown sugar
- 3 tablespoons all-purpose flour
- ½ cup lemon juice
- 2 tablespoons grated lemon zest
- ½ teaspoon ground cinnamon
- ⅛ teaspoon salt
- ⅛ teaspoon ground nutmeg
- 1 tablespoon unsalted butter, cut into pieces
- 1 teaspoon whole milk
- 1 teaspoon raw sugar

continued

Method

For the pie crusts

1. In the bowl of a food processor fitted with the steel blade attachment, combine flour and salt. Process for 1 minute to aerate the flour and combine with the salt.
2. Add the small chilled butter cubes and process just until the butter-flour mixture resembles coarse crumbs.
3. With the motor running, in a slow, steady stream, add the ice water (mixed with a teaspoon of apple cider vinegar) through the feed tube, until the dough begins to form a ball.
4. Remove from the processor bowl, divide the dough into two equal balls, and flatten to two round disks. Cover tightly in plastic wrap and refrigerate for 4 hours or overnight.
5. Remove the pastry disks from refrigerator about 15 minutes before rolling the dough.

Making the apple filling

1. Preheat oven to 425°F.
2. In a small saucepan, combine the raisins and brandy. Bring to a boil. Remove from the heat; let stand for 30 minutes.
3. Prepare a large mixing bowl. Zest 4 lemons and set aside; reserve the freshly squeezed lemon juice in a large mixing bowl that will contain the cut apples slices.
4. Peel the apples, cut in half, and core. Cut each half into three or four wedges. Toss the cut apples in the mixing bowl with the lemon juice to prevent oxidation.
5. When all the apples have been peeled and cut, drain off the residual lemon juice in the bowl and discard. Drain the raisins and add them to the apples and stir to combine, along with the vanilla extract.

6. Combine the brown sugar, flour, lemon zest, cinnamon, salt, and nutmeg. Sprinkle over apples and raisins and toss lightly.
7. On a lightly floured work surface, roll out one of the pastry disks to a 12-inch round. Carefully place the rolled bottom crust into a 9-inch pie plate.
8. Arrange the filling in the pie plate and dot the surface with small bits of butter.
9. Roll out remaining dough to fit the top of pie and place over filling.
10. Trim, seal, and decoratively flute the edges. Cut some steam slits in the top crust.
11. Brush milk over pastry and sprinkle with the raw sugar.
12. Place pie plate on a baking sheet.
13. Bake at 425°F for the first 20 minutes.
14. Reduce oven temperature to 375°F. Continue baking the pie for 30 to 40 minutes longer, or until the crust is golden and the apple filling is bubbling.
15. Cool baked pie thoroughly on a wire rack before cutting and serving.

You can make variations of the filling by using other dried fruits with the apples, such as cranberries or cherries, or by the addition of toasted walnuts or pecans, and by plumping the dried fruits with other spirits like dark rum, Grand Marnier, Cointreau, or a flavored vodka.

Beginning during my first Christmas season at Campion, I invited the senior managers and their spouses or significant others for a served gala dinner in the great hall of the mansion. Ordinarily, we hosted between twenty-five and thirty-five guests for this event. We cleared the mansion's entry hall of its major furnishing and set up five or six round tables with chairs. For each of these dinners I developed a four-course menu, often including a pasta course, an entrée along with some side dishes, a salad course, and a festive holiday dessert. I did most of the preparation work and cooking, often spending several evenings before the event prepping the various dishes. I solicited the help of a few of the able-bodied Campion Jesuits to be the servers and wine stewards for these holiday galas. The reward for the voluntary labor was that these Jesuits got to sit with the guests and enjoy the meal. In addition to the dinner, I regularly prepared little take-home gifts for the couples that included something that I had made or baked. One year I preordered some Mason jars and filled them with a homemade tomato sauce, along with a laminated copy of the recipe for the sauce. In another year my friend Lidia Bastianich sent me cases of her signature pastas and sauces, which I featured in the gift bags. The bags sometimes included items like panettone, a traditional Italian holiday cake, or milk and dark- and milk-chocolate oranges.

For one of these galas, I decided to feature crown roast of pork. Fr. Jim Mattaliano took on the assignment of finding a butcher who might be able and willing to prepare and tie the racks of pork. He went to a butcher shop that his grandparents had frequented in his hometown. The crown roasts were impeccably prepared—making the chef's job infinitely easier.

Here is a recipe for preparing and roasting a crown roast of pork with a delicious bread dressing made with pears and cranberries.

CROWN ROAST OF PORK WITH BARTLETT PEAR AND CRANBERRY STUFFING

Makes 12 servings

Ingredients

For the crown pork roast

- In advance, ask a butcher to prepare a crown pork loin roast, which will often weigh between 6 and 10 pounds, depending on the number (2 or 3) racks that are tied together. Specifically request that the butcher tie the rib roast (backbone removed) for you, making half-inch deep cuts between the ribs and trimming or Frenching the bones. An average serving is one or two ribs per person.

For the crown pork roast rub

- 3 cloves minced garlic
- 4 rosemary branches, leaves stripped from stems, finely minced
- 10 minced sage leaves
- 1 teaspoon minced thyme
- 2 teaspoons kosher salt
- 1 teaspoon freshly ground black pepper
- ½ cup extra-virgin olive oil

For the pear and cranberry dressing

- 10 cups dried sourdough or peasant bread cubes
- 4 peeled and diced Bartlett pears
- 2 cups whole fresh cranberries (frozen and thawed are also fine)
- 6 ounces pancetta (a single thick piece)
- 4 ribs peeled and diced celery
- 2 diced onions
- 1 teaspoon minced thyme
- 1 teaspoon dried sage powder
- 4 cloves minced garlic
- ½ fennel bulb, cut into small dice
- 1 cup boiling water
- 1 cup hot chicken stock
- 2 cups dry white wine
- kosher salt
- extra-virgin olive oil

Method

1. Preheat the oven to 375°F.

continued

To prepare and apply the rub and to begin the roasting process

1. In a bowl, combine the minced garlic, rosemary, sage, salt, and pepper with a half cup of olive oil. With your clean hands, apply the herb paste mixture to the pork roast and rub it well to cover the entire surface.
2. Place the seasoned roast on a rack in an open roasting pan, rib ends down.
3. Cook the roast, uncovered, at 375°F for two hours, then remove it from the oven in order to fill it with the prepared stuffing.

To prepare the pear and cranberry dressing

1. Cut the piece of pancetta into a small dice and place in a sauté pan in which a tablespoon of olive oil has been heated. Cook the pancetta until it is softened and lightly browned, and gives off some of its fat. Remove from pan and drain on paper towels.
2. In the same sauté pan, with the reserved pancetta fat and olive oil, cook the celery, onions, and fennel, seasoned with salt, until they are soft.
3. Add the chopped thyme, sage powder, and garlic and cook for an additional minute only.
4. Add the chopped pears, cranberries, and wine and cook until the wine and pear liquid reduces to about half its original volume. Remove the skillet from the heat.
5. In a very large mixing bowl, add the cubed bread and the content from the hot skillet (vegetables and liquid), and combine.
6. Gradually add the hot chicken stock and boiling water to saturate the bread. Work the mixture with your hands. Add more hot liquid as needed. Finally, add in the cooked pancetta and combine. Add additional salt and pepper, as needed.

To fill the crown roast and finish cooking

1. Reduce the oven temperature to 325°F.

2. Carefully invert the roast, rib tips up, then fill the center cavity (the crown) with the prepared stuffing. Any leftover dressing can be transferred to a baking dish and roasted, covered, for about 35 minutes at 325°F.
3. Cover the edges of the rib chops with pieces of aluminum foil to prevent burning. If the top of the stuffing gets too brown during the final roasting period, cover it loosely with aluminum foil.
4. Return the roast to the oven and set the timer for 1½ hours. Meanwhile, keep an eye on the stuffing. If the stuffing turns too brown, cover it with aluminum foil.
5. Continue roasting for about another 45 minutes to an hour, or until the internal temperature of the thickest part of the roast reaches 175°F.
6. Allow the roast to rest for about 20 minutes, lightly tented with aluminum foil, before carving and serving.

As we prepared to enter the second decade of the millennium, I was feeling more than ordinarily tired. I dismissed these feelings, acknowledging that I was balancing many different obligations that were keeping me engaged 24/7. The apostolic planning goal had been met and we were actively beginning implementation of some of the major strategic objectives. All the institutional reorganization tasks had been completed and all the senior management positions had been filled, including new directors of nursing, activities, and chaplaincy. A new initiative to support the continuing professional education of nursing staff had been implemented and the first candidates had successfully matriculated into nurse practitioner, master's, and bachelor's of nursing science degree programs. We had completed the searches and appointed new executive directors for Campion Health & Wellness and Campion Conference & Renewal. We had completed the annual site visitation survey by the Department of Public Health to assess compliance with federal standards of care, including detailed reviews of staffing, quality of care, resident satisfaction, and the cleanliness of facilities. All of the holiday liturgies and celebrations had been planned. Year-end solicitation letters had been mailed.

I was scheduled for the first of two cataract surgeries in early January 2020. As I was in the preop preparation area at the hospital awaiting my procedure, the nurse who was taking my blood pressure seemed a bit concerned by the very high reading she was recording. "Are you taking any medications to treat hypertension?" she asked. Surprised by her question, I replied that I had never been prescribed or taken blood pressure lowering medications, and that my measurements were predictably within normal ranges. She suggested that perhaps the elevation in pressure might be linked to anxiety about the upcoming surgical procedure, but she did advise that I should keep an eye on it.

I had never regularly monitored my blood pressure. However, when I returned to Campion postsurgery, I asked the charge nurse on the night shift to measure it. It had actually increased from the level reported by the nurse just before surgery. When I returned to the hospital the following morning to meet the ophthalmologist for a postsurgery examination, I mentioned my new hypertension concerns. She did another check in the office and my blood pressure was then registering in the range of a hypertensive crisis. I quickly arranged an emergency consult with my primary care physician, who started me on a medication protocol composed of a calcium channel blocker and a diuretic. He ordered a full blood panel screening and wrote an order for an overnight sleep study to screen for possible obstructive apnea. The bottom line from all of these fact-finding examinations and studies was that I was diagnosed with severe apnea, which, combined with my age and chronic stress, was most probably the driving force behind this silent health threat of hypertension.

Hypertension can cause serious damage to one's blood vessels and internal organs, including the heart. In my case, there were no notable symptoms or warning signs. I had attributed my fatigue, weariness, and disturbed sleep to working too long and too hard for my age. I had not realized just how much elevated blood pressure can affect the body, and how threatening over time it can be to one's overall functioning, effectiveness, and health. It was sobering to recall that everyone in both of my ancestral lines had died not of cancers, but of cardiovascular diseases.

I had to make some immediate life changes and reduce some of the risk factors. As I was someone progressively inching to the eighties, my physician reminded me that age and stress were not my friends, nor was my body mass index.

I had been anticipating completing my executive role and religious leadership responsibilities for the Jesuits at Campion Center during the summer of 2020. With the provincial's support and encouragement, I embraced what I termed a radical lifestyle change and moved to the Boston College community in early March, two days before the Jesuit community embraced the new restrictions imposed by the growing threats of SARS-CoV-2, the COVID-19 pandemic.

Boston College has proven to be Elysian fields for me, a welcoming, pleasant, and life-nurturing place in which to rest, renew, and revitalize. I first learned about these idyllic fields when I was a high school and college student, especially in reading the works of Homer and Virgil. Homer describes Elysium as a place where the favored ones of the gods enjoy tranquility and peace, not too distant from the Christian concept of heaven. In the *Odyssey*, the poet becomes rhapsodic when he speaks of Elysium as a place where no rain or snow falls and where the winds are soft and gentle, singing softly from the sea and offering new vigor and life to all who are blessed to find themselves in Elysium's embrace.

Of course, when I was a junior in Fr. John Chapman's Greek class, these words brushed right over my head. I had little appreciation then for Homer's description of Zeus's favor for his friends or about the place of safety, security, and repose that Homer's metaphor of Elysium represents. In Fr. Joe Trinkle's Latin literature class in my senior year at BC High, however, the imaginary world of Virgil's *Aeneid* made a deep and lasting impression. Joe Trinkle had been a successful commercial artist and illustrator before he embarked on his vocation as a Jesuit, and in introducing many of the major stories and characters in this epic poem, each week he would fill the sprawling blackboards of our classroom with colored chalk sketches. I recall vividly his depiction of the Elysian fields where he portrayed its blessed inhabitants engaged in blissful activities: sitting under trees composing music and poetry, dancing with carefree abandon, grooming beautiful horses, and polishing the gleaming brass fittings of their chariots.

There are probably few people who would view the onset of the public health crisis of COVID-19 and the restrictive precautionary measures involving quarantines, social distancing, and the total lockdowns that it has mandated as Elysian fields. Yet the pandemic has forced all of us to adjust to new realities, not knowing when and how we will all emerge from these uncertain times.

At Boston College, as a community we worked hard to take every reasonable precaution against infecting the Jesuits with whom we live. We maintained appropriate physical distancing from each other, without becoming socially isolated. We were able to gather in a small group daily for the celebration of the Eucharist, realizing that the majority of Roman Catholics did not have these same opportunities. In the dining room, we sat alone at individual tables meant to accommodate four diners. But we were able to maintain some semblance of social conversations across a crowded room.

Notwithstanding our efforts to remain socially engaged while physically distanced, I observed what these long months of confinement, isolation, and loneliness can do to the mental and physical health of fellow Jesuit brothers, especially those who are older and retired from active ministries.

Personally, I was able to convert an extended crisis into an opportunity. I quickly ventured—along with some of my doctors—into the world of telehealth conferencing. The ability to arrange online discussions with a health professional alleviated anxieties and provided direction as I adjusted to new medications and new medical devices, such as a CPAP machine to manage my apnea. The pandemic created opportunities to connect by telephone and FaceTime and Zoom with other Jesuits, family, and friends, where we were able to share our experiences and challenges. And as soon as I began to feel better, I returned to this writing project. For several months during the pandemic, I spent four or five hours each day engaged in the work of remembering and writing. Several of my Jesuit companions became intrigued by this project, especially by the gastronomic dimensions of the undertaking. I was frequently asked about what recipe I was composing or adapting on a given day. Truthfully, it has been somewhat amazing to me just how many details of my long and fruitful life I have been able to recall and chronicle.

And as I near the end of this epic story, I feel a closer affinity to Agatha Christie than I had ever felt before. I have been a fan of her detective and crime story novels and short story collections for many years. Hercule Poirot and Miss Marple became my friends. I felt that I, too, had been a passenger on the Orient Express. I must have gone to see *The Mousetrap* three or four times during various visits to London's West End.

As I was beginning to think again about resuming work on this memoir, I reread Agatha Christie's autobiography. She had begun work on her memoir in 1950 but did not finish it until almost fifteen years later, when she was nearing her seventy-fifth birthday. In her own mind, seventy-five was the right age to stop writing. She felt that at that stage of her life's journey, she was satisfied with all that she had accomplished. I must say that I share her sentiments, although I'm still not entirely ready to retreat to and settle down permanently in the Elysian fields.

I was also inspired to resume work on my own life's chronicle after finishing reading Agatha's own meandering tale of her travels and adventures, and the pure *joie de vivre* she felt. Her husband, Anthony, along with other friends and her editor, Philip Ziegler, completed editing and put the finishing touches on her autobiographical manuscript and published it the year after her death at the age of eighty-six in 1976. Like Agatha, in my memoir I have "plunged my hand into a lucky dip and come up with a handful of assorted memories."[16]

In particular, I found strong affinity with Agatha Christie's perspectives on the life course:

> *Life seems to me to consist of three parts: the absorbing and usually enjoyable present, which rushes on from minute to minute with fatal speed; the future, dim and uncertain, for which one can make any number of interesting plans, the wilder and more improbable the better since—as nothing will turn out as you expect it to do—you might as well have the fun of planning anyway; and thirdly, the past, the memories and the realities that are the bedrock of one's present life, brought back suddenly by a scent, the shape of a hill, an old song—some triviality that makes one suddenly say "I remember . . . " with a peculiar and quite unexplainable pleasure.*

Perhaps that is why people like me—at this advanced stage of life—may take the time to assemble and record a catalogue of personal memories. In my case they have been stitched together along with a thesaurus of culinary reminiscences, which celebrate my lifelong fascination with cooking and baking. By disciplining myself to sit down and record these assorted memories and recipes, this exercise has brought all of them back to life again.

In her summing up, Agatha Christie observed: "If the thing you want beyond anything cannot be, it is much better to recognize it and go forward, instead of dwelling on one's regrets and hopes." This is a lesson from which many of us could richly benefit.

For the final recipe in this story of a Jesuit's abundant life and culinary journey I wanted to offer something original that is both savory and sweet: a celebratory multilayer cake, based on a classic sponge cake that delighted Queen Victoria during

16 *Agatha Christie, An Autobiography* (London: HarperCollins, 1977).

the sixty-three years of her reign as sovereign of Great Britain. Binding together the layers of this cake is a rich caramel buttercream infused with fresh rosemary and finished with sea salt flakes. For decoration, I surround the frosted cake with fragments of glistening pecan praline and crown it with buttercream rosettes, topped with caramelized pecans.

SAVORY AND SWEET: A ROSEMARY SALTED CARAMEL BUTTERCREAM CAKE

Makes 8 to 10 servings

Ingredients

For the rosemary-infused salted caramel buttercream

- 4½ cups granulated sugar
- 7 tablespoons water
- 2 cups heavy cream
- 1 pound softened unsalted butter
- 2 sprigs fresh rosemary
- ½ teaspoon *fleur de sel*

For the sponge cake layers

- ½ stick melted and cooled unsalted butter
- 1½ cups sifted cake flour
- 9 room-temperature eggs
- 1½ cups granulated sugar
- 1 teaspoon pure vanilla extract
- a pinch of coarse salt

For the pecan praline and glazed pecan decorations

- 1 cup coarsely chopped pecans

- 16 pecan halves
- 2 cups granulated sugar
- 8 tablespoons water

Method

To prepare and bake the sponge cake layers

1. Preheat oven to 350°F.
2. Butter two 9-inch round springform cake pans and line the bottoms with parchment.
3. Butter the parchment liner and the sides, and flour the pans, tapping out any excess flour.
4. Separate the egg yolks and whites.
5. Whisk together the egg yolks and 1 cup of granulated sugar in a non-reactive stainless steel mixing bowl set over a saucepan of simmering water; mix until the sugar has dissolved and mixture is warm, 3 to 4 minutes. Do not let the bottom of the mixing bowl touch the water.
6. Remove from heat and pour into the bowl of a stand mixer fitted with the paddle attachment.
7. On medium speed, beat the egg yolks and melted sugar mixture until it becomes pale yellow and thick enough to form a ribbon. This will take 3 to 5 minutes. Beat in vanilla and salt.
8. With a handheld electric mixer, beat the room-temperature egg whites until they form soft peaks. Gradually add the remaining ½ cup of granulated sugar and beat on medium-high speed until stiff, glossy peaks form, about 2 minutes.
9. Fold ⅓ of the beaten egg whites into the creamed egg yolks and sugar, then gently fold in the remaining whites. Sift flour over top and gently start to fold in. When nearly all the flour has been folded in, pour the cooled, melted butter along the inside wall of the bowl and gently fold into the batter until it is just incorporated, and the batter is smooth. Do not overmix.

continued

10. Divide the batter between the two prepared springform cake pans and bake for about 25 minutes.
11. After removing the cakes from the oven, release the spring lever on the pans and invert the cakes, removing the metal bottom of the baking pans and the parchment liners. Turn the cakes right side up and cool completely on a wire rack before filling with buttercream.

To prepare the rosemary-scented caramel buttercream

1. In a saucepan, warm 2 cups of heavy cream; do not allow the cream to boil.
2. When warmed, pour the cream into a stainless steel bowl, add two intact stems of fresh rosemary, cover the bowl with plastic wrap, and allow the herbs to infuse and flavor the cream as it cools.
3. In a large, heavy-bottomed saucepan, place the 4½ cups of granulated sugar and 7 tablespoons of water. Slowly bring to the boil over a medium heat, stirring until the sugar has dissolved.
4. Once the sugar is completely dissolved in the water, turn up the heat and boil until the sugar begins to turn to a light golden caramel color. Once it begins to turn, remove the pan from the heat and pour it into a large stainless steel mixing bowl.
5. Drain the infused heavy cream and add the herbal cream to the hot caramel. Be careful: the addition of the cream will initially cause the caramel to bubble up. With a metal mixing spoon, stir to blend the cream with the caramel and set aside to cool. Then you can cover the bowl with plastic wrap and put into refrigerator to set.
6. When the caramel is thoroughly chilled and set, with a spatula, transfer the caramel to the bowl of a standing mixer. With the metal whisk attachment, begin to beat the caramel on low to medium speed.
7. While the motor is running, progressively add pieces of the softened butter to the bowl of the mixer until you have added the full pound of butter. Scrape down the sides of the bowl during this blending of the butter into the chilled caramel.

8. When all the butter is incorporated, add the ½ teaspoon of *fleur de sel* flakes and mix to blend. Remove the bowl from the stand mixer, cover with plastic wrap, and refrigerate until ready to use.

To make the pecan praline and caramelized pecan decorations

1. Line a baking sheet with a silicone pad or some parchment paper.
2. On one half of the tray, spread the roughly chopped pecans in an even, clustered layer. Keep the pecan halves nearby.
3. In a heavy-bottomed saucepan, dissolve the 2 cups of sugar in 8 tablespoons of water over low heat, stirring constantly, then increase the heat and boil the syrup until it turns a deep golden-brown color.
4. Allow the caramel to cool for a minute or two, then pour about half of it over the chopped pecans spread on one half of the baking pan.
5. Working quickly, add the remaining 16 pecan halves into the caramel and with metal tongs, remove them and arrange them, top side up, on the other half of the baking pan. Allow the pecan praline and the caramelized pecan halves to cool completely.

To assemble, frost, and decorate the sponge layer cake

1. With a long, serrated knife, carefully divide each of the sponge layers into two even disks.
2. On a cake stand or serving plate, arrange wax paper pieces under the first sponge disk (to help keep the serving plate clean during the frosting).
3. Remove the herb-and-salted caramel buttercream from the refrigerator and with a metal whisk, beat it again to loosen the buttercream for spreading.
4. In a pastry bag fitted with a star tip, add about ¼ of the buttercream for decorations.
5. Working with an offset spatula, spread a layer of the buttercream over

continued

the base layer of the sponge cake, and repeat for the second and third layers.

6. Spread all of the remaining buttercream on the top layer, spreading evenly and frosting the sides of the cake. Smooth out the top and sides.
7. Break the pecan praline into small pieces and decoratively distribute and press the praline along the sides of the cake.
8. Pipe rosettes of the buttercream around the top edge of the cake and in its center and finally decorate the cake with the caramelized pecan halves.

....

This indeed has been a very long tale of faith, food, and friendship—a testimonial to an exceptionally rich, interesting, and abundant life. As I pen these final words, I am reminded of a quote often attributed to Shakespeare: "A friend is one that knows you as you are, understands where you have been, accepts what you have become, and still, gently allows you to grow." Through these pages and recipes, you have come to know me a bit more intimately and can rejoice with me in whispering this hopeful and grateful prayer of the psalmist: "They still bear fruit in old age; they will stay fresh and green." (Psalm 92:14).

EPILOGUE

Every person has within themself some food which they give to their neighbor. For it cannot happen that, when we approach each other as human beings and join in conversation, we do not either take or give some food between us either by a response, or by a question, or by some gesture. . . . Therefore, as we said, every person has some food within them from which, if indeed it is good and "from the good treasure of their heart they bring forth good," they may supply pure food to their neighbors.

—ORIGEN, *HOMILIES ON LEVITICUS*, VII, 5

The Rev. Dr. Samuel Fernández, a patristic scholar and a visiting professor at Boston College from the Pontificia Universidad Católica de Chile, suggested the quotation from Origen, a brilliant third-century Christian theologian. In a casual conversation over lunch on the topic of my memoir-cookbook, Fr. Fernández made an instantaneous connection between my book's title and Origen's use of food analogies in his theological and homiletic writings.

I was intrigued by Fr. Fernández's observations and the ensuing discussion. Scholars agree that Origen formulated one of the first systematic expositions of Christian theology ever written. Yet Origen was a religious extremist; to some observers, a kook. He was an early vegan, teetotaler, fasted regularly, walked barefooted, and may have even castrated himself for the faith. Yet he also recognized—as do I—the marvelous interconnections among things like faith, food, and friendship.

Through this brief epilogue (ἐπί epi, "in addition" and λόγος logos, "word"), I would like to bring closure to this reflection on my life and ministry by offering a few final words of gratitude to those whose lives have been food and nurture for me.

I wish to acknowledge with love and gratitude the innumerable ways in which my family of origin has cared for me throughout my life. Although my Irish-born grandparents and my American-born parents were neither great cooks nor foodies, they provided my siblings and me with everything we could need. In reflecting back on what these poor immigrants and their children bequeathed to us, I recall St. Paul's wisdom: "As for the rich in this present age, charge them not to be haughty, nor to set their hopes on the uncertainty of riches, but on God, who richly provides us with everything to enjoy. They are to do good, to be rich in good works, to be generous and ready to share, thus storing up treasure for themselves as a good foundation for the future, so that they may take hold of that which is truly life" (1 Timothy 6:17–19).

My siblings, their spouses, children, grandchildren, and I have learned these lessons of faith, food, and friendship well from our parents and grandparents, and with happy hearts, I am consoled in knowing that we are generously passing on these imperishable gifts to others.

The Letter to the Hebrews offers this advice: "Remember those who led you, who spoke the word of God to you; and considering the result of their conduct, imitate their faith" (Hebrews 13:7). I will be forever indebted to the Society of Jesus and to my Jesuit brothers whom I met for the first time as a young boy in Boston's South End. Jesuits have been my teachers, mentors, role models, and most importantly, faithful companions for my entire life. There is another scriptural text that counsels "Start children off on the way they should go, and even when they are old they will not turn from it" (Proverbs 22:6). Jesuits succeeded in lighting a flame within me and, with God's grace, it continues to burn passionately and brightly.

This memoir has afforded me an unparalleled opportunity to remember only some of the individuals who have shaped and reshaped my life. I would also like to acknowledge with profound gratitude the hundreds of other family members, friends, and colleagues whose names and narratives are not formally mentioned or memorialized in these pages. I am humbled when I realize that to do so would require multiple additional volumes. My remembrance and prayer for each of you, nonetheless, is powerful and unceasing. I have not forgotten you.

I thank God for giving me such a vibrant community of family and friends as companions on life's journey. Each of you has been a blessing: loving, encouraging, admonishing, forgiving, guiding, supporting, and uplifting me amid all of life's vicissitudes. Because of you I did not have to make this journey alone, and you have always been there—icons of faith, food, and friendship. For each of you I pray:

"The Lord bless you and keep you; the Lord make His face shine upon you and be gracious to you; the Lord lift up his countenance upon you and give you peace." (Numbers 6:24–26, ESV).

A work of this scope and breadth does not come to fruition without a community of friends. Initially, I began several years ago to collect and record my memories and recipes as an informal exercise of life review, with no intention of publishing them. In conversations with some friends mentioned in this book, a strong consensus emerged among them that I should become a bit more purposeful and deliberate in dedicating time and effort to completing this project. Taking seriously their counsel and encouragement, I began to organize both my recollections and recipes. When the confluence of my convalescence and the pandemic opened up unanticipated, undistracted days of quiet, the project took wing. I wish to thank several individuals and couples whose generosity and support have especially helped bring this book to life. During a dinner shared together in their New York apartment in the spring of 2021, Chris Grisanti and his wife, Suzanne Fawbush, were insistent that together we should commit to find a publisher with expertise in working with this blended genre of memoir and cookbook who could help shape my manuscript—then more than eight hundred pages in length—into an interesting and readable book. They enlisted the help of other friends—Geoff Bible, Ed Herlihy, Kathy Foley, Joanne and Manny Chirico, Jincie and Ken Duane—and quickly identified the Greenleaf Book Group. How does one begin to express gratitude to such friends, believers, and generous supporters? The Bible teaches us about the power of a grateful heart. An attitude of thanksgiving has the capability to fill us with hope and joy. My heart could not be more full than it is in acknowledging the munificence and endorsement of friends like these. With St. Paul I say: "All this is for your benefit, so that the grace that is reaching more and more people may cause thanksgiving to overflow to the glory of God" (2 Corinthians 4:15).

Even before I transmitted the completed manuscript to the able hands of the team at Greenleaf Book Group, one of my Boston College Jesuit friends painstakingly poured over each page of the lengthy manuscript with a red pen in hand. Fr. John J. Paris, S.J., is the Michael P. Walsh Professor of Bioethics Emeritus at Boston College. With the keen eye of a seasoned author and editor, he offered both substantive and stylistic recommendations that improved the text. Alongside Fr. Paris was Fr. Harvey Egan, S.J., emeritus professor of systematic and mystical theology at Boston College, where he brilliantly taught for forty years. Harvey, the author of many acclaimed books, offered his counsel and experience of the publication process, and later provided valuable advice on design. Fr. Egan himself is an accomplished cook, with a fascination for and a breadth of experience in sampling international cuisines. Throughout the writing process, he was always ready to offer useful perspectives on recipe development and ingredients. And keeping a watchful eye on me as I regained my health during the final stages of the writing and editing process was our Boston College Jesuit community nurse, Kim Noonan. Kim monitored not only my vital functions but also kept pace with the latest recipes to find a place in the manuscript.

This all prepared me for creative engagement with the talented Austin-based production team at Greenleaf, and their subsidiary River Grove Books. Working initially with Justin Branch, director of business development and sales, was both instructive and helpful. Once I signed a contract in October 2021, Justin introduced me to the team assigned to my manuscript, beginning with Jen Glynn, Greenleaf's senior project manager, along with editor Sally Garland. Throughout the months, Jen and Sally have remained on top of an assertive production schedule.

I was indeed fortunate when Jen and Sally invited Anne Sanow to be my principal copyeditor. Anne has collaborated with numerous authors of fiction and nonfiction, and to my great benefit, also has a passion for cuisine and cooking. Currently based in New Orleans, Anne lives in a culinary mecca where a fusion of culinary styles thrive. I could not have asked for a better copyediting partner. Anne reads recipes with the precise eye of a seasoned writing professor and author and with the breadth of experience and sophistication of a knowledgeable cook. Without a doubt, the text is infinitely better because of her investment, expertise, and care. A thousand thanks, Anne.

We are all familiar with the idiomatic expression "don't judge a book by its cover," suggesting that something's intrinsic value or worth cannot be assessed by its outward appearance alone. I suspect that designer Chase Quarterman, Greenleaf's design supervisor, might be willing to challenge that old adage. Even though a power failure interrupted our first teleconference, our working relationship throughout the design process has been nothing but collaborative and immensely enjoyable. Chase has created a remarkable cover and design for this book. In this case, I think we can justifiably judge this book by its cover and design. Thank you, Chase.

Faith, food, and friendship have provided prisms through which to reflect on a long and abundant life. Maturation in faith and religious commitment is a lifelong process that continually relies on nurture and support. Stories of successes and failures, profit and loss, growth and decline punctuate all the seasons of our lives. In the end, however, what emerges as of greatest importance is the power and resiliency of human spirit (soul)—that place deep within each of us where we are most authentically ourselves. This, I believe, is the driving force for all life: physical, psychological, emotional, relational, and spiritual. And it is where we most intimately know and are able to fully embrace God.

This has certainly been the driving force of my entire life's journey. If this exercise in remembering and celebrating faith, food, and friendship has uncovered anything, it is this realization of the power and force of love. If this has been true for my life, it is possible that it has always been true. And if people search, they will touch the same truth in every age and culture, even though others may use different languages, symbols, rituals, and recipes to express it. The search will always culminate in deeper love and union, and in increasingly wider circles. Of all recipes, this will prove, in the end, to be the most important and enduring.

Only in love can I find you, my God.
In love the gates of my soul spring open,
allowing me to breathe a new air of freedom
and forget my own petty self.

In love my whole being streams forth out
of the rigid confines of narrowness and anxious self-assertion,
which makes me a prisoner of my own poverty and emptiness.
In love all the powers of my soul flow out toward you,
wanting never more to return,

but to lose themselves completely in you,
since by your love you are the inmost center of my heart,
closer to me than I am to myself.

But when I love you,
when I manage to break out of the narrow circle of self
and leave behind the restless agony of unanswered questions,
when my blinded eyes no longer look merely from afar
and from the outside upon your unapproachable brightness,

and much more when you yourself, O Incomprehensible One,
have become through love the inmost center of my life,
then I can bury myself entirely in you,
O mysterious God,
and with myself all my questions.

—KARL RAHNER, S.J.[17]

17 Karl Rahner, *Encounters with Silence*, trans. James M. Demske, S. J. (Westminster, MD: Newman, 1965), 3–10. Karl Rahner, S.J. (1904–1984), was a major theologian of the twentieth century and was one of the architects of the Second Vatican Council. His world-embracing vision influenced much of the Council's language and documents and provided theological support for openness and dialogue, as well as a recognition of God's love for all humankind.

ABOUT THE AUTHOR

Born and raised in a second-generation, working-class American Irish community in South Boston, Massachusetts, Fr. Smith came under the spiritual and intellectual influence of the Society of Jesus (the Jesuits) during his high school and undergraduate years at Boston College High School and Boston College. Since 1962, he has been a member of the Society of Jesus and was ordained to the priesthood in 1972.

His academic formation includes degrees in philosophy, theology, French language and literature, and counseling psychology. He completed a doctorate in clinical psychology and spent five decades as a clinician, professor, consultant, trustee, department chair, dean, chief executive officer, and chancellor. In addition to his academic formation and professional achievements, Fr. Smith is also an accomplished cook.

While pursuing studies in Paris in the 1960s at the Sorbonne, he completed training at Le Cordon Bleu. Later, while teaching in Rome and serving as a psychological consultant for the Vatican, he immersed himself in learning about regional Italian food and wine. Through his travel adventures in Europe, Asia, Central and South America, and the Middle East, Fr. Smith continued to expand his culinary knowledge and repertoire.

Made in United States
Orlando, FL
16 December 2024